OUT IN CULTURE

The Cassell Lesbian and Gay Studies list offers

a broad-based platform to lesbian, gay and bisexual writers for the discussion of

contemporary issues and for the promotion of new ideas and research.

COMMISSIONING:
Steve Cook and Roz Hopkins

CONSULTANTS:
Liz Gibbs, Keith Howes, Christina Ruse and Peter Tatchell

OUT IN CULTURE

OUT IN CULTURE

Gay, Lesbian, and Queer Essays on Popular Culture

Edited by Corey K. Creekmur and Alexander Doty

CASSELL

Published in the United States of America by Duke University Press © 1995

Cassell

Wellington House

125 Strand

London WC2R OBB

First published 1995

British Library Cataloguing-in-Publication Data
A catalogue record for this book is available
from the British Library.
ISBN 0–304–33488–X
Printed and bound in the United
States of America.

In Memory of Marlon Riggs

Contents

Introduction

Corey K. Creekmur and Alexander Doty

Out in Culture charts some of the ways in which lesbians, gays, and queers have understood and negotiated the pleasures and affirmations, as well as the disappointments and denials, of mass culture. As readings that challenge the hegemonic structure of mainstream opinion and representation—what has been called *compulsory heterosexuality* (Adrienne Rich), *the heterosexual matrix* (Judith Butler), or *the straight mind* (Monique Wittig)[1]—the essays collected here develop antihomophobic and antiheterocentrist critical approaches to some of the major forms of contemporary mass culture: film, television, popular music, and fashion.

Homosexual men and women have always had a close and complex relation to mass culture. Historians such as David Halperin, John D'Emilio, and Lillian Faderman have argued, in fact, that the identity that we designate *homosexual* arose in tandem with capitalist consumer culture.[2] But, like all marginalized minorities or (sub)cultures, gays and lesbians often found their cultural experience and participation constrained and proscribed by a dominant culture in which they are a generally ignored or oppressed, if logically integral, part.[3] Certainly, gays and lesbians can experience and make meaning of mass culture in ways the culture industries encourage: consuming it "straight" as "just mere" entertainment.

Historically, however, gays and lesbians have also related to mass culture *differently,* through an alternative or negotiated, if not always fully subversive, reception of the products and messages of popular culture—and, of course, by producing popular literature, film, music, television, photography, and fashion within mainstream mass culture industries. As a result, many gay and lesbian popular culture producers and consumers have wondered how they might have access to mainstream culture without denying or losing their oppositional identities, how they might participate without necessarily assimilating, and how they might take pleasure in, and make affirmative meanings out of, experiences and artifacts that they have been told do not offer queer pleasures and meanings.

Surrounding concerns like these are general cultural paradigms that have defined gay and lesbian experience, most often through the metaphor of *the closet*—a private (or "sub"-cultural) space one comes out of to inhabit public space honestly and with one's identity intact. As Diana Fuss argues, "The philosophical opposition between 'heterosexual' and 'homosexual,' like so many other conventional binaries, has always been constructed on the foundations of another related opposition: the couple 'inside' and 'outside.' "⁴ But the inevitability of the symbolic and social "limits," "margins," "borders," and "boundaries" maintaining these oppositions has been continually challenged by the unconventional participation of gays and lesbians in mainstream culture. For the writers collected in this anthology, a central issue is how to be "out in culture": how to occupy a place in mass culture, yet maintain a perspective on it that does not accept its homophobic and heterocentrist definitions, images, and terms of analysis. This issue involves the considerable difficulties not only of living as a lesbian, gay, or queer consumer inside mass culture but also of responding as active producers of intellectual work—as a writer or, in many cases, as a teacher—within a mainstream culture that seduces as often as it repels, and frequently does both at once.

For some time (at least since the model embodied by Oscar Wilde), this queerly "different" experience of mass culture was most evident, if coded, in the ironic, scandalous sensibility known as *camp*—perhaps gay culture's crucial contribution to modernism. An attitude at once casual and severe, affectionate and ironic, camp served to deflate the pretensions of mainstream culture while elevating what that same culture devalued or repressed, thus providing a strategy for rewriting and questioning the meanings and values of mainstream representations. Camp was also, for some time, an "insider's" attitude and knowledge, a means not only of disturbing dominant cultural values but also of disseminating information about who (or what) was in—that is, in the life (homosexual), in the know, au courant, avant-garde, or, to use a later term, hip.

From a camp perspective, anyone "out of it" is not only culturally conservative or reactionary but implicitly also straight, not homosexual. Through this dramatic redefinition of the outsider's status as being "in," camp may have been the first intellectual (although highly aestheticized) approach to indicate the potential for gays, lesbians, or bisexuals to reverse, or at least question, the terms of dominant cultural production and reading. Camp also illuminates the user's "queer" status in relation to dominant culture, for, throughout this century, camp has been one way in which many gays and lesbians have dealt with a mass culture that avoided and repressed the explicit representation, not to mention the affirmation, of homosexuality as a practice and, even more radically, as a perspective. In other words, camp has the ability to "queer" straight culture by asserting that there is queerness at the core of mainstream culture even though that culture tirelessly insists that its images, ideologies, and readings were always only about heterosexuality.

To take a privileged example from camp's (counter)canon, MGM's wholesome children's fantasy *The Wizard of Oz* and its child star, Judy Garland, could be elaborated in terms of their camp functions: *The Wizard of Oz* is a story in which everyone lives in two very different worlds, and in which most of its characters live two very different lives, while its emotionally confused and oppressed teenage heroine longs for a world in which her inner desires can be expressed freely and fully.[5] Dorothy finds this world in a Technicolor land "over the rainbow" inhabited by a sissy lion, an artificial man who cannot stop crying, and a butch-femme couple of witches. This is a reading of the film that sees the film's fantastic excesses (color, costume, song, performance, etc.) as expressing the hidden lives of many of its most devoted viewers, who identified themselves as "friends of Dorothy."

For all camp's potential as a strategy of resistance for certain gays and lesbians (who either learned gay camp or viewed certain aspects of their own culture campily, like butch-femme styles and roles), camp largely remained a private, subcultural form until the early 1960s, when Susan Sontag, among others, recognized its growing influence on a "hipper" general population, the generation that would soon be called the *counterculture*.[6] Camp's increasing exploitation in broader cultural contexts was perhaps facilitated by its tendency to remain coy about explicitly acknowledging its homosexual cultural connections. For example, from the 1950s to the early 1970s, the film critic Parker Tyler wrote in a style that can only be called flamboyant high camp. But his work never says outright what all but its most obtuse readers understood: that this was the work of a man whose gayness directly informed his cultural evaluations and prose style.[7] Richard Dyer also noted the tendency of the British journal *Films and Filming* consistently and covertly to appeal to gay readers in the 1960s, particularly through its selection of "beefcake" stills and references to cult stars like Judy Garland, without ever directly identifying itself as a gay magazine.[8] So, although camp is, in Philip Core's phrase, "the lie that tells the truth," it was for many decades still a veiled form of "the love that dare not speak its name" in film and popular culture criticism and reception.[9] As such, it was a strategy that was criticized as "closeted" and apolitical by many within the "gay liberation" movement of the 1970s. In its "closeted," less overtly political forms, camp has frequently been denigrated and maligned as self-oppressive and misogynistic ever since the Stonewall rebellion of 1969 made gay culture more publicly visible on the evening of Judy Garland's funeral.

By the late 1960s, influenced by the civil rights and women's liberation movements, the politics of gay liberation centered around the radical imperative of making the once-hidden visible. Among other things, gay liberation would encourage an explicit account of the once "secret" relation between gays and lesbians and mass culture. The groundbreaking work of critics like Robin Wood, Vito Russo, Jack Babuscio, Caroline Sheldon, and Richard Dyer, often writing for the emergent gay and lesbian press in the United States (*The Advocate, Christopher Street*), England (*Gay News*), and Canada (*The Body Politic*), demonstrated, in Wood's term, the "responsibility" of gay, lesbian, and bisexual writers to acknowledge the ways in which their sexual and political identities influenced their critical perspectives.[10] In other words, these critics' work on film and other media "came out" along with them as they replaced rhetorical strategies dependent on coded insider references with direct assertions of group identity (the marked use of the pronoun *we* replacing *they,* e.g.). Along with this, these critics began unapologetically to introduce into their writing autobiographical accounts of their erotic and emotional investments in such things as Hollywood cinema, physique and muscle magazines, Broadway musicals, and drag.

Even with this new critical visibility, however, camp was not discarded or lost: it was often brought forward as something explicitly gay, lesbian, bisexual, or, more recently, queer. Not that all post-Stonewall uses of camp are visibly or aurally queer. There remain "sub"-cultural, closeted forms of camp as well as mainstream uses that attempt to deny or repress camp's queerness. But, since the 1970s, "old camp" has existed alongside "new camp." At times, critics and activists will employ "new camping" in order to "out" the texts and pleasures of "old camp(ing)." That is, they will broadcast to anyone who will listen the information that Bette Davis means something special to certain gay men (see Jerry Tartaglia's video *Remembrance*); or that *Valley of the Dolls* is a queer camp text; or that the wacky play with gender, style, and sexuality in *Wayne's World* is (*a*) campy and (*b*) not straight (recall, e.g., Garth's "coming out" through his appreciation of Bugs Bunny in drag); or that they get a "queer feeling" (to quote from the film) when they see Katharine Hepburn dressed as a teenaged boy in *Sylvia Scarlett*.[11] So there really is no critical or political "bottom line" on the uses of camp these days. Like other queer reading practices, sometimes it reinscribes queerness on the margins of popular culture, sometimes it questions the notion of a mainstream culture or preferred (read straight, white, middle-class male) cultural readings, while at other times it places queerness at the heart of the popular.

While many gay men were committed to camp and other "sub"-cultural popular culture pleasures before the 1970s, lesbian audiences/consumers were developing their own rich cultural relation with film, television, music, fashion, and popular literature. Sometimes this relation was articulated through the strategies of camp, but more often it was through reading strategies involving identification (sometimes cross-gendered) and erotics. The evidence of these lesbian uses of popular culture before the 1970s remained largely within lesbian communities and was generally confined to letters, diaries, and conversations. Within the last decade or so, however, there have been attempts to record this oral and otherwise informal popular cultural history formally: Judy Whitaker's interview article "Hollywood Transformed" reveals a lesbian canon of stars and films; Andrea Weiss's *Violets and Vampires* considers lesbian uses of mass culture personalities and texts in different periods; Aerlyn Weissman and Lynn Fernie's film *Forbidden Love* explores the importance of "pulp novels" to lesbian culture; Lillian Faderman's *Odd Girls and Twilight Lovers* provides a history of contemporary lesbian culture; Jane Cottis and Kaucyila Brooke's video *Dry Kisses Only* offers an overview of lesbian representation and reading practices; and Cecilia Barriga's video *Meeting [of] Two Queens* combines clips from Garbo and Dietrich films to create the romance narrative that Hollywood never produced.[12]

As with gays, most lesbian involvement in popular culture production before the 1970s was invisible or closeted—Hollywood director Dorothy Arzner and stars like Alla Nazimova and Greta Garbo being among the most notable examples. But during this time there were a few "out" lesbian popular culture producers, like filmmaker Barbara Hammer, pulp novelist Ann Bannon, and "women's (womyn's) music" performer Chris Williamson. Overall, however, lesbians seemed less invested than gay men in popular culture production and criticism before the 1970s, perhaps because achieving positions of power and control within popular culture industries has always been difficult for women (whether lesbian or not), whereas closeted gay men, such as songwriters Cole Porter and Lorenz Hart or directors James Whale and George Cukor, often achieved prominence and power in the popular culture mainstream.

In the area of criticism and theory, Caroline Sheldon's "Lesbians and Film" (1977) was one of the earliest widely read accounts of lesbian politics, representation, production, and reception in relation to film.[13] This was followed in the United States by the work of feminist critics in the radical journal *Jump Cut*. These critics, already sophisticated in their ideological analysis of media representations of women, began writing openly lesbian critical commentaries about film and, later, television and video. The 1981 "Lesbians and Film" issue of *Jump Cut* was a call for more public work in lesbian popular culture criticism and production.[14] We have reprinted the introductory essay from this issue—along with Robin Wood's groundbreaking "Responsibilities of a Gay Film Critic" (1978)—in order to set up a critical-historical context for the essays that follow in this anthology.

The most recent essays collected here are the products of a complex historical moment: the increased visibility of gays and lesbians in popular culture as well as political life is continually being offset by the ongoing AIDS crisis and those who use it to strengthen homophobia; the success of gay and lesbian (or gender) studies in academe is threatened by a "politically correct" backlash and undermined by severe cutbacks in federal funding for queer-positive art and scholarship; the appearance of a new queer cinema (the work of Todd Haynes, Tom Kalin, Marlon Riggs, Issac Julien, Sadie Benning, Derek Jarman, Sheila McLaughlin, and Monica Treut, among many others) and the success of gay and lesbian film festivals is occurring alongside the misogyny and homophobia of popular Hollywood films like *The Silence of the Lambs, Basic Instinct,* and *JFK*.[15] For many members of a generation coming to political consciousness haunted by AIDS but collectively strengthened by AIDS activism, the term *queer* has become an attractive and oppositional self-label that acknowledges a new cultural context for politics, criticism, reception-consumption, and production. Queer writers not only resist mainstream definitions of sexuality and identity but put themselves in positions to question gay and lesbian orthodoxies that, for example, continue to marginalize black gay men or Chicana lesbians, or that isolate gay men from lesbians, or that have strict and narrow political positions on controversial issues like drag, pornography, sadomasochism, fetishism, and bisexuality.

This contemporary context for queer criticism has influenced the construction of this anthology. We originally conceived of this volume rather modestly as bringing together scattered, often difficult-to-find, popular press and "classic" academic essays in gay male film criticism and theory that might be useful as a teaching text. Some of these essays remain here, but we soon recognized that our search for previously published essays (reflected by the bibliography) was uncovering a surprisingly large body of material that also heralded an unprecedented period of new gay, lesbian, and queer media criticism. We also saw film studies opening itself up to include culture studies subjects—allowing the serious analysis of television, popular music, and fashion, for example—even as it was becoming more visibly queer at conferences and in journals. Our response was to reshape the anthology by soliciting exciting original work or reprinting more recent essays that would expand on or challenge the "tradition" of gay and lesbian theory and criticism located in the earlier work of Robin Wood, B. Ruby Rich, Julia Lesage, Richard Dyer, Thomas Waugh, and others. We became especially convinced that continuing our emphasis on gayness alone would not reflect the current state of queer cultural criticism, so approximately half the collection represents the work of a new generation of lesbian critics whose simultaneous commitments to feminism, lesbian studies, and queer studies are demonstrated in their work.

This anthology therefore collects essays that address a range of general issues and specific texts important to gay, lesbian, and queer cultural criticism. While many of the essays are drawn from recent academic lesbian, gay, and queer cultural studies, with its important inheritances from contemporary critical theory, especially feminism, some essays originate in the active, "alternative" gay and lesbian press, a widely read, if underappreciated, source for queer cultural commentary. While (mis)information about gays, lesbians, and bisexuals has begun to appear more frequently in virtually all media, the alternative press—represented by *The Advocate, Out, 10 Percent, Genre, Christopher Street, Soujourner, Deneuve,* the *New York Native, On Our Backs, Fuse,* the late *Outweek* and *OUT/LOOK,* and hundreds of local journals, newspapers, and 'zines—has been discussing and analyzing contemporary mass culture consistently and insightfully for decades. This anthology attempts to create a dialogue—even if a contentious one—between the "academic" and the "journalistic," two arenas of critical intervention that are unfortunately isolated simply because of their presumed functions, audiences, and rhetorical styles. So, within and between the essays collected here, there are many theoretical and political conflicts and ideological contradictions (some generational, some gender based, some centered on sexual definition) to keep things interesting. If some of the essays are more informative than analytic, or more polemical than theoretical, this only suggests the range of modes as well as topics in queer cultural commentary.

The earlier pieces by Robin Wood and, as a group, Edith Becker, Michelle Citron, B. Ruby Rich, and Julia Lesage represent a "coming out" for gay and lesbian film criticism. Subsequently, this type of criticism would achieve its academic legitimation through the connections with auteur theory, Marxism (and other forms of ideological analysis), and feminism suggested by "Lesbians and Film: An Introduction" and "Responsibilities of a Gay Film Critic." These seminal essays are followed by a group of works by Chris Straayer, Al LaValley, Valerie Traub, and Alexander Doty that offer broad historical and theoretical perspectives on lesbian, gay, and queer culture's relation to mainstream film. Specific "classic" films are then examined by Corey Creekmur (*My Darling Clementine*) and B. Ruby Rich (*Mädchen in Uniform*) in pieces that consider both these films' historical contexts and the textual means by which they represent femininity, masculinity, and homosexuality.

Stars and directors as "authors" of queer cultural meaning and pleasures are considered in Patricia White's essay on Agnes Moorehead and in the collection of essays by John Hepworth, Robin Wood, Sabrina Barton, Rhona J. Berenstein, and Lucretia Knapp on Alfred Hitchcock films. Why a dossier on Hitchcock and not a Hollywood director who identified as homosexual like George Cukor or Dorothy Arzner? Because Hitchcock's films, more than those of anyone else, have become the "test cases" for each new position in film theory and criticism whether auteurism, semiotics-structuralism, feminism, ideological analysis, or psychoanalysis. The essays in this dossier borrow from earlier theoretical work in order to establish the continuing importance of Hitchcock films as sites for working through issues in gay, lesbian, and queer film and cultural theory and criticism.

Areas outside of "mainstream" media making and viewing are the subjects of another set of essays. Michael Moon's work investigates the influences on and of a key figure in the gay avant-garde, Jack Smith. Pornography, a genre often connected to the avant-garde and the experimental in accounts of gay and lesbian film- and videomaking, is examined from queer historical, cultural, and theoretical positions in pieces by Thomas Waugh and Nayland Blake, the latter writing on "gay culture's Norman Rockwell," artist Tom of Finland. Fetishism, fantasy, and the lesbian cultural debates surrounding the dildo are the subjects of Heather Findlay's piece, which considers how advertising, psychoanalysis, erotic fiction and film, and the styles of these sex toys themselves have contributed to these debates.

Television and the mainstream press come under queer scrutiny in essays that consider the visual representation of AIDS in the print media (Jan Zita Grover), the dynamics of gender and sexuality that surround the figure of Pee-Wee Herman (Bruce LaBruce), and the complex politics of black gay representation (Essex Hemphill).

A second dossier collects essays emphasizing the often contradictory pleasures and purposes of popular music for gays and lesbians. Richard Dyer, gay culture's most wide-ranging critic, argues for the positive functions of a blatantly capitalist form, disco, within gay culture. On the other hand, Arlene Stein considers the ambivalent implications of the recent "crossover" of "women's music" into the commercial pop mainstream. Updating the camp tradition of gay diva worship, Michael Musto's essay justifies the love of Madonna's large queer fandom, while Anthony Thomas provides a historical account of the often "whitewashed" gay black influence on contemporary dance music. As a group, these essays demonstrate how one form of mass culture—popular music—generates a productive range of responses within an increasingly diverse community of cultural consumers.

The final selection of essays is concerned with that broad and important arena of gay, lesbian, bisexual, and queer life and art: style. Taken together, the pieces on drag by Mark Thompson and Jeffrey Hilbert provide historical and ideological perspectives on cross-dressing in gay communities. Marlon Riggs's essay considers the "feminine" gay black and his position within African-American culture and representation, while the work of Arlene Stein and Danae Clark examines the uses and meanings of a range of lesbian looks within lesbian communities and in mainstream consumer culture.

This collection concludes with a general bibliography of gay, lesbian, and queer work on mass culture. While this bibliography is not exhaustive, it does reveal that the short list once envisioned by us and by many who heard about this project turned out to be a very long one indeed. This bibliography is meant to be useful to a range of interested readers and researchers and in itself stands as a demonstration of the already impressive history and scope of gay, lesbian, and queer cultural criticism. Our hope is that this anthology both encapsulates and extends the work that has come before it.

Notes

1 These terms are elaborated in Adrienne Rich, "Compulsory Heterosexuality and Lesbian Existence," *Signs: Journal of Women in Culture and Society* 5, no. 4 (1980): 631–60 (reprinted in *Powers of Desire: The Politics of Sexuality,* ed. Ann Snitow, Christine Stansell, and Sharon Thompson [New York: Monthly Review Press, 1983], 177–205, and in Adrienne Rich, *Blood, Bread, and Poetry: Selected Prose, 1979–1985* [New York: Norton, 1986], 23–75); Judith Butler, *Gender Trouble: Feminism and the Subversion of Identity* (New York: Routledge, 1990); and Monique Wittig, "The Straight Mind," in *The Straight Mind and Other Essays* (Boston: Beacon, 1992), 21–32.

2 John Halperin, *One Hundred Years of Homosexuality and Other Essays on Greek Love* (New York: Routledge, 1990); John D'Emilio, "Capitalism and Gay Identity," in *Powers of Desire,* 100–13 (reprinted in *The Gay and Lesbian Studies Reader,* ed. Henry Abelove, Michele Aina Barale, and David Halperin [New York and London: Routledge, 1993], 467–76, and in John D'Emilio, *Making Trouble: Essays on Gay History, Politics, and the University* [New York and London: Routledge, 1992], 3–16); Lillian Faderman, *Surpassing the Love of Men: Romantic Friendship and Love between Women from the Renaissance to the Present* (New York: Morrow, 1981).

3 It has been frequently noted that the identification of *homosexual* as a sexual and, especially, as a social category preceded, and thus logically required the designation of, the category *heterosexual.*

4 Diana Fuss, "Inside/Out," in *Inside/Out: Lesbian Theories, Gay Theories,* ed. Fuss (New York and London: Routledge, 1991), 1.

5 *The Wizard of Oz,* directed by Victor Fleming (MGM, 1939).

6 Susan Sontag, "Notes on Camp," in *Against Interpretation* (New York: Farrar, Straus, Giroux, 1966), 275–92. Other works that discuss camp include Esther Newton, *Mother Camp: Female Impersonators in America* (1972; Chicago: University of Chicago Press,

1979); Andrew Ross, "The Uses of Camp," in *No Respect: Intellectuals and Popular Culture* (New York and London: Routledge, 1989), 135–70; Philip Core, *Camp: The Lie That Tells the Truth* (New York: Delilah, 1984); Oscar Montero, "Lipstick Vogue: The Politics of Drag," *Radical America* 22, no. 1 (January–February 1988): 35–42; Carole-Anne Tyler, "Boys Will Be Girls: The Politics of Gay Drag," in *Inside/Out: Lesbian Theories, Gay Theories,* ed. Diana Fuss (New York and London: Routledge, 1991), 32–70; Jack Babuscio, "Camp and the Gay Sensibility," in *Gays and Film,* ed. Richard Dyer (New York: New York Zoetrope, 1984), 40–57; Andrew Britton, "For Interpretation: Notes against Camp," *Gay Left* 7 (1978–79); Sue-Ellen Case, "Toward a Butch-Femme Aesthetic," *Discourse* 11, no. 1 (Fall–Winter 1988–89): 55–71 (reprinted in *Making a Spectacle: Feminist Essays on Contemporary Women's Theatre,* ed. Lynda Hart [Ann Arbor: University of Michigan Press, 1989], 282–299); Sue-Ellen Case, "Tracking the Vampire," *differences* 3, no. 2 (1991): 1–20; Al LaValley, "The Great Escape," *American Film* 10, no. 6 (April 1985): 29–34, 70–71 (reprinted in this volume); Seymour Kleinberg, *Alienated Affections: Being Gay in America* (New York: St. Martin's, 1980), 38–69, 118–56; Christine Riddiough, "Culture and Politics," in *Pink Triangles: Radical Perspectives on Gay Liberation,* ed. Pam Mitchell (Boston: Alyson, 1980), 14–33; Derek Cohen and Richard Dyer, "The Politics of Gay Culture," *Homosexuality: Power and Politics,* ed. Gay Left Collective (London and New York: Allison & Busby, 1980); Mark Booth, *Camp* (New York: Quartet, 1983); Butler, *Gender Trouble,* 128–49; Vito Russo, "Camp," in *Gay Men: The Sociology of Male Homosexuality,* ed. Martin P. Levine (New York: Harper & Row, 1979), 205–10; Robin Wood, "The Dyer's Hand: Stars and Gays," *Film Comment* 16, no. 1 (January–February 1980): 70–72; Jeffrey Hilbert, "The Politics of Drag," *The Advocate,* no. 575 (23 April 1991): 42–47 (reprinted in this volume); Lisa Duggan, "The Anguished Cry of an 80s Femme: 'I Want to be a Drag Queen,' " *OUT/LOOK* 1, no. 1 (Spring 1988): 62–65; Pamela Robertson, " 'The Kinda Comedy That Imitates Me': Mae West's Identification with the Feminist Camp," *Cinema Journal* 32, no. 2 (Winter 1993): 57–72; Michael Musto, "Old Camp, New Camp," *Out,* no. 5 (April/May 1993): 32–39; Richard Dyer, "It's Being So Camp as Keeps Us Going," *Only Entertainment* (London and New York: Routledge, 1992), 135–47.

7   Parker Tyler's writings about film include *Screening the Sexes: Homosexuality in the Movies* (Garden City, N.Y.: Anchor, 1973), *Magic and Myth of the Movies* (New York: Holt, 1947), *Sex, Psyche, Et cetera in the Film* (New York: Horizon, 1969), *Underground Film: A Critical History* (New York: Grove, 1969), *The Hollywood Hallucination* (New York: Creative Arts, 1944), and *The Three Faces of the Film: The Art, the Dream, and the Cult* (1960) (New Brunswick, N.J.: Barnes, 1967).

8   Richard Dyer, *Heavenly Bodies: Film Stars and Society* (New York: St. Martin's, 1986), 148.

9   Core, *Camp,* 5–17.

10   Robin Wood, "Responsibilities of a Gay Film Critic," *Film Comment* 14, no. 1 (January–February 1978): 12–17; (reprinted in *Movies and Methods,* ed. Bill Nichols [Berkeley and Los Angeles: University of California Press 2:649–60] and in this volume).

11   *Remembrance,* directed by Jerry Tartaglia (1990); *Valley of the Dolls,* directed by Mark

Robson (Twentieth Century–Fox, 1967); *Wayne's World,* directed by Penelope Spheeris (Paramount, 1992); *Sylvia Scarlett,* directed by George Cukor (RKO, 1936).

12 Judy (later Claire) Whitaker, "Hollywood Transformed," *Jump Cut* 24/25 (1981): 33–35 (reprinted in *Jump Cut: Hollywood, Politics and Counter-Cinema,* ed. Peter Stevens [New York: Prager, 1985], 106–18); Andrea Weiss, *Violets and Vampires: Lesbians in Film* (New York: Penguin, 1992); *Forbidden Love,* directed by Aerlyn Weissman and Lynn Fernie, National Film Board of Canada (1992); Lillian Faderman, *Odd Girls and Twilight Lovers: A History of Lesbian Life in Twentieth Century America* (New York: Columbia University Press, 1991); *Dry Kisses Only,* directed by Jane Cottis and Kaucyila Brooke (1990); *Meeting [of] Two Queens,* directed by Cecilia Barriga (1991).

13 Caroline Sheldon, "Lesbians and Film: Some Thoughts," in *Gays and Film,* 5–26.

14 "Special Section: Lesbians and Film," *Jump Cut* 24/25 (1981): 17–51.

15 *The Silence of the Lambs,* directed by Jonathan Demme (Orion, 1991); *Basic Instinct,* directed by Paul Verhoeven (Tri-Star, 1992); *JFK,* directed by Oliver Stone (Warners, 1992).

Responsibilities

of a Gay

Film Critic

Robin Wood

First, my title. I intend equal emphasis on all three terms: *gay film critic*. Critic: one concerned in problems of the interpretation and evaluation of art and artifacts. Film critic: one who makes the central area of that concern the cinema. Gay—not just the word and the fact it points to, but the word and fact asserted publicly: one who is conscious of belonging to one of society's oppressed minority groups, and who is ready to confront the implications of that for both his theory and his practice.

I can define what I mean here in relation to two types of gay critic who reject this equality of emphasis. First, the critic who for whatever reasons (many different ones are conceivable, of widely varying respectability) resists the public revelation of his gayness, arguing (either as defensive self-justification or as a sincerely held principle) that it has nothing to do with his view of art—the view conceived as "objective," and art conceived as something Out There that one can be objective about. I cannot afford to be too contemptuous of this type, as I belonged to it myself until quite recently, and in my case I was always half aware that the defensive self-justification was of the flimsiest. A gay subtext is intermittently discernible running through my early work; a number of people, including some who hadn't met me, have told me that they deduced that I was gay long before I came out. But if these early writings are worth analyzing at all from the gay viewpoint, it could only be as an analysis of self-oppression—an alternating pattern of peeping out of the closet door and then quickly slamming it shut, and pasting over the chinks with placards on which words like *marriage, family, health,* and *normality* were loudly displayed—and with self-oppression becoming, as it always must, the oppression of others. (See, especially, the treatment of homosexual relations in the account of *Les Biches* in the book on Chabrol I coauthored with Michael Walker, for the most embarrassing moments of which I must accept responsibility.)[1]

The other type of gay critic places the emphasis strongly, sometimes exclusively, on *gay,* and concerns himself strictly with works that have *direct* bearing on gayness, approaching them from a political-propagandist viewpoint: do they or do they not further the gay cause? He will find it necessary to review Fassbinder's *Fox,* but will probably ignore Godard's *Tout va bien.* My choice of examples here is not arbitrary. The objection to such criticism is not merely that it is aesthetically restrictive but that it implies an inadequate, and insufficiently radical, grasp of what the gay liberation movement stands for at its best, of its more general social significance. Godard's film, in which gayness is nowhere alluded to, seems to me to have far greater positive importance for gay liberation than Fassbinder's sour determinism, with its incidental reinforcing of gay stereotypes for the bourgeois audience ("the truth about the homosexual milieu," as the English establishment critics greeted it).

Positively, I am able to point to two British colleagues who amply fulfill, in their very different ways, my conception of the gay film critic's responsibilities: Richard Dyer and Andrew Britton. The latter's article on Eisenstein in *Framework* strikes me as exemplary in this respect.[2]

The change in my critical position and practice that many people have noted—some with favor, some with dismay—has been centrally determined by my coming out, and by the changes in my personal life connected with that. Critics are not, of course, supposed to talk personally. It is regarded as an embarrassment, as bad taste, and besides it is an affront to the famous ideal of "objectivity." The typical bourgeois establishment reaction to any form of personal revelation might be typified by a remark by Philip Strick in his ignominious review of my last book in *Sight and Sound*—a review that managed to trivialize every issue in sight—where my coming out in print was described as "telling us about his love life."[3] Yet I believe there will always be a close connection between critical theory, critical practice, and personal life; and it seems important that the critic should be aware of the personal bias that must inevitably affect his choice of theoretical position, and prepared to foreground it in his work.

I don't believe that any theory exists in a vacuum or as truth. Every theory is the product of the needs of particular people within a particular culture at a particular stage of its development, and can only properly be understood within its context. Our gravitation, as human individuals within, and determined by, our culture, toward one or other of the available critical positions, will depend on our personal needs, on the way we wish to lead our lives, on the sort of society we would like to build, on the particularities of our involvement in the social process.

Such a view presupposes a constantly developing, dynamic relationship between criticism and art, between individual and work. There is in a sense no such thing as "the films of Ingmar Bergman," existing as an entity that criticism could finally and definitively describe and interpret and place in the museum. Rather, the films exist as experienced and perceived by the viewer, with the precise nature of the experiencing depending on the viewer's position in society and within ideology. Our sense of the *use* of art generally, and of the particular uses to which particular works allow themselves to be put, will vary from generation to generation, shifting in accordance with our sense of personal and social needs.

What I propose to do is, first, define what gay liberation means to me, the kind of significance I attach to the movement, the kinds of social intervention I see it capable of making, and then reconsider certain films and directors (not necessarily or centrally concerned with gayness) that already meant a great deal to me before my coming out, in an attempt to indicate the nature of the shift in my critical practice, the somewhat different kinds of interest and emphasis I would now bring to an interpretation and evaluation of them.

As most commonly expressed in the newspapers, periodicals, etc., of our establishment (not to mention various gay society discussions I have attended), the aim of the gay liberation movement would appear to be read as that of gaining acceptance and equal rights for homosexuals within existing society. My basic argument is that such an aim is totally inadequate. Acceptance of the homosexual by society has its obvious corollary and condition: acceptance of society by the homosexual. To see the incongruity of this, one has only to consider the dominant ideological norms of the society within which we live. As far as love and sexuality are concerned, those norms are marriage (in the form of legalized heterosexual monogamy) and the nuclear family (with the alternative, at once complementary and incompatible, of exclusive romantic love). Between them they offer homosexuals the terms on which they might be acceptable: the aping of heterosexual marriage and family (with poodles instead of children) or *l'amour fou,* preferably culminating in suicide or alcoholism.

Of crucial importance to gay liberation is its very close, logical connection with women's liberation. The present status of both has been made possible by the increasing public acceptance of birth control, with its implicit acknowledgment that the aim of sex is not necessarily procreation, and its consequent undermining of the tyrannical and repressive norm of monogamy and family. The common logical aim of both movements must be, it seems to me, to attack and undermine the dominant ideological norms on all levels. This offers the gay critic a brief that is enormously more open and comprehensive than the examination of the ways in which homosexuals have been presented on the screen (though that might of course become a perfectly legitimate focus of her or his attention, provided the wider implications were always kept in view). The attack, for instance, could—indeed, should—be directed at the economic structures of capitalism that support the norms, as they are embodied in the structure of the film industry itself as well as in its products. Being neither a practiced political nor a sociological thinker, I am going to restrict myself to questions of sexuality and love.

When dealing with ideology, it is always necessary to ask not only what it *expresses* but what it *represses*. The opposed, largely contradictory, ideological positives our culture offers (monogamy and family, romantic love) have one obvious feature in common: the insistence on exclusivity and mutual possession, with "fidelity" thought of basically in sexual terms and sexuality mystified as "sacred." Beyond this, there is the furtive extramarital affair, with its penalties of tension, secrecy, distrust, recrimination, etc. What is repressed is the possibility that people might relate freely to each other, on a nonpairing basis, without imposing restrictions on each other's liberty. The dominant ideology has a word for this: *promiscuity,* a term loaded with pejorative connotations. According to ideology's double standards, there is some difference between male promiscuity and female promiscuity. A heterosexual man who is promiscuous acquires a certain glamour and is a Casanova; a woman who is promiscuous is a bitch, a tart, a slut, a whore. By and large, however, ideology has no place for promiscuity (or, as I prefer to call it, *relating freely to one another*) as an asserted lifestyle or a possible norm.

My shift in terminology is also a shift in meaning. *Promiscuity* is always exclusively sexual, and the notion of it within ideology has the function of separating sexuality from love. *Relating freely to each other,* on the other hand, involves potentially the whole person—*including* his or her sexuality, without which the relating wouldn't be free, but not *restricted* to it. (This is not to denigrate the pleasure of quite casual sexual relations, or to suggest that every relationship should be "complete," whatever that might mean.) Much the same distinction could be made if one substituted for *promiscuity* the term *permissiveness*—a term popularly understood almost entirely in sexual terms rather than in terms of free human relationships. The term has the added objectionability that it implies that someone or something ("society") is doing the permitting; and to acknowledge society's right to permit is to acknowledge its right to prohibit. In general, ideology's method of dealing with the unthinkable notion of free relationships is to trivialize or dirty it, so that it becomes difficult to imagine what it might actually entail or how it might work.

In *Life against Death,* Norman O. Brown defines the central characteristic of capitalist man as dissatisfaction, with anxiety as its inevitable companion: the

desire to own more, coupled with the fear of losing what one has.[4] Anxiety, or
insecurity, certainly seems fundamental to the possessiveness that characterizes
most of our sexual relationships. Parenthetically, as a person whose personal
insecurity reaches proportions one might describe as grotesque, I must stress
that I don't wish to appear to speak from some superior "liberated" position
wherein I have solved all life's problems within my own life. On the contrary, I
speak as one struggling and floundering frantically among the mess and confusion of sexual relationships as they currently exist; I am prey to all the contami-
nations of the jealousy, possessiveness, and exclusivity that I attack. One must,
however, recognize—otherwise there could never be any progress—that ideas
must always outstrip emotions. Our emotions have to be educated, and emotional education is the most painful of all processes, because the education is
resisted at every point by what we call our instincts but might more reasonably
think of as our ideological structuring. Only with ideas can we confront ideology.

I shall move in a while to two strongly contrasted directors with whose work I
have, as a critic, been associated—Bergman and Howard Hawks—attempting to
suggest ways in which their work might be reread from the perspective I have
outlined.[5] I shall not spell out in detail the differences between my approach now
and my books on these two directors, as this would be deducible for those who
have read them and boring for those who haven't, but I hope for the former
group a critical reflection back over my past work will be implicit. First, however,
I want to talk briefly about a film that, long among my favorites, has grown in
meaning and in richness for me over the past year: Jean Renoir's *The Rules of the
Game*. I have come to reread the film precisely in the context I have defined: our
entrapment in ideological notions of love and sexuality, with their emphasis on
pairing, choice, and exclusivity; and the continuously repressed but insistent
vision of the potential loveliness of genuinely shared relationships, in which none
of the participants feels excluded, in which love is recognized as a life principle
that transcends the exclusive romantic attachment. To anticipate, one can evoke
here one of Renoir's favorite words, and the force it gets from the context of his
work: *generosity*.

Two general or recurrent features of Renoir's work must be made present
here. One is the notion (influenced perhaps by the childhood described in *Renoir, My Father* and the background of French Impressionism) of life as continual flux.[6] He quotes Antoine Lavoisier's "In nature nothing is lost, nothing is
created, everything is transformed" as one of his favorite texts. The other is the
recurring relationship pattern in his films (at once an extension and a questioning of the "eternal triangle") of one to three—usually one woman to three men
(*The Golden Coach, Elena et les hommes, Diary of a Chambermaid, French Can-*

Can, and *Rules of the Game* itself, where there are in fact four men if one counts St. Aubin), though in *The River* there is one man to three women. The addition of a third option crucially affects the significance of the triangle, which in our culture has always been firmly associated with exclusivity and the necessity for choice (usually, the conflict is between marriage, family, and romantic love, the opposed and complementary ideological poles). If three, why not four, five—or twenty?

The film was initially received (and is still, by some people) as virulent social satire, an attack on a decadent ruling class on the eve of its inevitable dissolution. Confronted with this view, Renoir's own response was one of amazement: "But I love those people. . . . I would love to have lived in that world."[7] It is consistently analyzable, I think, in terms of a tension between the two impulses these responses suggest.

There's another way of looking at the film's rich ambiguity of effect: it can be read as a film about people who go too far, or as a film about people who can't quite go far enough. Many have commented on the difficulty of defining what, precisely, *are* the rules of the game. In fact, every character has his or her own rules, or a personal variation on an implied complex of rules. In only two characters do the rules appear clear-cut and rigid in their application: Schumacher (Gaston Modot) and Lisette (Paulette Dubost). One aspect of the film's astonishingly complex yet precise formal organization can be suggested by pointing to three things about them: (1) they are husband and wife; (2) the rules they enforce are the most strongly contrasted of any represented in the film, indeed diametrically opposed; and (3) it is the dual action of their application of their rules that produces the climactic catastrophe. The rules of Schumacher, the gamekeeper from Alsace (who is deliberately presented, in 1939, as an embryonic Fascist), are centered on strict and repressive notions of marital fidelity, the ownership of wife by husband, that give him the moral right to shoot both wife and lover in the event of discovered infidelity. The rules of Lisette, the Parisian ladies' maid, are centered on notions of free sexual play as long as it remains frivolous and unengaged. When it comes to seriousness, the priorities are narrowly social-ideological; Octave (Renoir) is too old for Christine (Nora Gregor), and couldn't afford to keep her in the luxury she's used to.

Between these two—with their equally defined and entrapping, if opposite, sets of rules—come the film's central characters, who all exist in states of varying uncertainty and confusion as to what the rules are. And Christine's uncertainty is significantly the most extreme. From her point of view, the ambiguity of the film can be put another way: the story of a woman trying desperately to understand what her role should be or the story of a woman who can't quite accept that all roles are traps and refuses them all—with the roles defined in terms of the relationships available with particular men. It is important to recognize that the society Renoir depicts is inhabited almost entirely by outsiders: the marquis is Jewish, Christine is from Vienna, André Jurieu (Roland Toutain) is from the modern world of airplanes and public heroes, Octave is a perpetual outsider wherever he is. The character who seems chiefly to embody our idea of a stable aristocratic society is the general, an old man whose constant refrain is that everything is passing away.

It is a society in which all order is at a stage of potential or imminent collapse; and this can be seen in terms of either a closing down or an opening up (the film encourages both readings). "I don't want fences, and I don't want rabbits," the marquis tells Schumacher, and the remark has very clear parallels with the paradoxes of the characters' sexual behavior throughout the film. I have no knowledge of the actual domestic commitments of rabbits—their familial organization may be as impeccably bourgeois as it appears in the books of one of my favorite authors, Beatrix Potter—but in popular imagery rabbits always have connotations of promiscuity; "breeding like rabbits" doesn't refer merely to the number of offspring but to presumed sexual habits. The emphasis throughout the hunt is on the mindless slaughter of rabbits, the detailed imagery evoking the strongest sympathetic response toward what is being destroyed.

The tension I have described can be illustrated succinctly with the beautiful little scene in which, after her discovery of her husband's adulterous relationship with Geneviève (Mila Parély), Christine confronts her rival in her room and enlists her in an ambiguously motivated complicity. On the one hand, Christine's reaction to the shock (she had previously believed completely in her husband's fidelity) is to play what she takes to be "the game" by rejecting all seriousness; she wants Geneviève to keep her husband occupied, not so that she can develop her relationship with André—whom she describes at this point as "too sincere"—but so that she can play around. On the other hand, the possibility of freely shared relationships is nowhere closer to the surface of the film than in this scene, which culminates in a moment of relaxed conviviality and exchange between two women (the demonstrations of how Tyrolean dances go) of a kind very rare in the cinema, where women are habitually seen from the male viewpoint as rivals for the man, their possible uniting repressed. The whole film can be read as structured on continuously shifting couplings (I don't intend the sexual meaning here) that cut completely across all the divisions of sex, class, social role; virtually all the characters have a "duet scene" at some point in the film. The obvious exception is André and Genevieve—the two Octave suggests near the beginning that it would be most convenient to pair off.

Renoir's method and the film's visual style are crucial to its meaning. His creative collaboration with actors—*all* the actors—is well known. The camera style emphasizes the structure patterns of the scenario by never allowing us more than transitory identification with one character at the expense of others. The constant reframings, in which the camera excludes some to include others, the continual entrances into and exits from the frame, the division of our attention between foreground and background—the style might be aptly described as perpetual visual promiscuity, quite breaking down the traditional one-to-one relationship of spectator to protagonist to which the cinema has habituated us. The Renoiresque principle of emotional generosity is everywhere frustrated in its free functioning by the characters' insistence on sexual pairing, and everywhere expressed and celebrated through the "promiscuity" of the camera style and the direction of actors.

Ultimately, *The Rules of the Game* is circumscribed within the ideological assumptions about pairing (Renoir never overtly questions this on a sexual level), yet it is precisely such assumptions that provoke every disaster in the film. It hovers continuously on the verge of a new acceptance. Hence the final ambiguity of effect. The film is at once an elegy to a lost society and one of the most progressive ever made. The world it creates is of the past, yet it everywhere points toward a possible future.

If I were to rewrite my early books now, the one on Bergman would certainly cause me the greatest problems, and be the one in need of the most drastic revision. When I wrote it, my sense of identification with its subject was extraordinarily intense. Beneath the apparently happy surface of a firmly traditional marriage-and-family situation, I was experiencing the sort of anguish and desperation that Bergman's films so compellingly communicate, and accepting it as unchangeable, as "the human condition." Now, it is precisely this tendency of the films to impose themselves as "the human condition" that most worries me. In a supremely revealing moment of the interview book *Bergman on Bergman*, the filmmaker asserts his innocence of any ideology, a substance by which his films are apparently completely uncontaminated.[8] He seems to be using the term in a sense somewhat different from that in which it is usually employed in current film criticism; he means by it a *conscious* structure of social-political ideas. Yet the innocence clearly extends beyond that. There is no awareness that an ideology might exist in one's work, and centrally structure and determine it, without one's being conscious of it. The lack of an explicit social-political dimension to Bergman's work has often been noted; ten years ago I quite failed to see the force of such an objection, my own work as a critic having precisely the same lack.

Another, related way of considering the limitations of Bergman's work is via Andrew Sarris's objection that the films are repeatedly flawed by eruptions of "undigested clinical material."[9] The obstinate recurrence of certain narrative and relationship structures in Bergman's work (structures that, I have argued elsewhere, are basically psychological, the characters representing projections of the artist's inner tensions) is plainly neurotic, and testifies to that central principle of neurosis: resistance wherein the neurosis defends itself against cure. What the films repeatedly assert, with impressive intensity and conviction, is that life under the conditions in which it is lived is intolerable, therefore. . . . At this point a shutter comes down. The "therefore" should continue: "therefore we must strive to change the conditions." The shutter asserts, "the conditions are something called 'the human predicament'; they can't be changed."

In Bergman's films, neurotic resistance goes hand in hand with the resistance to any concept of ideology. Since I wrote my book he has made what I consider two of his finest films, *The Passion of Anna* and *The Touch*—though neither seems to be in general very highly regarded, and my admiration for them is not without reservations. Both films contain important elements, both in style and in narrative structure, that suggest a desire on Bergman's part to open out his work, to pass beyond the stalemate in which it constantly threatens to get trapped. An extended analysis of these films would take the form of examining the conflict between these innovative elements and the resistance to them. More briefly, one can assert that nowhere more than in *Passion* has the intolerability of possessive relationships—the lies, subterfuges, resentments, frustrations, jealousies, eruptions of "psychic and physical violence," the ultimate mutual destructiveness—been more ruthlessly or vividly analyzed. Yet the films continue, doggedly, to assert all this as a fact of life, as the human condition, rather than as ideologically determined. Even *Passion,* with its relatively open structure and its excitingly spontaneous, exploratory style, can never seriously envisage the possibility that things might be changed.

In any assessment of Bergman's work I would not wish to give much prominence to *Face to Face,* which seems to me one of his very worst films, actively offensive in its self-indulgence. If I focus on it here, it is because it is his first work to deal openly with gayness, and because its treatment of gays provides so precise an index of the limitations of Bergman's work.

Near the beginning of a film devoted to portraying the inner anguish of an individual, defined in terms of personal psychology, the notion of "world revolution" is reduced in passing to a game for fourteen-year-olds; no possible connection is suggested between the two. Of the three gay characters, two are presented as stereotypical. (The treatment of the actor, Michael Stromberg, is more detailed and sympathetic in the published script, which one might read as a sign that Bergman was actually repressing his own sense of other possibilities in the finished film; the sympatheticness, however, takes the form of suggesting that the character shares in the general anguish.) The third, the character portrayed by Erland Josephsson, is presented favorably by Bergman, the penalty for which is that his gayness is essentially monogamous—a minimal adaptation of the dominant sexual ideology—and that he suffers. Any possible alternative to the dominant ideological assumptions about relationships is firmly put down. We are left with the familiar Bergman pattern: the heroine, tormented in adulthood by her experiences as a child, moves toward forgiveness and reconciliation across the generations. In Bergman's world, as nothing can be changed, all that people can hope for is to learn to forgive each other for the pain they inflict.

I suspect that, were I to reread my early books, the one on Hawks would embarrass me least. By and large, I continue to admire the same Hawks films I admired when I wrote it, for some of the same reasons, and my delight in them is undiminished. My way of seeing them, however, has changed and widened somewhat.

First, I want to consider the ambiguous relation of Hawks's work to the dominant ideology. In some ways the films are very firmly and obviously within the ideology: sexist (they celebrate masculinity, and, however aggressive the women may be, male dominance is always reasserted at the end) and racist (white Americanness is a taken-for-granted token of superiority, and foreigners are either comic or subservient, and frequently both). These are more Hollywood than Hawks, though of course one can't clearly separate the two; they could be paralleled in the work of most mainstream American directors. Though they have to be noted, it seems legitimate to place the emphasis on the Hawksian particularities, the features that distinguish him.

The films might be said to belong loosely to an alternative American tradition (represented at its best by *Huckleberry Finn* and at its worst by Hemingway) that says no to established society, to the development of civilization conceived as the supreme good. What is striking is the almost total absence in the films of home, marriage, and family—and not only concretely but as concepts. The opposition between the adventure films and the comedies has been perceived in various ways, but both have in common the rejection of established order. The adventure films create an alternative order, cut off from mainstream civilization, centered on the male group; the comedies subvert order, throwing everything into chaos. The two sets of films are by and large very different in tone and rhythm. The adventure films are leisurely, measured, with an overall serenity that grows steadily up to *Rio Bravo* and *Hatari!* and then decreases abruptly in the films of Hawks's old age; the comedies are fast, frenetic, tense, with hysteria constantly threatened and sometimes taking over. In both sets the concept of chaos is important, but it is quite differently defined. In the adventure films it is *out there* (the Andes mountains, the Arctic wastes, etc.) and menacing; in the comedies it is *inside,* a positive force awaiting its chance to disrupt the established order, appalling yet also exhilarating and liberating.

The role of women in Hawks's films is always problematic. In many respects they remain male fantasy figures; no one would wish to claim them for the feminist cause, despite their aliveness and independence. With very few exceptions (*Red Line 7000*, e.g.), the women are always hostile to each other, unable to unite, conceived as instant, automatic rivals for the male, as in *Only Angels Have Wings* and *To Have and Have Not*. Their great interest—apart from the intensely vivid and dynamic, if male-oriented, performances Hawks usually gets from his actresses—lies in the total absence, in the adventure films at least, of any logical role for them. The point becomes very clear if one juxtaposes them with John Ford's women, who have a very well-defined, thoroughly traditional role: they are wives and mothers, mainstay of the home, at once the motivation behind the building of civilization and the guarantee of its continuance and transmission. In Hawks there is no positively conceived civilization, no home, no marriage. Woman becomes problematic by her very presence—which in Hawks is always a very insistent presence, far removed from the little lady left waving tearfully goodbye at the start to await the hero's return at the end. Hawks's solution (always uneasy, never satisfying, but central to the vitality of the films) is to break down as far as possible the division between male and female; always, in the adventure films, by making the woman aggressive and "masculine."

Many critics have noted a gay subtext running through Hawks's work, constantly suppressed, yet always insisting on some form of ambiguous, half-grudging expression. It goes right back to the silent period. *Fig Leaves* contains a remarkable scene in which a man "acts" a woman in a mock courtship with his friend; *A Girl in Every Port* (which actually ends with the woman ousted and the male relationship reaffirmed at her expense) was the first of two films Hawks has described as "a love story between men." He has of course never acknowledged gayness in his films and would repudiate any suggestion of it; nonetheless, one might see the term *love story* as a giveaway.

There are obvious examples of male relations so close as to become at least sexually ambiguous: Thomas Mitchell's feeling for Cary Grant in *Only Angels Have Wings*, or Kirk Douglas and Dewey Martin in the other "love story between men," *The Big Sky*. There is also, from the forties on, a whole procession of young male actors, usually playing second fiddle or sidekick to the hero (but the relationship always characterized by an underlying tension or conflict—that conflict in which, according to *Bringing Up Baby*'s psychiatrist, the love impulse expresses itself), who are fairly obvious gay icons in appearance and behavior, if not always in offscreen actuality: Montgomery Clift, Dewey Martin, Ricky Nelson, the young James Caan.

In view of this continually present, half-suppressed, sexual ambiguity in both male and female roles, the notion of chaos in Hawks—and the films' ambivalent attitudes to it—takes on a new interest. It is closely connected to one of the most striking, consistent, and peculiar features of his work: the fascination with role reversal. This takes a great variety of forms. In *Gentlemen Prefer Blondes* and *The Ransom of Red Chief* (Hawks's episode in *O. Henry's Full House*), the reversal is between child and adult; in *Monkey Business* and *Hatari!* the sophisticated and the primitive change places, become reversible, the distinction blurred. Most striking here is Elsa Martinelli's initiation into the Warusha tribe, and the subsequent scene where her tribal paint is replaced with cold cream. *Hatari!* also reverses humans and animals; it opens with truck and jeep converging on a rhinoceros, and ends (almost) with baby elephants converging on a woman. Most bizarrely and puzzlingly, one has in *The Thing* the reversal of human and vegetable.

But most pervasive—and surely the crucial and explanatory instance—is the reversal, in film after film, of male and female. Existing within sexist ideology, the films never manage to assert equality: it is funny for men to dress as women, but generally attractive for women to dress as men (and they are in uniform, not drag). Yet the notion of potential reversibility is very strong. One small, intriguing point: the interchangeability of Angie Dickinson in *Rio Bravo* and James Caan in *El Dorado*. Both are conceived in terms of their relationship to John Wayne, a relationship based on both affection and antagonism; both are gamblers; both are seen doing the same bit of business with a pack of cards; both are identified partly by their idiosyncratic adornments (Dickinson by her feathers, Caan by a picturesque hat); both follow or stand by Wayne after they have been dismissed—in the long tradition of Hawks's heroines. And both have the same line of dialogue, addressed in both cases to Wayne: "I always make you mad, don't I?"

The logical end of the characterizing tendencies of Hawks's work is bisexuality: the ultimate overthrow of social order, and the essential meaning of the chaos the films both fear and celebrate. Ultimately it is always contained (Andrew Britton would say "repressed") within Hawks's classicism, which is also the classicism of presixties Hollywood. Yet it seems to me nevertheless the secret source of the oeuvre's richness, vitality, and fascination.

Notes

1 Robin Wood and Michael Walker, *Claude Chabrol* (New York: Praeger, 1970), 103–12.

2 Andrew Britton, "Sexuality and Power or the Two Others," *Framework* 6 (Autumn 1977), 7–11, 39; and "Sexuality and Power," *Framework* 7/8 (Spring 1978), 5–11.

3 Philip Strick, "review of Robin Wood, *Personal Views: Exploration in Film* [London: Gordon Fraser, 1976]," in *Sight and Sound* 45, no. 4 (Autumn 1976): 258.

4 Norman O. Brown, *Life Against Death: The Psychoanalytical Meaning of History* (Middleton, Conn.: Wesleyan University Press, 1959).

5 Robin Wood, *Ingmar Bergman* (New York: Praeger, 1969) and *Howard Hawks* (London: Secker and Warburg, 1968, revised edition London: BFI, 1981).

6 Jean Renoir, *Renoir, My Father,* trans. Rudolph and Dorothy Weaver (Boston: Little, Brown, 1962).

7 Jean Renoir, "A Certain Grace," in *The Rules of the Game: A Film by Jean Renoir,* trans. John McGrath and Maureen Titelbaum (London: Lorrimer, 1970), 13.

8 Ingmar Bergman, *Bergman on Bergman* (New York: Simon and Schuster, 1973).

9 Andrew Sarris, *Village Voice* 23 March 1967, 25.

Lesbians

and

Film

Edith Becker, Michelle Citron, Julia Lesage, and B. Ruby Rich

I t sometimes seems to us that lesbianism is the hole in the heart of feminist film criticism. We have been working in this area for a number of years, and while we believe that feminist criticism has developed new theoretical tools for examining cinematic images, structures, and themes, nevertheless we see a failure to confront lesbian issues.

It is important, and possible, to begin this work now. The space for such a discussion has been made possible by the evolution of the lesbian movement, both as an autonomous development and in conjunction with feminist, Left, and gay male struggles. The intellectual and political groundwork has been established, within the lesbian movement, and we can now draw on this for its application to film. Furthermore, there is now a clear audience and support for such film criticism. The creation of a lesbian film criticism is particularly urgent, given the intensified use of the lesbian as a negative sign in Hollywood movies and the continuing space assigned to lesbians as gratification of male fantasy in pornography and a distressing number of male avant-garde films. Equally important as an impetus for a new criticism is the rise of an independent lesbian cinema, underacknowledged and in need of attention.

Jump Cut has analyzed film practice in our society and its role in reinforcing oppressions based on race, sex, or class. Acknowledging connections between the individual psyche and social history, we find it useful to examine film as a cultural institution that excessively promotes as a norm the single option of heterosexuality. The articulation of sexuality is neither natural nor inevitable; it is shaped and determined by a given society within a particular historical moment. (See, e.g., Weimar Germany or fifth-century Greece for notable examples of difference.)

Lesbians are sharks, vampires, creatures from the deep lagoon, godzillas, hydrogen bombs, inventions of the laboratory, werewolves—all of whom stalk Beverly Hills by night. Christopher Lee, in drag, in the Hammer Films middle-period, is my ideal lesbian.

—Bertha Harris

This historically determined sexuality may be expressed personally between individuals or enforced publicly through institutions. It is always disguised as "natural" to mask its ideological function. What we consider entertainment depends in large part on our expectations of sexual identity and its depiction in film. Yet film's role in enforcing heterosexuality has hardly been challenged.

Feminist film criticism has analyzed film texts and film reception to explicate women's place within male culture and to extricate us from that place. Unfortunately, such criticism has too often accepted heterosexuality as its norm. The refusal to deal with a lesbian perspective has warped film criticism as well as the larger political and intellectual context, including discussions of ideology, popular culture, and psychoanalysis. A lesbian perspective, however, can connect in new ways our views of culture, fantasy and desire, and women's oppression, clarifying how these replicate a patriarchal power structure and how that, in turn, finds expression on the screen.

The seemingly simple replacement of the subject *woman* with the subject *lesbian* radically redefines feminist film criticism. When the topic is the *image of* the *lesbian* in film or the *function of* the *lesbian* in the text, whole different issues have to be approached. Whole new critical methodologies must be found to deal with these issues.

Mainstream Film and the Suppression of Positive Images

Lesbians are nearly invisible in mainstream cinematic history, except as evil or negative-example characters. There is the lesbian as villainess, exemplified in films such as *Windows* (1978). There is the lesbian as vampire, both metaphorically (as in Claude Chabrol's *Les Biches,* 1967, or Roberto Rossellini's *Rome, Open City,* 1944–45) and quite literally, as in the genre of lesbian vampire movies. There is the brutal bull dyke, ranging from the dyke in *Touch of Evil* (1958) who just wants to watch to the dyke in *Farewell My Lovely* (1944) who insists on action. As feminist critics we should pay attention to these negative images because they are not only about lesbianism but, in fact, are about the containment of women's sexuality and independence.

Furthermore, negative stereotypes about lesbians have a lot to teach us about the limitations of any "positive image" approach to the depiction of women in Hollywood film. These limitations come from the fact that positive images, like negative images, suppress contradiction and are thus static. For example, *Julia* (1977) does not develop the complexities of being a writer, or the contradictions of being a political organizer and mother, or the complexities of being lesbians (if in fact they are). We are just asked to admire the female protagonists. Another limitation could be demonstrated by imagining the substitution of lesbians into most of the stories we have on television or in film. For example, if one of Charlie's Angels were a lesbian, this would probably not change the blatant sexism or bourgeois ideology of the show, or its emphasis on individual solutions to social problems.

There are instances in which we could imagine the progressive nature of substitution. For example, the substitution of a lesbian couple for a heterosexual one could in fact substantially alter the narrative structures of film romance. Yet the economic pressures of marketing and film production guarantee that in a homophobic society, any authentic "positive image" of lesbian romantic love remains too great a risk ever to find direct expression on the screen. *Windows,* for instance, displaces lesbian attraction, turning its expression into violence. Mainstream cinema employs a traditional dichotomy of positive/negative, using allegedly lesbian villainesses to punish those characters who deviate from the norms of domesticity or romantic love. Heterosexuality is the positive, lesbianism the negative.

Ironically, then, the most explicit vision of lesbianism has been left to pornography, where the lesbian loses her menace and becomes a turn-on. Men maintain control over women by creating the fantasy images of women that they need. Pornography "controls" and uses lesbianism by defining it purely as a form of genital sexuality that, in being watched, can thereby be recuperated into male fantasy. As long as lesbianism remains a component of pornography made by and for men, lesbian sexuality will be received by most sectors of the dominant society *as* pornography. Still, pornographic codes are not omnipresent. They cannot be granted so much power that the depiction of sexuality is no longer an option for lesbian filmmakers.

Lesbians are women who survive without men financially and emotionally, representing the ultimate in an independent life style. Lesbians are the women who battle day by day to show that women are valid human beings, not just appendages of men. . . . Lesbians are the women who are penalized for their sexuality more than any other women on earth.

—Sidney Abbott and Barbara Love

If the love relationship between women is too often a negative image, it would seem logical to look to cinematic portrayals of women's friendships as an alternative. However, female friendship is itself limited in cinema. In the multitude of buddy films, pairs of men get to act out their adventure fantasies. Women's friendships in film, on the other hand, bear comparison with the types of sisters in patriarchal literature, described by Louise Bernikow in *Among Women* (New York: Harmony Books, 1980). Like those sisters, women friends are shown as either trying to get "the man's something" and fighting over who gets it (*All About Eve*, 1950), turning against each other (*The Women*, 1939), sacrificing self to familial devotion (*Little Women*, 1949), or accepting the judgment of Paris that splits women into narrowly defined "I'm this/you're that" sets of roles (*The Turning Point*, 1977).

In cinema, even women's friendships revolve around men. Just as the supposed visibility of *woman* and *lesbian* in film has turned out to be fraudulent, so cinematic friendships between women are equally illusionary (with the exception of rare token scenes in such films as *Mildred Pierce*, 1945, or *Coal Miner's Daughter*, 1980). None of the richness of women's real relations appears.

It is revealing to chart the pairings that are either acceptable or unacceptable in popular films, as shown in the accompanying figure. Both extremes of the spectrum—authentic portrayals of lesbianism or gay male relations—fall out of bounds for the dominant cinema. In categories 2 and 5, there is a discrepancy at work: the idealization of male friendships and debasement of female friendships. The only honorable categories left to the skewed middle of the chart are predictably male/female friendship, male/male friendship, and male/female coupling. Women don't fare very well in these three categories. Women may appear as a momentary diversion in the buddy films. Women have traditionally been kept in line through family ties and romantic love. In the films that depict male/female friendship, women form an alliance with men that mirrors the power balance in the larger society: in other words, the friendship is a mentor-student model (as in *Norma Rae*, 1979). Or the friendship may simply provide the foreplay for eventual romance (as in *The Electric Horseman*, 1980). Even worse is the male/female friendship that women form at the expense of their friendships with other women, whom the man now replaces (as in *Kramer vs. Kramer*, 1980).

The suppression of categories 1 and 2 suggests the reality of the very continuum between lesbians and other women that the dominant cinema usually takes pains to deny. Perhaps the real taboo is not sexuality between women, but the affirmation of *any* associations between women that are primary and exclusive of men. Or perhaps the potential for sexuality between women is itself so strong a threat that it blocks the depiction of even female friendship.

The world of women is banned from film. Female associations could include

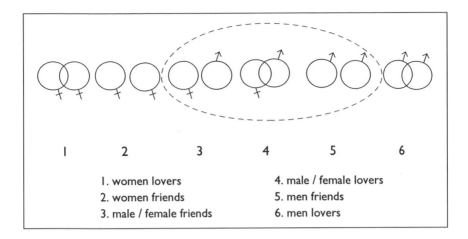

1. women lovers
2. women friends
3. male / female friends
4. male / female lovers
5. men friends
6. men lovers

intellectual relations, work projects, or emotional exchanges. Presumably, lesbians deserve visibility in these contexts, but mainstream cinema makes that impossible by separating off the *lesbian* as a being not only defined by, but limited to, her sexuality. Films don't show lesbians working together because that provides no voyeuristic interest for the male viewer. Straight women working together provide just as little interest. Traditionally women are represented in cinema almost exclusively as sexual objects for the use of the male character within the film and/or the man in the audience. Therefore, the depiction of women (whether heterosexual or lesbian) in primary association with each other would be profoundly discomforting and likely to provoke the use of *lesbian* as a derogatory label, because women are acting as self-defined beings, not reacting to men.

Given the absence of any real lesbian "image" on the screen, the lesbian audience over the years has had to make do by identifying with portrayals of strong female characters, adventurous male characters, or occasional women's friendships. It's often a case of settling for crumbs. One source of pleasure has been the rare scene of an actress with a cult reputation acting out that rumored sexuality on the screen, such as Marlene Dietrich kissing another woman in *Morocco* (1930).

My only books
Were women's looks.
—Nathalie Barney

The Film Subtext and Gossip

The most important viewing strategy has been to concentrate on the subtext, the "hidden" meaning, of commercial films. The notion of the lesbian subtext depends on the knowledge, suspicion, or hope that some participants in the film (director, actress, screenwriter) were themselves lesbians, and that their perspective can be discerned in the film even though disguised. Subtexting, then, depends for its cues on gossip.

Gossip provides the official unrecorded history of lesbian participation in film. Actresses and directors have had to hide their identity in order to preserve their careers in a homophobic society. For actresses, the star system has depended on a vast public's fantasy identification with the glamourous woman; the knowledge that the star was a lesbian would have ended her career. With the advent of the sound-film era and the massive industrialization of film production and distribution, a time when most women directors were drummed out of the field as a financial liability, being openly lesbian was obviously out of the question.

Knowing a director's sexual identity does not necessarily provide a formula for interpreting the work. A film by a lesbian director or writer may or may not advance "positive" lesbian characters; it may have no lesbian content at all. On the other hand, *not* to know details of lesbian participation in film production is a problem in constructing any solid lesbian history. One example is the case of Dorothy Arzner, Hollywood's only woman career director of the 1920s through the 1940s, whose style of dress and attention to independent woman characters in her films have prompted the search for a lesbian subtext in her work—despite the careful absence of any statements by Arzner herself that could encourage such an undertaking.

In the case of directors whose work isn't specifically feminist, whose lives are strictly closeted, or in the case of lesbian actresses enacting prescribed roles, the burden of proof for a lesbian analysis frequently depends on the interpretation of style. One example would be the silent film *Salome* (1923), produced by its star Alla Nazimova, whose lesbianism is discussed in Kenneth Anger's book *Hollywood Babylon* (San Francisco: Straight Arrow Books, 1975) and caricatured in Ken Russell's film *Valentino* (1977). *Salome*'s mannered acting, art nouveau costumes and set design, and all-homosexual cast combine to evoke the homosexual aesthetic of the Oscar Wilde, Aubrey Beardsley circle.

The lesbian viewer may also pay attention to the frequence of disjunction between actress and role within a film: that is, an actress with a lesbian reputation may act "out of character" and seem to address the audience from the standpoint of her off-screen persona despite her supposed on-screen heterosexuality. A glance, a costume, a gesture, is enough to give the cue.

Gossip feeds into audience expectation and interpretation. Long denigrated in our culture, gossip nevertheless serves a crucial purpose in the survival of subcultural identity within an oppressive society. If oral history is the history of those denied control of the printed record, gossip is the history of those who cannot even speak in their own first-person voice. While gossip transpires at the private level of conversation, subtexting is the route by which dominant cultural products can be used to serve subcultural needs, by annexing a mass product (movies) alien to lesbian identity.

Given the importance of subcultural identification, much lesbian film viewing and criticism depends on subtexting. Such readings can be valuable and accurate. They can resolve ambiguities otherwise inexplicable in the film text. Or they can construct alternate explications. Lesbian criticism casts a jaundiced eye on self-important heterosexual rituals and in so doing can illuminate the psychosexual structuring of cultural production with the particular clarity of the outsider. However, at other times, subtextual readings can be erroneous. This is a problem, not only for lesbian criticism, but for feminist film criticism in general. For instance, sometimes feminist readings exceed the subtextual and become fantasy projections, as in one woman's reading of *Star Wars* (1977) as a matriarchal vision. Other times, heterosexual elements of a film are ignored to preserve a lesbian reading, as in one reading of *Little Darlings* (1980) that sees the title characters as little dykes. More serious is the practice of praising films as indictments of the evils awaiting women who engage in heterosexuality, without recognizing to what extent such films actively further the oppression of women. Seeing *Looking for Mr. Goodbar* (1977), for example, as a warning against heterosexual dating games fails to take seriously the real misogyny and degradation of women central to the film. Subtextual readings are important to the formation of an alternate criticism but, to be convincing, must remember to keep the film in sight.

The Lesbian Filmmaker

Some feminist filmmakers have rejected the rigid sexual roles presented in commercial and documentary films and shown a great flexibility in depicting women's lives, desires, and fantasies. The weakened boundaries of sexual definition in these films mark an advance. For example, French director Nelly Kaplan in her earlier film *A Very Curious Girl* (1967) assigned a lesbian character the same traits as an exploitative man. In her more recent film *Nea* (1976), however, she has a mistreated wife reject her patriarchal husband in favor of a more satisfying lesbian relationship with his sister. The film is fascinating for its attempt to take on the issue of sexuality without hedging, though the sensationalistic aspects of some of the treatment are perhaps questionable.

What is a lesbian? A lesbian is the rage of all women condensed to the point of explosion. She is the woman who, often beginning at an extremely early age, acts in accordance with her inner compulsion to be a more complete and freer human being than her society— perhaps then, but certainly later—cares to allow her. She may not be fully conscious of the political implications of what for her began as personal necessity, but on some level she has not been able to accept the limitations and oppressions laid on her by the most basic role of her society—the female role.

—Radicalesbians

In the German film *The Second Awakening of Christa Klages* (1978) Margarethe von Trotta traces the revival of a friendship between a woman fugitive and her high school friend at a time of need. The heroine shifts in the course of the film from hiding out with her male sidekick (who gets killed) to running off to Portugal with her high school girlfriend in a relationship that is suggested as a lesbian one. Also, Hungarian director Marta Mészáros has consistently made films devoted to the rich friendship between women. Because of her very pessimistic depictions of heterosexual relations and her visual attention to the sensuality of women's bodies, the dynamic between women retains a sexual potential even though such a development is never played out within the films themselves.

Occasionally, in documentary film as well there has been a lessening of censorship regarding the lesbian presence. *We're Alive* (1975) presents women prisoners collectively shaping their own film and offering combined Left, lesbian, and feminist analyses of their own conditions. The film doesn't separate out the lesbian experience into a separate category. Such fluidity of sexual boundaries is an encouraging sign in feminist filmmaking.

Most feminist films, however, try to challenge male dominance without being self-conscious of their own suppression of lesbianism or, in some cases, homophobia. In *Girl Friends* (1978) the lesbian character is a negative cartoon introduced only to be rejected. Overt homophobia is rare in comparison with the more subtle suppression—total absence. For example, weren't *any* of the women in the Women's Emergency Brigade documented in *With Babies and Banners*

(1978) lesbians? Lesbianism is not a subject of interest to New Day Films, the single largest feminist distributor of documentary films in the United States. Lesbian issues are not addressed in the films, the word does not appear in their catalog, and only rarely does any woman even appear to be a lesbian in the interviews and portraits that form their film treatments of social issues. It would be foolish to expect heterosexual feminists to produce lesbian films, but if their films are meant to describe the reality of women's experience, they must include lesbians as a part of that reality.

It is to the lesbian filmmaker we must look for consistent lesbian visibility and the political and aesthetic questions such a visibility poses. What is the context of production for lesbian filmmakers? Independent lesbian filmmakers have problems that (a) all independents have: money, equipment and distribution; (b) all women have: technical deprivation, access, accountability to the demands of a political movement; (c) all lesbians have: self-denial, risk of censorship, retaliation.

Production problems confronting lesbians have both external and internal sources. The risk of economic blacklisting is an ever present one for the lesbian filmmaker, who may lie on a grant application only to find that, once the "real" film is made, she is cut off from funding sources for a future project. Or she may never know, when rejected for money for an accurately described script, whether homophobia was the reason for the lack of funding. Also, existing distribution markets for sixteen-millimeter independent films can hardly be seen to constitute a receptive environment for lesbian films. Libraries, schools, and cable television may be able to absorb broadly based feminist works, but they screen out lesbian work either because of their own homophobia or as a conservative response to their constituency.

External and internal problems cannot be artificially separated. Sometimes, self-censorship occurs as a pragmatic handling of political goals and market realities on the part of a filmmaker. For example, *The Power of Men Is the Patience of Women* (1978) is a German film dramatizing the problem of battered women, the importance of women's shelters, and collective alternatives. Director Cristina Perinciola decided to show clearly the double-headed axe (a symbol of lesbian identity) worn by one of the women in the film as a code for lesbian viewers, while at the same time to omit any other reference to lesbianism. This was a deliberate move to ensure the film was televised. It is an interesting solution for maintaining a visibility for the lesbian community given the political urgency of maximum exposure of the issue of wife beating (particularly through the medium of television, to reach women who may in fact not even be able to leave the house). Still, this is a stopgap measure and not an ideal solution.

Is it sapphism which nourishes her intelligence, or is it her intelligence which makes her a lesbian?

— Jean Roycrc

There is a persistent dilemma in lesbians' internalizing the societal homophobia with which all our lives are saturated. Such an internalization may result in conscious or unconscious self-censorship, self-denial, or, in extreme instances, self-hatred. The issue of inhibition is part of the ongoing struggle in forgoing a lesbian identity and, as such, is part of an ongoing discussion within the lesbian community.

The lesbian independent filmmaker has not found the worlds of Left political filmmaking or avant-garde film hospitable, regardless of what her own concerns politically or aesthetically may be. In the "political" camp, lesbianism has been rated a low "personal" priority on the political agenda. The Left has too often given a clear message that lesbianism isn't important.

In the "avant-garde" camp, lesbianism isn't treated any better than in Hollywood or pornography. Werner Nekes's *T(wo) Men,* Steve Dwoskin's *Chinese Checkers,* and Jim Benning's *11 × 14* all use the depiction of lesbian sexuality (usually a fraudulent one) as the hook to hold audience interest through their formal experimentations. Moreover, innovative lesbian films are likely to be marginalized or discounted within avant-garde film circles because of their charged content. With "content" still more or less a modernist taboo for avant-garde filmmakers, the lesbian filmmaker is likely to find her formal contributions made invisible. Moreover, avant-garde filmmaking remains one of the last strongholds of the "sensitive artist" tradition, which is by definition male and still mitigates strongly against feminists and certainly against lesbians.

Because lesbians' films don't fit into the existing distribution networks for independent Left or avant-garde films, there is still a large body of lesbian work that has yet to break out of its local audience into visible distribution.

Toward a Lesbian Cinema

Lesbians, historically bereft of cultural, political and moral contexts, have especially relied on imaginative literature to dream themselves into situations of cultural, political and moral power. Twenty years ago, without Molly Bolt, we were Rhett Butler and Stephen Gordon and the Count of Monte Cristo. It is, of course, much more to the point to be Molly Bolt—or Patience and Sarah or Mrs. Stevens. The trouble with this process (vulgarly referred to as "identifying with") is that while the new lesbian hero is certainly safer for our mental health than Rhett or the Count or Stephen—we do not have to associate power and adventure with the penis any longer; we do not have to call on God to cure us of "inversion" and wear male underwear any longer—and while we see her operating in what some might very loosely call a "cultural" context of tree-hugging, feminist folk/rock, vegetarianism and goddess-worship, her aggressive, strong, even magnificent image is by and large taken on by her beholder still inside the heterosexual/patriarchal definition of moral and political reality. Lesbian literature is not a matter of a woman plus a woman in bed.

—Bertha Harris

At this point, the paucity of lesbian visibility in films has made the presentation of a "positive" lesbian subject a serious priority for lesbian filmmakers. Earlier we talked about the problems in seeking "positive images" of lesbians in Hollywood films: this becomes a very different issue when discussing lesbian filmmakers and movement films. Affirmation has been and remains vital. The most common form this affirming of identity has taken in lesbian filmmaking is the coming-out film. Coming out has been a central ritual of the lesbian movement, and the films by lesbians quantitatively reflect this. Such films offer a public expression of personal experience and are one component of a lesbian culture that shapes, supports, and politicizes personal change and self-definition. We must not underestimate the need for films to affirm all aspects of lesbian identity, given the virulent hostility against lesbians in our society. Films are required to reclaim history, offer self-definition, and create alternative visions.

The expression of self implicitly includes a struggle against the dominant ideology. An oppressed group, once able to make films, will create positive images both to offer the new self-identity and also to combat the negative stereotypes promulgated by the dominant culture. Therefore, positive images cannot be cut off from the societal pressures that created the original stereotypes or the conditions that maintain them. A positive image of lesbian motherhood is constructed in *In the Best Interests of the Children* (1977), a documentary film made by Liz Stevens and Frances Reid. Such a portrayal of lesbian mothers cannot be cut off from the societal context, that is, the legal battle by lesbian mothers to retain custody of their children. The film was made to serve those custody suits. For this political reason, the filmmakers also chose to film in a traditional documentary mode for maximum credibility, accessibility, and persuasiveness with the particular audience (lawyers, juries, social workers) intended for the film. In this sense, the film has been very successful. It has also provided a boost in morale for many beleaguered lesbian mothers caught in the same legal traps. On the other hand, the documentary can be criticized for precisely this positive approach, that is, for presenting lesbian mothers as perfect, for not articulating their anger, and for leaving an overly optimistic impression of the current situation. However, this film should not have to bear the weight of our entire expectations of what a film about lesbian motherhood might be. Other films can, and should, be made.

Lesbian: A term understood to mean a woman who relates sexually and emotionally to other women.

—Barbara Ponse

One need is for films that deal with variation, complex identities, and contradiction—all outside the scope of the "positive image" approach. Lesbian films cannot be considered outside the context of the lesbian community. Within this community, we face daily contradictions (passing as straight at work but being out with friends, public oppression vs. private pleasure, or the seeming contradiction of multiple political commitments). The recognition and working through of conflict is a process that is essential to political and personal growth, and one that our films could be aiding. Unsolved problems, anger, unpleasant decisions, fights, and other messy material are all dealt with in our lives and could be portrayed on the screen as well. Barbara Hammer's film *Double Strength* (1978), for instance, approaches the question of lesbian relationships, love, and romanticism. Jan Oxenberg's films, in particular, pull humor out of a hatful of contradictions. Susana Blaustein's self-portrait, *Susana* (1980), wittily visualizes the conflict between her lesbian lifestyle and traditional Argentine family values that is precipitated by her sister's visit. We need more films that deal with the contradictions, details, and pleasures of lesbian life.

What about all the aspects of lesbian life that haven't yet made it into the movies? We have yet to see any film about that venerable mainstay of lesbian culture, the bars. Despite a network of lesbian and gay history projects, research has yet to inform lesbian filmmaking: for example, the slide show "Lesbian Masquerade: Women Who Passed as Men in Early San Francisco" could provide the basis for a wonderful film on the phenomenon of "passing women." Again, looking to history, the presence of lesbians in the suffragette movement has yet to be explored in film. Films are still needed to write lesbians back into history, to include the lives of lesbians on welfare, lesbians fighting nationalist struggles, lesbians of color, . . . lesbians contributing to struggles both inside and outside the lesbian movement per se. The lesbian imagination is certainly not limited to the traditionally political. Lesbian films could explore the interior of a lesbian household or formally study the textures of daily life.

Since lesbians are trying to live lives that reflect new value systems, there is a need for lesbian films that match those value systems both in the range of subject matter and stylistically. Lesbian literature offers an example of new visions, styles, textures, and tonalities. Just as lesbian writers have discovered new linguistic structures and narrative styles that both express the lesbian imagination and refute the dominance of patriarchal writing, so must lesbian filmmakers take on this task. A lesbian film style could reveal the interlocking structures in characters' lives and bring a nonoppressive approach to image making and reception. Fantasy and visionary art are sources of strength, used by lesbians "to dream themselves" into power. Utopianism has both positive and negative connotations, both true: it can be a flight from social change, but can also be a beacon of inspiration. More films need to take up the foundation laid by Monique Wittig, Verena Stefan, and Olga Broumas in literature.

For lesbian filmmakers, the tension between creating new forms and maintaining contact with the audience they serve is ever present. Often, contact has been maintained by the use of already acceptable forms. Yet it is important to develop new forms to suit the meaning of the films and not rely solely on existing narrative or documentary styles. Issues, styles, and priorities change as more lesbian films come into being. The work is already beginning.

Eroticism and Pornography

While lesbian filmmaking is not solely "a matter of a woman plus a woman in bed," nevertheless sexuality cannot and should not be avoided. For the lesbian community, the cinematic depiction of sexuality poses a particular problem. It is important to name this element of lesbianism for what it is, to articulate its nature, and to give positive models of lesbian sexuality for younger women coming out. But how can this be reconciled with the objectification of such sexuality in film and the visual arts (from Helmut Newton's high-class porn photography to advertisements for Twin Sisters scotch)? The visualization of nonvoyeuristic, authentic lesbian lovemaking should be attempted. But, paradoxically, the continued existence of pornography still clouds the depiction of sexuality.

The representation of women's bodies in art and film has been an issue of concern to feminist critics (see Lucy R. Lippard on body art in *From the Center: Feminist Essays on Women's Art* [New York: Dutton, 1976]). Owing to a history of patriarchal art, to the visual coding of our society, and to the presence of a male audience, it sometimes seems that the attempt for women to reclaim our bodies is doomed. In feminist film such an assessment has often led to a turning away from the depiction of heterosexual lovemaking, because of its inherent power relations and the difficulty in trying to create a new visual iconography to alter those relations.

The meaning of our love for women is what we have constantly to expand.

—Adrienne Rich

Lesbian filmmakers are faced with a different situation. The all-woman environment on the screen and in the audience defines sexuality within a lesbian context and therefore should pose no problem to the representation of lesbian lovemaking. It would seem that lesbian filmmakers have no need for puritanism. Even in this context, however, lesbian viewers may still feel themselves made vulnerable by the open sexuality on the screen. French novelist and filmmaker Christiane Rochefort is clear about the reason: "Because we don't want men to look at what we do, I cut the intimate scenes."

The problem is present for the audience as much as for the filmmaker. Feeling so often under siege in society, it is hard to relax in a safehouse. Films showing lesbian lovemaking are vital to the lesbian filmmaker and lesbian community, yet there are always concerns as to what use outside the intended context the film can be put. Aware of how men misappropriate lesbian films, some filmmakers have sought to restrict screenings of films with lesbian lovemaking to all-woman audiences, as in the case of Barbara Hammer's *Dyketactics* (1974). Although unrestrictive of audience, Belgian filmmaker Chantal Akerman tried in her early film *Je, tu, il, elle* (1974) to construct a fresh nonvoyeuristic image of lesbian lovemaking. Yet critics, on the whole, have discussed the film with pornography as their singular reference point, indicating the limitations of the artist's intention. What distinguishes both *Je, tu, il, elle* and *Dyketactics* from other depictions of lesbian lovemaking in film is their visual and editing styles, as well as the presence of the filmmaker as participant in the scene, which conveys an insider's point of view.

Since lesbian sexuality is different from heterosexuality, films about it done from a lesbian perspective rather than an outsider's perspective will have to be different in both form and content. By using visual and musical coding associated with pornography, the lesbian lovemaking scenes in Connie Beeson's *Holding* have been easily co-opted into theatrical marketing for a mass audience. At other times, paradoxically, mass audience films can be appropriated in part by the lesbian audience. The racist soft-core hit *Emmanuelle* (1974) contained scenes of lesbian eroticism that were accepted as satisfying by many lesbian viewers. They could be appropriated, perhaps, because they were suggestively erotic rather than explicitly pornographic: the women were neither naked nor in bed.

While it would be inappropriate to divert our attention here into a lengthy debate on the distinctions between pornography and erotic film, we could mention a few points. The objectification of women and the enactment of male/female power relations are basic to pornography. Furthermore, lesbian depictions within pornography are predicated on standards alien to lesbian sexuality, such as making a fetish of genital sex or displacing emotional involvement. Pornography's exploitative style (of lighting, camera angle, and editing) obstructs the possibility of erotic enjoyment. The differences between eroticism and pornography in film can only become clearer as more lesbian filmmakers present sexuality in their work. Nor is the filmmaker's attempt a vain one. The ideal remains of a visual image/style that could rupture even the patriarchal codes by which lesbian sexuality is read. Therefore it is important to keep co-optation from becoming intimidation.

Pornography is the extreme case, yet it points to a widespread phenomenon: the difficulty of defining the terms of lesbian experience when these very terms may mean one thing inside the women's community and something quite different in the gynophobic (woman-hating) society outside. Collective action inside is separatism outside; woman's anger inside is hysteria outside; autonomy inside is man hating outside. These contradictions cannot be avoided. They emerge whenever a period of struggle is in progress, whenever an oppressed people aggressively assumes the task of self-definition.

The Development of a Lesbian Identity

The lesbian struggle for self-definition has been in process for a long time in a variety of ways—organizationally, through publications, culturally, in music and poetry, in the bars—and in alliance with a number of other movements, particularly with gay male, Left, and feminist struggles. In the United States, any history must take into account the founding of the first lesbian organization in the country, the Daughters of Bilitis, in 1955, and its publication, *The Ladder*, published continuously from 1956 to 1972. The official position of the Daughters of Bilitis, brave for its time, stressed education to the general public about homosexuality, self-education, research projects in the social sciences, and lobbying for more tolerant legislation. Their emphasis on acceptance is very different from that of the best-known lesbian literary tradition, that of Nathalie Barney, Renée Vivien, and their coterie in Paris at the turn of the century. The

Paris circle's pride in and celebration of relations and sexual liaisons between women take no notice of heterosexual society, a luxury that its economic status permitted. These women were able to speak in their own voice early on, owing to class status, but it remained to the 1970s to offer equal opportunity.

These very different traditions, of political awareness and cultural pride, were finally brought together with the events leading into and out of the Stonewall resistance of 1969. At that event, in New York City, gay men and lesbians fought back against police, battling generations of police harassment. The political tradition of that night has been kept alive and furthered by annual Gay Pride Week events each June, with marches in cities all over the country; by organizations, like the Gay Liberation Front, and later the National Gay Task Force, or like the specifically media organization, the National Association of Lesbian and Gay Filmmakers; by actions, like those against the exhibition of *Windows* and the filming and opening of *Cruising* (1980); by national demonstrations, like the 14 October 1979 mass mobilization in Washington in defense of gay rights against the homophobic backlash and increasingly repressive legislation.

Within the Left, gays and lesbians have struggled against homophobia, both unconscious and deliberate. While many sectors of the gay and lesbian movement have a non- or anti-Leftist perspective, the presence of gays and lesbians in Left organizations and national solidarity movements, as well as the participation of gay and lesbian groups in Left coalitions, is significant.

The dominant context for the lesbian movement, of course, has been the women's movement, in which lesbian feminists have always been a major presence, from the earliest days of women's liberation to the present. However, that history has been scarred by continual eruptions between lesbians and straight women within the movement, resulting in purges and separate lesbian organizations. Nevertheless, leading in the formulation of feminist theory that critiques patriarchal society and its institutions of power, lesbians have been activists in all spheres of the movement: rape crisis work, battered women's shelters, women's health clinics, reproductive rights struggles, the organizing of women workers, and so on.

We have selected these events above not to provide a thumbnail history, but merely to put into context the discussion of lesbian aesthetics and film history, which cannot be divorced from the political and cultural ferment of its era. The development of a lesbian identity has been especially strong in art, poetry, literature, music, and philosophy. This development has occurred both within autonomous lesbian contexts and within the more generalized women's community, though any line of demarcation may be hard to fix.

Women's music offers an outstanding example of how women working together have created not only a pleasurable art form but the entire apparatus necessary to bring that art to its public, the women's community: women composers, musicians, technicians, producers (like the group of women who form Roadworks), recording companies (like Olivia Records), and distribution networks. Women's concerts and coffeehouses have provided a public space within which lesbian audiences can enjoy the creative articulation of a shared culture.

Though cultural, these spaces are also political. Without the journals, galleries, concerts, bars, publishing houses . . . there would be no basis for collective awareness or action, no evidence that things could be otherwise for lesbians in a society of mandatory heterosexuality.

Women have taken possession of the means of production in yet another way through the establishment of a number of publishing houses to ensure a free voice for feminist and lesbian writers. Similarly, lesbian journals have proliferated on both regional and national levels, as have feminist publications in general. On the regional level, the journals play a role in local political struggles, report on issues of interest to lesbians, publish local poetry and graphics, provide a directory for lesbian services, and advertise local businesses and bars. One national publication that follows this format of a news and culture blend is *Off Our Backs,* a magazine that has always maintained a strong political stance.

In 1976–77, four national journals were founded that have contributed to, discussed, and helped shape the renaissance in lesbian culture, theory, and politics: *Conditions,* "a magazine of writing by women with an emphasis on writing by lesbians"; *Chrysalis,* "a magazine of woman's culture"; *Heresies,* "a feminist publication on art and politics"; and *Sinister Wisdom,* "a journal of words and pictures for the lesbian imagination in all women." These journals all have a national readership, are handsomely produced, and focus much more on history, philosophical issues, and broad questions of aesthetics and culture than they do on current events or reporting. These journals are the mechanisms by which a network of feminist thought is spun across the country, establishing a common frame of reference.

The editors of *Heresies, Conditions,* and *Off Our Backs* have opened their publications to the concerns of black and Third World women's experiences. The issues of *Third World Women: The Politics of Being Other* (*Heresies* 8), *Conditions: 5: The Black Women's Issue,* and *Off Our Backs: Ain't I a Woman?* (vol. 10, no. 6) all confront the white feminist/lesbian movements to acknowledge the uniqueness and autonomy of our triply (by race, class, and sex) oppressed sisters. In the past, white movement women "have claimed that they could not find any women of color as an excuse for their all-whiteness," write the editors of *Conditions: 5.*

These excuses have dissolved as women "of color" substantiate their continued historical struggles through their diverse modes of artistic expression. If it is only in recent years that the publishers of these national women's journals have made the printing of these women's work a priority, how much longer will those who control the necessary, and more expensive, means for production and distribution of films remain racist, closed to black and Third World women? The relatively few films made by and about these women have yet to reach a mass distribution level. As the *Heresies* collective writes, because black and "Third World women are *other* than the majority and the power-holding class, and . . . have concerns *other* than those of white feminists, white artists and men" ("Editorial Statement," *Heresies* 2, no. 4, issue 8, 1.), their works remain ghettoized and are often found only within their original cultural community.

Naturally, black and Latina lesbians are not waiting for the rest of the movement to catch up: there have been black and Third World lesbian conferences in New York and Washington, D.C., in California, and groups such as the Combahee River Collective in Roxbury, Massachusetts, are engaged in ongoing work on the level of theory and practice. Happily, the lesbian and women's community as a whole is participating in the dialogue and not passively forcing Third World and black women to do all the work of education or confrontation.

There will always be differences in the perspectives of lesbians from differing races or class backgrounds. The ideal of a universal sisterhood does not necessitate the suppression of differences. Still, it is only now, with the greater participation of black and Third World lesbians, that we can discuss the degree to which a faulty universalization was previously practiced. While lesbians who are not white are less likely to perceive patriarchy as the *primary* enemy, their perspective on class and race oppression can only educate the lesbian movement about political realities.

As the lesbian movement progresses, and as lesbian filmmaking prospers, the kinds of lesbian films we are seeing are bound to change. As there is more of an interchange between filmmakers of all races, lesbian films will be more likely to reflect the connections in our society between homophobia, antifeminism, and the corresponding mechanisms of racism and class oppression. Lesbian films are passionately linked to the lesbian community, both in the sense of political struggle and in the banalities of daily life. It is that immediacy that gives the art its strength and the audience its pleasure. Lesbian filmmaking has begun to develop new editing strategies, tamper with traditional sound/image relations, and visualize new codes by which women's bodies can be seen. Only such a reassessment of film aesthetics can adequately serve the values of lesbian culture at this time. By moving beyond oppression to liberation, a true lesbian art form and an authentic lesbian aesthetic can emerge.

This is a filmmaking that is not reacting against older, heterosexual images of lesbianism. At the center of the new cinema, there must be a conscious sense of self. In turn, lesbian film theory must begin to dismantle some of the structures of current feminist film theory and film history in order to build a more inclusive foundation. Lesbian criticism can give voice to those things that have long remained silent and, in so doing, point out the extent to which previous feminist film criticism may still be bound into measuring by male or heterosexual standards. A true recognition of lesbianism would seriously challenge the concept of women as inevitable objects of exchange between men, or as fixed in an eternal trap of "sexual difference" based in heterosexuality.

Feminist theory that sees all women on the screen only as the objects of male desire—including, by implication, lesbians—is inadequate. This theoretical framework excludes lesbian experience, and it may in fact diminish the experience of all women.

I remember a scene. . . . This from a film I want to see. It is a film made by a woman about two women who live together. This is a scene from their daily lives. It is a film about the small daily transformations which women experience, allow, tend to, and which have been invisible in this male culture. In this film, two women touch. In all ways possible they show knowledge of what they have lived through and what they will yet do, and one sees in their movements how they have survived. I am certain that one day this film will exist.

—Susan Griffin

The Hypothetical

Lesbian Heroine

in Narrative

Feature Film

Chris Straayer

Feminist film theory based on sexual difference has much to gain from considering lesbian desire and sexuality. Women's desire for women deconstructs male/female sexual dichotomies, sex/gender conflation, and the universality of the oedipal narrative. Acknowledgment of the female-initiated active sexuality and sexualized activity of lesbians has the potential to reopen a space in which straight women as well as lesbians can exercise self-determined pleasure.

In this article, I am concerned mainly with films that do *not* depict lesbianism explicitly but employ or provide sites for lesbian intervention. This decision is based on my interest in the lesbian viewer and how her relation to films with covert lesbianism content resembles her positioning in society. In textual analyses of *Entre nous* and *Voyage en douce*—two French films that seemingly oblige different audiences and interpretation—I demonstrate how, rather than enforcing opposite meanings, the films allow for multiple readings that overlap. I use the term *hypothetical* to indicate that neither the character's lesbianism nor her heroism is an obvious fact of the films. I articulate a lesbian aesthetic that is subjective but not idiosyncratic.

In particular, I examine two sites of negotiation between texts and viewers, shifts in the heterosexual structure that are vulnerable to lesbian pleasuring: the lesbian look of exchange and female bonding. I place these in contrast to the male gaze and its narrative corollary, love at first sight. I then examine the contradictions that arise when the articulation of nonheterosexual subject matter is attempted within a structure conventionally motivated by heterosexuality. Finally, the question inevitably raised by women-only interactions—Where is the man?—inspires a radical disclosure of sex as historically and socially constructed and a redefinition of subjectivity.

Feminist Film Theory: Gender, Sexuality, and Viewership

Within the construction of narrative film sexuality, the phrase *lesbian heroine* is a contradiction in terms. The female position in classical narrative is a stationary site to which the male hero travels and on which he acts. The relationship between male and female is one of conquest. The processes of acting and receiving are thus genderized.[1]

There can be no lesbian heroine here, for the very definition of *lesbianism* requires an act of defiance in relation to assumptions about sexual desire and activity. Conventional film discourse can accommodate the lesbian heroine only as a hero, as "male." Yet maleness is potentially irrelevant to lesbianism, if not to lesbians.

The lesbian heroine in film must be conceived as a viewer construction, short-circuiting the very networks that attempt to forbid her energy. She is constructed from contradictions within the text and between text and viewer, who insists on assertive, even transgressive identifications and seeing.

The Hollywood romance formula of love at first sight relies on a slippage between sexuality and love. Sexual desire pretends to be reason enough for love, and love pretends to be sexual pleasure. While sexual desire is visually available for viewers' vicarious experiences, sexual pleasure is blocked. By the time the plot reaches a symbolic climax, love has been substituted for sex, restricting sex to the realm of desire. So structured, love is unrequited sex. Since this love is hetero love, homosexual viewers are doubly distanced from sexual pleasure.

The sexual gaze as elaborated in much feminist film theory is a male prerogative, a unidirectional gaze from male onto female, pursuing a downward slant in relation to power. In contrast, the lesbian look that I describe requires exchange. It looks for a returning look, not just a receiving look. It sets up two-directional sexual activity.

Considerable work by feminist film theorists has attempted to articulate operations of looking in narrative film texts and film spectatorship. In "Visual Pleasure and Narrative Cinema," Laura Mulvey described how the patriarchal unconscious has structured classical cinema with visual and narrative pleasure specifically for the heterosexual male viewer, gratifying his narcissistic ego via a surrogate male character who condones and relays the viewer's look at the woman character, and providing him voyeuristic pleasure via a more direct, nonnarrative presentation of the woman as image (rather than character). Woman's erotic image elicits castration anxiety in the male viewer, which is eased by visual and narrative operations of fetishism and sadism. As Mulvey states, "None of these interacting layers is intrinsic to film, but it is only in the film form that they can reach a perfect and beautiful contradiction, thanks to the possibility in the cinema of shifting the emphasis of the look."[2]

Although Mulvey's article remains invaluable in addressing patriarchal dominance as the ideological status quo formally enforced by/in the mainstream cinema/text, it does not account for other sexual forces and experiences within society. Mulvey's arguments have been constructively elaborated, revised, and rebutted by numerous other feminist film theorists. However, much of this work has brought about an unproductive slippage between text and actuality that presses this exclusive patriarchal structure onto the world. This excludes the reactions of "deviant" participants in the film event from theory's discursive event. Even though the spectator's psychology is formed within a culture that collapses sexual/anatomical difference onto gender, the same culture also contains opposing factors and configurations that generate a proliferation of discourses that instigates actual psychological diversity. It is this diversity rather than cinema's dominant ideology that we must examine in order to deconstruct the alignment of male with activity and female with passivity.

In a later article, "Afterthoughts on 'Visual Pleasure and Narrative Cinema' Inspired by *Duel in the Sun*," Mulvey suggests that female viewers experience Freud's "true heroic feeling" through masculine identification with active male characters, a process that allows this spectator "to rediscover that lost aspect of her sexual identity, the never fully repressed bedrock of feminine neurosis." With her "own memories" of masculinity, a certain "regression" takes place in this deft "trans-sex identification," and, like returning to her past daydreams of action, she experiences viewer pleasure. Nevertheless, "the female spectator's phantasy of masculinisation is always to some extent at cross purposes with itself, restless in its transvestite clothes."[3]

Such a confusion of clothing with sex, and of both with desire for action, accepts the limitations of sex-role stereotyping in the text. True, such desire on the part of female viewers usually requires identification with male characters, but this is a limitation of mainstream cinema, not a "regression" on the part of women.

By not addressing mechanisms of gay spectatorship, the above scheme denies such pleasure or suggests that it is achieved from the heterosexual text via transvestite ploys. Mainstream cinema's nearly total compulsory heterosexuality does require homosexual viewers to appropriate heterosexual representations for homosexual pleasure. However, the "transvestite" viewer-text interaction described by Mulvey and others should not be confused with gay or bisexual viewership.

Mary Ann Doane understands this cross-gender identification by female viewers as one means of achieving distance from the text. In "Film and the

Masquerade: Theorizing the Female Spectator," she argues that, because woman's preoedipal bond with the mother continues to be strong throughout her life (unlike man's), the female viewer—unless she utilizes specific devices—is unable to achieve that distance from the film's textual *body* that allows man the process of voyeurism. "For the female spectator there is a certain over-presence of the image—she *is* the image. Given the closeness of this relationship, the female spectator's desire can be described only in terms of a kind of narcissism—the female look demands a becoming." As a result, woman overidentifies with cinema's female victims, experiencing a pleasurable reconnection that is necessarily masochistic. Because her body lacks the potential for castration, "woman is constructed differently in relation to the process of looking."[4]

Doane goes on to describe an alternate strategy for women to overcome proximity and mimic a distance from the(ir) image—the masquerade of femininity: "Above and beyond a simple adoption of the masculine position in relation to the cinematic sign, the female spectator is given two options: the masochism of overidentification or the narcissism entailed in becoming one's own object of desire, in assuming the image in the most radical way. The effectivity of masquerade lies precisely in its potential to manufacture a distance from the image, to generate a problematic within which the image is manipulable, producible, and readable to woman."[5]

The primary question that followed Mulvey's "Visual Pleasure and Narrative Cinema" was, How can women's film viewing pleasure be understood? Although subsequent feminist film theory drawing on psychoanalysis successfully opened up that field for feminist purposes and raised significant new questions, the answers that it has provided—elaborations of particular processes of masochism and transvestitism—remain only partially sufficient to the original question. Much of this work has circumvented a crucial option in female spectatorship by avoiding the investigation of women viewers' erotic attraction to and visual appreciation of women characters.[6] Further work needs to examine how viewers determine films as much as how films determine viewers. And care should be taken that the theorized transvestite or bisexual viewer does not inadvertently suppress the homosexual viewer.

Eroticizing Looks between Women Characters

Visual exchanges between same-sex characters typically are nonsexual. The challenge becomes to eroticize these looks. This is the goal of homosexual viewers, who bring their desires to the heterosexual raw material and representational system of the text. Occasionally, they collaborate with texts to excavate

Figure 1. Frame enlargement from *Voyage en douce.*

subtexts and uncover ambivalence in the patriarchal "order." Since the heterosexual structure of the gaze is already established as sexual, it can be built on to
accomplish an erotic homosexual look.

Independently structured glances between women, however, are outside conventional definition and therefore threaten. The ultimate threat of eye contact
between women, inherent in all scenes of female bonding, is the elimination of
the male. Any erotic exchange of glances between women requires counter-
efforts to disempower and deeroticize them.

I now focus on two films, both open to lesbian readings, that are interesting for
their similarities and differences. *Voyage en douce* (directed by Michele Deville,
1980) is an erotic art film, bordering on "soft porn," about two women who take
a trip to the country together. They exchange fantasies and flirtations, then
return home to their male partners. *Entre nous* (directed by Diane Kurys, 1983)
is also about the interactions between two women, but their relationship leans
ostensibly toward the buddies genre. They too take a trip away from their husbands. The women demonstrate growing mutual affection, and, at the film's
conclusion, they are living together. Although the two films appear opposite—
one pseudolesbian soft porn serving a male audience, the other feminist and
appealing to a female audience—this dichotomy is deconstructed once viewers
are actively involved.

Figure 2. Frame enlargement from *Voyage en douce*.

Voyage en douce is particularly interesting in relation to looking because, instead of resolution, it attempts sustained sexual desire. According to the conventions of pornography, the erotic involvement of two women functions as foreplay for a heterosexual climax. This does not happen in *Voyage en douce*. Erotic looking and flirting between women is thematic in this film. The lesbian desire this stimulates is accentuated by a hierarchical looking structure that mimics the male gaze. Throughout the film, a blonde woman, Hélène, played by Dominique Sanda, is the more active looker and the text's primary visual narrator. It is primarily "through her eyes" that sexual fantasies are visualized on the screen. When taking nude photographs of her brunette companion, Lucie, played by Geraldine Chaplin, a camera prop "equips" Hélène/Sanda for this male role. (See figures 1 and 2.)

Hélène is also the primary pursuer in the narrative, while Lucie functions to stimulate, tease, and frustrate that desire. The film's episodic structure—another convention of pornography—alternates between the women's individual sexual stories and fantasies and their erotically charged interactions. Hélène pampers and grooms Lucie, appreciates her visually, and verbally reassures her about her beauty and desirableness. This serves to build both a generalized sexual desire and a more specific lesbian desire. In both cases, a series of narrative denials and delays establishes an "interruptus" motif. Early in the film, there is a point-of-

Figure 3. Frame enlargement from *Entre nous*.

view shot of a look from Lucie at Hélène's breast, which Hélène quickly covers. Later, when Hélène purposely exposes her breast to excite Lucie, Lucie is not responsive. When photographing Lucie, Hélène encourages her to remove her clothes. Lucie does so hesitantly and coquettishly, but, when Hélène attempts to take the final nude shot, she is out of film.

In several scenes, Hélène and Lucie exchange unmediated glances, as do the two women characters in *Entre nous*—Lena, played by Isabelle Huppert, and Madeline, played by Miou Miou. Such exchanges, which occur primarily within two-person shots, gain sexual energy from the women's physical proximity and subtle body contact. The fact that two women share the film frame encourages this lesbian reading; that is, the women are consistently framed as a "couple." This visual motif provides a pleasurable homosexual content that is frustrated by the plot.[7] However, the absence of a shot-reverse-shot, reciprocal point-of-view pattern in these two-shots excludes the viewer from experiencing the looking. Thus, the viewer's identification with the women's looking is necessarily more sympathetic than empathic.

In *Entre nous*, the addition of a mirror to such a shot establishes a second internal frame. The reciprocal point-of-view exchange achieved between these two simultaneous frames—a two-shot of the women looking at each other through

Figure 4. Frame enlargement from *Entre nous*.

the mirror—allows the viewer to be sutured into the looking experience while also experiencing the pleasure of seeing the two women together. It is notable that, during this shot, the women are nude and admiring each other's breasts. (See figure 3.)

A similar construction occurs temporally instead of spatially when, in a sequence in the garden, the camera temporarily identifies with the look and movement of Lena/Huppert approaching Madeline/Miou Miou through a subjective tracking shot and then holds steady while Lena enters the frame. The viewer is carried into the women's space via an identification with Lena's look, then observes their embrace from an invited vantage point. This is followed by a shot of Madeline's father and son watching disapprovingly—a look from outside. Standing together, hand in hand, these two males foreground the generation missing between them—Madeline's husband. Hence, their look both acknowledges and checks the dimensions of the women's visual exchange.

Voyage en douce also contains abundant mirror shots, some of which similarly conduct visual exchanges between the characters, while others seem to foreground hierarchical erotic looking. In particular, several mirror shots occur in which the two women examine Lucie's image while Hélène compliments or grooms her.

Female Bonding in Film

What becomes evident from these examples is that, when one searches for lesbian exchange in narrative film construction, one finds a constant flux between competing forces to suggest and deny it. As with sexuality in general, efforts to subdue lesbian connotations can stimulate innovations. Female bonding and the exchange of glances between women threaten heterosexual and patriarchal structures. When female bonding occurs in feature narrative film, its readiness for lesbian appropriation is often acknowledged by internal efforts to forbid such conclusions.

Conceptually, female bonding is a precondition for lesbianism. If women are situated only in relationship to men or in antagonistic relationship to each other, the very idea of lesbianism is precluded. This partially explains the appreciation that lesbian audiences have for films with female bonding. So often has female bonding stood in for lesbian content that lesbian audiences seem to find it an acceptable displacement at the conclusions of such "lesbian romances" as *Personal Best* (directed by Robert Towne, 1982) and *Lianna* (directed by John Sayles, 1982).

The widespread popularity of *Entre nous* among lesbian audiences can be attributed to basic narrative conditions, which are reiterated throughout the film. Most important is female bonding. The film begins with parallel editing between Lena's and Madeline's separate lives. This crosscutting constructs audience expectation and desire for the two women to meet. Once they have met, the two women spend the majority of screen time together. Lesbian viewers experience pleasure in their physical closeness. Although lesbianism is never made explicit in the film, an erotic subtext is readily available. The specific agenda held by lesbian viewers for female bonding warrants an inside joke at the film's conclusion when Lena and Madeline are finally living together. In the "background" a song plays: "I wonder who's kissing her now. I wonder who's showing her how."

The development of Lena and Madeline's relationship stands in sharp contrast to the development of Lena's marriage. During World War II, she and Michel are prisoners in a camp. He is being released and is allowed to take a wife out with him. He selects Lena by sight alone.

In many ways, female bonding is the antithesis of love at first sight. While love at first sight necessarily deemphasizes materiality and context, female bonding is built on an involvement in specific personal environments. Furthermore, the relationship acquires a physical quality from the presence of personal items that, when exchanged, suggest intimacy. Women frequently wear each other's clothes in both these films. Body lotion and love letters pass between Lena and Madeline as easily as do cigarettes.

Such bonding activity between women suggests an alternate use for the feminine masquerade. This mutual appreciation of one another's feminine appearance, which achieves intimacy via an attention to personal effects, demonstrates the masquerade's potential to draw women closer together and to function as nonverbal homoerotic expression that connects image to body. This "deviant" employment of the feminine masquerade is in contradistinction to Doane's elaboration of it as a distancing device for women. (See figure 4.)

The primary threat of female bonding is the elimination of the male. The unstated but always evident question implicit in such films—Where is the man?—acknowledges defensive androcentric reactions. Its underlying presence attempts to define female bonding and lesbianism in relation to men. Publicity that accompanies a distribution point of *Voyage en douce* from New Yorker Films describes the film as "what women talk about when men aren't around." In *Entre nous,* scenes approaching physical intimacy between the two women are juxtaposed with shots signaling the lone male. Depicting female bonding as the exclusion of men moves the defining principle outside the women's own interactions. The lesbian potential, an "unfortunate" by-product of the female bonding configuration, must be checked.

The Male Intermediary

One way to interfere with female bonding is to insert references to men and heterosexuality between women characters. In *Entre nous,* Madeline and Lena spend a considerable portion of their time together talking about their husbands and lovers. For example, they jointly compose a letter to Madeline's lover. Reassuring references to offscreen males, however, remain a feeble attempt to undermine the visual impact that the women together make.

To be more effective, the interference needs to be visual in order physically to separate the women's bodies and interrupt their glances. Male intermediaries are common in films with female bonding. In *Entre nous,* when Lena and Madeline are dancing together in a Paris night club (which opens with a *male* point-of-view shot at Madeline's ass), two male onlookers become intermediaries by diverting the women's glances and easing the tension created by their physical embrace. (See figure 5.)

Voyage en douce literally places a male between the two women. The soft porn approach of *Voyage en douce* relies on titillating the male viewer with lesbian insinuations. Ultimately, however, female characters must remain available to male viewers. In one scene, Hélène verbally instructs a young male, placed between the women, on how to kiss Lucie. The inexperienced boy reinforces the

Figure 5. Frame enlargement from *Entre nous.*

male viewer's sense of superior potency—the male viewer is represented but not replaced. In this scene, the boy connects the two women as much as he separates them. It is Hélène who is sensitive to Lucie's pacing and is manipulating her desire. The boy is an intermediary. Hélène's vicarious engagement, however, is confined to the realm of desire. The actual kiss excludes her. (See figure 6.)

Often, as in the following example from *Entre nous,* the connection that an intermediary provides is less obvious. Lena is on her way to meet Madeline in Paris when she has a sexual encounter with an anonymous male. A soldier who shares her train compartment kisses and caresses her. Later, while discussing this experience with Madeline, Lena "comes to realize" that this was her first orgasmic experience. The scene on the train reasserts Lena's heterosexuality. At the same time, this experience and knowledge of sexual pleasure is more connected to her friendship with Madeline, via their exchange of intimate information, than to her heterosexual marriage of many years. In fact, it is Madeline who recognizes Lena's described experience as an orgasm and identifies it to her. Because the film cuts away from the train scene shortly after the sexual activity begins, the film viewer does not witness Lena's orgasm. Had this train scene continued, her orgasm might have approximated, in film time, the moment when Madeline names it—and Lena gasps. In a peculiar manner, then, Madeline is

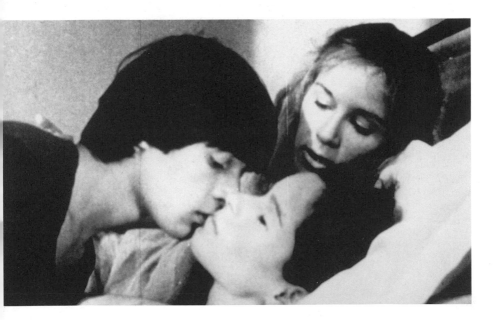

Figure 6. Frame enlargement from *Voyage en douce.*

filmically credited for the orgasm. Likewise, Lena's excited state on the train, her predisposition to sexual activity, might be read as motivated by her anticipation of being with Madeline.

A male's intrusion on female bonding, then, is just as likely to homoeroticize the situation as to induce corrective heterosexuality. In *Entre nous,* it is Lena's jealous husband who gives language to the sexual possibilities of their friendship. By calling the women's boutique a "whorehouse," he foregrounds the erotic symbolism that clothing provides. When he calls the women "dykes," he not only reveals the fears of a jealous husband but confirms the audience's perceptions.

While I would not go so far as to equate these two films, it would be naive to dismiss *Voyage en douce* simply as a "rip-off" of lesbianism for male voyeuristic pleasure while applauding *Entre nous* as "politically correct" lesbianism. In their different ways, *Entre nous* does just as much to stimulate lesbian desire as does *Voyage en douce,* and *Voyage en douce* frustrates it just as much as *Entre nous* does. The two films exhibit similar tensions and compromises. As far as any final commitment to lesbianism, *Entre nous* is no more frank than is *Voyage en douce.* Lesbian reading requires as much viewer initiation in one film as the other.

One could argue that any potential lesbianism in *Voyage en douce* is under-mined by heterosexual framing in early and late scenes with Hélène's male partner. Another interpretation of this framing device, however, sends conclusions in a different direction. Early in the film, Lucie crouches outside Hélène's door. Hélène sees Lucie through the railing under the banister as she climbs the stairs to her apartment. When Lucie declares that she is leaving her male partner, Hélène takes her into her apartment, where they plan a vacation together. At the film's conclusion, the two women return to Hélène's apartment. Then Lucie decides to go back to her husband, but Hélène decides to leave hers again. Inadvertently, Hélène locks herself out of the apartment without her suitcase. Instead of ringing the doorbell, she crouches in Lucie's earlier position as the camera moves down the stairs to observe her through the railing. One can read this shot as portraying the prison of heterosexuality or domesticity—as a cul-de-sac. Or one can read this pattern as indicating a cyclic structure.

Hélène's display of lesbian desire throughout *Voyage en douce* qualifies her as a hypothetical lesbian heroine as much as the women in *Entre nous*. Ultimately, these characters' lesbianism remains hypothetical and illusory because of their isolation. The acknowledgment of lesbian desire does not, in either film, acknowledge the *condition* of lesbianism within culture.

To summarize, *Voyage en douce* and *Entre nous* are narrative films that exist by right of a language informed by heterosexuality. However, because they are about women's relationships, they also challenge the conventions of this language. The contradictions that result from their use of a heterosexual system for nonheterosexual narratives give rise to innovations that interact with audience expectations to create multiple and ambivalent interpretations. The focus on two women together threatens to establish both asexuality and homosexuality, both of which are outside the heterosexual desire that drives mainstream film and narrative. Therefore, simultaneous actions take place in the text to eroticize the women's interactions and to abort the resulting homoerotics. These very contradictions and opposing intentions cause the gaps and ambiguous figurations that allow lesbian readings.

I have demonstrated three such figurations: the erotic exchange of glances, which contrasts with the unidirectional, hierarchical male gaze articulated by Mulvey; eroticized female bonding, which utilizes the feminine masquerade to achieve closeness, contrasting the use and purpose of the masquerade described by Doane; and the oppositely sexed intermediary who both separates and connects the same-sexed couple, accomplishing both heterosexuality and homosexuality within the contradictory text. These structures neither replace nor compromise the heterosexual film text and event recognized and analyzed in previous feminist film theory but rather offer additions and alternatives to account for homosexual viewership and desire.

Revising Binary Sexual Ideology

As a woman, the lesbian is defined and situated in culture as opposite to man, as a lack. The lesbian's physical/sexual interactions, however, insist on a different presence, one that operates outside male determination. It is her womanness, not her lesbianism, that confines her within the patriarchal formation of femininity. Therefore, were lesbians able to situate themselves as another sex, that is, as nonwomen (and nonmen), they could theoretically create a defining model to which men are irrelevant.[8]

In his introduction to *Herculine Barbin,* Michel Foucault contrasts the allowance of free choice and the coexistence of sexes within one body in the Middle Ages to the medical/legal relegation of the hermaphrodite to a single "true" sex in the eighteenth century:

Do we *truly* need a *true* sex? With a persistence that borders on stubbornness, modern Western societies have answered in the affirmative. They have obstinately brought into play this question of a "true sex" in an order of things where one might have imagined that all that counted was the reality of the body and the intensity of its pleasures.

For a long time, however, such a demand was not made, as is proven by the history of the status which medicine and law have granted to hermaphrodites. Indeed it was a very long time before the postulate that a hermaphrodite must have a sex—a single, true sex— was formulated. . . .

Biological theories of sexuality, juridical conceptions of the individual, forms of administrative control in modern nations, led little by little to rejecting the idea of a mixture of the two sexes in a single body, and consequently to limiting the free choice of indeterminate individuals. Henceforth, everybody was to have one and only one sex. Everybody was to have his or her primary, profound, determined and determining sexual identity; as for the elements of the other sex that might appear, they could only be accidental, superficial, or even quite simply illusory.[9]

Foucault's insights challenge the very "obvious" criteria used not only to delineate the sexes but to limit their number to two. By denying evidence of sexual continuums and conceptually precluding a more complex sexual variance in favor of a system of binary opposition, arbitrary and enforced standards for assignment of both sex and sexual behavior are made to seem adequate, primary, and natural.

No attempt to delineate clearly between two "true" sexes has been successful. The exceptions and ambiguities in anatomical and physiological assignments become even more pervasive when considering secondary sex characteristics, hormones, chromosome patterns, and behaviors. Erasing the hermaphrodite from our consciousness allows male and female terms to appear unambiguous and definite. In effect, the hermaphrodism existing within each of these terms is dismissed.

If we understand male and female sexes as constructs, we must ask ourselves what investment empowers them. Certainly, within classic narrative film, the language/expression/momentum of heterosexual desire relies precisely on this particular system of binary opposition.

Within contemporary psycholinguistic thought, the subject is always male. Because of her different psychological development and relationship to the mother, the female remains more strongly connected to the prelanguage imaginary. Any "I" she speaks is constructed for her by the male principle, just as female is defined not from itself but as male's other.

Lesbian sexuality generates an identity that is *not* defined by an opposition to maleness. Thus, the lesbian (of a lesbian) remains outside the male-female polarity. She demonstrates a radical possibility for attaining subjectivity through activity that asserts personal meaning and is understood via similarities as much as differences.

Lesbian "deviance" refutes the all-encompassing "natural" power of the male-female opposition as defining principle. Lesbianism demands a new operation of subjectivity in which active desires, pleasures, and other specific declarations of identity construct a field of multiple entry points. Within this new operation, a heterosexual woman's active sexuality would not be consumed but empowered. Rather than enforcing two "true" sexes, which allow one (male) subject, we must recognize the power of individual activities, in this case sexualities, to assert subjectivity.

I am not merely suggesting that sexual preference be added to anatomy as a determiner of the subject position, but rather that individual activity and assertion can construct subjectivity. Thus, for example, the experience and assertion of one's ethnic or racial identity would be acknowledged as an authentic subject component.

The proposal that lesbians might abandon the female "position" without adopting maleness uncovers a historical investment in and enforcement of a system of two sexes as well as two genders. This consistent maintenance of a historical construct explains the overloaded significance of the question, Where is the man? in response to relationships between women and lesbians. It raises the ultimate importance of investigating lesbian aesthetics.

Notes

1   See Teresa de Lauretis, *Alice Doesn't: Feminism, Semiotics, Cinema* (Bloomington: Indiana University Press, 1984), esp. the chapter on desire in narrative.

2   Laura Mulvey, "Visual Pleasure and Narrative Cinema," *Screen* 16, no. 3 (1975): 17.

3   Laura Mulvey, "Afterthoughts on 'Visual Pleasure and Narrative Cinema' Inspired by *Duel in the Sun,*" *Framework* 15–17 (Summer 1981): 13.

4   Mary Ann Doane, "Film and the Masquerade: Theorizing the Female Spectator," in *Femmes Fatales: Feminism, Film Theory, Psychoanalysis* (New York: Routledge, 1991), 22, see also 24. Doane's "Masquerade Reconsidered: Further Thoughts on the Female Spectator," also in *Femmes Fatales*.

5   Doane, "Film and the Masquerade," 31–32.

6   Such an investigation was called for over a decade ago by Michelle Citron, Julia Lesage, Judith Mayne, B. Ruby Rich, and Anna Maria Taylor. See their discussion in "Women and Film: Discussion of Feminist Aesthetics," *New German Critique* 13 (Winter 1978): 88–91.

7   See Lucie Arbuthnot and Gail Seneca, "Pre-text and Text in *Gentlemen Prefer Blondes,*" in *Film Reader 5* (Evanston, Ill.: Film Division/School of Speech, Northwestern University, 1982), 13–23. Arbuthnot and Seneca describe the pleasure afforded the lesbian viewer by such framing together of women characters.

8   Although my own position differs on some points from hers, Monique Wittig is the foremost contemporary theorizer of a lesbian "third sex." For her arguments that oppression constructs sex, that the concept *lesbian* is beyond the categories of sex, and therefore that "lesbians are not women," see her "One Is Not Born a Woman," *Feminist Issues* 1, no. 2 (Winter 1981): 47–54, and "The Category of Sex," *Feminist Issues* 2, no. 2 (Fall 1982): 63–68. For a useful discussion of Wittig's antiessentialist materialism, see Diana Fuss, *Essentially Speaking: Feminism, Nature, and Difference* (New York: Routledge, 1989), 39–53.

9   Michel Foucault, introduction to *Herculine Barbin: Being the Recently Discovered Memoirs of a Nineteenth-Century French Hermaphrodite,* trans. Richard McDougall (New York: Pantheon, 1980), vii–viii.

The

Great Escape

Al LaValley

I t's no secret to patrons of urban repertory film houses that for years a large part of the audience has been gay men. To the "gay rep" of Hollywood classics—films like *All About Eve, The Women, Sunset Boulevard, A Star Is Born, Now, Voyager,* and the star vehicles of Greta Garbo, Joan Crawford, Bette Davis, Judy Garland, and Marilyn Monroe—have been added newer gay cult favorites (*Cabaret, Mahogany, The Rose, American Gigolo*), as well as the more openly gay films (*Victor/Victoria, Making Love, Taxi zum Klo*), and even occasionally a few of the more political gay-produced documentaries (*Word Is Out, Track Two*). A soupçon of gay porn often completes this varied menu.

Gay men, however, generally don't go to the Hollywood movies, whether old or new, for gay themes, either overt or covert. They know full well that the history of Hollywood's treatment of gays has always been largely negative. There exists another gay history of the movies that has little to do with gay themes and characters, yet constitutes a major part of gay consciousness, both before and after the watershed Stonewall riots of 1969. In the many years of absence of any real representation of themselves on screen, gays created this history out of straight or nominally straight films. They found aspects of what could be called a gay sensibility, partly brought to celluloid by homosexual artists—set designers, makeup men, costumers, writers, actors, and directors—but also inherent in the aesthetics and genres of the Hollywood film itself.

Here they found hints of a utopian and alternate world, one more congenial to their sexuality and repressed emotions. If the narratives of these films ultimately condemned these differences, gay men knew how to shuck off last reel repentances, marriages, and moral condemnations as necessities of both the Production Code and the dominant heterosexual industry and audience. They treasured film not so much for its narrative fulfillments as for its great moments, those interstices that were often, ironically, the source of a film's real power: Davis declaring her independence to her mother in *Now, Voyager,* Garbo dressed as a young man flirting with John Gilbert at a country inn in *Queen Christina,* Crawford pleading for understanding from Walter Huston in *Rain.*

There is no single gay sensibility expressed on film; instead, one finds various strands of allied themes and perspectives, some shared and others not. All, however, proceed from the marginal and outcast condition of gays, and all are strategies of rebellion and subversion, born with the emergence of gay identity in the late-nineteenth century, the same period that gave birth to film.

The major gay discourses that have informed films for gay audiences are constellations of images, narratives, themes, stars, character behavior, and styles that embody the dominant quality of the gay sensibility and act as subversive shaping structures in gay cult films—even though they may not fully dominate (in fact, they rarely do). These discourses reveal the hidden and repressed facets of society, and gay audiences are apt to foreground them, whereas straight audiences, often oblivious to homosexual signals or frightened by them, tend to repress them.

Aestheticism

This is the earliest important gay discourse. Oscar Wilde is responsible for giving it its major gay characteristics, in *The Picture of Dorian Gray* and in *The Importance of Being Earnest.* In both works, art functions as a utopian second world opposed to the middle-class boredom and dullness of the "real" world. By espousing art, the artist also endorses an indulgence in individualistic and dandyish behavior, a dedication to beauty, sensuality, style, wit, and the exotic—and by implication homosexual behavior. Unfortunately, Wilde is also responsible for collocating wit and villainy, too, in his sinister picture of Basil Hallward in *Dorian Gray* and in Dorian's own slashing of his ugly portrait on which his sexual (read: homosexual) sins have been visited. From these two figures flow all the creepy young and old aesthetes and dandies of many films, so well characterized by George Sanders and Hurd Hatfield in the film of *Dorian Gray.* Sanders made a career of such nasties, the apex being Addison De Witt in *All About Eve.*

Firmly in this tradition of aesthetes are a gallery of Hitchcock's central figures (indeed, Hitchcock himself may be in this tradition): Robert Walker's Bruno in *Strangers on a Train,* Joseph Cotten's Uncle Charlie in *Shadow of a Doubt,* Farley Granger and John Dall as the young murderers of *Rope.* Here, too, belong Clifton Webb's Waldo Lydecker in *Laura,* Franchot Tone's crazy, murderous sculptor in *Phantom Lady*, and the megalomaniacal publisher Earl Janoth, played by Charles Laughton, in *The Big Clock*. Although it's possible to find these figures loathsome and repellent, most of them are also riveting and fascinating. Their colorfulness dominates the films and eclipses the pale heroes, such as Dana Andrews in *Laura* or Ray Milland in *The Big Clock*. Their promise of the exotic, the outré, and their way with words—one thinks of Webb uttering his haughty bons mots to Laura, "Get me out of this party or I shall run amok"—make them figures of a distinctive gay style and taste.

The idea of art as a story of gay self-discovery and celebration seems old-fashioned today. Instead, the aesthetic discourse has shifted from concern with figures in the film to a preoccupation with figures behind the film. Now, the director behind the scenes is the hidden artist being celebrated. Hence the gay fascination with such stylists as Bertolucci, Fellini, Weir, Russell, Fassbinder, Coppola, Cimino, Visconti, Roeg, and even the homophobic De Palma.

At the heart of gay cult, the aesthetically stylized genre of the musical reigns supreme. For years most major cities with large gay populations have had theaters that specialize in showing (mainly MGM) musicals for the gay audience. Those of Vincente Minnelli and the Arthur Freed unit have the largest following. The attraction is multifaceted. In these films, life seems lifted to a utopian level of wish fulfillment, charged with bold colors, elegant style, dance, costume, and song. The narrative, as well as the musical numbers, is often stylized. Performance is an integral theme, often lifting the characters out of the everyday rut. In *The Pirate*, Judy Garland dreams about the sexually dynamic Macoco and comes alive; furthermore, the false Macoco is far more sexual and vibrant in Gene Kelly than is the real Macoco in the flabby and sexless Walter Slezak.

Garland is the queen of the MGM musicals and the queen of gay cult. Still youthful enough in the forties to invoke the wistfulness and innocence of *The Wizard of Oz*, but old enough to evince the emotional depths and passions of a ballad, she was even then beginning to have bouts with depression and drugs that gave an occasional edginess and a quick switching of moods to her performances. Garland became fully alive only when performing, particularly when singing, and in these films, often paired with Gene Kelly (whose sexually charged athleticism and good looks offer a more direct appeal), she plumbs emotional and sexual depths not available in ordinary life.

Another highly stylized genre is the bitchy comedy of manners. Here Bette Davis is the queen and *All About Eve* the key gay cult film. Theatricalization and the grand manner of the older Broadway theater contribute to the aesthetic attraction, wedding realism to high artifice, giving style some justification. Davis as grande dame—lording it over her toadies, friends, and fans, and dishing everyone in sight—is an archetypal model for the bitchy gay queen: "Fasten your

seat belts. It's going to be a bumpy night." Most Davis films have moments
of such caustic domineering wit, when she suddenly winds up and lets those
around her have it. They make Davis a major gay icon, the figure who has had
enough, and who, when she starts speaking her mind, finds herself overflowing
with anger, vituperation, and an unexpected eloquence. As such, she captures
gay frustration and wish fulfillment.

Camp

Camp is a gay version of irony and critical distance. Of the four discourses, it's
the only one with solid gay roots—in Samuel Butler's satire, Edward Lear's
nonsense poetry, and Oscar Wilde's absurdist wit. Camp always involves the
collision of two or more opposing sets of signals—Crawford's wide, masculine
shoulders conflicting with her feminine image, Busby Berkeley's straight-faced
use of women for mechanical designs, even Carmen Miranda's tutti-frutti hat.
Sometimes the conflict is intentional—Gloria Swanson's exit line and the grim
reality of her situation in *Sunset Boulevard*—but the disparity is still camp. The
sense of too-muchness, the excess, or inappropriateness produces a sudden self-
consciousness in the viewer, but one that needn't dissolve the basic meaning of
the gesture. Camp can explode that basic gesture (look how crazy Norma Desmond is), but also enhance and celebrate it (her gesture is a triumph over a dull,
debased reality).

And camp comes in many varieties: high (*Sunset Boulevard*), low (Maria
Montez in *Cobra Woman*), conscious (*The Rocky Horror Picture Show*), and
unconscious (the banana number from *The Gang's All Here*). Parker Tyler once
even argued that Garbo is camp in her love scenes because their grandeur and
excess stand out from the often tawdry plots that surround them and supposedly
generate them.

Camp is addicted to the grotesque, where it often seems misogynistic. Here,
consciously or not, the more contained idiosyncrasies of a star—Davis's bitchy
wit, Crawford's stern determination—are heightened, isolated, and played off
against their previously more realistic embodiments. Aging, in fact, constitutes
still another camp factor in the interplay of images, as *What Ever Happened to
Baby Jane?* shows. Davis's later acting career often slides into caricature, but it
isn't necessarily campy; Crawford in her later roles usually is. The process begins with *Mildred Pierce,* where she's often admired by feminists for her strong
role. Gays are apt to note the camp aspect first, for it's here that she first begins to
look like a man as well as act like one, fierce with determination and the obsession
for success, her face an expressionless mask. In 1945 Crawford still thought

herself a knockout in a swimsuit and maternally tender to her children, so the result on film is a campy collision of images and signals. The camp aspect is even more heightened in a late film like *Berserk*, where she is still trying to appear sexy in tights and tries to seduce by coy glances a man one-third her age.

Often celebrating as it deconstructs, camp can allow outmoded emotions to flourish not just for their sentimentality or kitschy quality, but for their seeds of rebellion against a drier, more conformist modernity. In this respect, camp treasures an excessive theatricality and outrageousness as an avenue to heightened emotion.

Drag and camp are closely united. Extreme camp figures already seem like drag queens. Mae West—with her tough talk, her sense of the put-on, and her role reversals where she takes the masculine initiative—resembles a man (these qualities inevitably give rise to the rumor that she really was one in disguise). Gavin Lambert has cited Barbara Stanwyck in *Double Indemnity*, with her painted Kewpie-doll mouth and her blonde wig, as another example. And along with Crawford in her shoulder pads, there's also Garland in her tux outfit and Carol Channing in virtually any role.

Loud, somewhat obscene women, who violate the decorum one is taught to expect socially from women (Ethel Merman, Martha Raye, Phyllis Diller, Hermione Gingold, Joan Rivers), all come close to being what Esther Newton calls Mother Camp figures, the bawdy outrageous female impersonators who host drag shows in urban nightclubs.[1] Newton, a feminist, claims that camp itself grows out of absurdities and incongruities in the patriarchal family, reflected in the perverse juxtaposition of the sacred, idealized mother and the profane, obscene woman that the Mother Camp figure embodies. If that's the case, it's easy to see why Divine, a three-hundred-pound transvestite, playing Dawn Davenport in *Female Trouble*, is both an image of the violation of motherhood and a symbol of authentic release when she strangles her Hare Krishna child. The mixed response of audiences to the famous child-beating scene in *Mommie Dearest* is occasioned by a similar duality and clash between socially feminized roles and authentic wishes.

In recent years, both camp and drag have acquired a more universal taste, as illustrated by the general popularity of female-impersonation shows, John Waters's movies with Divine, Warhol's drag queens, Craig Russell in *Outrageous!*, and even the cult following of *The Rocky Horror Picture Show*. The last example, despite its transvestite hero from Transylvania who has sex with both Brad and Janet, is still largely attended by a straight teenage audience. Here, as in most mainstream films, the threat of gender confusion is reduced by big budgets and large-scale financing and distribution; the anarchic potential of drag is lessened;

there's always much less a sense of rebellion and examination of gender roles and more a sense of mere surface play. Compare, for instance, the softer picture of Divine as a put-upon suburban housewife in the commercial *Polyester* with her Bad Mama Manson style in the low-budget independent *Pink Flamingos* and *Multiple Maniacs*, films where the drag queen is both rebel queen and conscious camp figure, a King or Queen Ubu.

In their less commercialized forms, drag and camp can be on the cutting edge of both sexual and social reality by their power to overturn images, to confuse and distort, and to make the ordinary surreal. Drag queens like Divine give an effect of uncontrollable and anarchic energy shattering bourgeois sexual and social morality, hence, the jet-propulsion quality of the earlier Waters narratives, as they move to scenes of mad confrontation with their enemies: Divine holding court and sentencing the Marbles to death in *Pink Flamingos;* Divine strangling her child, performing on a trampoline in a frenzy, and shooting the audience in *Female Trouble.*

Rebellion

Gays have no special claim on rebellion against society; many are economically very well off and seem firmly embedded in society's structures. Yet they are also outsiders, frequent victims of society's discrimination and marginal figures within its movements of power; as such, almost all gays feel some thrill at rebellion. The intensity of the thrill and the deflection from its principal social target may depend on the depth of dislocation of each individual gay man. When rebellious gays have become artists and foregrounded their rebellion, it's often appeared in outrageous form.

During the fifties, motorcycle gangs and leather became key icons of rebellion in the movies, and were easily assimilated into gay culture, as Kenneth Anger's *Scorpio Rising* showed. Cocteau was probably first on film with the collocation of violence, leather, and cycles in *Orpheus* (1950), where the emissaries of Death ran down the poet Cégeste (played by Cocteau's lover, Edouard Dermithe). However, it was not the underground, but Marlon Brando and James Dean, who most fully embodied the rebellious bad-boy image of the fifties, particularly in *The Wild One* and *Rebel Without a Cause* and *East of Eden*. Brando's famous reply to the question "What are you rebelling against?"—"What have you got?"—expressed the amorphous, uncrystallized quality of revolt, its taunting cynicism and pose of boredom with ordinary life. Both Brando's and Dean's rebelliousness contained a smoldering sexuality, far more active than anything the underground had yet produced. Here, flagrant sexuality and rebellion invoked a new self and society, not just the opportunity to act with more of the usual male swagger.

One of the attractions of film noir was its hidden sense of rebellion, the way it sexualized the urban ambience, as gay cruising does now. Any chance encounter—Fred MacMurray dropping into a Los Feliz house to see about insurance—could suddenly become an erotic adventure. Possibly the rudiments of the gay porn movie lie here. And this is why the recent *Cruising*, despite its homophobia and its often ignorant ideas on male sexual encounters, drew a gay audience. The sexual ambience of the urban gay world was vividly portrayed, and it was peopled with real gays involved in real sex acts—at least until certain cuts were belatedly made. Pacino dons his leather cap, beckoning himself to murderous acts, but for gays the film's attraction lies in its alternative and exciting sexuality, beyond the confines of the norm, in its promises of the city of night.

Even nominally homophobic movies stressing this theme can become gay cult, seeming to protest too much, so that their homophobia appears to mask an underlying homoeroticism. In *American Gigolo*, sexy bad boy of the urban nightworld, Richard Gere clearly says, "I don't do fags," and the movie goes to great and absurd lengths to make homosexuals the murderers of a woman, but the style, the ambience, and the use of Gere still seem strikingly gay. *Midnight Cowboy*, another film about hustling, has more trouble thematically avoiding the homosexual overtones of its central relationship, mainly because Jon Voight occasionally hustles men and seems to overreact both in the gay movie theater scene and, especially, in the hotel room where he strikes out with excessive cruelty at the sad, aging homosexual.

The city seen as a large cruising ground, filled with mystery and excitement, is perhaps best remembered in the resolutely heterosexual *Taxi Driver*, with its long takes of Travis Bickle in his cab. Although it's violence and crime that Bickle imagines, his world is also much charged with sexuality. One wonders if Martin Scorsese saw Fred Halstead's pioneering and highly controversial gay porno film *LA Plays Itself*, where such ambient cruising shots from a car were first highlighted. *Taxi zum Klo* seems to echo both movies, with its shots of Frank Ripploh driving in the rain, caught in a kind of dream drift by the allure of the nighttime city and its sexual promise.

Horror is another genre that traditionally plays with submerged sexuality, the monster frequently, as in the Jekyll and Hyde movies, being a more unconscious and sexual version of the repressed hero. Gays understand in horror films the duality of their own emotional lives, the straight social mask they are often compelled to wear and beneath it the illegitimate strong sexual desires that constitute their real self.

Melodrama also powerfully articulates unconventional sexual longings and flirts with a sense of the outré and the excessive, of emotions sliding beyond the norm into grotesquerie and madness. The gay fascination with madness is partly repressive—anger, guilt, and pain directed at the self and internalized—but it's also a courting of an ecstatic state beyond convention. The mad climactic scenes of two films, *A Streetcar Named Desire* and *Sunset Boulevard,* have become treasured gay cult moments because they suggest vindication of one's private emotional vision even in defeat, a soaring beyond the limits society and even nature impose. They are statements of the heightened affirmation of individual difference, simultaneously tragic, ecstatic, pitiable, and even campy. Both Norma Desmond and Blanche du Bois refuse to cave in to the pressures of a debased exterior world; they descend into madness, preserving their richer private and emotional world in highly theatrical exits. It's these moments, so uniquely individualized, not the stars, that have become celebrated moments of gay film history.

The most recent example of the mad grotesque—Faye Dunaway's impersonation of Joan Crawford in *Mommie Dearest*—lacks the triumphant exit and memorable final line, but, in the famous "no more wire hangers" scene, approaches both the horror genre's duality and the excess of madness. Even though she is gratuitously made up here with grotesque facial paint, she is powerful because one can hear a tormented soul authentically exploding from the pressures of a system that has encased her in the noble role of stardom, which she partly believes.

The Natural Man

This discourse, the prevailing one today, says that homosexuality is healthy and good, an alternative expression of a basic sexual instinct, a view given explicit treatment in *Making Love.* Socially, this discourse stresses natural, affective male bonding and utopian visions of male camaraderie. It lies behind virtually all the political films made by gay liberation filmmakers.

Today's open films usually center on a coming-out ritual, the discovery of this natural man and wider self. Not only is this strong in *Making Love*—where the ending actually gives Zack two beloveds, a new man and his ex-wife Claire—but it hovers in the background in gay-made films like the British *Nighthawks* and the German *Taxi zum Klo.* These two end with gay teachers coming out to their students, their private identities taking on broader public meaning. Before gay lib, a number of films suggested a similar drama or revelation, but beat a quick retreat when things got too uncomfortable. *Tea and Sympathy* and *Cat on a Hot*

Tin Roof both featured young protagonists with problems that finally only *looked* homosexual; each was cured by a good woman, the understanding Deborah Kerr or the ravishing Elizabeth Taylor.

During the fifties and sixties, attacks on the Production Code's ban on homosexuality often came from filming the increasingly explicit plays of Tennessee Williams. Hollywood's version of *Cat on a Hot Tin Roof* may have hemmed and hawed about what went on between Brick and his friend (finally nothing!) and swamped even this revelation by a grandiloquent final third on the nature of mendacity and materialism, two easy targets, but at least the homosexual subject was touched on. Earlier, the censors had trimmed Blanche's tragic monologue in *A Streetcar Named Desire* about the suicide of her homosexual poet husband, but the real homoerotic content of both the play and the film came through in Williams's quirky love-hate relationship with Stanley Kowalski, as well as in Brando, the young stud star. Partly it was a conflict of adoration for Brando as the natural man against the cruel and callous character he had to play, also partly a mixture of fear for rough trade and the attraction to it, the belief that some sort of Greek beauty is embodied in it.

Many of Williams's films—*Sweet Bird of Youth, The Fugitive Kind*—contained a similar stud figure, dropped into society and causing a frenzy, but also sending out homoerotic overtones by his striking central erotic presence. William Inge's *Picnic* did much the same; today the homoerotic content of stud William Holden's dance seems hard to miss. Even Inge's original screenplay, *Splendor in the Grass,* while supposedly based on a real case of heterosexual repression known to Inge in his youth, seems an authorial statement with much of Inge in the Natalie Wood role: the hysterical overreaction when barred from the forbidden love object—in this case natural man-stud Warren Beatty—psychotherapy for hysteria, and its minimal muted rewards, lamely marked as growth and adjustment. Ostensibly the film struggles to celebrate the Freudian cure, the waning of the Wordsworthian vision as an aspect of maturity, but down deep it recreates the yearning to act homosexually, to possess and be possessed by the natural man. No accident that Brando and Beatty overawed the respective playwrights and were cast by them in their first major roles.

These are covert gay films, but many straight genre films that feature all-male groups cannot deflect homoeroticism easily either. It's as though homosexuality or bisexuality were a repressed, more natural state, pushing its way to the surface as soon as women recede into the background or become invisible. All the major types of buddy films contain this vision in varying degrees: war, gangster, schoolboy, prison, cop, and cowboy. The homosexuality is usually deeply repressed and highly deflected; these films may reflect a fear of women as much as they do an attraction to men. Nevertheless, the desire for stronger male ties and loyalties often animates the drama of vengeance in cop, detective, and Western films and gives them a satisfying air of closure.

Most buddy films deflect the danger of homoeroticism by incorporating romance or women in ultimately marginal roles. Perhaps in *Butch Cassidy and the Sundance Kid,* Newman and Redford needed little cover, but Katharine Ross's peripheral presence and her absence from the *Liebestod* ending has made the film a locus classicus for arguing about repressed homosexuality in buddy films. And Parker Tyler has enjoyed pointing out how odd it was that in *The Great Escape* the escapees from a Nazi prison camp never once mentioned their spouses or their need for women, how they also coupled up in twosomes for the escape, and how the film lingered on the relationship between the glamourous James Garner and the unattractive and handicapped Donald Pleasance.

Gangster, prison, war, and detective movies, and much of film noir, move in a largely male world, where women, when present, are apt to be fearful—a world marked by the sexual excitement and enticement of violence. The early gangster movies were surprisingly explicit on the homosexual issue. *Little Caesar, Public Enemy,* and *Scarface* all attempted to link the isolation of their heroes to sexual neuroticism and an implicit homosexuality, in which male bonding superseded the acquisition of the prized women. Paul Muni leaves Karen Morley dangling on the telephone as he laments the loss of his sidekick; James Cagney can't make it with Jean Harlow and shoves a grapefruit in Mae Clarke's face while he breaks up over his partner's death; and Edward G. Robinson is so obsessed by the desertion of his fancy dancing man to respectability and marriage that he is lured to his own death.

Few of these action movies, however, are gay cult films, not just because of their celebration of institutional violence, but because of their macho style of action, the unreflective shoot-'em-up pleasure, by which they seem to avoid any delving into the base of their narrative. Their treatment of women as mere sex objects similarly marks a failure to explore sexuality, and a reliance instead on macho chest thumping and bravado as carriers and signifiers of heterosexuality. When the movies are softer and celebrate camaraderie or make the city a place of exotic sexual promise, or when they become so stylized, moody, elegant, and formal that they leave their genres behind altogether, they are definitely gay cult items. *Gallipoli,* for instance, undermines the war genre, and *Heaven's Gate* and *Days of Heaven* undermine the Western.

One might have expected Stonewall to make star cults outmoded among gays. In a sense it did: the natural man discourse, with its strong political and social vision and its sense of a fulfilled and open self, has supplanted both the aesthetic and the campy discourses, which for years gave gays a history and an identity. A delirious absorption in the stars is now something associated with pre-Stonewall gays or drag queens, yet neither gay openness nor the new machismo has completely abolished the cults. New figures are added regularly: Diana Ross, Donna Summer, Jennifer Holiday from the world of music, for example. There's a newer, more open gay following for male stars: Richard Gere, Christopher Reeve, even teen hunks like Matt Dillon. Perhaps most intriguingly of all, Joan Crawford has been resurrected through the newest gay cult favorite, *Mommie Dearest*, where camp and feminist interests intersect wildly.

Clearly, the range of gay tastes charted here cannot be found in any single gay man. Newer political gays are apt to frown on any use of the movies aside from the natural man and new social vision, which the political films they are making endorse. At the other extreme, there is a body of old movie queens who loathe the new gay films and still want to live in a world dominated by MGM musicals, Bette Davis, Joan Crawford, and melodramas. In between lies the large body of gay men who will go to see *Taxi zum Klo* or *Track Two*, but adore *Mommie Dearest* and old Bette Davis or MGM musical films as well. In their fascination with these films, they are responding to aspects of them—rebellion, camp, theatricality, emotional implications—that much of straight movie criticism condemns or fails to see.

Yet it is precisely these elements, many of them the product of gays in the movie industry itself, that sketch the contours for a changed society that is less patriarchal, open to a wider range of emotions, more playful and fun loving, and less sexist.

Note

1   Esther Newton, *Mother Camp: Female Impersonators in America* (1972; Chicago: University of Chicago Press, 1979).

There's Something Queer Here

Alexander Doty

But standing before the work of art requires you to act too.
The tension you bring to the work of art is an action.
—Jean Genet[1]

I'm gonna take you to queer bars
I'm gonna drive you in queer cars
You're gonna meet all of my queer friends
Our queer, queer fun it never ends.
—"The Queer Song," Gretchen Phillips[2]

The most slippery and elusive terrain for mass culture studies continues to be negotiated within audience and reception theory. Perhaps this is because within cultural studies, "audience" is now always already acknowledged to be fragmented, polymorphous, contradictory, and "nomadic," whether in the form of individual or group subjects. Given this, it seems an almost impossible task to conduct reception studies that capture the complexity of those moments in which audiences meet mass culture texts. As Janice Radway puts it:

No wonder we find it so difficult to theorize the dispersed, anonymous, unpredictable nature of the use of mass-produced, mass-mediated cultural forms. If the receivers of such forms are never assembled fixedly on a site or even in an easily identifiable space, if they are frequently not uniformly or even attentively disposed to systems of cultural production or to the messages they issue, how can we theorize, not to mention examine, the ever-shifting kaleidoscope of cultural circulation and consumption?[3]

In confronting this complexity, Radway suggests that mass culture studies begin to analyze reception more ethnographically by focusing on the dense patterns and practices "of daily life and the way in which the media are integrated and implicated within it," rather than starting with already established audience categories.[4] Clearly the danger of making essentializing statements about both audiences and their reception practices lurks behind any uncritical use of categories such as *women, teenagers, lesbians, housewives, blue-collar workers, blacks,* or *gay men.* Further, conducting reception studies on the basis of conventional audience categories can also lead to critical blindness about how certain reception strategies are shared by otherwise disparate individuals and groups.

I would like to propose *queerness* as a mass culture reception practice that is shared by all sorts of people in varying degrees of consistency and intensity.[5] Before proceeding, however, I will need to discuss—even defend—my use of *queer* in such phrases as *queer positions, queer readers, queer readings,* and *queer discourses.* In working through my thoughts on gay and lesbian cultural history, I found that while I used *gay* to describe particulars of men's culture and *lesbian* to describe particulars of women's culture, I was hard-pressed to find a term to describe a cultural common ground between lesbians and gays as well as other nonstraights—a term representing unity as well as suggesting diversity. For certain historical and political reasons, *queer* suggested itself as such a term. As Adele Morrison said in an *OUT/LOOK* interview: "Queer is not an 'instead of,' it's an 'inclusive of.' I'd never want to lose the terms that specifically identify me."[6]

Currently, the word *gay* doesn't consistently have the same gender-unifying quality it may once have possessed. And since I'm interested in discussing aspects of cultural identification as well as of sexual desire, *homosexual* will not do either. I agree with those who do not find the word *homosexual* an appropriate synonym for both *gay* and *lesbian,* as these latter terms are constructions that concern more than who you sleep with—although the objects of sexual desires are certainly central to expressions of lesbian and gay cultural identities. I also wanted to find a term with some ambiguity, a term that would describe a wide range of impulses and cultural expressions, including space for describing and expressing bisexual, transsexual, and straight queerness. While we acknowledge that homosexuals as well as heterosexuals can operate or mediate from within straight cultural spaces and positions—after all, most of us grew up learning the rules of straight culture—we have paid less attention to the proposition that basically heterocentrist texts can contain queer elements, and basically heterosexual, straight-identifying people can experience queer moments. And these people should be encouraged to examine and express these moments *as* queer, not as moments of "homosexual panic," or temporary confusion, or as unfortunate, shameful, or sinful lapses in judgment or taste to be ignored, repressed, condemned, or somehow explained away within and by straight cultural politics—or even within and by gay or lesbian discourses.

My uses of the terms *queer readings, queer discourses,* and *queer positions,* then, are attempts to account for the existence and expression of a wide range of positions within culture that are *queer* or non-, anti-, or contrastraight.[7] I am using the term *queer* to mark a flexible space for the expression of all aspects of non- (anti-, contra-) straight cultural production and reception.[8] As such, this cultural "queer space" recognizes the possibility that various and fluctuating queer positions might be occupied whenever *anyone* produces or responds to culture. In this sense, the use of the term *queer* to discuss reception takes up the standard binary opposition of *queer* and *nonqueer* (or *straight*) while questioning its viability, at least in cultural studies, because, as noted earlier, the queer often operates within the nonqueer, as the nonqueer does within the queer (whether in reception, texts, or producers). The queer readings of mass culture I am concerned with in this essay will be those readings articulating positions *within* queer discourses. That is, these readings seem to be expressions of queer perspectives on mass culture from the inside, rather than descriptions of how "they" (gays and/or lesbians, usually) respond to, use, or are depicted in mass culture.

When a colleague heard I had begun using the word *queer* in my cultural studies work, she asked if I did so in order to "nostalgically" recapture and reassert the "romance" of the culturally marginal in the face of trends within straight capitalist societies to co-opt or contain aspects of queer cultures. I had, in fact, intended something quite different. By using *queer,* I want to recapture and reassert a militant sense of difference that views the erotically "marginal" as both (in bell hooks's words) a consciously chosen "site of resistance" and a "location of radical openness and possibility."[9] And I want to suggest that within cultural production and reception, queer erotics are already part of culture's erotic center, both as a necessary construct by which to define the heterosexual and the straight (as "not queer"), and as a position that can be and is occupied in various ways by otherwise heterosexual and straight-identifying people.

But in another sense recapturing and reasserting a certain nostalgia and romance is part of my project here, for through playfully occupying various queer positions in relation to the fantasy/dream elements involved in cultural production and reception, we (whether straight, gay, lesbian, or bi identifying) are offered spaces to express a range of erotic desire frequently linked in Western cultures to nostalgic and romantic adult conceptions of childhood. Unfortunately, these moments of erotic complexity are usually explained away as part of the "regressive" work of mass media, whereby we are tricked into certain "unacceptable" and "immature" responses as passive subjects. But when cultural texts encourage straight-identified audience members to express a less-censored range of queer desire and pleasure than is possible in daily life, this "regression" has positive gender- and sexuality-destabilizing effects.[10]

I am aware of the current political controversy surrounding the word *queer*. Some gays, lesbians, and bisexuals have expressed their inability to also identify with *queerness*, as they feel the term has too long and too painful a history as a weapon of oppression and self-hate. These nonqueer lesbians, gays, and bisexuals find the attempts of radical forces in gay and lesbian communities (such as Queer Nation) to recover and positively redefine the term *queer* successful only within these communities—and unevenly successful at that. Preferring current or freshly created terms, non-queer-identifying lesbians, gays, and bisexuals often feel that any positive effects resulting from reappropriating *queer* are more theoretical than real.

But the history of gay and lesbian cultures and politics has shown that there are many times and places where the theoretical can have real social impact. Enough lesbians, gays, bisexuals, and other queers taking and making enough of these moments can create a more consistent awareness within the general public of queer cultural and political spaces, as these theory-in-the-flesh moments are concerned with making what has been for the most part publicly invisible and silent visible and vocal. In terms of mass culture reception, there are frequent theory-in-the-flesh opportunities in the course of everyday life. For example, how many times do we get the chance to inform people about our particular queer perspectives on film, television, literature, or music during conversations (or to engage someone else's perhaps unacknowledged queer perspective)? And how often, even if we are openly lesbian, gay, or bisexual, have we kept silent, or edited our conversations, deciding that our queer opinions are really only interesting to other queers, or that these opinions would make people uncomfortable—even while we think family, friends, and strangers should, of course, feel free to articulate various heterosexual or straight opinions in detail at any time?

Of course, queer positions aren't the only ones from which queers read and produce mass culture. As with nonqueers, factors such as class, ethnicity, gender, occupation, education, and religious, national, and regional allegiances influence our identity construction, and therefore are important to the positions we take as cultural producers and readers-consumers. These other cultural factors can exert influences difficult to separate from the development of our identities as queers and, as a result, difficult to discuss apart from our engagement in culture as queers. For example, most people find it next to impossible to articulate their sexual identities (queer or nonqueer) without some reference to gender. Generally, lesbian- and gay-specific forms of queer identities involve some degree of same-gender identification and desire or a cross-gender identification linked to same-gender desire. The understanding of what *gender* is in these cases can range from accepting conventional straight forms, which naturalize *feminine* and *masculine* by conflating them with essentializing, biology-based conceptions of *woman* and *man;* to imitating the outward forms and behaviors of one gender or the other while not fully subscribing to the straight ideological imperatives that define that gender; to combining or ignoring traditional gender codes in order to reflect attitudes that have little or nothing to do with straight ideas about femininity/women or masculinity/men. These last two positions are the places where queerly reconfigured gender identities begin to be worked out.[11]

"Begin to be," because most radically, as Sue-Ellen Case points out, "queer theory, unlike lesbian theory or gay male theory, is not gender specific." Believing that "both gay and lesbian theory reinscribe sexual difference, to some extent, in their gender-specific constructions," Case calls for a queer theory that "works not at the site of gender, but at the site of ontology." But while a nongendered notion of queerness makes sense, articulating this queer theory fully apart from gendered straight feminist, gay, and lesbian theorizing becomes difficult within languages and cultures that make gender and gender difference so crucial to their discursive practices. Through her discussions of vampire myths, Case works hard to establish a discourse that avoids gendered terms, yet she finds it necessary to resort to them every so often in order to suggest the queerness of certain things: placing *she* in quotation marks at one point, or discussing R. W. Fassbinder's film character Petra von Kant as "a truly queer creature who flickers somewhere between haute couture butch lesbian and male drag queen."[12]

Since I'm working with a conception of queerness that includes gay- and lesbian-specific positions as well as Case's nonlesbian and nongay queerness, gender definitions and uses remain important here to examining the ways in which queerness influences mass culture production and reception. For example, gay men who identify with some conception of "the feminine"[13] through processes that could stem from conscious personal choice, or from internalizing long-standing straight imperatives that encourage gay men to think of themselves as "not men" (and therefore, by implication or by direct attribution, as being like "women"), or from some degree of negotiation between these two processes, are at the center of the gay culture cults built around the imposing, spectacular women stars of opera (Maria Callas, Joan Sutherland, Beverly Sills, Renata Scotto, Teresa Stratas, Leontyne Price), theater (Lynn Fontanne, Katharine Cornell, Gertrude Lawrence, Maggie Smith, Angela Lansbury, Ethel Merman, Tallulah Bankhead), film (Bette Davis, Joan Crawford, Judy Garland, Marlene

Dietrich, Vivien Leigh, Bette Midler, Glenda Jackson), popular music (Midler, Garland, Eartha Kitt, Edith Piaf, Barbra Streisand, Billie Holiday, Donna Summer, Diana Ross, Debbie Harry, Madonna), and television (Carol Burnett, the casts of *Designing Women* and *The Golden Girls*, Candice Bergen in *Murphy Brown*, Mary Tyler Moore and the supporting cast of women on *The Mary Tyler Moore Show*).[14] For the past two decades in the gay popular press, book chapters and articles on the connections between gay men and women stars have been a commonplace, but only occasionally do these works go beyond the monolithic audience label *gay men* to suggest the potential for discussing reception in a manner attuned to more specific definitions of sexual identity, such as those constructed to some degree within the dynamics of gender and sexuality.[15]

Given this situation, one strand of queer mass culture reception studies might be more precisely focused on these networks of women performers who were, and are, meaningful at different times and places and for different reasons to feminine-identified gay men. One of the most extended analytic pieces on feminine gay men's reception of women stars is the "Homosexuals' Girls" chapter of Julie Burchill's *Girls on Film*. But Burchill is clearly writing critically *about* a particular queer reception position; she is not queerly positioned herself. Indeed, Burchill's analysis of how "queens" respond to women stars seems written to conform to very narrow-minded ideas about audience and reception. For Burchill, all "feminine homosexual" men's investment in women stars is rooted in envy, jealousy, misogyny, and cruelty—and she concludes this even as she relates a comment by one of her gay friends: "You may have a flaming faggot's taste in movies, kid, but your perspective is pure Puritan."[16]

Clearly, we need more popular and academic mass culture work that carefully considers feminine gay and other gendered queer reception practices, as well as those of even less-analyzed queer readership positions formed around the nexus of race and sexuality, or class and sexuality, or ethnicity and sexuality, or some combination of gender/race/class/ethnicity and sexuality.[17] These studies would offer valuable evidence of precisely how and where specific complex constructions of queerness can and do reveal themselves in the uses of mass culture, as well as revealing how and where that mass culture comes to influence and reinforce the process of queer identity formation.

One of the earliest attempts at such a study of queers and mass culture was a series of interviews with nine lesbians conducted by Judy Whitaker in 1981 for *Jump Cut*, "Hollywood Transformed." These interviews touched on a number of issues surrounding lesbian identity, including gender identification. Although careful to label these interviews "biographical sketches, not sociological or psychological studies," Whitaker does make some comments suggesting the potential for such studies:

Of the nine women who were interviewed, at least six said they identified at some time with male characters. Often the explanation is that men had the interesting active roles. Does this mean that these lesbians want to be like men? That would be a specious conclusion. None of the women who identified with male characters were "in love" with the characters' girl friends. All of the interviewees were "in love" at some time with actresses, but they did not identify with or want to be the male suitors of those actresses. While the context of the discussion is film, what these women are really talking about is their lives. . . . Transformation and positive self-image are dominant themes in what they have to say. Hollywood is transcended.[18]

After reading these interviews, there might be some question about how fully the straight ideologies Hollywood narratives encourage are "transcended" by these lesbian readers' uses of mainstream films, for as two of the interviewees remark, "We're so starved, we go see anything because something is better than nothing," and "It's a compromise. It's a given degree of alienation."[19] This sense of queer readings of mass culture as involving a measure of "compromise" and "alienation" contributes to the complexity of queer articulations of mass culture reception. For the pathos of feeling like a mass culture hanger-on is often related to the processes by which queers (and straights who find themselves queerly positioned) internalize straight culture's homophobic and heterocentrist attitudes and later reproduce them in their own queer responses to film and other mass culture forms.

Even so, traditional narrative films such as *Sylvia Scarlett, Gentlemen Prefer Blondes, Trapeze, To Live and Die in L.A., Internal Affairs*, and *Thelma and Louise*, which are ostensibly addressed to straight audiences, often have greater potential for encouraging a wider range of queer responses than such clearly lesbian- and gay-addressed films as *Scorpio Rising, Home Movies, Women I Love*, and *Loads*.[20] The intense tensions and pleasures generated by the woman-woman and man-man aspects within the narratives of the former group of films create a space of sexual instability that already queerly positioned viewers can connect with in various ways, and within which straights might be likely to recognize and express their queer impulses. For example, gays might find a form of queer pleasure in the alternately tender and boisterous rapport between Lorelei/Marilyn Monroe and Dorothy/Jane Russell in *Gentlemen Prefer Blondes,* or in the exhilarating woman bonding of the title characters in *Thelma and Louise*. Or lesbians and straights could queerly respond to the erotic elements in the relationships between the major male characters in *Trapeze, To Live and Die in L.A.,* or *Internal Affairs*. And any viewer might feel a sexually ambiguous attraction—is it gay, lesbian, bisexual, or straight?—to the image of Katharine Hepburn dressed as a young man in *Sylvia Scarlett*.

Of course, these queer positions and readings can become modified or can change over time, as people, cultures, and politics change. In my own case, as a white gay male who internalized dominant culture's definitions of myself as "like a woman" in a traditional 1950s and 1960s understanding of who *a woman* and what *femininity* were supposed to be, my pleasure in *Gentlemen Prefer Blondes* initially worked itself out through a classic gay process of identifying, alternately, with Monroe and Russell, thereby experiencing vicarious if temporary empowerment through their use of sexual allure to attract men—including the entire American Olympic team. Reassessing the feminine aspects of my gay sexual identity sometime in the 1970s (after Stonewall and my coming out), I returned to the film and discovered my response was now less rooted in the fantasy of being Monroe or Russell and gaining sexual access to men, than in the pleasure of Russell being the "gentleman" who preferred blonde Monroe, who looked out for her best interests, who protected her against men, and who enjoyed performing with her. This queer pleasure in a lesbian text has been abetted by extratextual information I have read, or was told about Russell's solicitous and supportive offscreen behavior toward Monroe while making the film.[21] But along with these elements of queer reading that developed from the interaction of my feminine gay identity, my knowledge of extratextual behind-the-scenes gossip, and the text itself, I also take a great deal of direct gay erotic pleasure in the "Is There Anyone Here for Love?" number, enjoying its blatantly homohistoric and -erotic ancient Greek Olympics mise-en-scène (including Russell's large column earrings), while admiring Russell's panache and good humor as she sings, strides, and strokes her way through a sea of half-naked male dancer-athletes. I no longer feel the need to mediate my sexual desires through her.

In 1985, Al LaValley suggested that this type of movement—from negotiating gay sexual desire through strong women stars to directly expressing desire for male images on screen—was becoming increasingly evident in gay culture, although certain forms of identification with women through gay connections with "the feminine" continue:

One might have expected Stonewall to make star cults outmoded among gays. In a sense it did: The natural-man discourse, with its strong political and social vision and its sense of a fulfilled and open self, has supplanted both the aesthetic and campy discourses. . . . A delirious absorption in the stars is now something associated with preStonewall gays or drag queens, yet neither gay openness nor the new machismo has completely abolished the cults. New figures are added regularly: Diana Ross, Donna Summer, Jennifer Holliday from the world of music, for example. There's a newer, more open gay following for male stars: Richard Gere, Christopher Reeve [and, to update, Mel Gibson], even teen hunks like Matt Dillon [Christopher Atkins, Johnny Depp, Jason Priestley, and Luke Perry].[22]

One could also add performers such as Bette Midler, Patti LaBelle, and Madonna to LaValley's list of women performers. While ambivalent about her motives ("Is she the Queen of Queers. . . . Or is she just milking us for shock value?"), Michael Musto's *Outweek* article "Immaculate Connection" suggests that Madonna is queer culture's post-Stonewall Judy Garland:

By now, we finally seem willing to release Judy Garland from her afterlife responsibility of being our quintessential icon. And in the land of the living, career stagnation has robbed Diana [Ross], Liza [Minnelli], and Barbra [Streisand] of their chances, while Donna [Summer] thumped the bible on our heads in a way that made it bounce back into her face. That leaves Madonna as Queer Queen, and she merits the title as someone who isn't afraid to offend straight America if it does the rest of us some good.

Musto finds Madonna "unlike past icons" as she's "not a vulnerable toy":[23] this indicates to him the need to reexamine gay culture's enthusiasms for women stars with greater attention to how shifting historic (and perhaps generational) contexts alter the meanings and uses of these stars for particular groups of gay men.

Examining how and where these gay cults of women stars work in relation to what LaValley saw in the mid-1980s as the "newer, more openly gay following for male stars" would also make for fascinating cultural history. Certainly there have been "homosexual" followings for male personalities in mass culture since the late nineteenth century, with performers and actors—Sandow the muscleman, Edwin Booth—vying with gay enthusiasms for opera divas and actresses such as Jenny Lind and Lillian Russell. Along these lines, one could queerly combine star studies with genre studies in order to analyze the gay appreciation of women musical performers, and the musical's "feminine" or "effeminized" aesthetic, camp, and emotive genre characteristics (spectacularized decor and costuming, intricate choreography, and singing about romantic yearning and fulfillment), with reference to the more hidden cultural history of gay erotics centered around men in musicals.[24]

In film, this erotic history would perhaps begin with Ramon Navarro (himself gay) stripped down to sing "Pagan Love Song" in *The Pagan*. Beyond this, a gay beefcake musical history would include Gene Kelly (whose ass was always on display in carefully tailored pants); numbers like "Is There Anyone Here for Love?" (*Gentlemen Prefer Blondes*) and "Y.M.C.A." (*Can't Stop the Music*) that feature men in gym shorts, swimsuits (Esther Williams musicals are especially spectacular in this regard), military (especially sailor) uniforms, and pseudonative or pseudoclassical (Greek and Roman) outfits; films such as *Athena* (bodybuilders), *Seven Brides for Seven Brothers* (Western Levis, flannel, and leather men), *West Side Story* (Hispanic and Anglo T-shirted and blue-jeaned delinquents, including a butch girl); Elvis Presley films (and those of other "teen girl" pop and rock music idols—Frank Sinatra, Ricky Nelson, Fabian, Cliff Richard, the Beatles, and so on); and the films of John Travolta (*Saturday Night Fever, Grease, Staying Alive*), Patrick Swayze (*Dirty Dancing*), and Mikhail Baryshnikov, who in *The Turning Point* and *White Nights* provided the impetus for many gays to be more vocal about their "lowbrow" sexual pleasure in supposedly high-cultural male bodies. If television, music video, and concert performers and texts were added to this hardly exhaustive list, it would include David Bowie, Morrissey, David Cassidy, Tom Jones, and Marky Mark, among many others, and videos such as *Cherish, Express Yourself,* and *Justify My Love* (all performed by Madonna), *Being Boring* (The Pet Shop Boys), *Love Will Never Do Without You* (Janet Jackson), *Just Tell Me That You Want Me* (Kim Wilde), and *Rico Suave* (Gerardo), along with a number of heavy-metal videos featuring long-haired lead singers in a variety of skintight and artfully opened or ripped clothes.[25]

I can't leave this discussion of gay erotics and musicals without a few more words about Gene Kelly's "male trio" musicals, such as *On the Town, Take Me Out to the Ball Game,* and *It's Always Fair Weather.*[26] Clad in sailor uniforms, baseball uniforms, and Army uniforms, the male trios in these films are composed of two conventionally sexy men (Kelly and Frank Sinatra in the first two films, Kelly and Dan Dailey in the last) and a comic, less attractive "buffer" (Jules Munshin in the first two, Michael Kidd in the last) who is meant to diffuse the sexual energy generated between the two male leads when they sing and dance together. Other Kelly films—*Singin' in the Rain, An American in Paris,* and *Anchors Aweigh*—resort to the more conventional heterosexual(izing) narrative device of using a woman to mediate and diffuse male-male erotics.[27] But whether in the form of a third man or an ingenue, these devices fail to fully heterosexualize the relationship between Kelly and his male costars. In *Singin' in the Rain,* for example, I can't help but read Donald O'Connor maniacally unleashing his physical energy to entertain Kelly during the "Make 'Em Laugh" number as anything but a case of overwrought, displaced gay desire.[28]

Kelly himself jokingly refers to the queer erotics of his image and his many buddy musicals in *That's Entertainment!* when he reveals the answer to the often-asked question, "Who was your favorite dancing partner . . . Cyd Charisse, Leslie Caron, Rita Hayworth, Vera-Ellen?" by showing a clip of the dance he did with Fred Astaire ("The Babbit and the Bromide") in *Ziegfeld Follies*. "It's the only time we danced together," Kelly remarks over the clip, "but I'd change my name to Ginger if we could do it again." As it turned out, Kelly and Astaire did "do it again" in *That's Entertainment 2,* and their reunion as a dancing couple became the focus of much of the film's publicity campaign, as had been the case when Astaire reunited with Ginger Rogers in *The Barkleys of Broadway.*[29]

While there has been at the very least a general, if often clichéd, cultural connection made between gays and musicals, lesbian work within the genre has been less acknowledged. However, the evidence of lesbian viewing practices—in articles such as "Hollywood Transformed," in videos such as *Dry Kisses Only* and *Grapefruit*, and in informal discussions (mention *Calamity Jane* to a group of thirty- to fortysomething American lesbians)—suggests that lesbian viewers have always negotiated their own culturally specific readings and pleasures within the genre.[30] Although it never uses the word *lesbian*, Lucie Arbuthnot and Gail Seneca's 1982 article "Pre-text and Text in *Gentlemen Prefer Blondes*" is perhaps the best-known lesbian-positioned piece on the musical. While couched in homosocial rhetoric, this analysis of the authors' pleasures in the film focuses on Lorelei/Monroe's and Dorothy/Russell's connection to each other through looks, touch, and words (*lovey, honey, sister, dear*). Noting that a "typical characteristic of [the] movie musical genre is that there are two leads, a man and a woman, who sing and dance together, and eventually become romantically involved," Seneca and Arbuthnot recognize that in *Gentlemen Prefer Blondes* "it is Monroe and Russell who sing—and even harmonize, adding another layer to the metaphor—and dance as a team." Since the men in the film are "never given a musical role," the authors conclude "the pre-text of heterosexual romance is so thin that it scarcely threatens the text of female friendship."[31]

One note hints at a possible butch-femme reading of the Russell/Monroe relationship, centered on Russell's forthright stride and stance: "The Russell character also adopts a 'masculine' stride and stance. More often, Monroe plays the 'lady' to Russell's manly moves. For example, Russell opens doors for Monroe; Monroe sinks into Russell's strong frame, allowing Russell to hold her protectively."[32] Released in 1953, during the height of traditional butch-femme role-playing in American urban lesbian culture, *Gentlemen Prefer Blondes* could well have been read and enjoyed by lesbians at the time with reference to this particular social-psychological paradigm for understanding and expressing their sexual identity.[33] The film continues to be read along these lines by some lesbians as well as by other queerly positioned viewers. Overall, Seneca and Arbuthnot's analysis of *Gentlemen Prefer Blondes* qualifies as a lesbian reading, as it discusses the film and the musical genre so as to "re-vision . . . connections with women" by focusing on the pleasures of and between women on the screen and women in the audience, rather than on "the ways in which the film affords pleasure, or denies pleasure, to men."[34]

Working with the various suggestive comments in this article and considering actual and potential lesbian readings of other musicals can lead to a consideration of other pairs and trios of song-and-dance women performers (often related as sisters in the narratives), certain strong solo women film and video musical stars (Eleanor Powell, Esther Williams, Carmen Miranda, Lena Horne, Eartha Kitt, Doris Day, Julie Andrews, Tina Turner, Madonna), and musical numbers performed by groups of women, with little or no participation by men.[35] Of particular interest in this latter category are those often-reviled Busby Berkeley musical spectacles, which appear in a different light if one considers lesbians (and other queers) as spectators, rather than straight men. I'm thinking here especially of numbers like "The Lady in the Tutti-Frutti Hat" in *The Gang's All Here*, where Carmen Miranda triggers an all-woman group masturbation fantasia involving banana dildos and foot fetishism; "Dames" in *Dames*, where women sleep, bathe, dress, and seek employment together—some pause to acknowledge the camera as bearer of the voyeuristic (straight) male gaze, only to prohibit this gaze by using powder puffs, atomizer sprays, and other objects to cover the lens; "The Polka-Dot Ballet" in *The Gang's All Here*, where androgynized women in tights rhythmically move neon hoops and large dots in unison, then melt into a vivid, hallucinogenically colored vaginal opening initially inhabited by Alice Faye's head surrounded by shiny cloth; "Spin a Little Web of Dreams" in *Fashions of 1934*, where a seamstress falls asleep and "spins a little web of dreams" about a group of seminude women amid giant undulating ostrich-feather fans who, at one point, create a tableau called "Venus with Her Galley Slaves"; and parts of many other numbers (the two women sharing an upper berth on the Niagara Limited who cynically comment on marriage in *42nd Street*'s "Shuffle Off to Buffalo," e.g.).[36]

Since this discussion of queer positions and queer readings seems to have worked itself out so far largely as a discussion of musical stars and the musical genre, I might add here that of the articles and books written about film musicals only the revised edition of Jane Feuer's *Hollywood Musicals* goes beyond a passing remark in considering the ways in which this genre has been the product of gay film workers, or how the ways in which musicals are viewed and later talked about have been influenced by gay and lesbian reception practices.[37] From most accounts of the musical, it is a genre whose celebration of heterosexual romance must always be read straight. The same seems to be the case with those other film genres typically linked to gays, lesbians, and bisexuals: the horror/fantasy film and the melodrama. While there has been a rich history of queers producing and reading these genres, surprisingly little has been done to express this cultural history formally. There has been more queer work done in and on the horror film: vampire pieces by Richard Dyer, Bonnie Zimmerman, and Sue-Ellen Case; Bruna Fionda, Polly Gladwin, Isiling Mack-Nataf's lesbian vampire film *The Mark of Lilith* (1986); Amy Goldstein's vampire musical film *Because the Dawn* (1988); a sequence in *Dry Kisses Only* that provides a lesbian take on vampire films; an article by Martin F. Norden on sexuality in *The Bride of Frankenstein;*

and some pieces on *The Rocky Horror Picture Show* (although most are not written from a queer position), to cite a few examples.[38]

But there is still much left unexamined beyond the level of conversation. Carl Dreyer's lesbophobic "classic" *Vampyr* could use a thorough queer reading, as could Tod Browning's *Dracula*—which opens with a coach ride through Transylvania in the company of a superstitious Christian straight couple, a suit-and-tie lesbian couple, and a feminine gay man, who will quickly become the bisexual Count Dracula's vampirized servant. Subsequent events in the film include a straight woman who becomes a child molester known as "The Woman in White" after the count vampirizes her. It is also amazing that gay horror director James Whale has yet to receive full-scale queer auteurist consideration for films such as *Frankenstein* (the idea of men making the "perfect" man), *The Bride of Frankenstein* (gay Dr. Praetorius; queer Henry Frankenstein; the erotics between the blind man, the monster, and Jesus on the cross; the overall campy atmosphere), *The Old Dark House* (a gay and lesbian brother and sister; a 103-year-old man in the attic who is actually a woman), and *The Invisible Man* (effete, mad genius Claude Rains spurns his fiancée, becomes invisible, tries to find a male partner in crime, and becomes *visible* only after he is killed by the police).[39] Beyond queer readings of specific films and directors, it would also be important to consider how the central conventions of horror and melodrama actually encourage queer positioning as they exploit the spectacle of heterosexual romance, straight domesticity, and traditional gender roles gone awry. In a sense, then, *everyone's* pleasure in these genres is "perverse," is queer, as much of it takes place within the space of the contraheterosexual and the contrastraight.

Just how much everyone's pleasures in mass culture are part of this contrastraight, rather than strictly antistraight, space—just how *queer* our responses to cultural texts are so much of the time—is what I'd finally like this essay to suggest. Queer positions, queer readings, and queer pleasures are part of a reception space that stands simultaneously beside and within that created by heterosexual and straight positions. These positions, readings, and pleasures also suggest that what happens in cultural reception goes beyond the traditional opposition of homo and hetero, as queer reception is often a place beyond the audience's conscious "real-life" definition of their sexual identities and cultural positions—often, but not always, beyond such sexual identities and identity politics, that is—for, in all my enthusiasm for breaking down rigid concepts of sexuality through the example of mass culture reception, I don't want to suggest that there is a queer utopia that unproblematically and apolitically unites straights and queers (or even all queers) in some mass culture reception area in the sky. Queer reception doesn't stand outside personal and cultural histories; it is part of the articulation of these histories. This is why, politically, queer reception (and production) practices can include everything from the reactionary to the radical to the indeterminate, as with the audience for (as well as the producers of) "queercore" publications, who individually and collectively often seem to combine reactionary and radical attitudes.

What queer reception often does, however, is stand outside the relatively clear-cut and essentializing categories of sexual identity under which most people function. You might identify yourself as a lesbian or a straight woman yet queerly experience the gay erotics of male buddy films such as *Red River* and *Butch Cassidy and the Sundance Kid;* or maybe as a gay man your cultlike devotion to *Laverne and Shirley, Kate and Allie,* or *The Golden Girls* has less to do with straight-defined cross-gender identification than with your queer enjoyment in how these series are crucially concerned with articulating the loving relationships between women.[40] Queer readings aren't "alternative" readings, wishful or willful misreadings, or "reading too much into things" readings. They result from the recognition and articulation of the complex range of queerness that has been in popular culture texts and their audiences all along.

Notes

1 Jean Genet, *Gay Sunshine Interviews,* ed. Winston Leyland (San Francisco: Gay Sunshine, 1978), 73.

2 Gretchen Phillips, "The Queer Song," performed by Two Nice Girls, *Chloe Likes Olivia* (Rough Trade Records, 1991). Lyrics quoted by permission.

3 Janice Radway, "Reception Study: Ethnography and the Problems of Dispersed Audiences and Nomadic Subjects," *Cultural Studies* 2, no. 3 (October 1988): 361.

4 Ibid., 366.

5 Stuart Hall's article "Encoding/Decoding" informs much of my general approach to queer cultural readings of mass culture. This important essay is in *Culture, Media, Language,* ed. Stuart Hall, Andrew Lowe, and Paul Willis (Birmingham, U.K.: Center for Contemporary Cultural Studies, 1980), 128–38.

6 Adele Morrison as quoted in Steve Cosson, "Queer," *OUT/LOOK* 11 (Winter 1991): 21.

7 Although the ideas that comprise *straightness* and *heterosexuality* are actually flexible and changeable over time and across cultures, these concepts have been—and still are—generally understood within Western public discourses as rather clearly defined around rigid gender roles, exclusive opposite-sex desires, and such social and ideological institutions as patriarchy, marriage, "legitimate" childbearing and -rearing, and the nuclear, patrilineal family. And all of this has been/is placed in binary opposition to *homosexuality* or *queerness.* However, if we consider the notion of *queerness* in relation to the terms of the still commonly evoked utopian binary of sexuality (with its implicit dynamics of hetero-

sexual gender stability vs. homosexual [cross-]gender instability), it becomes clear that queerness, not straightness, describes an enormous space of cultural production and reception. For it is *deviance* from the demands of strict straight/heterosexual paradigms (however they are defined in a given time and place) that most often defines and describes our sexualized and/or gendered pleasures and positions in relation to movies, television, videos, and popular music. Indeed, many so-called straight mass culture texts encourage "deviant" erotic and/or gendered responses and pleasures in straight viewers.

8 These thoughts about queer spaces in mass culture are most immediately indebted to Robin Wood's "Responsibilities of a Gay Film Critic," in *Movies and Methods II,* ed. Bill Nichols (Berkeley and Los Angeles: University of California Press, 1985), 649–60; and Marilyn R. Farwell's "Heterosexual Plots and Lesbian Subtexts: Toward a Theory of Lesbian Narrative Space," in *Lesbian Texts and Contexts: Radical Revisions,* ed. Karla Jay and Joanne Glasgow (New York: New York University Press, 1990), 91–103. Concerned with the politics of film critics/theorists (Wood) and the creation of uniquely lesbian narrative spaces for characters in literature (Farwell), these articles lucidly combine academic theory with gay- and lesbian-specific cultural concerns to suggest how and where being gay or lesbian makes a difference in cultural production and reception.

9 bell hooks, "Choosing the Margins as a Space of Radical Openness," in *Yearning: Race, Gender, and Cultural Politics* (Boston: South End, 1990), 153.

10 While I use the term *regression* here in relation to queerness and mass culture, I don't want to invoke conventional psychoanalytic and popular ideas about queerness as a permanently infantilized stage past which heterosexuals somehow progress.

11 In "On Becoming a Lesbian Reader," in *Sweet Dreams: Sexuality, Gender and Popular Fiction,* ed. Susannah Radstone (London: Lawrence & Wishart, 1988), Allison Hennegan offers many incisive examples of the complex workings of gender in the construction of queer identities and cultural reading practices, as well as indicating the reciprocity between sexual identity formation and reading cultural texts. Speaking of her adolescence, Hennegan states: "That I turned to ancient Greece need come as no surprise. If there's one thing everyone knows about the Greeks it's that they were all That Way. . . . That women's own voices were virtually silent, bar a few precious scraps of lyric poetry and the occasional verbatim transcript from a court hearing, did not then worry me. What I was looking for were strong and passionate emotions which bound human beings to members of their own sex rather than to the other. That the bonds depicted existed primarily between men didn't matter. In part this was because I spent at least half my adolescence 'being male' inside my own head: 'gender identity confusion' in today's terminology, or 'male identified,' but neither phrase is right or adequate. I never for one moment thought I was a man nor wished to be. But somehow I had to find a way of thinking of myself which included the possibility of desiring women. And those who desire women are men" (p. 170).

12 Sue-Ellen Case, "Tracking the Vampire," *differences* 3, no. 2 (Summer 1991): 2, 3, 8, 12.

13 Some gay men will prefer the terms *effeminate* or *woman identified* where I use *feminine* in this section and throughout the text. I find the former term still too closely connected to straight uses that simultaneously trivialize and trash women and gay men, while the latter

term might appear to place gay men in the position of essentializing theoretical transsexuals. Where I use *effeminate,* it should be understood as describing culturally dictated heterosexist ideas about gays and gender (which queers might also employ).

14 Although most of these performers have an international gay following, this list is rather Anglo-American. To begin to expand it, one would add names like Zarah Leander (Germany), Isa Miranda (Italy), Dolores del Rio, Maria Felix, Sara Montiel (Latin America and Spain), and Josephine Baker (France). As is the case in the United States and Great Britain, while some national and regional queer cultural work has been done regarding (feminine) gays and women stars, much more needs to be done. Television series cited in this section: *Designing Women* (1986–93, CBS), *The Golden Girls* (1985–92, NBC), *Murphy Brown* (1989–present, CBS), *The Mary Tyler Moore Show* (1970–77, CBS).

15 Among the work on women stars that concerns feminine gay reception (with the "feminine" aspects usually implied) are Parker Tyler, "Mother Superior of the Faggots and Some Rival Queens," in *Screening the Sexes: Homosexuality in the Movies* (Garden City, N.Y.: Anchor, 1973), 1–15 (on Mae West); Quentin Crisp, "Stardom and Stars," in *How to Go to the Movies* (New York: St. Martin's, 1989), 11–30; Gregg Howe, "On Identifying with Judy Garland" and "A Dozen Women We Adore," in *Gay Life,* ed. Eric E. Rofes (New York: Doubleday, 1986), 178–86; Seymour Kleinberg, "Finer Clay: The World Eroticized," in *Alienated Affections: Being Gay in America* (New York: St. Martin's, 1980), 38–69; Michael Bronski, "Hollywood Homo-sense," in *Culture Clash: The Making of Gay Sensibility* (Boston: South End, 1984), 134–43; Jack Smith, "The Perfect Filmic Appositeness of Maria Montez," *Film Culture* 27 (1962–63): 28–32. I might also include critic John Simon's *Private Screenings* (New York: Macmillan, 1967) on this list, for its Wildean bitchy-witty critiques of stars such as Elizabeth Taylor, Barbra Streisand, Anna Karina, and Monica Vitti, which are embedded in film reviews. Simon may be a self-declared straight, but his style and sensibility, in this collection at least, are pure scathing urban queen—which works itself out here, unfortunately, to include a heavy dose of misogyny.

16 Julie Burchill, *Girls on Film* (New York: Pantheon, 1986), 109.

17 More work is being done in these areas all the time. Some of the more recent essays include Richard Fung, "Looking for My Penis: The Eroticized Asian in Gay Porn Video," in *How Do I Look? Queer Film and Video,* ed. Bad Object-Choices (Seattle: Bay, 1991), 145–60; Kobena Mercer, "Skin Head Sex Thing: Radical Differences and the Homoerotic," in ibid., 169–210; Mark A. Reid, "The Photography of Rotimi Fani-Kayode," *Wide Angle* 14, no. 2 (April 1992): 38–51; Essex Hemphill, "*In Living Color:* Toms, Coons, Mammies, Faggots and Bucks," *Outweek* 78 (26 December 1990): 32–40; Marlon Riggs, "Black Macho Revisited: Reflections on a Snap! Queen," *Independent* 14, no. 3 (April 1991): 32–34; Manthia Diawara, "The Absent One: The Avant-Garde and the Black Imaginary in *Looking for Langston,*" *Wide Angle* 13, nos. 3/4 (July–October 1991): 96–109; Anthony Thomas, "The House the Kids Built: The Gay Imprint on American Dance Music," *OUT/LOOK* 2, no. 1 (Summer 1989): 24–33; Jackie Goldsby, "What It Means to Be Colored Me," *OUT/LOOK* 3, no. 1 (Summer 1990): 8–17; Kobena Mercer and Isaac

Julien, "Race, Sexual Politics and Black Masculinity: A Dossier," in *Unwrapping Masculinity*, ed. Rowena Chapman and Jonathan Rutherford (London: Lawrence & Wishart, 1988), 97–164.

18 Judy Whitaker, "Hollywood Transformed," *Jump Cut* 24/25 (1981): 33. Gail Sausser's "Movie and T.V. Heart-Throbs" chapter of *Lesbian Etiquette* (Trumansburg, N.Y.: Crossing, 1986) offers another expression of lesbian reception practices, their connection to gender identity, and the evolution of both through time: "I loved romantic movies when I was a teenager. I unconsciously identified with all the heroes who got the girl. Since I came out, however, my identifications have changed. Now I yell, 'No, no, not him!" at the heroine and root for her female roommate. What a difference a decade (or two) makes" (p. 57).

19 Whitaker, "Hollywood," 34.

20 Films mentioned in this section: *Sylvia Scarlett,* directed by George Cukor (RKO, 1936); *Gentlemen Prefer Blondes,* directed by Howard Hawks (Twentieth Century–Fox, 1953); *Trapeze,* directed by Carol Reed (United Artists, 1956); *To Live and Die in L.A.,* directed by William Friedkin (New Century, 1985); *Internal Affairs,* directed by Mike Figgis (Paramount, 1990); *Thelma and Louise,* directed by Ridley Scott (MGM, 1991); *Scorpio Rising,* directed by Kenneth Anger (1962–63); *Home Movies,* directed by Jan Oxenberg (1972); *Women I Love,* directed by Barbara Hammer (1976); and *Loads,* directed by Curt McDowell (1980).

When I say certain mainstream films elicit a "wider range of queer responses" than films made by, for, or about lesbians, gays, and bisexuals, I am not commenting on the politics of these films or their reception, only about the multiplicity of queer responses. And while the lesbian and gay films listed here are much more direct and explicit about the sex in them being homo, the sexual politics of these films are not necessarily more progressive or radical than that of the mainstream films.

21 The strength of the Monroe-Lorelei/Russell-Dorothy pairing on and off screen was publicly acknowledged shortly after the film's release when, as a team, the two stars went through the ceremony of putting prints of their hands and feet in the forecourt of Grauman's Chinese Theatre in Hollywood.

22 Al LaValley, "The Great Escape," *American Film* 10, no. 6 (April 1985): 71. (LaValley's essay is reprinted in this volume.)

23 Michael Musto, "Immaculate Connection," *Outweek* 90 (20 March 1991): 35–36.

24 In the revised edition of *The Hollywood Musical* (London: BFI and Bloomington: Indiana University Press, 1993), Jane Feuer has added a brief section focusing on MGM's Freed Unit and Judy Garland that suggests ways of developing gay readings of musicals with reference to both production and queer cultural contexts. Mentioned in Feuer's discussions, Richard Dyer's chapter "Judy Garland and Gay Men," in *Heavenly Bodies: Film Stars and Society* (New York: St. Martin's, 1986), 141–94, is an exemplary analysis of how and why queers and queer cultures read and, in certain ways, help to create star personas.

25 Films mentioned in this section: *The Pagan,* directed by W. S. Van Dyke (MGM, 1929); *Athena,* directed by Richard Thorpe (MGM, 1954); *Seven Brides for Seven Brothers,* di-

rected by Stanley Donan (MGM, 1954); *West Side Story,* directed by Robert Wise and Jerome Robbins (United Artists, 1961); *Saturday Night Fever,* directed by John Badham (Paramount, 1977); *Grease,* directed by Randall Kleiser (Paramount, 1980); *Staying Alive,* directed by Sylvester Stallone (Paramount, 1984); *Dirty Dancing,* directed by Emile Ardolino (Vestron, 1987); *The Turning Point,* directed by Herbert Ross (Twentieth Century–Fox, 1977); and *White Nights,* directed by Taylor Hackford (Paramount, 1987).

26 Films cited: *On the Town,* directed by Gene Kelly and Stanley Donen (MGM, 1950); *Take Me Out to the Ball Game,* directed by Busby Berkeley (MGM, 1949); and *It's Always Fair Weather,* directed by Gene Kelly and Stanley Donen (MGM, 1955). For a more extended discussion of Gene Kelly and the "buddy" musical, see Steven Cohan's chapter "Les Boys," in *Masked Men: American Masculinity and the Movies in the Fifties* (Bloomington: Indiana University Press, forthcoming).

27 Films cited: *Singin' in the Rain,* directed by Gene Kelly and Stanley Donen (MGM, 1952); *An American in Paris,* directed by Vincente Minnelli (MGM, 1951); and *Anchors Aweigh,* directed by George Sidney (MGM, 1945).

28 In *The Celluloid Closet: Homosexuality in the Movies,* rev. ed. (New York: Harper & Row, 1987), Vito Russo uncovers material on *Singin' in the Rain*'s production history that reveals that the erotics between Kelly and O'Connor were referred to in the original script: "One line of dialogue in Betty Comden and Adolph Green's screenplay for *Singin' in the Rain* (1952) was penciled out by the censors because it gave 'a hint of sexual perversion' between Donald O'Connor and Gene Kelly. When O'Connor gets the idea of dubbing the voice of Debbie Reynolds for the high-pitched, tinny voice of Jean Hagen in a proposed musical, *The Dancing Cavalier,* he illustrates his idea for Kelly by standing in front of Reynolds and mouthing the words to 'Good Morning' while she sings behind him. When the song is over, O'Connor turns to Kelly and asks 'Well? Convincing?' Kelly, not yet catching on, takes it as a joke and replies, 'Enchanting! What are you doing later?' The joke was eliminated" (pp. 98–99).

29 Films cited: *That's Entertainment,* directed by Jack Haley, Jr. (MGM, 1974); *Ziegfeld Follies,* directed by Vincente Minnelli (MGM, 1946); *That's Entertainment 2,* directed by Gene Kelly (MGM, 1976); and *The Barkleys of Broadway,* directed by Charles Walters (MGM, 1949).

30 Whitaker, "Hollywood Transformed"; *Dry Kisses Only,* directed by Jane Cottis and Kaucyila Brooke (1990); *Grapefruit,* directed by Cecelia Dougherty (1989); *Calamity Jane,* directed by David Butler (Warners, 1953). Some lesbians also take what they would describe as a gay pleasure in musicals, and perform readings of individual films and of the genre in terms they identify as being influenced by their understanding of the ways gay men appreciate musicals. These kinds of gay approaches might take the form of specific star cult enthusiasms (for Judy Garland, Barbra Streisand, or Bette Midler, e.g.) that individual lesbian readers feel aren't important in lesbian culture, or of an appreciation for certain aesthetic or critical approaches (camp, e.g.) that seem unpopular, inoperative, or not "politically correct" in the lesbian culture(s) within which the individual reader places herself.

31 Lucie Arbuthnot and Gail Seneca, "Pre-text and Text in *Gentlemen Prefer Blondes,*"

Film Reader 5 (1982): 20, 21. This essay is reprinted in *Issues in Feminist Film Criticism,* ed. Patricia Erens (Bloomington: Indiana University Press, 1990), 112–25.

32 Ibid., 23.

33 Alix Stanton's "Blondes, Brunettes, Butches and Femmes" (seminar paper, Cornell University, 1991) offers a more extended consideration of butch-femme roles and cultures in relation to readings of *Gentlemen Prefer Blondes* (and *How to Marry a Millionaire,* directed by Jean Negulesco, Twentieth Century–Fox, 1953).

34 Arbuthnot and Seneca, "Pre-text and Text," 21. For another approach to the lesbian aspects of this film, see Maureen Turim's "Gentlemen Consume Blondes," in *Issues in Feminist Film Criticism,* 101–11 (originally in *Wide Angle* 1, no. 1 [1979]; also reprinted in *Movies and Methods, Volume II,* ed. Bill Nichols [Berkeley and Los Angeles: University of California Press, 1985]: 369–78). As part of an addendum to the original article, Turim considers lesbianism and *Gentlemen Prefer Blondes* in light of certain feminist film theories about straight male spectatorship. Turim sees the main characters as male constructed "pseudo-lesbians," and the film's use of them as being related to "how lesbianism has served in male-oriented pornography to increase visual stimulation and to ultimately give twice as much power to the eye, which can penetrate even the liaisons which would appear to deny male entry" (pp. 110–11).

35 While not a lesbian-specific reading, Shari Roberts's "You Are My Lucky Star: Eleanor Powell's Brief Dance with Fame" (from "Seeing Stars: Female WWII Hollywood Musical Stars" [Ph.D. diss., University of Chicago, 1994]) is suggestive of how and where such a reading might begin, with its discussion of Powell's (autoerotic) strength as a solo performer and its threatening qualities: "If . . . Powell represents a recognition of women as independent, working women, her films also reflect society's related fear of this 'new' woman, and potential gender confusion. . . . This anxiety is demonstrated with homophobic and cross-dressing jokes in the Powell films" (p. 7).

36 Films mentioned in this section: *The Gang's All Here,* directed by Busby Berkeley (Twentieth Century–Fox, 1943); *Dames,* directed by Ray Enright (Warners, 1934); *Fashions of 1934,* directed by William Dieterle (Warners, 1934); and *42nd Street,* directed by Lloyd Bacon (Warners, 1933).

37 Feuer's "Gay Readings of Musicals" section in *Hollywood Musicals* concentrates on gay male production and reception of musicals.

38 Articles mentioned in this section: Richard Dyer, "Children of the Night: Vampirism as Homosexuality, Homosexuality as Vampirism," in *Sweet Dreams,* 47–72; Bonnie Zimmerman, "*Daughters of Darkness:* Lesbian Vampires," *Jump Cut* 24/25 (1981): 23–24; Sue-Ellen Case, "Tracking the Vampire," *differences* 3, no. 2 (Summer 1991): 1–20; Martin F. Norden, "Sexual References in James Whale's *Bride of Frankenstein,*" in *Eros in the Mind's Eye: Sexuality and the Fantastic in Art and Film,* ed. Donald Palumbo (New York: Greenwood, 1986), 141–50; Elizabeth Reba Weise, "Bisexuality, *The Rocky Horror Picture Show,* and Me," in *Bi Any Other Name: Bisexual People Speak Out,* ed. Loraine Hutchins and Lani Kaahumanu (Boston: Alyson, 1991), 134–39.

39 Films mentioned in this section: *Vampyr,* directed by Carl Theodore Dryer (Gloria Film, 1931); *Dracula,* directed by Tod Browning (Universal, 1931); *Frankenstein,* directed

by James Whale (Universal, 1931); *The Bride of Frankenstein,* directed by James Whale (Universal, 1935); *The Old Dark House,* directed by James Whale (Universal, 1932); and *The Invisible Man,* directed by James Whale (Universal, 1933). In light of the discussion of musicals in this essay, it is interesting to recall here that Whale's biggest success apart from his horror films was directing Universal's 1936 version of *Show Boat.*

40 Films and television series mentioned in this section: *Red River,* directed by Howard Hawks (United Artists, 1948); *Butch Cassidy and the Sundance Kid,* directed by George Roy Hill (Twentieth Century–Fox, 1969); *Laverne and Shirley* (1976–83, ABC); *Kate and Allie* (1984–90, CBS); and *The Golden Girls* (1985–92, NBC).

Supporting

Character

The Queer Career of Agnes Moorehead

Patricia White

The main character of Robert Aldrich's *The Killing of Sister George* is a role-playing lesbian in more than one sense. In "real life" June Buckridge (Beryl Reid) is "George," a bawdy, domineering, cigar-smoking butch, whose younger lover Childie keeps house and collects dolls. As the country nurse "Sister George" on a television soap opera, she is a character actress beloved by the public. Produced in 1968, on the verge of Stonewall and just in time to receive an X under the ratings system that finally replaced the Production Code, *The Killing of Sister George* is one of the first Hollywood films to represent lesbianism openly. But, in making its main character a character actress, the film suggests that lesbians may always have been present in popular culture, accepted and loved by audiences in genres that never admitted of the existence of homosexuality.

The film thematizes the continuity between the off-screen "masculine," tweed-suited dyke type and the on-screen "asexual," tweed-suited nurse type—thus George is able to appropriate her lesbian moniker from her television character—and demonstrates that the very construction of the "asexual" is, of course, a heterosexist one. At one point the drunken George makes a pass at a group of nuns in a taxicab—a scene that at once demonstrates her butch sexual courage and visibility and wittily restates the theme of covert and overt types. George ought to be able to recognize a sister when she sees one. In the film's lesbian bar scene, filmed on location and thus with extraordinary subcultural verisimilitude at London's Gateways Club—George and Childie dress up as Laurel and Hardy. This additional level of role-playing makes reference to a practice of comic typing that conceals homoerotic logic within a wildly popular mass cultural form.

When chic BBC executive Mercy Croft takes a fancy to Childie and has the

Sister George character killed off the soap, following a familiar script of homo-phobic narrative exigency, the question of the actress's visibility as a lesbian is preempted. The supporting actress is offered instead the leading role in her very own series—as Clarabell the Cow. In Frank Marcus's play from which the film was adapted, Sister George was a character on a radio soap opera; the movie parallels the demotion from human to animal with the step down from on-camera ham to voice-over cow. Yet the role, however demeaning and misogynist, affords a certain finesse of George's disguise. At the end of the film, George, who had at first scornfully turned down the role of Clarabell, begins to practice her "moos." But even in her humiliation lies a certain triumph—her "unrepresent-able" butch persona will still enter the homes of countless television viewers, her voice recognizable to her fans.

Agnes Moorehead was a familiar and popular television personality in the role of Endora on "Bewitched" when in one of the last of some sixty film roles she provided the voice of the goose in the animated feature *Charlotte's Web*. It was not a degrading part, as Clarabell Cow was meant to be—she co-starred with her "beloved friend" Debbie Reynolds, and Paul Lynde contributed to the barnyard fun. The role drew on her roots in radio—what one reviewer described as her trademark "crackling, snapping, sinister, paranoic, paralyzing voice."[1] And, be-fore her stardom as television's preeminent witch, Moorehead reigned as one of the most widely recognized and highly regarded supporting actresses in Hol-lywood cinema. Like George, she played "types"; she was the silver screen's definitive spinster aunt (figure 1). In accounting for the adaptability of her per-sona across a range of popular media, I believe that another element of Moore-head's star image must be considered. In an interview with Boze Hadleigh, "A Hollywood Square Comes Out," Lynde, a special guest star on "Bewitched" who played an "uncle" as aptly and as memorably as Moorehead played an "aunt," remarks, "Well, the whole world knows Agnes was a lesbian—I mean classy as hell, but one of the all-time Hollywood dykes."[2]

Regardless of whether the lady really was a lesbian, the characterization com-plements her persona. It represents a gendered node within what Eve Sedgwick has described as the modern Western "epistemology of the closet."[3] If the "whole world" knows about Agnes, the so-called general audience may exercise what Sedgwick calls "the privilege of unknowing"—after all, it's only entertainment. I would like to argue that it is no mere queer coincidence that Agnes Moorehead can be dubbed both one of the all-time Hollywood supporting actresses and one of the all-time Hollywood dykes. Moorehead is a prime candidate for gay hagi-ography. Her best known incarnation, Endora, is a camp icon; she passes even the cinephile test, having been featured in films by auteurs such as Welles, Sirk, Ray, and Aldrich. But, more important, Moorehead's ubiquity and longevity as a

Figure 1.
Moorehead's film debut in *Citizen Kane*
established her credentials and her persona.

character actress are such that she can be identified with the very media in which she triumphed, with the regime of popular entertainment itself, and with the continuities and ruptures in gender and sexual ideology that can be read off from it. At once essential to classical realism and marginal to its narrative goals, the supporting character is a site for the encoding of the threat and the promise of female deviance. As New York lesbian performance artist Lisa Kron writes in a biographical note, reflecting on the animal and grandmother roles she was asked to play in college, "It begins to dawn on her that 'character actress' is really a code word for lesbian."[4] The negative valence of many of Moorehead's roles is marked—Endora herself is the butt of a constant barrage of mother-in-law jokes. Her persona is less "heartwarming" than many a golden age supporting actress—from Anne Revere to Mary Wickes to Marjorie Main. Although the ideological stake in subordinating female difference is apparent, this negativity may also be Moorehead's most subversive edge.

My discussion of Moorehead takes up three overlapping areas of inquiry: the narrative function of supporting characters in the heterosexual Hollywood regime (as well as the ideological weight that they carry in television's world of family values); the importance of typification in these roles and in lesbian recognizability more generally; and the understanding of star images as complex, contradictory signs, as exemplified in the work of gay film theorist Richard Dyer as well as in the reception practices of gay culture.

What is it that supporting characters are meant to "support" if not the imbricated ideologies of heterosexual romance and white American hegemony permeating Hollywood cinema? They prop up a very particular representational order. As Stephen Heath describes the operation of narrativity, "The film picks up . . . the notable elements (to be noted in and for the progress of the narrative which in return defines their notability) without for all that giving up what is thus left aside and which it seeks to retain—something of an available reserve of insignificant material—in order precisely to ring 'true,' true to *reality*." Retained to speak a social "truth," the supporting character represents "an available reserve of insignificant," if "realistic," types of women—workers, older women, nonwhite women. Lacking a love interest—Hollywood deems only one type of love of interest—she doesn't get "picked up" by the story: in the most basic narratological terms, she is the witch, not the princess. By film's end she has literally been left aside, just as she is compositionally marginal in the frame. For, as Heath economically puts it, "Narrative contains a film's multiple articulations as a single articulation, its images as a single image (the 'narrative image,' which is a film's presence, how it can be talked about, what it can be sold and bought on—in the production stills displayed outside a cinema, for example)."[5] Supporting characters are sacrificed to the narrative image of heterosexual closure; their names rarely appear in the television-guide blurbs about old movies, nor are their photographs included on the videotape box that delivers a "picture" to a potential viewer.

Yet attention to the function of certain types of female characters can throw into relief the single-mindedness with which the Hollywood system re-presents heterosexuality. For example, the discourse of lesbian desire introduced by housekeeper Mrs. Danvers (Judith Anderson) in Hitchcock's *Rebecca* significantly undercuts the film's conventional romantic "resolution." And, while melodramatic pathos depends on Jane Wyman's long separation from Rock Hudson in Sirk's *Magnificent Obsession,* an alternative reading—or a different focus of spectatorial regard—might note that she spends this off-screen time in the company of her devoted nurse/companion, played by Agnes Moorehead, who offered Wyman support in four films besides. A film may be dismissive of a minor player, portray her fate as gratuitous, but it may take less time and care to assimilate her to its ideological project than it would in the case of the female protagonist. In Hedda Hopper's column "Bit Player Outshines the Stars," Moorehead remarks, "I sort of look at myself sideways on the screen."[6] While this comment indicates a failure of narcissistic identification, even, perhaps, a cringing at the conservatism to which her image is often harnessed, it also suggests an astute reading of her liminal, and at times disruptive, narrative function. It replicates, too, the oblique sightline traced on Hollywood cinema by many queer spectators.

Nurses, secretaries, career women, nuns, companions, and housekeepers connote, not lesbian identity, but a deviation from heterosexualized femininity. Gay male critics often register an affinity with such characters. Inasmuch as character actresses are enjoyed, admired, or pressed into camp service by a queer mode of reading, it is apparently character itself that is supported. Thelma Ritter, a great ironic interpreter of this type of role, was a particular favorite of gay film historian Vito Russo, for example. In his book on the gay sensibility, Michael Bronski singles out the woman friend that "many top female stars were paired off with . . . before they ended up getting the leading man" as a cinematic type with particular appeal. Portrayed by the likes of Joan Blondell and Eve Arden, "the sidekick's role was generally to act as a confidante and to give the audience a pungent analysis of the plot. Sidekicks were sarcastic, unromantic, and sensible. They were cleverly self-deprecating . . . but could also turn the wit on men. Too smart ever to get the man, sidekicks had to settle for being funnier than everybody else. For gay men who would never walk off into the sunset with a leading man, the sidekick was a dose of real life." Bronski attributes a sort of metacritical role to confidante characters and a self-conscious reading practice to their fans, but he reads these images in relation only to male characters and spectators. He goes on to cite Russo's work on sissy roles and the actors who specialized in their portrayal in Hollywood films of the thirties and forties. Bronski asserts, "Woman sidekicks were never played as lesbians, just 'old maids,' but the non-romantic male was always implicitly gay."[7]

Given the virtual conceptual blank that is lesbianism in the culture at large, it is no accident that the social types standing in for lesbians in Hollywood cinema are misogynistically coded as "asexual." They are trivialized and rendered comical rather than threatening. Although sex and ideology certainly mark the stereotypes of sissy and old maid differently, in particular in relation to tropes of gender inversion, Bronski's statement limits the operation of the connotative in the female images and thus compounds the invisibility to which lesbians are already consigned.

In contrast, one lesbian writer confidently attributes sexuality to a much later incarnation of the "old maid" type. In a cover article for *Lesbian News* entitled "The Truth about Miss Hathaway," Marion Garbo Todd defends the spinster secretary character played by Nancy Kulp on the sixties American sitcom "The Beverly Hillbillies" from the following assessment in the fan magazine *Television Collector:* "Miss Jane Hathaway could have been the prototype for the term 'Plain Jane.' Tall and lanky, with an asexual manner, the epitome of a spinster." Todd retorts, "Where does this 'plain Jane' stuff come from? How can the word plain be used to describe the handsome Miss Hathaway? 'Tall and lanky' is not the right phrase for her body; 'long and sensuous' is much more accurate. Her long neck, aquiline nose, wavy hair, and large bright eyes made her very beautiful. She had smile lines to swoon over, and her voice was a delight. . . . In her tasteful skirt suit, short hairdo, and horn-rimmed glasses, she could have been the lead character in any lesbian pulp novel."[8]

Visual codes are recognized, enumerated, and deployed to cast Kulp in a leading role in a different genre. In her groundbreaking work on studio-era lesbian director Dorothy Arzner, Judith Mayne notes that, in her films, secondary women characters can be seen sporting the dapper dress and masculine manner that Arzner herself affected. Lesbianism is made visible within the text through ironic inflection of an "asexual" type.[9]

As Richard Dyer writes, in an essay on "typical" lesbian and gay representations, "A major fact about being gay is that it doesn't show. . . . There are signs of gayness, a repertoire of gestures, expressions, stances, clothing, and even environments that bespeak gayness, but these are cultural forms designed to show what the person's person alone does not show: that he or she is gay. Such a repertoire of signs, making visible the invisible, is the basis of any representation of gay people involving visual recognition, the requirement of recognizability in turn entailing that of typicality."[10] Thus, historically and culturally specific codes in lesbian and gay communities function similarly to the codes of recognition in popular cultural forms. In this light, the often-heard demand for nonstereotypical, "well-rounded" gay and lesbian characters in film may go against the very conditions of our visibility. Dyer detects the prevalence of the sexological discourse of "in-betweenism"—the notion that homosexuals betray characteristics of the opposite gender—in a range of typical visual representations, including self-representations, of effeminate men and mannish women. Citing *The Killing of Sister George,* he sees both George's tweeds and her rival Mercy Croft's chic and tailored predatory look as variations on this "dyke" type.[11] The vexed question of lesbian stereotyping can be related to the potentially subversive implications of more general practices of visual typing in female supporting characters.

The widespread apprehension of the Sister Georges or Miss Jane Hathaways as asexual or, worse, man starved—precisely invisible as lesbian—has to do, perhaps paradoxically, with the visual overdetermination of "woman" as sexual in film. The supporting character necessarily diverges from this ideal—not incidentally, a white one—of woman in film. The cinematic system of the look constructs the singular female star as image and guarantee of masculine desire and spectatorial fascination. As images of a different version of femininity than that of female stars, supporting characters may not ultimately be so supportive of the status quo, for they can inflect with female desire the image of woman embodied in the leading lady, with whom they are narratively paired and iconographically contrasted, often within the same frame.

One of the most consequential operations of Hollywood's containment and social enforcement of difference is the near-exclusive restriction of nonwhite and visually and audibly recognizable ethnic types precisely to supporting roles. Mary Ann Doane remarks that the "woman's film" genre is really the "white woman's film": "When black women are present, they are the ground rather than the figure; often they are made to merge with the diegesis. They inhabit the textual sidelines, primarily as servants."[12] The complexity, code crossing, and incoherence of racialized sexual and gender ideology is performed by the on-screen conjunction of, and contrast between, black and white women. The mammy stereotype, often denounced as "asexual," may be inflected as "lesbian" in its close articulation with the presentation of the white heroine's desire. Such a character, or a known performer such as Ethel Waters in a mammy role, might not merge altogether with the diegesis for African American, lesbian, and gay viewers.

A process of erotic doubling between a woman of color and the white star may also serve to figure lesbianism—for example, between Anna May Wong and Marlene Dietrich as traveling companions in *Shanghai Express,* in which the signifier *prostitution* sexualizes the contiguity of the two women. Or the racist projection of sexuality onto the "other woman" may indicate erotic tension between the stereotyped woman of color and the "repressed" and only presumptively heterosexual white heroine. Bette Davis's character performs two passionate acts in *The Letter*—she kills her lover in the opening sequence and goes into the night to meet her death at the hands of his Asian widow at the end. While the man in the triangle is never shown, the "other" woman's body is insistently present, bizarrely underscored by the excessive makeup and costuming used to transform white supporting actress Gale Sondergaard. This common casting practice foregrounds the way in which the representation of racial difference turns on the attributes of whiteness in the classical Hollywood cinema. In *Beyond the Forest*, the Davis character's long, center-parted black hair is uncannily mirrored in the background by that of her mocking Latina maid, played by Mexican actress Dona Drake. At a crucial point in the story, the heroine disguises herself in the jeans and flannel shirt worn by her servant. That the masquerade involves an element of gender transgression ironically makes visible the irreducible difference between women—race, class, and power—that appears to give such doubling its frisson.

Judith Mayne goes on to discuss how images of Dorothy Arzner—often two-shots of her looking at a conventionally feminine actress—have been used to illustrate feminist critical texts that emphatically do not mention her lesbianism. When these lesbian looks, these exchanges of the gaze between contrasting female types—generally between supporting and lead actresses—are echoed in Arzner's films, Mayne argues, they can be read as her authorial signature. In a two-shot from Raoul Walsh's *The Revolt of Mamie Stover,* the look of Agnes

Figure 2. Moorehead and Jane Russell in *The Revolt of Mamie Stover*.
Courtesy Museum of Modern Art.

Moorehead in her bathrobe prevents Jane Russell's sexuality from being perceived as intended for the male spectator alone (figure 2). Yet the early feminist
analysis of this film, too, ignored its lesbian visual economy. In another two-shot,
Agnes Moorehead and Debbie Reynolds embody the visual relation between a
supporting actress "type" and a bona fide female star (figure 3). On-screen and
off, the couple conforms to the stereotype of older, sapphic sophisticate who
preys on innocent younger woman, in this case the singing nun.

While great Hollywood supporting actresses such as Thelma Ritter or Mer-
cedes McCambridge could perhaps be read as working-class butch or fifties in-
betweenist types, Agnes Moorehead's persona fits a more upper-class sapphic
stereotype.[13] As a promotional item describes her, "Rated as one of the best
dressed stars of screen and radio, her preference runs to tailored suits"—to recall
Lynde's words, she was "classy as hell" (figure 4). On-screen, the spinster type
refuses both the masculine signifiers that make lesbianism visible in heterosexual terms and the hyperbolization of the feminine that is the very definition of *womanliness*. The type is a product of a misogynist and heterosexist

Figure 3. Moorehead
and her beloved friend
Debbie Reynolds in
The Singing Nun.
Courtesy Museum of
Modern Art.

imagination—yet within it the spinster can at once "pass" as straight and be recognizable as lesbian.

It is impossible to unpack the ambivalent character of the narrative category of *support* and the negotiable aspects of visual typification apart from a consideration of the performer as text. Donald Bogle, in *Toms, Coons, Mulattos, Mammies and Bucks,* his influential book on African American stereotypes, presents the most sustained argument for how particular performers become visible in these roles and transform types. As he states in an interview, "There was another life and point of view that was being suggested to me by Hattie McDaniel's rather hostile edge."[14] It is Ritter's nurses, Arden's sidekicks, Franklin Pangborn's sissies, and McDaniel's maids that capture the imagination. The more roles an actress appears in, the more unforeseen the effects that are introduced in a particular text by her casting. Star texts are ongoing, modified by shifting ideological imperatives, shaped by audience response. On series television, the weekly appearance of the performer works like typecasting in studio films. It is in this sense that I want to speak of Moorehead's *queer career.*

In his work on stars, Dyer argues that, in narrative films, novelistic concep-

Figure 4.
"Her preference runs to tailored suits."

tions of character are articulated with stars as already signifying images—which essentially function within the same bourgeois ideology of the self-consistent individual. How might this approach apply to Moorehead, who, as a character actress, however familiar, is not strictly a "star"? As Dyer notes, "Type characters are acknowledged to have a place . . . but only to enable the proper elaboration of the central, individuated character(s). In this respect, no star could be just a type, since all stars play central characters."[15] Moorehead does not have a fully individuated star image (at least not before "Bewitched"), yet neither can her on-screen type be considered merely an extension of her off-screen "self" (which would reintroduce the category of the individual in another way). She has a subversive edge that does not get "rounded off." What was distinct was the fact of her *acting*, which allowed her to represent and to "quote" a type at the same time.

Agnes Moorehead's long career encompassed a gallery of types connoting female difference. Her early success was achieved on radio as, among other things, a stooge to male comics. After she went to Hollywood with Orson Welles and the Mercury Theater, she continued her radio work as an all-purpose female voice, impersonating Eleanor Roosevelt and scores of other women on the "March of Time." Outside the Hollywood regime of the gaze, it seems that a deviant version of femininity could represent the norm. On-screen, she never portrayed a central character, receiving top billing only in the posthumously released horror flick *Dear Dead Delilah*. Instead, she played second fiddle, variations on the unmarried woman: nurses (*Magnificent Obsession*), nuns (*The Singing Nun, Scandal at Scourie*), governesses (*The Youngest Profession, The Un-*

tamed), ladies' companions (*Mrs. Parkington, Her Highness and the Bellboy*), busybodies (*Since You Went Away, All That Heaven Allows*), hypochondriacs (*Pollyanna*), maids (*Hush, Hush, Sweet Charlotte*), and, of course, aunts.

In *The Magnificent Ambersons*, Jack Amberson rebukes his nephew for tormenting the Moorehead character: "You know George, just being an aunt isn't really the great career it may sometimes seem to be." But this, her second film, launched the actress on a trajectory that proved otherwise. Despite her fifth billing, she was named best actress by the New York Film Critics and went on to play aunts again in *Jane Eyre, Tomorrow the World, The Lost Moment, Summer Holiday, Johnny Belinda,* and *The Story of Three Loves,* and on Broadway in *Gigi* just before her death. For variety, she portrayed women in professions that lesbians might suitably pursue: a WAC commander (*Keep Your Powder Dry*), a prison superintendent (*Caged*), a literary agent (*From Main Street to Broadway*), a drama teacher (*Jeanne Eagels*), a mystery writer (*The Bat*), a judge (*Bachelor in Paradise*), and, in a blond wig, a "sort of school marm and madam rolled into one," offering firm support to Jane Russell's Mamie Stover.[16] When she played married women, she was generally a nagging wife, most notably in the radio play *Sorry, Wrong Number,* written expressly for her talents. Critics note the "waspish and neurotic," "mean-spirited, shrewish," "possessive, puritanical, and vitriolic," "bitter, nasty, frustrated," and "meddlesome" traits of her "old crones," "harridans, spinsters and bitches," "termagants and passionate viragos." Her many mother parts did not always evince maternal qualities. Besides Samantha, her screen offspring included Citizen Kane, Jesse James, and Genghis Khan. Her role in *The Story of Mankind* was a brief appearance as Queen Elizabeth I; she commissioned a portrait of herself costumed as the red-haired virgin queen.

The Agnes Moorehead of the "Bewitched" era (the show ran on ABC from 1964 to 1972) can aptly be described with the title of her one-woman show, in which she toured extensively in the fifties—"The Fabulous Redhead." On "Bewitched," she was a flippant, vividly costumed, outrageously madeup, impeccably coiffed, castrating witch with a mortal hatred for her daughter's husband, whose name she somehow could not recall. This is the Moorehead-as-"character" association that the contemporary viewer brings to her earlier film roles. Moorehead turned her Actress-with-a-capital-A stage image—regal bearing, exaggerated gestures and enunciation, and taste for high fashion—to high camp effect in her interpretation of Endora, flagrantly foregrounding "performance." Offscreen, she was nicknamed "Madame Mauve" because of her inordinate fondness for lavender, which she insisted on having everything "done" in—from her luggage and Thunderbird to her dressing room lightbulbs and maids' uniforms.[17]

Before the fifties stage and sixties television brought color to her roles, Agnes

Moorehead was considered an actress of "character." Her Victorian-sounding name (her father was a minister), aristocratic profile, penchant for accents and other vocal trademarks, her manners, even manneredness, contributed to the public perception of Moorehead as a "serious" actress. As one critic notes, she is associated with "heavy dramatics on the grand scale. For many, Agnes's performances represent the near epitome of screen theatrics."[18] Although she was "typecast," versatility was regarded as part of her artistry.[19] A studio publicity item raved, "The accomplished character actress of stage, screen and radio is given here one of her rare opportunities to bid for romantic interest. The result is a revelation of a new facet of the versatile actress's many-sided repertory, strikingly effective."[20] The implication is that her ability to portray a heterosexual is a true sign of talent.

Moorehead was distinguished by four Academy Award nominations for best actress in a supporting role, although she never won the Oscar. As six-time loser Thelma Ritter cracked, "Always the bridesmaid and never the bride."[21] A profile in a nostalgia magazine muses about the fact that Moorehead never snagged the award: "It is an interesting speculation that one of the reasons she always lost was that she played neurotic aunts, stepmothers, spinsters who reflected the dark side of the human condition."[22] That the old maid should evoke such a grandiose conception as the dark side of the human condition attests to Moorehead's considerable achievement—she makes the spinster positively sinister. In an essay on the functions of feminist criticism, Tania Modleski chastises a male literary critic who, "casting about for an example of the trivial, strikes irresistibly upon the image of the spinster." "From a feminist point of view," Modleski argues, "nothing could be *more* 'historically and ideologically significant' than the existence of the single woman in patriarchy, her (frequently caricatured) representation in patriarchal art, and the relationship between the reality and the representation."[23] Moorehead's image captured some of this, perhaps lesbian, significance, if only in the mirror image of anxiety. The profile goes on to suggest how closely the spinster image was identified with the actress: "Never married, she, nevertheless, had an adopted son; a close friendship with Debbie Reynolds, with whom she co-starred in several of her last pictures; and a religious faith as a Methodist." This "nevertheless" means to blur over a logical relation between spinster and lesbian that the syntax sets up: "Never married, she had a close friendship with Debbie Reynolds." The statement is interesting for another reason: its blatant, symptomatic contradiction of fact, for Agnes Moorehead was married at least twice (Reynolds mentions three unions). I presume that the actress's much-vaunted privacy and cultivated "mystery" were not intended to conceal this facet of her "many-side repertory."

Moorehead's image reconciles the serious with the trivial—having "character"

with being "a character"—and thus occupies the domain of camp. As Susan
Sontag notes, "Camp is the glorification of 'character.' . . . Character is understood as a state of continual incandescence—a person being one, very intense
thing. . . . Wherever there is development of character, Camp is reduced."[24]
Camp is a crucial and far from trivial dimension of Moorehead's reception, but,
with its emphasis on style, it is an insufficient analytic category for a feminist
consideration of what is at stake in the "content" of her image. Looking at how
that image was articulated in and utilized by certain of her films can illuminate
the contradiction that she embodies, as a figure simultaneously necessary to the
Hollywood system and suppressed by it. She is taken seriously, featured in so
many films as to seem ubiquitous. At the same time, her parts are marginal ones,
the characters she portrays trivialized or vilified. If her roles as written often
smack of misogyny, as performed they suggest a different negativity—a negativity that cannot be represented within the terms of classical cinema and that
shares the semiotic field of lesbianism.

Fanny Minnafer in Orson Welles's *The Magnificent Ambersons* is the role that
established at once Moorehead's reviled spinster image *and* the difficulty of
reconciling that image with the Hollywood plot. Lacking economic independence, Aunt Fanny lives with the fading Amberson clan as an observer rather
than as a participant. *The Magnificent Ambersons* is a self-conscious film, and her
restlessness and discontent contribute greatly to its mood. She accuses her
nephew George, "You wouldn't treat anybody in the world like this, except old
Fanny. 'Old Fanny,' you say, 'it's nobody but old Fanny so I'll kick her. Nobody'll
resent it, I'll kick her all I want to.'" But the film inscribes Fanny's position on the
periphery—lurking in the shadows to whisper her suspicions to George, looking
on from the edge of the frame or the background of the composition—as a
vantage point for the spectator. She actually prevents the formation of two heterosexual couples by her interference. In material excised from the film's release
version, Fanny is shown at the end among a veritable colony of spinsters at the
boarding house. Her discourse pervades the film, even if she triumphs only as
the representative of its themes of frustration and barrenness.

One commentator characterizes the challenge for Moorehead as an actress,
"to channel her tremendous energy so that it would emerge in accord with the
film rather than as an intriguing distraction."[25] Elements of her tour-de-force
characterization of Aunt Fanny erupt as fascinating "distractions" in such later
roles as Mrs. Reed in *Jane Eyre* and Countess Fosco in *The Woman in White*. The
question of Moorehead's discordant difference and of her relation to the fulfillment of the romance plot is marked in another literary film, *The Lost Moment*
(1947). In this adaptation of Henry James's *The Aspern Papers*, Moorehead plays
the elderly aunt who in her youth was the recipient of love letters from a famous

poet. A mere octogenarian in the novella becomes a hideously madeup 105-year-old in the film. It is as if the plausibility of Moorehead's participation in such a romance even in the past demands extremes of disguise.

Moorehead thoroughly embraced that inexplicable quality of her characters that prompted others to react with dislike, even phobia. In *Since You Went Away* (directed by John Cromwell, 1944), David O. Selznick's sentimental story of women on the homefront during World War II, Agnes portrays a local busybody, a character who embodies a displaced anxiety about the unheroic activities in which women might become involved while the menfolk are away at war. Joseph Cotten's character repeatedly insults her, joking that the sound of her voice grates on him even when he's far away from her. The penetrating, persecuting female voice signifies here not only as a quality of Moorehead's character, Emily Hawkins, but as Moorehead as an actress, who often worked with Cotten. Ultimately, the disparate desires of the women in the film are rallied into patriotic solidarity when they castigate the Moorehead character for petty war profiteering. The film scapegoats her to consolidate both nationalist and gender ideology, a project that could be seen as operating across the forties, the period in which Moorehead's image was established.

In *Good Dames,* his book on five female "character stars" (supporting actresses rarely receive individual biographies), James Robert Parish comments on Moorehead's performance in this film:

The role itself was a variation of the cinema type portrayed throughout the 1940s by the very adept Eve Arden. The difference in these two actresses' approach to such a part is that whenever Agnes is required to make a flip remark on the screen, it comes across in total seriousness as a reflection of her character's basic, unregenerate meanness. Her piercing eyes and overall body movements provide the viewer with no other interpretation. In contrast, Arden can toss off the most devastating remark, and it emerges as a pert observation, juicy and smart, but essentially nonvicious.[26]

Although Moorehead did play essentially nonvicious roles, she was more convincing—and less recuperable—in her moments of unregenerate meanness. The subversiveness of the best character stars, such as Arden and Ritter, can be neutralized by their being enthusiastically adopted as cuddly curmudgeons. Moorehead's unlikableness, on the razor-thin edge of misogynist dismissal, contravenes this tendency. It is hard to embrace Moorehead without being spattered with acid.

Madge Rapf in the Bogart/Bacall vehicle *Dark Passage* (1947), directed by Delmar Daves, is a curious sort of femme fatale, whose fate is a telling example of the retribution that the Moorehead character could bring down. Moorehead's being cast against character in a "sexual" role is in part responsible for the film's surreal effects.[27] As Dana Polan comments in an important analysis, "The narrative of *Dark Passage* is one in which dramatic coincidences occur so often as to break down any question of plausibility."[28] When Madge happens to knock at the door of the apartment where, through an unlikely chain of circumstances, escaped convict Vincent Parry (Bogart) is hiding, he instantly recognizes the voice of his nemesis. Madge had testified against him at his murder trial. As he observes, "She's the type that comes back, and back again." This not only indicates how she functions in the film as the return of the repressed but is a fitting comment on Moorehead's career.

Madge's character is attributed with the evil, inconsistency, and unintelligibility of motive of an ordinary femme fatale, without the movie conceding that sexuality is her tool for leading men to destruction. Instead, her fatal quality seems to be the simple fact of her existence, rendered as "interference" through Moorehead's "nagging" connotations. As Vincent describes her, "Madge knows everybody, pesters everybody." Her ex-fiancé, Bob, snaps at her, "You're not satisfied unless you're bothering people. I'm annoyed whenever I see you." Responding to her concern that Parry will try to kill her, Bob remarks, with an extraordinary mixture of outright malignance and contemptuous dismissal, "You're the last person he wants to see, let alone kill. . . . You're not the type that makes people hate." Her insignificance is thus marked in rather significant terms. It is as if the other characters recognize the difficulty of integrating her in the plot. Vincent muses, "Maybe she'll get run over or something." And his wish is granted.

In this profoundly illogical film, the logic of misogyny works with classic simplicity; it can be placated only by Madge's abjection, by the spectacle of her death. When Vincent comes to her apartment to accuse *her* of murdering his wife, she defies him to prove it. At her crowning moment of Moorehead histrionics, she "accidently" and quite improbably falls through a picture window, with a flounce of floor-length drapes. The camera dwells on her body's descent, a markedly excessive cinematic flourish. Polan has commented on the ambiguity and threat embodied in domestic space in forties films: "Significantly, in several films, murder, suicide, and accidental death through windows blur (and not only for the characters but also for the spectator), thereby suggesting the ambivalence of sense." He captures something of the spectator's bewilderment in this instance: "In *Dark Passage,* for example, it is never clear (even with motion-analyzing equipment and freeze-framing) how Madge manages to fall through her apartment window to her death."[29]

Dark Passage plays out the film noir's generic fear of feminine difference. The hero is vindicated, and woman is both criminal and victim. However, here it is not the alluring but the annoying woman who is punished, an extreme case of the anxiety that the Moorehead character could provoke. Madge, as a "bad," super-fluous woman, is marked for death from the beginning. But for all that it is an almost mundane exigency of plot, her killing seems to require a supernatural force, thereby foregrounding the ideology that demands it. And Madge's fall doesn't immediately benefit the hero; it has something of the quality of a self-willed disappearance. Madge threatens, "You will never be able to prove any-thing because I won't be there."

Here, I would like to quote the late, legendary underground gay filmmaker and Hollywood camp tastemaker Jack Smith:

I'm being haunted now by a performance in a movie. It was in *Dark Passage*. Agnes Moorehead plays this pest. . . . In a huge close-up you see the twitch of her little purse of a mouth. [Movies] can reveal a certain personality type—a certain kind of pest or what have you—and then you have something to remember when you see a person in life. . . . That happened to me just recently. This raging pest from the Gay Men's Health Crisis just called and said she'd be right over. . . . The poor creature, her life was so empty that she had to join the Gay movement to pester AIDS victims in order to have a social life. Right away I looked at her and thought of Madge in *Dark Passage*."[30]

Smith relates the star and the practice of cinematic typification to real life and to a gay context, using her quality of "intensity" to make sense of some aspect of the tragically implausible but all too real and very dark passage that is living with AIDS.

John Cromwell's *Caged* (1950) features Moorehead as Mrs. Benton, the effi-cient and smartly tailored head of a woman's prison, but here her philanthropic impulse is benevolent and welcome. In such an environment, among female deviates, Moorehead's persona is not pitted against other women but appears at its most benign. This is also the most overtly lesbian of her films—it establishes a genuine genre—and Moorehead receives second billing. Like *The Killing of Sis-ter George* or the lesbian classic *Maedchen in Uniform* with its conflict between stern headmistress and compassionate teacher, this feminist drama opposes two "dyke" types in a struggle for control over the young heroine (Eleanor Parker). The sympathetic, reform-minded prison superintendent tries to protect inno-cent Marie Allen from the corruptions of life inside. "You'll find all kinds of women in here, just as you would outside," Benton promises. Hope Emerson portrays Evelyn Harper, the sadistic matron in uniform who provides small comforts for her girls in exchange for payment. Of this remarkable six-foot, two-inch, 230-pound character actress (who, incidentally, provided the voice of Elsie the Borden cow), gay porn editor and film critic Boyd MacDonald writes, "Per-haps only members of a sexual elite—that is, outlaws—can instinctively appreci-ate the grandeur of an Emerson."[31] In one scene, Harper, grotesquely dressed up for her night off, describes in detail her upcoming "date" in order to taunt the imprisoned women. This attribution of heterosexuality, like the photograph of a "husband" displayed on Moorehead's desk, can easily be read as an out-and-out charade.

When Benton attempts to fire Harper, the latter leaks a scandalous tale to the press: "Matron charges immorality," headlines blare. "Blames superintendent." The article is accompanied by a singularly apt sketch of Benton/Moorehead's face encircled by a huge question mark. The unspoken questions dogging Moorehead's persona are here explicitly tied to a story full of "filthy lies" that euphemistically signify lesbianism.

In this classic struggle between good and evil, Harper is finally stabbed by a prisoner. But, in the meantime, Marie has gone bad—the beginning of her defiance marked when her kitten is crushed in a riot provoked by Harper's attempt to snatch Fluff away from her. Marie finally accepts the attentions of the vice queen Kitty, who arranges for her parole. Forced to relinquish her wedding ring when she went to prison, Marie tosses it away when it is returned on her release. Benton tells her devoted secretary to keep Marie's file active: "She'll be back." Ultimately, different tropes of lesbian seduction—nurturance and dominance—represented by different types of character actresses, Moorehead and Emerson, work in consort to keep the female community intact. In *Caged*, Moorehead's character can represent the film's moral center because here she presides over a homosocial world and, fittingly, over an extraordinarily talented female supporting cast.

While the pleasures of reading Moorehead's ornery forties persona are obviously augmented by her syndication canonization in "Bewitched," both her situation and its comedy on that show are made possible by the character of her prior Hollywood career. Writing on the popularization of camp taste in the sixties and on *Whatever Happened to Baby Jane?* in particular, Andrew Ross claims, "The camp effect . . . is created . . . when the products (stars, in this case) of a much earlier mode of production, which has lost its power to dominate cultural meanings, become available . . . for redefinition to contemporary codes of taste."[32] Of Robert Aldrich's follow-up to *Baby Jane*, *Hush, Hush Sweet Charlotte*, produced the year "Bewitched" debuted, Bosley Crowther ranted, "Agnes Moorehead as [Bette Davis's] weird and crone like servant is allowed to get away with some of the broadest mugging and snarling ever done by a respectable actress on the screen. If she gets an Academy Award for this performance . . . the Academy should close up shop!"[33] The slatternly Velma Cruther significantly reverses an important element of Moorehead's image—her fastidiousness. In a cycle in which the biggest female stars travestied their former images, it is appropriate for one of the great supporting actresses to play a classic supporting role, the loyal servant, in a spectacularly unsupportive manner—to indulge in upstaging and scenery chewing that puts Davis herself to shame. Velma may be killed off for her snooping by a fall nearly as dramatic as that in *Dark Passage,* but icons never die.

One of Moorehead's last films, scripted by Henry Farrell, who wrote *Baby Jane,* continues this self-conscious exploitation of her image. Set in the thirties, *What's the Matter with Helen?* (directed by Curtis Harrington, 1971) features Debbie Reynolds and Shelley Winters as the mothers of two convicted thrill killers in the Leopold and Loeb mode, who move to Hollywood to escape their past. Reynolds, intrigued by the story, which was originally titled *Best of Friends,* persuaded her friend Agnes Moorehead to play powerful radio evangelist Sister Alma. The "matter" with Helen concerns not only her psychopathic murderous tendencies but her fanatical devotion to the evangelist's message and, surprise, her lesbian love for her best friend. The role and the project thus summed up a number of strong components of the Moorehead persona: radio, religion, the famous personality, lesbianism, the relationship with Reynolds.

Endora represents the culmination of Moorehead meddlesomeness. In the premiere episode of "Bewitched," she repeatedly evicts Samantha's husband from the honeymoon suite, and she literally casts a dark shadow over heterosexual relations each week when her credit "and Agnes Moorehead as Endora" appears on a black cloud of smoke blotting out "Derwood" and Samantha's embrace. What's-his-name's anxiety about his wife's powers are well founded: she belongs to a matriarchal order of superior beings (figure 5). "Bewitched" supported a veritable gay subculture among its "funny" witch and warlock character actors. A recent "Bewitched"-kitsch revival attests to the show's influence on the queer nation generation. In a recent interview with the Los Angeles lesbian and gay newsweekly the *Advocate,* star Elizabeth Montgomery even agreed that the show's premise was "the ultimate closet story."[34]

If Moorehead's earlier characters were outside the central action, Endora is transcendently ex-centric. As Pat Mellencamp writes, in the situation comedy, "expectation of pleasurable performance . . . rather than narrative suspense [is the] currency of audience exchange."[35] Endora has an enunciative role in the series. Casting spells on small-minded mortals, she disrupts the couple's petty suburban lives and generates the weekly plot. She appears and disappears with a flutter of the wrist—her ability to materialize when least expected or to drop out of the picture altogether is almost a commentary on the disappearing act that "incidental" characters performed in countless Hollywood films.

From stern spinster to fabulous redhead to silly goose, Agnes Moorehead's queer career attests to the ideological, narratological, and iconographic congruence among old maid, witch, and lesbian. Her star image also appeals to

Figure 5.
Endora and Samantha
(Elizabeth Montgomery).
Publicity still for
Bewitched.

lesbian and gay audiences because it connotes acting itself—artifice, impersonation, and exaggeration. I do not wish to suggest that the characters that Moorehead portrayed "really were" lesbians, nor to imply that lesbians can simply
recover our presence in Hollywood cinema by identifying actresses who really
were lesbians, although gossip in its many forms is a legitimate text to be read
(figure 6). Rather, the peculiarities of Moorehead's image and the enthusiasms
that it has generated illustrate how supporting characters were essential but also
potentially disruptive to the construction of sexual difference in classical cinema.
They were the types who were meant to remain invisible so that the codes of
Hollywood's heterosexual contract would also remain invisible. By resituating
such performers in patriarchal domesticity, American television often ended up
broadcasting forms of queer performativity. Gay criticism and culture have been
alert to the pleasures and resistances embodied in star signs. Feminist film theory
has explicated the patriarchal construction of woman *as* image—and demonstrated the difficulty of articulating female desire and difference in relation
to that construction. An exploration of the paradoxical conditions of lesbian
representability in popular culture might fruitfully draw on both approaches.

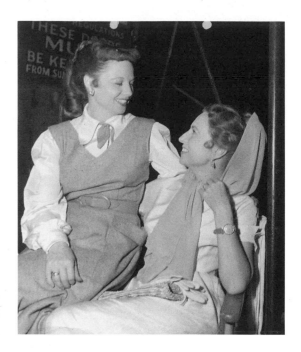

Figure 6.
Moorehead with
unidentified companion.

Whether playing it straight or camping it up, Agnes Moorehead is quite a character, "the type that comes back, and back again," as an insistent reminder of the price of heterosexual presumption.

Postscript

The television "personality" remains a privileged locus of lesbian and gay iconic signification, as a recent, metatextual example shows. On the top-rated ABC sitcom "Roseanne," Nancy, a supporting character played by Sandra Bernhard—a notorious real-life, role-playing queer—declared that she is a lesbian. Yet, in putting forward an overt lesbian characterization, in this age of outing and the representational politics of acting up, the show draws on a covert one. At first surprised by her friend's announcement, Roseanne then recalls a code in which the coming-out message is intelligible: "Nancy always did like that Miss Jane Hathaway on 'The Beverly Hillbillies.' That about says it all."

Notes

For Montana Silkwood. Thanks to Lisa Cohen and Cynthia Schneider for their helpful comments.

I Quoted in Warren Sherk, *Agnes Moorehead: A Very Private Person* (Philadelphia: Dorrance, 1976), 73.

2 While filming *How Sweet It Is* on an ocean liner, Lynde recounts, "At night, we'd sit around and dish. [Director] Jerry [Paris] told me those rumors that everybody's heard about Debbie [Reynolds] and her *close friend* Agnes Moorehead. . . . I'd heard those rumors, but Jerry filled in some details that. . . . Oh, I'd better not, I'm not even sure if the story's really true" (*Outlook* 6 [Fall 1989]: 26). Hadleigh claims that Reynolds threatened to sue Eddie Fisher if he included the story in his autobiography.

Reynolds herself reports the "innuendo" that she and Moorehead were lovers without explicitly denying it (see Debbie Reynolds with David Patrick Columbia, *My Life* [New York: Pocket, 1988], 388). Moorehead repeatedly discussed "why I adore Debbie Reynolds" (interview with Sidney Skolsky, *New York Post*, 2 August 1964), avowing, "It's really the loneliest sort of life. . . . I did become good friends with Debbie Reynolds" (*New York Post*, 11 January 1969). The friendship is generally considered a salient fact about Moorehead. The two women "became close friends, in a mother-daughter type relationship" (James Robert Parish, *Good Dames* [New Brunswick, N.J.: Barnes, 1974], 122).

As corroboration goes, there is no more than ample documentation of the *rumor* in the gay press: "Hollywood knew her as its reigning lesbian, queen of Sapphic love. ('Who was Carrie Fisher's mother?' the old joke went. 'Debbie Reynolds. Who was her father? Agnes Moorehead')" (*NYQ*, 22 December 1991, 41). Dick Sargent, the second actor to play Samantha's mortal husband on "Bewitched," who recently came out in *People* and on "Entertainment Tonight" as well as in the gay press, was unable to confirm the tales about Moorehead's lesbianism. The knowledge that Darrin, the show's representative of put-upon normalcy, was played by a gay actor literalizes what the *Advocate* calls the "gay allegory" of "Bewitched" (30 July 1992, 69). In a gracious interview with the lesbian and gay news weekly on the occasion of her serving with Sargent as grand marshall of the Los Angeles lesbian and gay pride parade, star Elizabeth Montgomery notes, "Don't think that didn't enter our minds at the time. We talked about it on the set . . . that this was about people not being allowed to be what they really are . . . and all the frustration and trouble it can cause. It was a neat message to get across" (ibid., 69). Asked about Moorehead's lesbianism, Montgomery replies, "I've heard the rumors, but I never talked with her about them. . . . It was never anything she felt free enough to talk to me about. I wish . . . that Agnes felt she could trust me. . . . We were very fond of one another, but it never got personal." In characteristically grande dame fashion, Moorehead herself wrote, "I have played so many authoritative and strong characters that some people are nervous at the prospect of meeting me. . . . There is a certain amount of aloofness on my part at times, because an actor can so easily be hurt by unfair criticism. I think an artist should be kept separated to maintain glamour and a kind of mystery. . . . I don't believe in the girl-next-door image. What the actor has to sell to the public is fantasy, a magic kind of ingredient that should not be analyzed" (quoted in the *New York Times* obituary, 1 May 1974, 48).

Outside of gay publications, what often appears in place of any remarks about Moorehead's sexuality is an emphasis on her religious beliefs (see Herbie J. Pilato, *The Bewitched Book* [New York: Delta, 1992], 24–26). That Moorehead was devout is not in question.

But religion seems to appear as a defense against a homosexual reading, as the very emblem and safeguard of spinsterishness. Ann B. Davis, who played Alice, the housekeeper who resembled a physical education teacher, on "The Brady Bunch" (and before portrayed Schultzy on "The Bob Cummings Show"), has also enjoyed a surge in appreciation. In a recent update, she is reported as having shared a home since 1976 with an Episcopal bishop and his wife. "The three are dedicated to prayer and Bible study." She "never married" and admits, "I basically don't do that well with children, although my sister [identical twin Harriet] says I'm a great aunt" (*People,* 1 June 1992, 86).

Material on Moorehead cited throughout this essay was found in clippings files at the New York Public Library for the Performing Arts and the Museum of Modern Art Film Study Center.

3   Eve Kosofsky Sedgwick, *Epistemology of the Closet* (Berkeley: University of California Press, 1990).

4   Lisa Kron, *Program,* "101 Humiliating Stories," performed at P.S. 122, New York City, January 7–31, 1993.

5   Stephen Heath, *Questions of Cinema* (Bloomington: Indiana University Press, 1981), 135, 121.

6   Agnes Moorehead clippings file, New York Public Library for the Performing Arts.

7   Michael Bronski, *Culture Clash: The Making of Gay Sensibility* (Boston: South End, 1984), 102. See also chapter 1, "Who's a Sissy?" of Vito Russo, *The Celluloid Closet* (New York: Harper & Row, 1981).

8   Marion Garbo Todd, "The Truth about Miss Hathaway: The Fascination of Television's Perennial Spinster," *Lesbian News* 16, no. 10 (May 1991): 40.

9   See Sarah Halprin, "Writing in the Margins" (review of E. Ann Kaplan, *Women and Film: Both Sides of the Camera*), *Jump Cut* 29 (February 1984): 32, cited in Judith Mayne, "Lesbian Looks: Dorothy Arzner and Female Authorship," in *How Do I Look?* ed. Bad Object Choices (Seattle: Bay, 1991), 115. Mayne's argument about Arzner also appears in chapter 3, "Female Authorship Reconsidered," of her book *Woman at the Keyhole* (Bloomington: Indiana University Press, 1990).

10   Richard Dyer, "Seen to Be Believed: Some Problems in the Representation of Gay People as Typical," *Visual Communication* 9, no. 2 (Spring 1983): 2. See also his "Stereotyping" in *Gays in Film,* ed. Richard Dyer (London: BFI, 1978; rev., 1984), 27–39; and T. E. Perkins, "Rethinking Stereotypes," in *Ideology and Cultural Production,* ed. Michèle Barrett et al. (New York: St. Martin's, 1979), 135–59.

11   Dyer, "Seen to Be Believed," 8.

12   Mary Ann Doane, "Dark Continents: Epistemologies of Racial and Sexual Difference in Psychoanalysis and the Cinema," in *Femmes Fatales: Feminism, Film Theory, Psychoanalysis* (New York: Routledge, 1991), 233.

13   Ritter was a member of the early lesbian community on Fire Island documented in Esther Newton's study *Cherry Grove, Fire Island: Sixty Years in America's First Gay and Lesbian Town* (Boston: Beacon, 1993). McCambridge's career encompasses a series of telling roles: the unforgettable Emma Small in *Johnny Guitar,* an uncredited bit in Welles's

Touch of Evil as a leather-jacketed onlooker at Janet Leigh's rape, a guest spot as mom to an effeminate warlock on "Bewitched," another as the woman who wanted to marry Dr. Smith on "Lost in Space," and the voice of the devil in *The Exorcist*.

That Ritter and McCambridge were radio performers like Moorehead suggests an interesting dialectic between lesbian representability and literal visibility.

14 Lisa Jones, "The Defiant Ones: A Talk with Film Historian Donald Bogle," *Village Voice* (June 1991): 69. See Donald Bogle, *Toms, Coons, Mulattoes, Mammies and Bucks: An Interpretive History of Blacks in American Films* (1973; New York: Continuum, 1992).

15 Richard Dyer, *Stars* (London: BFI, 1979), 117; see also 109–10.

16 The comment that character actors are a "brassiere for the star, literally holding him or her up," is difficult to resist quoting in this case (Hortense Powdermaker, *Hollywood: The Dream Factory* [New York: Little, Brown, 1950], 206, quoted in Barry King, "Articulating Stardom," in *Stardom: Industry of Desire*, ed. Christine Gledhill [New York: Routledge, 1991], 179).

17 See Sherk, *Agnes Moorehead*, 70. In Charles Laughton's bio of Moorehead for *Don Juan in Hell*, in which they toured extensively in the early fifties, he writes about her days as a drama student in New York: "She was kind of mad around this time, not because she had to pull in her belt notches, but because she hadn't enough money to buy mauve lace, and mauve taffeta and mauve velvet and mauve feathers and geegaws which are a necessity to Agnes Moorehead's breathing."

18 James Robert Parish, *Good Dames*, 78.

19 The Agnes Moorehead fan club's publication was originally entitled "Versatility," as noted in an issue of "Moorehead Memos," a later incarnation of the club's newsletter.

20 Unidentified clipping, Agnes Moorehead Clipping File, Museum of Modern Art Film Study Center, n.p.

21 Quoted in Mason Wiley and Damien Bona, *Inside Oscar* (New York: Ballantine, 1986), 241.

22 *Classic Images* 136 (October 1986): 18.

23 Tania Modleski, *Feminism without Women* (New York: Routledge, 1991), 50.

24 Susan Sontag, "Notes on Camp," in *Against Interpretation* (New York: Farrar, Straus, Giroux, 1975), 283.

25 James Robert Parish, *Good Dames*, 84.

26 James Robert Parish, *Good Dames*, 90.

27 In another revealing comparison, Parish notes that *Dark Passage* gave Moorehead an "opportunity to portray . . . a woman close to her own age without disguising costumes, makeup or foreign accents. . . . Here was a jealous, sex-starved characterization that the electric Dame Judith Anderson would have been proud to play in her heyday" (ibid., 94). Charles Higham and Joel Greenberg acknowledge that "Agnes Moorehead's prying, vicious Madge Rapf is a definitive portrait of bitchery" (*Hollywood in the Forties* [New York: Barnes, 1968], 39).

28 Dana Polan, *Power and Paranoia: History, Narrative, and the American Cinema, 1940– 1950* (New York: Columbia University Press, 1986), 195.

29 Ibid., 274.

30 Jack Smith, "Remarks on Art and the Theatre," in *Jack Smith,* ed. Ira Cohen, Historical Treasures no. 33 (New York: Haumann, 1993), 133–35.

31 Boyd MacDonald, *Cruising the Movies: A Sexual Guide to Oldies on TV* (New York: Gay Press, 1988), 21.

32 Andrew Ross, *No Respect: Intellectuals and Popular Culture* (New York: Routledge, 1989), 139.

33 Bosley Crowther, *The New York Times,* 4 March 1965, section 1, 36.

34 *Advocate,* no. 608 (30 July 1990): 69.

35 Patricia Mellencamp, "Situation Comedy, Feminism, and Freud: Discourses of Gracie and Lucy," in *Studies in Entertainment,* ed. Tania Modleski (Bloomington: Indiana University Press, 1986), 91.

The Ambiguities

of "Lesbian"

Viewing Pleasure

The (Dis)articulations of Black Widow

Valerie Traub

To ask, What is a "lesbian"? is generally to elicit a direct, descriptive response: A lesbian is such and such. But the very simplicity of this question is, in fact, disarming, for part of the theoretical and existential problem of defining the "lesbian" is the variability and fluidity of the category to which "she" belongs. To answer the question is to *fix* that which is fundamentally unstable, to immobilize what is in fact a shifting field of only temporarily meaningful significations. Whatever a "lesbian" "is" is constantly negotiated—a matter of conflicting and contradictory investments and agendas, desires and wills. Although "love" and "desire" for other women is a historical constant within a consistent minority of the population, how that love and desire are experienced and expressed—individually and culturally—are historically changing phenomena. The terms by which "lesbian" is interpreted, and thus given cultural meaning and presence, alter in relation to the shifting fortunes of gender ideologies and conflicts, erotic techniques and disciplines, movement politics, fashion and consumer trends, media representations, and paradigms of mental illness and physical disease—to name just a very few.

And yet, despite this historical variability in what a "lesbian" "is," a particular construction of the "lesbian" has achieved the reified, if unconscious, status of the "real." To put this in historical perspective, at the turn of the century, the ascending theoretical paradigm regarding both the female and the male "homosexual" was that of psychoanalysis, which, as Jeffrey Weeks and Michel Foucault have argued, marked both a new mode of categorization and discipline, and a historical point of departure for a newly "identified" segment of the population.[1] Yet, despite the subsequent delegitimization of the psychoanalytic paradigm by the feminist and gay liberation movements in the sixties and seventies, the terms of psychoanalysis have continued to define, pervasively if unintentionally, what a "lesbian" "is"—not only within the rarified atmosphere of academic or medical discourses, but within popular culture and, more insidiously, within the "lesbian" subcultures within which I live. In novels and films, mainstream and alternative—and, more important, in our reactions to them—"lesbian" continues to be thought through and within a psychoanalytic nexus of signification. "Lesbians" are both outside of and implicated within this nexus, as we are simultaneously marginalized *by* it and unwitting reproducers *of* it.

To unpack the workings of this paradigm, let us begin with Freud's notorious remark about the impossibility of female desire:

There is only one libido, which serves both the masculine and the feminine sexual functions. To it itself we cannot assign any sex; if, following the conventional equation of activity and masculinity, we are inclined to describe it as masculine, we must not forget that it also covers trends with a passive aim. Nevertheless the juxtaposition "feminine libido" is without any justification.[2]

And let us follow Freud with the observations of the feminist Lacanian Julia Kristeva:

Obliteration of the pre-Oedipal stage, identification with the father, and then: "I'm looking, as a man would, for a woman"; or else, "I submit myself, as if I were a man who thought he was a woman, to a woman who thinks she is a man." Such are the double or triple twists of what is commonly called female homosexuality, or lesbianism. . . . Intellectual or artist, she wages a vigilant war against her pre-Oedipal dependence on her mother, which keeps her from discovering her own body as other, different, possessing a vagina.[3]

Despite the historical and political divide between Sigmund Freud and Julia Kristeva—turn of the century Vienna and postmodern France, intransigent patriarchalism and self-reflective feminism—their comments represent a continuous lineage of thought that has become so ubiquitous as to be an ideological commonplace. It is this mode of thinking that demands interrogation if the question of women's desire(s), including "lesbian" desire(s), is to be explored. Not only do Kristeva's remarks, like Freud's, fail to describe my experience of "lesbian" sexuality, but her formulation of "lesbian" desire reproduces Freud's insistence on the necessity of binary categories of gender. Film theorist Laura Mulvey has demonstrated how Freud, in the above passage, shifts the active/masculine equation from a "conventional" metaphoric concept to a naturalizing, biologically based use.[4] By means of this shift, Freud first metaphorizes the libido as serving both "masculine" and "feminine" sexual functions, but then denies a "feminine" specificity to it, relegating women's active desire to the "unnatural" imposture of "masculinity." Mulvey shows that for Freud, "the feminine cannot be conceptualized as different, but rather only as *opposition* (passivity) in an antinomic sense, or as *similarity* (the phallic phase)." Kristeva's logic remains caught in the same trap: "lesbian" can only be thought of as opposition (to women, to heterosexuality) or similarity ("as a man"). Through-out, Kristeva's rhetorical strategy reproduces Freud's; she invokes "lesbian" only to assert its status as "masculine" imposture: the "difference" existing *within* women's desires is, perversely, male.

The following essay attempts to explore the question of women's desire(s) in terms other than those binary designations offered by Freud and Kristeva, and to refuse, in the words of David Halperin, "to collaborate in the reification of modern sexual categories."[5] My methodology is both informed by and contesta-tory of psychoanalysis, as I employ psychoanalytic insights to deconstruct nor-malizing codes and prescriptions. Specifically, I attempt to expose the way bi-nary categories of gender determine in advance our conceptualization not only of gender identity and behavior but erotic positions and practices, and to show how the conflation of gender and erotic desire serves this binary teleology.[6] As I have argued in more detail elsewhere, the very term "sexual difference" conflates two related but different trajectories of subjectivity—gender identification and erotic desire—which, even in the most radical feminist and psychoanalytic the-orizing, results in an elision of erotic practice.[7]

I offer the 1987 film *Black Widow*—ostensibly a mainstream, heterosexual "woman's film" starring Debra Winger and Theresa Russell—as an example of the way such gendered dualisms simultaneously make possible and inhibit the representation of "lesbian" desire.[8] By employing multiple transpositions of identity to produce homoerotic tension between the two female leads, *Black Widow* solicits a "lesbian" gaze at the same time that it invites male heterosexual enjoyment. "Lesbian" viewing pleasure, however, like male and female hetero-sexual pleasure, is constructed around a set of overdetermined relations between gender and sexuality; it does not exist outside of, but in complex relation to, the "deployment of sexuality" dominating contemporary discourse.[9] "Lesbian" ap-propriation of the "gaze" comes only at the price of acquiescence to a system of sexual (gender and erotic) regularization that reproduces dominant taxonomies of sexual (gender and erotic) difference.

The terms by which *Black Widow* elicits "lesbian" desire are precisely those that repress its specificity. Investing in a binary teleology that upholds a struc-tural heterosexuality at the same time it (con)figures "lesbian" desire, the film in-stantiates the following ideological commonplace: if a woman desires a woman, it must be because she (1) really wants to be a man, or (2) really wants to be the *other* woman. Seemingly oppositional, the two are actually inversions of one another: based on an assumption of the "lesbian's" gender dysfunction, the structure of the opposition preserves the seemingly essential heterosexuality of desire.

Given this ideological constellation, the fact that *Black Widow* (directed as it is primarily toward heterosexual entertainment) invites, even produces, "lesbian" pleasure, seems to me to offer a rarefied instance of the maintenance of heterosexual hegemony within the particular North American erotic pressures of the 1980s. These pressures include, but are certainly not limited to, male anxiety about erotically assertive women, the refeminization of women in response to male anxiety, and the newly rematerialized threat of death involved in all erotic liaisons: within the context of AIDS, the film noir narrative trope of sexual danger takes on a more urgent significance. Specific cinematic codes of gender and eroticism, co-joined with spectator desires for "lesbian" representation (whether for political or erotic reasons), create the conditions for erotically ambiguous but ideologically replete viewings.

Insofar as I attempt both a textual reading of the contradictions and ambiguities in *Black Widow,* and an audience-directed analysis of "real" "lesbian" responses to the film, my interpretation stands at the crossroads of two trends in feminist film theory: one path follows, in minute detail, the signifying powers of the text; the other begins with the interpretative interventions and appropriations of the film spectator.[10] Within both paths, the analysis is complicated by the fact that intentionalities and responses are both conscious and unconscious. If E. Ann Kaplan is correct in her assumption that "any reading is a result of a delicate, perhaps unconscious, negotiation between the historical positions/ideologies any text is seeking to present, and the frameworks/codes/local ideologies and individual psychoanalytic constructs that spectators bring to texts,"[11] then any "film event" is a complex and oftentimes contradictory interaction between conscious and unconscious intentionalities of both text and audience. The "female spectator" or "lesbian viewer" thus is simultaneously a hypothetical point of address to which the film "speaks" and a subject position ascribed to "real" female audience members. Crucial to such an understanding of spectatorship is the awareness that, as much as "lesbians" independently walk into the theater, they are also constructed within the space the film affords them. That this space is precisely a locus of ambiguity—both potential and constraint, affordance and limitation, a space opened for representation and a space denied—suggests that the contradictions *within Black Widow* bear some relation to the status of "lesbian" representation more generally. Ambiguity not only informs this film but constitutes the very possibilities of "lesbian" desire within a predominantly heterosexual (and heterosexist) ideology.

In the classical narrative cinema, to see is to desire.
　　　　　—Linda Williams, "When the Woman Looks"[12]

The female spectator . . . temporarily accepts "masculinization" in memory of her "active" phase. . . . The female spectator's phantasy of masculinization [is] at cross-purposes with itself, restless in its transvestite clothes.
　　　　　—Laura Mulvey, "Afterthoughts on 'Visual Pleasure
　　　　　　　　and Narrative Cinema' "[13]

Feminist psychoanalytic and film theorists such as E. Ann Kaplan, Luce Irigaray, and Laura Mulvey have argued that in phallocentric modes of representation only two positions are possible: the active male subject and the passive female object of the gaze.[14] Mulvey in particular hypothesized that such a phallocentric binarism governs the representation of women in classic Hollywood cinema. Under attack from feminists who challenged her static and totalized description of patriarchal power, as well as her negative view of pleasure itself, Mulvey offered the following amendment to her theory: the position of the female spectator is analogous to that of the female transvestite; adopting a "masculinized" position, the female subject of the gaze is forever at odds with a desire that is never her "own." In seeking to define a more dynamic model of women's agency, Mulvey problematically falls back on the psychoanalytic construct of a masculinized desire.

Other feminist film theorists have focused on those moments *within* filmic texts, in the words of Linda Williams, "when the woman looks." Williams's reading of the horror genre as well as Mary Ann Doane's analysis of "women's films," however, suggest that women characters are punished for adopting the male prerogative of the look; and Carol Clover's reading of slasher films argues that the female gaze works primarily as a "congenial double for the adolescent male" viewer, "a male surrogate in things oedipal, a homoerotic stand in."[15] In short, across genre, the female gaze acts only as an equivocal assumption of power.

Indeed, it could be argued that to the extent film depends on visual stimulation, the genre as a whole enacts the specular economy criticized by Irigaray, in which subject and object are always rigidly demarcated, the logic of castration (depending on the sight of what is *not there*) enforcing the representation of the female body as lack. As a way out of this predominantly visual economy, Irigaray proposes instead a tactile erotics, based on physical and psychological contiguity or "nearness." However, as much as women's eroticism may be infused with tactility, many feminist film theorists do not want to accede the pleasure of the gaze to men alone. Contesting the notion that eroticization of the female body is necessarily phallocentric, they argue that the problem is not in specularity itself, but in the reified status of subject and object in the phallo-centric visual economy.

Drawing on the psychoanalytic paradigm of fantasy in which viewing positions are multiple and mobile, such theorists describe the dynamics of identification, and hence, the gaze, as "bisexual," "transactional," or "double."[16] One such theorist, Teresa de Lauretis, implies that a different modality of power might be possible within a homoerotic gaze.[17] In the context of theorizing a gaze unbound by rigid gender polarities, the figure of the "lesbian" is, it seems to me, a priv-ileged site of inquiry. As both subject and object of desire, she embodies the potential desiring modality of all viewing subjects, her body displacing the bi-nary economy enforced by heterosexual ideology. And yet, not quite: insofar as she is still constrained by the structural asymmetries of gender, the "lesbian" *subverts,* but cannot *overturn,* the hegemony of binary codes. More important, the terms by which she enacts her subversion may not be of her own making.

The appropriation of *Black Widow* by "lesbian" audiences enacts the dynamic of women looking at a woman looking at another woman; despite whatever masculinist assumptions about female bodies may structure its visuals, *Black Widow* persistently insists that the gaze within the film is female. The protago-nist, Alex (Winger), an "androgynous," "asexual" Justice Department investiga-tor, searches for, finds, and eventually conquers her antagonist—a "feminine," "sexy" woman, "Reni" (Russell), who compulsively marries wealthy men in order to kill them. By means of her investigation, Alex's subjectivity is trans-formed through identification with and desire for the "black widow."

My use of quotation marks around the terms "androgynous" and "feminine," "asexual," and "sexy" signifies my discomfort with these binary designations— for even "androgynous" poses an intermediary position that keeps the opposi-tional poles intact. Though preferable to "masculine"—which is how many re-viewers describe Alex (when they aren't using adjectives like "frumpy," "clumsy and untidy," "bookish and sloppy," "drab," and "dowdily work-obsessed")[18]— "androgyny" hardly describes Alex's character; insofar as it connotes either someone who could "pass" as male or female, or who deliberately seeks to blur gender distinctions (e.g., Annie Lenox, Grace Jones, Boy George, or David Bowie), "androgyny" is a sexual style foreign to Alex. Indeed, the question posed by the figure of Alex—at once powerful in stance and vulnerable in look, a computer "jock" yet conventionally "sexy" in a black evening dress—is the same question inhering in the figure of the desiring female spectator: how to develop a vocabulary that does not relegate women's desires to previously constituted poles of femininity = passivity versus masculinity = activity? In the terms of de

Lauretis, Alex represents "the signified of a sexual difference not reducible to the terms of a phallic or Oedipal polarity."[19] The strong, effective, attractive, desiring woman finds no proper name or description in our current gender/erotic categories. Even the "lesbian" terminology of the "rough-fluff" maintains the binary schema that Alex's persona defies.

Likewise, Reni, in each of her manifestations—Catharine/Marielle/Margaret/Reni—is universally acknowledged as a "femme." But, as much as it may conjure up prescribed images of facial structure and bodily physique, this term says nothing about her intelligence, strength, willfulness, courage. She controls every one of her relationships with men, precisely by allowing them an illusory sense of control. If Reni is a "femme," then the correlation between "femininity" and passivity holds no purchase. And if Alex is perceived as "asexual," perhaps this says more about male expectations of female accessibility than about her own desires. Indeed, her "asexuality" is defined through the questionable auspices of her boss, who has been rebuffed in his attempt to seduce her, and through reviewers who assume that Alex's lack of interest in *this* man (and this *man*) implies a total disinterest in sexuality.

Structurally, *Black Widow* attempts to revise its genre's investment in a gendered heterosexuality that positions woman as object to be sought and either punished or saved. A revision of the film noir's narrative of the male investigator's pursuit of a "femme fatale," Alex's role as investigator inverts the cinematic structure of gendered representation. And yet, not entirely: for, in retaining a woman (quite literally, a fatal "femme") as the object of investigation, *Black Widow* rejects an easy inversion of the film noir mode (an inversion that would keep intact both gender opposition and heterosexuality) and instead creates the conditions for a homoerotic structuring of pursuit and desire.[20]

Superficially, the film's main characters represent inversions of the same problem. Reni, who in each of her manifestations embodies the quality of "to-be-looked-at-ness," murders men;[21] conventional in gender identification, easily objectifiable within mainstream cinematic codes, she is literally a sexual outlaw, using her charms to lure men into her trap. Conversely, Alex largely ignores men as objects of desire, and defies cinematic objectification during the first half of the film by wearing comfortable, loose clothes; but in her role as Justice Department investigator, she is positioned as the obedient daughter upholding and protecting the Father's laws. To this extent, the women are inverted mirror images that together pose the problem of women and the law: the law of gender, the law of (hetero)sexuality, the law of matrimony, the Law of the Father.

Yet, despite the affirmation of the Law implied by the film noir structure, the status of men in the film—and hence, heterosexuality—is problematic. With one exception, the men surrounding Alex—boss, coworkers, cops—are condescending, paternalistic, convinced of their superiority, unable to understand either her pursuit of the murderer (whom they term a phantom) or her refusal of their advances (which they term frigidity). Reni's first three husbands—wealthy, powerful, if a bit gullible—are interchangeable victims; their differences in occupation and personality only serve to highlight Reni's success in transforming her identity to correspond to their fantasies of the desirable woman. Indeed, Reni's verbal responses to these men are so palpably fake, so clichéd, that the message seems to be, Echo a man and he'll marry you. The man most fully realized as a character—Reni's Hawaiian fiancé and fourth husband, Paul (Sami Frey)—is interesting not because of his erotic dynamism but because of his lack of it; as many reviewers remarked, this lack seriously undercuts the believability of the two women's alleged sexual competition.[22] Indeed, rather than calling the shots, Paul is first manipulated by Reni into sleeping with Alex (a ploy to make Reni seem even more desirable), and then used by Alex to force Reni into a confession.

What points most insistently to the failure of heterosexuality in the film is the ability of the women to recognize in one another precisely those qualities that the men cannot. Despite her boss's certainty that the murders, if they *are* murders, are not committed by a woman—"the whole MO, a complex series of seductions and murders, that's not something you see a woman do"—Alex takes Reni's capacity for violence seriously; she sees the pattern in the murders because she wills herself into Reni's way of thinking. Likewise, Reni respects Alex; although flattered by Alex's obvious fascination with her, she never underestimates Alex as an opponent, never dismisses the threat Alex poses. No man distrusts Reni; no man believes Alex. From the perspective of the male gaze within the film, Reni is angelic and Alex neurotic.

"The black widow—she mates and she kills. Your question is 'Does she love?' It's impossible to answer that—unless you live in her world."

—Reni

According to those reviewers who disliked *Black Widow*, its primary failure was its inadequate contextualizing of Reni's motive for murder.[23] Again and again, the reviewers discuss the film in terms of its *lack*: what it doesn't show, what it doesn't explain. The film does provide a number of possible motives— desire for wealth and power, self-hatred, a confusion of love and death—but it undercuts the totalizing drive to find *one* explanation. Alex's tall tale of her own abused childhood (complete with father beating her with a spatula), offered as a possible parallel to Reni's, is a self-conscious parody: as her facade begins to break down at the excesses of her story, she laughingly exclaims to her boss, "I can't believe you really went for it! Don't you know, no one knows why anyone does anything!"

It just may be that the film's reluctance to provide a compelling motivation for murder is related to a more deeply buried reticence about articulating Reni's erotic desire. As her relationship with Alex takes precedence over the detective story midpoint in the narrative, the question becomes less why Reni kills—she simply does—but whether she is capable of love or desire at all. The film noir's investment in containing female desire by imposing punishment gives way to the prior question of woman's desire per se. Whereas Reni's status as murderer fatally affects her relationships with men, it tends to affect only minimally the eroticism of the film, which is focused, instead, on the women. By the end of the film, the question takes on further specification: What *constitutes* love/desire for a woman "like" her? Despite Reni's assertion that she loved each of her husbands, her strategic withholding of sex from Paul suggests that whatever "authentic" erotic desire she feels for men is submitted to her greater desire to compel them to submit to her will to kill. What is *not* comprehensible within the heterosexual outlines of the plot is why Reni tenderly holds Alex's handkerchief to her face after searching her room, why she aggressively, even brutally, kisses Alex during her wedding reception, and why, at the end of the film, speaking to Alex across a prison grill, she says, "Of all the relationships I'll look back on in fifty years' time, I'll always remember this one." To the extent that the film *chooses not* to contextualize these actions, Reni remains a mystery.

To know Reni, you have to enter her world. But what *is* her world? Located precisely at/as the aporia of the film, Reni's erotic subjectivity is the space most vividly *dis*articulated, actively voided of possible "content." A "lesbian" narrative is needed to make the plot comprehensible, but such an option is never offered within the film. Spectator desires for narrative congruity and coherence thus battle with the heterosexist framework that disallows "lesbian" desire as a possible reality. From a "lesbian" perspective, Reni's offer of Paul to Alex is not merely a coercive gesture; in inverting the male homosocial system by which women are exchanged between men, Paul's body becomes a courier, communicating indirectly those desires that Reni and Alex cannot express. What is at stake, then, in the representation of "lesbian" desire in *Black Widow* is the very intelligibility of the narrative; correspondingly, what is at stake in *Black Widow* is the very possibility of "lesbian" representation within a masculinist and heterosexual field.

Mirror, mirror, on the wall,
Who's the fairest of them all?

From the film's first shot, in which "Catharine," her face not only reflected in but split by a mirror, applies makeup to her eyes and then hides them behind dark glasses, the film plays with standard cinematic tropes of sight and identity: eyes, glasses, mirrors, photographs. Concerned not only with what one sees, but who is doing the looking, the film foregrounds "gazing" at the same time it disrupts any stable notion of identity—as if to say, what you see is not necessarily what you get.

In a crucial early scene, Alex engages in an evening of mimetic identification with the representations "Reni" has, at that point, created of herself. Projecting slides of photographs of "Catharine" and "Marielle" onto her living room wall, transposing the different images on top of each other, Alex intends to prove their essential similitude—the different women are, indeed, one and the same. But the moment of Alex's unification of the object of her search is also the moment that initiates Alex's disunity: superimposing herself on top of the transpositions, walking to her bathroom mirror, comparing her body parts—hand, face, hair—to the images on her wall, Alex calls up her similarity to and difference from the other woman/women. The consensus of reviewers is that Alex thereby confronts her failure to conform to patriarchal standards of "femininity": measuring herself against the image projected by Russell—who is ipso facto granted a higher rating in the beauty department than Winger—she finds herself "wanting." As one of the more feminist reviewers writes, in what is her major criticism of the film: "Alex, in gazing at the 'other' woman, is turned back into an awareness of what she herself lacks. Her obsession with Catharine is thus based on her seeing Catharine as alien to herself, but more importantly, it is symptomatic of her devaluation of herself as an 'incomplete' woman."[24]

The film does attempt to represent Alex's obsession with Reni as dissatisfaction with her "lack," as jealous (heterosexual) desire to *be* the "other" woman, and it structures the Hawaiian menage à trois precisely to foreground Alex's supposed inadequacy: Reni wins, Alex loses Paul. But does Alex even *want* Paul? After their night together, we see Alex gazing into a mirror—but this is no Scarlett O'Hara, her "femininity" at last fulfilled by the force of male passion. Like a similar shot of Reni looking in the mirror after the death of her first husband, Alex's face is utterly inscrutable. Indeed, the clichéd motivation (all she needed was a good fuck) recedes in light of Winger's compelling portrayal of a professional who will not hesitate to use others sexually if her investigation warrants it.

For an audience erotically invested in Winger's powerful persona, unaware that she is lacking in *anything*, the projection scene reads as a refusal of those gender dichotomies that organize erotic desire.[25] A return to Lacan's mirror stage of psychic development, it signals the moment before the symbolic phallus intervenes to position subjects within an arbitrary system of two genders corresponding to only two desires. The mirror stage is important for two reasons. On the one hand, the mirror reflects back to the infant for the first time an image of itself as a unified, coherent subject. On the other hand, to the extent that this image is external, inverted, mediated by the mirror and thus alienated, its promise of a unified self is illusory, a lie. The inception of the subject is also the instance of the subject's radical displacement from "itself," prefiguring the "necessary" injunction that the subject embody a normative gender and erotic position. Alex's return to this stage marks a desire for the moment before woman's body is alienated from itself, and from the bodies of other women. Rather than close down the possibilities of female identity and desire, Alex's fascination with Reni reopens them: activating the sense of "wanting" as verb rather than adjective, as desire rather than merely lack, this scene instantiates the articulation of a desire with no (proper) name.

And yet the structure of the narrative, like Lacanian psychoanalysis, insists that if Alex wants Reni, she must also want to *be* Reni. From the projection scene on, Alex begins to identify with the object of her gaze: the quality of her obsession (her boss complains, "She's obsessed with killing, and you're obsessed with her") is such that by the end of the film she has borrowed the clothes, hair dresser, and male lover of the woman she pursues. More important, Alex has also become a "black widow," desiring, trapping, "mating with," and annihilating her prey.

Visually the film plays with this identification; with increasing regularity after the projection scene, Alex and Reni are alternatingly dressed in blue and red. If one wears blue, the other is in red, as if to emphasize their difference; but insofar as *each* wears both red and blue, difference slides into interchangeability. In fact, from one scene to the next, the women slip into one another: a view of Alex slumped over her bathroom sink is followed by a cut of Reni in a similar posture slumped over her bed; Alex's detective research in the projection scene immediately precedes Reni's research of an anthropological video; Reni's night with Paul succeeds Alex's night with him. Alex, initially coded in binary terms as "masculine" (she really wants to be a man), becomes increasingly "feminized" (she really wants to be the *other* woman). Thus, despite (and because of) the erotic tension between the women, the film reasserts the essential heterosexuality of desire. *Black Widow* manipulates the components of "lesbian" visual pleasure, and thereby constitutes such pleasure, by asserting the isomorphism of gender identification and erotic desire, and their complicity in the filmic gaze itself. The trap in which Freud, Kristeva, Lacan, and Mulvey are caught is the same web *Black Widow* seeks to weave.

From a psychoanalytic perspective, Alex's desire to transform her identity into a mirror image of Reni raises two related issues: narcissism and preoedipal conflict. However, rather than comply with the film's rehearsal of psychoanalytic dogma, and rather than assimilate female desire to daughterly ambivalence toward the mother and overidentification with the father, let us expose the essentialism on which this interpretation is based. It is not that "lesbians" are fundamentally narcissistic, but that they too are trapped within dominant erotic constructs. Heretofore, gender difference has served as the primary indicator of erotic tension, with "lesbians" neurotically unable to deal with such "difference." However, the belief that homoerotic desire depends on gender similitude obscures both the implication of gender in larger systems of power, and the role of *other* differences in erotic arousal. The poles of gender are only one, and not necessarily the most crucial, of tensions structuring erotic excitement: arousal may be as motivated by the differences *within* each gender as by gender difference itself.[26]

More instructive at this point than psychoanalysis's naming and fixing of the "lesbian" is *Black Widow*'s inability to do so. The destabilization of identity in the film points to the paradox of "lesbian" representation within a heterosexist field of reference. As Judith Roof makes clear, within normative heterosexism "lesbians" cannot be represented except in terms of their unrepresentability.[27] Who *is* "Reni"? Can we even properly call her by that name? A professional dissembler, Reni's multiple impersonations (the sophisticated wife of a New York publisher, the flouncy "airhead" married to a Texas toy mogul, the studious anthropologist on the board of a Seattle museum, the leisured playgirl in Hawaii) defy the certainty presumed by the act of naming. If I've chosen to call her "Reni" because it is the persona she inhabits during her relationship with Alex, the arbitrariness of this choice is demonstrated by the fact that the reviewers consistently call her "Catharine" (interestingly enough, as if her originary persona were more surely "her"), of which "Reni" is a shortened version. And who is "Alex," who has not only shortened her name from Alexandra, but, once engaged in her search, has been reincarnated in the form of middle-class vacationer Jessica (Jessie) Barnes? Her second transformation—her "makeover" under Reni's tutelage—underscores the point that it is not only Reni who manufactures, and fractures, identity. Of course, Alex and Reni are not "free" to "choose" their personas: as Reni's hyperfemininity and Alex's new bikini and hairstyle attest, they both must work within existing codes of female behavior. Indeed, the film seems to falter when confronted with possibilities outside of the dominant ideology: who will Alex become after she leaves the courthouse in the final frame of the film, walking into the bright sun, but grim-faced and obviously upset by Reni's certain criminal conviction? Will she return (in her blue and white flowered sundress) to her bleak Justice Department "job with green windows"? Will she continue to adopt Reni's identity, becoming her own rendition of the "femme fatale"? Will she "come out" as a "lesbian"? What *are* her options? The film does not, apparently cannot, say.

Such refusals to articulate are constitutive of the film as a whole. *Black Widow* is constructed around two mirroring incoherencies—Reni's desire for Alex and Alex's desire for Reni—and it is only within these gaps that the representation of anything "lesbian" can emerge. Moments of textual excess—moments not required by the logic of plot, but instead functioning to upset the coherency of the narrative—instantiate "lesbian" desire in the film. A series of scenes eroticize the relationship between the women: a CPR practice session involving mouth-to-mouth resuscitation, performed in bathing suits (in which Alex jokes, "You're not taking this personally, are you?"—both an indication and undermining of the sexual tension between the two); a picnic during which Reni seductively lies under watchful Alex's gaze; and an underwater scuba-diving scene, during which, owing to the mysterious failure of Alex's oxygen tank (we suspect foul play), the two experience the enforced intimacy of sharing breath. After all, "lesbian" pleasure is not totally denied in patriarchal culture; rather, it is subtly controlled and disciplined under the male heterosexual gaze.

The most intense moment of textual superfluity—and the greatest incoherency—is the "kiss" exchanged between the two women immediately after Reni's marriage to Paul. Insofar as the act of kissing has been widely constructed as a synecdoche of the movements of the erotic body, indeed, the sine qua non of erotic desire, its exchange between women most powerfully signifies "lesbian": indeed, the "kiss" is utterly incomprehensible without an acknowledgment of the women's desire(s).[28] However, I want to argue that the "kiss" is also the moment when the film most forcefully *dis*articulates "lesbian" desire: neither sensual nor friendly, the kiss in its brutality comes close to the iconography of rape, a taking of possession, an assertion of both knowledge and power—Reni wants Alex to know that *she* knows *Alex* knows she is a murderer. An explicit warning, it is also the "black widow's" sign of mating—and thus a kiss of death. The "kiss" both does and actively does not signify "lesbian," and as such metonymically figures the film as a whole.

Such incoherencies are evident as well in the publicity for the film. The newspaper ad released by Twentieth Century–Fox provides a visual representation of the film's strategies simultaneously to inscribe and deny "lesbian" significations. Within the upper half of the frame, on either side of a column of bright light, the lit faces of Winger and Russell loom large against a mysterious dark background, dwarfing the anonymous, darkened male figure surrounded by light at the bottom of the frame. Their symmetrically inverted faces are stark and bare, their hair barely visible, their torsos occluded. Suspended in the darkness, the two women embody a mirror image of sexual determination and threat; all visual meaning is gathered in the striking similitude of the shape of and attitude expressed by their eyes, lips, noses, and facial structure. The single male victim, on the other hand, enters, as if from the outside, fully clothed, a trenchcoat providing defense against the threat of the overarching, dual, female gaze.

Visually, this ad poses the primary relationship as female. Yet intervening between them is not merely the vulnerable man, but a stark, tall column of light, overwritten with these equally stark words: "She mates and she kills. No man can resist her. Only one woman can stop her." Rewriting similarity as antagonism, the written text interjects an essential difference between the dual female images: one is a siren, one a savior, though their lack of physical differentiation makes it impossible to tell which is which. Just as the white column, rising from the figure of the male, interrupts the contiguity of the women, forcing phallic light between the mysterious darkness they represent, the written text imposes a heterosexual interpretation through its triangulation of desire.

Six of the ten reviews I read mentioned the attraction between the women, and two lamented that the film didn't push further in that direction.[29] None of the reviews questioned, however, what "lesbian" would mean in the context of *Black Widow,* nor did any of them ask *why* the film didn't pursue that direction—what social, psychological, economic, and generic exigencies combined to prohibit a more explicit filmic representation. This reluctance of "liberal" reviewers to interrogate the film's presumptions bespeaks of more than the usual superficiality of such reviews. I suggest that to the extent the film is seen to gesture toward "lesbian" desire, it invokes more anxiety than pleasure in even the "liberal" heterosexual viewer. Rather than embodying an ethic of tolerance and inclusiveness, *Black Widow* demonstrates not only the failure of heterosexuality—encapsulated in the last scene by Paul's stony face as Reni kisses him on the cheek—but the instability of sexual "identity" as such. Neither Alex nor Reni are figured as "lesbian" by birth, and, according to the gender and erotic codings the film endorses, both of them obviously could "be" heterosexual if they chose. But, despite the moonlit scenes with Paul, neither woman does so choose, at least not clearly and unequivocally. Defying essentialist categories of erotic identity, the film thus verges on exposing the vulnerability of all erotic subjects. Deep in the heart of desire is an anxiety that not only animates, but constitutes it.

However much *Black Widow* represents "lesbian" desire, its commitment to the conflation of gender and sexuality results in desire's effacement. Whatever positive signification the "kiss" may hold for either woman is subsumed by a generic logic and psychic aggression, a heterosexual teleology, that finally puts the beloved behind bars. In this sense, "lesbian" representation in *Black Widow* is precisely *dis*articulated; through the play of desire and identification, their intersections and conflations, "lesbian" desire is constructed only to be imprisoned.

The final look exchanged between the two women is of neither betrayal nor triumph, but longing. It is not a matter, therefore, of arguing that Reni or Alex "is" "a" "lesbian" or *Black Widow* is a "lesbian film," but rather that both black widow(s) and *Black Widow* pose the problem of "lesbian" representation within a dominantly heterosexist and patriarchal system. *Black Widow* articulates "lesbian" desire, rendering it visible, only to reencode it as invisible, inarticulate.

That *Black Widow* constructs its representation of "lesbian" desire precisely to contain it, that it enforces the impossibility of "lesbian" representation by invoking its possibility, is not the whole story. There is something in excess of the film's strategies of containment: the presence of "real lesbians" in the audience, appropriating and deriving pleasure from the very nuances and fissures the film exposes, wresting the love story away from the heterosexual teleology demanded by the film noir. Insofar as the film cannot be read separately from the transaction taking place as it unrolls before an audience, *Black Widow* becomes an event of cultural production, a moment in which "lesbian" subjectivities themselves are constructed. If "lesbian" viewers enter the cinema with their identities "intact," the boundaries of those identities are refigured by means of the interaction with "lesbian" desire they both witness and engage in. By (im)posing the (im)-possibilities of "lesbian" desire, the film literally *invites* "lesbians" in both senses of the word: it allures/attracts them, and offers an opening in which to become the image the film represents. As such, the film enacts its own dominant metaphor: a "black widow," it both seduces and seeks to suppress the desire it solicits.

The status of *Black Widow* as a "lesbian" cult film, however, suggests that its attempt to imprison "lesbian" subjectivity fails. But perhaps imprisonment was not really its goal, for, despite the logic of punishment entailed by Reni's crimes and the film noir formula, the primary mode of discipline enacted by *Black Widow* is *correction:* the film succeeds remarkably well in interpellating the "lesbian" subject according to its binary schema of identification and desire. The dominant logic of "the gaze" would suggest that, insofar as Reni and Alex are constructed, respectively, as object and subject of the gaze, the audience should identify with Alex and, through her, desire Reni. And yet the majority of "lesbians" I know who saw the film defied spectator conventions, constructing Alex as an erotic object to suit *their* desires.[30] At the same time, their construction enacts precisely the conflation of gender and eroticism endorsed by the film and by which the dominant ideology homogenizes "lesbian" desire as "narcissistic": identification *with* Alex leads to desire *for* Alex.

To particularize the set of identities that comprise the "lesbian" at this historical juncture: "Lesbian" viewers encountered *Black Widow* at a time when "lesbian chic" was in ascendence; no longer an object of suspicion, the "Vogue dyke" became a viable object of desire.[31] Indeed, I would argue that *Black Widow* appealed to "lesbian" viewing communities in part because of its mainstream, crossover status. Alex, coded as "deviant" in gender role, provides a point of entry—of identification—into the film, and from there, desires for more mainstream pleasures (i.e., the conventionally beautiful woman whom Alex becomes) take over. For an audience hungry for more complex cultural representations of their lives than stereotypes of unattractive "manhaters" afford, *Black Widow* proves an enticing mixture.

And yet the diverse subject positions of those who call themselves (or are called by others) "lesbian" obviate the possibility of assigning *one* position to the "lesbian" spectator. Differences in class and race fracture the illusory unity of the "lesbian subject," as the filmic object of the gaze is rendered inaccessible (for economic reasons) or undesirable (for cultural or political reasons). Insofar as *Black Widow*'s portrayal of Hawaii is structured from the perspective of Western tourism, its eroticism functions on the basis of the elision of race and class differences. Indeed, as "Hawaii" in *Black Widow* equals four-star hotels, scuba diving, and stunning volcanic eruptions, the film's attitude toward its subject is summed up by Paul: with no irony, he explains to Reni that because he loves the volcano so much, he intends to build a hotel there.

Race and class stratification within the "lesbian" spectator are further complicated by differences in gender identification and erotic practice. The "lesbian" who identifies as "butch" may respond differently to Alex or Reni than would a "femme" or "rough-fluff," and not all "butches," "rough-fluffs," or "femmes" would respond alike.[32] The bisexual who had chosen a monogamous gay relationship may respond to other erotic cues than would the woman who has multiple partners. The feminist who has adopted a "lesbian" identity as a political necessity may feel differently about her desires than would the woman who feels she has been "gay" from birth. Needless to say, those involved in S/M have different erotic tastes from those preferring what has come to be called (reductively, I think) "vanilla" sex. And finally, it must be said that, dominant ideology to the contrary, "lesbian" desire is extant within many putative heterosexuals. Indeed, despite the linguistic imperative underlying the division between "homo" and "hetero," "lesbian" desire is not oppositional to female heterosexual desire—though what its relation might be (contiguous, tangential, interstitial, disterminate) is yet to be theorized beyond the psychoanalytic narrative that poses "lesbian" desire as that which must be repressed.

The range and diversity of identifications and practices of "lesbians" raise again the question with which I began my analysis of *Black Widow:* What *is* a "lesbian"? What *is* "lesbian" desire? I hope to have shown that such questions can be answered meaningfully only in historically contingent terms. I want to suggest too that, in its singularity and self-identity, "lesbian" is a politically necessary but conceptually inadequate demarcation: to my mind, less a person than an activity, less an activity than a modality of pleasure, a position taken in relation to desire. Its problematic ontological status suggests that it is better used as an adjective (e.g., "lesbian" desire) than a noun signifying a discrete order of being. Neither inhering essentially within subjects nor forceably imposed on them, "lesbian" is a point of reference around which erotic "difference" can and must rally politically, but on which it should never stand for long. Rather than affirm "lesbian" desire definitionally (e.g., Alex "is" a "lesbian"), I propose instead the more laborious process of exploring the contradictions inherent in the "lesbian's" construction, for it is the convergences, intensifications, slippages, and displacements between gender and eroticism that make possible a vision of a nonbinary mode of erotic pleasure—for *all* erotic subjects.

A final moment of excess: just as Alex leaves the courthouse, two women, one in red, one in blue, walk across the screen. Outside of Hollywood's codes of stardom, these women signify the ordinary, the everyday, as they go about their business. To any "lesbian" viewer, at this historical moment, their stride, affect, dress, and hairstyle suggest "dyke." Why does *Black Widow* end with an image so seemingly superfluous to its diegesis? But *are* they superfluous? As Alex/Jessie walks off into her unknown destiny, as Reni/Catharine/Marielle/Margaret languishes behind bars, these women—an alternative image of Alex and Reni together—signal visually what the film has suppressed narratively: "lesbian" desire is available, reproducible, and, despite efforts to deny it, everywhere.

Notes

I would especially like to thank Brenda Marshall, Darlene Dralus, and the students involved in my course "Representations of Women's Identity" for sharing their responses to this film. Thanks also to Kris Straub, Julia Epstein, Jay Clayton, Ellen Garvey, Susan Zimmerman, Serena Anderlini, and Michael Kreyling for their responses to an early draft. Finally, the Vanderbilt University Research Council graciously extended funds to sustain me during the writing of this essay.

1 Jeffrey Weeks, *Sexuality and Its Discontents* (London: Routledge & Kegan Paul, 1985); and Michel Foucault, *The History of Sexuality*, vol. 1 (New York: Random House, 1976).

2 Sigmund Freud, "Femininity," in *New Introductory Lectures on Psychoanalysis*, trans. and ed. James Strachey (New York: Norton, 1965), 116.

3 Julia Kristeva, "About Chinese Women," in *The Kristeva Reader,* ed. Toril Moi (New York: Columbia University Press, 1986), 149.

4 Laura Mulvey, "Afterthoughts on 'Visual Pleasure and Narrative Cinema' Inspired by *Duel in the Sun,*" in *Feminism and Film Theory,* ed. Constance Penley (London: Routledge, Chapman & Hall, 1988), 71.

5 David Halperin, "One Hundred Years of Homosexuality," *Diacritics* 16, no. 2 (Summer 1986): 40.

6 Despite his attempt to separate sexual aim (passive/active) and object (hetero/homo), Freud consistently conflated gender and eroticism through his concept of bisexuality. At times referring to the integration of "masculine" and "feminine" attributes (i.e., activity, passivity), at times referring to the nascent capacity for both hetero- and homoerotic object choice, at times referring to both, "bisexuality" in Freudian usage allows gender and eroticism not only to nudge against, but slip into one another.

7 See Valerie Traub, "Desire and the Differences It Makes," in *The Matter of Difference: Materialist Feminist Criticism of Shakespeare,* ed. Valerie Wayne (London: Harvester, 1991). Other feminist theorists are calling for a specification of and differentiation between gender and eroticism, the most sophisticated being Eve Sedgwick, "Across Gender, across Sexuality: Willa Cather and Others," *South Atlantic Quarterly* 88, no. 1 (Winter 1989): 53–72, "Epistemology of the Closet (I)," *Raritan 7,* no. 4 (Spring 1988): 39–69, and "Epistemology of the Closet (II)," *Raritan* 8, no. 1 (Summer 1988): 102–30; and Teresa de Lauretis, "Sexual Indifference and Lesbian Representation," *Theatre Journal* 40, no. 2 (May 1988): 155–77. In the final stages of writing this article, I came across an excellent essay by Jackie Stacey, "Desperately Seeking Difference," in *The Female Gaze: Women as Viewers of Popular Culture,* ed. Lorraine Gramman and Margaret Marshmont (London: Women's Press, 1988), 112–29. Stacey analyzes desire or, as she terms it, "fascination" between women in *All About Eve* and *Desperately Seeking Susan* in terms surprisingly close to mine. In fact, she anticipates my critique of psychoanalytic binarism, having isolated the same passage of Kristeva to make her point: "This insistence upon a gendered dualism of sexual desire maps homosexuality on to an assumed antithesis of masculinity and femininity. . . . In arguing for a more complex model of cinematic spectatorship, I am suggesting that we need to separate gender identification from sexuality, too often conflated in the name of sexual difference" (p. 121). She even footnotes *Black Widow* as a film in which homoerotic connotations are more explicit than in the films she analyzes.

8 Directed by Bob Rafelson, screenplay by Ronald Bass, released by Twentieth Century–Fox. Within the context of this film, I use "lesbian" to describe a desire for other women, whether or not it is ever acted on. In this, I differ from the dominant trend of using "gay," not only because it generally refers to men, but because its usefulness is increasingly limited to the description of an identity evolving out of a self-conscious minority community. My concept of "lesbian" is also distinguished from the feminist concept of the "woman-identified-woman," which fails to include eroticism as a necessary component. For the most articulate spokesperson for the woman-identified-woman definition, see

Adrienne Rich, "Compulsory Heterosexuality and Lesbian Existence," *Signs* 5, no. 4 (1980): 631–60. Like Catharine Stimpson, I see the "lesbian" as a matter of the body, but unlike her, I insist on the importance of fantasy as much as action in the modality of desire (see "Zero-Degree Deviancy: The Lesbian Novel in English," *Critical Inquiry* 8, no. 2 [Winter 1981]: 363–79). There exists a long history of debate over definitions of "lesbian," much of it unproblematically asserting the existence of a type of *being* based on certain *credentials* (love for women, political alliance, genital sexual activity). To my mind, what is more crucial than the proving or maintaining of "lesbian" credentials is consistent public affirmation of the rights of "lesbians," a practice with which all persons, regardless of erotic practice, can be involved.

9 For an explanation of this phrase, see Foucault, *The History of Sexuality.*

10 See Janet Bergstrom and Mary Ann Doane, "The Female Spectator: Contexts and Directions," *Camera Obscura* 20/21 (May/September 1989): 5–27. Elizabeth Ellsworth's analysis of "lesbian" reviewers of *Personal Best* has been extremely helpful to my formulation of "lesbian" interventions in dominant media (see "Illicit Pleasures: Feminist Spectators and *Personal Best,*" in *Becoming Feminine: The Politics of Popular Culture,* ed. Leslie Roman, Linda Christian Smith, with Elizabeth Ellsworth [London: Falmer, 1988], 102–19).

11 E. Ann Kaplan, "Response," *Camera Obscura* 20/21 (May/September 1989): 197.

12 Linda Williams, "When the Woman Looks," in *Re-Vision: Essays in Feminist Film Criticism,* ed. Mary Ann Doane, Patricia Mellencamp, and Linda Williams (Los Angeles: American Film Institute, 1984), 83–99.

13 Mulvey, "Afterthoughts," 78–79.

14 Luce Irigaray, *This Sex Which Is Not One,* trans. Catharine Porter (Ithaca, N.Y.: Cornell University Press, 1985), and *Speculum of the Other Woman,* trans. Gillian Gill (Ithaca, N.Y.: Cornell University Press, 1985); Laura Mulvey, "Visual Pleasure and Narrative Cinema," in *Feminism and Film Theory,* 57–68; and E. Ann Kaplan, *Woman and Film: Both Sides of the Camera* (Methuen: London, 1983).

15 Carol Clover, "Her Body, Himself: Gender in the Slasher Film," *Representations* 20 (Fall 1987): 212, 213; Mary Ann Doane, "The Woman's Film: Possession and Address," in *Re-Vision,* 67–82, *The Desire to Desire: The Woman's Film of the 1940s* (Bloomington: Indiana University Press, 1987), and "Film and the Masquerade: Theorizing the Female Spectator," *Screen* 23, nos. 3/4 (September/October 1982): 74–88. See also Tania Modleski, *The Women Who Knew Too Much: Hitchcock and Feminist Theory* (New York: Methuen, 1988).

16 Elizabeth Cowie, e.g., encourages us to view film as fantasy, "a *mise en scène* of desire which can be seen to have multiple places for the subject of the fantasy, and for the viewing subject who, through identification, may similarly take up these multiple positions"; Janet Bergstrom speaks of a "textual address which is bisexual (in Freud's sense) and in which identifications are neither stable nor predictable"; and D. N. Rodowick expresses the relation between "masculine" and "feminine" identifications as "transactional" (*Camera Obscura* 20/21 [May/September 1989]: 97, 129, 272). Teresa de Lauretis argues that the

female gaze consists of a "double identification" in *Alice Doesn't: Feminism, Semiotics, Cinema* (Bloomington: Indiana University Press, 1984), 144, and *Technologies of Gender: Essays on Theory, Film, and Fiction* (Bloomington: Indiana University Press, 1987).

17 de Lauretis, "Sexual Indifference." Analyses of representations of "lesbians" in film by Mandy Merck, " 'Lianna' and the Lesbians of Art Cinema," and Linda Williams, " 'Personal Best': Women in Love," in *Films for Women,* ed. Charlotte Brundson (London: British Film Institute, 1986), 166–78, 146–54, and B. Ruby Rich, "From Repressive Tolerance to Erotic Liberation: *Mädchen in Uniform,*" in *Re-Vision,* 100–30, while containing interesting descriptions of these films, are not much concerned with the dynamics of the gaze. Of interest in regard to representations of "lesbians" in theater are essays by Jill Dolan, "The Dynamics of Desire: Sexuality and Gender in Pornography and Performance," *Theatre Journal* 39, no. 2 (May 1987): 156–74; and Sue-Ellen Case, "Toward a Butch-Femme Aesthetic," in *Making a Spectacle: Feminist Essays on Contemporary Women's Theatre,* ed. Lynda Hart (Ann Arbor: University of Michigan Press, 1989), 282–99.

18 Marina Heung (*Film Quarterly* 41 no. 3 [Fall 1987], 54–58), Richard Combs (*Sight and Sound* 56 no. 3 [Summer 1987], 220–221), and Mike McGrady (*Newsday* 6 February 1987, Part III, 3) called Alex "frumpy"; Heung added "clumsy and untidy." Charles Sawyer (*Films in Review* 38 [April 1987], 227–228), termed her "bookish and sloppy," while for David Denby (*New York* [16 February 1987], 72), she was "drab," and for Louise Sweet (*Monthly Film Bulletin* 642 [July 1987], 201–203), "dowdily work-obsessed."

19 de Lauretis, *Alice Doesn't,* 82.

20 *Black Widow* is not a feminist film. It makes no attempt to denaturalize the eroticization of the female body, instead visually offering it up for display. In keeping with the film noir paradigm, it also thematically destroys the woman who would destroy men. As Belinda Bulge says in "Joan Collins and the Wilder Side of Women," "The *femme fatale* of *film noir* ultimately loses control of the action, as both narrative and camera exert mastery over her. At the end of the film she is symbolically imprisoned by the visual composition of her image, just as, in many of the narratives, she is imprisoned, or killed, for her crime. The destruction of the *film noir* 'spider woman' constitutes a moral lesson: the power of the independent woman is an evil that will destroy her" (*The Female Gaze,* 109).

21 The phrase is Mulvey's ("Visual Pleasure," 62).

22 David Edelstein wrote in the *Village Voice* (17 February 1987, 70), "Frey sits on the screen like a blob of snail butter. Whenever he's around, the movie can't seem to focus. His Hawaiian Tropics tan is like a cloaking device (it washes him out), and he sounds as if he learned his lines phonetically." In *Vanity Fair* (50, no. 2 [February 1987], 54–57, 117–18), Arthur Lubow reports that Winger ate a pizza with garlic before their (discarded) love scene; she unconsciously sabotaged it, the writer implies, because she knew the film should be Alex and Catharine, not Alex and her frog prince. "What I can't figure out is why she didn't have paella the next day and clams oreganata the next. She should have stopped taking showers."

23 Such was the view of *Magill's Cinema Annual 1988* (Pasadena: Salem Press, 1988), 75–78, Marina Heung (*Film Quarterly* 41 no. 3 [Fall 1987], 54–58), David Denby (*New York* [16 February 1987], 72), Mike McGrady (*Newsday* 6 February 1987, Part III, 3),

Richard Combs (*Sight and Sound* 56 no. 3 [Summer 1987], 220–221), David Edelstein (*Village Voice* 17 February 1987, 70), and David Lida (*Women's Wear Daily* 6 February 1987, 20).

24 Heung, 56.

25 Winger's persona transcends film boundaries; in part, her popularity rests on the fact that, irrespective of her particular dramatic role, her voice, features, bodily physique, and stance configure her as a powerful woman.

26 Despite his psychoanalytic normalizations, I have found Robert Stoller's work helpful in this regard (see *Observing the Erotic Imagination* [New Haven, Conn.: Yale University Press, 1985], 53).

27 Judith Roof, "The Match in the Crocus: Representations of Lesbian Sexuality," in *Discontented Discourses: Feminism/Textual Intervention/Psychoanalysis,* ed. Marleen S. Barr and Richard Feldstein (Urbana: University of Illinois Press, 1989), 110–16.

28 According to the recent film *Pretty Woman,* for prostitutes, kissing is *verboten* precisely because it imports emotion into a commercial transaction. According to Cindy Patton, kissing is rarely depicted in pornography because "it brings emotion into the pornography, potentially disrupting the thrill of untrammelled sex" and because "kisses are non-gendered, reciprocal, and non-role defined" ("Hegemony and Orgasm—or the Instability of Heterosexual Pornography," *Screen* 30, nos. 1 and 2 [Winter/Spring 1989]: 100, 112). And yet even "kissing" must be internally differentiated, as the dexterity and autonomy of the female tongue in oral "tonguing" turns the "kiss" into a surrogate for, and deferred promise of, fellatio.

29 Those six were Heung, Sawyer, Denby, Edelstein, and Roger Ebert (*New York Post* [6 February 1987], 24). Denby says, "The scenes between the two women don't go far enough," (72) and Ebert writes (quite provocatively), "From the moment Winger and Russell meet, there's a strong undercurrent of eroticism between the two women. We feel it, they feel it, and the movie allows it one brief expression—when Russell roughly reaches out and kisses Winger. But Ron Bass, who wrote the screenplay, and Bob Rafelson, who directed, don't follow that magnetism. They create the unconvincing love affair between Winger and the tycoon to set up a happy ending that left me feeling cheated. What would have been more intriguing? Why not follow a more cynical, truly diabolical course— something inspired by the soul of *film noir*? Why not have Winger fall completely under the spell of the black widow, and stand by while the tycoon is murdered so the two women can live happily ever after? And then end on an eerie note as Winger begins to wonder if Russell can trust her with the secret?" (24).

30 For other instances of "lesbian" intervention in visual codes, see Danae Clark, "Commodity Lesbianism in Advertising and Commercial Television" (paper presented at the Society for Cinema Studies Conference, Washington, D.C., May 1990). See too Jonathan Dollimore's identification of radical strategies of cultural negotiation, "the transformation of dominant ideologies through (mis)appropriation and their subversion through inversion," in "The Dominant and the Deviant: a Violent Dialectic," *Critical Quarterly* 28, nos. 1/2 (1987): 179–92.

31 See, e.g., Arlene Stein, "All Dressed Up, But No Place to Go? Style Wars and the New

Lesbianism," *Outlook:* National Lesbian and *Gay Quarterly* 1, no. 4 (1989), 34–42; also included in this volume.

32 "Butch," like "femme," is a historically constructed erotic *style*. Isomorphic with neither maleness nor masculinity, it is not an imitation of men, but a subversion through inversion of dominant masculinist codes. "Butch" implies a critique of the authenticity of masculinity, signifying that maleness and masculinity are also historically constructed categories.

From Repressive

Tolerance to

Erotic Liberation

Mädchen in Uniform

B. Ruby Rich

What in God's name does one call this sensibility if it be not love? This extraordinary heightening of all one's impressions; this intensification of sensitiveness; this complete identification of feeling? . . . *I* was Manuela, as she is Manuela, and everything that has happened to her has in essence, and other circumstances, happened to me. This incredible feeling of sisterhood.

—Dorothy Thompson, on meeting Christa Winsloe[1]

There are moments when one historical period seems to beckon to another, offering the semblance of lessons to be learned or errors to be avoided. Certainly, that is true today for those of us reviewing the fate of progressive political organizations in the Weimar period preceding Adolph Hitler's coming to power in the inflation-torn and authority-hungry Germany of 1933. In particular, the history of women's-rights groups and homosexual-emancipation organizations is one that needs to be better known and analyzed. It is a testimony to our ignorance of the period that Leontine Sagan's film *Mädchen in Uniform* (1931) is generally assumed to be an anomaly, a film without a context, or else a metaphor, a coded tale about something *else*, something other than what appears on screen. If we are to understand *Mädchen in Uniform* fully, then it is important to keep in view the society within which it was made: the celebrated milieu of Berlin *avant-la-guerre*, Berlin with dozens of gay and lesbian bars and journals, the Berlin of a social tolerance so widespread that it nearly camouflaged the underlying legal restraints (which were to grow, rapidly, into massive repression). I would stop short of claiming an outlandish Rosetta Stone status for the film, no matter how tempting, lest the reader lose faith. Yet it might be emphasized, *Mädchen in Uniform* is an exemplary work, not only for what it presents to us on the screen but also for the timely issues that its analysis must confront. It is the film revival most central to establishing a history of lesbian cinema.

Mädchen in Uniform was filmed by Leontine Sagan in Germany in 1931, based on the play *Yesterday and Today* by Christa Winsloe (alias the Baroness von Hatvany), republished as a novel, *The Child Manuela*, also by Winsloe. The film, like the play, enjoyed a tremendous initial popularity, both within Germany and internationally; yet it has been nearly invisible in the past few decades within the academic study of German cinema. The film has frequently fallen into a seeming limbo between the silent German Expressionist cinema and the notorious products of the Third Reich studios. Despite its remarkable sound quality (praised by Lotte Eisner as the work in which "the prewar German sound film reached its highest level")[2] and in spite of its evocative cinematography (which Kracauer cited as transmitting "the symbolic power of light"),[3] *Mädchen in Uniform* faded from the textbooks, the revival houses, and even eventually from distribution entirely. During the early seventies, however, Sagan's classic was resoundingly redeemed by the cycle of women's film festivals, gathering a solid following and the critical attention it had long lacked. The result, today, is that the film is back in distribution in a beautifully reconstructed print (in contrast to the butchered, mistitled print that made the rounds of the early festivals) and is accorded a secure spot in the history of pre-Reich cinema.

In part, the film's reputation rests on unusual stylistic components. Sagan's montage-inflected structure manages to break away from the usually stagey and claustrophobic mise-en-scène of early sound films. Her montages, no doubt Soviet influenced, establish a persuasive counterpoint to the more theatrical scenes and mold them into a cinematic rhythm. Dramatically, her use of a large cast of nonprofessional actresses lends the film a fresh and documentary-like tone, while the performances of the lead actresses won widespread praise.

Sagan was a pioneer in her use of sound, not only as a functional synchronous accompaniment, but also as a thematic element in its own right. However, most important to the film's reputation through the years has been its significance as an antiauthoritarian and prophetically antifascist film. And, to be sure, the film has suitable credentials for such a claim. Any film so opposed to militarism, so anti-Prussian, so much in support of the emotional freedom of women, must be an antifascist film. Furthermore, it was made through the Deutsche Film Gemeinschaft, a cooperative production company specifically organized for this project—and was the first German commercial film to be made collectively. Add to such factors the fact that the film was made on the very eve of Hitler's rise to power, just prior to the annexation of the film industry into Goebbel's cultural program, and the legend of Sagan's protosubversive movie is secure. In emphasizing the film's progressive stance in relation to the Nazi assumption of power, however, film historians have tended to overlook, minimize, or trivialize the film's central concern with love between women.

Today, we must take issue with the largely unexamined critical assumption that the relations between women in the film are essentially a metaphor for the real power relations of which it treats, that is, the struggle against fascism. I would suggest that *Mädchen in Uniform* is not only antifascist, but also anti-patriarchal in its politics. Such a reading need not depend on metaphor, but can be more forcefully demonstrated by a close attention to the film text. As I propose to read it, *Mädchen in Uniform* is a film about sexual repression in the name of social harmony; absent patriarchy and its forms of presence; bonds between women that represent attraction instead of repulsion; and the release of powers that can accompany the identification of a lesbian sexuality. The film is a dual coming-out story: that of Manuela, the adolescent who voices "the love that dares not speak its name" and who, in distinguishing between fantasy and desire, dares to act on the latter; and that of Fräulein von Bernburg, the teacher who repudiates her own role as an agent of suppression and wins her own freedom by accepting her attraction to another woman. In this reading, the film remains a profoundly antifascist drama, but now its political significance becomes a direct consequence of the film's properly central subject, lesbianism, rather than a covert message wrapped in an attractive but irrelevant metaphor. If *Mädchen in Uniform* is the first truly radical lesbian film, it is also a fairly typical product of late Weimar society, a society in which "homosexuality . . . became a form of fashionable behavior" linked to "the Weimar idea of making a complete break with the staid and bankrupt past of one's parents' generation."[4] As such, it offers a particularly clear example of the interplay between personal and collective politics—and the revolutionary potential inherent in the conjunction of the two.

The film centers on the relationship between two women. Manuela (Hertha Thiele) is a young student newly arrived at a Potsdam boarding school that caters to the daughters of German officers who, in the mid-twenties, are largely impoverished, as is the school itself. With her mother dead, her father unable to look after her, and her aunt/guardian icily uncaring, Manuela is left craving affection. Fräulein von Bernburg (Dorothea Wieck) is the school's most adored teacher, champion of a maternalistic humanitarianism opposed to the school's Prussian codes. Harsh, ascetic, militaristic, the boarding-school environment is enforced by a totalitarian principal (Emilie Unda) dedicated to toughening up her charges.

Manuela quickly develops a passionate attachment to Fräulein von Bernburg, who simultaneously nourishes and discourages her admirer. Manuela's infatuation is even more intense than the crushes that her fellow students have on the esteemed Bernburg. Furthermore, she carries matters to an unprecedented level by announcing her passion publicly, to all the school. The declaration occurs when Manuela, drunk and in male attire, celebrates her thespian success in the school play by offering the news of her affections as a convivial toast. For such a transgression, Manuela is confined to solitary in the infirmary by the school principal, who forbids students and faculty alike from so much as speaking to her.

The mounting crisis impels Fräulein von Bernburg to confront the principal and challenge her authority, a climax that coincides with the desperate Manuela's own decision to solve the problem by committing suicide. Distraught at having to give up her beloved teacher, Manuela climbs the school's forbidding staircase (a central leitmotif in the film) and is about to throw herself from its uppermost railing when her schoolgirl companions, disobeying the injunction, come to her rescue. Their arrival is paralleled by the rush of Fräulein von Bernburg to the scene, confirming her affection for Manuela and her identification with the students' action. The aversion of imminent tragedy is a triumph for the forces of love and community, signaling the coming of a new order. The event seals the fate of the evil principal, who retreats down the hall into the shadows even as Fräulein von Bernburg remains in the light, united through crosscutting with Manuela and the students grouped above her on the staircase.

As should be clear from the summary, the action of *Mädchen in Uniform* transpires entirely within an all-woman environment and, indeed, a thoroughly "feminine" atmosphere. However, the very first establishing shots of the film serve to inform us of the real power of absent patriarchy and remind us that an all-woman school in no way represents a woman-defined space. The montage of visual icons in the first few frames establishes an exterior world of military preparedness, steeples and archways, bugle calls and the marching rhythm of soldiery. And this world of regimentation extends to the neat rows of students who, two by two, file past the gateway into the domain of the school. The link between the exterior authority and the interior order is explicitly visualized only once, but it informs our reading of the entire film (particularly as represented by the emblematic use of off-screen sounds and on-screen symbols, like the staircase).

On her first day of school, Manuela listens to the principal's speech outlining her required duty and identity: "You are all soldiers' daughters and, God willing, you will all be soldiers' mothers." The girls are there to be taught the Prussian values in order that they might transmit the "correct line" to their future progeny. They are destined to be the transmitters of a culture, not its inheritors. The learning is not for them as women in their own right, but for their function as reproducers of bodies and ideologies. The extent to which the absent patriarchy (which at no point in the film takes the shape of actual men on screen) dominates

the women's world is a theme constantly reiterated by Sagan in her many visual-
izations of classically Romantic leitmotifs. Barred shadows cross the women's
paths, a sternly overbearing staircase encloses their every movement, a frantic
montage marshals their steps into a militaristic gait, and even the school songs
reinforce the authority of a demanding fatherland with a handful of schoolgirls
in its grasp. The film's very title underlines this theme, with its play of meanings
on the word *uniform* meaning (as a noun) the clothing of a regimented educa-
tional/military/professional institution, or (as an adjective) the regulated, all-
alike behavior of uniformity dictated by the rules of the patriarchal order.

The ultimate incarnation of the absent but controlling patriarchy is the school
principal. Her identity as the "phallic woman" is suggested by her reliance on
an everpresent cane with which she measures her steps and signals her authority, and by the phallocentric codes of *Kinder, Kirche, Küche* (children, church,
kitchen) that she is dedicated to instilling. Her mandates and bearing call to mind
a vision of Frederick the Great, to whom she has been compared. Perhaps
coincidentally, her jowly face and disassociated affect are equally reminiscent of
that other prophetic cinematic persona of demented authority, Doctor Caligari.
Like the mad Doctor, this principal is accompanied by an obedient assistant, a
dark hunchbacked figure who carries out her orders. Unlike Caligari's missions
of murder, the principal's agenda is more properly "feminine" in its details of
manipulation and reconnaissance. The henchwoman is a warped figure; like the
principal shuffling with her cane, the assistant presents an image of womanhood
carrying out patriarchal dirty work and physically warped by her complicity. Her
hands huddled close to her chest, her eyes pinched and shoulders stooped, the
assistant becomes a physical marker of emotional damage. In *The Cabinet of Dr.
Caligari* madness and hypnotism were held responsible for complicity in murder; Sagan is willing to pinpoint a more precise cause in the dogma of an authoritarian ideology. Just as nuns have long provided an easy example of a woman's
order subject to entirely male authority (in the form of priest, pope, or God the
Father, Son, the heavenly bridegroom), so, too, the institution of the woman's
boarding school is shaped to the mold of the militaristic patriarchal society,
poured like molten liquid into its empty spaces to keep it whole.

How, then, does the power structure within the school itself function? Specifically, what are the roles assumed by the beloved Fräulein von Bernburg, champion of the emotions, and the hated principal, enforcer of discipline? Traditionally, critical readings of the film have identified Fräulein von Bernburg as a
sort of freedom fighter, a humanitarian standing up to the forces of repression,
and have targeted the principal much as I have described her, a tyrant ruling over
a regime of denial. I would take issue with this romanticized view and trade its
simplistic hero/villain dichotomy for a different model, that is, a system of re-

pression based instead on the "good cop, bad cop" pattern, with the principal as the "bad cop" and Fräulein von Bernburg as the "good cop."

To comprehend the logic of such a system in the case of the boarding school, it is necessary to return to the point made earlier in the principal's opening speech. As she made clear, the young women are being bred ("educated") as transmitters of the patriarchal German culture ever present in encoded form within the world of the school. In order to ensure this training, preserve the young women's "honor," and most effectively carry out their special socialization, it is necessary for society to shape women within an all-female setting; in fact, prior to feminist movements, this was no doubt the primary reason for "separatist" institutions. What, however, is the danger to the patriarchal society presented by such an institution? It is a sexual danger: the threat that the heterosexuality required of these women may, in the cloistered pressure-cooker atmosphere of the boarding school, become derailed into a focus on their own sex. The possibility that heterosexuality on the part of women may become transferred ("warped" as the father might say) into homosexuality presents a powerful threat to a system geared for procreation and the rearing of male offspring: "Gender is not only an identification with one sex; it also entails that sexual desire be directed toward the other sex."[5] The danger of the boarding school is that a concentration on the former entails a corresponding relaxation of the latter. Perhaps it is because the women's boarding school is the Achilles heel of patriarchy that it figures in so much lesbian literature and cinema.

In *Mädchen in Uniform*, the code name for this sexual threat is *emotionalism*. When Fräulein von Bernburg early in the film catches two schoolgirls exchanging a love letter, she confiscates the paper and, to their relief and delight, rips it up without reading a word; smiling but strict, she warns them to desist in the exchange of such letters because they can lead to "emotionalism." Again, later in the film, the student ringleader, Ilse, uses the same expression with the same negative message. She is engaged in declaiming a series of mock toasts during the postplay banquet, all phrased in the language of the school's official ideology, and thus she reprimands Manuela for the acting style of her male impersonation: "Remember, next time, less emotionalism."

In line with the model of repression that I suggest, Fräulein von Bernburg's task as the "good cop" seems to be to keep "emotionalism" in check and to make her charges more comfortable in their oppression. She acts as a pressure valve and as the focus of dissident energies in order that the overall system will not be endangered. Fräulein von Bernburg has two guises, then, for coping with the social and sexual schism. Socially, she polices the heart, that is, the emotional life of her students. As she puts it at one point to Manuela, "You mustn't persuade yourself it isn't nice here." It is her presence in the school's cabinet of power that keeps the girls from rebelling against an order that would otherwise be totally abhorrent. Likewise, it is her presence as a confidante that permits her to discern and block any tentative moves in the direction of revolt, as, for example, when she persuades the headstrong Ilse not to run away from the school. Thus she functions as mediator between the top and the bottom of the school hierarchy.

It is made clear, however, that the methods by which Fräulein von Bernburg exercises her functions are sexual. For instance, she succeeds in persuading Ilse to stay by slapping her on the ass and speaking to her seductively. This is her second guise: she capitalizes on the standard form of transference that leads adolescent girls to develop crushes on their teachers. Her positioning of herself as the exclusive object of schoolgirl affection may be seen as a tactic of repressive tolerance carried out in the arena of sexuality. Under the camouflage of her tolerance is the reality of repression. If the girls focus their sexual desires on her—where they can never be realized—then the danger of such desires being re-focused on each other (where they *could* be realized) is averted. The figure of the teacher remains ever more powerful, more attractive, more worthy of adoration, than any mere fellow student. It is, in fact, very nearly a relationship of adoration in the religious sense, with forms of expression that are thoroughly ritualized and contained, as, for example, the evening bedtime scene makes clear.

The scene is set in the dormitory on Manuela's first night in the school. It is filmed with the soft focus and radiant light of a Romantic painting, for example, a Friedrich. The lights are dimmed by Fräulein von Bernburg to make the scene more seductive. All the girls are poised on the edge of their beds, kneeling in identical white gowns, heads upraised to receive the communion of her lips touching their foreheads, which she holds firmly as she administers each ritual-istic kiss. This extreme fetishizing of the kiss by the nature of the teacher's gestures and the film's style is emblematic of the unspoken codes of repressive tolerance. The kiss is permitted, to each alike, but it is at once the given and the boundary. Nothing more may be allowed or even suggested, although the ten-sion of that which is withheld suffuses the scene with eroticism and grants the teacher her very power. The kiss is both minimum and maximum, a state of grace and a state of stasis. The entire equilibrium is founded on this extreme tension, which is snapped when Manuela, overwhelmed by the atmosphere and her feelings, breaks the rules. She throws her arms around Fräulein von Bern-burg's body in a tight embrace and receives not a punishment but a kiss—a kiss, not merely on the forehead, but full on the lips.

Of course the school's system of sexual repression does not crumble from this one transgression; it is much too securely established. Less so is Fräulein von Bernburg, whose situation is a difficult one. It is apparent that the sexual repres-sion she forces on the students she also forces on herself. Yet Manuela causes a surplus of feeling that she cannot control. Sagan carefully presents Fräulein von Bernburg almost entirely in terms of Manuela. The first time she appears in the film, she is looking at the newly arrived Manuela on the stairway. The extent to which she begins to identify her own desires and sensitivities with Manuela's takes the shape of a literal superimposition. When Sagan presents a scene of Manuela as student in Fräulein von Bernburg's classroom, it is the anguish of the conflicted pair that she portrays through an extraordinary dissolve that predates the more widespread (and more pernicious) use of the motif by Ingmar Bergman in *Persona*.[6] In the scene while struggling vainly to retrieve a memorized passage from a mind gone blank in the beloved teacher's presence, Manuela's vision begins to blur. Fräulein von Bernburg's sight, subjectively rendered, blurs as well, as her face becomes superimposed and fused with Manuela's staring back at her. It is she, as teacher, who breaks the locked gaze, averts her eyes, and reprimands Manuela with a "not prepared again," thus reasserting her authority and utilizing her rank to shield her emotions.

The next meeting of the two takes place in Fräulein von Bernburg's office soon after, where she has called Manuela in order to give her one of her chemises (in response to an attendant's expressed pity for the young girl's lack of undergarments, due to her lack of a caring mother). By giving Manuela one of her own chemises, she attempts to channel her concern and affection into the quasi-permissible form of a maternal gift that, however, is clearly an erotic token. The conversation that transpires between the two provides further evidence of the code of repressive tolerance exercised toward the students' incipient homosexuality. From the start, it is clear that "emotionalism" rules the encounter, as Fräulein von Bernburg begins by reprimanding Manuela, who has burst into tears at the gift of the chemise: "What an excitable child you are." Manuela confesses she is not crying out of unhappiness, and finally is coaxed to explain by the teacher's concern: "Is there a reason you can't confide to me?" It is the loneliness of the nights that plagues her, the moments after the goodnight kiss: "I stare at your door and would like to get up and go to you, but I'm not allowed . . . I like you so awfully much." She is tortured by the passage of time: "I think of when I get older, and have to leave the school, and you'll kiss other children." Her expression of love, desire, and jealousy is quite explicitly phrased (although, in the older prints of the film, it was largely unsubtitled). Unprepared for such a declaration and unwilling to face the consequences of receiving such information, Fräulein von Bernburg lays down the law of the land: "I think of you, too, Manuela. . . . But you know I can't make exceptions. The others would be jealous."

Her response is telling. She doesn't say that she does not share the girl's feelings of attraction; if anything, she implies that she does. She does not invent a boyfriend to assert a defensive heterosexual identity. She asserts only that she is under obligation to love all the girls equally in order to maintain her position as object of their affection; therefore, she cannot break that egalitarianism in order to reciprocate Manuela's passion. The system that she must serve—as its token humanitarian—represses her own sexuality as well as that of the students. She is as much the victim as the promulgator of its repression, unlike the principal, whose phallic identity cancels out any homoeroticism. However, despite her struggle to repress her own emotions, Fräulein von Bernburg does act. The gift of the chemise is a turning point: it leads to the crisis of the school play, which is the central moment of the film, the moment that changes its direction from repressive tolerance to one of erotic liberation, the choice taken by Manuela throughout and by Fräulein von Bernburg, more complexly, at the film's end.

The school play, a favorite device of the boarding school genre, necessitates the pleasurable moment of cross-dressing in male attire. Manuela plays the lead role of Don Carlos in the 1787 play of the same name by Friedrich Schiller, scion of the *Sturm und Drang* school and leader with Goethe of Weimar classicism.

The choice of this play by Sagan and Winsloe to be the play-within-the-film is particularly significant.[7] *Don Carlos* is identified with the youthful Schiller, in that it represents the peak of his early idealistic period (indeed, after it, Schiller went into a period of doubt and reevaluation that kept him from writing plays again for a full decade). *Sturm und Drang* was a literary movement that presaged German Romanticism in its emphasis on the individual in conflict with a rationalist, unjust order. Both Schiller and Goethe stressed emotional harmony and a community of sympathy as the basic social values to put forward in opposition to the oppressive rationalism of the Enlightenment; *Don Carlos* is considered the very embodiment of that theme. Based on the life of Don Carlos, son of the Spanish King Philip II, the play counterposes the son's liberal idealism with the brutal tyranny of his father's reign. In the play, Don Carlos forms an alliance with the older and wiser Marquis Posa, who conspires with him to advance a human order and overthrow the ruler. In Schiller's play, the marquis—learning that their plans are suspected—saves the prince by drawing all guilt on himself, consequently suffering execution by the king's decree in order to save the prince. The play ends tragically, with Don Carlos refusing to relish his fatally bought freedom, showing his true face to the king, and thus suffering a similar death at the hands of the bloodthirsty Inquisition.

Thus far, then, *Don Carlos* would seem the perfect corollary to the film's much advanced theme of humanitarian idealism counterposed against a fascist reign. In such an interpretation, Manuela would essentially play herself, while the Marquis Posa would represent the Fräulein von Bernburg role and the king would represent the principal. Schiller, like Winsloe/Sagan, thus assumes the

mantle of protoantifascist for his eloquent, romantic opposition to the mad-
dened illogic of absolute order. The principal's invited guests seem prone to this
same interpretation, for they cluck disapprovingly over their tea that "Schiller
sometimes writes very freely."

However, the subsequent scenes following this admonition, as well as the
choice of the scene from *Don Carlos,* suggest the same sort of alternate reading
that I have been suggesting for *Mädchen in Uniform* as a whole. The scene
immediately following the tea-talk is one of the schoolgirls, giddy from a dose of
spiked punch, dancing in each other's arms, disobeying the rules, and generally
enacting their guardians' worst fears. The scene chosen from *Don Carlos* is not
one dealing in political matters, but rather the rarified scene in which Don Carlos
at last wins an audience with the queen and declares his forbidden love to her.
Reprimanded for his rashness in compromising them both by coming to see her,
Don Carlos tells the queen, "Even if it means death, I shall not go from here: One
moment lived in Paradise is not too dearly bought with death." These are the
lines spoken by Manuela (as Don Carlos) in the scene we see of the school play.
A significant key to the narrative of *Don Carlos* is the fact that the prince's
beloved is his father's newly acquired wife: she is, literally, his mother, which
makes their love forbidden as, in the words of Schiller's play, "the world and
nature and the laws of Rome condemn such passions." Sagan clearly annexes
this sentiment by choosing the scene in which Don Carlos proclaims his love for
Elizabeth, the name both of the Queen Mother and of Fräulein von Bernburg.
With Manuela cross-dressed as the passionate suitor (in a performance heralded
by all for its remarkable sincerity!), the sequence represents the central theme of
forbidden love encoded within the sanctity of German high culture.

Drunk with punch and the euphoria of her success, Manuela decides to extend her role into real life: she rises to deliver an impassioned toast in which she
declares her love for Fräulein von Bernburg and announces the gift of her chemise as proof of its reciprocation. She abandons caution to proclaim, "I know she
likes me." She echoes and surpasses Don Carlos in her insistence on sharing the
news: "Nothing else matters. . . . I'm not afraid of anything. . . . Yes, everyone
should know." In a coming out that is the opposite of Don Carlos's vow of
silence, she concludes with a celebratory generosity: "Long live Fräulein von
Bernburg, beloved by all."

Despite the school's aura of eroticism, it is this act of pronouncement that
constitutes the unpardonable transgression. It is the *naming* of that which may
well be known, this claiming of what is felt by the public speaking of its name,
that is expressly forbidden.[8] For her speech, which is witnessed by the dread
principal, Manuela is immediately imprisoned, significantly enough within the
confines of the infirmary—in a reference to the pseudoscientific view of homo-

sexuality as a species of mental imbalance, a disease, but one that nevertheless can be punished as a crime. Indeed, the first view of Manuela in the hospital traces her position in bed below heavy bars of light emblazoned on the shadowed wall above her head. The immediate wish of the principal is to blot out history, to expunge the traces of the "scandal" and pretend that nothing ever happened. It is a wish that is initially reflected in Manuela's own coming to consciousness, as she emerges from her hangover with the complaint that she cannot remember what has happened or what she has done. So powerful is the taboo that amnesia is the consequence of its transgression.

The public speech, in fact, can be seen as an extremely powerful transgression, one that, unlike the private actions between Manuela and Fräulein von Bernburg, publicly disrupts and subverts the prevailing order of the school. The principal's regime could tolerate the widely ackowledged schoolgirl crushes and libidinous undercurrents as long as they remained marginalized and subservient to the dominant ideology. The homoeroticism had been portrayed graphically ever since the time of Manuela's arrival: Ilse told her how envious other girls were, asking if it were true that "the Golden One" really "kisses you good night, oh god, oh god . . ."; the laundrywoman explained the heart and initials on her school uniform, "E.V.G.", by laughing that "the girl who wore this dress must have been infatuated with Fräulein Elizabeth von Bernburg, thus the initials"; and pairs of girls were repeatedly shown holding hands, embracing by windows, or passing love notes. An unendorsed de facto eroticism could be contained within the reigning patriarchal order, but a double challenge could not be abided: the challenge of Manuela's public naming of that eroticism and the challenge of Fräulein von Bernburg's material action in presenting the chemise over and above the limits of egalitarianism. For this reason, amnesia was a possibility only for Manuela. Everyone else remembered quite well what had occurred.

Unable to turn back the clock, the principal opts for quarantine: Manuela is sentenced to solitary confinement, as though homosexuality were a communicable disease spread by social contact. As Manuela becomes distraught in the final phase of the film, Fräulein von Bernburg struggles, more consciously than her young student, to come to terms with her sexuality and acknowledge her feelings for her own sex. In their final meeting with Manuela, held clandestinely in defiance of the principal's prohibition, she tries to tell the girl the exact nature of a "crime" she seems unable to understand: "you must be cured . . . of liking me so much." At the same time, she makes a telling complaint about Manuela's speech. She does not reproach Manuela for what she has brought on herself, as we might expect, but instead says: "What you have done to me, you know." There is more meaning to the statement than the fact of Manuela's speech, which to be sure has damaged her standing at the school but yet is not wholly different from countless other private declarations she no doubt has withstood. Rather, Fräulein von Bernburg may well be referring to the terrible inner conflict into which Manuela's speech has thrown her. It is a conflict not unlike that felt by so many in-the-closet homosexuals of both sexes in this country following the opening up of sexual boundaries during the Stonewall eruption and the succeeding gay liberation movement of the late sixties and early seventies. This period carried for many an undesired pressure to identify a previously privatized sexuality (in Fräulein von Bernburg's case, to make that identification not only to others, but to herself as well). From the moment of this reproach, the teacher's struggle to "come out" and emerge from the raging conflict within her becomes the central theme of the film. It is a theme concerned with finding the courage to oppose an unjust authority, a courage shared, finally, with the other students of the school.

Fräulein von Bernburg's inner struggle reaches its peak immediately after this meeting with Manuela, which has concluded badly, with the girl rushing out of the room in desperation and the teacher's race to call her back blocked by the arrival of the principal. In fact, her confrontations with the principal have been escalating ever since the "theatrical" incident. She has begun assuming more radical stances in opposition to the principal's edict. Earlier, arguing over her permissiveness toward Manuela, she had declared: "What you call sin, I call love, which has a thousand forms." She was speaking in general terms of her philosophy of maternal nurturance versus the principal's punitive discipline, but the more explicit meaning of the statement also holds true. Intent on subjugating the teacher to her authority, the principal now threatens her: "I will not permit revolutionary ideas." Fräulein von Bernburg then breaks rank in the only truly decisive way possible, responding: "I resign." Herewith, she makes her choice to reject her role as the "good cop" and seek a genuine humanitarianism *outside* the corrupt system of the school, which in turn means seeking also her genuine sexuality as she has come to recognize it.

As the teacher and the principal enact their battle of will and authority, Manuela prepares to throw herself over the stairwell. It is this point that the film's second superimposition of the faces of Manuela and Fräulein von Bernburg takes place. Again, it is Fräulein von Bernburg who "experiences" the blurred vision and "sees" Manuela's face projected through her own image. This time, however, having made her choice to break with the patriarchal order, she does not avert her gaze or try to separate herself from the vision. Instead, she recognizes this "vision" as a psychic signal of her bond with Manuela.

What does the superimposition mean in this context? The principal had earlier warned the teacher to "dissolve" her contact with Manuela, suggesting the nature of this shot. The blurring of definition and melding of identities has usually had a negative impact when applied to women in cinema. In Ingmar

Bergman's *Persona*, for example, the loss of individual identity is the threat that haunts women's intimacy like a destructive specter: getting too close to another woman means losing oneself. In addition, there is always the companion myth of narcissism. The superimposition shots here may also be a tacit recognition by Sagan of the myth of homosexuality as a narcissistic doubling, an attempt to solidify one's identity by the addition of its likeness in another. Rather than balking at the vision, however, Fräulein von Bernburg recognizes the merged faces as a signal of power by combination. She does not read the superimposition as erasure (the patriarchal warning) or negative bonding (the mirror phase prolonged), but rather as positive depiction of the strength exercised by such a *redoubling* of energy and identity. She trusts the sign and acts on it. Shouting Manuela's name, she rushes from her office (and the startled principal) to the stairwell, intent on rescuing Manuela, where of course she discovers that the schoolgirls have arrived ahead of her and saved the day.

There are only these two superimpositions in the entire film, and significantly they are both assigned to Fräulein von Bernburg at times in which Manuela is in distress. It is Fräulein von Bernburg, and the force she has come to represent, who prevails in the film's final scene: the rescued Manuela is cradled by the schoolgirls as the defeated principal, bereft of her authority, slowly retreats down the long, gloomy hall. The darkness of the hall deepens in her wake, her cane taps faintly on the floor, the sound of bells and finally bugles can be heard in the distance. As the bugle calls signify, it is a provisional victory, and yet the patriarchal order *has* been ruptured within the school by the liberation of eros among the women.

In terms of the interpretation that I have been suggesting, as well as the more traditional interpretation of antifascism, the ending of the film is extremely important. Yet the nature of the ending has been frequently obscured in cinema histories. Many reports of the film have cited a supposed "other" ending in which Manuela successfully commits suicide, and some critics have even cited the existence of a "Nazi" suicide ending and "export" version like this one. Yet, as several German sources testify, such was not the case.[9] However, the original play *did* have Manuela kill herself and ended with the principal setting a cover-up in motion at the play's end; but this is one of many differences between the play and the film that I will discuss later. In point of fact, the film *Mädchen in Uniform* concludes with an ending of rescue. What does this ending signify? Such an ending confers a unity on the film's two themes—the widely acknowledged one of antiauthoritarianism as well as the previously ignored one of erotic liberation—and shapes them into a consistent and harmonious whole.

It has frequently been argued that the preferred ending for a proto-Nazi film was suicide, that is, the ultimate abandonment of hope that leads the individual to throw herself/himself into the depth of oblivion or, conversely, into the hands of a superhuman savior. That was the scenario against which a film like *Kuhle Wampe* (by Slatan Dudow with script by Bertolt Brecht) rebelled, by refusing to end on a note of despair and insisting instead on the persistence of faith in the future. So, too, Sagan. Her anti-Naziism is nowhere more apparent than in the ending, which posits not only the maintenance of hope but also the vindication of resistance as a very different "triumph of the will" from Leni Riefenstahl's brand. In Riefenstahl's film of the same period *The Blue Light* (1932), the heroine (played by Riefenstahl) finally throws herself from a cliff, despairing, isolated from others of her kind, done in by an unsympathetic society. Not so Manuela: the schoolgirls of the boarding school integrate her sensibility into their own consciousness; instead of closing ranks against her, they come to her (and, by extension, their own) rescue. The cliffhanger ending is at once a powerful statement of political resistance, both individual and collective, and a validation of lesbianism as a personal and public right.

The principal earlier had condemned Fräulein von Bernburg's feelings and actions as "revolutionary," and so they may indeed be. In a patriarchal society that depends on women for the reward and procreation of its (his) own kind, a break in the link is disastrous: "What would happen if our hypothetical woman not only refused the man to whom she was promised, but asked for a woman instead? If a single refusal were disruptive, a double refusal would be insurrectionary."[10] The ending of the film serves to validate Fräulein von Bernburg's difficult development from humanitarian disciplinarian to a free, stronger, and woman-identified woman. The progression of the scenario depends on her inner struggle and final evolution in response to the catalyst of Manuela's passion. At the film's end, Fräulein von Bernburg stands triumphant with the schoolgirls witnessing the principal's melancholy retreat. She wins this position *not* by maintaining her power in the hierarchy but by rejecting it, *not* by tightening the reins of her repression but by casting them down, *not* by co-option but by refusal. Her place on the staircase at the end may be seen, then, as a reward for her "coming out" and acknowledging her sexuality, just as Manuela's rescue at the end represents a social legitimation of her passion. *Mädchen in Uniform* presents a positive vision of lesbianism that has been largely disregarded for years, a film victim of a subtle critical homophobia that has insisted on perceiving the literal as the merely metaphoric.

An analysis of the film today clarifies the meaning and can easily annex Sagan's work to our contemporary tradition of lesbian culture. But historical differences nevertheless persist between the perspectives of Sagan making a film cooperatively in Berlin on the eve of the Third Reich and most of us today. Differences are apparent even in the shifts of meaning between Christa Winsloe's original play and its metamorphosis into *Mädchen in Uniform*. Yet most surprising, perhaps, are the similarities that slowly become recognizable on reexamining both the film and its period—similarities that in some cases are crucial for us to recognize as we proceed into the eighties.

Sagan's movie is in many respects a more radical work of lesbian celebration than Winsloe's play, while at the same time it focuses far more on the codes of patriarchal power than the stage production. The stage play (both the original, *Yesterday and Today,* and the international version, *Girls in Uniform,* which was widely performed after the film's release)[11] actually fits quite tidily into the model of the "lesbian fairy tale" that Elaine Marks traces to its Sapphic origins in her important essay on lesbian literature:

Although there is no evidence in Sappho's poems to corroborate the notion that she did indeed have a school, religious or secular, for young women, the gynaeceum, ruled by the seductive or seducing teacher has become, since the eighteenth century, the preferred locus for most fictions about women loving women. . . . The younger woman, whose point of view usually dominates, is always passionate and innocent. If, as is usually the case when the author of the text is a woman, it is the younger woman who falls in love, the narrative is structured so as to insist on this love as an awakening. The older woman as object of the younger woman's desire is restrained and admirable, beautiful and cultivated . . . the exchanges between the older and the younger woman are reminiscent of a mother-daughter relationship. The mother of the younger woman is either dead or in some explicit way inadequate. Her absence is implied in the young woman's insistent need for a goodnight kiss. The gynaeceum, particularly when it is represented by a school, also controls time. Time limits are set by the school calendar whose inexorable end announces the fatal separation, which may involve a death. Temporal structures reiterate the almost universally accepted notion that a schoolgirl crush is but a phase in the emotional development of the young woman, something that will pass. The dénouement in these lesbian fairy tales is often brought about by a public event during which private passions explode.[12]

If the contours of Marks's paradigm bear a striking resemblance to the film (which in fact was viewed as an adolescent tale far more than a lesbian one), its elements fit the play even more so. For example, in the play a subplot involves Manuela's pursuit by a diligent, if unwanted, male suitor: her equestrian instructor, no less. In the play, Fräulein von Bernburg is not unmotivated in her feelings for the girls: she secretly wants to be the head of the school herself. She does not resign in the final confrontation with the principal, but merely tries to increase her power base through the face-off; and Manuela throws herself out a window before anyone has had the chance to rescue her. Since the play can end with only Manuela having stepped out of line and dead for her actions, it is far more easily recuperable into the tradition of lesbianism as tragic, powerless, passive, and, in particular, fatal to its adherent. As Marks emphasizes, the "constraints" of the genre signify the "marginal status of lesbians and lesbianism."[13]

While incorporating the classic elements of the "fairy tale" in *Mädchen in Uniform,* Sagan goes further. She changes a few areas of the story line and utilizes the visual and editing codes particular to cinema in order to extend the meaning of the original text.[14] One of the film's strongest features is its success in making palpable the functioning of patriarchal codes despite the absence of any male or militaristic figures. The use of the central staircase is one such case, with a symbolism both visual (its barred railings and threatening abyss) and philosophical (its use by the girls prohibited from using the formal front staircase). The stairwell suggests a confining enclosure, carceral in its grates of iron and shadow, as well as the functional confinement of virtually all the girls' activities. At one point, the schoolgirls drop an object from the top in order to test a formula for calculating the time a falling body takes to reach bottom. The staircase is thus both a representation of the prevailing order and its power of organization and also a portent of tragedy in its depth and shadows. The camera frequently views the marching of the girls through the iron forms, further emphasizing their molding into Prussian "women of iron." And, of course, the very first meeting between Manuela and Fräulein von Bernburg occurs on the staircase, their bodies positioned midway between forbidding shadows at screen left and a bright window screen right.

In addition to such visual compositions, Sagan inserts a series of montages that provide a bridge between the fairly theatrical scenes involving the central characters and the documentary-style observations of schoolgirl behavior. The large cast of schoolgirls—all nonprofessional actresses—functions as an alternate discourse to set against the patriarchal regimentation. The students horse around, express homesickness, carry on multiple intrigues with each other, play jokes, dress and undress, and relate to each other in a tone that shifts between childishness and eroticism.[15] At one point, a locker room scene of bedtime activities is immediately followed by a montage that marshals the disorganized activities into a marching order of mouths in extreme close-up barking orders, feet hurrying to obey, identical lines of students filing past, and so on. The montage ends with a shift to the famous dormitory scene of Fräulein von Bernburg's goodnight kisses, a scene that is itself ambiguous in its resolution of eroticism with regimentation.

Most significant are the montage sequences that frame the encounters between Manuela and Fräulein von Bernburg, and indeed, frame our entire encounter with the film. The montage that opens the film communicates a view of the exterior towers of Potsdam; the old stone putti and the statue that resembles a tiny soldier and the sounds of church bells and bugles portray an atmosphere of patriarchal readiness within which the school building itself is located. Traces of the same montage appear as narrative interruptions at key moments in the evolution of Manuela and Fräulein von Bernburg's relationship. For example, just after Manuela has thrown her arms around the teacher in the goodnight scene, Sagan inserts a rapid cut to the towers and statues. Later, when Fräulein von Bernburg gives the student her chemise, Sagan similarly terminates the scene with a cut to the stone towers and the sound of bells tolling. The montages appear to be cautionary, clues to the audience that emotions between women are never free of the shadow of patriarchal aggression. Their intrusion into the film is an antidote to viewing this all-female space as a "free zone" within a patriarchal society, which can be seen to dominate not only in the concrete form of the staircase or principal, but in the equally threatening form of external authority that waits just outside the school gates.

Even at the film's end, when the two women and their student supporters seem most victorious, the ominous sound of the bugles reappears to accompany the principal's retreat. While Siegfried Kracauer contends that the prominence of the motif at the end of the film proves that "the principle of authority has not been shaken" within the school,[16] I would suggest otherwise: the motif reminds the audience just how provisional the victory is, and just how powerful are the patriarchal forces with which any new order within the school must contend. It is a warning that separation from the dominant order does not automatically grant freedom from its dominance. It should have been a warning to lesbians then living in Germany that the time for strong collective action was on them, as the forces of fascism gathered outside the windows. Instead, the Third Reich indeed came to power, and most of those responsible for *Mädchen in Uniform* left the country.

Who were they? Little has been written and little is known about the women behind this work. Their sexuality has been as thoroughly veiled as the lesbian theme of the film itself. Rumors, anecdotes, and bits of stories form the customary trail of unofficial history. Blanche Wiesen Cook is instructive regarding what *not* to look for. Commenting on *Mädchen in Uniform*, Ann Elisabet Weirach's *The Scorpion,* and other works of this period and genre, Cook warns against accepting the tragic tales of unrequited love and tragic abandonment as autobiographical fictions: "The truth is that these passionate little girls were not always abused and abandoned. They did not commit suicide. They wrote books about passionate little girls, death, and abandonment."[17] Not infrequently the lives of the authors and their models display a depth and breadth of options not readily visible in their constructed tales—when, that is, their lives are recoverable at all.

Leontine Sagan was born in Austria in 1889 and was married at some point to a doctor from Vienna. She trained as a stage director and actress and worked with such directors as Bernofskey and Max Reinhardt, teaching for a time at Reinhardt's drama school. As an actress, she appeared alongside Salka Viertel in an early production of the Ibsen play *John Gabriel Borkman* and also in a rare production of Franz Blei's *The Wave*. The circumstances of her taking on the direction of *Mädchen in Uniform* are not now available, although she was certainly a popular figure in the Berlin theater scene. She left Germany soon after and went to England, where Alexander Korda sought to capitalize on her success by engaging her to direct *Men of Tomorrow*, a sort of "boys in uniform" film about Oxford; not surprisingly, the success was not repeated. Judging by the published script and cast list for a production of *Mädchen in Uniform*, Sagan also worked in theater in London. The play, retitled *Children in Uniform*, listed as being "produced by Leontine Sagan" at the Duchess Theatre, London, opening 7 October 1932. Soon after, Sagan left England. She moved to the United States for several years and thence to South Africa, where she co-founded the National Theater. She died in 1974 in Johannesburg. As far as is known, she never made another film.

The two leading actresses of *Mädchen in Uniform*, Hertha Thiele and Dorothea Wieck, starred together in another film shortly afterward. Directed by Frank Wysbar in 1933, *Anna and Elisabeth* returned to the traditional view of intimate attachments between women as debilitating and demonic: Hertha Thiele played a young girl with miraculous powers who drove Dorothea Wieck to attempt suicide because Thiele failed to resurrect her husband! The women are portrayed as having an unnaturally close, almost supernatural, relationship; lesbianism is explicit only as the power of darkness. Both actresses were still alive in the early 1980s, and much additional material has been made available by Karol Gramann, the *Frauen und Film* editor who interviewed Thiele.[18]

Christa Winsloe is the best remembered of the *Mädchen in Uniform* women, perhaps simply because her intimates wrote memoirs. Erika Mann, who herself played one of the teachers in the film, remembered Winsloe (the Baroness von Hatvany) in her memoirs of 1939 in a fashion that would please Blanche Cook. Smiling and confident, dressed in white shirt and tie, Christa Winsloe looks out at us from a photograph captioned "once a Mädchen in uniform." Erika Mann recalls Christa's life as a "beautiful and amusing society woman" who ran an expensive household in Munich and hosted salons in Budapest and Vienna as the wife of Baron Ludwig Hatvany, a Hungarian writer and "grand seigneur." She made animal sculptures and held exquisite dinner parties, at one of which Mann remembers her announcing her plan to write a play about her own childhood boarding-school experiences. Trying to explain the play's phenomenal success, Mann suggests:

How was it? . . . Because Christa Hatvany had guarded in her heart, and now redis-covered, a simple, strong and genuine feeling, and because she could so express it that hundreds of thousands of people [*sic*] recognized the pain and ecstasy of their own child-hood, their own first love, which had, in their own hearts, been overlaid, but never stifled. The poignant feeling of recognition.[19]

If Mann holds to the favorite view of lesbian as a phase through which "hun-dreds of thousands" of women pass during adolescence, she at least manages to hold out a phrase of reservation regarding the impulse that is yet "never stifled."

Certainly it was never stifled in Christa. Nor in Dorothy Thompson, the U.S. journalist who was married to Sinclair Lewis when, in 1932, at her own ten-day Christmas party, she fell in love with Christa, who was then on the verge of getting a divorce from the Baron. Dorothy Thompson's diaries of the time reveal her struggle to name her experience, to try to understand how she can be "hap-pily married, and yet wanting that curious tenderness. That pervading warm tenderness—there are no words for it."[20] When the party guests had left, Doro-thy followed Christa to Budapest. In March, the two met in Italy, where they shared a villa at Portofino for several months. On leaving the villa, Dorothy brought Christa back to the U.S. with her. In August, the two women traveled back to Austria together. When apart, they wrote constantly. In early 1934, Sinclair Lewis had to be out of town for several months, and Dorothy stayed in New York with Christa. "They were a couple," said their friend John Farrar. "If you asked Dorothy for dinner, you asked Christa too."[21]

After two years, however, relations between the two began to break down, with Dorothy answering one of Christa's letters: "I feel that something between us has broken. . . . I had a strange dream last night. I dreamed I was putting out into a very rough sea in a frail ship, and the crew were all women. I was afraid, and woke up, sweating."[22] By this time, Thompson was persona non grata in Germany, having been expelled on her last trip by Adolph Hitler himself be-cause of an uncomplimentary interview (and, no doubt, her habit of laughing at Bund rallies). Christa couldn't return to her home, so went instead in 1935 to live in southern France. Their continued intimacy was so strong that, in 1940, when the Nazi occupation of France made it impossible for Christa to withdraw money from her Munich bank, Dorothy began sending her money every month to live on.

Christa Winsloe's life had a sad end, but nothing at all like a Marks fairy tale formula: she was murdered on 10 June 1944 by a common criminal named

Lambert, who pretended to be operating as a member of the French resistance. His claim led to ugly speculation that Winsloe had been a Nazi spy and to an old friend's writing Dorothy Thompson at the end of the war (1946) to inform her of the death and to beg help in clearing Christa Winsloe's name. The friend explained the rumors by Christa's liaison at the time with a French-Swiss girlfriend, Simone Gentet, who was alleged to be a spy:

Christa once described her as a hysterical, dissolute morphine addict and alcoholic, but she certainly knew nothing of Simone's other activities, should the rumor be true . . . we know with such absolute certainty that Christa was the most violent enemy of National-Socialism and that she would never have made the slightest compromise. On the contrary, we were always worried that the Gestapo would grab her and we still believed this is what happened to her because she had helped many Jewish friends get out of the country.[23]

Thus, the author of *Mädchen in Uniform* was killed by a man claiming to be a resistance fighter but whom her friends believed to be a Gestapo agent, an ambiguity that lends to her death the same confusion that continues to surround the relationship between homosexuality and the Nazi era.

As an example of their conflation, Rossellini's *Rome, Open City* established an early tradition of identifying homosexuality with fascism through his narrative of hearty male resistance fighters betrayed by a lesbian morphine addict and her Gestapo lover. Bertolucci continued the tradition by consistently portraying fascists as suffering from sexual repressions of "perversions" in his films (with time out in *The Conformist* for a lesbian resistance fighter in the person of Dominique Sanda, although he did equip her with a male mentor and suggest that her attraction to women was her weakness). The connections have not depended on cinema, either Italian or German, for promulgation. The stereotype of Nazi campiness, of ss regalia as s-&-m toys, of the Gestapo as a leather-boy thrill, of the big bull dyke as concentration camp boss, etc., all seem to have a firm hold in our culture's fantasy life and historical mythology—this despite the facts of the Third Reich's large-scale massacre of homosexuals as pollutants of Aryan blood and a stain on the future master race. Hitler apparently agreed with Manuela's boarding-school principal in seeing homosexuality and lesbianism as "revolutionary." He did not hesitate to purge his own ranks, as on the infamous "night of the long knives" of June 1934, when Ernst Röhm (the sA chief of staff and a well-known homosexual) and his followers were murdered to make the sA, as Hitler put it, "a pure and cleanly institution."

Why the Nazis wanted to eliminate homosexuals along with Jews, Communists, and various national minorities is a question that seems fairly well answered and understood now in the light of Nazi ideology and the "final solutions" it proposed for the united, fascistic, patriarchal Aryan race. Why gay men or any women should have joined the Nazi party at all is quite another question. What circumstances led to the existence of a Röhm? What sort of outlook could have lent credence to Christa Winsloe's murder as an act of resistance, or alternately, as an act of Nazi vengeance? What sort of lesbian community inhabited Berlin during the Weimar Republic and the rise of the Third Reich? What sort of women's movement was there to combat the Nazi ideology of woman's place? What were social and legal attitudes toward homosexuality? Who liked *Mädchen in Uniform*, and why? To answer these questions fully lies outside the possibilities of this article, but to address them at least in part is crucial to our understanding of the film and to our recognizing just how exemplary was Leontine Sagan's combination of personal liberation and collective action.[24]

Germany had a radical women's movement in the early years of the century, beginning with the country's first large rally for women's suffrage in 1894. The movement for women's rights was part of a larger movement for overall reform known as the *Lebensreformbewegung* (the Life Reform Movement), which encompassed groups working on behalf of women and homosexuals as well as youths, natural health, clothing reform, and nudity. There do not seem to have been lesbian political organizations as such, but many lesbians were active in women's suffrage and feminist groups (notably Anita Augspurg and Lida Gustava Heymann, who fought for suffrage and opposed World War I as "a men's war fought between men's states"), and many others worked with the Scientific-Humanitarian Committee founded by Magnus Hirschfeld (the key figure in homosexual rights struggles). As early as 1904, Anna Ruling had addressed the Committee at a meeting on the common struggles of women's and homosexuals' rights groups, complaining that women's organizations were "not lifting a finger . . . doing nothing, absolutely nothing" in support of homosexual emancipation.

In 1909, however, a bill was proposed to criminalize lesbianism, which up until then had not been subject to the Paragraph 175 laws against male homosexuality. Seeing the bill as a clear retaliation against the gains of the women's movement, Dr. Helene Stöcker (who in 1905 had founded the League for the Protection of Maternity and Sexual Reform) spoke at a meeting held jointly with the Committee to support its petition drive against the proposed bill and to denounce the criminalization of lesbianism as "a grave error." The arguments on behalf of both women and homosexuality were diverse and at times contradictory, with variations in ideology so wide that some elements could be supportive of the new Russian Revolution as a model while other elements drifted into support of National Socialism. Stöcker's argument for keeping lesbianism legal rested on the defense of "individual freedom in the most private part of private life—love life"; Hirschfeld rested his arguments on scientific theories of human sexuality/psychology and on a human-rights-type plea for tolerance; certain other groups based their homosexuality on theories of male supremacy and past models of soldiery and lovers-in-arms leading to an early Nazi identification; while other groups initially supportive of sexual freedoms for women, like those in the "sexual hygiene" movement, turned antiabortionist for racial reasons and ended up merging with the proto-Nazi "racial hygiene" groups.

Varying definitions of private and public life—and private versus public rights—are key to the differences. Hirschfeld, unlike many others, threw all his energies into effecting social education and legal changes (although with a tone of apology and tolerance begging foreign to our styles today). The years of the Weimar Republic witnessed a flowering of women's rights and of struggles for homosexual emancipation, as well as a bursting forth of a large lesbian and gay subculture quartered largely in Berlin. And the sexual theories of the time are fascinating. In 1919, Hirschfeld opened the doors of his institute of Sexual Science and won substantial support for the theory of "a third sex" that was neither male nor female: he called homosexuals *Uranians* and based much of his strategy on this notion of a literally alien species.

The move to criminalize lesbianism had been dropped with the advent of the Republic and the end of World War I, which had seen women move so totally out of the former spheres as to make such a bill ineffective as a stay-at-home device. Therefore, much of Hirschfeld's Committee's efforts went toward the repeal of Paragraph 175 (prohibiting male homosexual practice). The Coalition for Reform of the Sexual Crimes Code (founded in 1925) worked to legalize acts between "consenting adults." The German Communist party, following the lead established by revolutionary Soviet laws in support of homosexual rights, had a strong presence on the Reichstag committee for penal code reform—which succeeded in recommending for approval the repeal of Paragraph 175 (but, unfortunately, its approval came on 16 October 1929, when the crash of the U.S. stock market changed the whole nature of the political scene in Germany, leading to the tabling of the resolution and the quick rise of the Nazi forces). As anti-Semitism, misogyny, and homophobia grew alongside the move to the Right in Germany, Hirschfeld became an ever more popular target. Attacked in 1920, his skull fractured in 1921, fired on in 1923, attacked verbally by a Nazi delegate to the Reichstag in 1927, he had the dubious honor of seeing the library of his institute become one of the first victims of book burning on 10 May 1933, just four months after Hitler became chancellor.[25]

The cycle of free expression followed by total persecution experienced by Magnus Hirschfeld was symptomatic of the treatment of the larger gay population and culture he had come to symbolize. Jim Steakley provides a partial answer to the obvious reaction (how could such a thing happen?), pinpointing the Weimar contradiction "between personal and collective liberation"—a contradiction manifested in the simultaneous existence of a widespread social tolerance of homosexuality (including the flourishing of gay culture, the growth of bars, and de facto police acquiescence, at least in Berlin) alongside repressive laws and the frequent failure of most legal actions on behalf of lesbians or gay men.[26] The history of Berlin's gay male subculture is fairly well known today; according to Steakley, there were some forty gay bars and between one and two thousand prostitutes in the city by 1914, as well as perhaps thirty homosexual journals published during the course of the Weimar years. However, the same "invisibility" that granted lesbians immunity from the criminal laws has also granted the Weimar lesbians a less welcome immunity from the history books.

Recent research has begun to yield materials that can outline for us the contours of the lesbian community that was so lively during the same period, especially in the larger cities of Berlin and Munich. Louise Brooks (who starred as Lulu in G. W. Pabst's *Pandora's Box,* which offered a glimpse of Berlin's decadent ways) has reminisced about the mood of Berlin, recalling, for example, a lesbian bar, the Maly, where "there was a choice of feminine or collar-and-tie lesbians."[27] Alex de Jonge provides a more embroidered account in a male visitor's account of the Silhouette, which was "one of Berlin's most fashionable night spots." He, too, describes the scene of role-dressed couples on a night out, but makes an important point: "You could see women well known in German literature, society, the theater and politics. . . . There was no suggestion of vice about the place. It was a usual phenomenon in German life."[28] While the Silhouette admitted men if accompanied by a lesbian regular, other women's bars did not; de Jonge mentions Die Grotte and Entre Nous as two of the "more exclusive" places, about which he therefore can provide no information.

Ilse Kokula has provided one of the most complete accounts of the period in her brief but tantalizing summary, "The Uranian Ladies Often Meet in Patisseries."[29] She expands on the meaning of *Uranian* by tracing its root as an epithet of Aphrodite taken to mean "celestial" or spiritual, and she reiterates Hirschfeld's popular theory of "a third sex." The estimate of homosexuality in Weimar Berlin is placed at fifty thousand out of a population of two and a half million (although the methodology behind the statistics is not specified). While bars, hotels, and saunas serviced gay men, there were also, more surprisingly, various services for lesbians seeking to meet each other. For example, there were *Vermittlungsbüros,* or agencies that fixed up single lesbians. There were personals columns in which lesbians advertised for partners. One such ad from the period listing the following: "Fräulein, decent, 24 years old, looking for pretty Fräulein as girlfriend." There were also a number of social clubs for lesbians that met in cafés and *Konditoreien* (patisseries), such as one group of "Israelite" (Jewish) lesbians who met from 4:00 to 6:00 in the afternoon to talk and play chess. Balls were held regularly, run by and for lesbian women. There was a general attitude of self-recognition, with many lesbian couples eager to convince the world how well-adjusted they were and to combat the stereotypes of depravity and tragedy.

From 1918 on, lesbian journals were part of the culture, usually presenting a perspective that was part political and part educational; they had such titles as *Frauenliebe* (womenlove), *Ledige Frauen* (unmarried women), and *Die Freundin: Weekly Journal for Ideal Friendship between Women.* *Die Freundin* was published continuously during 1923–32 by the *Damenklub* (women's club, or bar) Violette—itself a coded name, as violets were considered a sign of lesbianism at that time. Some of Ilse Kokula's information is evidently derived from firsthand sources, as she is able to comment that many older lesbians still remember the cafés "with great pleasure," and that one such woman, Kati R., remembers that the secret lesbian balls continued into the 1950s and 1960s, with as many as two hundred women attending. What emerges, then, is a picture of lesbian life as a widespread phenomenon, surprisingly aboveground and organized around its own publications, clubs, and rituals. This is reflected in virtually none of the films or official histories of the time.

Despite such a spirit of freedom and such an ambience of lesbian permissiveness, at no point, either in its own time or in ours, has *Mädchen in Uniform* been critically (i.e., publicly) discussed as a lesbian text. And yet the histories specify its initial succès de scandale, implying an at least unofficial recognition of the film's true meaning. Why has this meaning been so hidden, so difficult to retrieve? The extent of the obstacles in the path of the gay historian seeking to reinterpret film texts has been emphasized recently by Vito Russo's uncovering of the original New York State censor's notes on the American release of *Mädchen in Uniform.*[30] Almost line for line, scene for scene, the shots and subtitles that I have specified as revolutionary and most fundamentally lesbian were the sections of the film that the censors wanted to cut. Initially condemned, the film was approved by the censors for release in August 1932 only after all evidence of lesbianism had been cut. Their notes were specific; for example, "Reel Four: Eliminate all views of Manuela's face as she looks at Miss Von Bernburg in the classroom." The censors at least understood the power of the superimpositions! But, in a cruel irony of manipulation, the contemporary critics reviewed the butchered film positively, using its now antiseptic contents to ridicule all who had been holding the film up as an example of "neuroticism . . . a celluloid *Well of Loneliness.*"

Ever since, most critics have been eager to harness its tale of schoolgirl struggle to an assumed "universal" of humankind's fight against fascism, rather than some perverse championing of inverted emotions. With hindsight, however, we can equally read the film as a celebration of and warning for its most sympathetic audience: the lesbian population in Germany in 1931. Like Manuela and Fräulein von Bernburg, the lesbian community was proud and outspoken, romantic and idealistic, equally opposed to a bourgeois morality as well as to outdated models of woman's proper place. The schoolgirls may have been stand-ins for the lesbian women they could grow up to become (if they passed through Erika Mann's famous "phase" intact). If the boarding school was chosen as a literary and cinematic motif because it was more socially acceptable than the grown-up reality, then how ironic that it is all that remains for us. We need more research into our history. We need more information on films of the period that have been almost entirely forgotten, like *Anna and Elizabeth* or *Different from the Others*.[31] We need to heed carefully Blanche Cook's warning not to judge the authors entirely by their texts, lest literary conventions of the time blind us to the unexpected. We need to recognize *Mädchen in Uniform* not only as a beloved fairy tale but also as a powerful expression of its own time—an individual record of a collective aspiration.

Mädchen in Uniform has been extremely influential for other writers and films as well as for lesbian viewers down to the present day. Colette herself wrote the text for the subtitles of the French release print.[32] None other than Hollywood mogul Irving Thalberg was a fan of the film. He quizzed Salka Viertel, as she worked on the screenplay of *Queen Christina*, as to whether she had seen Sagan's film. "Does not Christina's affection for her lady-in-waiting indicate something like that?" he asked, and urged her to "keep it in mind" because, "if handled with taste it would give us very interesting scenes."[33]

Stephen Spender came to New York in February 1982 to speak about "Experiencing the Cinema in Berlin."[34] The film he most vividly remembered was *Mädchen in Uniform*, which he and Christopher Isherwood had gone to see during their 1931–32 residence in Berlin. Spender recalled that they had slipped away from some other event to see what he described as "the most remarkable film we'd ever seen," due in large measure to the "extraordinary impression" made on them by Hertha Thiele; indeed, he went so far as to describe the film as "full of extraordinary images based on this girl's face." Of special relevance to us is Spender's description of a Berlin caught up in a cinematic fever inspired by the Soviet films that showed two or three times a week. "Unlike futurist art," said Spender, the Soviet and progressive Weimar films "really did make you think they would change your life." With a certain nostalgia for a time *before* everyone became "suspicious about photography," Spender pinpointed the importance for him of *Mädchen in Uniform* and the progressive films with which he identifies it: "The great thing about photography in this period was that it seemed an expression of freedom." It is only in today's historical considerations that this film and others like it have come to be graded on formal qualities disassociated from any political meaning. Spender's remarks are useful in reminding today's viewers (and scholars) that Sagan was working at a time when "the camera was linked to the idea of a revolution that was still possible."

Like Spender, we can acknowledge what Colette, Thalberg, Viertel, and Garbo all seem to have known: that *Mädchen in Uniform* was a film about women's love for each other. And what Louise Brooks knew: that such love was no rarity in Weimar Berlin. And what Alex de Jonge knew: that it was no vice. And today we can also begin to consider what Jim Steakley knew: that there was a disturbing gap at the time between "personal" and "collective" liberation.

Mädchen in Uniform emerges from such a review of Weimar's lesbian subculture not any longer as an anomaly, but as a survivor. The film assumes a new importance when seen not as a curiosity but rather as a clue, an archaeological relic pointing back to an obliterated people and pointing ahead, for us, to a much-needed perspective on our current situation.

The first lesson of *Mädchen in Uniform* is that lesbianism has a much larger and finer history than we often suspect, that the film indicates as much, and that we need to do more work on reconstructing the image of lesbian culture that has been so painfully erased. The second lesson is that in looking backward and inward we cannot afford to stop looking forward and outward. The bells and bugles that sound periodically throughout the film, casting a prophetic pall on the love of Manuela and Fräulein von Bernburg, are waiting just outside the gates for us as well. As I have suggested, the ending of the film can be interpreted as a warning to heed the forces mounting outside our narrow zones of victory and liberation. Such an interpretation, if it was perceived at the time, went unheeded by the film's lesbian audience in 1931. Today, the work in building a lesbian culture cannot afford to ignore the context of such labor in a society veering so strongly in the opposite direction.

Today, we must begin to consider the contemporary gap between "personal" (or lifestyle) freedoms and "collective" (or legal political) rights. We must begin to examine what the links and coalitions are, in our own time, between lesbian, gay male, and feminist organizations. We must learn strategy and remember that when the pre-Weimar misogynist, F. Eberhard, wanted to attack the women's movement, he accused the emancipated women of being lesbians and, therefore, depraved. The women's groups of the late Weimar period exhibited a distressing willingness to take such attacks to heart and try to accommodate themselves accordingly. Polite co-optation sapped the strength of the groups. Too late, many lesbians must have learned that patisseries do not grant asylum.

Struggle was postponed to a fatally late date owing to false perceptions of homosexuality as a "private" issue that was being adequately handled and of lesbians/gay men as somehow more protected than others because of the history of social tolerance. The celebrants of the staircase must listen hard to the rallying cries outside the school and take heed. Today, we cannot afford to ignore history, nor to repeat it. While lesbianism and feminism are certainly "revolutionary" (to quote the principal yet again), the history of Weimar politics demonstrates that they are not *inherently* so unless linked to a pragmatic political strategy and set of principles. In the eighties our struggles for sexual freedom and gender flexibility must be integrated with the ongoing fights against economic injustices, racism, growing militarism, and all such forces that have an impact on every individual in our society. We have to do better.

Notes

1 Jonathan Katz, *Gay American History* (New York: Avon, 1976), 843. Acknowledgment is due here to two people who contributed the very heart of this article: Karola Gramann, who has written me extensively from Frankfurt and shared her own knowledge and research on *Mädchen in Uniform;* and Bill Horrigan, who brought numerous sources to my attention and even located copies of rare materials like the original playbill and published play script—his materials improved my work immeasurably. In addition, I owe thanks to Ramona Curry, who provided encouragement and translations, and to Rennie Harrigan, who offered background information and suggested avenues of research. The section of this article that deals with specific textual analysis of the film was originally presented as a paper at the Fourth Annual Purdue Film Conference, March 1979, on a panel devoted to early German cinema. Thanks to Jim Franklin for his encouragement at that time. This article was first published in *Jump Cut,* no. 24/25 (March 1981): 44–45, as part of a special section on lesbians and film; without the context and spirit of that special section and my coeditors on it, this article could not have been written. A shorter version was published in *Radical America* 15, no. 6 (1982): 17–36.

2 Lotte H. Eisner, *The Haunted Screen* (Berkeley: University of California Press, 1969), 326.

3 Siegfried Kracauer, *From Caligari to Hitler* (Princeton, N.J.: Princeton University Press, 1947), 227.

4 Alex de Jonge, *The Weimar Chronicle: Prelude to Hitler* (London: Paddington, 1978), 138.

5 Gayle Rubin, "The Traffic in Women: Notes on the 'Political Economy' of Sex," in *Toward an Anthropology of Women,* ed. Rayna R. Reiter (New York: Monthly Review Press, 1975), 180.

6 The comparison with *Persona* is pointed out by Nancy Scholar as well, in an article that marks the seventies revival of the film (see her "*Mädchen in Uniform,*" in *Sexual Stratagems: The World of Women in Film,* ed. Patricia Erens [New York: Horizon, 1979], 219–23).

7 It should be noted that *Don Carlos* appears to be yet another innovation of the film, as opposed to a borrowing from the play. In the published play script of *Girls in Uniform*, the production (which takes place entirely off-stage) is described as a light French drama of courtly love with Manuela featured as a knight in armor. Apart from the clearly delineated statements on forbidden love that I outline in the text, the choice of *Don Carlos* also serves to throw into relief the differing consequences for the outlaw lover of both periods. In the Schiller drama, death by auto-da-fé awaited heretics of the reigning order. By the time of *Mädchen*, however, the lover marked by the heresy of lesbianism already faced a modern narrative expectation: in the absence of a functioning Inquisition, she is expected to perform her own execution via suicide. The quotation recited by Manuela about death as the payment for paradise thus accrues additional meaning.

8 For a fuller discussion of this issue, see my article "The Crisis of Naming in Feminist Film Criticism," *Jump Cut* 19 (December 1978): 9–12, and a considerably revised version, "In the Name of Feminist Film Criticism," *Heresies* 9 (Spring 1980): 74–81.

9 Variations on the theme of a double ending have been repeated by a number of critics, including Nancy Scholar and Sharon Smith, *Women Who Make Movies* (New York: Hopkinson & Blake, 1975); Caroline Sheldon, "Lesbians and Film: Some Thoughts," in *Gays and Film*, ed. Richard Dyer (London: British Film Institute, 1977), 5–26; and Parker Tyler, *Screening the Sexes* (New York: Holt, 1972). While American and English critics display a striking unanimity on this point, the German critics of the period of the film's release make no such acknowledgment. Both Eisner and Kracauer specify the averted suicide at the end of the film they are discussing, while neither makes reference to any such "home market" alternate ending. In private correspondence, Karola Gramann wrote me that she was unable to find anyone in Germany who had seen the alleged suicide ending. However, in a 1980 interview with the still lively Hertha Thiele (living in East Berlin and still active in theater), Gramann discovered that a suicide ending was indeed filmed—but never included in the final film, for the reason that the scene was too pathetic looking to the filmmakers. As best as can be determined, no one in Germany ever saw the film with such an ending.

10 Rubin, "The Traffic in Women," 183.

11 Quotations and data are derived from personal copies of the original playbill (Blackstone Theatre, Chicago, "beginning Sunday Night, March 11, 1933") and the published play (Christa Winsloe, *Girl in Uniform: A Play in Three Acts* [Boston: Little, Brown, 1933]).

12 Elaine Marks, "Lesbian Intertextuality," in *Homosexualities and French Literature*, ed. George Stambolian and Elaine Marks (Ithaca, N.Y.: Cornell University Press, 1979), 357–58.

13 Ibid., 357.

14 I refer here to Leontine Sagan alone, but that is inaccurate. Carl Froelich is listed as "supervisor," but other sources of the period make claims for co-director or even director status for Froelich, although there is no firm evidence to support such a claim. It should be noted that Froelich stayed in Germany after Hitler's ascendancy and directed films that met the standards of the Third Reich. In addition, there is a fascinating detail for speculation. According to Erwin Leiser's *Nazi Cinema* (New York: Macmillan, 1974), Carl Froe-lich directed a film about Frederick the Great, *The Hymn of Leuthen,* which showed for the first time on 3 February 1933, four days after Hitler became chancellor of the Reich—suggesting that the intelligence that created *Mädchen* must have belonged to Sagan and not to Froelich. Given the analogy of the principal to the Frederick stereotype, however, the progression is fascinating. It has been said (by none other than the Reich actor Emil Jannings) that a historical line may be drawn "from Frederick the Great to Bismarck to Hitler." Given that, here is the fascinating detail: a 1942 film on Frederick (Veit Harlan's *The Great King*) detailed the episode of the Prussian king's defeat at Kunersdorf in 1759 and in particular shows the disdain that Frederick manifested for one regiment that "pre-ferred life to victory" and had not thrown itself into suicidal combat. Stripped of stripes and insignia for this action, the regiment's colonel commits suicide. The name of the colonel and his regiment? Bernburg. Such a detail makes one wonder what Froelich's contribution could have been, as Sagan seems so clearly to have had her way thematically.

15 At one point, in the first locker room scene, the model of heterosexuality comes under discussion and, obliquely, attack. There is a photo of a male actor in Ilse's locker, a male pinup some girls are giggling over, and finally, highlighted, an illustration in Manuela's book that depicts a woman being rapaciously carried off by a swashbuckling man on horseback—a rather dark statement on the power principles of heterosexual fantasy and reality.

16 Kracauer, *From Caligari to Hitler,* 229.

17 Blanche Wiesen Cook, "'Women Alone Stir My Imagination': Lesbianism and the Cultural Tradition," *Signs* 4, no. 4 (1979): 722.

18 Information on *Anna and Elizabeth* is taken from David Stewart Hull, *Film in the Third Reich* (Berkeley: University of California Press, 1969), 37–38; and also from private corre-spondence with Karola Gramann. The 1980 interview with Thiele appears in *Frauen und Film* 28 (1981): 32–41.

19 Erika Mann and Klaus Mann, *Escape to Life* (Boston: Houghton Mifflin, 1939), 50–51.

20 Katz, *Gay American History,* 841.

21 Marion K. Sanders, *Dorothy Thompson: A Legend in Her Time* (Boston: Houghton Mifflin, 1973), 190.

22 Ibid., 193.

23 Ibid.

24 The three basic texts to consult on issues of feminism and homosexuality in Weimar Germany are Richard Evans, *The Feminist Movement in Germany 1894–1933* (Beverly Hills, Calif.: Sage, 1976); Lillian Faderman and Brigitte Eriksson, *Lesbian Feminism in Turn-of-the-Century Germany* (Tallahassee, Fla.: Naiad, 1979); and James D. Steakley, *The Homosexual Emancipation Movement in Germany* (New York: Arno, 1975). Relevant information in this article is culled almost entirely from these sources. For a superior review and perspective piece, see Carol Anne Douglas, "German Feminists and the Right: Can It Happen Here?" *off our backs* 10, no. 11 (December 1980): 18–20. Douglas dis-cusses at length the political cross-currents I have barely managed to summarize here.

25 Interestingly enough, Hirschfeld appeared in a film he must have taken a part in producing. *Different from the Others* (directed by Richard Oswald in 1919) starred Conrad Veidt as a homosexual blackmail victim who is "saved" by the intervention of a philanthropic doctor played by Hirschfeld himself. It was widely banned, but evidently more for reasons of anti-Semitism (directed against Hirschfeld) than homophobia, if such a distinction can indeed be made. The film was remade in 1927 as *Laws of Love,* again starring Veidt, but minus Hirschfeld, whose absence in this version led to Veidt's character's suicide.

26 Steakley, *Homosexual Emancipation Movement,* 78–79.

27 Louise Brooks, "On Making Pabst's *Lulu,*" in *Women and the Cinema,* ed. Karyn Kay and Gerald Peary (New York: Dutton, 1977), 81.

28 de Jonge, *Prelude to Hitler,* 140.

29 Ilse Kokula, "Die urnischen Damen treffen sich vielfach in Konditoreien," in *Courage* 7 (Berlin, July 1980); copy courtesy of Karola Gramann.

30 Vito Russo, *The Celluloid Closet: Homosexuality in the Movies* (New York: Harper & Row/Colophon, 1981), 56–59. Russo's book came out after this article's initial publishing. It is an important work, beautifully researched and filled with primary data, but unfortunately marred by a bitchy misogyny. Nevertheless, the photograph of a very butch Dorothy Arzner arm-in-arm with Joan Crawford on the 1937 set of *The Bride Wore Red* is itself worth the price of the book.

31 See note 25 above. A print of *Different from the Others* survives in an East German archive. A print of *Anna and Elizabeth* survives in an archive at Koblenz. A special form of *Different from the Others* was made for screenings in Montreal and New York City in 1982; *Anna and Elizabeth* has yet to be seen here.

32 The French subtitles and a preface explaining Colette's role in writing them can be found in *Colette au cinéma,* ed. Alain and Odette Virmaux (Paris: Flammarion, 1975). Unfortunately, the entire *Mädchen in Uniform* section has been omitted from the English-language edition, trans. Sarah W. R. Smith (New York: Ungar, 1980).

33 Salka Viertel, *The Kindness of Strangers* (New York: Holt, 1969), 175. Viertel's memoirs are discreetly restrained on virtually all topics of sexuality and therefore shed no light on the nature of her relationship with Greta Garbo. Viertel wrote the screen treatments for Garbo's films and was her frequent companion. In his dirt-digging *Hollywood Babylon* (New York: Dell, 1975), Kenneth Anger wrote that "Garbo's genuine reserve held the gossips at bay for the most part. There was however, occasional speculation about how close her friendship really was with writer Salka Viertel" (p. 246).

34 The event was the International Center of Photography's symposium "Avant-Garde German Photography: 1919–1939," held at the Guggenheim Museum. Quotations are based on notes.

Acting Like

a Man

Masculine Performance in *My Darling Clementine*

Corey K. Creekmur

In memory of Gerald Mast

J ohn Ford's first post–World War II Western, *My Darling Clementine* (Twentieth Century–Fox, 1946), starring Henry Fonda in his first role since 1943, has been frequently analyzed by auteurist as well as genre critics and consistently judged one of the central works in its director's oeuvre and a classic, even paradigmatic, American Western.[1] While the traditional critical categories of author and genre both insist that a particular work be understood within a broader context, such categories nevertheless remain, in Rick Altman's words, "restrictive . . . complex methods of reducing the field of play of individual texts," simultaneously deflecting specific interpretations while encouraging others.[2] Until quite recently, critical readings of the films of John Ford and the Western genre have been especially complicitous in their implicit enforcement, through a rigid deployment of a series of culturally gendered antinomies, of a version of what Adrienne Rich has termed *compulsory heterosexuality* and have thus worked, despite their many obvious contributions, to suppress alternative, nonheterocentric interpretations of Ford's Westerns. Here again, the "conglomerate of all kinds of disciplines, theories, and current ideas" that Monique Wittig calls "the straight mind" demonstrates its ongoing inability to "conceive of a culture, a society where heterosexuality would not order not only all human relationships but also its very production of concepts and all the processes which escape consciousness, as well."[3] In the specific case of *My Darling Clementine,* previous commentary on the film has not allowed or at least not encouraged us to see the meeting of the film's two main characters (and stars) in this way: in a bar full of men, Wyatt Earp (Henry Fonda) cruises Doc Holliday (Victor Mature), who responds by buying him a glass of champagne and then asking him out on a date.[4]

Of course, in 1946, in a John Ford Western, or more generally in a classical Hollywood film, such a remarkable dramatization of an in fact *unremarkable* event (the conventional gay pickup) could be neither manifest nor widely comprehensible to a general audience. Although at the same time, but in cinema's underground, the dreaming Kenneth Anger was picking up uniformed sailors in his *Fireworks* (1947), former naval officers Ford and Fonda were hardly coming out but instead coming home, returning to their old jobs of representing American history through dramatic reconstruction. (Ford and Fonda's previous collaborations were *Young Mr. Lincoln, Drums along the Mohawk* [both 1939], and *The Grapes of Wrath* [1940]. They would later make *The Fugitive* [1947] and *Fort Apache* [1948] and have a well-known falling out during the production of *Mister Roberts* [1955], ironically their "return" to the navy.) Henry Fonda, in particular, was returning to acting after seeing action in the Pacific as an assistant operations and air combat intelligence officer; John Ford had served as lieutenant commander and chief of the Field Photographic Branch of the Office of Strategic Services, which evolved into the Central Intelligence Agency, from August 1941 to October 1945; Victor Mature had been in the coast guard, and the film's principal screenwriter, Winston Miller, had just been discharged from the marines. *My Darling Clementine* is certainly, as many critics have noted, a displaced, even allegorical narrative about men returning to domestic responsibilities after successful intervention in global affairs; Fonda's Wyatt Earp begins the film as a civilian recently retired from his position as marshall of Dodge City, a career change marked by the fact that he no longer carries a gun. Like other more explicit postwar films (William Wyler's *The Best Years of Our Lives* or Frank Capra's *It's a Wonderful Life* [both also 1946]), *My Darling Clementine* addresses the anxieties of its contemporary audience—in this case an audience that had been successfully mobilized around a single goal but that now wondered how their energies might be redirected and dispersed in the revitalization of social and civic life back home.[5]

Although previous readings of the film have successfully historicized many of the film's functions for its contemporary audience, these readings have tended to rely, as I've noted, on a system of rigid binary oppositions in order to demonstrate the workings of the film, especially within the conventions of its genre. Stemming from Frederick Jackson Turner's frontier thesis (1893) and its influential perpetuation in Henry Nash Smith's *Virgin Land* (1950), and given their most explicit codification for the analysis of the Western film by Jim Kitses in *Horizons West* (1970), these antinomies (such structural pairs as culture/nature, civilization/wilderness, garden/desert, community/individual, and East/West) are understood, in Stephen Neale's poststructuralist formulation, to "articulate the space of the functioning of what is defined in the genre as the Law, and the space which is defined as outside it, as Other."[6] *My Darling Clementine,* like most of the classical Hollywood cinema, attempts a reconciliation between the apparently incompatible values represented by such structural oppositions. The film's sacrifice of Doc Holliday, the Eastern man, and Chihuahua, the Western woman, and its complementary elevation of Wyatt Earp, the Western man, and Clementine Carter, the Eastern woman, as its ideal couple is one way in which *My Darling Clementine* plays out what Robert Ray calls the "classical thematic paradigm" of American cinema or demonstrates Raymond Bellour's observation that "the problematic of marriage" subtends the Western genre "from one end to the other."[7]

But Ford's film also attempts to work through a concern that cannot be adequately understood as the simple reconciliation of opposites, especially those represented as male and female, or as aggressive "natural" masculinity and passive "civilized" femininity, idealizations frequently cited and rarely questioned in discussions of Ford's films. Although the film eventually (although with often misrecognized uncertainty) constructs an ideal heterosexual couple, much of its plotting is directed toward securing a place not between two opposed poles but along a continuum; before the ideal man can be paired with the ideal woman, the film works to locate and define a normative masculinity adequate to the normative femininity defined, with much less difficulty, by the Eastern-bred WASP Clementine. Clementine's only challenge to her position is of course the Mexican prostitute Chihuahua (Linda Darnell), but Chihuahua's abject class and race—curiously misrepresented when Earp threatens to send her "back to the Apache reservation"—effectively eliminate her as anything but an erotic threat, and, as I will argue, she is not the film's sole erotic object.

Before examining the models of masculine identity delineated by the film, it is worth observing that the narrative's general exchange of Clementine from Doc's past into Wyatt's future also encourages a reading of the film in terms of the structures of triangular desire identified by Rene Girard and elaborated by Eve Kosofsky Sedgwick in her influential demonstration of the logical interdependence of male homosociality, homosexuality, and homophobia in English literature. Emphasizing a point from Girard, Sedgwick writes that, "in any erotic rivalry, the bond that links the two rivals is as intense and potent as the bond that links either of the rivals to the beloved."[8] Once noted, the erotic tensions structuring the relations between Doc and Wyatt in relation to Chihuahua and then Clementine seem in fact rather obvious, but two sequences in the film might be emphasized in this regard. Even before Doc and Wyatt have met, Wyatt unknowingly prepares for Doc's arrival by forcibly removing Chihuahua from the saloon and thereby establishing an all-male enclave for their first encounter. Chihuahua is absent for the making of Doc and Wyatt's "date," and the two men are next seen together at the theater in a box seat, each with one leg—the outside, Wyatt's right and Doc's left—propped up as if to form a single crotch out of the two bodies. Chihuahua's sudden arrival between the men explicitly breaks their symmetry: she literally comes between the male figures, reintroducing tension into their relationship.

From a later scene, after Doc attempts to save Chihuahua in an emergency operation, Wyatt's question to the bartender, "Mac, have you ever been in love?" has been uncritically assumed by critics as obviously referring to his interest in Clementine, who assisted Doc as a nurse. Wyatt's question, however, immediately follows his admiring toast to "Doctor John Holliday" and his gaze at the renewed Doc—as well as Clementine—as they leave the saloon. Wyatt's indirect declaration of love might also suggest his attempt to comprehend his relationship to Doc, and only the "unexamined heterocentricity" sustaining previous accounts of the scene can secure the meaning (or object) of Wyatt's question with certainty. Tag Gallagher, for example, sees "jubilation" in Wyatt's question, "for Clem's failure with Holliday leaves her available for Wyatt,"[9] but this account apparently cannot recognize that this failure might leave *Holliday* available for Wyatt as well, a possibility in accord with Wyatt's earlier comment to the rebuffed Clementine, "If you ask me, you're giving up too easily," a statement that affirms Doc's value rather than hers as a romantic prize. The bartender's non sequitur response to Wyatt's question ("No, I been a bartender all me life") in fact comically acknowledges that desire sometimes escapes the boundaries of conventional heterosexual content, linking itself to forms of identity and identification indirectly related to gender. (Here, the film's continual play with names should be noted: characters are misnamed yet effectively identified as "Mr. Bon Ton," "Mr. Gambler," "Mr. Tin Star Marshall," "Mr. Shakespeare," "Yorick," etc.) At this point, only Clementine's presence continues to suggest a rivalry between the male characters, even though their mutual admiration has just been declared.

Curiously, the original posters for the film advertised an explicit triangle between Doc and Wyatt over Chihuahua (played by the film's only major female star). Linda Darnell's large, glamorous image is placed between smaller images of Fonda and Mature with their guns drawn and is surrounded by these misleading words: "Into the West came Clementine. . . . To set it loving—harder . . . killing—quicker! For she was everything the West was . . . Young, Fiery, Exciting!" By fully collapsing the film's female characters together, even though the film itself seems clearly to isolate them as virgin and whore, the advertising perhaps reveals the film's actual construction of both women as ultimately equivalent obstacles to and deflections of the narrative's other, less obviously constructed desires.

Previous efforts to define Wyatt Earp (and his brothers) as the film's protago-
nist(s) in opposition to Old Man Clanton (and his sons) as antagonist(s) have
had to explain most of the film's extended middle as another, subsidiary conflict,
the struggle between Wyatt, as an official hero, and Doc Holliday, as an outlaw
hero, over control of Tombstone. The pressure of the film's central sequences
is then directed toward reconciling the explicit opposition between Wyatt and
Doc so that they can collectively avenge the murders of the two younger Earp
brothers and Chihuahua (Doc's mistress and patient) in the final showdown at
the O.K. Corral. However, by emphasizing the film's oblique work toward its
conclusion rather than the conclusion itself, the usefulness of seeing Wyatt and
Doc, or the Earps and the Clantons, as simply opposed is put into question.
Doc, Wyatt, and Old Man Clanton, as played by Victor Mature, Henry Fonda,
and Walter Brennan, are better understood to represent positions on a continuum of social definitions of masculinity, especially as defined or demonstrated
by action and appearance. The necessity of eliminating both Doc and Old Man
Clanton from the narrative is not simply to clear the social space for the (antici-
pated) marriage of Wyatt and Clementine but to fulfill the prerequisite need to
secure Wyatt's place along a line of gender definitions that has indistinct grada-
tions.

One model for this continuum can be derived from theories of male sex-role
identity being constructed by psychiatry and the social sciences before and at the
time of the film's release. During and after the First World War, as Elaine Showalter has demonstrated, the widespread incidence of male hysteria, or "shell
shock," radically undermined the previously secure categories of masculinity
and femininity within English and American psychiatry; through the next two
decades, the central question for research on male neurosis was, as Joseph H.
Pleck puts it: "What makes men less masculine than they should be, and what
can we do about it?"[10] Lewis Terman and Catherine Miles's influential study *Sex
and Personality* (1936) argued that, "for each sex, there is a psychologically
normative or ideal configuration of traits, attitudes, and interests that members
of that sex demonstrate to varying degrees."[11] This view, that the essential problem for some males might be not "having enough" masculinity, a deficit that
could appear as effeminacy or homosexuality, was widely adopted by American
psychology until after the war, when the simple opposition between masculinity
and not enough masculinity was upset by the introduction, by such figures as
Talcott Parsons and Nevitt Sanford, of the notion of *hypermasculinity*, a term
introduced in part to account for residual wartime male aggression.[12] (The
redefinitions of male heterosexuality and homosexuality as locations along a
behavioral continuum rather than as a simple opposition or "inversion" would
be successfully reinforced with the publication in 1948 of the first Kinsey Re-

port, *Sexual Behavior in the Human Male;* Kinsey's controversial six-point scale determined tendencies toward "exclusive" heterosexual or homosexual behavior based on "both psychologic reactions and overt experience.")[13]

The suggestion that masculinity could be threatened by either deficiency or excess is helpful for understanding *My Darling Clementine*'s effort to secure a place for Wyatt Earp not in opposition to but somewhere *between* Doc Holliday and Old Man Clanton. At a simple visual level, these positions are suggested by the facial hair of these figures: Clanton is fully bearded throughout the film, and Doc is always clean-shaven (although in his past, as Clementine points out after noticing a college photograph in his hotel room, he wore a moustache). Wyatt, however, begins the film with a beard, which he will have removed, leaving only a trim moustache. His moustache (a rare "prop" for Fonda) places him between Victor Mature's pretty, smooth face (emphasized through the film's frequent high-contrast lighting) and Walter Brennan's unusually rugged face. But Wyatt's possible mobility or instability within this position is suggested by his initial appearance—he can easily become hypermasculinely bearded—and, more important, by his second encounter with the barber, when he is excessively dandified and sprayed with the "sweet smellin' stuff" that his brothers and Clementine will mistake for the "scent of the desert flower." Wyatt's uncomfortable question when looking at his image in the barber's mirror—"You don't think that's kind of . . . ?"—can be reasonably completed only with a word that we nevertheless cannot imagine this character speaking: "effeminate?" (I have no idea what the vernacular cowboy equivalent for *faggy* might be.)

Wyatt's normative masculinity, in short, must be stabilized through the effective resistance to threats of deficiency or excess represented by identification with either Doc or Clanton. The primal violence that excludes the Clantons from Tombstone and perversely binds them as an all-male family is counteracted by Wyatt's ability to maintain social control through clever suggestion or restrained violence (in all but the final gunfight he only superficially wounds opponents) and to head *his* all-male family through fraternal respect. (The father of the Earps, who Wyatt says will "be all busted up" and "never get over" the murder of his youngest son, is frequently evoked but remains off-screen, his absence thereby allowing his sons to function as an egalitarian group.) In much more complex ways, Doc's effeminacy functions as a seductive threat to Wyatt's masculinity. Wyatt's initial comment on seeing Doc—"nice lookin' fella"—is exactly the sort of comment that, to use Sedgwick's terms, male homosocial bonds—traditionally enacted in segregated spaces like clubs, locker rooms, and saloons—allow within the extreme limits of either explicit homosexual desire or homophobia. Wyatt's long, measured walk between the space marked by (hypermasculine) pinups of bare-chested boxers on the saloon wall behind the poker

table and Doc's position at the end of the bar (emphasized by deep focus cinematography) might be understood as a traversal of this middle ground of normative heterosexual masculinity, with the pinups and the approach to Doc gestures
toward, but not actual acts of, transgression.

Wyatt's initial comment (surely as much about "beautiful hunk of man" Victor Mature as Doc Holliday)[14] and his eventual casual acceptance of Doc's offers
to buy him a drink ("Champagne it is, Mac") and escort him to the theater
("Yeah, fine") are bridged by threats and displays of power, traditional techniques of masculine assertion in the Western (or, for that matter, in the policing
of bars) that serve to neutralize the scene's expressions of physical admiration;
Wyatt comfortably introduces his younger brother as a "good-lookin' fella" as
well, immediately after the threatening presence of his other brother's gun has
been established. Ford, however, creates an unusual tension in the scene, violat-
ing the 180-degree rule by placing his camera on both sides of the bar and
cutting between these positions: Wyatt and Doc reverse their location on screen
in a kind of waltz ("Camptown Races" accompanies the scene) that brings them
together visually and physically even as they are articulating their ideological
differences. A slightly low camera angle from behind the bar even makes it look
as if the two are holding hands.

Doc's threats are of course no match for Wyatt's more playful flirtations,
where his missing gun, opened vest, and introduction of his brothers serve more
as teases than explicit enforcements of power. Wyatt's control throughout the
film is maintained by such playful actions or quiet suggestiveness (consider the
moments when he runs the drunk Indian or the gambler out of town, the latter
explicitly contrasted with Doc's physical threat to the gambler at Wyatt's card
table on his arrival), unlike Clanton's borderline sadism or Doc's hysterical masochism (which Wyatt characterizes as "a sucker's game"). I will soon argue that
the sudden appearance of the ham actor in this scene is the most important way
in which the tensions that I am describing will be deflected and redistributed in
the film. But Wyatt's attraction and repulsion in relation to Doc are also dramatized through his acquiescence to drinking champagne, followed immediately by
Doc's first coughing fit and grasp for his silk handkerchief, the film's most
insistent signs of Doc's "sickness," decadence, and inadequacy as a man; later fits
will prevent him from completing Hamlet's soliloquy and explaining himself to
Clementine and finally get him killed, with the foppish hanky fluttering in the
breeze. Frank McConnell, attentive to the costuming in the film, never directly
says what his descriptions of Doc imply: Doc's "unhealthy, suicidal involution" is
figured through his "elegant, overstylized gambler's clothes," an "overemphasized elegance" summarized by his handkerchief, "an odd, graceful, almost dandified accouterment for a gunfighter, and as such the perfect visual expression of

Doc's refined, cynical and somehow diseased culture." McConnell's rapid accumulation of terms connoting combined excess ("overstylized," "overemphasized"), femininity ("elegance," "graceful"), and sickness ("unhealthy," "diseased") belies the rhetorical hesitation ("*almost* dandified," "*somehow* diseased") in naming "homosexuality" as the stereotypical summary explanation for Doc's character.[15]

The gunfight at the O.K. Corral that eventually brings Wyatt, Doc, and Clanton together is certainly, as most critics note, the film's final, overt demonstration of the necessity of legitimized violence in the exercise of social control. But the confrontation is also explicitly a reaction on the part of all three characters to their work of mourning—Wyatt for two brothers, Clanton for a son, and Doc for Chihuahua but especially for his lost skills and status as a doctor who failed to save her. The ways in which the psychic work of mourning translates itself into social action continue to locate Wyatt on a masculine continuum between the other male characters.

Clanton's mourning is initially feminized, as the old man sits in formalized grief (traditionally assigned to women) before the body of his slain son; but this position is immediately revealed to be a masquerade when he raises and fires his (previously hidden) shotgun. Clanton's mourning is merely a momentarily convenient excuse for continuing the blood lust that characterizes his family throughout the film; his weeping is a brief act of drag that his erected and fired shotgun instantly concludes. (McBride and Wilmington hint at Clanton's behavioral transvestism, noting that, "when his sons are wiped out in the gunfight at the O.K. Corral, he cries 'My boys! Ike . . . Sam . . . Phin . . . Billy . . .' *like a sagebrush Medea,* and then tries to pick off a few more Earps before Ward Bond mows him down with a righteous blast from the hip" [my emphasis].)[16] Doc's mourning—reinforced by his wearing only black throughout the film—is consistently depicted as melancholia, the "morbid pathological disposition" that Freud describes as characterized by "a profoundly painful dejection, abrogation of interest in the outside world, loss of the capacity to love, inhibition of all activity, and a lowering of the self-regarding feelings to a degree that finds utterance in self-reproaches and self-revilings, and culminates in a delusional expectation of punishment."[17]

Whereas mourning is a conscious negotiation of the loss of a loved object in the world, melancholia shifts that impoverishment to one's own ego and thus encourages pathological narcissism. Showalter quotes a description of World War I shellshock victims that summarizes Doc's character: "They were subject to queer moods and queer tempers, fits of profound depression alternating with a restless desire for pleasure. Many were easily moved to passion where they lost control of themselves, many were bitter in their speech, violent in opinion, fright-

ening."[18] When Wyatt speaks at the grave of his murdered brother at the beginning of the film (in a paradigmatic Fordian moment, recreating scenes from
Judge Priest [1934] and *Young Mr. Lincoln,* where men, however, speak to dead
women), he successfully translates his grief into social responsibility; he and his
brothers remain in Tombstone so that "maybe when we leave this country,
young kids like [James] will be able to grow up and live safe." Although Wyatt will
finally refer to the showdown with the Clantons as "strictly a family affair," his
revenge is stoically performed as a civic act authorized by his official position.

For the film's contemporary postwar audience, a demonstration of how to
bury one's dead, accept this loss as a necessary sacrifice to social progress, and
then get on with things would seem especially compelling. Doc's losses, however,
are more ambiguous and less successfully negotiated and are expressed through
self-loathing, alcoholism, and the rejection of "normal" human interaction (he
finally dismisses both Chihuahua and Clementine); Doc's emphatic assertion to
Clementine—"The man you knew is no more. There's not a vestige of him left.
Nothing"—is perhaps his most direct statement identifying his loss as narcissistic, although she assumes that he is referring to his physical illness alone. The
difference between Doc and Wyatt in this regard is suggested by their parallel
glances into mirrors in the film: whereas Wyatt's shock at his dandified haircut in
the barber's mirror is treated with comic discomfort, Doc's view of his face
reflected in the glass of his framed medical diploma results in disgust and rage
when he smashes the image with a shot glass. Doc's melancholia is consistently
linked in the film with his insufficient masculinity, as Clanton's aggression is
linked with his hypermasculine role as a feared, primal father. Taken as representatives of psychic and behavioral options for men returning from war, Henry
Fonda's Wyatt Earp is not simply and finally the narrative's physical survivor but
also its psychological "winner," the figure who remains physically and psychically intact: he is the film's actual "mature victor."

I have suggested that, for the film's historical male audience, *My Darling
Clementine* in part demonstrates how to act, how to return successfully from the
war by reestablishing and centering a masculinity recently placed in potential
crisis. But the curious intrusion into the film, and into the scene that I have isolated as the moment when an alternative to the narrative's eventual heterosexual
imperative first asserts itself, of the ham actor Granville Thorndyke (Alan Mow-
bray) and the town mascot Old Dad (played by Francis Ford, John's brother)
suggests that the film is interested in complicating the limited understanding of
"acting" that I have been using.

My Darling Clementine, in fact, might be considered as a dramatized treatise on
performance or as an acted essay on acting as both behavior and profession. In
commentary on the film, Thorndyke has been, along with the barber shop, the

unfinished church, and the nascent schoolmarm Clementine, exclusively under-stood to represent the bringing of civilization to the wilderness. But Doc's ironic delight in the incongruity of "Shakespeare in Tombstone" might also be due to his recognition of another whose masculinity is problematic in this cultural land-scape: Thorndyke is not only flamboyant in dress and manner—and, unlike Wyatt, clearly familiar with champagne—but, more significantly, typed as effemi-nate by his very profession of actor (in 1953, a *Photoplay* article asked, "Are Actors Sissies?" but its negative answer hardly eliminated the doubts motivating the question). His sentimental farewell to Old Dad, for which he draws on Joseph Addison and Shakespeare, is the film's most outrageously melodramatic yet most touching declaration of love: "Great souls by instinct to each other turn, Demand allegiance, and in friendship burn. Good night, sweet prince."

As the film's explicit representative of an activity commonly deemed unmanly, Thorndyke nevertheless performs, at the remove of the narrative, the very work of, among others, Henry Fonda, Victor Mature, and Walter Brennan. The film, however, only encourages us directly to identify Thorndyke with Doc, who, in an extraordinary moment in the American Western, takes up Hamlet's soliloquy, momentarily mesmerizing Wyatt, until he is stopped by his second coughing fit. This scene can certainly be appreciated as high camp (Victor Mature reciting Shakespeare in a Western), but it also achieves an effective condensation of many of the film's key concerns: Doc, whose deficient masculinity renders him continually insufficient to complete tasks that it will be Wyatt's duty to accom-plish, can, in fact, *act*, if that term means simply to imitate, feign, or represent. Doc actually finds himself close to Hamlet's position, torn between an inability to act (perform a deed) and his disgust with his talent for acting (or pretending).

In an influential essay first published in 1952, Maynard Mack argued that *Hamlet*'s image patterns revolved around three words, *show, act,* and *play,* with *act* "the play's radical metaphor." According to Mack, *Hamlet*'s nagging ques-tion is, "How does an act (a deed) relate to an act (a pretense)?"[19] Throughout *My Darling Clementine,* this question is consistently inflected with questions concerning "proper" masculinity and so might be reformulated as, How does acting like a man relate to acting by a man? In other words, how should mas-culine behavior—in a film as well as social life—be performed? The film's desire, one suspects, is to hide these questions beneath the naturalistic performance that it sanctions, Henry Fonda's unobtrusive modulation of his body and voice in the role of Wyatt Earp. Ford is continually willing to film Fonda simply standing, sitting, or walking, often from behind. Fonda's performance is a construction built up from small physical gestures that frequently resemble an adolescent boy's attempts to gauge the potential of his recently altered body: his lazy walk, his playful balancing act on the chair (which Peter Stowell exactly calls the "performance of an integrated personality"),[20] and his manipulations of his hat all seem, on reflection, to serve as denials of the histrionics so abhorrent to Hamlet yet apparently endemic to those who, like Thorndyke and Doc, inhabit Hamlet's role. (In many of its details, Fonda's performance repeats, or perhaps comments on, his prewar performance in *Young Mr. Lincoln;* both characters sit with their legs splayed, dance with awkward charm [to the same music], speak calmly [unlike Hamlet] over graves, fling hats aside, and collect unusual objects in their hats. Both characters might be said to be playfully mastering their post-adolescent bodies.)[21]

In its mobilization of the pressures and prejudices of its culture to define Wyatt—and Fonda—as ideal representatives of normative masculine heterosexuality, *My Darling Clementine* must finally rescue, through disavowal, its hero and principal actor from the unmanly profession of acting itself; Fonda's easy, laconic naturalism—a balance of mature control and boyish play—defines proper masculine behavior for the film's audience, which has seen alternate models of masculinity condemned and eliminated. In fact, Fonda's stardom, against Walter Brennan's lifelong (if successful) status as a supporting actor and Victor Mature's contemporary status as a kitsch icon, is perhaps Hollywood's (or nostalgia's) own replaying of *My Darling Clementine*'s narrative reward for the figure who most successfully obtains his secure masculinity by nevertheless acting, as we say with revealing rhetorical hesitation, "like a man."

Notes

Research for this paper was supported by a Ball Brothers Foundation Visiting Fellowship that allowed me to examine materials in the John Ford Collection at the Lilly Library, Indiana University; I thank William R. Cagle, Lilly librarian, and his staff, especially Heather R. Munro, manuscripts reference assistant, who placed two of Ford's Oscars in my hands. Versions of this essay have been presented at the University of Pittsburgh, the University of Winnipeg, the Mass Culture Workshop at the University of Chicago, and the Society for Cinema Studies conference, and I am indebted to comments and support from all these sites. Special thanks for early and late encouragement goes to Alex Doty and Constance Penley, Emma and Vienna in my fantasy remake of *Johnny Guitar.*

1 A transcription of the film and additional information on its production and critical reception can be found in Robert Lyons, ed., *My Darling Clementine* (New Brunswick, N.J.: Rutgers University Press, 1984). I have also examined a "Final Script" for the film by Samuel G. Engel and Winston Miller, dated 11 March 1946; this script contains numerous revised pages by Engel dated 22, 25, and 30 March 1946 and "Added Scenes and Retakes" dated 8 and 10 July 1946. The bibliography on John Ford and the Western since the rise of auterist and genre criticism is lengthy. Studies of Ford and *My Darling Clementine* con-

sulted for this study include Lindsay Anderson, *About John Ford* (New York: McGraw-Hill, 1981); John Baxter, *The Cinema of John Ford* (New York: Barnes, 1971); Peter Biskind, *Seeing Is Believing: How Hollywood Taught Us to Stop Worrying and Love the Fifties* (New York: Pantheon, 1983), 34–43; Peter Bogdanovich, *John Ford* (Berkeley: University of California Press, 1968); Michael Budd, "Genre, Director, and Stars in John Ford's Westerns: Fonda, Wayne, Stewart, and Widmark," *Wide Angle* 2, no. 4 (1978): 52–61; William Darby, "Musical Links in *Young Mr. Lincoln, My Darling Clementine,* and *The Man Who Shot Liberty Valance,*" *Cinema Journal* 31, no. 1 (Fall 1991): 22–36; Stefan Fleischer, "A Study through Stills of *My Darling Clementine,*" *Journal of Modern Literature* 3, no. 2 (April 1973): 241–52; Tag Gallagher, *John Ford: The Man and His Films* (Berkeley and Los Angeles: University of California Press, 1986), 225–34; Douglas Gomery, "Mise-en-scène in John Ford's *My Darling Clementine,*" *Wide Angle* 2, no. 4 (1978): 14–19; Joseph McBride and Michael Wilmington, *John Ford* (New York: Da Capo, 1975), 85–96; Frank McConnell, *Storytelling and Mythmaking: Images from Film and Literature* (New York: Oxford University Press, 1979), 118–21, 272–75; Bill Nichols, "Style, Grammar, and the Movies," in *Movies and Methods,* ed. Bill Nichols (Berkeley and Los Angeles: University of California Press, 1976), 607–28; J. A. Place, *The Western Films of John Ford* (Seacaucus, N.J.: Citadel, 1974), 58–70; Andrew Sarris, *The John Ford Movie Mystery* (Bloomington: Indiana University Press, 1975); Peter Stowell, *John Ford* (Boston: Twayne, 1986); and Peter Wollen, *Signs and Meaning in the Cinema* (Bloomington: Indiana University Press, 1972), 94–102. Two error-filled biographies, Dan Ford, *Pappy: The Life of John Ford* (Englewood Cliffs, N.J.: Prentice-Hall, 1979), and Andrew Sinclair, *John Ford* (New York: Dial/James Wade, 1979), have been superseded by Tag Gallagher's critical biography.

Rather pedantic "corrections" of the historical errors made by Ford specifically and Westerns in general can be found in Jon Tuska, *The American West in Film* (Westport, Conn.: Greenwood, 1985), esp. 183–96; and Wayne Michael Sarf, *God Bless You, Buffalo Bill* (Rutherford, N.J.: Fairleigh Dickinson University Press, 1983), esp. 29–73. Both authors largely blame Stuart N. Lake's *Wyatt Earp, Frontier Marshal* (Boston: Houghton Mifflin, 1931) (a screen-credited source for *My Darling Clementine* and the basis for Fox films in 1934 and 1939) for initiating many of the historical errors in the Wyatt Earp legend perpetuated by Hollywood films. For a recent, meticulously researched account of the events and figures in Ford's fiction, see Paula Mitchell Marks, *And Die in the West: The Story of the O.K. Corral Gunfight* (New York: Simon & Schuster, 1989).

2 Rick Altman, *The American Film Musical* (Bloomington: Indiana University Press, 1985), 5.

3 See Adrienne Rich, "Compulsory Homosexuality and Lesbian Existence," in *Blood, Bread, and Poetry: Selected Prose, 1979–1985* (New York: Norton, 1986), 23–75; Monique Wittig, "The Straight Mind," in *The Straight Mind and Other Essays* (Boston: Beacon, 1992), 27–28. Wittig also uses the term *heterosexual contract,* and Rich uses *unexamined heterocentricity* to effectively indicate the comfortable obliviousness characteristic of the criticism that I discuss here. With different inflections, Judith Butler's term *heterosexual matrix* might also be useful here (see Judith Butler, *Gender Trouble: Feminism and the Subversion of Identity* [New York: Routledge, 1990], 12, 151 n. 6).

4 To my knowledge, only John Baxter directly acknowledges the film's homoerotics, although this is his entire discussion of the matter: "A homosexual attachment is implied, no doubt subconsciously, between Holliday and Wyatt, encapsulated in the latter's admiring response to his first glimpse of Doc, 'A fine-looking man,' [*sic*] but supported by Wyatt's solicitude for Holliday in his illness, his resentment of the other's mistress Chihuahua (Linda Darnell) and his nervous decision to take over Holliday's discarded *fiancee* who is, in a sense, the feminine aspect of Holliday's personality" (*The Cinema of John Ford*, 101). My different understanding of the film's "homosexual attachment" should be clear in what follows. Although I am concerned with the film's immediate cultural context rather than the historical accuracy of its representations, a letter from Stuart Lake (author of *Wyatt Earp, Frontier Marshall;* see n. 1 above) to Micky Nielan of Twentieth Century–Fox dated 12 January 1946, and passed on to Ford on 16 January 1946, is suggestive in relation to my reading. Lake writes, "One interesting item is that in the book—which is still a steady seller—I did not tell the whole story. The key to one whale of a dramatic situation, I left out for very sound reasons. With the deaths of several persons since that time I know that I am the only living person who knows about it—they were very, very few even back in 1881—and those same deaths have freed me from the need to hold it secret." Lake claims that he has "had a couple of offers to write the unpublished chapters" but that the war has prevented him from this work; I have been unable to determine whether he ever did and so can only speculate about the nature of the secret he withheld (closeted?) until the deaths of Earp's contemporaries (John Ford Collection, Lilly Library, box 1, Correspondence 1906–46).

5 For "allegorical" readings of the film, see, e.g., Peter Biskind: "before Tombstone (read, the home front) and the West (read, the Western world) can be made safe for kids (read, democracy), [Wyatt] has to pick up the gun once again, in much the same way that both corporate liberals and conservatives alike basically agreed on the necessity of remilitarizing America for the cold war" (*Seeing Is Believing*, 35–40). Or see Tag Gallagher: "Wyatt Earp (the U.S.) gives up marshalling in Dodge City (World War I), but takes up arms again to combat the Clantons (World War II) to make the world safe" (*John Ford*, 225). On Wyler's and Capra's films in their context, see Kaja Silverman's chapter "Historical Trauma and Male Subjectivity," in *Male Subjectivity at the Margins* (New York: Routledge, 1992), 52–106. Robert Ray also analyzes *It's a Wonderful Life* with reference to *My Darling Clementine* in *A Certain Tendency of the American Cinema, 1930–1980* (Princeton, N.J.: Princeton University Press, 1985), 179–243.

6 Stephen Neale, *Genre* (London: British Film Institute, 1980), 56. See Jim Kitses, *Horizons West* (Bloomington: Indiana University Press, 1969), 7–27. Robert Ray quotes Kitses and provides a list of schematic oppositions in order to analyze Ford's *The Man Who Shot Liberty Valance* (1962) (see *A Certain Tendency of the American Cinema*, 200). Other references here are to Frederick Jackson Turner, *The Significance of the Frontier in American History* (1893), ed. Harold P. Simonson (New York: Continuum, 1963); and Henry Nash Smith, *Virgin Land: The American West as Symbol and Myth* (Cambridge, Mass.: Harvard University Press, 1950; reprint, 1970). For a recent and compelling reinterpretation of Turner's thesis and the Western, see Virginia Wright Wexman's chapter "Star and Genre:

John Wayne, the Western, and the American Dream of the Family on the Land," in *Creating the Couple: Love, Marriage, and Hollywood Performance* (Princeton, N.J.: Princeton University Press, 1993), 67–129.

7 Ray, *A Certain Tendency of the Hollywood Cinema*, 25–88; Raymond Bellour's claim, using William Wyler's *The Westerner* (1940) as his example, appears in "Alternation, Segmentation, Hypnosis: Interview with Raymond Bellour," conducted by Janet Bergstrom, in *Feminism and Film Theory*, ed. Constance Penley (New York: Routledge, 1988), 187. See also Bellour's contributions to *Le Western* (Paris: 10/18 U.E.G., 1966; 2d ed., 1969) and his essay on Wyler's film in *Le cinema americain, analyses filmiques* (Paris: Flammarion, 1979).

8 Eve Kosofsky Sedgwick, *Between Men: English Literature and Male Homosocial Desire* (New York: Columbia University Press, 1985), 21. Sedgwick is building on Rene Girard, *Deceit, Desire, and the Novel: Self and Other in Literary Structure* (Baltimore: Johns Hopkins University Press, 1965). For an interesting application of Sedgwick to film, see Michael Moon, "A Small Boy and Others: Sexual Disorientation in Henry James, Kenneth Anger, and David Lynch," in *Comparative American Identities: Race, Sex, and Nationality in the Modern Text*, ed. Hortense J. Spillers (New York: Routledge, 1991), 141–56.

9 Gallagher, *John Ford*, 229.

10 See Elaine Showalter, *The Female Malady* (New York: Penguin, 1985), 167–94; Showalter notes that, "when military doctors and psychiatrists dismissed shell-shock patients as cowards, they were often hinting at effeminacy or homosexuality" (p. 172). See also Joseph H. Pleck, "The Theory of Male Sex-Role Identity: Its Rise and Fall, 1936 to the Present," in *The Making Of Masculinities*, ed. Harry Brod (Boston: Allen & Unwin, 1987), 22.

11 Pleck, "Male Sex-Role Identity," 23; see Lewis Terman and Catherine Miles, *Sex and Personality* (New York: McGraw-Hill, 1936).

12 See Talcott Parsons, "Certain Primary Sources and Patterns of Aggression in the Social Structure of the Western World," *Psychiatry* 10 (1947): 167–81; T. W. Adorno, E. Frenkel-Brunswick, D. J. Levinson, and R. N. Sanford, *The Authoritarian Personality* (New York: Wiley, 1950); R. N. Sanford, *Self and Society* (New York: Atherton, 1966); and Walter Langer's OSS-initiated study of Hitler, *The Mind of Adolf Hitler* (New York: Basic, 1972).

13 Alfred C. Kinsey, Wardell B. Pomeroy, and Clyde E. Martin, *Sexual Behavior in the Human Male* (Philadelphia: Saunders, 1948). For recent discussions of Kinsey's report and homosexuality, see Kenneth Lewes, *The Psychoanalytic Theory of Male Homosexuality* (New York: Simon & Schuster, 1988), esp. chap. 6; and John H. Gagnon, "Gender Preference in Erotic Relations: The Kinsey Scale and Sexual Scripts," in *Homosexuality/Heterosexuality: Concepts of Sexual Orientation*, ed. D. P. McWhirter, S. A. Sanders, and J. M. Reinisch (New York: Oxford University Press, 1990), 177–207. On definitions of homosexuality constructed for the military in World War II, see Allan Bérubé, *Coming Out under Fire: The History of Gay Men and Women in World War Two* (New York: Free Press, 1990), esp. 149–74. For the importance of World War II in creating homosexual identities, see John D'Emilio, *Sexual Politics, Sexual Communities: The Making of a Homo-*

sexual Minority in the United States, 1940–1970 (Chicago: University of Chicago Press, 1983); and John Castillo, *Love, Sex and War: Changing Values, 1939–45* (London: Collins, 1985). For an account of how the war could be "blamed" for homosexual "deviance" in the cold war era, see Lee Edelman, "Tearooms and Sympathy; or, The Epistemology of the Water Closet," in *Nationalisms and Sexualities,* ed. Andrew Parker, Mary Russo, Doris Sommer, and Patricia Yaeger (New York: Routledge, 1992), 263–84, esp. n. 22.

14   Robert Coughlan, "Victor Mature: 'Beautiful Hunk of Man' from Hollywood Is New Matinee Idol," *Life,* 7 April 1941, 65–74. Mature is also called a "beautiful hunk of man" in a profile by John R. Franchey, "Life Owes You Nothing," *Photoplay,* May 1942, 57. The casting of Doc was an ongoing concern for Ford and Darryl F. Zanuck during the pre-production of the film. Interoffice memos in the John Ford Collection at the Lilly Library reveal that the following actors were considered: Tyrone Power, James Stewart, Mark Stevens (according to Zanuck "a young man" but "by no means a pretty boy"), John Russell, John Hodiak, and Douglas Fairbanks, Jr. ("as it's a flamboyant role it is quite possible he could kick hell out of it," Ford notes). On 8 January 1946, Zanuck wrote Ford:

I am pleased that you like Victor Mature. Personally I think the guy has been one of the most under-rated performers in Hollywood. The public is crazy about him and strangely enough every picture that he has been in has been a big box office hit. Yet the Romanoff round table has refused to take him seriously as an actor.

A part like Doc Halliday [*sic*] will be sensational for him as I know you will get a great performance out of him and I agree with you that the peculiar traits of his personality are ideal for a characterization such as this.

In response, on 12 January 1946, Ford wrote Zanuck:

I had Victor Mature in. Had a long talk with him and he promises to continue on the wagon, watch his diet and generally reduce. He claims that he can take off twelve pounds easily and that mostly on his face. He is an enthusiastic kid and I sincerely hope that he makes it. You know that I will do my utmost for him and I can guarantee that he will turn out a swell job.

Am very happy about doing it in black and white. I had a long talk with Henry Fonda and he seemed delighted that he isn't going to play Wyatt Erp [*sic*] in technicolor with rouge on his lips. He is also genuinely interested in the Mature casting. Thinks it is, to use Rufus LeMaire's words, "sensational."

All these memos are in the John Ford Collection, Lilly Library, box 1, Correspondence 1906–46; some correspondence related to the production and final cut of *My Darling Clementine* is collected in Rudy Behlmer, ed., *Memo from Darryl F. Zanuck: The Golden Years at Twentieth Century–Fox* (New York: Grove, 1993), 101–7. I quote these documents in order to emphasize the unusual attention to Mature's face, physique, and "peculiar traits," as opposed to Fonda's unproblematic casting and even relief at not having to paint his face for a color film. A "fag joke" insinuating Mature's homosexuality appeared on the Jack Benny radio program in the early forties (see Alexander Doty, *Making Things Perfectly Queer: Interpreting Mass Culture* [Minneapolis: University of Minnesota Press,

1993], 72–73). The same joke is quoted by Margaret T. McFadden, "'America's Boy Friend Who Can't Get a Date': Gender, Race, and the Cultural Work of the Jack Benny Program, 1932–1946," *Journal of American History*, 80, no. 1 [June 1993]: 129).

15 McConnell, *Storytelling and Mythmaking*, 119–20, 275.

16 McBride and Wilmington, *John Ford*, 93.

17 Sigmund Freud, "Mourning and Melancholia" (1917), in *The Standard Edition of the Complete Psychological Works of Sigmund Freud,* trans. and ed. James Strachey (New York: Norton, 1966), 14: 239–58.

18 Elaine Showalter, *The Female Malady*, 190.

19 The critical literature on *Hamlet* is of course extensive; I have relied on the overview collection *Hamlet: Critical Essays,* ed. Joseph G. Price (New York: Garland, 1986), which includes Maynard Mack, "The World of *Hamlet*," 39–58 (originally published in *The Yale Review* 41 [1952]: 502–23). For information that places Ford's actor in his historical context, see Lawrence W. Levine's chapter "William Shakespeare in America" in *Highbrow/Lowbrow: The Emergence of Cultural Hierarchy in America* (Cambridge, Mass.: Harvard University Press, 1988), 11–81. On the origins of connotations linking homosexuality and male actors, see Kristina Straub's illuminating study *Sexual Suspects: Eighteenth-Century Players and Sexual Ideology* (Princeton, N.J.: Princeton University Press, 1992) as well as Kaier Curtin's *"We Can Always Call Them Bulgarians": The Emergence of Lesbians and Gay Men on the American Stage* (Boston, 1987).

20 Stowell, *John Ford,* 103.

21 Another odd connection between the films is now extratextual but nevertheless intriguing. As Ford told Peter Bogdanovich, "They cut some nice things out of it (*Young Mr. Lincoln*). For example, I had a lovely scene in which Lincoln rode into town on a mule, passed by a theatre and stopped to see what was playing, and it was the Booth family doing *Hamlet;* we had a typical old-fashioned poster up. Here was this poor shabby country lawyer wishing he had enough money to go see *Hamlet* when a very handsome young boy with dark hair—you knew he was a member of the Booth family—fresh, snobbish kid, all beautifully dressed—just walked out to the edge of the plank walk and looked at Lincoln. He looked at this funny, incongruous man in a tall hat riding a mule, and you knew there was some connection there. They cut it out—too bad" (Bogdanovich, *John Ford,* 72–73). On the Booth family and Hamlet, see Gene Smith's fascinating *American Gothic: The Story of America's Legendary Theatrical Family—Junius, Edwin, and John Wilkes Booth* (New York: Simon & Schuster, 1992). John Wilkes Booth's famous brother Edwin, "the Prince of Players," had just completed an unprecedented one hundred performances as Hamlet in New York City when John shot Lincoln in, of course, Ford's theater.

Dossier on Hitchcock

Introduction

Alexander Doty

Note from Alfred Hitchcock to Joan Crawford: "In my very rare homosexual moments I often glance through the pages of *Vogue*, where the other day I saw a magnificent picture of you."[1]

Since the personal lives of directors and the connection of these lives to artistic intent are at the heart of popular uses of auteurism, let us ask the burning question now: Was Alfred Hitchcock queer? He probably would not have called himself queer, except in the sense of being odd. But if "being" queer (homosexual, gay, bisexual, or lesbian) is a case not only of naming yourself but of being named by your pleasures, desires, and even your anxieties, then Hitchcock was queer. His note to Joan Crawford, cited above, reveals that he understood his pleasure in looking at pictures in *Vogue* as "homosexual": that is, he seems to realize you do not have to identify as queer to take queer pleasures in mass culture. But, even aside from such biographical details as the note to Crawford and those anecdotes in Donald Spoto's *The Dark Side of Genius* that discuss the director's encounters with homosexuality (and homosexual actors),[2] Hitchcock's films speak volumes about his encounters with straight culture's contradictory and often incoherent ideas about queerness. These queer encounters were often further complicated in Hitchcock films by being worked out in relation to traditional cultural notions of masculinity and, especially, femininity. The intersection of gender and homosexuality in Hitchcock films is the starting point for Robin Wood's "rereading" of Spoto's biography in this section, and is central to the project of Tania Modleski's chapter on *Murder!* in *The Women Who Knew Too Much* and to Theodore Price's *Hitchcock and Homosexuality*.[3]

Examining the relation between the masculine, the feminine, and the male homosexual in Hitchcock films is also crucial to Sabrina Barton's " 'Criss-Cross': Paranoia and Projection in *Strangers on a Train*" (in this volume). Barton finds *Strangers on a Train* particularly interesting "for its suggestion that a masterful [straight] male subject position is at once produced and continually threatened by its own paranoid homophobic and misogynistic plots." But while this film (and by extention other Hitchcock films) "does not seem to critique the privilege of the bourgeois male subject" outright, "it takes a more than perverse pleasure in exposing the mechanisms of, and [the main male character's] complicity in, the displaced violence [against women and gays] required to ensure that privilege." On the other hand, Barton admits that *Stranger on a Train*'s narrative encourages the audience to see the main character's ex-wife as "the voracious tramp" and the male antagonist as "the deranged homosexual."

As one line of feminist debate about Hitchcock's films has centered around the question, Is Hitchcock a misogynist? an important question for some queer critics has been, Is Hitchcock homophobic? That is, do we get a sense from his films that he subscribes to conventional pejorative cultural ideas about queerness? In part this question is connected to concerns about "positive images" and nonstereotyped representations that are perhaps most fully explored in Vito Russo's *The Celluloid Closet*.[4] John Hepworth's "Hitchcock's Homophobia" (in this volume) finds the director guilty of a typically vicious Hollywood homophobia that ruins films like *Rope, Strangers on a Train,* and *Psycho:* "Any thoughtful examination of Hitchcock's cinema reveals that among his various blind spots, gay sexuality was his supreme bête noir, and that Hitch was a supreme fag baiter." Exacerbating this problem for Hepworth are (pre-1982) critics like Eric Rohmer, Claude Chabrol, and Robin Wood, who seem to share Hitchcock's "idiotic prejudice[s]" about homosexuality in their critical work on the director's films.

Responding to Hepworth's charges in a letter included here, Wood updates his position on Hitchcock but still questions Hepworth's use of certain "subtextual" codes to read characters as "gay" in Hitchcock's films. Expanding on this rebuttal in "Murderous Gays: Hitchcock's Homophobia" (which includes a rereading of *Rope*), Wood again wonders which characters in Hitchcock's oeuvre are, or are "supposed to be," gay. In a provocative move, Wood suggests that even those audiences and critics who deplore Hitchcock's homophobia may themselves be using "heterosexist myths" and stereotypes in order to name certain characters as gay or lesbian. Ultimately, Wood calls for critics to contextualize their discussions of Hitchcock's "supposed to be" gay and lesbian characters by placing them in relation to the troubled heterosexuals and heterosexual relationships that abound in Hitchcock films.

Comparing queerness and heterosexuality in Hitchcock films is central to

Rhona Berenstein's " 'I'm not the sort of person men marry': Monsters, Queers, and Hitchcock's *Rebecca*" and Lucretia Knapp's "The Queer Voice in *Marnie*," the final essays in this section. Both essays find that strong lesbian narrative lines coexist with heterosexual ones in *Rebecca* and *Marnie*. And, while lesbianism may be demonized in both films, heterosexuality is not made to appear a particularly appealing alternative. Berenstein and Knapp are especially interested in how mother-daughter relationships and the bonds between women in *Rebecca* and *Marnie* erotically challenge and disrupt these film's heterosexual(izing) narrative projects. While the heterosexual(izing) process seems to predominate by film's end, both Berenstein and Knapp suggest that the queer "outlaw woman" (Rebecca, Marnie) in each film has not been fully contained, vanquished, or "straightened out."

Taken together, these five essays, along with D. A. Miller's "Anal *Rope*," suggest how queer theory and criticism has learned from and built on other critical and theoretical positions: auteurism, semiotics/structuralism, Marxism/ideological analysis, feminism, psychoanalysis.[5] So it seems fitting that the director and the films that often became catalysts for working out earlier film theories should become important to articulating the tangled and volatile relation between queerness and mass culture.

Notes

1 Chip Duckett, "Out Front," *Out* (June–July 1993): 8.
2 Donald Spoto, *The Dark Side of Genius: The Life of Alfred Hitchcock* (New York: Ballantine, 1983).
3 Tania Modleski, "Male Hysteria and the 'Order of Things': *Murder!*" in *The Women Who Knew Too Much* (1988; New York and London: Routledge, 1989), 31–42; Theodore Price, *Hitchcock and Homosexuality: His 50-Year Obsession with Jack the Ripper and the Superbitch Prostitute—a Psychoanalytic View* (Metuchen, N.J.: Scarecrow, 1992).
4 Vito Russo, *The Celluloid Closet: Homosexuality in the Movies,* rev. ed. (1981; New York: Harper & Row, 1987).
5 D. A. Miller, "Anal *Rope*," *Representations* 32 (Fall 1990): 114–33 (reprinted in *Inside/Out: Lesbian Theories, Gay Theories,* ed. Diana Fuss [New York and London: Routledge, 1991], 119–41).

Hitchcock's

Homophobia

John Hepworth

I t's reasonable to assume that one of the functions of art is to try to dissolve those cultural and psychological factors that impede the evolution of a given society. Unfortunately, artists tend to grapple only with the factors that stifle their own evolution; their assessment of these problems may have only indirect benefits for society-at-large. Unlike a political activist, an artist's struggle is deeply personal struggle. By the same token, any failure to transcend such bêtes noires which he shadowboxes or a demon from whom he attempts to wrestle a blessing. Any broader social emancipation that may result is actually a by-product of this personal struggle. By the same token, any failure to transcend such *bêtes noires* also gets passed along and—particularly if the artist has sufficient cultural clout—further burdens and bewilders that society.

It follows that to sit through a film by a major filmmaker who demonstrates that he is unable to free himself of certain ersatz "truths" is to experience a sort of collective cultural harassment. Each of us sitting in the theater undergoes a sinking sensation: "Uh oh, he's going to give us the same bullshit after all." In movies, the audience is confronted with the consequences of an artist's failure in a particularly intense way. Any film that reaffirms cultural mystifications is bad art at its most disheartening. When a filmmaker we have come to respect actually espouses such mystifications, we're understandably dismayed and confounded. I found myself confronted by these very feelings while recently watching Alfred Hitchcock's *Strangers on a Train*.

With due respect to the critics who have fought to establish the value of Hitchcock's work, I came away from *Strangers on a Train* more convinced than ever that it was time to point out some of the Grand Old Man's limitations lest we be saddled with them indefinitely. I'm thinking especially of Hitchcock's homophobia and the cretinous psychological pseudo-explanations with which he attempted to justify, his apparent fear and hatred of gay men and women.

Hitchcock's unique vision as a filmmaker springs from his instinctive awareness of the dilemmas confronting the "one-dimensional man" who lives in an increasingly abstract and "uncreaturely" world. In Hitchcock's movies modern society always seems on the verge of disintegrating into a random collection of meaningless cultural fictions and pop hallucinations. The demons that Kafka unleashed in literature Hitchcock flung onto the screen. *The Birds* is the ultimate Hitchcock film because it so graphically embodies his vision of the random destructiveness of modern life taken to its absolute. (It likewise demonstrates the importance—the sacredness—of loyalty and community in Hitchcock's vision; indeed, these are often the only elements of reality in his vision of a culture abounding in illusion.)

Hitchcock's sensibility is predominantly poetic and even spiritual; he is one of the least intellectual or political of the great filmmakers. This sensibility, coupled with the fierce, almost apocalyptic nature of his vision, produced a surprisingly uneven body of work—everything from the defiant genius of *Vertigo* and the dazzling beauty of *North by Northwest* to the abysmal vulgarity and stupidity that exist in *Strangers on a Train* and *Psycho*. If Hitchcock's best work gives us a vision of modern life that is both invigorating and disturbing, then his worst films are a slapdash collage of silly clichés.

François Truffaut has correctly observed that "Hitchcock belongs among such artists of anxiety as Kafka, Dostoyevsky, and Poe." This is the crux of any discussion of the variability of Hitchcock's work. Despite the intellectual detachment and sophistication that Hitchcock cultivated in his films and his image, he was first and foremost an *intuitive* filmmaker. His tremendous strengths and appalling weaknesses stem from the uses of these intuitions. He was strong when he allowed himself to be completely lyrical and true to his inspirations, weak whenever he attempted to be an intellectual or a psychologist. Not surprisingly, we find ourselves with *two* Alfred Hitchcocks: the artist in whose work we hear the resounding of W. H. Auden's heroic phrase, "We must love one another or die," and the pseudointellectual psychologist capable of the crudest deductions.

Hitchcock at his full stature is Hitchcock the poet who understands the crucial significance of love. *The Thirty-Nine Steps, The Lady Vanishes, Notorious, I Confess, The Wrong Man, Vertigo, North by Northwest, Marnie,* and *The Birds* are all works of rare nobility, suppleness, and insight. Like Renoir and Welles, Hitchcock is one of the great lyric poets of the cinema. Because his best work *is* so totally intuitive, it is difficult to explain why *Vertigo* and *North by Northwest* are so moving. Their value as art has little or nothing to do with either intellect or psychology. Nor, one feels, are their values accidental.

Yet whenever Hitchcock tried to assume the pose of a man-of-the-world or a thinker, the falseness of this whimsical stance utterly took hold of his work, and the results are invariably bungled, silly, and sometimes surprisingly nasty, as if Hitchcock, like some poker player suspected of bluffing, desperately keeps raising the stakes.

Sabotage, Rebecca, Strangers on a Train, Spellbound, Psycho, Topaz, Torn Curtain, and *Frenzy* range in quality from the mediocre to the abominable, indicating that when his intuition failed him he had little or nothing to fall back on. A striking illustration of how fanciful Hitchcock's thinking could be was his contention that the more popular one of his films was at the box office, the better it must be artistically. It is inconceivable to imagine Hitchcock making such political films as *Citizen Kane* or *Touch of Evil* or Renoir's *La bête humaine, Boudu sauve des eaux,* or *La règle du jeu.* Compared to these films, the crude shallowness of *Torn Curtain* and *Topaz*—even allowing for elements of adventure and melodrama inherent in Hitchcock's style—show precisely how politically naive Hitchcock could be. This brings us to the *really* silly side of Hitchcock: his homophobia.

Whenever Hitchcock reaches for his pet theme of "psychological disorders" you can almost invariably expect him to deal with *sexual* disorders, and this in turn usually means crazy—and I mean crazy—dykes and faggots, like creepy Judith Anderson burning down dear old Manderley in *Rebecca* or heartless Robert Walker, gutless Anthony Perkins, and sneaky Barry Forster murdering people at the drop of a hat in *Strangers on a Train, Psycho,* and *Frenzy.*

Any thoughtful examination of Hitchcock's cinema reveals that among his various blind spots, gay sexuality was his supreme bête noire, and that Hitch was a supreme fag baiter. Whenever he dealt with homosexuality (and he did surprisingly often), his artistic sense deserted him entirely, and the *other* Alfred Hitchcock emerged. The infuriating nastiness of Hitchcock's most homophobic films lies in his willingness—even eagerness—to strike low blows and hold up crowd-pleasing scapegoats. This is Hitchcock the demagogue. This is the Hitchcock whom Charles Higham correctly denounces as "a practical joker, a cunning and sophisticated cynic" given to "pitiless mockery."[1] This is the Hitchcock whom David Thomson rightly castigates as "a man of very mundane, shallow moral and social attitudes" and of whom he observes "there is an artistic timidity in Hitchcock that, having put the audience through it, must allow them to come to terms with the experience. But his own personality is withdrawn, cold, insecure, and uncharitable."[2] In the case of *Strangers on a Train,* one might add that he is frankly vicious. Try sitting through the scene in which *sweet* Ruth Roman pleads with bitchy, *sadistic* Robert Walker (wearing a flamboyant dressing gown) without getting a bit hot under the collar. Or listen as Walker, all diabolical sultriness (becoming a sort of cat in heat on Quaaludes) cruises Farley Granger with such prissy gems as "I've had a *strenuous* evening" and "I'm afraid I don't know what a '*smoocher*' is." It seems incredible that no one has yet stepped forward to denounce Hitchcock's homophobia. (Vito Russo in *The Celluloid Closet* has to an extent now done the job, but still he sees *Rope* and *Strangers on a Train* as instances of Hollywood's homophobia, and not as an integral part of Hitchcock himself.) Of course, the willingness to overlook this aspect of Hitchcock's work must have something to do with the fact that until recently homophobia was considered a fairly respectable trait, at least among the majority of critics and viewers. But that an artist of Hitchcock's caliber should have abused gays so wantonly and played so deliberately to the gallery seems incongruous and even startling. Homophobia was the conventional wisdom of the day, and he believed and endorsed it; in a surprising number of films he crammed it down the public's throat.

Yet how can one make sense of the fact that even highly intelligent and educated Hitchcock critics like Robin Wood, Eric Rohmer, or Claude Chabrol also condone his homophobia? Robin Wood's observations on *North by Northwest* and that film's characterization of Leonard (played by Robert Landau at his sneaky, creepy best) offer an interesting case in point. Leonard is Philip Vandamm's (James Mason's) private secretary. He is also gay and, significantly, one of the most reprehensible villains Hitchcock ever produced. At the climax of the film, Leonard responds to Cary Grant's impassioned plea for help (he and Eva Marie Saint are about to fall to their deaths) by hesitating for an instant and then cold-bloodedly stepping on Grant's hand. He is at that moment of the film nothing less than a monster. Under other dramatic circumstances this might be acceptable (fiction contains many such monsters), except that in this instance we come to understand that for Hitchcock, Leonard is a monster *because* he is gay. Wood comments on Leonard in his book, *Hitchcock's Films:* "Before the Mount Rushmore climax, we have Thornhill's [Grant's] attempt to rescue Eve [Saint] from Vandamm's house, Vandamm's discovery of her nature, and his plans to dispose of her over the sea. Leonard is built up here as the incarnation of destruction and negation. His motive is sexual jealousy—jealousy of Eve, his rival for Vandamm. He discloses the truth about Eve in a melodramatic and vindictive way by 'shooting' Vandamm with her blank-loaded revolver."[3] Clearly Leonard is another entry in Hitchcock's gallery of fiendish faggots.

Wood's study of Hitchcock is extraordinarily insightful and stimulating with the glaring exception that he neither challenges nor disputes Hitchcock's homophobia. The extent to which he accepts it is evident in these comments on *Psycho:* "The attic, Norman's own bedroom, represents the sick man's conscious mental development; strange confusion of the childish and the adult, cuddly toys, grubby unmade bed, a record of the *Eroica* symphony; the unexplained nature of all this carries the suggestion that what we see are mere superficial hints of the underlying mysteries, a suggestion confirmed by the clasped, untitled book which Lila [Vera Miles] never opens (a Bates family album?). Consequently we accept Norman more than ever as a human being, with all the human being's complex potentialities. The cellar gives us the hidden sexual springs of his behavior: there Lila finds Mrs. Bates. It is a fruit-cellar—the fruit is insisted upon in the mother's macabre joke about being 'fruity': the source of fruition and fertility become rotten."[4]

So Wood is prepared to accept homosexuality as "the source of fruition and fertility become rotten," and though he's perfectly correct in interpreting Hitchcock's homophobic "fruit" diagnosis of the case, how could he possibly bring himself to accept it? That an artist of Hitchcock's talent and a critic of Robin Wood's perceptiveness should prove themselves such inveterate yahoos on the subject of gay sex says a good deal about the respectability that homophobia enjoyed until fairly recently. (Wood's book was published in 1965.) It tells us how deeply the homophobic mystique has entrenched itself in Western culture and how pathologically squeamish that culture is in regard to sexual gratification (a squeamishness often camouflaged by a moral pose). Finally, it suggests how this "raw nerve" in the sexist psychology of Western society can conceivably condemn gays as the last minority to be permitted liberation. Rather than reject Hitchcock's homophobia as the dreadful false note in the work of an important artist, a sort of scatterbrained incursion into the world of eroticism and sensuality and sexual variance—a world Hitchcock knew nothing about and obviously felt threatened by—Robin Wood in *Hitchcock's Films* unfortunately goes right along with him.

Eric Rohmer and Claude Chabrol's *Hitchcock,* written in 1957 and recently translated (1979) by Stanley Hochman, is also considered one of the key works on Hitchcock. In his foreword to the book, Hochman mentions that "most critics have generally acknowledged the importance of this youthful work, even when, like Robin Wood, they ultimately rejected aspects of the rigorously Catholic analyses."[5] Figuring prominently among these aspects of "rigorously Catholic analyses," one is stupefied to encounter Rohmer and Chabrol's unqualified agreement with Hitchcock's homophobic hypothesis (which, when you get right down to it, is a sort of sexual polemic that attempts to do for homosexuality what *Reefer Madness* tried to do for marijuana).

Although it can hardly be said that Wood rejects Chabrol and Rohmer's hard-line "Catholic" endorsement of Hitchcock's homophobia, Wood nevertheless seems positively Unitarian by comparison. Here are Rohmer and Chabrol discussing *Murder*, a 1930 British Hitchcock film: "In *Murder*, the homosexual kills when he is unmasked. Unlike the protagonists in *Rope*, or Bruno Anthony [Robert Walker] in *Strangers on a Train*, he considers himself abnormal and is aware that his vice is a defect. But he is also incapable of loving, and he is interested only in escaping the consequences of his crime. When Hitchcock gets around to probing the problem of homosexuality in the two other films, we will become aware that his condemnation of homosexuality is justly based on the impossibility of true homosexual love; since this love is only an imitation, it is condemned to nonreciprocity. Diana loves the homosexual, since she allows herself to be convicted in his stead, but the homosexual doesn't love her, since he permits her to do so."[6]

The use of the term *the homosexual*—one assumes the poor wretch *has* a name—gives us a good idea of just how clinically Chabrol and Rohmer view "the problem," and their Hardy Boys clinical approach is not unfaithful to Hitchcock's own. On the back cover of *Hitchcock,* we have *Library Journal's* assurance that the book is "a classic deserving inclusion in all film collections." This depends on how much youthfulness one is prepared to accept. The following paragraph is far too youthful for my taste, but it does reveal what amounts to Hitchcock's homophobic militancy. Speaking once again of *Murder:* "Obviously this is an absolutely classic detective plot but it is heightened by a very important and characteristic detail: there is no doubt that the assassin's true secret is not that he is a half-breed in the ordinary sense but a sexual half-breed, a homosexual. Hitchcock makes no attempt to hide his intentions: he shows us the character's feminine characteristics (he pats his hair, studies himself in the mirror, pirouettes, becomes hysterical) and even shows him to us dressed as a woman! Once this is understood, the film is seen in an unexpected light: it is the first panel of a triptych that includes *Rope* and *Strangers on a Train*, a triptych that illustrates the problem of homosexuality from three points of view: moral in *Murder,* realistic in *Rope*, and psychoanalytic in *Strangers on a Train*."[7] That Chabrol and Rohmer are so impressed by the profundity of Hitchcock's idiotic prejudice further illustrates how fashionable such notions once were.

Psycho and *Frenzy* are only slightly toned down extensions of the earlier homophobic "triptych"; they remain surprisingly faithful to Hitchcock's recurring fascination for crazy killer faggots. Actually, the soft-pedaled, almost subliminal homophobia in *Psycho* is more destructive and insidious than the more blatant expressions of *Strangers on a Train* and the other earlier works. In fact, one can almost dismiss these as quaint, whereas *Psycho*, being a less crude, less explicit formulation of the same homophobic hysteria, tends to sneak its message across rather more subtly.

At the beginning of *Psycho*, Norman Bates is depicted as a very sympathetic character, but he rapidly becomes merely pathetic, then disturbed, defensive, and finally, more and more spectacularly demented until he is reduced to little more than a raving thing. By the end of the film he has become little more than a convenient plot device. Norman Bates/the Mother is a sleazy gimmick in the scenario of a psychological horror movie: the faggot as Frankenstein's monster. *Psycho* is a remarkably tasteless movie. In the final sequence, we are shown Norman Bates unmasked, and lo and behold, we are back with our hysterical, hair-patting sexual half-breed in (psychotic) drag and Hitchcock is back in full fag-baiting stride.

In the police station just before the final sequence, the audience is invited to share several jokes about Norman. When the guard brings Norman a blanket "because he feels a chill," we don't see Norman, but we hear him as the guards are shown leaving his cell. The audience invariably laughs nervously when they hear Norman's lisping high-pitched "Thank you." Hitchcock is asking us to contemplate the darkly comic spectacle of this refugee from a fruit cellar who now speaks with a woman's voice.

Moments earlier, John Gavin, representing something like American manhood incarnate and struggling to overcome his distaste, asks, "Why was he . . . *dressed* like that?" Another of the men present blurts out, "He's a transvestite." But Simon Oakland, who plays the wily psychologist obviously delighted by the complexities of the whole business, is a real stickler for detail; he replies, "Not *exactly.*" This ridiculous scene isn't the flaw that some critics feel spoils an otherwise thrilling movie. Ludicrous as it is, it is crucial to the story that Hitchcock is telling, and above all it is crucial in that Hitchcock takes the scene absolutely seriously. It's another "psychological panel" in his work, and it proves just how absurd his notion of homicidal transvestism really is.

Unfortunately, *Psycho* ends up telling most of the audience exactly what they want to hear on the subject of "fruits," and the cultural harassment of one section of the audience becomes cultural fodder for another.

As Donald Spoto points out in his fascinating book *The Dark Side of Genius: The Life of Alfred Hitchcock,* Hitchcock came from a background of orthodox victorian Catholicism. As an artist his films make sense essentially in spiritual and poetic terms. He was a filmmaker in the tradition of Dreyer, Bresson, Mizo-gouchi, and, in a sense, Welles. He was certainly enough of an artist to keep his spiritual convictions from interfering in any way with the integrity of his best work. In his mediocre "neurotic" films, however, it seems fair to assume that his strict Catholic views do exert their influence. His persistent equation of homosexuality with moral depravity *and* pathological derangement is something that only an amateur moralistic psychoanalyst could devise. It's astonishing that a man of Hitchcock's genius could have embraced and expounded such tripe. His view of homosexuality remained every bit as inflexible as that of the Catholic Church itself, and as late as *Frenzy* (1971), we still see the disturbed gay man (Barry Foster) who is eventually treacherous, loathesome, pathetically comic, and who comes complete with a mother fixation and a barely disguised crush on Jon Finch (a toned-down replay of Robert Walker's sinful passion for Farley Granger in *Strangers*). What follows, of course, are horrendous necktie stranglings of women. Had Hitchcock actually argued that under certain circumstances and with certain personalities, sexual *repression* can lead to violence, his work would hold up under scrutiny, but he argues emphatically that sexual *perversion* (often gay sexuality per se) can, and seemingly always does, lead to violence.

As we look back from the vantage point of the early 1980s, we can see precisely how consistently sexist, racist, and homophobic the American cinema has been. Vito Russo's *The Celluloid Closet* amply documents the rivers of gay blood that Hollywood has had occasion to wash its hands in. From our standpoint today it's decidedly unnerving to examine such evidence, to calculate the extent to which we have come to exist in a cultural fantasy devised by a racist, heterosexist economic elite. Popular culture has, in retrospect, assumed the character of a deliberate political contrivance from which, in this century, virtually no aspect of public life has been exempt. Racism, sexism, and homophobia all serve the same ends, as Paul Goodman so diligently tried to get across, and their repeated, often congruent occurrence in popular fiction is not the result of some tragic fortuitous misunderstanding, but a consistently implemented, expedient cultural program. So be it; let the buyer beware. But to encounter such wanton disregard for truth and justice in the work of an artist of Hitchcock's talent and integrity is disappointing to say the least. He was a difficult and paradoxical filmmaker whom it seems necessary both to bury *and* to praise.

That a film such as *Cruising* was denounced at the time of its production and distribution is important, but because William Friedkin is a hack, nothing he has made—or ever will make—will have long-term significance. But Hitchcock is an artist whose work is continually screened and constantly finding new audiences. It is because Hitchcock's art *is* art that it is necessary to stress its limitations, weaknesses, and occasional lapses into unqualified balderdash.

In his essay "An Open Letter to Surrealists Everywhere," Henry Miller makes the following observation: "In every age, just as in every life worthy of the name, there is the effort to reestablish that equilibrium which is disturbed by the power and tyranny which a few great individuals exercise over us. . . . It has to do with the adoption of a creative attitude towards life. One of the most effective ways in which it expresses itself is in the killing off of the tyrannical influences wielded over us by those who are dead. It consists not in denying these exemplars, but in absorbing them, assimilating them, and eventually surpassing them."[8]

A nonsectarian "Amen!" to that, and goodnight, Hitch, wherever you are. Thank you for always hating TV commercials, thank you for *Notorious, Marnie,* and *The Wrong Man,* and for that glorious joyride through hell called *Vertigo.*

Notes

1   Charles Higham, *The Art of the American Film 1900–1971* (New York: Anchor, 1973), 227.

2   David Thomson, *A Biographical Dictionary of Film* (New York: William Morrow, 1976), 249.

3   Robin Wood, *Hitchcock's Films,* 2nd revised edition (London: A. S. Barnes, 1969), 110.

4   Ibid., 120.

5   Eric Rohmer and Claude Chabrol, *Hitchcock: The First Forty-Four Films,* trans. Stanley Hochman (New York: Ungar, 1979), vii.

6   Ibid., 27–28.

7   Ibid., 27.

8   Henry Miller, "An Open Letter to Surrealists Everywhere," in *The Cosmological Eye* (New York: New Directions, 1939), 152–53.

Letter to the Editor

My attention has been drawn to the article "Hitchcock's Homophobia" by John Hepworth (Issue 64) in which both Hitchcock's films and my book on them are under attack.

While it is important that the reactionary aspects of my early work be exposed and condemned, I think Hepworth should, in fairness, have acknowledged the radical change in my position (both critical and personal) since *Hitchcock's Films* was written. In view of the fact that my work for the past decade has been consistently dedicated to the raising of feminist and gay issues within the field of film criticism (centered on, but by no means restricted to, my "official" coming-out article, "Responsibilities of a Gay Film Critic," *Film Comment,* January 1978), I think many readers may be surprised by Hepworth's description of me as "an inveterate yahoo on the subject of gay sex."

As for Hitchcock, Hepworth reads a gay subtext in his films far more widely than I do, seeming to assume that "sexually disturbed" equals "homosexual." It had certainly never occurred to me that Barry Foster in *Frenzy* was supposed to be gay (his "barely concealed crush on Jon Finch" looks, to an Englishman, like an idiosyncratic British working-class bonhomie). Nor have I ever considered Norman Bates in *Psycho* as a gay character. I'm afraid I cannot accept the (dubious) compliment that I was "perfectly correct in interpreting Hitchcock's homophobic 'fruit' diagnosis of the case." When I wrote *Hitchcock's Films* in the early sixties (which feels like half a century ago), struggling, under extreme social pressures, to sustain an identity as a happily married family man and schoolteacher within a British middle-class environment, I had no contact with gay culture whatever and absolutely no acquaintance with the slang connotations of "fruit": no double entendre was intended. (It is, in fact, *Mrs.* Bates, not Norman, who is alleged to be "fruity," in a context that has nothing to do with homosexuality.)

I think there *is* a homophobic element in what one might call the Hitchcock "complex," but it is not very helpful to decontextualize it as Hepworth does: it makes sense only in relation to Hitchcock's treatment of *heterosexual* relationships. Hitchcock was unable to detach himself clearly from patriarchal structures and assumptions, yet his work as a whole amounts to one of the most acute and devastating analyses we have of the strains, anxieties, violence, and psychic destructiveness necessary to maintain patriarchal domination. This doesn't *excuse* the homophobia, but it certainly helps explain it. It also explains why a character like Bruno in *Strangers on a Train* is clearly the center of the film's energies, a far more attractive and fascinating character than the shallow, bland, and opportunistic "hero."

Finally, may I draw Hepworth's attention to one character in the Hitchcock oeuvre who is strongly signified as gay and is presented entirely positively—indeed, as the film's most admirable character? Louis Jourdan in *The Paradine Case* is the only character to retain his integrity, even at the cost of suicide: a suicide motivated not by the fact of being gay but by his feeling dishonored by the allegation (via the film's nominal "hero," Gregory Peck) that he has betrayed and murdered the man to whom he was devoted.

Robin Wood

John Hepworth Responds

I appreciate Robin Wood's desire to set the record straight, but strongly resent his unfair suggestion that he's been misrepresented.

Of Psycho's Norman Bates, Wood did write, "The cellar gives us the *hidden sexual springs of his behavior* (my italics): there Lila finds Mrs. Bates. It is the *fruit*-cellar (his italics)—the fruit is insisted upon in the mother's macabre joke about being 'fruity': the source of fruition and fertility become rotten." I have a difficult time squaring this with Wood's statement in his letter that "I had no contact with gay culture whatever and absolutely no acquaintance with the slang connotations of 'fruit': no double entendre was intended. (It is, in fact, Mrs. Bates, not Norman, who is alleged to be 'fruity,' in a context that has nothing to do with homosexuality.)" For at least two generations virtually any eight-year-old in the English-speaking world could explain in a second what the word "fruit" signifies. Along with "homo," "faggot," and "queer," the word "fruit" has long been a popular appellation for a homosexual. What *non*-homosexual "hidden sexual springs" did Wood have in mind when he argued the significance of the whole rotten fruit business?

Wood's letter clearly states, "While it is important that the reactionary aspects of my early work be exposed and condemned, I think Hepworth should, in fairness, have acknowledged the radical change in my position (both critical and personal) since *Hitchcock's Films* was written." Yet almost in the same breath, Wood asserts, "Nor have I ever considered Norman Bates in *Psycho* as a gay character. I'm afraid I cannot accept the (dubious) compliment that I was 'perfectly correct in interpreting Hitchcock's homophobic "fruit" diagnosis of the case.' " Which is it to be—have I or haven't I misinterpreted Wood? There is something muddled about Wood's damning-with-faint-praise evaluation of my article. It shouldn't be so difficult for a film scholar and gay activist to decide whether or not the article has value.

The Murderous

Gays

Hitchcock's Homophobia

Robin Wood

I t has been often noted that the figure of the psychopath that recurs through-out Hitchcock's work is sometimes coded (with more or less explicitness) as gay (or in one case lesbian). There is the "half-caste" transvestite of *Murder!;* the two young murderers of *Rope;* Mrs. Danvers, of whose (presumably late) husband we learn nothing, in *Rebecca;* Bruno Anthony in *Strangers on a Train.* Some have sought, with far less incontrovertible evidence, to extend the list to include the Uncle Charlie of *Shadow of a Doubt* and Norman Bates; in which case we may as well add the Bob Rusk of *Frenzy.* These latter instances seem to rest on little except popular (and generally discredited) heterosexist mythology: one is prob-ably gay if one shows traces of effeminacy, had a close relationship with one's mother, or hates and murders women. However, in questioning whether the term *gay* is applicable to all of these characters, I don't wish to suggest that they are not all closely interlinked, or that they don't relate to some permanent com-ponent of the Hitchcock psyche (as embodied in the films), of which both repressed homosexuality and its inevitable corollary homophobia may form a significant part.

It is necessary at this point to make explicit certain assumptions (which, de-riving from the Freudian psychoanalytical tradition, are not unarguable or uni-versally accepted, though I personally find them convincing) that will form the basis of the argument I wish to build. They will already be familiar to my readers (notably from the essay on *Raging Bull* in *Hollywood from Vietnam to Reagan*);[1] I apologize for the repetition, but cannot take the familiarity for granted. What is at issue here is not simply the meaning and nature of Hitchcock's homophobia, but its relation to the treatment of heterosexual relations in his films. These, then, are the principles on which the ensuing speculations are based:

Constitutional Bisexuality   According to Freud, the human infant is already a sexual being, but the sexuality is at this stage indeterminate, both in its means (the various erogenous zones) and its ends (object choice). Freud used the term *polymorphous perversity* to describe this (it seems to many of us) highly desirable and enviable state of being. It is not a felicitous choice of words: surely, if the infant's "polymorphous" eroticism is natural and innate, it is the "normal" (i.e., socialized) adult who is "perverse" (literally "turned aside"). For practical, social/political purposes in relation to our culture in its current phase of evolution, the crucial implication of this is that we are all, innately, bisexual, at least in potential. This potential is, of course, very infrequently realized in our adult lives, greatly to our psychic impoverishment and to the detriment of relations between the sexes.

Masculinity/Femininity   Not identical with, but closely related to and paralleling, Freud's discovery of constitutional bisexuality, is his perception that, in the infant, the characteristics our culture labels *masculine* and *feminine* are by no means the exclusive property of male and female respectively: little girls have as much claim to "masculinity" (activeness, forcefulness, assertiveness, aggression, dominance, etc.) as little boys, and little boys exhibit the "feminine" traits (passivity, gentleness, submissiveness, sensitivity, emotional expression, etc.) as part of their natural human legacy. There is, that is to say, no reason whatever to suppose that these apparently—culturally—opposed characteristics are in any way "naturally" tied to the facts of anatomical difference or develop organically out of it. The relation of this to bisexuality is not entirely clear (though one can scarcely doubt that there *is* one): it is a readily observable fact of our culture that heterosexual men can exhibit markedly "feminine" qualities, and that gay men can be aggressively "masculine." We can, however, assert that a complete human being would be one capable of expressing both transgender and bisexual tendencies: our society would become one within which infinite variation, infinite choices, were possible.

Repression   If not nature, then culture: there has to be *some* way of accounting, not only for the sorting out of human beings into heterosexual/homosexual, masculine/feminine, but also for the disappearance, from most people's conscious lives, of even the traces of tendencies regarded as inappropriate to their socialized makeup. Patriarchy cannot endure ambiguity (or infinite possibilities of variation): it requires "real men" and "real women" for the maintenance of its power and of the central social unit through which its power is transmitted and perpetuated, the family. This hatred of ambiguity applies equally to sexuality and gender, uniting the two streams of development (or, more precisely, *arrested* development). But of course it is not enough to say to the infant "Don't be bisexual" or "Don't be masculine (or feminine)": even if she or he obeyed, the threat of conscious desire and conscious choice would remain. Hence patriarchal cultures have evolved (with innumerable local variations, the terrain of anthropologists) those social and psychic processes that Freud described so brilliantly (if not always accurately, and with his regrettable tendency to universalize the culturally specific): the Oedipus and castration complexes and their resolution, the "oedipal trajectory" that guides the boy to his identification with the father (actual and symbolic) and the girl to her identification with the mother. If it is *successful* (a word that, in this context, becomes painfully ironic), the completion of the trajectory involves the repression of the individual's homosexual tendencies, which become *literally* unthinkable. For men, it also involves the repression of *femininity*, that collection of human attributes (often morally admirable) that is henceforth associated with the "weaker" sex and despised as inferior and "unmanly." It is very dangerous to regard evolution as natural, inevitable, unchangeable, and irreversible. True, it embodies a response to human needs, but those needs are always culturally and historically specific, not an irreducible and immutable "fact of life." Often, the needs change or disappear altogether, and we are left with an evolved response to them that is archaic, culturally useless, or actively harmful in its regressiveness. One can certainly argue that this is now the case with the whole bag and baggage of repression, the oedipal trajectory, castration complexes, "traditional" family structures, gender construction, homophobia. It is amazing that it has taken civilization so long explicitly and consciously to challenge this entire process of social/psychic structuration, and very exciting to be alive in an age when the challenge has at last been uttered (by women, by gays, and, increasingly, by heterosexual men).

Homophobia   What is repressed is never annihilated: it survives in the unconscious as a constant potential threat, capable of resurfacing in response to changing circumstances or particular stimuli. Hence the explanation of that otherwise inexplicable malady homophobia. In every homophobe, the repressed homosexual tendencies are dangerously close to the surface of the unconscious, yet their existence must never be acknowledged. The homophobe's fear and hatred of homosexuals is essentially a projection outward of his fear and hatred of tendencies within himself of which he dare not permit himself to become aware. Every expression of homophobia is therefore revealing: one may look in confident expectation for the traces of homosexuality.

Men's Hatred of Women   Again, the parallel holds. There is always a close relation between the heterosexual male's attitude to gays and his attitude to women:

to put it simply, one will expect a homophobe to treat women very badly. As with bisexuality, so with the man's femininity: what is repressed is not destroyed but constantly threatens to return, and must be disowned and repudiated. The word *love* is always problematic, because it means so many different things (in different cultures, and to different individuals within the same culture). One might suggest, however, that authentic love must always have as a major component the ability to identify. Only a man who freely accepts and expresses his own femininity can truly love a woman: otherwise, "love" becomes perverted into the drive to dominate, possess, and if necessary destroy. In extreme cases, the psychic violence—the acts of repression demanded by the oedipal trajectory—that males in our culture are conditioned to inflict on themselves in the interests of socialization and "normality," will find their external manifestation in acts of physical violence against women.

The above is offered as a (provisional) blueprint for the exploration of Hitchcock's films and, through them, of our civilization in its contemporary phase of evolution. It is not intended completely to *explain* the films: if it did so, they could not be considered great or particularly significant works (beyond the significance necessarily inherent in any cultural artifact). The films—and the "Hitchcock" they embody, related to but not necessarily identical with Alfred Hitchcock the human individual—relate very intimately to the blueprint but do not neatly fit it: therein, precisely, lie their greatness and fascination. Their importance resides in the intensity and complexity with which they dramatize the impossible strains, tensions, and conflicts inherent in my psychoanalytical outline. It is this that gives them their cultural centrality.

In every case history that he explored, Freud discovered, at some level of the analysis, the traces—the scars—of repressed homosexuality, and it seems clearer to us than it was to him that the repression (not the homosexuality itself) was intimately related to the sources of the disorder—in many instances *was* the source. To explore Hitchcock's films is to explore issues that are of crucial and increasingly urgent importance to the future of our civilization; the films *demand* a resolution that they themselves can never reach, leaving us with that often noted "nasty taste" in the form of unresolved tensions.

The Dark Side of Gender Construction

Donald Spoto's *The Dark Side of Genius: The Life of Alfred Hitchcock* is an extremely unpleasant book but is a very useful one: far more useful, to my mind, than its predecessor, *The Art of Alfred Hitchcock*.[2] The project embodied in the two books (considered together) seems somewhat perverse (though only "normally" so, within the terms of our culture): the idolization of the "art" of Hitchcock followed by the thoroughgoing denigration of the man who created it. To borrow a title from Molly Haskell, Spoto moves abruptly "from reverence to rape," illustrating yet again the very close psychic proximity of those two apparently opposed human activities. Spoto's book is undoubtedly ungenerous to the point of the meanminded: he certainly sees to it that "the evil that men do lives after them, / The good is oft interred with their bones." He acknowledges the nice things that Hitchcock did, but perfunctorily, glossing over them in a sentence or two; the nasty things are lingered over, described in detail and with relish. If one refuses to be alienated by this (and it takes a degree of conscious determination and resistance), then the biographical material Spoto presents becomes quite fascinating in its resonances (in relation to the films, to the culture, and to the relation between the two).[3] The book's central problem lies in Spoto's failure to provide a theoretical and psychoanalytical framework adequate to *explain* the material: there is plenty of "pop" psychologizing, always at the level of the individual, but no attempt at a psychoanalytical theory of culture that would encompass both the life and the films.

Before attempting to reread some aspects of the material Spoto presents, I need to add one further psychoanalytic observation to the schema set forth above, one that, while not without a general relevance, is more obviously specific to the Hitchcock "case." When I wrote *Hitchcock's Films,*[4] I suggested that the sense of precariousness and unpredictability, that something terrible, uncontrollable, and perhaps inexplicable may erupt at any moment within the most seemingly normal and secure environment and circumstances—the phenomenon that achieves its most explicit embodiment in *The Birds*—is central to the Hitchcockian worldview. I did not recognize at that time that what I was describing was the paranoid mentality (my own, perhaps, at that period of my life, when my personal identification with the Hitchcock worldview—as I perceived it—was at its most intense and least distanced). I wrote at length on the implications of paranoia, using Freud's account of the Schreber case, in the essay on *Raging Bull* cited above, and I don't wish to reiterate my points here in detail. All that requires to be reiterated is Freud's finding (confirmed by both Jung and Ferenczi) that *in all cases* "a defence against a homosexual wish was clearly recognizable at the very centre of the conflict which underlay the disease, and that it was in an attempt to master an unconsciously reinforced current of homosexuality that they had all of them come to grief." It seems logical, in fact, to interpret male paranoia in terms of a *double* bind, its source not only in the repression of homosexuality but in the repression of femininity, its consequence the hatred, fear, and distrust not only of other men (as potential, hence threatening, love objects) but of women also (as the embodiments of the femininity that must be disowned), the consequence of that consequence the possible eruption of violence against both sexes. *Raging Bull* perhaps offers the cinema's most radical and comprehensive examination of this, but Hitchcock's work as a whole (and his life, insofar as it is relevant to the work) seems richly suggestive in relation to these ideas.

The testimonies and biographical data that Spoto presents, with reference to Hitchcock's attitude to homosexuality and homosexuals, add up to evidence that is characteristically complex and contradictory: the attitude certainly was not simple, the available (admittedly rather meager) evidence suggesting an ambivalence that parallels and is closely related to the ambivalence toward women, exactly as the repression of homosexuality parallels the repression of femininity. On the one hand we are told that Hitchcock was at ease with gay people: Spoto's source, identified only as "an actress who knew him well," is quoted as saying, "Some people might be surprised by this . . . but Hitchcock was always quite comfortable with homosexual or bisexual people. He always told his actors that they really had to be part masculine and part feminine in order to get inside any other character. Subjectivity, he felt, and feeling, transcended gender."[5] The remarks take on a particular resonance, not only in relation to the films themselves, but in relation to the whole complex controversy about spectator identification that has raged in film theory since Laura Mulvey's "Visual Pleasure and Narrative Cinema" was published in 1975.[6] Spoto also conjectures, reasonably enough, that, with his sexually repressive childhood as background, Hitchcock was intrigued by all forms of deviancy. There is also Spoto's account of the meeting with Murnau, with Hitchcock "not even comfortable in the presence of women, let alone homosexual men."[7] Being at ease and being intrigued are not exactly synonymous, and being uncomfortable is congruent with neither: one can already discern, in the incompatible but not necessarily inaccurate descriptions, the characteristic tension between identification and distance. The ambivalence is confirmed by Spoto's accounts of Hitchcock's methods of dealing with, and attitudes toward, the gay men with whom he inevitably shared a prolonged proximity: gay actors.

During 1925–27 Hitchcock directed two films starring Ivor Novello, *The Lodger* and *Downhill:* Novello was noted publicly for his extreme, somewhat "feminine," good looks, and privately for his relative openness about being actively gay. During the same period, two things occurred that proved of great significance both in Hitchcock's personal and professional development, the significance having as much to do with the construction, and exploitation, of a public image as with a private life style: (*a*) he put on a great deal of weight; (*b*) he married Alma Reville. One does not wish to reduce the complexities of such occurrences to a single motivation: obviously, one can have ten different, perhaps contradictory, motivations (conscious and unconscious) for getting married. But one contributing psychoanalytical explanation is tempting and plausible (if purely conjectural): that, on some level, they can be interpreted as defenses against the feelings aroused by Novello. Why, in fact, *did* Hitchcock put on so much weight? No clear medical evidence has been produced, as far as I know. There seems to be abundant testimony that Hitchcock, throughout his life, longed to be attractive to women and experienced agonies of frustration over his fatness. The psychoanalytical evidence seems to point in the opposite direction, to a hysterical resistance to being physically attractive to *anyone.*

In 1952 Hitchcock directed *I Confess,* starring Montgomery Clift. There are perfectly plausible ways of rationalizing Hitchcock's consistent hostility to Clift: the "Method" acting, the neuroticism, the heavy drinking. More than plausible, they are clearly *sufficient,* if one wishes to look no further. Yet one wonders. Novello and Clift were certainly not the only homosexual men with whom Hitchcock worked, but they were certainly the two most physically attractive.

It is at this point that my present theme—Hitchcock's reactions to gay actors— bleeds inevitably into my next: his notorious practical jokes. All of these were clearly acts of aggression; they appear to have been distributed roughly equally, against women (including Hitchcock's own daughter) and against men, though it seems plain that men were the victims of the two ugliest. One may invoke here (it is central to my thesis, sketchy as that thesis admittedly is) Michael Kaufman's essay in *Beyond Patriarchy,* "The Construction of Masculinity and the Triad of Male Violence"—against women, against other men, against oneself.[8] Kaufman's theme is precisely that this triad of violence *characterizes* what we in our culture call *masculinity:* it is not the exception but the rule, if not necessarily on the physical level then on the psychic.

Novello and Clift were both the objects of Hitchcock's "jokes"—the essential seriousness of which one scarcely needs Freud to illuminate: Novello in a very mild way, Clift arousing Hitchcock's "sense of humor" at its most vicious. With Novello the joke took the form of photographing him (in *The Lodger*) with a flowerpot behind him, so that it appeared that the flowerpot was on his head, making him look ridiculous: it is easy to read this as a defense against Novello's beauty. With Clift the "joke" consisted in daring him, already very drunk, to drink a whole beaker of brandy in one gulp: Spoto tells us that the actor "fell to the floor, face down, in a perilous alcoholic stupor." A somewhat extreme revenge for the crime of "Method" acting.

The cruelest of all Hitchcock's practical jokes had for its victim a property man. Spoto is tantalizingly unspecific about this—presumably no more precise information is available. The man is nameless, and no offense that could even remotely justify the joke is presented; it is also not clear when the incident occurred, though it was somewhere in the late twenties. Hitchcock bet the property man a week's salary "that he would be too frightened to spend a whole night chained to a camera in a deserted and darkened studio." Before departing Hitchcock offered him a beaker of brandy (the link with the Clift "joke," across a period of about twenty-five years, is obvious), which the man eagerly accepted. It was "laced . . . with the strongest available laxative." What one most wants to know, of course, is whether the unfortunate victim was gay, sexually attractive, or both.

Yet together with these displays of aggression against gay men goes a tendency to identify with them. I shall return to this in discussing certain characters in the films, but certain casting choices are also intriguing. There is a continual sense that Hitchcock identified masochistically with his villain victims, and two instances are supported by specific hints. There is the sacristan murderer (O. E. Hasse) of *I Confess:* Hitchcock, at the last minute, gave his wife the name "Alma" and wrote in dialogue that has startlingly personal overtones ("Where is my Alma?"—he has just killed her!—"I loved her. It made me cry to see her work so hard"). And there is the case of Alexander Sebastian in *Notorious,* who, Hitchcock says, was the one who really loved Ingrid Bergman (as, according to Spoto, did Hitchcock himself). Spoto suggests that O. E. Hasse was gay; he also reveals that the actor Hitchcock originally wanted for Sebastian was Clifton Webb.

Many of the victims of the practical jokes were women, and one must connect these relatively harmless (though frequently unkind, embarrassing, and malicious) acts of aggression with the violence (physical and psychic) against women enacted in the films, and with the *real* ordeal inflicted on Tippi Hedren during the filming of *The Birds* (an ordeal that, as Spoto describes it, evinces a powerful obsessional drive on Hitchcock's part). That there is another side to this—an ambivalence of which the tension merely carries to its extreme a predominant characterizing feature of our culture—will I hope already have been suggested by my accounts of *Blackmail* and *Notorious:* in the films, at least—and it is the films, not the private life, that should be our concern—Hitchcock manages frequently to dramatize an identification with his female characters that must deny all but the most singlemindedly sadistic male viewer any simple pleasure in the violences to which they are subjected. The repression of men's femininity is scarcely less damaging than the repression of their homosexuality (and I have posited a strong if not entirely clear connection between the two). Hitchcock's greatness as an artist may ultimately be found to reside in the fact that both of these parallel repressions were in his case—from the point of view of "normality" and "socialization"—only partially "successful."

In the shower murder sequence of *Psycho,* with what/whom does Hitchcock—

hence, through the communicative processes of cinema, the compliant spectator—identify, the hacking, stabbing, phallic knife or the terrified woman? I
think the answer must be "both"—with the addendum that the latter identification is, by virtue of the terms the film has set up, by far the more powerful,
making terror rather than sadistic pleasure the dominant impression. (One could
extend this, clearly enough, to the most impressive, and most profoundly disturbing, scene in *Frenzy*, the rape and murder of Brenda Blaney/Barbara Leigh-
Hunt.) The "triad of male violence," as reproduced in Hitchcock's work, is never
simple: hence its fascination and distinction. The violence against women and
the homophobia must be seen as the products of a terror and panic that are the
logical response, within the terms of our culture, to its construction of gender,
of one of its "unsuccessful" graduates. Against these phenomena must be set
Hitchcock's frequently passionate identification with his female characters, and
his more troubled and ambivalent, partial identification with his gay characters.

But which, in fact, *are* Hitchcock's gay characters? It seems to me a matter far
harder to determine than has often precipitously been claimed. I suggested earlier that the claims largely rest on heterosexist myths about homosexuals (which
Hitchcock may of course have shared). What immensely compounds the problem is the fact that, prior to the sixties, it was impossible openly to acknowledge
even the existence of homosexuality in a Hollywood movie; consequently, homosexuality had to be coded, and discreetly, and coding, even when indiscreet, is
notoriously likely to produce ambiguities and uncertainties.

Is Louis Jourdan in *The Paradine Case* supposed to be gay? He has none of the
iconography of "gayicity," but gayicity has always been a heterosexual construction, in one way or another. Despite the passionate erotic commitment of
Alida Valli, he has remained totally faithful to his "master," Colonel Paradine, his
commitment seeming as passionate as hers, leading to his suicide when accused
of murdering him. As a gay man, I find it far easier to accept him, on this
evidence, as gay or bisexual than, for example, Joseph Cotten in *Shadow of a
Doubt* or Anthony Perkins in *Psycho*. But if this reading is correct (or at least
plausible), he is certainly the gay character in Hitchcock who is neither neurotic
nor villainous, a reason, perhaps, not so much for denying that the character is
gay as for assuming that it didn't occur to Hitchcock that he might be. Such a
reading seems clearly to be outside Hitchcock's understanding of the film: he
wanted Robert Newton for the role, and compares the plot to *Lady Chatterley's
Lover*, which he appears to understand as little as he understands his own film,
seeing Mrs. Paradine as a "nymphomaniac" who degrades herself. But he is here
talking somewhat obsessively about his original concept, which seems totally at
odds with, and much less interesting than, the film he and Selznick actually

made. The attribution of gayness doesn't seriously alter the film's central tragic irony—that a strong and passionate woman has rebelled against patriarchal subservience to the extent of murdering her husband because of her love for a man who can't possibly reciprocate it—but it would certainly intensify it. There can be no doubt that Valli and Jourdan (gay or not) constitute the (hopelessly split) moral center of the film, highlighting the emptiness of the "normality" represented by Gregory Peck and Ann Todd and presided over by the monstrous patriarchal figure of Charles Laughton.

Mrs. Danvers appears to be the only lesbian in the Hitchcock canon. There was to have been a lesbian couple in *The Long Night,* the project on which Hitchcock was working when he died, and his screenwriter, David Freeman, tells us that Hitchcock had qualms about making them villains. The qualms were not shared by Mr. Freeman, who remarks that today "the love that dared not speak its name has become the love that won't shut up."[9] One must take this as his sophisticated and enlightened response to two thousand years of systematic oppression, persecution, and, in certain periods, mass slaughter of gays by the heterosexual power hierarchy, of which the oppression at least continues; or perhaps just as another uneasy giveaway manifestation of homophobia. In any case, Hitchcock's attitude seems to have been more sensitive than his screenwriter's, even though we have it only in the latter's description.

As for "Danny" herself, she is of course both neurotic and a villainess: one cannot gloss over the fact that she tries to drive Joan Fontaine to suicide. Yet how we read her depends to a degree on how we read the film as a whole: is it about the construction of the "good wife" and the ideologically correct heterosexual couple? Or is it about the male's fear of an adult and autonomous female sexuality, which makes it impossible for him to relate to any woman who resists definition as his "little girl"? If the latter, then Rebecca becomes—implicitly—the film's real heroine (and victim), and Mrs. Danvers's devotion to her takes on rather more complex connotations. At the end of the film generic conventions, and their inherited meaning accumulated through a long tradition, become so powerful as virtually to supersede questions of personal authorship (Hitchcock, Selznick). Throughout the literature and cinema of melodrama, women victimized within patriarchy have, recurrently, two recourses: passive—the retreat from patriarchal rationality into madness; and active—fire, as supreme symbol of revolt (Brunnhilde burns down Valhalla). At the end of *Rebecca* (as in *Jane Eyre*) they are magnificently combined: Mrs. Danvers goes insane and burns down Manderley, the symbol of the patriarchal order within which Maxim tried to contain the first Mrs. de Winter and now hopes to live with the second (suitably subordinated if regrettably adult).

It seems to be generally accepted that Bruno Anthony in *Strangers on a Train* is supposed to be gay. "Supposed to be" strikes me as the appropriate way of putting it, because once again the attribution seems to rest more on popular heterosexual myths about gay men than on any actual evidence the film (caught in the constraints of censorship) can provide: he hates his father, is overindulged by his silly mother, seems rather to enjoy murdering women, and dresses flamboyantly. It is probable that Hitchcock thought he was gay. What must be said is that Bruno forms a link in a chain of fascinating, insiduously attractive Hitchcock villains who constantly threaten to "take over" the films in which they appear, not only as the center of interest but even, for all their monstrous actions, as the center of sympathy: Uncle Charlie in *Shadow of a Doubt*, Willy, the U-boat commander, in *Lifeboat*, Brandon in *Rope*, Norman Bates in *Psycho*, the Bob Rusk of *Frenzy*. Only one of these (Brandon) is defined, as unambiguously as censorship allowed, as gay, and no one, as far as I know, has yet attributed homosexuality to Willy. Gayness, that is to say, is by no means an *essential* attribute of the Hitchcock villain. What connects the various links in the chain is either a form of fascism (whether political or personal), or psychopathology, or both: Willy is a Nazi, Charlie and Brandon both subscribe to what one might call pop-Nietzscheanism, and all but Willy are presented as, to varying degrees, psychologically disturbed. All these characters strike me as very personal to Hitchcock, as partial identification figures who must also be repudiated. They enact that obsession with power/domination/control and the dread of its loss (impotence) that pervades his work at every level, from the thematic to the methodological; they also dramatize his sense of horror at this syndrome, his awareness of its harm, both to the self and to others. As for the threat of these characters unbalancing their respective films, it seems to me to be effectively and convincingly countered in all but *Strangers on a Train* (and perhaps *Frenzy*), which remains as a result one of the least satisfying films of Hitchcock's maturity (if also one of the most "brilliant"). Hitchcock clearly has no interest whatever in the characters played by Farley Granger and Ruth Roman, and this lack is inevitably communicated to the audience; their relationship has no emotional weight, their aspirations no moral value. Everything gravitates toward Bruno as the film's magnetic center of attraction: he becomes not only its most complex and detailed character but also its most vulnerable, in his struggle for control and the escalation of his failure to maintain it. I find it difficult to decide exactly how much this has to do with Hitchcock's fascination with sexual/gender ambiguity and how much with the failure of the scenario to provide opportunities to develop an effective counterweight or counteridentification (such as Young Charlie in *Shadow of a Doubt*, the various subsidiary characters and alternative ideological positions of *Lifeboat*, the force of James Stewart's horror and self-horror in *Rope*).

Who Killed David Kentley?

Rope seems to me both generally underrated and in certain crucial aspects widely misperceived. Although it is now universally acknowledged that its two murderers are characterized as gay, very little work has been done on the implications of this: it is treated as if it were a mere incidental. Behind this neglect I suspect lies an overt hostility on the part of gay critics and a "liberal" queasiness on the part of heterosexual ones: no one is likely to praise the film for its promotion of "positive" images of gayness, and on certain obvious levels it can clearly be read as reinforcing harmful derogatory myths of homosexuality (the tendency to associate it with neurosis on the one hand and fascism on the other). It seems to me important, however, to make careful distinctions between a film's (presumed) immediate social effect (i.e., how we deduce, forty years after the event, that it was received by that ill-defined and ultimately indefinable body the general audience), and what we can learn from it now if we attend to it carefully. It is possible to deplore it from the former point of view while finding it immensely valuable from the latter, though we should also be aware that the opposition is a very dangerous one: it may rest on gross bourgeois-intellectual snobbishness as to the nature of the general audience and its responses.

As I want to begin by making a point about the film's famous technique, I must first correct a common erroneous assumption. (I am not the first to correct it, but as the error persists it seems worth correcting again.) Repeatedly, one hears that *Rope* was shot entirely in ten-minute takes. As the film is approximately eighty minutes long, this entails the presumption that it consists of eight shots. Including the credit shot (roughly three minutes; it has to be included because it is clearly "within the diegesis," establishing the environment and culminating in the camera's pan left to show the closed curtains from behind which issues David Kentley's death scream), there are eleven shots. Only three of these (nos. 2, 6, and 9) are over nine minutes long; one (no. 10, culminating in the flinging open of the chest lid by Rupert Cadell/James Stewart) is under five minutes; the last is under six. The remainder are all between seven and eight minutes.

This does not of course detract in the least from the film's technical tour de force; it is the nature of that tour de force that I want to examine. One can define it by saying that *Rope* is the film that most strikingly justifies the antipathy to Hitchcock's work evident in the writings of that most eloquent exponent and theorist of the long take, André Bazin. For *Rope* represents the thorough refusal of all those potentialities of long take/camera movement style that Bazin celebrated in the work of Welles and Wyler. For Bazin, the long take, absence of editing, and use of depth of field played a key role in the cinema's potential objectively to "reveal" reality (see the remarks on Flaherty and Stroheim in "The Evolution of the Language of Cinema"),[10] and to realize itself as the ideal "democratic" art: the spectator is left free to choose which aspect of the image he will concentrate on, his response no longer dictated by the manipulations of Eisensteinian (or Hitchcockian) montage. For Hitchcock, the experimentation of *Rope* is never in the least conceived as in *opposition* to his already highly developed montage technique, but as a possible alternative to and equivalent for it, another means of exerting a total control over the gaze and the emotional response of the viewer. The spectator of *Rope* has no more freedom of choice than the spectator of *Psycho* (who has in any case more freedom than this somewhat simplistic opposition allows for: Hitchcock does not reduce his audiences to mindless zombies). I shall return to this when discussing Hitchcock's relation to Brandon/John Dall.

Rope can be read as associating homosexuality with the unnatural, the sick, the perverse—with "evil" and fascism. Nothing prohibits such a reading; Hitchcock and/or his writers may have thought that was what the film was saying. But what Hitchcock thought the film was saying is of little relevance: *Rope* belongs to a certain point in the evolution of homosexuals as social beings, of societal attitudes to them, of the material and social realities of homosexual existence, and it must now be read within a complicated cultural/historical context.

We may take as a starting point the famous disparaging remark attributed to Renoir, that Hitchcock made a film about two homosexuals and never showed them kissing. The remark is puzzling: Renoir, who had worked at that time in the Hollywood cinema, could scarcely have been unaware of the constraints of censorship. But even beyond that, the remark may miss the point: *Do* Brandon and Philip kiss (off-screen)? *Could* they? They are gay, and they live together, but are they technically lovers? Today, everyone seems ready to answer in the affirmative, and to regard as very naive people who didn't "get" this in 1948. The affirmative answer is quite possibly the correct one: I am not saying that it is wrong, only that we can't be so certain and may be thinking unhistorically.

The problem doubtless derives from the fact that a Hollywood movie made in the late forties could not possibly answer a question that it couldn't even raise. Even the matter of the apartment's sleeping accommodation is kept carefully ambiguous: at one point we are told that the telephone is "in the bedroom," which seems to imply that there is only one (and Janet/Joan Chandler's response, "How cozy," can certainly be taken as the film's most loaded comment on the issue); later, however, we hear of a *second* bedroom (neither is ever shown). It's not simply that *Rope* cannot tell us that the two men sleep together; it also cannot tell us clearly that they *don't*, since that would imply that they might. A parallel instance: five years after *Rope*, Preminger made *The Moon Is Blue*, and ran into massive censorship problems centered on the film's use of the word *virgin*. It is not of course that the word itself was ever regarded as obscene (surely not by the Catholic Legion of Decency!); it is rather that for an unmarried young woman to assert that she is a virgin is instantly to imply the possibility that she might not be.

I offer here another excursion into personal history as (I hope) the most vivid way of reconstructing, for *Rope*'s modern audience, something of the social context within which it was made and received. When *Rope* was released in England in 1948 I was seventeen. I had been having elaborate erotic fantasies about men for at least seven years, and at the age of fifteen I had discovered the word *homosexual* (in a book about Tchaikovsky), and suddenly realized with amazement that there must be other people in the world like myself. I grasped this intellectually; it didn't occur to me that I might ever meet (or perhaps already know) such people. Homosexuality then was not only "the love that dare not speak its name," it was the love whose name could not be spoken, because to speak it would be to acknowledge its existence. *Rope* completely fascinated—even obsessed—me: I went to see it at least three times, which was not common for me in those days. Although I was vaguely aware of the long takes (they had received a lot of publicity), I don't think it was only its technique that fascinated me. I identified almost obsessively, and somewhat morbidly, with Brandon. I had better be careful with the word *identified* here: I have never wanted to strangle anyone (at least not without a strong motive). The identification was super-ficially provoked, no doubt, by the fact that at that time I stuttered very badly (and I found the performance of John Dall, whom I had never seen before, so convincing that I remember believing, until the point in the film where Rupert comments that Brandon "always stutters when he's excited," that it was the *actor*, not the character, who had the speech defect and had heroically controlled it sufficiently to become a movie star). But, deeper than that, the source of the identification was a combination of Brandon's surface assurance and my own awareness of his extreme vulnerability (of which the stutter is of course a betray-ing symptom)—the arrogant assumption of control and power continuously undermined by the impossibility of maintaining it. On the simplest level I was perfectly aware that, in a Hollywood movie, no one can get away with murder, that Brandon would inevitably be exposed, caught, and punished: within such a context, his arrogance and assurance cease to be alienating and become per-versely touching, because one has recognized the illusoriness of their founda-tions. But the vulnerability is also fully dramatized, in the constant tension of Brandon himself and, more important, within his relationship with Philip.

I think it is significant that, despite the fact that I knew I was gay myself, it never occurred to me for a moment that the characters in the film might be: it was, at that time, literally *unthinkable*. If I couldn't believe, emotionally, in the existence of other homosexuals in real life, how could I believe in their existence within a Hollywood film? Yet I am quite certain now that my *unconscious* understanding that Brandon was gay strongly underlined the identification with him, and that it explains the fascination the film held for me. That the identification was largely masochistic, and tended to reinforce all my negative attitudes toward myself, is probably true. Yet no other film had ever given me a character with whom I could identify in quite that way, certainly not a *leading* character. Was I also aware, on some even more deeply unconscious level, that Hitchcock partly identified with Brandon? I could never have formulated it like that at the time, but I don't see how I could *not* have been: the whole film is structured on it.

Rope could not possibly "deal with" the subject of homosexuality, but it seems to me to offer a very precise account of its status and the mental "set" that would logically accompany it at that stage of our history. Of course, Brandon and Philip's milieu is far more sophisticated than was mine. Even allowing for this, however, it is certainly not a milieu in which homosexuality would be acknowledged, let alone accepted. Do Brandon and Philip acknowledge (off-screen) that they are homosexual? Again, the film cannot tell us. Ultimately, perhaps, it doesn't matter. Brandon and Philip may or may not be "lovers" in the technical sense. What the film conveys so impressively, and so accurately, is the intensity with which they hate each other. Doubtless in 1948 there were homosexuals who were able to love: given the social conditions, one might see it as a heroic achievement, a triumph of the human spirit over almost insuperable ideological odds. For, brought up and conditioned to detest ourselves, how could we love each other—each seeing in the other a reflection and constant reminder of his own sickness and evil?

Hence the fascism, hence the murder. Brandon has to see himself as a superior being because he knows that, however intelligent he might be, as a homosexual he is by definition an inferior one. Is the film about homosexuality as a perversion, or about society's perversion of homosexuality? As Brandon and Philip cannot love each other, and must be deeply ashamed of any sexual activities they have performed together, and hate each other for precisely the experiences that should have brought them most intimately together, they commit a sexual act that society, if it forbids and punishes it, at least condones to the extent that it can be represented on the cinema screen before a mass audience: the murder of David Kentley. In 1948 we could not watch Brandon and Philip kiss, or even be told that they ever did so, but we could watch them share the intimate experience of jointly strangling another young man. If the nature of the murder as sexual act (whether as projection of their hatred for the pleasure they share or substitute for the pleasure they dare not) is not clear from the outset, it becomes so from their reminiscence of it as Brandon tries to open the champagne bottle later in the same take. Philip asks him how he felt; Brandon, his hands struggling with the cork in a manner that evokes at once strangulation, masturbation, and impotence (Philip eventually has to open the bottle for him), replies that his real excitement came at the moment when David's body "went limp"—that is, at the "evidence" of orgasm. The image of the champagne bottle can be read as the clearest—though heavily coded—information as to what Brandon and Philip actually "do": self-masturbation rather than intercourse. The action vividly suggests the inherent shame and frustration that characterize the relationship—a kind of socially imposed impotence. Ultimately, it was society that was responsible for David Kentley's death, and if the film does not and cannot say this, it can, however inadvertently, supply the evidence that enables *us* to say it.

Metteurs-en-Scène

Rope shares with a number of subsequent Hitchcock films (*Under Capricorn* and *Vertigo,* e.g.) the structural strategy of a transference of identification whereby we are led to identify with a position that is later undermined and subjected to criticism and, to varying degrees, condemnation, the difference being that here, because we know that Brandon is a murderer, the identification is rendered problematic, qualified by a partial revulsion, from the outset. In each case the initial identification is with a character seeking power and domination over others (which distinguishes these films from *Psycho,* which employs a similar strategy to different ends: the difference depends on whether the first identification figure is male or female). I have already tried to suggest that my own identification with Brandon was not merely personal: I identified with him because Hitchcock did, and because he constructed the film around that. Brandon, though extreme, is a "typical" Hitchcock identification figure because he exemplifies the desire-for-power/fear-of-impotence syndrome that characterizes so many other *male* Hitchcock identification figures, be they nominally "heroes" (Peck in *The Paradine Case,* Wilding in *Under Capricorn,* Stewart in *Vertigo*) or "villains" (Uncle Charlie, Bruno Anthony). But in Brandon's case there is a unique factor not shared by his fellows: as with Hitchcock, the particular form through which his drive to dominate expresses itself is mise-en-scène.

Consistently, Brandon sees the murder and the ensuing party as a "work of art"; it is crucial to the film—and to Hitchcock—that from the outset he is aware of its limitations and imperfections. Almost his first remark is that it's a pity they had to draw the curtains: the murder should have taken place in broad daylight. If he is readier than Hitchcock to improvise (his sudden inspiration of shifting the meal to the chest containing David's body, turning it, with the twin candelabra, into an altar), the Hitchcockian distrust in such rashness is immediately dramatized in Philip's response. The murder also, necessarily, lacked the essential component that gives works of art (and in a very special way Hitchcock's films) their meaning: an audience. The party guests perform a dual function: they are both actors to be manipulated and the audience Brandon desired—unfortunately, an audience who missed the premise and are therefore frustratingly unable to appreciate the full artistry. Brandon is motivated throughout (and, significantly, it is the cause of his downfall) by that desire for acknowledgment that William Rothman argues is central to Hitchcock's work.[11] In its way, *Rope* is as much a "testament" movie as *Rear Window*. For Hitchcock as for Brandon, acknowledgment inevitably entails exposure: the audience can only acknowledge Hitchcock's art by becoming aware of precisely those things of which they are supposed to remain unconscious, the extent to which they have been manipulated, whether by montage or by *Rope*'s continuous reframings.

I do not wish to assert that Hitchcock identifies with Brandon *because* the latter is gay—although I have argued that this is central to the character's psychology and the source of his Hitchcockian obsession with domination. The point is rather that the gayness is no impediment: Hitchcock was able, with apparent ease, to identify with gay characters, just as he was able to identify with female characters, his "unsuccessful" socialization making it possible for him to cross boundaries that must remain closed to males who "successfully" complete the oedipal trajectory. Another way of saying this is to argue for the positive nature of the self-evident neuroticism that characterizes—that *drives*—Hitchcock's work (and that also defines its limitations). Neurosis, by definition, damages the psyche, stunting its free growth, its blossoming; yet it must also be read as an instinctual rebellion against the sexual and gendered regulation of our culture. One can certainly question whether to be nonneurotic (i.e., to complete the oedipal trajectory unproblematically) would be any less disqualifying: it would be very unlikely to produce art of any interest or distinction.

As I said above, identification with Brandon (ours, Hitchcock's) must from the outset be heavily qualified: he is a murderer and a fascist, and we are in 1948, only a few years after the full revelation of the appalling social consequences of his philosophy. In other words, the identification brings with it, automatically, feelings of resistance and disturbance, shame and guilt. The film provides the necessary corrective, countering the potential morbidity and masochism, in a number of ways and through a number of subordinate characters of whom Mr. Kentley (not unlike Hitchcock in age and build) is clearly the most important. What is crucial to this process, though, is the film's systematic transference of identification from Brandon to Rupert Cadell. Inaugurated by the functioning of the star system (James Stewart must take immediate precedence over John Dall), this is completed, it seems to me, precisely at the moment when Rupert (with the connivance of Hitchcock's camera) usurps the role of *metteur-en-scène*—his reconstruction (take no. 9) of how David was murdered, in which the camera effectively comes under his control, illustrating by its movements every step in his discourse.

It is important that Rupert is a very imperfect character who needs to learn about himself as much as he needs to learn about his pupils. As with all too many learned academics, there is a marked discrepancy between what he teaches and how he lives; now Brandon has lived what Rupert has taught, and Professor Cadell must face the consequences, in the form of David Kentley's body in the chest. Rupert's complicity is intricate and complex: he has espoused and professed theories that he himself (and we believe him in this) would never have been capable of putting into practice. Is this because Brandon and Philip are gay and he is not? He tells them, in his impassioned denunciation, that they are incapable of loving, and this is surely true. Again, the film's unresolvable, even undiscussable ambiguity: Is it saying that homosexuals are "really" like this, or that this is what society makes of them? In fact, however, the film is notably reticent on the subject of Rupert's own sexuality (he is a bachelor). If it cannot tell us explicitly that Brandon and Philip are homosexual, it conspicuously abstains from telling us that Rupert isn't—apart from the fact that he is played by James Stewart, which of course carries its weight (Hitchcock originally wanted Cary Grant for the role).

It is Rupert's complicity—the fact that his horrific recoil must also be a *self-recoil*—that makes his exposure and denunciation of the crime so powerful and ratifies the film's moral authority. It corresponds to our (and Hitchcock's) fascinated, horrified involvement with Brandon, and the necessity to cast off and repudiate that involvement. The film never lets Rupert, or ourselves, off the hook: as Victor Perkins demonstrated, it moves toward the completion of the figure of the triangle, with Rupert finally taking his appropriate position at its apex.[12] Nevertheless, the moment when he flings open the window and fires the shots is among the most liberating in all of Hitchcock's work: the fresh air, after the moral, psychic, and physical claustrophobia of the preceding narrative, seems almost tangible.

Notes

1 See Robin Wood, "The Homosexual Subtext: *Raging Bull*," in *Hollywood from Vietnam to Reagan* (New York: Columbia University Press, 1985), 245–258.

2 Donald Spoto, *The Dark Side of Genius: The Life of Alfred Hitchcock* (Boston: Little, Brown, 1983), and *The Art of Alfred Hitchcock* (New York: Dolphin/Doubleday, 1979).

3 Like all biographical data, Spoto's "facts" and his interpretation of them doubtless can and will be challenged. I accept them here as a working hypothesis.

4 Robin Wood, *Hitchcock's Films* (London: A. S. Barnes, 1965, 2nd enlarged edition, 1969).

5 Spoto, *Dark Side of Genius*, 86.

6 Laura Mulvey, "Visual Pleasure and Narrative Cinema," *Screen* 16, no. 3 (Autumn 1975), 6–18.

7 Spoto, *Dark Side of Genius*, 68.

8 Michael Kaufman, "The Construction of Masculinity and the Triad of Male Violence," in *Beyond Patriarchy: Essays by Men on Pleasure, Power, and Change,* ed. Michael Kaufman (New York: Oxford University Press, 1987), 1–29.

9 David Freeman, *The Last Days of Alfred Hitchcock* (Woodstock, N.Y.: The Overlook Press, 1984), 240.

10 André Bazin, "The Evolution of the Language of Cinema," in *What Is Cinema?* Vol. 1, trans. Hugh Gray (Berkeley: University of California Press, 1967), 23–40.

11 See William Rothman, *Hitchcock: The Murderous Gaze* (Cambridge, Mass.: Harvard University Press, 1982).

12 See V. F. Perkins, "*Rope,*" in *The Movie Reader,* ed. Ian Cameron (New York: Praeger, 1972), 35–37.

"Crisscross"

Paranoia and Projection in *Strangers on a Train*

Sabrina Barton

Isn't it a fascinating design? You could study it forever.
Hitchcock on *Strangers on a Train*

Like the hero, the camera, and the spectator, feminist film theory has fixed its gaze on Hitchcock's blonde: we can't take our eyes off her. And with good reason. Hollywood's dream machine thrives on her fetishized surfaces. It is precisely because she is the object of the "male" gaze that she must also be taken as an object of feminist study. Singled out for theoretical scrutiny by Laura Mulvey and Raymond Bellour in the mid-seventies, the Hitchcock blonde has since come to stand for the "to-be-looked-at-ness" of cinematic femininity in general.[1] Investigations of cinematic subjectivity and spectatorship regularly return to what are now, as a consequence, the canonical Hitchcock texts, all linked by the spectacle of the blonde: Grace Kelly in *Rear Window,* Kim Novak in *Vertigo,* Janet Leigh in *Psycho,* Tippi Hedren in *The Birds* and *Marnie,* and Eva Marie-Saint in *North by Northwest.*[2] To understand the function of Hitchcock's blonde is thus to understand something fundamental about the imperatives of desire and representation in classical Hollywood cinema.

In an effort to depart from the rigid gender alignments of our by now all too familiar male gaze/female object model of classical Hollywood cinema, and in order to reconsider the constitution of the female subject, feminist criticism has recently taken a surprising turn: the interrogation of the male subject. For example, during a feminist film conference at Cornell University in the fall of 1988 called "Feminist Film Theory and Cultural Critique," many of the papers chose to take another look at representations of male subjectivity, especially gay male subjectivity, under the aegis of directors as different as Friedkin, Fassbinder, and Jarman, in order to consider various formations of "masculinity."[3] Though drawing sharp comments from some members of the audience disturbed by the predominance of "man talk" at a feminist conference, this shift of focus has rapidly become a favored feminist strategy for a more complicated understanding of the role of sexual difference in theories of the cinema.

Feminist film criticism's interest in male subjectivity parallels feminist literary criticism's explorations of the fissures in patriarchy, in homosociality, and in the phallus.[4] By refuting the conventional gender ideology promoted by most texts, and by examining ways in which male subjects are as constructed and, potentially, as fragmented and attenuated as female subjects, recent readings make available important forms of female empowerment. I would like to take up the question of representations of male subjectivity in film as a strategy for rethinking the singularly unempowered role assigned to the female subject in certain areas of film theory. In so doing, I hope to reopen the case of the director around whose preponderate oeuvre the debate over cinematic constitutions of female subjectivity has taken place, Alfred Hitchcock.

My focus will be on *Strangers on a Train,* a film obviously, even narrowly, focused on male subjectivity.[5] Just as *Vertigo* self-consciously explores blonde specularization—that is, the reducing of a female subject (Judy) to a mirroring blonde object (Madeleine)—*Strangers on a Train* explores the structuration of a male subject, an exploration from which what I will call the "blonde-function" is notably absent in any recognizable form. As a result, the film demarcates the position and function of "Woman" within patriarchy's plots in a way that rapt attention to a spectacular blonde object can (and perhaps is intended to) obscure. Unlike the narrative design of canonical Hitchcock films, *Strangers on a Train* offers no men in pursuit of blondes, nor blondes in pursuit of men. The first few minutes of the film, with its self-announcing singleminded interest in the movements between two men, at once explains this film's previous absence from feminist attention and indicates its relevance to the current feminist debate about representations of masculinity.

After the credit sequence, the camera lowers its angle, hovering around knee level, and crosscuts (in time to Dmitri Tiomkin's score) between two pairs of men's legs departing from taxis and walking briskly through Washington, D.C.'s, Union Station toward a train. While this camera angle remains a familiar cinematic device for the male scrutiny of female legs, Hitchcock's witty, stylized opening instead directs the audience to track the promenading of men. There are no diegetic glances, male or female, within the sequence to provide an alibi for the camera's fixation. Hitchcock's formal technique, crosscutting, proleptically indicates the film's narrative interest in the crisscrossing and doubling of desire between men that will be developed and played out in *Strangers on a Train*.

The narrative trajectory is propelled by the efforts of the two male protagonists to deny or acknowledge their "chance" crossing of paths on the train, a crisscrossing that will shortly result in the murder of Guy's wife, Miriam. When Bruno, voicing Guy's desire to be free from Miriam, proposes over lambchops that they "swap murders . . . crisscross" (the deal would be that Bruno murder Guy's lower-class, blackmailing wife in exchange for Guy murdering Bruno's domineering father), Bruno's proposition narrativizes the symmetrical relation between the two men textually inscribed by the opening crosscutting ("crisscross"). The homosexual valence of this symmetry is emphasized by Bruno's quick exclamation at their first meeting, "I like you—I'd do anything for you!" A profusion of doubling motifs crops up during their encounter—including Guy's tennis doubles, Guy's "bigamy" joke, Bruno's drink order ("scotch and plain water—a *pair—doubles*"), the pair of crisscrossed tennis rackets on Guy's lighter—all reinforcing the linkage of the two men by inviting us to read Bruno Anthony as Guy Haines's double.

The film's concern with the slippage of male identity is further underlined by Guy's lighter, which he "forgets" in Bruno's train compartment: the initials "A to G" may refer to Ann or An/thony. The eroticization of Bruno's threat, and the paranoia it triggers in Guy, completes this film's hyperbolically Freudian and homophobic account of how the paranoid subject, suffering from the repression and distortion of homosexual desire, projects a persecuting double.[6] With the loss of the lighter to Bruno, Guy loses crucial evidence of his heterosexual identity and of his innocence: he may now be blackmailed by the threatening other who commits his murder ("It's *your* murder," Bruno will later remind Guy).[7] The murder of Miriam makes possible Guy's social advancement but at the same time equates Guy with his partner in crime, an equation that anticipates the film's central concern: the destabilization and restabilization of Guy's subjectivity.

While *Strangers on a Train* does not seem to critique the privilege of the bourgeois male subject, it takes a more than perverse pleasure in exposing the mechanisms of, and Guy's guilty complicity in, the displaced violence required to ensure that privilege. On the one hand, the film's two deaths (Miriam and Bruno) are represented as necessary, even deserved by the two scapegoated stereotypes (and stereotypical scapegoats)—the voracious tramp and the deranged homosexual—who threaten Guy's stable identity. But, on the other hand, the film makes visible the secret of Guy's success, the mechanisms of paranoia and projection through which the other is cast out and punished. To describe the film as simply being about Guy's "dark underside"[8] is to miss *Strangers on a Train*'s special interest to the feminist film critic for its suggestion that a masterful male subject position is at once produced and continually threatened by its own paranoid homophobic and misogynist plots, the plots familiar from so much classical Hollywood cinema.

Crisscrossing/Coupling

Those familiar Hollywood plots obsessively center around a male oedipal resolution and the formation of the heterosexual couple. Raymond Bellour argues that a process of "alternation" distributes similarities and dissimilarities across every register of the text to produce and naturalize the couple. For example, in *The Big Sleep* the lighting, shot/reverse shot editing, and dialogue duration of a twelve-shot sequence generate the aura of "inevitability" around the Bacall/Bogart coupling and clearly define Bogart's "masculinity" and Bacall's "femininity." The primary goal of coded repetitions and differences is "to ensure the natural continuity of the narrative—that is, to sustain its artifice, but without ever making it too obvious."[9] The not-too-obvious obviousness of a narrative flow into heterosexual coupledom anchors mainstream American cinema.

What, then, do we make of the fact that the first twelve shots of *Strangers on a Train* work to produce the obviousness and inevitability of a same-sex male couple? This question is especially interesting in light of Thierry Kuntzel's claim that a film's opening serves as a microcosm or "matrix" for the film as a whole, the manifest "dream" from which the rest of the film unfolds, repeats, and resolves itself.[10] Before exploring Guy and Bruno's relationship as a couple, I will look first at how crisscrossing codes generate this coupling effect. Although conventional exposition is deferred until *Strangers'* second segment, the layering of crisscrossing codes already "narrates" an inevitable meeting/clash between these two anonymous strangers. In this way, narrative desire resonates within the elaborate enunciation—the "fascinating design"—of Hitchcock's *Strangers on a Train*.

Overall, the chart reveals a strikingly balanced alternation of camera angles, framing, movement, and shot duration between the Bruno and the Guy "sides" of the opening sequence. The crisscrossing symmetries of the first twelve shots produce the two male protagonists as mirroring doubles (a doubling echoed by the pairs of porter legs that share the frame with Guy and Bruno). Freud explains scenarios of uncanny doubling in terms of a rift within the subject. *Strangers on a Train* divides the hero's "normal" (Guy) self from the murderous, sexual (Bruno) self that the ego represses and projects outward as "other." Doubling motifs divide the "two" selves, while crosscutting motifs reveal that they are destined for one another.

At the same time, however, the heavily codified symmetries of the opening matrix work to render the dissymmetries all the more telling, dissymmetries that reassuringly invite us to distinguish between the doubles. Most obvious is the detail of mise-en-scène that immediately asserts the basic difference between the two men: their shoes. This figure condenses the thematics of sexuality and class about to unfold. One of the men (who turns out to be the hero, Guy Haines) wears inconspicuous brown lace-ups suitable to his status as the mild-mannered, upwardly mobile tennis celebrity whose political aspirations include marriage to a Senator's daughter (Ann Morton). The other (his antagonistic Other, Bruno Anthony) sports decadent two-toned, wing-tipped shoes whose semiotics in this film signal his eccentricity and effeminacy, traits associated with his membership in the decaying upper classes. Taste in shoes is determining in this film: Guy wouldn't be caught dead in Bruno's shoes; Bruno will be both caught and dead. And when Miriam warns Guy, "You can't throw me away like an old shoe," she is mistaken. As her analogy predicts, old wives *are* like old shoes—easily discarded.

A more subtle dissymmetry lies in the inscription of Bruno's priority in this segment, the imbalance of power that the rest of the film will struggle to correct. The exterior space of the film's establishing shot of Union Station, over which the credits roll, is appropriated by Bruno when he steps from his cab, compelling the camera to assume its low-angle position. In shot 8, Bruno will again have priority in entering the interior space of the train. (Bruno uncannily is always already in the place Guy intends to be: train stations, tennis courts, the museum, the senator's party, the amusement park.) As a result, when Guy steps into the exterior space from his cab (shot 2) and enters the interior space of the train (shot 10), his movement has a secondary status. At one point, Guy even loses "his" shot (shot 8), which the strict alternation of shots—1/2, 3/4, 5/6—has led us to expect. Instead of a cut, the camera watches Guy enter Bruno's shot 7 "dissolving" him into an insert of crisscrossing train tracks from the moving train's "point of view." This literalized "tracking" shot alludes to Guy not only in its serial placement but also in its movement from left to right (just as the camera has been "tracking" Guy from left to right): the splitting tracks metaphorize the hero's splitting self. A second dissolve returns us to Bruno walking from right to left along the aisle of the train, confirming that the previous figure of splitting was an adequate substitute for Guy. Alternation has been sustained. The double dissolves that frame shot 7 function as a hinge at which the segment divides itself, a division marked by the absence of the hero.

Shot:	Punctuation	Angle	Framing	S/M	Characters	Speech	Duration
I	[estab. shot)	l to /	(L to) MC	(S to)M	B		++
2	cut	\	MC	MC	G		+
3	cut	\	MC	S	B		-
4	cut	/	MC	S*	G		-
5	cut	\	M	S*	B		—
6	cut	/	M	S*	G		—
7	cut	l	MC to L	M	B		++
8	dissolve	l to /	M to L	M	X		+
9	dissolve	l to \	MC	M	B		+
10	cut	l to /	MC	M	G		+
11	cut	/	C	M	G & B		-
12	cut	l	ML	S	G & B	B: "Excuse me"	-

Key to Chart:

I am using Bellour's chart of specific and nonspecific cinematic codes from "The Obvious and the Code" (in *Narrative, Apparatus, Ideology: A Film Theory Reader,* ed. Philip Rosen [New York: Columbia University Press, 1986]), with the exception of his "elements of narration" category, which does not strictly apply to this opening segment.

Angle = / (low camera angle from upper right); \ (low angle from upper left); l (straight-on)

Framing = L (long shot); ML (medium long); M (medium); MC (medium close); C (close-up)

Static or Moving Camera = S (static); S* (camera adjusts to keep character centered but "feels" static); M (moving)

Characters = presence or absence of G (Guy) or B (Bruno) in frame

Speech = presence or absence of dialogue

Time = ++ (longer), + (long), - (short), — (shorter) relative duration of shot

Punctuation = the join between shots

Guy (in another reverse image of his other) walks along the train aisle from left to right and sits directly across from Bruno, kicking Bruno's flamboyantly shod foot as he does so: Guy, not Bruno, makes the first move, a move we view voyeuristically from our low-angle vantage point. This point of contact not only anthropomorphizes the earlier figure of the train tracks—that is, a figure of splitting and crisscrossing—it also rhymes with a prior crisscrossing between Guy and Bruno traced solely by the reversal of camera angles in the first four shots. A chart of the camera angles' movement reveals an inaugural chiasmus or "X," a figure for the subsequent series of textual and thematic crisscrossing exchanges between Guy and Bruno:

Segment 1. (shot 2) G. ————————————————————— B. (shot 1)
            (3) B. ————————————————————— G. (4)
                (5) B.   G. (6)
                    (7) B.   X. (8)
                            B. (9). G. (10)
                            B. & G. (11)
                            B. & G. (12)

Guy's transgressive "kick" sets the plot in motion by triggering the quick splicing together of both pairs of feet in shot 11, which culminates in the tableaux of Guy and Bruno, face to face, finally sharing a single frame in shot 12. The sequence of filmic crisscrossing that opens the film thus resolves itself in a bit of physical crisscrossing (in fact, a bit of footsie), sustaining the film's fetishistic fascination with shoes. However, Guy's desire is coded as "accident," while Bruno's apology for Guy's accident indicates the instantaneous transfer of guilt to the other. The carousel scene at the end of the film will complete the rewriting of Guy's "accident" as Bruno's perversion: there the scapegoated homosexual villain intentionally kicks at Guy until the carousel collapses and the pair are explosively hurled apart.

The threat implicit in the initial crisscrossing sequence culminates in a question concerning identity: "Is your name Guy Haines?" The audience, like Bruno, lacks an iconic James Stewart or Cary Grant to secure instant identification. The opening matrix of *Strangers on a Train* generates an uneasy confusion over who these two guys are, a confusion central to the film's thematics of destabilized male identity. The second narrative sequence answers Bruno's question by identifying the two main characters and introducing the murder-swapping plot. Once again, Bruno dominates shot and dialogue duration, further occluding Guy's own desire and agency. However, editing codes function to sustain a crisscrossing symmetry between the two men: out of the sixty-seven shots in this segment on the train, fifty-eight (roughly 86 percent) are paired into twenty-nine sets of reverse angles. When Bruno proposes that they "swap murders—crisscross," shot/reverse shot editing becomes especially pronounced with the camera flipping back to Guy each time he tries to interrupt, as if itself destabilized, as if itself caught between two points of view. Perhaps because it encodes Hollywood heterosexuality ("Classic Hollywood cinema abounds in shot/reverse shot formations in which men look at women"),[11] *Strangers'* use of shot/reverse shot becomes frenetic as it places Guy in the "feminine" position. The segment concludes with Bruno alone in his train compartment, once again naming with hushed pleasure the formation that binds him to Guy: "Crisscross," he murmurs. Later, when Bruno reminds Guy of his role in Miriam's murder—"we planned it together on the train: crisscross"—the camera will resume its intensive shot/reverse shot structuration. Guy's complicity, denied at the level of narrative, infiltrates the textual codes.

The crisscrossing game of Guy's tennis playing, which emblematizes the textual codes of this film and of Hollywood cinema generally, is only the most explicit instance of the crisscrossing games that Guy must win: the illicit crisscrossing of desire (or coupling) between himself and Bruno; the crisscrossing murder-swapping plan; and the homosocial crisscrossing between Guy and the senator (i.e., the swapping of the father's daughter for the surrogate son's advancement).[12] Guy's identity as an acceptable Hollywood hero turns on winning these games. The film as a whole suggests that winning requires the playing out of the very misogynist and homophobic impulses that render male normality a contest (contested) in the first place.

Destabilization

While much of Hollywood's misogynist and homophobic plotting is so conventionalized as to manage to pass itself off as "natural," *Strangers on a Train* is striking for how explicitly it links plots against the female and homosexual other to the paranoid projections of a contested male subject. Guy's initial encounters with Miriam and Bruno produce increasingly intense forms of paranoia: our hero, who supposedly hasn't *done* anything, rapidly becomes a nervous wreck before our eyes. (Unlike Cary Grant's easy mastery in *North By Northwest* over the stranger he meets on a train, Eva Marie-Saint, Guy lacks a blonde function and therefore lacks mastery.) To underline the degree to which Guy's dilemma is essentially psychic and self-induced, the film lets us overhear a police detective reveal that they "don't have a thing on him." In contrast to the standard doubles plots of, say, Clint Eastwood's *Tightrope* or television evil-twin movies, Hitchcock never represents Guy's dilemma as the problem of what act of violence his evil double will commit next. Rather, the film's suspense turns on Guy's ability to act "normal." Should Guy report to the office? Should he keep practicing for Forest Hills?—these are the urgent questions Guy discusses with the Mortons after they learn of Miriam's death. *Strangers on a Train* explores not the mystery of Miriam's murder but the mystery behind Guy's "normal" subjectivity.[13]

The role of paranoia and projection in eliminating the "abnormal" is clarified by Laplanche and Pontalis in their exploration of Freud's dual structure of paranoia as either a "not wishing to know" or a "not wishing to be": the first is understood as a "*refusal to recognize (méconnaissance)* which has as its counterpart the subject's ability to recognize in others what he refuses to acknowledge in himself"; the second is understood as "a quasi-real process of expulsion: the subject ejects something he does not want and later rediscovers it in the outside reality."[14] The narrative trajectory of *Strangers on a Train* may be mapped according to these two senses of paranoia: first Guy, refusing to recognize his own murderous desire, recognizes that desire in Bruno; the film then charts Guy's disavowal, rediscovery, and expulsion of (himself as) Bruno. Paranoid projection grounds the masculine subject and at the same time reveals the violence and precariousness of that grounding. On the train, Bruno reads our repressed, paranoid hero like an open book (Guy warns him that maybe he "read[s] too much"). Next, when Guy visits the music store where Miriam works, she, like Bruno, is uncannily able to read or penetrate Guy's secrets. After listening to her mocking refusal to grant him a divorce and her insinuating remarks about his new friends, his new money, and his new liaison with Ann Morton, Guy becomes enraged and abusive: he calls her a "doublecrosser," implicitly threatening her with the crisscross scheme. The music store's glass listening booth serves as a figure for Guy's vulnerability to Miriam's knowing look. Although Guy retreats there for privacy, the booth puts him on display, just as he has found his interiority suddenly on display before Bruno's "close reading" and Miriam's penetrating glasses. Together, the glasses and the glass booth trigger Guy's panicked sensation of lost mastery. Like the space of the listening booth, the supposedly sealed-off space of Guy's subjectivity has become utterly transparent and vulnerable to the gaze from the outside. (A young couple, always visible in the adjoining booth, serves as our spectator-surrogates, watching with curiosity the pantomime of the unfolding narrative.)

The destabilization of Guy continues when he leaves the music store for another glass booth, this time a phone booth from which he calls Ann—a booth that again makes his inner voice "transparent." In what the startled Ann describes as a "savage" voice, he shouts over the noise of a train that he'd like to break Miriam's "foul useless little neck. . . . I said I could strangle her!" Hitchcock's next cut, from Guy in the phone booth to Bruno at home, filmically dramatizes a psychic projection from self (Guy) to other (Bruno), a projection of the desire to strangle.

Instantly, Guy's murderous desire gets transmitted, as if through an accidental crisscrossing of wires, to Bruno. In this extraordinary cut from the phone booth to a close-up shot of a pair of hands held in a strangling position, the word *strangle* is literally projected—the murderous signifier cast out by Guy and metonymically transferred into the hands of the double, Bruno, who commits the crime. A subsequent motif of close-ups on Bruno's hands (while he waits outside Guy's house, stalks Miriam at the amusement park, struggles to regain Guy's lighter) reinforces a reading of Bruno's hands as the auxiliary device of Guy's agency. The editing of this shot—the jarring suddenness of the cut from Guy's voice to Bruno's hands, heightened by the musical score's dissonant orchestral accompaniment—enacts Guy's psychic disavowal of the cast-out image. This moment also alludes to the spectator's complicity in the process of cinematic projection. The glass booth and the telephone stand in for film's image and sound apparatus, whose projections enable the audience's own disavowal of projected desires: we do not seek or speak our desires, but passively sit back and let them speak us. Like Guy, we never need to dial direct.[15]

However, in *Strangers on a Train* the male spectator harbors an excessively paranoid relation to his projected images. The scene depicting Guy's anticipatory dread of Miriam's murder is aptly characterized by Laplanche and Pontalis's formulation of paranoia as "comparable to the cinematographic"; that is, Guy "sends out into the external world an image of something that exists in him in an unconscious way."[16] Arriving home late from a tennis match, Guy steps from his cab into a disorientingly canted camera frame and dark, shadowy lighting; he then hears the weird echoing sound of Bruno's voice invisibly calling, as if ventriloquized and projected outward: "Guy . . . Guy. . . . " But when Guy turns from his doorway back toward the darkened courtyard, instead of innocent bewilderment we see the haunted expression that insists on his guilt. Although he hasn't yet been told, the film suggests that unconsciously Guy already "knows" his wife has been strangled to death. Guy is a man who knows too much, and his repressed knowledge quite literally emanates from him.

Guy's attempts to stabilize himself through conversations with his fiancée, Ann, are repeatedly interrupted by his association with Bruno. For example, at the museum just before Bruno appears, Guy confesses to Ann that he feels like he's living in a "glass bowl": his words performatively summon his double and refer back to the earlier figures of his own transparency. Ann's failure to mediate the threat this "other man" poses to Guy's masculinity (her failure as a blonde function) complicates Bellour's account of cinema's preoccupation with Woman as "the mirror-effect of the narcissistic doubling that makes possible the constitution of the male subject through the woman's body."[17] Ann fails to mirror Guy because the site of "the woman's body" is already occupied by Bruno.[18] The priority of the other man suggests that the heterosexual version of "narcissistic doubling" by way of a blonde function may founder before same-sex narcissistic identifications.

Freud's work on paranoia repeatedly betrays the tenuousness of his own opposition between homosexual desire and "normal" heterosexual functioning: "So long as the individual is functioning normally and it is consequently impossible to see into the depths of his mental life, we may doubt whether his emotional relations to his neighbors in society have anything to do with sexuality. . . . But delusions never fail to uncover these relations." "Uncover[ing]" relations with one's neighbors will disclose a sexual, often homosexual, content. Unable to conceal "the depths of his mental life," Guy no longer "function[s] normally" as a heterosexual male. Hitchcock's film dramatizes Freud's insight into the imposture of "functioning normally," even as it subscribes to Freud's own investment in that imposture. Freud also pointed out that it is through the "attempt to master" so-called abnormal unconscious desires that we "come to grief."[19] *Strangers on a Train* seems fascinated by the inevitability of coming to grief, by the inevitability of paranoia in a society that requires the repression of all "abnormal" desires.

The mise-en-scène of *Strangers* charts the abnormal within the normal as we follow Bruno following Guy, repeatedly erupting into the well-lit Washington, D.C., public spaces Guy eagerly inhabits in an effort to distance himself from his double. Bruno materializes as a dark, spectral silhouette at a museum, at the steps of the Jefferson Memorial, the tennis courts, even the senator's house, contaminating these clean havens of patriarchal order. Shadows repeatedly cut across—cut and divide—Guy's body. As Bruno remarks, "You're not yourself, Guy." Hitchcock's films persistently uncover the "nonself" within the "self," the gothic deviancy lodged within realist normalcy.

The gothicism associated with Bruno can be elucidated by considering Eve Sedgwick's work on the "eroticized, paranoid double." In her reading of James Hogg's gothic classic, *Confessions of a Justified Sinner*, Sedgwick discusses the threat that "slipperiness of identity" poses for the male subject in the homosocial order.[20] The character of Bruno, with his decaying aristocratic legacy, his effeminacy, his insanity, his incestuous relationship with his mother, and his positioning as the persecuting double of Guy, is right out of the gothic tradition. In fact, Hogg's account of an ambitious tennis player pursued by a persecuting double may even be a source for the film's revision of Guy's profession from architect (in Highsmith's novel) to tennis player. Hogg's emphasis on his protagonist's paranoid horror of his double's "hideous glances"—identifying the problem of male subjectivity with a problem of visual mastery—makes the following passage a strikingly cinematic anticipation of Guy's subjection to Bruno's "hideous glances": "To whatever place of amusement he [George] betook himself, and however well he concealed his intentions of going there from all flesh living, there was his brother . . . also, and always within a few yards of him, generally about the same distance, and ever and anon darting looks at him that chilled his very soul. . . . All whose eyes caught a glimpse of these hideous glances followed them to the object toward which they darted."[21] This passage vividly captures the coercive effect of "hideous glances" on object and spectator alike.

Those soul-chilling "darting looks" that violate the boundaries of the self neatly characterize the threat that Jacqueline Rose argues is inherent in cinema's scopic system. In her critique of Bellour's account of the masterful male gaze, Rose claims, like Freud, that "normal" self/other relations are destabilized by the narcissistic projections that may so easily flip into fears of persecution: "Paranoia is latent to the reversibility of the ego's self-alienation. Furthermore, since the projective alienation of the subject's own image is the precondition for the identification of an object world, all systems of objectification can be related to the structure of paranoia. Aggressivity is latent to the system, but it will also be discharged where the stability of the system is threatened."[22] If a "projective alienation of the subject's own image" underwrites the differentiation of ego and object world—the organization of self and other—then the systematic expelling of otherness can backfire; polarization is always susceptible of reversal; the subject may suddenly become an object of her or his own outcast images; and any destabilization will unleash the paranoia and aggressivity "latent to the system." Narcissism, difference, and the look are not so easily managed.

In *Strangers on a Train* the threat of reversibility inherent in the cinematic system is played out, so to speak, in a tennis court sequence where the back-and-forth shots (shot/reverse shots) emblematize the subject's attempts at mastery. The sequence begins with a shot of Guy watching (what else) a doubles match while awaiting his turn to practice for Forest Hills. The camera then reverses to show us, directly across the courts, the bleachers full of spectators who, like Guy, are watching the game. A reverse angle back to Guy shows his expression suddenly become anxious and paranoid. Still another reverse angle of the spectators' heads rhythmically following the back-and-forth movement of the ball invites the film audience to laugh at their coerced looking, superior in our privileged alignment with the gaze of the camera.

All this occurs within seconds until, with a shock, we see what Guy sees: Bruno's single head fixed and staring right at us. The spectator/camera/Guy are all caught in an act of imaginary mastery—visible and vulnerable after all. Like Guy's crisscrossed relation to Bruno, we are placed in a mirroring relation to the automation-like tennis spectators across the court whose "freely" shifting look, like ours, is an illusion, an illusion punctured for us by the reversal of the look from Bruno. As Rose argues, when "the subject is looked at from the point of its own projections," it causes "the look . . . itself [to] be externalized."[23] This moment of reversal and externalization invariably elicits gasps and surprised laughter from the *Strangers* audience: we enjoy being startled by a vertiginous glimpse of ourselves constituted as objects rather than subjects of the gaze. But only for a moment. As the camera zooms in toward Bruno, we instantly register that his look is slightly to the side of the camera—he sees Guy but not us—an obliquity that recuperates our sense of visual mastery, safely outside that mise-en-abîme of interspecularity. The predicament of violent reversal inherent in crisscrossing glances later resurfaces in another unusual shot/reverse shot during the Morton party sequence. In an upstairs bedroom, after Bruno has caused a scene, Guy calls him a "mad, crazy maniac." When Bruno pleads, "But Guy, I like you," Guy punches him.[24] Bruno's plea triggers a cut to his point of view, just in time to record Guy's oncoming fist as a blow to the camera's/spectator's/Bruno's "face," a collision registered by a brief fade to black, obliterating our view altogether. An instantaneous reverse angle has Bruno's chin snapping back from the camera's/spectator's/Guy's point of view. Guy's aggressivity—his fist—works to suture his point of view to that of the apparatus.

A reversal of power between men is thus accompanied by the surfacing of the means of enunciation. ("Aggressivity . . . will also be discharged where the stability of the system is threatened," per Rose.) At stake in violent struggles against the double is the goal of securely realigning the hero with the discursive apparatus. However, *Strangers on a Train*'s crisscrossing motifs make visible the always reversible hinge of psychic and cinematic mastery. And the opacity of the blackened screen lingers as a figure for the failures of point of view.

The Dangerous Game of Restabilization—"You're not yourself, Guy"

The problem of not being oneself, of failing to master a stable subject position with a unitary point of view, is a problem that Lacanian theory views as endemic to a fissured ego structure ceaselessly projecting the self onto external objects or screens. *Strangers on a Train* shows how seamlessly Guy's "normal" irritation with Miriam slides into murderous projection, and it is this very continuity from "normal" to violent projection that discloses the mechanism by which unstable male subjectivity gets renarrativized as a paranoid fear of the female or homosexual other.

The paranoid male subject, as represented in *Strangers on a Train*, thus counters the conventional evocation of a male subject who (in theory, at least) enjoys a safely distanced fetishistic or voyeuristic relation to the image. That invincible figure is usually opposed to women who "lacking castration anxiety [are] also deprived of the possibility of fetishism"—woman can only *be* the fetishized object or image.[25] But woman holds no monopoly on an unstable proximity to signification; sexual differentiation marks only the most dramatic of an endless series of efforts on the part of all subjects to position a self within our culture's signifying systems. Nonetheless, an ideological form like film is likely to reflect not a shared psychic predicament but our gendered positions under patriarchy—woman's exclusion, powerlessness, difference. Feminist film theory ought therefore to remain suspicious of claiming "loss and difference" for femininity. After all, the feminist strategy of valorizing the disruptive potential of woman's proximity to the image repeats an association that has already been happily offered up by the film itself.

Without losing sight of the profound asymmetries in Hollywood's representations of gender, we can explore the fissures in "masculinity" revealed by these representations in order to help free femininity from bearing the entire burden of split subjectivity. Disruption is not a glamourous thing that a woman "does" through her own agency. But perhaps disruption—or the ruptured representation—of subjectivity is something a marginalized female or male subject may recognize and read.[26] After all, the two marginalized subjects in *Strangers,* Miriam and Bruno, are the insightful and playful readers who question Guy's unitary point of view, reminding us that the "normal" male subject also harbors a dangerously reversible (or crisscrossed) relation of ego to image.

Not surprisingly, Guy's climactic Forest Hills match near the end of the film seems calculated to produce him as a clear winner. Earlier crosscutting and tennis sequences are repeated for this resolution, but with a difference. Guy is now a player, not a spectator, and (the sports announcer tells us) he has changed his style and become fast, aggressive, hardhitting. Watching him from the stands is not Bruno but Ann, her head not fixed but obediently following Guy's shots. Bruno is excluded, in spite of the resurgence of the crosscutting technique that first established the link between the two men, for, in contrast to the opening sequence, this latter alternation between Bruno (trying to plant Guy's incriminating lighter at the scene of the crime) and Guy (who must win his match and get on a train to stop Bruno) works mainly as scaffolding for an elaborate narrative suspense that all but absorbs the "fascinating design" of formal crisscrossing codes. Furthermore, instead of the visual and aural matching in the opening segment, these codes reinforce narrative difference: shots of Guy are associated with open space, rapid cutting, vigorous narrative action, bright lighting, and lively music; Bruno's shots are associated with claustrophobic space, longer takes, thwarted action, dark lighting, and sonorous music: Guy will go free, Bruno will not.

And yet, in a perfectly Hitchcockian twist, the entire sequence is played under the sign of "sameness." Entering the stadium, the camera glides over an awning inscribed with a line from Kipling: "And treat those two imposters just the same."[27] The line ironizes the tidy polarization of Hollywood closure to come. At the very moment that every textual register in the film encourages us to root for Guy's victory over the match, over Bruno, and over the senator's daughter, a literary citation reminds us that these so-called opposites (named in the poem "Triumph" and "Disaster") are "the same." The hero is called an "imposter": his mastery—his "triumphant" phallus—an imposture.

Learning how to assume the props and posturing of masculinity is, in fact, the subject of Kipling's poem "If—," whose rhetorical structure is an address from a father to his son. The poem offers a lesson in negotiating the tricky balance—the "if"—of "normal" patriarchal subjectivity. *If* the boy can succeed: "Yours is the Earth and everything that's in it, / And—which is more—you'll be a Man, my son!" (lines 31–32). To possess everything, including the "more" of Manhood, depends in this poem on a logic of paranoia, on a rigid guarding of self from other, on holding everything in and treating all others alike (with the same degree of suspicious distance) so that "neither foes nor loving friends can hurt you." The moral of the poem becomes the moral of the epilogue of *Strangers on a Train:* when a minister on a train repeats Bruno's destabilizing question—"Aren't you Guy Haines?"—Guy and Ann silently leave the compartment. Guy has learned not to talk to strangers.

However, the silence of conjugal closure echoes with the screams of the carousel sequence that precedes and produces it. Guy's restabilized identity only barely emerges from the disordering confusion of "those two imposters." "That's him," says the ticket taker at the carousel, identifying the criminal, Bruno. "Yes, we know," respond the policemen, meaning Guy. As if in response to this failure of reference (who is "him"?) a policeman's wild gunshot misses its indistinct double target and instead kills the operator hidden within the apparatus of the carousel. The troubling question of male identity ("Aren't you Guy Haines?") once again bespeaks the instability of the subject constituted in language.

The question also bespeaks the instability of the spectator's own processes of identification within the language of cinema. It is curious, then, that apparatus theory has tended to promote the concept of a spectator who achieves a sublime imaginary unity before the flickering screen. Joan Copjec diagnoses that critical claim as itself a paranoid masculine fantasy of a "phallic machine" that can reproduce stable male subject positions. She cites Freud's observation that "it is highly probable that all complicated machinery and apparatus occurring in dreams stand for the genitals—and as a rule the male ones." Copjec also argues that the disruptive complications of sexual difference have been evaded, in part by collapsing Jean-Louis Baudry's two distinct terms—*appareil* and *dispositif*—into the single and phallic concept of *apparatus,* which elides the more mobile, multiform concept of *arrangement* that *dispositif* offers.[28] It seems to me that the "fascinating design" of Hitchcock's apparatus (the film text, the carousel) similarly strains against, yet also reveals, multiform sexual arrangements.

The carousel apparatus initially seems an innocent enough pleasure, evoking an early form of the cinema: the amusement park setting, the purchasing of tickets, the revolving images, the spritely music on the soundtrack, the painted props, the interested spectators. Then the hidden agent of amusement (the director?) is eliminated by a random gunshot. With his death, our spectator surrogates lose their illusion of control and begin to scream in terror: the game is a dangerous one. The visual and aural confusion that follows breaks up orderly spectatorial positioning and produces the film's highest pitch of excitement: pleasure-in-order gives way to a (pleasurable) panic-in-disorder.

The film has already hinted at the allure of disordered cinematic subjectivity by revealing the instability inherent in shot/reverse shot. The carousel scene pursues the logic of an inherent instability to its extreme. The vertiginous 360-degree whirling circularity of the merry-go-round "describes" the breaking of the 180-degree rule that governs both shot/reverse shot and orderly continuity editing.[29] The film's figure for an "unrealistic" spinning camera—for out-of-control apparatus and 360 degrees of taboo space—represents the collapse of the linear, 180-degree editing logic that divided Guy from Bruno; that collapse discloses the "other scene" of crisscrossing: intercourse. The camera moves in for a tight framing of Guy and Bruno writhing around on the floor of the merry-go-round, lying on top of one another, clenched together, with phallic poles and a horse's hoof pumping up and down, in and out of the frame (the foot fetish returning as a sign of homoerotic desire). Hitchcock fragments the space surrounding the grappling men through disorientingly blurred and spliced together rear-projection footage. Subject/object relations are disjoined; distorting close-ups animate the inanimate machine horses; screams mingle in a cacophony of diegetic and nondiegetic music; textual codes explode into confusion.

The erotic charge of this sensational confusion lies in the fusing of images of "disordering" homosexuality with disordered cinematic representation. The carousel scene betrays "the temptation" that normative textual codes are "intended to overcome: the temptation to refuse cultural re-integration, to skid off-course, out-of-control, to prefer castration to false plenitude."[30] In the carousel scene, transgressive desire disorders the film's symbolic law and allows two men to spin out of control. Desire unbinds a figural and sexual energy that is at once celebratory and apocalyptic.

Ultimately, the film's horror of destabilization ensures the scene's restabilizing resolution. The film allows dangerous unbinding in order to motivate rebinding; it allows disordered desire in order to motivate the reordering of desire.[31] *Strangers on a Train* associates the ruptured cinematic codes with Bruno, and then proceeds to eliminate both at once. Bruno is literally buried in the confusion effects he "caused," in the cracked, dismantled machinery of the carousel apparatus. Although all subjects are at once located and dislocated within signification, *Strangers* reinstates an opposition: Guy is back on track, while Bruno is literally "dislocated" ("I think his neck is broken").

In terms of the film's closure, then, the apparatus does function with some success as a machine for restabilizing masculinity. As if to emphasize this, the carousel sequence alludes to Hollywood's most popular genre for the cinematic construction of masculinity: the Western. The scene includes good guys and bad guys, guns, horses, a chase, a fistfight, screaming women, the law, a mother and her son. The film's attention to the son on the merry-go-round, a young boy who advances from spectator to player when he begins to hit Bruno in imitation of Guy, establishes a rhetorical situation analogous to that of the Kipling poem: the boy-spectator must learn how to "be a Man," only in this case through the witnessing of violent male spectacle.[32] Cultural representations supply the tropes through which male identity gets constituted.

This moment repeats and reverses a prior scene between Bruno and a young boy. While trailing Miriam about the amusement park, Bruno encounters a young boy wearing a cowboy suit and hat who points a toy gun at him and says, "Bang! Bang!" In response, Bruno bursts the boy's balloon with his cigar, transforming pretend violence into real violence with a bang. Bruno mimes the little boy's violent gesture just as the boy himself is miming the gestures and costume of masculinity produced by the Western. The film erodes the distinction between innocent and intentional violence, between playacting and aggressive acts. Bruno's "pretend" strangulation at the Morton's party quickly turns murderous; Guy's "innocent" idiom—"I could strangle her"—assumes performative efficacy. The boy's toy gun alludes to Bruno's "perfect murder" game at the Morton party ("Bang, bang, bang, blood all over the place"); the toy gun also refers to Guy's playacting of his "perfect murder" of Mr. Anthony—he creeps up the stairs holding Bruno's gun like a prop or toy that will later turn lethal in the hands of his double. Once again, the game is dangerous. But out of dangerous games emerge heroes and villains.

Narrative codes complete the work of reestablishing difference between Guy and Bruno (narrative once again proving itself able to recuperate textual perturbance). Most important, Guy saves the little boy-spectator whom Bruno almost pushes off the ride, thus securing an instant polarity of family protector versus child murderer. Responding to the mother's terrified appeal, "My little boy!" Guy's heroics sever his relation to Bruno as he inserts himself into the paternal slot of an oedipal triangle. Bruno's deviance is reasserted in a final trope as he, snarling, grasps the eroticized horse's hoof and kicks Guy's hands. The weird metonymic relation scripts Bruno as the sole bestial aggressor, no longer in the pedosymmetry with Guy established by the film's opening sequence.

The spectacle of the exploding carousel marks the dismantling of the apparatus by an eruption of homosexual panic. I want to argue that the carousel scene also refers back to a fissure within the apparently smoothly functioning apparatus of the murdered-woman plot. I am thinking of the moment when a woman, Miriam, sees herself trapped within a murderous male projection, Guy's/ Bruno's, just before his strangling hands cause her eyeglasses to fall to the ground and crack. Bruno's casual postmurder joke to Guy—"Nobody saw—only Miriam"— will later redound with a vengeance. Miriam's look, signified by her cracked glasses, returns in the trope of the broken carousel.

Broken Spectacles

As the murdered-woman sequence begins, however, Miriam's looks seem far from disruptive; she blindly mistakes Bruno's murderous stalking for innocent flirtation. Hitchcock plays the sequence for comedy. By displacing the film's horror of doubleness onto a feminine object, he invites the audience to feel that Miriam is asking for it. Miriam herself is "double," or pregnant; sexually, she is doubly guilty, out with two young men; and she has just doublecrossed Guy. Miriam's voraciousness—she hungrily eats and lasciviously looks throughout this sequence—seems implicitly to cause her own murder. Women who eat too much, like women who see too much, deserve to die.

In his role as murderer, Bruno functions as a projected figure for the male director, actor, and spectator: he enacts the revenge of the threatened and paranoid male subject on both sides of the camera. Before following Miriam and her doubled dates into the Tunnel of Love, Bruno pauses to buy popcorn, like the paradigmatic moviegoer, from an old-fashioned machine whose spinning wheel and flickering lights allude to the film projector itself.[33] When the camera films the shadows hugely projected by Miriam grappling with her dates inside the Tunnel, it is as if sexual gropings in the darkness of the theater were themselves indistinguishable from the projected screen images. The camera then cuts outside in time for Miriam's off-screen scream, cuing the audience to project—to imagine and desire—her murder; we repeat Guy's own projection of Miriam's murder. By linking Guy's paranoia and projection to tropes for cinematic projection, this scene hints at a causal link between male paranoia and movies' murdered-women plots.

The murder sequence concludes on the island when Bruno as director holds Guy's lighter under the female object's chin, creating his desired effect of underlighting. He then as spectator asks, "Is your name Miriam?" And, finally, as actor—the actor who enacts Guy's desire—he begins to strangle her. Guy's desire—"I could strangle her"—writes the script that is played out or projected through Bruno.[34] Hitchcock films even the murder as another shadow show, another staging of projected images. The strangulation is filmed from the mirroring lens of a huge replica of Miriam's glasses that Hitchcock designed to achieve this effect.

Instead of using a spectacular blonde object, Hitchcock has literalized the function of woman as a specular screen for male projections. In contrast to *Vertigo,* where the blonde's body becomes the fetish, in *Strangers on a Train* the fetish is not Miriam as spectacle but Miriam's spectacles. What becomes visible as a result is the disjunctive space between Miriam as a screen for projected images (that is, the "blonde function"), and Miriam as a subject and viewer in her own right. Again unlike *Vertigo*'s victimized female object of male desire, Miriam has fun with her playacting ("I can be very pathetic as the deserted little mother in the courtroom," she threatens Guy) and has fun with her flirtations (her seductive gazing at Guy and Bruno). As a woman with spectacles, rather than a blonde spectacle, Miriam continues, even after her death, to make visible male paranoia and projection. For example, Barbara's Miriam-like eyeglasses will later betray Guy's complicity to his fiancée, Ann.

Strangers on a Train is punctuated with examples of female spectators who enjoy an alarming facility around and pleasure in representation: Mrs. Anthony's irreverently surreal painting of St. Francis onto which Bruno projects a monstrous portrait of his father; Miriam's "pretty story" as she mockingly threatens to perform the role of "deserted little mother" in the courtroom; Barbara's eager launching into the discourse of detective fiction, referring to Guy as a "suspect" who might be "thrown in the can and left all night" (she openly voices her pleasure in narratives in which "a man loves you so much he'd kill for you" until sharply reprimanded by her father, the senator); Mrs. Cunningham and Mrs. Anderson at the Morton party gleefully spinning out conventional plots for husband murdering; Miriam's scream of laughter in the Tunnel of Love, indicating her irreverent distance from the games of love and murder in which she is supposed to be the helpless object; Ann's sharp glances as she recognizes the congruences between Guy and Bruno, and between Barbara and Miriam, and pieces the puzzle together; and even the old woman in the back of the car the police appropriate to chase Guy to the train station: "Excuse us ma'am, we're chasing a man," to which she responds with delight "Oh really? How exciting!" What links these different examples together is a refusal of the high seriousness and masochistic identification often associated with woman's reading of patriarchal narrative.

But, as Guy's rage at Miriam indicates (rather like Scottie's rage at Midge when she parodically paints herself as a blonde function sporting spectacles, in *Vertigo*), in *Strangers on a Train* active female spectating is no joke. Interestingly enough, Hitchcock's own appearance in the film seems to imply a less paranoid solution to the problem of the threatening other. He climbs onto the train, carrying the figure for his own double—a double bass. Like the tennis-celebrity Guy, Hitchcock is a public figure; he is precisely *not* a stranger on a train. His paranoid sense of being seen, recognized, and pursued is borne out by the critical tradition that has followed on his death. Yet his appearance contradicts the solution that the film's ideology promotes for Guy (and a link is established when Guy crosses the director's path on the steps of the train). While Guy, like the addressed son of "If—," is to cultivate a suspicious silence and a quest for invisibility as a guarantee, as Kipling put it, of being a "Man," Hitchcock's appearance parodically deconstructs masculine identity. Unlike Guy's disavowed, gendered, sexualized other, the director's "other," the bass fiddle, is simply a shape or figure that he carries with him—a shape resembling his own, a figure indeterminately masculine or feminine.

I am, certainly, overreading a joke. But the image of Hitchcock with his humorous double not only condenses the film's thematics of male paranoia and projection, but also works to associate the director with his own female other. The musical instrument, like the pair of spectacles, is linked with Miriam in the music store. Thus, the film's two primary figures for vision and voice both allude to the woman who saw too much, who said too much, who ate too much. Hitchcock's repressed double may be this projected "overweight" woman, whose hungers he finds intolerable. We do not, of course, see the director wearing glasses; his "spectacles" are the camera itself that, when it chooses to film the director, makes visible the mechanisms of projection whose invisibility is conventionally so important to the "complicated machinery" of classical Hollywood cinema. Where, by the way, are Miriam's broken spectacles at the film's end? Those missing spectacles function as a loose end, an unrecuperated figure for female insight, for the possibility of reasserting distance from the image and for reading the paranoid projections of male subjectivity.

Notes

1 Laura Mulvey, "Visual Pleasure and Narrative Cinema," *Screen* 16, no. 3 (Autumn 1975): 6–18; Raymond Bellour, "*The Birds*," *Cahiers du Cinéma* 216 (October 1969): 24–38 (English translation from the BFI Educational Advisory Service), "Hitchcock the Enunciator," *Camera Obscura* 2 (Fall 1977): 69–91; "Psychosis, Neurosis, Perversion," *Camera Obscura* 3–4 (Summer 1979): 105–132.

2 Some examples: Jacqueline Rose, "Paranoia and the Film System," in *Feminism and Film Theory*, ed. Constance Penley (Minneapolis: University of Minnesota Press, 1988), 141–158. Robert Stam and Roberta Pearson, "Hitchcock's *Rear Window:* Reflexivity and the Critique of Voyeurism," *Enclitic* 7, no. 1 (1983): 136–45; Tania Modleski, *The Women Who Knew Too Much: Hitchcock and Feminist Theory* (New York and London: Methuen, 1988).

3 Papers interested in male subjectivity were Timothy Murray's "Dirty Stills: Retrospection, Hieroglyphs, and Filmic Phantoms," Kaja Silverman's "Male Subjectivity at the Margins," and Sharon Willis's "Disputed Territories: Masculinity and Social Space." Article versions of the latter two pieces appear in *Camera Obscura* 19 (January 1989): 54–84, 4–23, Silverman's under the title "Fassbinder and Lacan: A Reconsideration of Gaze, Look, and Image." Murray's "Le cliché taché: Rétrospection et décomposition cinématographique," trans. Eliane Dal Molin, was published in *Le Théâtre du Québec: Mémoire et appropriation*, L'annuaire théâtral, 5/6 (Fall 1988/Spring 1989), 307–18, with a longer version, "Dirty Stills: Arcadian Retrospection, Cinematic Hieroglyphs, and Blackness Run Riot in Olivier's *Othello*" in *Like a Film: Ideological Fantasy on Screen, Camera and Canvas* (New York: Routledge, 1993), 101–23.

4 See, e.g., Eve Kosofsky Sedgwick's work on male homosociality (*Between Men: English Literature and Male Homosocial Desire* [New York: Columbia University Press, 1985]) and recent feminist accounts of the novel, including Mary Poovey's work on the contradictions of patriarchal ideology (*Uneven Developments: The Ideological Work of Gender in Mid-Victorian England* [Chicago: University of Chicago Press, 1988]) and Nancy Armstrong's analysis of how eighteenth-century "female" subjectivity becomes nineteenth-century "male" subjectivity (*Desire and Domestic Fiction: A Political History of the Novel* [New York: Oxford University Press, 1987]); see also critiques of phallocentrism in psychoanalysis such as Jane Gallop's *Reading Lacan* (Ithaca, N.Y.: Cornell University Press, 1985) and Luce Irigaray's *This Sex Which Is Not One*, trans. Catherine Porter (Ithaca, N.Y.: Cornell University Press, 1985).

5 My thinking about this film owes much to discussions with Phil Barrish as well as with Amanda Anderson, Debra Fried, and the Writing About Film staff led by Lynda Bogel (Fall 1988). I also want to thank Tim Murray and Sasha Torres for their advice about revisions and Constance Penley for her interest in my project.

6 Sigmund Freud, "Psycho-analytic Notes on an Autobiographical Account of a Case of Paranoia" (1911), in *The Standard Edition of the Complete Psychological Works of Sigmund Freud*, trans. and ed. James Strachey (London: Hogarth, 1953), 12:59–79.

7 On the link between homosociality and blackmail in narratives concerned with male doubles, see Eve Kosofsky Sedgwick's "Toward the Gothic: Terrorism and Homosexual Panic," in *Between Men: English Literature and Male Homosocial Desire* (New York: Columbia University Press, 1985), 97–117.

8 Donald Spoto, *The Art of Alfred Hitchcock: Fifty Years of His Motion Pictures* (New York: Hopkinson & Blake, 1976), 209–10.

9 Raymond Bellour, "The Obvious and the Code," in *Narrative, Apparatus, Ideology: A Film Theory Reader*, ed. Philip Rosen (New York: Columbia University Press, 1986), 100.

10 Thierry Kuntzel, "The Film-Work, 2," *Camera Obscura* 5 (Spring 1980): 7–68.

11 Kaja Silverman, *The Subject of Semiotics* (New York: Oxford University Press, 1983), 225. By contrast, the scene between Guy and Miriam in the music store is filmed primarily in two-shot framing, both figures contained in a single camera frame, with far fewer cuts. A "pop" explanation of shot/reverse shot suture is found in Roger Ebert's account of the "Seeing Eye Man"—"Function performed by most men in Hollywood feature films. Involves a series of shots in which (1) the man sees something, (2) he points it out to the woman, (3) she then sees it too, often nodding in agreement, gratitude, amusement, or relief."

12 In contrast to Hitchcock's use of a "fascinating design" to channel the crisscrossing of desire between men (thus satisfying personal and professional censors), Patricia Highsmith's novel *Strangers on a Train* (New York: Harper & Bros., 1950), from which the film derives, makes the attraction and aggression between Guy and Bruno much more explicit.

13 A recent Hitchcockian treatment of doubles is David Cronenberg's *Dead Ringers* (1988) in which destabilized male subjectivity, paranoid projection, and murderous rage are all triggered by the intrusion of a female (Geneviève Bujold's) sexually aggressive look. Unlike *Strangers,* however, *Dead Ringers* retains its focus on the logic of a self-destructive male pathology: instead of murdering the woman, the identical twins—a literalized split self—destroy each other.

14 J. Laplanche and J. B. Pontalis, *The Language of Psychoanalysis* (New York: Norton, 1973), 354. I am indebted to Mary Ann Doane's *The Desire to Desire: The Woman's Film of the 1940s* (Bloomington: Indiana University Press, 1987) for stimulating my interest in paranoia and gender and for calling my attention to the Laplanche and Pontalis definition.

15 See Debra Fried's "The Men in *The Women,*" in *Women and Film,* ed. Janet Todd (Holmes & Meier, 1988), 43–69, for an account of phones as markers of the apparatus.

16 Laplanche and Pontalis, *Language of Psychoanalysis,* 354.

17 Raymond Bellour, "Psychosis, Neurosis, Perversion," 118–19.

18 Although Ann will ultimately replace Bruno and become Guy's conjugal "double," I think it is important to notice (to denaturalize or "deobviousize") the difficulty of the process along the way.

19 Freud, "A Case of Paranoia," 60.

20 Sedgwick, *Between Men,* 105.

21 James Hogg, *The Private Memoirs and Confessions of a Justified Sinner* (1824), ed. John Carey (London: Oxford University Press, 1969), 35–36.

22 Jacqueline Rose, "Paranoia and the Film System," in *Feminism and Film Theory,* ed. Constance Penley (New York: Routledge, 1988), 144.

23 Ibid., 147.

24 Interestingly, following his angry assault on Bruno, Guy tenderly reties Bruno's tie ("Here, let me," he says) as if the tie between them, between the self and the other, were a possible one, briefly opening up a space for a different articulation of masculinity. But the drive to resecure Guy's heterosexual "manhood" ultimately produces the expulsion of the homosexual other.

25 Doane, *The Desire to Desire,* 169.

26   Patricia Highsmith, who wrote lesbian fiction under the pseudonym Claire Morgan, might be considered such a reader.

27   "If—," in *Rudyard Kipling's Verse: The Definitive Edition* (London: Hodder & Stoughton, 1940), 576–77.

28   As Joan Copjec notes, Baudry actually uses the term *dispositif* (a disposition or arrangement) rather than *appareil* (apparatus) in his second essay on the workings of cinema, but both were translated as "apparatus" (Joan Copjec. "The Anxiety of the Influencing Machine," *October* 23 [Winter 1982], 57. Baudry himself retains an investment in the cinematic machine as capable of completing the subject (see Jean-Louis Baudry, "The Apparatus: Metapsychological Approaches to the Impression of Reality in the Cinema," in *Narrative, Apparatus, Ideology: A Film Theory Reader* [New York: Columbia University Press, 1986], 299–318). The subject of the "dispositif" is less positioned than dispositioned, less singular than multiple: "Patriarchy can only be an effect of a particular arrangement of competing discourse, and these competing discourses include "the multiformity of the construction of sexual differences" (Copjec, "Anxiety" 58–59). It is crucial for feminist film theory to recover this distinction since a cinematic *dispositif* or *arrangement,* as Constance Penley explains, implies not the "singular subject of the optical apparatus" but the subject (and here she quotes Derrida) of a "system of relations between strata . . . of the psyche, of society, of the world" ("Feminism, Film Theory, and the Bachelor Machines," in *The Future of an Illusion: Film, Feminism, and Psychoanalysis* [Minneapolis: University of Minnesota Press, 1989], 70).

29   As Kaja Silverman explains, the 180-degree rule is "predicated on the assumption that a complete camera revolution would be 'unrealistic,' defining a space larger than the 'naked eye' would normally cover" (*The Subject of Semiotics* 201).

30   Ibid., 232.

31   Kuntzel's insights into textual disorder in *The Most Dangerous Game* inform my reading of this scene: "Let's not be mistaken: narrative-representational film only allows discharge of energy, excess, disorder, confusion, on condition that all of these ruptures of code take on meaning—and *value*—with respect to the global economy of narration and representation" (Kuntzel, "The Film-Work," 48).

32   This is the familiar form of address in films preoccupied with the formation of male subjectivity. See, e.g., the role of the boy-spectator and his mimetic imitation of a television superhero (whom his father also therefore imitates) in *Robocop* (1987), a self-conscious reworking of the father/son thematic in *Shane*—most obviously in Shane's signature "gun-twirling" gesture so admired by Joey.

33   Debra Fried's helpful observation.

34   To complete the fantasy, her death enables a displaced version of a male couple, Miriam's doubled boyfriends, to go off together into the night.

"I'm not the sort

of person men

marry"

Monsters, Queers, and Hitchcock's *Rebecca*

Rhona J. Berenstein

There is an early scene in Alfred Hitchcock's *Rebecca* (1940) in which Maxim de Winter (Laurence Olivier) asks a young woman (Joan Fontaine) to marry him.[1] She offers Max a rather odd response to his query: "I'm not the sort of person men marry." Her comment incites at least two questions that are central to this narrative, to this tale of female desires. First, what sort of person do men marry? Second, why isn't Fontaine's character of that sort? The latter question sparks my urge to rewrite Fontaine's strange answer to Max as, "I'm not the sort of person who marries men." While such a transformation of dialogue can be cavalierly effected some fifty-one years after *Rebecca*'s release, Fontaine's affiliation with queer women—women whose sexualities defy the conventions of thirties and forties heterosexuality—is implied throughout the film. The tracing of the clues that point again and again to a queer subtext aligned with monstrosity will be outlined in the following pages.

Sue-Ellen Case has written that the "queer is the taboo-breaker, the monstrous, the uncanny. Like the Phantom of the Opera, the queer dwells underground, below the operatic overtones of the dominant; frightening to look at, desiring, as it plays its own organ, producing its own music." Case's queers— and her elaboration of queer theory—are associated with "the idiomatically-proscribed position of same-sex desire."[2] Queerness is characterized by the breaking of boundaries, by an incision into the ontological justification and valorization of heterosexuality. Whereas for Case queers revel in same-sex desire, in this discussion of Hitchcock's *Rebecca* the term *queer* will be applied both to the text's circulation of lesbian desires and to its movements between same-sex and other-sex desires. *Queer* thus refers to the same-sex components of the lesbian and bisexual desires exhibited by *Rebecca*'s heroines. It also refers to the disruptive qualities of the movement between same-sex and other-sex desires in bisexual examples.[3] In writing of the lesbian specters that dwell in Robert Wise's *The Haunting* (1963), Patricia White asserts, "The film, resisting the visualization of desire between women, displaces that desire onto the level of the supernatural."[4] Like the ghost story described by White, Hitchcock's Gothic romance sets the terms for a queer attraction and displaces that attraction onto the levels of metaphor and the supernatural. In applying White's comment to *Rebecca,* a close reading of the queer desires that punctuate that film demands both tracing the movie's elaboration of female subjectivity and exploring its construction of Rebecca's haunting monstrosity.

A Gothic romance is not an unusual text in which to seek and find a heroine. Like other woman's films of the forties, *Rebecca* focuses on the interrogation and representation of female subjectivity, and it appeals to female spectators. As a Gothic narrative, it also includes the elaboration of nightmare states, an attention to the protagonist's fears, and the representation of evil.[5] In *Rebecca,* a wealthy widower, Maxim de Winter, meets a younger woman (Fontaine) who is visiting Monte Carlo as a paid companion to an American, Mrs. Van Hopper (Florence Bates). Overhearing one of her employer's conversations, Fontaine learns that Maxim's wife drowned at sea the previous year. Fontaine and Max spend time together in Monte Carlo, and, although he remains a figure marked by restraint and mystery, he proposes to her. After their honeymoon, they return to his estate in England: Manderley. Fontaine feels out of her element amid the wealth and splendor of her new home. Her displacement is compounded by her belief that her predecessor, Rebecca, still holds her husband's and the staff's (especially, the housekeeper, Mrs. Danvers's) loyalties and that she will never be able to measure up to the first Mrs. de Winter. Mrs. Danvers (Judith Anderson) is especially cruel to the new bride, pointing out her inadequacies on a regular basis, and frequently asserting Rebecca's superiority to her successor. Eventually, however, Fontaine stands up to Danvers and takes her proper place as mistress of the mansion. Soon after, Rebecca's boat and body are discovered at sea. Maxim had falsely identified the woman's body that lies in the family crypt. In a dramatic confession, Max admits to his bride that he didn't love Rebecca, that, in fact, he hated her, and that they fought bitterly the night she died. Asserting that she fell and struck her head, thereby killing herself, Maxim admits that he placed her body in the boat, sailed it out, and sank it. The revelation that he didn't love Rebecca thrills Fontaine. The remainder of the film is spent investigating Rebecca's death. When a London doctor informs Max and the authorities that his first wife had cancer, her demise is dismissed as suicide. Hearing of Rebecca's illness and the suicide theory, Danvers sets the mansion on fire, destroying most of the de Winter possessions and killing herself.

According to Diane Waldman, "the central feature of the Gothics is ambiguity, the hesitation between two possible interpretations of events by the protagonist. . . . In the Gothic [romance film of the forties], this hesitation is experienced by a character . . . who is female."[6] In true Gothic fashion, *Rebecca* traces Fontaine's hesitations, her troubling questions that punctuate the film with ambiguity and ambivalence: Does Maxim love his second wife, or does he not? Will he always be preoccupied with Rebecca, or will he leave her in the past? Does he love Rebecca, or does his preoccupation suggest something other than love? Can Fontaine fulfill the expectations he has of a wife, or will she forever remain a child in his eyes? On the surface, these questions suggest that her husband serves as the focus of her inquiries, as the principle sign of ambiguity, since it is his actions and motives that Fontaine has trouble deciphering. These queries are, however, more complex than a surface reading would allow. Fontaine's efforts to find out more about Maxim's moods and feelings, to understand him better, are also attempts to find out about another woman, Rebecca. Rebecca is an elusive, sexually attractive, and powerful figure in this film—even in her absence. The second Mrs. de Winter's fascination with her predecessor permeates the text, thereby causing Fontaine to spend the course of the film investigating questions posed in relation to two characters: Max and Rebecca. Thus, although Fontaine and Max's coupling is marked by ambiguity, the text is equally haunted by an ambiguous representation of Rebecca.

Rebecca contributes to the ambiguities in Fontaine and Maxim's relationship by intervening in that relationship. She mediates, and in certain instances obstructs, the film's primary heterosexual couple. A close look at two early scenes indicates that Rebecca is a force that Fontaine and Max contend with, even in her absence. For example, in the scene directly following Fontaine's opening voice-over, Maxim meets his second wife. The ghost of Rebecca is figured as the crashing waves to which there was a dissolve from her bedroom window. The sequence begins with a high-angle panning shot of the ocean, which then moves up the side of a cliff and rests on a figure (Maxim) standing on the cliff's edge. There is a cut to an extreme close-up of Max's face as he stares at the ocean. As he begins to step forward, the music reaches a crescendo. It ends abruptly, and a female voice is heard shouting, "No, stop!" Maxim turns his head in the direction from which the voice came, and there is a cut to a long shot of him in the foreground, a woman in the mid-ground further down the hill, and the ocean on the left of the screen.

Until this point, both the shot constructions (framing, angles, etc.), as well as Max's physical posture, direction of his gaze, and general expression, suggest that it is toward the ocean, toward Rebecca, who is repeatedly associated with water throughout the film, that he is geared. He peers at the sea, he steps toward it, and he seems to float over it owing to the high angle of the shot. Once Fontaine's voice interrupts his reverie, however, the orientation of the scene shifts. He turns to face her. The configuration of the long shot suggests that Max and Fontaine are simultaneously aligned with each other, while their bodies remain oriented to the ocean. Their bodies appear to have turned fully toward each other only in the close-ups that follow this establishing shot. For Max, this scene ends with a realignment from Rebecca to Fontaine. After yelling at his future wife and causing her to depart, there is a cut to a close-up of his face as he watches her leave. He turns to look at the water and turns again to gaze at the spot from which Fontaine departed. Finally, he exits the frame. The camera rests in this position for a few moments; the screen is filled with the ocean and the sound of crashing waves.

Fontaine and Max's first meeting ends abruptly. She is chased away, he eventually departs in her direction, and the scene closes with an image of Rebecca's metonymic stand-in: water. Rebecca's participation in this sequence is, however, suggested by more than her oceanic associations. She occupies a position on the cliff as a memory, as a figure who once stood on that precipice with her new husband. The space in which Fontaine meets Max is the space in which, we later find out, his first bride confessed horrible things to him, in which she destroyed his dreams of matrimonial bliss. On the cliff, Rebecca agreed to "play the part" of the perfect wife, but their happiness was a sham. That Maxim and Fontaine meet at the site of the destruction of his first honeymoon does not bode well for their union. Rebecca haunts this scene as an absent signifier of failed heterosexual matrimony.

In a later scene, in which Fontaine and Max stand on a Monte Carlo promontory overlooking the ocean, Rebecca mediates their coupling once again. Fontaine has just finished sketching Max, and they begin to discuss Manderley and her childhood trip with her father to the region where it is located. Their discussion begins rather innocently. They mention the weather, how cold it must be in England, and how nice it is to be able to swim in the ocean. After this part of the conversation, Fontaine describes the perils of the undertow and tells of a man's drowning the previous year. Max squirms and grimaces in response to her words. He pulls away from her, as she continues, "I've never had any fear of drowning, have you?" Max pivots and turns as Fontaine continues to speak. He walks further and further into the background. Finally, Fontaine turns to where he once was, as the ocean frames her face in close-up. Eventually, he notes, "Come, I'll take you home." She nods nervously and acquiesces to his demand.

This description of the sketching scene suggests, as do later driving scenes, that, whether she appears in the form of a body of water or when verbally invoked and implied, Rebecca interferes in Fontaine and Max's relationship. In this example, she intervenes in their coupling by visually enveloping them and by serving as the unnamed demon responsible for Max's altered mood. Since, near the end of the scene, both Max and Fontaine are physically positioned in relation to the sea, and since that positioning delays Fontaine's realization that she has upset him and that he has departed from her side, Rebecca intrudes by drawing Fontaine's attention away from Max. Rebecca's presence in absentia thus sends a troubling ripple through Max and Fontaine's early interactions. She mediates their coupling by posing a threat to it: she threatens to haunt Maxim's present in the form of memories and irrevocably to insert herself into Fontaine's life as a menacing, intruding, and attractive figure.

Fontaine's relationship to her predecessor is unique—Rebecca is not just any heroine. First of all, she never once appears in the film. Second, she's dead. Rebecca's physical absence is, however, rendered palpable and in that sense present throughout the film. The deceased Mrs. de Winter haunts *Rebecca* as a ghost, a monstrosity whose power resides in not being seen. Tania Modleski puts it well when she notes, "Rebecca herself lurks in the blind space of the film, with the result that, like the shark [in *Jaws*] and unlike the second Mrs. de Winter, she never becomes 'domesticated.'"[7] The spectral status of Rebecca is ambiguous since it depends simultaneously on her figural invisibility and on a sustained discussion of her appearance, behavior, and corporeality. At times, the dialogue about Rebecca and a recognition of her position as the text's monster are combined. For example, when the second Mrs. de Winter asks Frank (Reginald Denny), Maxim's assistant, about his impressions of Rebecca, he responds, "I suppose she was the most beautiful *creature* I ever saw" (emphasis added). Later in the film, when Max describes the events of the night Rebecca died, he refers to her as a "spirit" and the "devil." Each of these descriptions aids in the establishment of her monstrosity, a monstrosity intimately linked, especially in Frank's comment, to her abnormal body.

The construction of Rebecca as a frightening figure bears a striking similarity to the position of monsters in the classic horror film: the monster is unnatural, diseased, and often has a privileged relationship with death. Rebecca's association with this type of monstrosity is accomplished both through dialogue, such as her description as a "creature," and through metaphoric and metonymic associations of her with the unrestrained and destructive forces of nature (primarily the sea) and with the foreboding and mysterious dominance of Manderley. The mansion that rests on Manderley's grounds is, like all Gothic homesteads, haunted. It is a space repeatedly associated with Rebecca through the appearance of her initials on napkins, stationery, and other items on which Fontaine stumbles as she moves through the house. The mansion serves both as the space that Rebecca haunts and as the space that is her: she embodies Manderley and lurks in its dark corners. In the beginning of the film, Fontaine describes the house as "secretive and silent," terms that both personify the mansion and align it with the eternally silent, deceased Rebecca. Like the monster of classic horror, the mansion is larger than life: even the doorknobs are positioned at a height that makes Fontaine look child-like in her attempts to turn them. It is mysterious and indecipherable: Fontaine is disoriented by its spaciousness. And it is foreign, especially to Fontaine, whose socioeconomic background has not prepared her for such wealth. Fontaine's relationship to her environment is, therefore, not unlike her relationship to Rebecca—a woman who is aggrandized, whose mysteriousness haunts Fontaine, and whose social class renders her alien to her successor.

Rebecca's affinity with Manderley and nature is suggested early in the film. The movie opens with a female voice-over that accompanies a mobile camera as it moves smoothly down a winding road and around the charred remains of a mansion. Fontaine's voice describes a dream she had of returning to Manderley. She notes how nature's "long, tenacious fingers" have encroached on the drive, how the moonlight tricks her into believing that "light came from the windows" of a house characterized by "perfect symmetry," and how, at the scene's close, she is left with the mansion's "staring walls." This sequence encapsulates two primary narrative threads that are woven through the text. First, the personification of nature ("long, tenacious fingers") and of the house ("staring walls") and the description of the house's perfection (as Maxim later notes, everyone told him Rebecca would make the "perfect wife") invoke Rebecca's absent presence and imply her association with the mansion and nature. Second, Fontaine's doubling with Rebecca in this segment establishes a theme that is elaborated on throughout the film. That doubling is implied through an ambiguous use of pronouns. Fontaine notes early in her voice-over, "Like all dreamers, I was possessed of a sudden, supernatural power and passed like a spirit through the barrier before me." Later in the monologue, she asserts, "We can never go back to Manderley again, that much is certain." In referring to herself as a spirit, in introducing herself in a manner that the film overwhelmingly associates with Rebecca, Fontaine's "I" might be construed as Rebecca's as well, as a signifier of subjectivity for the absent body that haunts the remainder of the narrative. When Fontaine shifts from the pronoun "I" to "we," she shifts from a singular subjective position to a subjectivity marked as plural, and thus suggestive of a coupling. The ambiguity of her words, the uncertainty of her pronouns (to which characters are they meant to refer?), implies two possible couples: Fontaine and Max and Fontaine and Rebecca.

That Fontaine and Rebecca's doubling and coupling are suggested at the beginning of the film is significant; not only do the doubling and coupling indicate the primacy of the women's relationship throughout *Rebecca*, but they also attest to the power of their bond to survive the end of the narrative. The remainder of the film, the part directly following Fontaine's voice-over, is a flashback. The events represented in *Rebecca* occurred before Fontaine's introductory dream, before the opening's alignment of Fontaine with Rebecca. Their alignment survives the death and destruction elaborated on in the film and outlasts Fontaine and Max's departure from Manderley. But it is not solely the survival of Fontaine and Rebecca's alignment that the opening dream suggests. Fontaine's compelling voice-over constructs the mansion and the woman whom it represents as figures to which the second Mrs. de Winter powerfully returns, even in her dreams. Fontaine's reverie signifies Rebecca's central position as a persistent object of fascination for her successor.

The flashback portion of the film thus functions, among other things, to establish Fontaine and Rebecca's alignment, to set the terms for a queer attraction. The shift from the opening segment to the flashback section of the narrative is achieved through a zoom into one of the mansion's windows—the one in Rebecca's bedroom—and a dissolve to a shot of crashing waves. The link between Rebecca and water that this transition establishes is reinforced in the scene between Fontaine and Max, mentioned earlier, in which she describes the perils of the undertow and recounts that a man drowned the previous year. The ocean, characterized as dangerous and destructive, is, as we later find out, home not only to this drowned man's body but to Rebecca's as well. In this scene, and in the film as a whole, Rebecca is both represented by and resides in the ocean. She possesses a destructive and monstrous link to the forces of nature.

The queer dimensions of Rebecca's monstrosity are implied at various moments in the narrative. In a scene in the boathouse in which Maxim reveals his true feelings for his first wife, he notes, "I never had a moment's happiness with her. She was incapable of love, or tenderness, or decency." A good portion of Olivier's dialogue is transcribed from the novel on which the film is based. However, in Daphne du Maurier's original text, Maxim goes on to articulate what is only suggested in the film: "She was not even normal."[8] Rebecca's abnormality finds metaphoric representation in the revelation that her body was wracked by disease, by a cancer that was propelling her to a speedy death. In contrast to Max's assumption that she was pregnant, that hers was a reproductive (read natural) female body, Rebecca was gestating a growing tumor, not a growing child. The novel makes her reproductive abnormality more explicit. Dr. Baker, in his review of her medical records, declares, "The X-rays showed a certain malformation of the uterus, I remember, which meant she could never have had a child, but that was quite apart, it had nothing to do with the disease."[9] The deductive leap from Rebecca's abnormal reproductive system to a queer sexuality is minimal: the association of homosexuality with sterility has a long heritage. Moreover, the description of Rebecca's physical state recalls the stereo-typical equation of lesbianism with an unnatural—that is, nonreproductive—female sexuality.

Rebecca's alignment with queerness is further suggested in another segment of the scene between Fontaine and Maxim in the boathouse. As Max recounts the events of their honeymoon in Monte Carlo, he tells of one of their discussions: "Do you remember that cliff where you first saw me? . . . That was where I found out about her. . . . She stood there laughing, her black hair blowing in the wind, and told me all about herself. Everything. Things I'll never tell a living soul. I wanted to kill her." Max's reaction to Rebecca's comments may refer to his horror at a confession of heterosexual infidelity. However, there is also a "coming-out" quality to Max's description—he "found out about her"; Rebecca told him "all about herself." This quality, combined with the unrepeatable nature of her words, suggests that hers is not a "lawless sexuality," to borrow Modleski's phrase, of a normal kind.[10] An admission of heterosexual infidelity in 1940 (or in 1938, when the novel was released) may have been horrid, but it could have been revealed to "another living soul." Queer behavior, on the other hand, was more likely to have been treated as unrepeatable, as thoroughly unutterable.

Writing of the male homosexual subtext in Robert Louis Stevenson's *The Strange Case of Dr. Jekyll and Mr. Hyde* (1886), Elaine Showalter notes, "The metaphors associated with Hyde are those of abnormality, criminality, disease, contagion, and death. . . . In the most famous code word of Victorian homosexuality, they [other male characters] find something *unspeakable* about Hyde."[11] While *Rebecca* appeared in print and celluloid well after the end of the last century, many of the metaphors that adhere to Hyde's character, as Showalter describes them, apply to Rebecca as well. Moreover, the unspeakable status of queerness in *Dr. Jekyll and Mr. Hyde* has endured well into this century, as Eve Kosofsky Sedgwick points out in *Epistemology of the Closet*.[12] That the mystique surrounding Rebecca's sexuality is characterized as unutterable reinforces its correspondence with late nineteenth and early twentieth-century treatments of homosexuality. Homosexuality was represented through the enforcement of a discourse of silence—it was that which was not, should not, and could not be spoken. In the novel, Rebecca's abnormal (in this instance, nonheterosexual) qualities are, however, elaborated on in a manner that flirts with speaking the unutterable. Near the end of the book, Mrs. Danvers tells Jack Favell (George Sanders), the cousin with whom Rebecca supposedly had an affair, that she was in love neither with him nor with Maxim; Mrs. Danvers continues, "She despised all men. She was above all that."[13] Here again, a stereotypical characterization of lesbians is invoked: Rebecca was a man hater. More significant perhaps in the context of the film is the fact that Favell is played by George Sanders, an actor whose general performance style and particular character in *Rebecca* suggest a dandy, a feminized man who bears a striking resemblance to lasting stereotypes of male homosexuals. In speaking of the nineteenth century, Showalter notes, "The image of the English male homosexual that prevailed for much of this century was that of the effeminate aesthete or the decadent dandy."[14] The fact that Favell, *Rebecca*'s "decadent dandy," is the only significant male figure around whom intimations of an affair with Rebecca revolve suggests that even her heterosexual interests may not have been very serious or very "straight."

The ambiguous representation of Rebecca's sexuality is compounded by an equally complex construction of her as an icon of femininity. Speaking of the novel on which the film was based, Alison Light argues that "Rebecca becomes the figure which reveals the girl's [Fontaine's] unfulfilled desires. She is what is missing from the marriage; she is body to the girl's endless cerebration, the absent centre around which the narrative and definitions of femininity turn."[15] Fontaine, indeed, spends much of the film attempting to replicate the actions, decisions, and wardrobe of her predecessor. In spite of Maxim's entreaties that she remain a child and that she never wear pearls and black satin (signifiers of adulthood and of the upper class), Fontaine insists on growing up and taking Rebecca's place—she wears pearls and black satin, begs Max to allow her to give a costume ball, and wears the same costume worn by Rebecca the previous year. Despite her repeated failures in becoming her predecessor, Fontaine dwells on the fact that she lacks what is attributed to Rebecca: "brains, beauty and breeding."

The ambiguities surrounding Rebecca as a model of femininity are compelling. As Light indicates, Rebecca is aligned with femininity in the novel, but she is also aligned with masculinity, as Mrs. Danvers' remarks make clear: "She had all the courage and spirit of a boy, had my Mrs. de Winter. She ought to have been a boy." And as Max notes of her appearance the night she died, "She looked like a boy in her sailing kit, a boy with a face like a Botticelli angel." Fontaine's character also assumes a masculine position in the book, but one associated less with independence and beauty, as is the case with Rebecca, than with the vulnerabilities of male childhood: "I was like a little scrubby schoolboy with a passion for a sixth-form prefect"; and elsewhere, "I would feel like a whipping boy who must bear his master's pains." It is noteworthy that the masculine traits attributed to the second Mrs. de Winter possess strong hints of male homosexuality. In the first example, Fontaine's character describes herself as a young boy attracted to an older boy. In the second, she positions herself as the victim in a male-identified sadomasochistic-type scenario. In both instances, she (as a "he") responds to men in positions of authority. The masculine traits attributed to Rebecca by Danvers are as powerful as those possessed by Fontaine's authoritative men. As

Danvers notes, "She did what she liked, she lived as she liked. She had the strength of a little lion."[16] The first Mrs. de Winter's impressive status suggests that Fontaine's position in relation to Rebecca is not unlike her position vis-à-vis the prefect and the master.[17] Rebecca and her successor are thus aligned through their shared, yet differential, relationships to masculinity—once again, a conventional reading of lesbianism springs to mind: lesbians are masculine women. Fontaine's position as the passive partner in these homosexual pairings invokes another connotation associated with lesbianism: she plays the "femme" to the master's, the prefect's, and Rebecca's "butch."

While the novel is more explicit in its associations of Rebecca and Fontaine's character with queerness, the film's very repression of the subject actually reinforces its presence as a relentless undercurrent. On screen, the most stringent ambiguities surrounding Rebecca's femininity are indicated by Maxim's requests that Fontaine not change, that she not become more like Rebecca. Frank's comment that she was a "beautiful creature" similarly problematizes the idealization of her feminine stature. Fontaine's refusal to heed these ambiguous warnings indicates that her fascination with Rebecca somehow exceeds Maxim's desires for Rebecca. Fontaine's insistence on assuming Rebecca's place in Manderley and the repeated doubling of her with the first Mrs. de Winter intimate Fontaine's intention to adopt Rebecca's position in the text—the position of the sexual renegade: the monstrous queer.

Rebecca's intrusion into her successor's life thus contributes to the fragmentation of Fontaine's desires. For the sake of clarity, those desires can roughly be divided into the following categories: (1) her desire for a romantic coupling with Maxim; (2) her desire for a familial union with (a) Max as a father figure and (b) Rebecca as an idealized mother; and (3) her romantic desire for Rebecca, for an absent female body. Fontaine's heterosexual desire has received the most critical attention in readings of the film. For example, Mary Ann Doane notes that in *Rebecca* "the diegetic film's continuous unfolding guaranteed a rather fragile binding of the drives in the heterosexual unit of the harmonious couple."[18] Although Doane goes on to address the manner in which that union is rendered tenuous in the film, the heterosexual couple serves as the central pivot of her analysis.

Fontaine's familial desires have also been noted by critics. Her relationship to Maxim is heavily coded as that between a daughter and her father. (For example, Max requests that she not grow up, that she stop biting her nails, and that she not catch cold.) Donald Ranvaud notes that Max becomes her "acquired father-figure," the man who rescues her from her lower socioeconomic position and, in classic fairy-tale fashion, removes her from the jaws of the beast—in this instance, her horrid employer, Mrs. Van Hopper.[19]

That Rebecca serves as Fontaine's idealized mother has been argued quite forcefully by Tania Modleski: "Hitchcock's films [present] images of ambiguous sexuality that threaten to destabilize the gender identity of the protagonists and viewers alike. Although in *Psycho* the mother/son relationship is paramount, I will argue that in films from *Rebecca* on it is more often the mother/daughter relationship that evokes this threat to identity and constitutes the main 'problem' of the films." Modleski describes *Rebecca* as a female oedipal drama in which Fontaine must vanquish the threat of her maternal rival in order to take up her proper position within an oedipal scenario, her proper position with her husband/father. As she notes, "It becomes obvious that the two desires cannot coexist: the desire for the mother impedes the progress of the heterosexual union. Ultimately, then, the heroine disavows her desire for the mother, affirming her primary attachment to the male."[20]

Modleski's reading is a compelling but partial one. Its strength resides in the recognition of the central function of the figure of Rebecca to the narrative, to the development of Fontaine's character, and to the film's primary heterosexual relationship. Her reading is, however, limited by her conflation of Rebecca's role as a maternal figure with her position as an object of female sexual desire. Modleski achieves this conflation by remarking on the issue of lesbianism ("there is something more at stake here, something potentially more subversive") and working that issue through in a rapid manner. Noting the limitations of the Electra complex for its too-rigid conceptualization of the girl's perception of her mother as an object of rivalry for her father's attention, Modleski argues the existence and power of the "desire of women for other women." She goes on to assert that Fontaine repeatedly seeks the affections of Mrs. Danvers (the bad mother), a woman obsessed with and sexually attracted to Rebecca. After establishing Fontaine's links to two mother figures (Rebecca and Danvers), Modleski writes the passage quoted above: "The desire for the mother impedes the progress of the heterosexual union."[21] The logic of Modleski's argument obscures a critical slippage. The rhetorical move is from the concept of lesbianism, to the elaboration of Fontaine's maternal feelings for Danvers, to Danvers's sexual attraction to Rebecca—queer desire is displaced from the daughter onto the bad mother. It is not Fontaine who sexually desires Rebecca, the argument suggests, but Mrs. Danvers who does so. Fontaine's rejection of Rebecca need not be read as the rejection of "something subversive" but as functioning instead to promote the viability of the Electra complex. (If she is not attracted *to* Rebecca, then it stands to reason that her disavowal depends on Rebecca's status as a rival for Maxim's affections.)

Assuming, however, that Modleski is sincere in her criticism of the Electra complex as an adequate theorization of relationships among women, her argument must be revised. That revision requires the reworking of Rebecca's function within the film. Modleski's comment might thus be reworded, "The desire for the mother [as a sexual object] impedes the progress of the heterosexual union." Such a revision is consonant with both psychoanalysis and feminist notions of bisexual spectatorship, which rely on an assumption of preoedipal proximity between daughter and mother, a proximity used to theorize women's overidentification with other women and, in the case of the female viewer and her gaze, with images.[22] This reading is, however, limited in that it suggests that the desire of one woman for another is explicable either as a form of regression or as an idealized relationship, both of which depend on overidentification as a premise. Modleski's concept—shared by other feminist film theorists and critics—that the desire for the mother impedes the progress of the heterosexual couple can be rephrased as follows. Desire marked by same-sex identification with the mother impedes the progress of desire marked by sexual difference, that is, desire for a man. For the heterosexual couple to succeed, there must be a shift away from same-sex identification, from sameness per se, to sexual difference. Adult female subjectivity and sexuality are, from this theoretical position, characterized by the female subject's accession to a position marked by difference, and it is only lesser forms of sexuality that posit sameness as their modus operandi.[23]

Since psychoanalysis privileges sexual difference, a male-female binary opposition, to account for identification processes, queer relationships are, by definition, theorized as either less than (regressed) or more than (overidentified) and thus always operate *in relation to* a heterosexual norm. The heterosexism inherent in this reading of psychic processes is apparent. It is also insidious in that it depends on the notion of identification for its explanatory power and results in a consequent elision or reduction of queer sexual desires. In the realm of film analysis, the female spectator's gaze at female characters becomes a gaze marked by same-sex identification. While this viewing process may or may not subsume sexual desires, those desires are not the organizing principal of the gaze, as is the case for the traditionally conceived heterosexual male viewer.[24] If sexual desires are equated with identificatory processes that are uniform for all women, how are queer female subjectivities to be differentiated from heterosexual female subjectivities? In prevailing uses of psychoanalysis to theorize the female spectator's gaze, they are not. All women's potential for bisexual identification is addressed by this concept, not queer women's potentials for same-sex sexual desire.[25]

In order for queer sexual desires to be removed from the domain of heterosexual identification processes, Rebecca's status as a maternal figure must be separated from her role as an object of female sexual desires.[26] Such a move involves a critical amputation of psychoanalysis, but it is one suggested by Modleski's reading itself. That is, since Danvers is constructed as a bad mother who is sexually attracted to another woman (Rebecca), Fontaine's interest in Rebecca might also be considered an adult woman's attraction to another. *Rebecca* may, therefore, be a drama that depends on the illusion of Oedipus and/or Electra to maintain the status quo but that ripples with a sapphic menace that continuously threatens to erupt through the narrative's surface.

Despite the enduring power of the queer undercurrents that charge *Rebecca*'s textual universe, as the film's heroine, Fontaine must eventually adhere to the conventions of most Hollywood cinema and assume a culturally desirable—adult heterosexual—position. Modleski provides an interesting reading of the function of Fontaine's fascination with Rebecca as it relates to the position that she must eventually adopt. In order for her to detach from the mother and attach to Maxim, Modleski argues that "she must try to make her desire mirror the man's desire." That this is no easy task is suggested both by the fact that Maxim never expresses his desire for Rebecca and by the fact that, in the end, it is revealed that he only briefly desired her. Since Fontaine assumes, despite indications to the contrary, that Max desires his first wife, she replicates that desire. As Modleski asserts, "The project of the film is to get Maxim to turn his gaze away from Rebecca and toward the heroine."[27] In order to accomplish this project, Fontaine reproduces (her fantasy of) his interest in the first Mrs. de Winter. This interpretation traverses the edge of queerness (Fontaine romantically desires Rebecca) but does not call that edge by its proper name. While the project of *Rebecca* may be, in part, to realign Max's attention from his first to his second wife, that realignment depends on the second wife's fascination with the first. The project of the film is both to shift Maxim's gaze from the object of his hatred (for it happens that his preoccupation with Rebecca is characterized not by a longing for his dead wife but by a loathing of her) and to shift the heroine's gaze from the object of her desire. Two shifts are required for the narrative to be resolved heterosexually, but only Fontaine's gaze demands a realignment of romantic desire.

Fontaine's fascination with Rebecca is often mediated by the film's most obvious queer character, the wicked witch of the west wing, Mrs. Danvers. Danvers traverses the novel and film with a male appellation, *Danny,* and thus shares the masculine attributes associated with Rebecca and her successor in the book. Danvers's marginal sexual orientation has been duly noted by critics. "Though no one mentioned the underlying lesbianism of the Rebecca-Danvers relationship, Hitchcock sensed it," asserts Leonard Leff in *Hitchcock and Selznick.*[28] And, referring to the censorship concerns that that relationship fostered in the Production Code Administration offices, he continues, "In the final cut, Breen told Selznick, 'there must be no suggestion whatever of a perverted relationship between Mrs. Danvers and Rebecca. If any possible hint of this creeps [in], . . . we will of course not be able to approve the picture.' "[29] Breen's reaction is important on two counts. First, it indicates that the film's "perversion" is not confined to Danvers and her bizarre behavior; it refers more generally to Danvers and Rebecca's relationship with each other. Second, Breen's response suggests that his office somehow overlooked the endurance of Danvers's romantic attachment to her mistress in the final cut since it is represented in various forms. For example, in an early scene, Mrs. Van Hopper, speaking of Max's feelings for his first wife, notes, "He simply adored Rebecca." Later in the film, when Beatrice (Gladys Cooper), Maxim's sister, explains Danvers's rudeness to Fontaine, she asserts, "She [Mrs. Danvers] simply adored Rebecca." Through verbal parallels, Danny's feelings are equated with those of a husband/lover. Although she is attracted to Rebecca, Danvers is also represented as similar to the object of her desire.[30] Dressed entirely in black, Danny haunts Manderley's hallways. Her rigid stance and odd facial expressions mark her as an unnatural figure.

In addition to her extreme attachment and likeness to Rebecca, Danvers serves as another type of threat: the queer who lures unsuspecting victims into her state of perversion, the homo that recruits. Danvers's abnormality and threatening qualities coalesce in the domain that most explicitly links monstrosity with femininity and sexuality—Rebecca's bedroom. While Danvers focuses on Fontaine's difference from the first Mrs. de Winter through most of the film, in Rebecca's suite she insists on Fontaine's likeness to her predecessor. As Modleski phrases it, in the bedroom scene Danvers asks Fontaine to "substitute her body for the body of Rebecca."[31] Fontaine's willingness to accommodate this substitution is a testament both to Danvers's hypnotic and manipulative powers and to Fontaine's interest in being as close as possible to Rebecca.

The second Mrs. de Winter's initial visit to Rebecca's suite serves as a potent site for the consideration of Fontaine's attraction to the first Mrs. de Winter. In this sequence, the heroine's movements and her position within the frame reinforce the doubling of Fontaine with Rebecca, the substitution of one body for the other, in that the former takes up the latter's place in the room (both in terms of her physical position as well as in terms of Danny's seduction of her). Moreover, her movements and facial expressions are quite forcefully arranged *in relation to* her desires for Max and Rebecca. Fontaine's performance is thus mediated by her simultaneous attraction to her husband and his former wife, by the alternation between the homosexual and the heterosexual attractions that characterize her queer desires.

When Fontaine enters Rebecca's rooms, her shadow is reflected on a wall at the left of the frame, immediately aligning her with the suite's previous, ghostly occupant. She opens a window, and there is a cut to a medium shot of her at Rebecca's vanity touching a brush. As she fondles Rebecca's possessions, Fontaine is startled by a photograph of Max that rests on the table. She turns away from his image, and the camera pans with her as she walks to the right of the frame, toward the bed. The shutters clatter, and Danvers, in silhouette, fills the frame. Fontaine's attraction to Rebecca is already suggested in this brief segment. Supported by camera movement, Fontaine touches Rebecca's personal property, literally gasps at the sight of Maxim's photograph, physically turns away from him, and walks toward the space that signifies Rebecca's sexuality— her bedroom.

As the scene continues, Fontaine is pulled further and further away from the lure of Max's image and closer to Danvers's enamored reminiscences of Rebecca. In a two-shot, Danvers removes Rebecca's fur coat from a closet. She rubs her own face with the sleeve; she then reaches out to Fontaine and does the same to her cheek. The sexual overtones of this gesture are clear. Not only does Danvers caress herself with a garment worn by Rebecca, but she touches Fontaine in precisely the same way, instigating a circulation of Rebecca's "touch." From a queer perspective, Danvers's actions, removing the coat from Rebecca's wardrobe, can be read as a humorous form of outing. In her book on the homosexual closet and homo/hetero gender relations, Sedgwick coins a phrase in reference to a sequence from Proust's *Remembrance of Things Past* that is also an apt description of Danvers's gesture: "the theatricalization of a closet-figured-as-spectacle."[32] Viewed from this angle, Danvers pulls her paramour out of the proverbial closet by removing and caressing a coat worn by Rebecca. Fontaine is implicated in this process in that she too cops a feel.

The queer connotations of this scene continue in the next two-shot, when Danvers pulls out a drawer filled with Rebecca's undergarments (made especially for her by the nuns of St. Claire).[33] As Danvers bends over and fondles them, Fontaine stands rigidly, trying to retain her composure but unable to keep her eyes off the clothing. Fontaine's attention is again drawn to Rebecca's clothes, in this instance her delicate underwear. Danny then closes the drawer and leans with her back against the wall. Fontaine stands in an identical position on the opposite side of the frame and listens intently as Danvers recounts, "I always used to wait up for her no matter how late." As she utters these words, both women, separated by the space that fills the center of the frame, have their faces slightly lifted. Danny completes her sentence, and she and Fontaine simultaneously turn their heads to the background, where Rebecca's vanity can be seen. Danvers describes how she used to keep Rebecca company while she undressed, bathed, and prepared for bed.

The positioning and performances of the women are extremely stylized in this sequence. While standing on opposite sides of the frame with their heads lifted, they listen to the space between them as if it were palpable, as if it were occupied by a figure communicating with them. When they shift their gazes to the background, they look at the place once filled with Rebecca's body. Their movement is thus orchestrated in relation to Rebecca—they attend to an absent presence. As the scene continues, Fontaine sits at the vanity, and Danny mimics brushing her—Rebecca's—hair. The camera then pans to the photo of Max. Although Maxim's image might be said to draw the women away from Rebecca, in that the camera moves toward it, Danny's attention is not displaced and Fontaine's only briefly realigned. The women barely acknowledge him. As the scene continues, Danvers shows Fontaine Rebecca's pillowcase, which Danny embroidered herself, and she pulls out a black see-through negligee that she touches gently. Danvers urges the heroine to move closer to look at the lingerie. As Fontaine moves, so does the camera, which pans around the outside of the bed. Fontaine stares at the black negligee. As she does so, she is entrapped both within the frame and within the confines of the bed's posts; she is locked into the space that most explicitly signifies Rebecca's sexual activities.[34] This shot is broken by Fontaine's attempt to get away from Danvers and the negligee. Fontaine walks rapidly toward the door, followed by Danny. There is a zoom into the two women's faces as the heroine is frightened by Mrs. Danvers's eerie words: "Sometimes I wonder if she doesn't come back here to Manderley and watch you and Mr. de Winter." Fontaine runs out of the room and out of Rebecca's domain.

This scene is marked by a series of movements between Fontaine and Maxim's photo, between Danvers and Rebecca, Danvers and Fontaine, and Fontaine and Rebecca. Attraction and repulsion circulate simultaneously in each of these pairings. In relation both to Rebecca and to Max, Fontaine's romantic desires are coupled with fear. Leff argues that the scene's mood is intentional: "Hitchcock's staging, alternately widening and narrowing the spaces between the characters in the large, airy room, mirrored the attraction-repulsion theme that tortures the young heroine not only in the sequence but throughout the film."[35] Thus, neither heterosexual nor queer romance finds smooth representation in this sequence. While in the remainder of the film Max often functions as a visual and narrative force to be reckoned with, here he is as trapped by the frame of a photograph as Fontaine is by the four posts of Rebecca's bed. Fontaine does finally escape the room, but her powerful fascination with her predecessor indicates that the scene is a central pivot of the text. Thus, although marked by Maxim's presence, this scene is overwhelmingly about relationships among women.

The representation of female bonding in film is, according to Chris Straayer, potent. As she notes, "Females together on the screen signal simultaneously a lack of sexuality and a forbidden sexuality, both of which upset the film's heterosexual mechanisms. Within those mechanisms, female bonding poses a narrative blandness. Since both filmic and narrative desires are fueled by sexual desire, films often introduce sexual signals to eroticize such framing which contains two women. Once eroticized, however, female bonding threatens to subvert or, worse, circumvent that heterosexual scheme entirely. The primary threat of female bonding is the elimination of the male."[36] The scene in Rebecca's bedroom puts into play the threats posed by Straayer's comments: the sexualization of female couplings, the subversion of heterosexuality, and the elimination of the male. A second bedroom scene, in which Danny nearly coaxes Fontaine to jump out a window to the terrace below, similarly relies on a threat to heterosexual romance and to the narrative primacy of the male. Although Fontaine does not jump to the pavement, does not join Rebecca's body in the water adjacent to the mansion, the scene revolves around the very real possibility that she will do so, that she will abandon her husband and jump. In a sense, Rebecca herself prevents Fontaine from suicide. Precisely at the moment that Fontaine is about to fulfill Danvers's wishes, Rebecca's boat and body are discovered. There is no need for her to dive from the window; Rebecca is no longer in the water below. Rebecca, the film's absent body, has come to her.

In her article on the hypothetical lesbian heroine, Straayer notes that, "when one searches for lesbian exchange in narrative film constructions, one finds a constant flux between competing forces to suggest and deny it."[37] *Rebecca* is a film that forcefully illustrates Straayer's argument. Punctuated by clues that repeatedly point to Rebecca's, Danvers's, and Fontaine's queer desires, the novel and film weave nonheterosexual lures into their narrative fabrics. *Rebecca*'s sapphic menace is constructed on the coattails of homophobic stereotyping: Rebecca is monstrous, diseased, nonreproductive, destructive, unnatural, masculine, and a man hater. She is also strikingly beautiful, powerful, and alluring enough to sustain the attentions of her housekeeper and her successor and to jeopardize the success of the film's primary heterosexual union. That the queer's most influential and engaging attributes belong to a character who is physically absent from the film underscores both the potency of her threat and the limitations of patriarchal structures of representation—structures in which queerness is relegated to discourses of invisibility and silence.

Despite Rebecca's physical absence from the film, she occupies a palpable position in the narrative, and her presence is felt by others. Moreover, her spirit survives not only in the form of a ghost that haunts the mansion but also in the form of a woman who dreams of returning to Manderley. Fontaine's fascination with Rebecca and her repeated doubling with her suggest that the first Mrs. de Winter survives the story (and her own death) in the figure of her successor. As Patricia White notes, Fontaine's sexuality in the film is "latent, not necessarily, not yet, lesbian."[38] There is every reason to believe that Fontaine's burgeoning sexuality does or will one day indicate her adoption of Rebecca's status as a sexual renegade, a woman simultaneously inside and outside the boundaries of dominant social convention.

Rebecca's disruptive sexuality traverses the film at once dependent on heterosexual romance (she did marry Maxim) and in opposition to it (she does attract Fontaine and Danvers). While social convention and economic imperatives may have led Rebecca (and Fontaine's character) to marry Maxim de Winter, to be the "sort of person men marry," Rebecca's matrimonial status was tenuous at best, and Fontaine's fares no better. Given different social conditions and options, Rebecca and Fontaine may not be the sort of people who marry men. That Rebecca's textual position is as attractive to readers and viewers as to Fontaine is suggested by Harriet Hawkins in her analysis of the novel: "The female reader will readily identify with the insecure narrator's sense of inadequacy in contrast to the unattainable perfection of the woman who had everything. . . . Yet— *mutatis mutandis*—the character most female readers would most *like* to be like is, of course, the confident, the fearless, the popular, the accomplished, the adored, [and I might add, the queer,] Rebecca."[39]

The ambiguous monstrosity of *Rebecca*'s queer subtext is consonant with the social constraints of the historical and cultural milieu in which the novel and movie appeared. "Here is a much-needed book which examines straightforwardly the dramatic problems of women involved too intimately in one another's lives—a powerful novel of a little known social menace," notes the back-cover synopsis of *Queer Patterns*, a mass-produced, 1935 paperback by Lilyan Brock that traces the lesbian sexual awakenings of the stage actress Sheila Case. "Read this book, and gain an enlightened understanding of the lost women whose strange urges produce one of the great problems of modern society." Despite the ominous tone of this back-cover quotation, the novel simultaneously supports and opposes the characterization of queerness as a menace—both threatening and destructive, and misunderstood and romantically appealing. Hitchcock's film version of Du Maurier's 1938 novel *Rebecca* bears a striking resemblance to this description of Brock's book. Whereas *Queer Patterns* is a "straight-forward" examination of lesbianism, *Rebecca*'s queerness is represented on a subterranean level—it dwells in a textual underground, as Sue-Ellen Case might phrase it. But *Rebecca*, like *Queer Patterns*, might also be described as a story in which women are "too" intimately involved with each other, as Modleski's argument suggests. Like *Queer Patterns, Rebecca* represents the intimate involvement of thirties women in an ambiguous manner: lesbianism both threat-ening and appealing, monstrous and attractive.

The ambiguous representation of women's relationships was a common fea-ture of American society in the early part of this century (and remains so today, as the recent film *Thelma and Louise* [1991] intimates). Historical accounts of the thirties indicate that it was a period in which the late nineteenth- and early twentieth-century gains of the educated and prominent New Women were nega-tively transformed. Between 1890 and 1920, New Women often lived in all-female communities, dedicated themselves to procuring women's rights, and amassed significant political powers. By the twenties and thirties, Carroll Smith-Rosenberg asserts, "Women and men alike had disowned the New Woman's brave vision" of a more equitable distribution of gender relations. The darker side of American culture's treatment of female independence emerged in that period as "charges of lesbianism had become a common way to discredit women professionals, reformers, and educators."[40] Possibly in an attempt to avoid such charges, the marriage rate increased, the age at which women married de-creased, and the percentage of women to attain college, graduate, and profes-sional degrees dropped significantly. New Women, women who stood for female independence, education, and equality, were, by the thirties, the foci of ambig-uous social representations—earlier commended, they were now criticized; ear-lier perceived as mildly threatening, they were now deemed a social and sexual menace. These perceptions of women and their social position informed the popular imagination of the United States in the thirties. *Rebecca* emerged along-side this ambiguous heritage of representing independent women.

In light of the historical context, it is not surprising that the act of tracing *Rebecca*'s "queer patterns" is an act of excavation, an attempt to render Rebecca corporeal in a text that continuously undermines her figural presence.[41] It is also not surprising that Rebecca's status within the film's universe, a status reminis-cent of the New Woman's move toward marriage and away from independence, is represented as monstrous, sexually threatening, and disruptive of conven-tional heterosexuality. Despite her horrifying attributes, however, she is a figure that commands attention—which is no easy feat, considering her invisibility. Rebecca is a character never allowed to show herself, to speak for herself. Queer-ness is, like the first Mrs. de Winter, allowed to circulate through *Rebecca*, but not permitted to declare itself. In speaking it, in asserting that a sapphic menace permeates the text, I hope that I have brought Rebecca de Winter one step closer to defining her own identity, to materializing amid Manderley's ruins. Maxim did not quite know what he was saying when he described Rebecca's appearance the night she died, but his words come closer than any others in the film to naming the unspeakable: "She looked ill, queer." Queer, indeed.

Notes

I would like to thank Gaia Banks, Alexander Doty, Anne Friedberg, Alison McKee, and Linda Williams for their helpful insights and editorial suggestions on an earlier version of this article.

1 Fontaine's character remains nameless throughout the narrative. Unlike the first Mrs. de Winter, whose name serves both as a character's forename and as the film's title, the second Mrs. de Winter relies on her marital appellation for identification. As a result, I will alternately refer to her as Fontaine and as the second Mrs. de Winter.

2 Sue-Ellen Case, "Tracking the Vampire." *differences* 3, no. 2 (Summer 1991): 3.

3 I alternate between the terms *queer* and *lesbian* in this discussion. *Queer* is meant to refer to the display of both lesbian and bisexual tendencies in *Rebecca*'s female characters. However, in combining bisexual and homosexual proclivities in one term, the lesbian specificities of certain characters (e.g., Danvers) and of certain stereotyped behaviors (e.g., Rebecca's man hating in the novel) go unnamed. As a result, I use the term *lesbian* in those instances in which it is important that specifically homosexual connotations be privileged.

4 Patricia White, "Female Spectator, Lesbian Specter: *The Haunting*," in *Inside/Out: Lesbian Theories, Gay Theories*, ed. Diana Fuss (New York and London: Routledge, 1991), 157.

5 Peter Brooks, *The Melodramatic Imagination* (New York: Columbia University Press, 1985), 9–10.

6 Diane Waldman, "'At last I can tell it to someone!': Feminine Point of View and Subjectivity in the Gothic Romance Film of the 1940s," *Cinema Journal* 23, no. 2 (Winter 1983): 31.

7 Tania Modleski, *The Women Who Knew Too Much: Hitchcock and Feminist Theory* (New York: Methuen, 1988), 53.

8 Daphne Du Maurier, *Rebecca* (New York: Avon, 1938), 271.

9 Ibid., 367.

10 Modleski, *Women Who Knew Too Much*, 48.

11 Elaine Showalter, *Sexual Anarchy: Gender and Culture at the Fin de Siècle* (New York: Penguin, 1990), 112.

12 Eve Kosofsky Sedgwick, *Epistemology of the Closet* (Berkeley and Los Angeles: University of California Press, 1990).

13 Du Maurier, *Rebecca*, 340.

14 Showalter, *Sexual Anarchy*, 178.

15 Alison Light, "'Returning to Manderley'—Romance Fiction, Female Sexuality and Class," *Feminist Review* 16 (Summer 1984): 12.

16 Du Maurier, *Rebecca*, 242, 278, 35, 12, 243.

17 The sex and gender ambiguities surrounding these quotations are strong. In speaking of herself as a "scrubby schoolboy," Fontaine's character is articulating her position in relation to Maxim. In the second example, when she describes herself as a "whipping boy," her "master" is her employer, Mrs. Van Hopper. The shifting connotations of both

examples—male homosexual, lesbian, and heterosexual—vie for position. Actually, the lesbian connotations of Fontaine's relationship with Van Hopper are suggested by Fontaine herself in the film. That is, while Fontaine notes at one point that she is Van Hopper's "paid companion," that position is later referred to as "a friend of the bosom."

18 Mary Ann Doane, *The Desire to Desire: The Woman's Film of the 1940s* (Bloomington: Indiana University Press, 1987), 166.

19 Donald Ranvaud, "Rebecca," *Framework* 13 (Autumn 1980): 21.

20 Modleski, *Women Who Knew Too Much,* 5, 51.

21 Ibid., 51.

22 Modleski adopts this perspective in the introduction to her book. In her discussion of female bisexuality, she draws on and revises Doane's theorization of the woman-mother-image trajectory (Mary Ann Doane, "Film and the Masquerade: Theorising the Female Spectator," *Screen* 23, nos. 3–4 [September–October 1982]: 74–87). Unlike Doane, Modleski asserts that overidentification is less a problem for the women who experience it, than it is for a patriarchal culture that does not know how to accommodate it.

23 This issue is a complex one. In her recent *Epistemology of the Closet,* Eve Kosofsky Sedgwick makes an important point regarding the historical contribution of assumptions that homo desire, unlike conventional definitions of hetero desire, has since the end of the last century been addressed in terms of identification. As she notes, "I do not, myself, believe same-sex relationships are much more likely to be based on similarity than are cross-sex relationships. That is, I do not believe that identification and desire are necessarily more closely linked in same-sex than in cross-sex relationships, or in gay than in nongay persons. I assume them to be closely linked in many or most relationships and persons, in fact. . . . Yet these *are* assumptions that underlie, and are in turn underwritten by, the definitional invention of 'homosexuality' " (p. 159). In a footnote, she adds, "The fact that 'homosexuality,' being . . . posited on definitional similarity, was the first modern piece of sexual definition that simply took as nugatory the distinction between relations of identification and relations of desire, meant that it posed a radical question to cross-gender relations and, in turn, to gender discourse in which a man's desire for a woman could not guarantee his difference from her—in which it might even, rather, suggest his likeness to her" (pp. 159–60). That psychoanalysis has historically grappled with precisely this issue of sameness/difference should not be overlooked. However, psychoanalysis has thus far failed to account for it other than by means of hierarchicalizing desire and placing heterosexuality at the top of the list.

24 To posit the viability of sexualized queer gazing is difficult within the realm of psychoanalysis since queer gazes are not constructed on the basis of sexual difference and thus can only be problematically theorized via the primary concepts attributed to the heterosexual male gaze: fetishism, voyeurism, and scopophilia.

25 I am indebted to Sue-Ellen Case for drawing my attention to this important distinction between theorizations of female spectatorial identification processes (as developed in some feminist film theory) and lesbian sexual desires. I was first introduced to this distinction in Case's "Tracking the Vampire."

26 I do not take issue with Modleski's argument that Rebecca serves a maternal function,

a function that operates as a major threat to destabilize gender identity in the film. I do, however, believe that there is, as Modleski implies, more at stake in the text—namely, queer desires' threat to destabilize heterosexual sexual (and not just identification) systems.

27 Modleski, *Women Who Knew Too Much*, 50, 48.

28 Hitchcock, of course, seemed to have a special talent for sensing and developing homosexual themes, as indicated by his *Rope* and *Strangers on a Train*.

29 Leonard Leff, *Hitchcock and Selznick* (New York: Weidenfeld & Nicolson, 1987), 70.

30 Danny's similarity to Rebecca and her alignment with lesbianism are further established at the film's end, when she burns to death in the mansion. Her demise recalls B. Ruby Rich's assessment of lesbianism in mainstream cinema: "The tradition of [representing] lesbianism as tragic, powerless . . . and in particular fatal to its adherent" (B. Ruby Rich, "*Mädchen in Uniform:* From Repressive Tolerance to Erotic Liberation," *Jump Cut* 24/25 [March 1981]: 47); included in this volume. Rebecca's death, prior to the film's opening, also supports this estimation of the fate of queers in classical Hollywood cinema. Rich's remarks also find support in Lilyan Brock's 1935 novel, *Queer Patterns* (New York: Eton). The heroine, Sheila Case, is brutally murdered by an insane ex-boyfriend, and a minor lesbian character, Jo Trent—hopelessly in love with an unreciprocating Sheila—throws herself in front of a truck to end her misery.

31 Modleski, *Women Who Knew Too Much*, 48.

32 Sedgwick, *Epistemology of the Closet*, 242.

33 Other than in relation to her cousin Jack Favell (who, as noted earlier, is represented as a feminized man), Rebecca is repeatedly associated with other women, e.g., Danvers, Lady Caroline de Winter, Fontaine, the nuns of St. Claire, and the drowned woman whom Max identified as his wife.

34 This scene is filled with a fascination with Rebecca's possessions—hair brushes, coat, underwear, negligee—that borders on fetishism. However, unlike the traditional conceptualization of fetishism as the male subject's substitution of various objects as a means of disavowing female castration. Rebecca's belongings serve to render that which is lacking, specifically their owner, powerfully present in absentia. The fetishization of Rebecca's personal property does not quash Danvers's and Fontaine's castration anxieties—why indeed would they have castration anxieties?—but serves, instead, to fuel Danvers's enamored reminiscences of the woman she adores and to reinforce Fontaine's feelings of fear and desire for Max's alluring and powerful first wife.

35 Leff, *Hitchcock and Selznick*, 71.

36 Chris Straayer, "The Hypothetical Lesbian Heroine: *Voyage en douce* (Michele Deville, 1980), *Entre nous* (Diane Kurys, 1983)," *Jump Cut* 35 (1990): 54; also included in this volume.

37 Ibid.

38 White, "Female Spectator, Lesbian Specter," 153.

39 Harriet Hawkins, *Classics and Trash: Traditions and Taboos in High Literature and Popular Modern Genres* (London: Harvester Wheatsheaf, 1990), 146.

40 Carroll Smith-Rosenberg, *Disorderly Conduct: Visions of Gender in Victorian America* (New York: Knopf, 1985), 246, 281.

41 Despite the fact that Rebecca is denied a corporeal existence in the film, she is given a form and body in publicity discourses that surrounded the text. In an advertisement for *Rebecca*, an image of Fontaine's and Olivier's faces dominates the upper-right-hand corner of the poster. Their faces are suspended over an image of a book with *Rebecca* printed on its cover. They gaze past the book to the left of the poster. In the lower-left-hand corner stands a white figure. She is a curvaceous woman whose dress is as white as her flesh and whose features are perceptible but indistinct. The lower half of her body melts into an image of Manderley. Although ghost-like, Rebecca is given a physical presence in this poster—she stands guard over Manderley and draws her co-stars' gazes to her side of the advertisement.

The Queer Voice

in *Marnie*

Lucretia Knapp

Mother, Mother, I am ill,
Send for the doctor over the hill.
Call for the doctor, call for the nurse,
Call for the lady with the alligator purse.

Mumps said the doctor,
The measles said the nurse,
Nothing said the lady with
The alligator purse.

O ne of the most intriguing and haunting "voices" in Alfred Hitchcock's film *Marnie* is this jump-rope rhyme familiar to many girls. This song, which refers to Marnie (Marnie is identified with the famous first scene in which we see her from behind, carrying a purse), occurs at the beginning and at the end of the film and in each case is associated with Marnie's visits to her mother. Like other Hitchcock films, such as *Rear Window, The Lady Vanishes,* and *Shadow of a Doubt,* subtle songs contain significant clues.[1]

The ambiguity of the rhyme questions gender and creates a riddle concerning "the lady." The song offers four discursive positions for women, the daughter, the mother, the nurse, and the lady, but only one position for men, the doctor. The lady is intriguing because she doesn't fit within the dualistic economy of male/female, doctor/nurse, and mumps/measles. The words play on gender identification, and therefore the gap in logic creates a mystery, a possible other position for the lady. Like Marnie, the lady from the rhyme doesn't fit within the oedipal triangle of man, woman, and child. She is the scary spinster with the purse; she is the mysterious other.

Marnie is the story of a woman who has an obsessive need to steal and who makes her living as a thief. Her every move is studied, a performance of survival through manipulation. Marnie steals from patriarchy and returns to a women's space, where her mother lives in a world of fatherless families. Marnie wears the man's desire and distracts him from realizing that he's made a bad deal. Easily and successfully, this trickster hits the man in his most vulnerable spot, the pocket.

After stealing a large amount of money from a company where she was employed as a secretary, Marnie changes identity, goes to ride her beloved horse Forio, and then visits her mother. At her mother's home, it becomes apparent that the color red triggers something in Marnie's past, causing a seizure. Although Mark Rutland is aware of her past thievery, he hires Marnie and then blackmails her into marriage. At Rutland's she meets Lil, Mark's sister-in-law, who takes an immediate interest in Marnie. Mark becomes obsessed with uncovering the causes of her symptoms, reforming her passion for thievery, and curing her lack of heterosexual desire. After her beloved Forio is injured and Marnie kills him, Mark drags Marnie to her mother's home. Finally Marnie discovers she had killed one of the many men that her mother had slept with. In the end, Marnie leaves with Mark.

Like the woman in the rhyme, Marnie is an outsider and is often shown in the film carrying the purse. The striking first image of the film is a close-up, not of Marnie but of her purse. Dialogue that links Marnie to the lady who says "nothing" occurs later in the film, when Mark and Marnie are at the racetrack. He asks her what she believes in, and Marnie vehemently asserts, "Nothing."[2] Her speech then is that of an outsider, of someone who is hiding something. Just like the lady with the alligator purse, Marnie's not talking, especially not to Mark. This rhyme and the word *nothing* seem to indicate that, whatever it is, she's not telling.

The rhyme, like the film, is compelling owing to the questioning presence of the troubling lady. *Marnie* is particularly fascinating because the figure of the outlaw as a motif is resonant for an exploration of how the lesbian is situated both as a viewer and as a figure in film theory. The outlaw in *Marnie* is a figure that exists in two worlds—a white patriarchal world and a cultural world of women. Masquerading as part of the system, this figure flouts patriarchal authority while using its own laws against it.

My main purpose in this essay is to redirect attention to those lesbian moments in *Marnie* that have been considered insignificant by other film theorists.

Hitchcock's work has provided a cornerstone of feminist theory, yet only recently has the homosexual aspect of his films been examined by theorists such as Robin Wood and D. A. Miller.[3] It seems only appropriate that Hitchcock, the mastermind of celluloid phobia, would find homophobia or homosexuality a costume for some exotic twist. Although Wood and Miller have talked about gay male figures, the issue of lesbianism in Hitchcock's films is relatively unexplored.[4] My interest lies in the possibilities of lesbian positions of spectatorship, or how a lesbian reading may focus on other moments or gazes within films, and specifically in *Marnie*. I will situate the possible positions of the lesbian spectator, first by suggesting that gay presence in feminist film theory has been much like gay presence in traditional Hollywood cinema—there but not there or, quite often, oddly cloaked. Looking at the female space and the female voices in *Marnie* (which have been repressed or overlooked by Raymond Bellour, e.g., who sees in the film nothing but a male oedipal drama) can bring to the viewer another understanding of Marnie and the lesbian spectator. I will assess the limitations of film theory, such as Mary Ann Doane's and Tania Modleski's valorization of the bisexual space and its precursor, the preoedipal, and suggest why these terms are not solely sufficient in theorizing lesbian or gay positions in life or in the theater. I will also consider why the mother has been such a stumbling block in the oedipal scenario in film and in film theory.

I am defining lesbian viewers as those with a consistency of identification (though necessarily in flux like all identifications), one that is part of a lesbian culture, a culture that shares signs, codes, and messages. As part of a subculture, some gays were and still are identified through dress. An obvious example is the lesbian butch, whose male attire no longer signifies gender but desire. In the late seventies some people wore the color green and/or blue jeans on Thursdays in order to show gay support and, even more important, gay visibility. Homophobia was also made visible as many individuals, fearing that they would be suspected of homosexuality, selected another uniform. Women who were athletes or spinsters could trigger the attention of a gay eye. For instance, certain characters on television were suspect, especially lone women. Miss Hathaway on "The Beverly Hillbillies" was quite self-sufficient and not married, and her oddness (being a bird watcher, nerdy, and single) made her a bit queer.[5] I find my own "tomboyish" identification with Peter Pan to be quite significant, especially considering that the character who played Peter was a girl masquerading as a boy.[6]

There are many variables to lesbian identities and many lesbian codes that vary or alter with time—that is, dress, haircuts, sturdy shoes, softball, and cheering for Martina. My desire is to read *Marnie* from such a lesbian perspective. Like Miss Hathaway, Marnie is a spinster, self-sufficient and banking on her future. And, like some lesbians, she finds it necessary to hide her identity at work. However, I will not argue Marnie is a lesbian character, although her resistance to compulsory heterosexuality could, for someone like Adrienne Rich, define her as such.

During the opening presentation for a lesbian and gay film festival in Urbana, Illinois, Richard Dyer wittily engaged with the question of why gays would be attracted to certain Hollywood films with unflattering portrayals such as *The Killing of Sister George, Personal Best,* or even *Desert Hearts.* Dyer argues that, although these films do not accurately portray gays or gay lifestyles, we enjoy watching them because of their campiness and because of something in the film that we identify with. Although *Marnie* does not neatly fit in this category, the film does share some similar stereotypes. *Marnie* is an example of a film rich with campiness and a text that is both corrupt with social and cultural bias while suggesting an existence for Marnie other than a heterosexual one.

Tania Modleski, in *The Women Who Knew Too Much,* examines the fascination that Hitchcock's films have held for some feminists and suggests that many of his films follow not the traditional oedipal scenario but rather a female oedipal path (although she doesn't find this to be true of *Marnie*).[7] My interest in Hitchcock's films is likewise driven by his constant obsession with gender play. Not only are feminine bodies quite abundant in Hitchcock's films, but the transversing of both masculine and feminine characteristics makes Hitchcock's characters questionable, alluring, but, almost always, the traps within the narratives.

Modleski suggests that the ambiguous sexuality in Hitchcock's films "destabilize[s] the gender identity of protagonists and viewers alike." Similarly, I find Hitchcock's films to be a bed of paradoxes and ambiguities in which identity is questioned and explored. In her account of the mother in Hitchcock films, Modleski points out that "the misogyny and the sympathy actually entail one another—just as Norman Bates's close relationship with his mother provokes his lethal aggression towards other women."[8] Although I agree with her assessment of the relation between misogyny and sympathy in regard to the mother in *Psycho,* Modleski stops short of examining the homophobia in which this relation is inextricably intertwined. This sympathy for Mom is seen for both Norman and Marnie as "unnaturally perverse" and deadly. The closeness to Mom or the corrupt space that she occupies is to blame for the lack of "normal" heterosexual desire (which can be read as gayness). Proximity to the mother or the feminine has always been a problem in heterosexual theory. Male gayness has been blamed on acquisition of the feminine or a frighteningly close relationship with the mother. Today, the preoedipal has become a kind of lesbian landmark for heterosexual theorists—that is, for those who most obsessively seek it, a place of comfort through eventual transcendence. In fact, the preoedipal seems to carry the dubious honor of being the red herring both in the oedipal configuration and in film theory.

In *The Mother/Daughter Plot* Marianne Hirsch redirects attention within the familial structure away from the oedipal of the traditional narrative to preoedipal and maternal structures. Hirsch suggests that, although feminist retellings of *Oedipus* have brought to the forefront a female plot and voice, when it comes to revisioning the oedipal narrative, feminists such as Muriel Rukeyser and Teresa de Lauretis have concerned themselves only with the flamboyant Sphinx character and not with the maternal figure of Jocasta. Hirsch suggests that the maternal is ignored in both male and feminist narratives because "[feminists] are attracted by the enigmatic, powerful, monstrous, and terrifying Sphinx; [but] omit the powerless, maternal, emotional, and virtually silent Jocasta."[9] Although Hirsch claims to be interested in both the Sphinx and Jocasta, her heterosexual, maternal compass seems to be pulling her in one direction only.

Like Nancy Chodorow and Julia Kristeva, numerous theorists of heterosexuality have been obsessed with a mother/daughter relationship often conflated with quasi-lesbian imagery because, I would argue, it serves as an ideal without confronting the cultural complexities of real lesbianism. It is a lesbianism of an unconscious sort, a sexuality that is immature because it is hypothetical, not long lasting. The lesbianism that these theorists invoke exists purely in a phantasmatic space. Hirsch, on the other hand, is concerned not with the idealized preoedipal space and the lesbian bond but with a more adult space of detachment between the mother and daughter. But the fate of the lesbian in Hirsch's adult space is invisibility. Although Hirsch's preoedipal is not the idealized one of most heterosexual theorists, it is, nonetheless, a problematic space for lesbian subjectivity.

Although Hirsch talks a lot about Adrienne Rich and even mentions the term "compulsory heterosexuality," she does so without talking about lesbian subjectivity. Hirsch rethinks the maternal but she does not find a place for lesbian daughters or lesbian mothers. My interest in Marnie and her mother goes beyond the heterosexual (oedipal) bond between the mother and the daughter. I am interested in Marnie as a daughter but also, perhaps primarily, as an outlaw. And although I am interested in the mother in *Marnie,* my interest is not in maternal subjectivity but in how she too is an outlaw of sorts (a woman who works outside the law) and a very ambiguous figure for Marnie's affection.

Therefore, my concern is not just with the feminine perspective but with a queer perspective that is even more removed from oedipal heterosexuality. In *A Lure of Knowledge,* Judith Roof questions "whether there is a difference between heterosexual and lesbian narratives of [the] mother" and how these "difference[s] might characterize mainstream representations of female heterosexual and lesbian desire."[10] Roof discusses the types of mothers that are mentioned in lesbian novels, mothers who have illegitimate children, who are not a part of the patriarchal world. Thus she describes women who, like Marnie's mother, live outside of patriarchy and thereby "detach[es] maternity from heterosexuality.[11] Roof is engaged by the abundance of heterosexual women theorists who are obsessed by the preoedipal within their work and through this "the lesbian ideal" mother/daughter relationship—and the lack of such an "ideal" relationship in lesbian novels. In some ways, then, Roof and Hirsch are both moving beyond the preoedipal to explore the mother/daughter relationship, though their interests are very distinct. Hirsch is concerned with the heterosexual mother and Roof with the lesbian but not just as daughter.

Although I find *Marnie* rich with queer moments, Raymond Bellour focuses exclusively on a limited heterosexual reading of *Marnie* that covers only the first ten minutes or so of the film and is only concerned with the male inheritance of the gaze.[12] Like Bellour, many theorists have been oblivious to the women's world in *Marnie* and to how it functions to disrupt the heterosexual narrative. The analysis of the gaze and oedipal narrative in Bellour's account marginalizes the two components of the film that threaten to upset the heterosexual space, particularly the female space and the female voice. The female space and female voice have been significant in feminist film theory as a means to explore women's existence or assumed invisibility within a dominant text. Although in *The Acoustic Mirror* Kaja Silverman cites *Marnie* as a film that is obsessed with the woman's voice, she argues that in Hollywood film there is no chance for the female voice to be heard because it is completely repressed. Discussing a number of "talking cure" films, Silverman refers to the last scene of *Marnie* when Marnie visits her mother's home with Mark, and states that Marnie's "voice often seems to circumvent her consciousness altogether. At these times she seeks not so much the language of the unconscious as the language of unconsciousness."[13]

Silverman's account has theoretical similarities with Laura Mulvey's groundbreaking article "Visual Pleasure and Narrative Cinema" in that both agree that women are not represented in cinema, although Mulvey is mainly concerned with the visual while Silverman focuses on the aural content of traditional narrative film.[14] Alternatively, the "other" space and the various voices within the film offer Marnie an escape from the oedipal story. Within this "other" space, there are three principal voices: the rhyme recited outside the mother's home, the occasional contradictory dialogue that moves against the traditional cinematic narrative, and Marnie's own voice, which accompanies her visual "seizures" into the past. These voices make reference to something other than heterosexuality; there is a quirkiness or queerness to the way they operate in the film.

Silverman recounts film theory's historic debates over authorship, citing Bellour's major participation in the quest for the auteur and reviewing his analysis of *Marnie* in his much quoted essay "Hitchcock, the Enunciator." Silverman reiterates Bellour's account of the male possession of the gaze, suggesting why the interconnectedness of authorship and subjectivity should be reconsidered: "The agency of that identification is the image of Marnie, which is passed from the camera to Strutt, Rutland, and Hitchcock-as-fictional-character during the opening three scenes of the film. Ironically, it is only through this radically dispersed and decentered 'hom(m)osexual' economy that Hitchcock-as-director comes to be installed as the point of apparent textual origin, and as the seemingly punctual source of meaning."[15] While Silverman acknowledges the "hom(m)o-sexual economy," she overlooks queer exchanges between the women. Thus, the identification of the possibility of lesbian desire within the heterosexual world is marginalized or, more emphatically, overlooked.

Although the oedipal narrative is quite obvious in *Marnie,* another subtle narrative wreaks havoc with the heterosexual plot. Curiously, Bellour disregards some of the most striking scenes that involve Marnie's relationships with Lil and her mother in order to discuss the significance of the male as hero, enunciator, or viewer.[16] The explicitly Freudian text is almost too obvious, as if Bellour's discovery is no more than Hitchcock's trap. Bellour's analysis of the purse is just one example of this.

As the film opens we see an extreme close-up of a purse tucked under a woman's arm. This "fetishized" object signifies Marnie's "problem" (her thievery) and her shifting identity (her changing costume). From the outset of the film, then, through the close-up of the purse, the artifice of other accessories such as her hair (Marnie changes her hair from black to blonde just at the point when she starts to become a saved good girl), and the sequence of shots that deny the viewer access to her face, Marnie's identity is problematized. We meet her through her "feminine" accessories: the contents of her suitcase, purse, white gloves, compact, nail file, and lingerie. The fetishization itself suggests the difficulty Marnie will have in positioning herself within an oedipal narrative. Her identity, which is not quite heterosexual and law abiding, is also displaced into a series of male fetishes. However, Marnie's identity, when coupled with a homo-erotic fetish, coheres in a more convincing manner.

In Bellour's examination of the opening shots of *Marnie* and the fetishized purse, he discusses how the position of "the subject of enunciation" is distributed, like a linear inheritance, among men. He overly simplifies the process of identification and equates the active gaze with a strict division of gender. The possession of the gaze and the possible active positions for the lesbian viewer are more complex. Bellour assumes that women only identify through or with the man's "fear" or fetish. With this narrow definition of identification, the inanimate outcome for women viewers is in the shape of a purse (or as "a man").

Emily Apter, in the conclusion of her book *Feminizing the Fetish,* makes an interesting observation about how male authors, in order to distinguish a difference between the two genders, construct a feminization of the fetish that says more about the man's fear, a male construction of feminization, than about women. Unlike Joan Riviere's argument about the "masquerade of femininity," in which the masculinity of the masculine intellectual "homosexual" woman is being covered over or masqueraded by femininity, Apter is speaking about a "double fetishism whereby male writers are seen to be pretending to be women pretending to be men."[17]

The feminine or homoerotic fetish may be difficult to detect in Hitchcock's films, considering the many layers of male fetishization that are inherent in his work. Hitchcock's scenes are curio boxes neatly arranged with fetishized collectibles—that is, stuffed birds, Norman's taxidermied mother, and phallic ships. In *Marnie,* the maternal is horrifically fetishized as the blood that washes over Marnie's eyes. Mark amasses objects, stuffed animals, and even a token that represents his dead wife, though it is quickly broken. In Marnie's mother's home, fetishized objects are of a domestic kind—knickknacks, vases, and flowers. Just as Marnie seems to be a feminized version of the name Mark, Hitchcock seems to break the fetish up into masculine (dead animals, artifacts) and feminine (domestic) objects. Likewise, fetishism has been regarded as a male terrain that is associated with an active—therefore masculine—gaze of voyeuristic desire. Women have generally been seen as the objects of fetishization, the objects of male desire, and not as the active agents of desire, especially for other women. The male, misogynist fetishization that surrounds Marnie is the veil between a homoerotic fetish and the viewer.

In Riviere's article, masculinity isn't questioned, just femininity. The fetish for Riviere is the masculine equivalent of women's masquerade. Apter, in trying to posit a less gender-specific fetish, suggests how femininity may be more than a camouflage for the masculine (or lesbian). As Apter explains, "In this sense we might reread the theory of the masquerade as corrected, so to speak, by sartorial female fetishism, which supplants the notion of femininity as empty content or infinitely layered veil, to replace it with a theory of materialized social construction."[18] Thus, the fetish is seen as a construct, not a cover for the essentialist concept of the masculine.[19]

The fetish or fetishism in *Marnie* can be read in varying ways. Marnie functions by constantly assuming and then denying identities. When trying to define Marnie, we can say what she isn't but not, exactly, what she is. A lesbian perspective opens up the possibility of reading the ambiguities in a film like *Marnie,* seeing what is in a film in a different way and therefore constructing a different text than the heterosexual eye might observe. Bellour stirs up masculine myths of authority, in which the male gaze and the fetish remain solid and absolute. More useful is the idea of the fetish as a continuously distorting form through which the complexities of projection are metaphorically sustained. Thus, "the fetish" is not produced out of that which woman lacks but functions as a cover for what she desires.[20]

I am suggesting not that there isn't a male fetish in the film but that there is a female fetish, and more specifically a lesbian fetish. For instance, the purse also functions as the fetishized object of a possible homoerotic gaze, specifically, when we hear exaggerated, hypnotic music and see a close-up of Marnie's face as she watches the secretary place the key to the safe in her purse. In certain instances, then, Marnie's gaze is in charge of the fetish. The more typical male-fetishized purse is almost necessary in order to make the women's desire read-able or suggested within the heterosexual text. The purse becomes the initial suture of varied exchanges between Mark's secretary and Marnie. (In the scenes with Mark, Strutt, and Hitchcock, Marnie doesn't return their gaze.) Between the two women the purse is an excuse for looking, a mutual object of interest, and the focal point of Marnie's active gaze. Freud developed the notion of the fetish primarily in terms of the heterosexual male; he does mention a clothes fetish in connection with women, although still in heterosexual terms. Unlike Freud's fetish (which is a replacement for the missing phallus, or desire for the masculine), the fetish suturing the gazes exchanged between Marnie and the secretary is desire for the feminine among women. Later, other objects, such as the safe, will become the distracting points of attention between the active gaze of Marnie and the secretary's returning smile.

When considering the idea of the fetish among women, or more specifically among lesbians, I can't help but reconsider the only exceptional fetish that Freud would attribute to women, clothing, although Freud's clothing was tailored in heterosexuality.[21] It seems that clothing, desire, and gender do not necessarily go hand in hand, and when they don't, it can make people nervous. No wonder some adults become anxious when little girls start eyeing cowboy boots instead of patent-leather shoes. When a lesbian or a gay man hides desire or attire, "being in the closet" seems a significant analogy indeed.

It will come as no surprise that Bellour is interested in reading Forio, the horse, as Marnie's desire for the phallus. I find Marnie and Lil's relationship a more intriguing scenario vis-à-vis the horse. Marnie and Lil's relationship within the often overlooked hunt scene opens up more possible sites of spectatorship. Bellour, again, sees Marnie only in relation to men, when a crucial part of the film is her relation to women. Although I wouldn't consider Garrot (the man who hands Marnie her horse) a very active or memorable character, Bellour points out how he is, because of his gender, an extension of Hitchcock and Mark. His gaze, according to Bellour, supposedly acts as some type of trigger. However, it is Lil and Marnie who will fight over the necessity to pull the trigger.

While riding in a hunt Marnie suffers a seizure from her chronic problem, the sight of red. This suggests Marnie's difficulty in both occupying and visually functioning within a certain space. The apparent difficulty drives Marnie to flee from the hunt. Unable to scale a wall, she tumbles from her injured horse. In the book *Marnie*, by Winston Graham, Mark comes to the rescue, but in Hitchcock's film Lil steps in as hero. (The other time this happens is when Marnie has a nightmare and calls for her mother. As Mark looks on, Lil touches Marnie and gives her comfort.) Although Lil's curiosity can get the best of her and Marnie, she also comes to Marnie as a protector, comforter, and sympathizer.[22] Just as Marnie must shoot Forio as an active way of protecting that which she loves, Lil is also willing to take on this active role for Marnie.

Lesbianism, Costume, and Spectatorship

As Bellour's analysis is obsessed with dress and accessories (the purse), film theory in general has been obsessed with gender, dress, and desire. The questions of women's desire and women's position as spectators have been a continuing locus of difficulty within feminist film theory. Some theorists still rely on clothing analogies in order to distinguish between male and female spectators and desires in ways that suggest how much lesbians have been a forgotten part of much feminist theoretical viewing. Mulvey's "Visual Pleasure and Narrative Cinema," the classic statement of sexual difference in the cinema, defined the only possible identification for the woman viewer as masculine, or masochistic. Although her work was groundbreaking for feminist theorists, her analysis did not take into account the diffuse complexities of the viewer.

Still struggling to pass through a grid of gender dichotomy, Mary Ann Doane varied the active male and passive female schema by giving the woman viewer another option, that of transvestism.[23] Doane's analysis of the female spectator and, again, the dependence on clothing seems to hint that desire is indeed sex specific, either male or female, and that therefore the "real" woman's identification must be narcissistic while to identify with the active subject is to be "something other than" woman, to be in drag.

In order to account for the possible position(s) of a lesbian viewer, it is necessary to attend to lesbian codes of desire and to a lesbian culture that is both within and outside a heterosexual one. Lesbian desire cannot be so simply defined within an "either-or" of gender choices. Teresa de Lauretis, in "Oedipus Interruptus," constructs a process of spectatorship that doesn't rely on simple definitions of masculine and feminine. She suggests that "each person goes to the movies with a semiotic history, personal and social, a series of previous identifications, by which she or he has been somehow engendered." De Lauretis talks of "the project of feminist cinema" as one that "does not destroy vision altogether, but constructs another (object of) vision and the conditions of visibility for a different social subject." Lesbian spectatorship opens up just such conditions of visibility, those possible positions of reading that are more complex than donning a hat, a purse, or both.[24]

Doane's analysis of the woman spectator as transvestite suggests that women can only imagine active agency with men's clothing. Desire is thought in heterosexual terms and thus contained by a dichotomous structure of male and female, masculine and feminine. However, pumps and loafers are not adequate assessments or reasonable representations of desire, for when we look at the larger picture, opposites don't always attract. Doane suggests that clothes make the man and women are forced into drag. Such an account of spectatorship seems similar to Freud's analysis of the lesbian: if a woman desires a woman, she takes up the position of man. The concept of transvestism is not as threatening to patriarchy as the image of the lesbian is, for transvestism still implies masculine privilege. However difficult she is to imagine, when a woman desires a woman, she is not a man. The lesbian spectator can move into the active position of desire as a woman. In theoretical terms, the lesbian spectator challenges a desire that has always been envisioned as sex specific. Still, in Hitchcockian waters gender seems to be the body that is not so easily kept afloat.

In other films, Hitchcock invests in the tension created between heterosexuality and homosexuality. Of course, a mother is usually mentioned or portrayed as a dominant or domineering figure—for example, in *North by Northwest*, *Strangers on a Train*, and of course *Psycho*. Hitchcock most explicitly plays on homosexuality in the film *Rope*, in which the "initiation ritual" (the murder of a male friend) by two young men is an act with strange sexual overtones that they are proud of and both hide and flaunt before their guests. Robin Wood points out in *Hitchcock's Films Revisited* that, although in 1948 the general audience may not have thought as much, today most read the boy-school characters Brandon and Philip as homosexuals. In "Anal *Rope*," D. A. Miller states, "Until recently, homosexuality offered not just the most prominent, it offered the only subject matter whose representation in American mass culture appertained exclusively to the shadow kingdom of connotation, where insinuations could be at once developed and denied." Miller discusses how the homosexuality in *Rope* is never explicitly shown through kissing, for example, but is hinted at by the "coital nuances of the dialogue" and through stereotypes, such as the prep boys school. Connotations, such as gazes and phrases also exist in *Marnie,* although Marnie does and does not conform to lesbian stereotypes. She is the spinster, the outlaw, and a part of the women's community, but she has the invisibility of the femme.[25]

Wood believes that the only lesbian character in a Hitchcock film is Mrs. Danvers from *Rebecca.* I argue that a lesbian would have more to identify with in *Marnie* than in *Rebecca.* Marnie is a less coherent character and therefore offers suggestions of a more complex reading. Marnie is a more appealing spinster, more resourceful, and more easily imagined as having or hiding an erotic life. I would suggest that Marnie opens up possibilities to the lesbian spectator because she doesn't desire a heterosexual life and a heterosexual male wants to cure her (which isn't new to many lesbians). And like Marnie, lesbians go through the process of "passing" through the heterosexual world while coming out and finding themselves.[26]

Teresa de Lauretis, in "Sexual Indifference and Lesbian Representation," addresses the subtleties of gestures in works in which central characters are not explicitly lesbian. Those who move within the margins are more inclined to notice what may otherwise go undetected to the heterosexual eye because of the shared experience of "passing." In the case of *Marnie,* attention to the set, background, and peripheral characters becomes central to my argument. Marnie is fascinating in her passing because of the tensions that she incorporates, looking feminine but having masculine desires (success in the public world, riding competence, theft). The tension between what she is and what she isn't, between stereotype and invisibility, gives Marnie an interesting complexity.

Marnie's voice allots a space that moves against the heterosexual tale of the film. The oedipal narrative of the film does conclude with the male replacing the mother. However, owing to visual and audible points of tension, this narrative is resisted. Marnie's voice is not brought to the surface by the male "analyst," Mark, but is activated by the mother's voice and by Marnie's association with her own repressed sounds and images (images that never appear on screen). This contradictory "voice" leaves Mark outside, with access only to the oedipal framework at the end of the narrative.

The discrepancies within the film create tensions on various levels that are never convincingly resolved. An amateur zoologist, Mark wants to "cure" Marnie's "deviant" behavior through scientific means. He reads books such as *Sexual Aberrations of the Female Criminal,* a more than passing hint at lesbianism. The male protagonist wants to recuperate Marnie into a patriarchal narrative progression, which she resists. Once again, a lesbian spectator may be particularly adept at reading these tensions, at attending to Marnie's resistance.

There are many incongruencies between the film's visuals and its soundtrack, and they create a space for Marnie outside the dualistic economies of patriarchy. Marnie speaks to the situation of the young girl enmeshed within an ambivalent mother/daughter relationship. Although the majority of the film takes place outside of this space, the mother/daughter world is a compelling aspect of the film and is regarded as Marnie's source of trauma. The mother/daughter realm is the film's Pandora's box and the key to Marnie's story. Just as Marnie has the ability to "pass" within patriarchy (through clothing and the falsification of her name), there are moments within the film that suggest a women's voice, whereby silence is broken and Marnie's position within a women's space is felt.

The women's space, the mother's world, is presented as a dark cloud that hangs over the heterosexual narrative. When the mother isn't physically shown, characters are constantly reminding each other and the viewer of her presence, through general comments about mothers. For example, when Rutland's secretary is talking to a friend, Maude, about weekend plans, she says with regret, "I only thought you said if your mother wasn't coming with us." At another moment in the film, during a discussion with Lil, Mark says, "You should try to be Marnie's friend." She replies, "I always thought a girl's best friend was her mother!" After Mark and Marnie are married, upset with all the money Mark has wasted on a ring and honeymoon, his banker cousin snivels, "He didn't even ask mother [to the wedding]." (This cousin is one of many "single" people in *Marnie*—Mark's secretary, Lil, Marnie, Marnie's mother, Jessie's mother, Mark, Mark's father—and is, to use Miller's term, inflected with connotations of queerness because of his close bond with mother.) And when Marnie becomes worried that she will be found out for her robberies, Mark states, "Didn't your mother ever tell you about sticks and stones?" The mother is someone from whom there is no escape. She is the ruler of the women's sphere, the witch from the fairy tale who is burned in real life. Marnie's journeys always lead back to the mother. To Marnie, her mother represents both anger and pleasure. It is by way of the mother's *voice* that Marnie eventually has access to her past. But the arrival will be greatly hindered by Marnie's ambivalence and the mother's fear.

The space where Marnie's mother lives is a community of women, where little girls inhabit the street, skipping, jumping, and singing rhyme. Marnie's mom tells her that she's thinking of sharing a household with a neighbor girl, Jessie, and her mother. Like a thief within patriarchy, Marnie moves between this women's community and the world of men, stealing from patriarchy and then returning to the mother.

After one of her thefts, Marnie stops to visit her mother. We see, looming in the distance, a giant ship, docked in the harbor, a phallic metaphor par excellence, which also encapsulates the fear and the threat that the mother poses within the oedipal narrative. When Marnie arrives, a small girl, Jessie, whom

Marnie obviously considers to be a rival for her mother's affection, greets her at the door. One facet of this mother/daughter relationship, then, is sibling rivalry. On seeing the color red, Marnie struggles to stifle a seizure, thus the "repressed memory." Because this reaction initially happens in the mother's home, the first seizure is linked not only to Marnie's mother but to sibling jealousy. The red comes to signify entry into the past, a connection with the mother (birth and menstruation), and the emotion of anger. Marnie quickly removes the indecent color by replacing the gladioli on the television with a present of white chrysanthemums, thus trying to veil the emotions that surround her early relationship with her mother.

Marnie's disruptive returns to her mother's home, her seizures and thefts, all attest to her internal and external conflicts. At the end of the film, Marnie will learn of her mother's past and realize how she did care for her, although the ambivalence will never be resolved. The voice is, this time, shared by the mother and daughter and moves against the possibility of a successful father-figure replacement. Once Marnie marries Mark, he will try to displace the mother or take Marnie away from the women's space. In Marnie's case, in order legitimately to enter patriarchy or remain true to the traditional oedipal narrative, the mother must be replaced by Mark, the amateur analyst. Mark doesn't have access to their shared space, though, and therefore he cannot adequately dislodge the mother from Marnie's story. The maternal bond is a threat because it opens up the possibility for a desire that is not informed by, or in harmony with, the masculine.

After Marnie leaves her mother, at the beginning of the film, she takes on a new appearance. She applies for and gets a job as a secretary at Mark's publishing company. While in the reception area, Mark's sister-in-law passes and the women exchange looks, Lil's competent, sensuous, and searching gaze makes Marnie drop her eyes, as if returning the look might disclose some secret. Marnie's glance is curious in that she overreacts to Lil. The gaze is especially significant because the interest between the two women is much like that of the traditional heterosexual gaze of the cinema. When Lil approaches the main office, she looks back at Marnie and says to Mark, "Who's the dish?" This "other" voice of desire suggests a momentary displacement of the heterosexual narrative. At one crucial moment, after Marnie has lied about her mother, Lil catches wind of some trouble. She tells Mark that if he needs any help he can count on her because she doesn't have any scruples. Fed up with Lil and her advances toward him, Mark, with hostility in his voice, asks her what she's waiting for (in regard to love), and Lil answers, "I'm queer for liars." But Marnie is the liar in the film. Although we are led to believe that this daughter substitute for Mark is out for daddy, her words indicate that she's possibly after the outlaw, or the other woman without scruples, the liar. Unlike the traditional Hollywood film in which the two women fight over the man, Marnie's interests lie elsewhere. Both Lil and Marnie are lone women, surrounded by the patriarchal Rutland world, and the strong tensions that exist between them are like the intensity or ambiguity that can surround jealousy or desire.

Just as the mother/daughter bond is a threat to patriarchy, much is invested in the desire for jealousy among women. As Irigaray states in *This Sex Which Is Not One,* "Commodities can only enter into relationships under the watchful eyes of their 'guardians.' . . . And the interests of businessmen require that commodities relate to each other as rivals."[27] In some ways, Lil and Marnie are the familiar rivals of the gothic novel. Within traditional cinema, invested in male desire, women are also often pitted against each other for the affection of the man. There are moments in Hollywood film, though, when the rivalry is disrupted, and through the tension another voice, a voice of contradiction, is heard. These two traditional female figures of the cinema, the blonde and the brunette, are both bad girls. Marnie holds Lil's curiosity throughout the film; Lil is an obsessed detective searching out Marnie's identity.

I have discussed the rhyme and the contradictory dialogue as two instances of the other voice in *Marnie.* The third example in the film is Marnie's narration that occurs during her seizures. Before Marnie is blackmailed into marrying Mark, he asks her to work overtime. A high camera angle shows the small figure of Marnie, approaching an industrialized, gothic mansion. In Mark's office, a space of fetishized history, zoology, and cultural artifacts, Marnie has her next seizure. The onslaught of the memory is now produced within both the mother's space and Mark's world. There are some signals that trigger Marnie's memory, or the little girl's experience. Initially, when Marnie is in Mark's office, the lightning frightens her. Soon her terror escalates as a tree smashes through a large wall of glass. Two signals, then, are the lightning and the metaphor of rape, which are indicative of the small girl's narrative or memory. Mark's forced entry, or coercion into the past, reveals a brutality that is determinedly resisted by Marnie. Later the rape during Marnie's honeymoon pushes her toward suicide but also toward further recollection of the childhood trauma that she has repressed.

At the climax of the film, desiring to cure her once and for all, Mark takes Marnie to see her mother. Once she is inside the door, Marnie's fear of lightning activates a seizure. When Mark puts his arms around Marnie to gallantly soothe her, Marnie's mother tells him to "get your hands off of my kid." Mark thinks that he is going to displace the mother but instead he takes up the place of the sailor. The memory of the mother's protective voice and Marnie's desire for something other than the protection of the man uncover Marnie's past.

Although the young Marnie appears to cry because of her fear of lightning, Marnie's words express memories of sexual abuse. Like the gap in time between lightning and thunder, the visual image and the soundtrack of the film do not match. The two ways of reading the scene are like a double exposure, with one perspective always distorting the other. Watching the visuals, you aren't sure whether the sailor is harming her, but you see him touching Marnie and kissing the young girl's neck. We are so attuned to direct most of our attention to the visual that the contradiction of Marnie's voice, in contrast to the image, can possibly go unnoticed. "I don't like him to kiss me. Make him go, Mama." The detached voice of Marnie, childlike and screaming, is clearly one of terror that contrasts with the more vague visuals. The "truth" is further dismantled within the image itself. When the sailor first comes out of the bedroom, in the left corner, there is a glimpse of the mother following the sailor. The viewer can assume, then, that the mother is present. This semi-comfort in knowing that Marnie isn't alone with this man is undercut as the scene continues and we move into a wider shot. It is disconcerting to see the mother reenter the living room, once again, as if she had never been there. The disjunction within the image can lead one to think, "Maybe what I saw isn't what I saw."

Marnie's voice explains the mother and daughter's need to protect each other (not necessarily successfully)—the necessity of hiding their story and also the difficulty in telling it. It explains why Mark is never a part of their narrative, because he denies the feminine world and believes in, and is part of, the male fetish and the oedipal scenario. Through tensions within the film that threaten the law of the father, the women's desire constantly challenges and therefore blocks a true recuperation of the heterosexual couple at the end of the film. Marnie's desire is not so much a commitment to Mark or marriage as a desire to avoid going to jail: "Oh Mark, I don't want to go to jail. I'd rather stay with you." As she steps out from her mother's home, a little girl wearing green, who resembles her, makes eye contact with Marnie. In this way, we have the sense that Marnie's spirit has not been curtailed by the man, that the happy ending may not be Marnie's ending after all.

In conclusion, I think that it is critical not only to realize the possibilities of lesbian pleasures in heterosexual texts as well as homosexual or homoerotic texts, but specifically to consider the possible lesbian interest in certain homophobic texts. Why should a text in which a nonheterosexual woman is looking for her past be of interest to a lesbian? *Marnie* affords a lesbian viewer a significant position whereby the status of outlaw becomes a meaningful investment. Lesbians do, after all, function inside as well as outside of a heterosexual world. It is probable that what has drawn theorists to Hitchcock is the very thing that has been swept under the rug. Thus Hitchcock's films are of great interest because, for him, there is nothing sacred about the heterosexual narrative, and he enjoys disrupting social norms with people's fears. What could be a more effective fear to taunt paranoid heterosexuality than homophobia?

A lesbian reading of *Marnie* may open up areas of interest that a heterosexual perspective may overlook or find insignificant, like the voices in *Marnie* or the exchanges between Marnie and Lil. *Marnie* offers the possibility of a lesbian reading, and the lesbian spectator has multiple levels of entry owing to the very ambiguous characters and scenes in the film. On my own informal and unscientific survey, lesbian spectators react with outpourings of anger or comical assertions that, although they know it won't happen in the film, Marnie should pair up with Lil.

That the film centers around the maternal bond, that it is the major problem for Marnie, speaks to the strength of the (maternal) repression and the fear that surrounds it. In *Marnie* patriarchy is so threatened by the women's community and the homoerotic that it fights fully to pull her back into the fatherland. The women's space is seen through a glass darkly, a crippled world where the ambiguous feelings of the mother push you away, after having already swallowed you. At the end of the film, however, it is Mark who has swallowed Marnie.

As Marnie and Mark leave Miss Edgar's home, we see a group of children outside the door. Two boys stand like guards, their backs turned strangely to the viewer. Three girls face Marnie and the viewer, and then we hear the rhyme: "Mumps said the doctor, Measles said the nurse, *Nothing* said the lady with the alligator purse." Or, "Something?"

Notes

I wish to thank Laura George and Judith Mayne for their helpful criticisms. This article is in memory of a very talented artist, Mary Evelyn Knapp.

1 In *Rear Window* a nursery rhyme, "My Hat It Has Three Corners," refers to a murderous "loaded" number 3 and a hat box, where a portion of the dead Mrs. Thorwald is buried. In a less subtle and more literal sense, a tune in *The Lady Vanishes* contains the crucial message of a political spy. In *Shadow of a Doubt* the humming of a song indicates to the young woman Charlie that charming Uncle Charlie is actually a murderer of rich women.

2 Like the psychoanalytic lack, Marnie's "nothing" signifies not simply an absence but a presence that is not easily defined. Teresa de Lauretis suggests the necessity of the concept of castration as a lack not of a phallus but of the feminine body, thus a desire or drive for the feminine ("Perverse Desire: The Lure of the Mannish Lesbian," *Australian Feminist Studies* [Autumn 1991]: 15–26). Judith Roof similarly suggests a lack that engenders a desire to desire the Other (or woman) (*The Lure of Knowledge* [New York: Columbia

University Press, 1991]). I am hesitant in using the term *lack* because it seems impossible not to associate it with the phallus. However, what we all have in common is the concept of desire for woman.

3 Of course, extensive work has been done in the area of gay theory by film theorists including Judith Mayne, Teresa de Lauretis, Alexander Doty, and Patricia White. See esp. D. A. Miller, "Anal *Rope*," *Representations* 32 (1990): 114–33; Robin Wood, *Hitchcock's Films Revisited* (New York: Columbia University Press, 1989), 232.

4 One recent exception was a panel on Hitchcock and homosexuality at the "Homosexuality and Holiday" conference, Center for Lesbian and Gay Studies, Graduate Center of the City University of New York, March 1992.

5 Lesbian novelist and columnist Marion Garbo Todd makes a humorously similar evaluation of Miss Hathaway in "The Fascination of Television's Perennial Spinster," *Lesbian News* 16, no. 10 (May 1991): 32–51.

6 Amid suggesting the destabilizing effect of the transvestite or cross-dresser, Marjorie Garber recalls one of the most beloved transvestite figures of all times, Peter Pan, and why it is that this character was played by a woman (*Vested Interests* [New York: Routledge, 1992], 165–85). I find this character extremely fascinating because he/she was a significant hero that came into my childhood via television in the late fifties and therefore is a compelling figure in regard to my developing lesbian viewership.

7 Tania Modleski, *The Women Who Knew Too Much* (New York: Routledge, 1988).

8 Ibid., 5.

9 Marianne Hirsch, *The Mother/Daughter Plot* (Bloomington: Indiana University Press, 1989), 2. It may be that many a lesbian would be drawn to the flamboyant Sphinx because she is not heterosexually defined.

10 Roof, *The Lure of Knowledge*, 91.

11 Ibid., 106.

12 Raymond Bellour, "Hitchcock, The Enunciator," trans. Bertrand Augst and Hilary Radner, *Camera Obscura* 2 (1981): 66–91.

13 Kaja Silverman, *The Acoustic Mirror* (Bloomington: Indiana University Press, 1988), 65.

14 Laura Mulvey, "Visual Pleasure and Narrative Cinema," in *Visual and Other Pleasures* (Bloomington: Indiana University Press, 1989), 14–26.

15 Silverman, *The Acoustic Mirror*, 204.

16 In Winston Graham's novel *Marnie,* on which the film is based, a male character named Terry is Mark's rival. The character Marnie explains this relationship: "Terry and Mark really were madly jealous of each other and ever willing to fight over anything; I'd be a new excuse" (*Marnie* [New York: Carroll & Graf, 1961]). As is so often the case in soap operas, the replacement of characters is noticeable. But, from the book to the film, it is not only a replacement of looks that is noticeable but a replacement of gender, as Lil takes over the traditionally male position of rival. Considering this gender difference and the desire of Terry in the book, this switch is significant.

17 Emily Apter, *Feminizing the Fetish: Psychoanalysis and Narrative Obsession in Turn-of-the-Century France* (New York: Cornell University Press, 1991), 249. See also Joan Riv-

iere, "Womanliness as Masquerade," in *Formations of Fantasy,* ed. Victor Burgin, James Donald, and Cora Kaplan (London: Methuen, 1986), 39–40.

18 Apter, *Feminizing the Fetish,* 98.

19 Teresa de Lauretis questions lesbian feminists' refusal of psychoanalytic theory as a means for discussing lesbian sexuality and suggests refiguring lesbian desire through the concept of Freud's negative theory of perversion or the concept of the fetish. De Lauretis finds the reappropriation of the masculinity complex necessary for lesbian theorists in order to move out of the preoedipal realm. For de Lauretis the castration complex is a necessary concept. She uses the character of Stephen in *The Well of Loneliness* to argue that lack is very much concerned with desire for the feminine. In Stephen's case lack signifies a desire for a feminine body and a desire for a feminine lover, a nonnarcissistic desire. However, just as de Lauretis believes Freud's masculine complex to forget the feminine lesbian, de Lauretis's fetish positions the butch lesbian as active and the femme lesbian as the passive participant in the fetish. Although I am drawn to the concept of lesbian desire and, through that, the lesbian fetish, I am somewhat perplexed by de Lauretis's rethinking of certain Freudian terms, specifically castration. De Lauretis believes that to "reject the notion of castration is to find ourselves without symbolic means to signify desire" ("Perverse Desire," 17). Although de Lauretis speaks of the desire as not masculine and substitutes the phallus for the fetish, it is difficult to consider the concept of castration without bringing to mind the phallus. My question is, Can you talk about lack without talking about castration? Although I find de Lauretis's fetish compelling, I question the use of the character of Stephen as an appropriate figure at the mirror, for what happens when Marnie looks in the mirror? Typically, unless a woman is considered "masculine" or "butch," her desire is invisible, just as the femme lesbian and Marnie are haunted by their invisibility within film, theory, and psychoanalysis. Elizabeth Grosz proposes the possibility of the lesbian fetish by suggesting that it is the masculine lesbian who fetishizes and what she fetishizes is the phallic woman (the mother in Freudian terms) or lesbian, which reduplicates the Freudian model in which only the male fetishizes. This brings to mind Riviere's homophobic text in which the masculine (lesbian) woman becomes feminized or fetishized. I find this analysis problematic because it assumes the relationship of the preoedipal lesbian and phallic mother and the masculine lesbian woman (Elizabeth Grosz, "Lesbian Fetishism?" *differences* 3 [1991]: 39–53).

20 As I mentioned before, I do not suggest a lack of something as de Lauretis and Roof do, but I am equally concerned with lesbian desire and desire for woman (or the feminine).

21 Emily Apter discusses how Freud considered the fetish to be a part of "the male erotic imagination spurred by castration anxiety or repressed homosexuality" (*Feminizing the Fetish,* 102). Apter explains that the only fetishistic desire that Freud granted to women was a desire for clothing.

22 In *The Celluloid Closet,* by Vito Russo, the sentence "what the well-dressed lesbian will wear" is the text that accompanies a photo of a costume sketch of Candice Bergen dressed as Lakey, the lesbian in the 1966 film *The Group* [New York: Harper & Row, 1985], 144). Dressed in a black suit, a black derby capping her head, Lakey looks similar to other well-

dressed "lesbian" characters such as Theodora in the 1963 film *The Haunting* and Lil in *Marnie*. In fact, in the hunting scene in *Marnie,* while out chasing foxes, both Lil and Marnie are dapperly dressed in black derbies, riding britches, and boots. But Lil and Theo, the lesbian in *The Haunting,* share the mystery of being the dark-haired characters. They are obsessed with the blonde woman's past and present identities and would prefer it if the male characters just left them alone. Each film is obsessed with how the psyche is constructed, and both Marnie and Elizabeth have a past that is tied to the mother, a past that they want to forget. The desire of the viewer to know about each woman's secret is enhanced by the pursuit of the dark-haired, well-dressed, and strong-willed woman. Patricia White has discussed how lesbian characters have been known to haunt film theory as well as horror films and is herself entranced by the characters Elizabeth and Theo ("Female Spectator, Lesbian Specter: *The Haunting,*" in *Inside/Out: Lesbian Theories, Gay Theories,* ed. Diana Fuss [New York: Routledge, 1991], 142–72).

23 Mary Ann Doane, "Film and the Masquerade: Theorizing the Female Spectator" (1982), reprinted in *Femmes Fatales: Feminism, Film Theory, Psychoanalysis* (New York: Routledge, 1991), 17–32.

24 Teresa de Lauretis, "Oedipus Interruptus," *Wide Angle* 7 (1986): 36, 38. De Lauretis makes this same point in "Sexual Indifference and Lesbian Representation," in *Performing Feminisms: Feminist Critical Theory and Theatre,* ed. Sue Ellen Case (Baltimore: Johns Hopkins University Press, 1990), 17–39.

25 Miller, "Anal Rope," 119, 118. In *Marnie* Mark brings Marnie to meet his family, and after Lil shakes Marnie's hand she rubs her wrist. In a gay (generally gay male) stereotyped gesture, Lil's wrist goes limp as she declares, "Oh Dear, I think I rather sprained my wrist this afternoon." After Lil beckons Marnie to her side to pour the tea, Mark makes something of the fact that Lil likes her tea with a slice of lemon, as though she has "weird" tastes.

26 Wood, *Hitchcock's Films Revisited,* 232. D. A. Miller, in "Anal Rope," also argues that homosexuality in Hitchcock's films is more complex.

27 Luce Irigaray, *This Sex Which Is Not One,* trans. Catherine Porter (Ithaca, N.Y.: Cornell University Press, 1985), 196.

Flaming

Closets

Michael Moon

In memory of Jack Smith

Lost in the woods around Cummington, Massachusetts, one summer after-noon in 1981, my friend Mark and I walked in endless circles and talked desultorily, exchanging fragments of our life stories. He told me the following anecdote by way of partially explaining why he had become sexually active only late in youth. When he was twelve, he said, his mother went out shopping one Saturday afternoon and left him and his two older brothers, who were thirteen and fourteen, at home by themselves. The oldest boy proposed they have what he called a Scheherazade party in their mother's absence, and the other two readily fell in with the plan. He had recently been talking about what sounded to each of them like a funny and possibly exciting game of "playing harem," and the boys decided to seize the opportunity to try it out. Giggling, they put on a phonograph record of Rimsky-Korsakoff's *Scheherazade* and launched into si-multaneous and uproarious stripteases to the music. Once they were undressed, one of the boys ran into their parents' room and returned with three of their mother's scarves, which they tied around their by now erect penises as they resumed their hilarious "harem girl" dances. At this point their mother, having realized she had forgotten her wallet, unexpectedly returned home. The three "dancing girls" found themselves surprised by a parental whirling dervish who shouted and cursed at them, threw the phonograph record off the turntable, and then, her fury still unvented, hurled a chair through one of the living-room windows. Mark said years later that he was so embarrassed and frightened by the episode that he didn't again indulge in any form of sexual experimentation—even solo masturbation—for nine years afterward.

To the question of why Mark's mother was so upset and angry there is of course no shortage of answers or explanations: a parent's violent responses to her pubescent sons' enactment of their sexuality; a woman's—a mother's—rage at a scene of the male sexuality by which she had long felt (if only unconsciously or inarticulately) oppressed; the blind homophobic fury of an at least nominally heterosexual woman at the (to her) astonishingly casual homosexual play of her three sons. It would have been little comfort to Mark and his brothers, and perhaps even less to their mother, to have been told that their behavior in this situation paralleled in some striking ways the plot of the most celebrated Scheherazade party of them all, the 1910 Diaghilev–Ballets Russes production, but I think it is of considerable interest to the student of the dynamics of homoeroticism and homophobia as constitutive elements of modern culture to notice how aspects of the scenario of Diaghilev's influential pseudooriental extravaganza in some ways correspond to Mark's story. In the Ballets Russes *Scheherazade*, the shah is told by his brother that he (the shah) is being duped by his wives, that all of them are unfaithful to him. The shah, in a pet, pretends to go off hunting, and leaves his chief wife, the sultana Zobeida, and the rest of the harem to themselves. As soon as he is gone, his wives receive their various "slave" lovers, Zobeida's being the so-called Golden Slave (one of Nijinsky's most celebrated roles). The shah returns unexpectedly, surprising his wives with their lovers, and, in a rage, orders his janissaries to slaughter the whole group. In a scene awhirl with flashing scimitars and falling bodies, Zobeida holds herself motionless, until, seeing her lover killed, she stabs herself to death. Her astonished husband bursts into tears, and the curtain falls.[1]

Diaghilev's *Scheherazade*, starring Nijinsky and the legendary Ida Rubinstein (as the "unfaithful wife" Zobeida) and choreographed by Fokine, was one of the most famous premieres in an age of opening-night coups de théâtre. Marcel Proust, who attended with the composer and conductor Reynaldo Hahn, his erstwhile lover, wrote afterward that the spectacle was the most beautiful he had ever seen.[2] Peter Wollen, drawing on Edward Said's *Orientalism* and related work of Perry Anderson and Arno Mayer, has deftly analyzed the implications of early twentieth-century cultural productions such as *Scheherazade*, the fashions they inspired and the social and political attitudes they underwrote, and the fantasies that were disseminated through them.[3] These latter included racist and imperialist fantasies of white bourgeois global domination of "oriental" peoples, and depended, for the glamourous and erotic aura they exuded for many white Europeans and Americans, on other fantasies, imbricated with them, about inhabiting environments of extreme opulence in which the members of "master races" could enact with impunity "forbidden" sexual impulses on the dominated bodies of others.

Wollen focuses his analysis of *Scheherazade* on Léon Bakst's set and costume designs, which, historians of fashion agree, revolutionized consumer perceptions throughout the bourgeois world. Bakst's use of brilliant hues of blue and green and red and orange side by side was immediately imitated in cultural productions of all kinds, in painting, jewelry design, and interior decoration. Cecil Beaton, then an acute young observer of the haute monde, wrote of the Paris of 1910 in the aftermath of *Scheherazade* that "a fashion world that had been dominated by corsets, lace, feathers and pastel shades soon found itself a seraglio of vivid colours, harem skirts, beads, fringes and voluptuousness."[4] "Fringes and voluptuousness" is suggestive: in the new seraglio "look" derived from Bakst's designs, signifiers of the ostensibly trivial order of bright-colored shawls, beads, and "fringe" suddenly became ubiquitous, and included within their semiotic range a "voluptuous fringe" that lay, in a manner of speaking, just the other side of the looking glass from their wearers' ordinary lives, a phantasmagoric "oriental" margin populated by lascivious odalisques and their slave lovers, jealous masters and their terrible household executioners. When the fashionable world of 1910 donned turbans, "harem pants," oriental shawls, and beads in "shocking" quantities and color combinations, they can be seen to have been participating in a mass fantasy of joining a "voluptuous fringe" where ordinary social life took on a "barbaric splendor" and sexuality imaginarily escaped the constraints of bourgeois domestic life and took on a "savage" and many-hued intensity.

Riots did not break out at the premiere of *Scheherazade*—that famously happened to the Ballets Russes three seasons later, at the first night of *Le sacre du printemps*. Violence was apparently largely confined to the stage in *Scheherazade*, in the general slaughter that followed the shah's vengeful entry into the scene of orgy in his own harem. In his analysis of the potent implicit political effects of the fashions—and not least of all the fashions in fantasy—a spectacle like *Scheherazade* fostered, Wollen emphasizes the enormous impact of Bakst's designs on popular perceptions and attitudes in this century. Interested as I am in the history of gay male subjectivity in the modern epoch, I want to consider another aspect of the "riot of fantasies" that converged on *Scheherazade* and that it in turn reproduced and disseminated. Besides its fosterage of colonialist racist attitudes of the kind Wollen reads out of it, there are other significant ways in which the repressive violence I have spoken of as being in one sense limited to the space of the stage in *Scheherazade* extended far beyond it. The ones I want to emphasize here are the misogynist and homophobic implications of the murderous disciplinary violence the piece symbolically carried out on its "stars," Rubinstein and Nijinsky, in their respective characters of Zobeida and the Golden Slave.

In a series of performances around the time of *Scheherazade*, ranging from

Saint Sebastian to Salome, Ida Rubinstein powerfully enacted a series of fin-de-siècle fantasies about the ostensibly "evil" potential of various modes of behavior attributed to women in some of the dominant representational regimens of the turn of the century. These ranged from phallic femininity (woman as castrator, femme fatale) to anorexic withdrawal (woman as victim, wraith). Self-styled high priestess of decadent performance in the early years of this century, Rubinstein offered to audiences sensational specularizations of some of their most resonant fantasies of gender conflict, including such complex ones as her impersonation of a "feminized" (i.e., castrated) male in her role as the protagonist of d'Annunzio and Debussy's *The Martyrdom of Saint Sebastian* (1911). *Saint Sebastian* boasted, as had *Scheherazade* the year before, not only Rubinstein's presence but also the choreography of Fokine and the set and costume designs of Bakst.[5] In his study *Idols of Perversity* Bram Dijkstra speaks of Rubinstein as having served as "an ambulant fetish expressive of the ideologically manipulated desires of [her] society." He emphasizes two of the possible bases for this fetishization of her poses on the part of male viewers: "Clearly, the fetishized emaciation of iconic figures such as Rubinstein made it possible for males to respond to them in either a sadistic or masochistic fashion, depending on whether they were seen as subjects in control of their own destinies (and hence a threat to the aggressive self-identity of the men observing them) or as ultrapassive objects of aggressive desire."[6] Although he analyzes lesbian artist Romaine Brooks's painting of Rubinstein at some length, Dijkstra limits his consideration of the possible meanings of her career almost entirely to male-centered ones. The crucial element of Rubinstein's public persona that Dijkstra fails to consider is her position as a powerful emblem for some of her lesbian admirers (these appear in his text only under the rather bland designation "her women friends") of a will to exhaust the entire repertory of binary roles through which femininity was conceived in the turn-of-the-century West. Placing predictable heterosexual male projections onto her performances to one side, one can readily imagine at least some of the ways that the more or less open secret of the lesbian sexuality she figured for some members of her audience (especially, we may assume, for lesbians themselves and for some gay male admirers) contributed to the highly charged atmosphere of her public appearances. For example, besides those aspects of her work described by Dijkstra as being in some ways compatible with contemporary male-identified fantasies of both extreme (phallic) feminine potency and no less extreme feminine passivity, the self-assertive and exhibitionistic aspects of her work also permitted her to present herself, at least liminally, as both a subject and an object of lesbian desire rendered visible to an extraordinary degree.

In her role as Zobeida in *Scheherazade* Rubinstein initially functions as a "threatening" embodiment of transgressive female heterosexual desire. But in the work's famous ending, which many members of its first audience, including Fokine, seem to have found its most overwhelming gesture, Rubinstein's motionless stance amid the scene of massacre around her seems to have represented an almost unbearably ambiguously charged moment. For the duration of that prolonged moment Zobeida resists enacting either her rage at her husband and master or her grief over the slaughter of her lover and her other companions, and instead gathers to herself the storm of energy swirling around her by temporarily but nonetheless forcefully adopting the position and appearance of being its still center.

Only a modicum of these tensions are resolved by the abrupt gesture with which Zobeida shatters her powerful but unsustainable pose: stabbing herself to death. The performative energies of Rubinstein's repertory of symbolic roles—the male-identified potent castrator (Judith) and violated suicide (Lucrece) as well as those of possible subject and object of lesbian desire—collapse incoherently as Zobeida, the temporary imaginary embodiment of all these roles, falls dead. Similarly, the positions—of being tremendously empowered and being oppressed literally to death—between which Rubinstein rapidly oscillated in the climactic moments of *Scheherazade* are left unresolved in the case of her gay male counterpart, Nijinsky, when, after an extraordinary enactment of flight and defiance, his "slave" character is seized and executed. "How odd it is that Nijinsky should always be the *slave* in your ballets," Diaghilev's friend and musical adviser Walter Nouvel quipped to the impresario at the time *Scheherazade* was being planned. "I hope one day you'll emancipate him."[7] Of course, Diaghilev never did, and Nijinsky's struggle to emancipate himself was to all appearances an excruciating failure. He was to break off his relationship with Diaghilev in 1913 and to stop dancing publicly altogether by 1919, thereafter to live on in confinement, diagnosed as schizophrenic, until 1950.

At the time of *Scheherazade*, however, he was still successfully negotiating the powerful projections of sexual contradiction onto his performances that are as notable an aspect of the record of his career as a different set of these are of his colleague Rubinstein's.[8] Fokine, for example, praised the way the dancer's "peculiar" "lack of masculinity" made him the perfect interpreter of the role of the Golden Slave. "Now he was a half-human, half-feline animal, softly leaping great distances, now a stallion," Fokine writes in a characteristic evocation of Nijinsky's supposed resolution of highly charged contradictions in his performances, in his body, and his dancing.[9] Both subhuman and superhuman, he is simultaneously perceived as an effeminate cat and a tremendous stud, but not as "masculine" in any ordinary sense. Fokine presents his decision to eliminate ordinary "masculinity" from the expressive range of Nijinsky's dancing in *Scheherazade* as an inevitable consequence of what he saw as the peculiar strengths of

Rubinstein's imperious appearance, and he does so with a stunning non sequitur. "Next to the very tall Rubinstein," he writes, "I felt that [Nijinsky] would have looked ridiculous had he acted in a masculine manner." The astonishing success of *Scheherazade* no doubt had more than a little to do with the extraordinary energy with which it found terms for specularizing—rendering both visible and spectacular—the "scandals" of the sexualities of its two stars and of their respective ways of revealing and concealing these in performance. Fokine to the contrary, much more complicated relations had to be "adjusted" between the two principals in *Scheherazade* than Rubinstein's height in comparison with Nijinsky's relative shortness: the whole array of conflicting sexual projections that could be made onto them and their performances had to be brought into effective relation to each other.

The main outline at least of the *Scheherazade* scenario as it was eventually performed by the Ballets Russes had been the idea of artist and theatrical designer Alexandre Benois, and he afterward wrote of Nijinsky's performance in terms remarkably similar to Fokine's "half-this, half-that" ones: impersonating the Golden Slave, Benois said, Nijinsky had become in rapid turns "half-cat, half-snake, fiendishly agile, feminine and yet wholly terrifying."[10] As with Rubinstein's performance, but in rather different terms, Nijinsky's was perceived as being both intensely phallic and no less intensely "feminine." The most significant difference between the affective ranges of Rubinstein's and Nijinsky's performances is that while her role permitted her to enact a fairly wide range of positions, including certain ones that were deemed "masculine," it was precisely these "ordinary" masculine positions that were excluded from Nijinsky's role. What Fokine calls Nijinsky's "peculiar" "lack of masculinity"—the constant interplay in his most characteristic performances of flashes of hypervirile and hyperfeminine effects, which make sensational impressions but can never be gotten to "add up" to "ordinary" masculinity—represents the piece's powerful negative electrical charge, at its opposite pole from the positive charge the piece locates in Rubinstein's power to enact "masculinity," at least liminally, alongside other performative modes.

Judging from available contemporary descriptions of the performance, one does not get the sense that there was any moment in Nijinsky's performance in which he was permitted to signal anything like Rubinstein's "majestic" and overwhelming gesture of prolonged motionless resistance to the murderous violence that furiously manifests itself in the piece's last scene. The strain of being a visible and intensely mystified embodiment of the open secret of male homosexuality in Paris and London in the decade or two after the epochal downfall and death of Oscar Wilde no doubt played a significant part in what was diagnosed as Nijinsky's schizophrenic disintegration in his late twenties, at the end of World

War I.[11] Rubinstein, as the daughter and heiress of a rich St. Petersburg family, was able to use her successes with the Ballets Russes as Cleopatra and Zobeida to launch herself as a star in subsequent productions that she herself financed; as I have said, Nijinsky's attempts to become similarly autonomous were a disastrous failure for a variety of reasons, not the least of which, I suspect, was the relation of his fame to the specularization of the imputed "lack of masculinity" that restricted him to the margins of identities of which "ordinary masculinity" was an indispensable component.

Between Diaghilev's, Nijinsky's, Rubinstein's, and Bakst's "Scheherezade party" of 1910 and Mark's and his brothers' of the early sixties lies a half century in which the construction of gay male subjectivity on a number of fronts has exhibited some striking—and sometimes terrible—consistencies.[12] Some of the most effective forms of resistance to homophobic oppression that gay men have developed and practiced during the same period have shown a similar kind of consistency. One of these has been the sometimes elaborately planned, sometimes spontaneously performed "Scheherazade party," staged over and over again in this century in locations ranging from the theater of the belle époque to, fifty years later, a suburban American living room. Rather than dismissing it as trivial, I want to insist on its having been an important aspect of the widely various repertory of political acts gay men have practiced and by means of which we have resisted this century's depradations against us. I take the "Scheherazade party"—the conspicuous energies with which it is enacted as well as the phobic violence with which it is repressed, violence of either the explosive variety that Mark experienced or the corrosive kind that gradually disabled Nijinsky—as an emblematic expression of a perilously highly charged compromise, the energies of which both "sides" in the ongoing war for and against gay visibility, homophobic and homophile, have been effectively exploiting for most of this century.

Jack Smith, who died of AIDS on 18 September 1989, was one of the most accomplished and influential but least known producers of the extremely theatricalized, densely materialist version of urban gay male social and artistic practice that has to this point been recognized, studied, and theorized chiefly under the extremely reductive rubric of "camp."[13] In 1962 Jack Smith threw a "Scheherazade party" that has probably had more political and artistic impact, at least in the English- and French-speaking worlds, than any since the Ballets Russes's of fifty years before. Filming for seven consecutive weekends on the roof of an old movie theater, since demolished, on the Lower East Side of Manhattan, Smith and a group of friends, apparelled in various kinds of drag—"harem," vampire, Marilyn Monroe—enacted for the camera a series of scenes from an imaginary transvestite orgy. They swayed to unheard music, "vamped" each other, casually and unhurriedly exposed parts of their bodies—here a female breast, there the limp penis of one reveler casually draped over the shoulder of another seated before him. Smith edited the results, added a soundtrack of old seventy-eights of German tango bands and Latin American pop songs, and screened the film in the spring of 1963 under the title *Flaming Creatures*.[14] It provoked a violent response. A small coterie of admirers, including Jonas Mekas and Susan Sontag, praised Smith for helping inaugurate a new sexually and artistically radical film practice in this country. Other viewers enjoyed the film's dreamy insouciance about matters of sexuality and gender, but many hated and attacked it. Theaters that showed *Flaming Creatures* were raided, and prints of the film were seized by the New York police. A few favorable published responses aside, the history of the reception of the film has amounted in large part to a history of the effort to suppress it, both here and abroad. A print of the film was seized by U.S. customs as it was being returned from a screening in Vancouver, and showings in Ann Arbor and Austin were "busted" by local police in the late sixties. Film scholar Karel Rowe screened the film at Northwestern in 1972 and unexpectedly found himself the object of a miniriot as infuriated "jock" students, disappointed in their expectations of seeing an ordinary porn film, pounded on the projection booth and demanded refunds.[15]

Smith stopped releasing films only a few years after *Flaming Creatures*, professing disgust that, as he put it, his witty and beautiful "comedy" had been reduced to a banal "sex issue of the Cocktail World."[16] Ironically, Susan Sontag became in a sense more "famous" for *Flaming Creatures*, about which she wrote a laudatory and defensive review in the *Nation* in 1964, than did its maker, Jack Smith. For every person who actually saw Smith's film, perhaps a hundred know it only from Sontag's description of it. Sontag's often cited essay "Notes on Camp" appeared (in *Partisan Review*) the same year as the *Flaming Creatures* review; and from the vantage point of twenty-five years after their first appearance, one may well be struck rereading her essays by the extreme degree to which they depoliticize the sexual and artistic practices that are their subjects. For example, Sontag praises *Flaming Creatures* for its "joy and innocence" (*"Flaming Creatures* is that rare modern work of art: it is about joy and innocence"), and while I can see speaking of it as a *joyous* film, the other half of the formulation makes one want to paraphrase Mae West: "*innocence* had nothing to do with it."[17] *Flaming Creatures* not only exemplifies a remarkable range of experience and sophistication about the ways people inhabit gender and sexuality, it also manifests an acutely intelligent political awareness and engagement. The maker of *Flaming Creatures* knew how to make a cultural product "guaranteed" to explode closets, he knew where and how to detonate it, and he was aware that setting people's closets on fire is not simply a liberatory act: inevitably, some people would get burned, including, quite possibly, the incendiaries themselves. Setting closets on fire in the way that a number of writers and filmmakers including Smith did throughout the decade leading up to the Stonewall rebellion, not for the homophobic purpose of intentionally injuring or destroying their inhabitants but in order to bring more people out, to try to put an end to the institution of the closet itself, was a serious and dangerous political project.

Exploding the closet by making "outrageous" forays against the heterosexual monopoly on filmic representation was in Smith's work not unrelated to other political activities he advocated and practiced, such as his resistance to what he called "landlordism," the ruinous remaking of Manhattan in the image of real estate interests in the seventies and eighties, and his commitment to tending and arranging the large collection of "trash" that he assembled and used as his basic performance material. Smith tried to get theater audiences to put themselves in the place of New York City's homeless twenty years before others did: for his *Capitalism of Atlantis* (1965), he wanted spectators brought in blindfolded while a loud recorded voice exhorted them to imagine themselves passed out from exhaustion on a hot sidewalk and being assaulted by cops and dragged into custody.[18] Smith also had utopian ideas about the "trash" culture he saw us as inhabiting; he told Sylvère Lotringer in a *Semiotext(e)* interview that "in the middle of the city should be a repository of objects that people don't want anymore, which they should take to this giant junkyard. . . . This center of unused objects would become a center of intellectual activity. Things would grow up around it."[19] Smith's first performance piece, a "nightclub act" he did in collaboration with filmmaker Ken Jacobs in Provincetown in 1961, was called *The Human Wreckage Review.*[20] For the almost thirty remaining years of his career, Smith was involved in a fiercely unsentimental project of reclaiming his own and other queer people's energies (all kinds of queer people, including gay ones) from the myriad forms of human wreckage into which our society has tended to channel it.

In 1967, near what was to be the end of the period of his most intense involvement with film, not only as a filmmaker but also as perhaps the most frequently featured performer in underground film during that movement's most productive decade, Smith was asked in an interview what pleasure he had taken in his film performances. "I never could afford psychoanalysis," he answered, and went on to say, "it was very brave of me to take psychoanalysis in that form."[21] The reply is in one sense instantly recognizable as a bit of period humor, but I propose to take it as more than that; I wish to affirm Smith's judgment that he "was very brave" to attempt to carry out a self-analysis—one from which I believe many other people in comparably marginal situations who have seen his work, or that of his imitators, have benefited—in a public and highly improvisatory manner, rather than the private and privileged circumstances under which analysis is normally carried out. As he treats all his other performances as opportunities for "acting out," so does Smith treat the film-journal interview as yet another venue for both enacting and examining common anxieties—common, at least, to people like him, then and since, experimenting with renegotiating their wholly or partially closeted artistic and political existences.

To a question in the same interview about his plans for the immediate future, Smith replies not with the statement about new projects in the offing that the interviewer expects, but with the wistful, pseudopersonal utterance, "Well, I have got to try to pull myself together."[22] The comedy of the director/film star who is so neurotic, so hysterically self-absorbed, that he compulsively responds to "public" interviewing with "private" psychotherapy-style answers fits the alternately glacially ironic and self-distancing but also aggressively "deviant" and exhibitionistic milieu of New York pop culture of the sixties, a culture that first centered around Smith but soon shifted to Warhol.

It may be useful to interrogate the kinds of attributions that have generally been made to Smith and his work—"playfulness" and "innocence" as well as simple "irony" and "self-mockery"—in order better to understand how his performance career, during and after the period in which he made and/or starred in numerous films, represents an alternative to psychoanalytic theory and therapy—in some ways consonant and in other ways in strong conflict with it. However "playful" one may choose to take Smith's undeniably ironic relation to his own performances to be, I think it is also undeniable that his career represents a highly serious, perhaps in some ways a painfully overserious, attempt to work out an exemplary role for himself and others on the sexual and artistic fringes. Asked in the interview just quoted what kind of film roles he might like to play that he had not yet done, Smith replied, "Well, I think I would like to play . . . Christ. But . . . maybe I never will—maybe the interest has all gone out of that, or maybe it would be too repetitious of Dracula" (in Andy Warhol's film version of which he had recently starred as "Batman-Dracula").[23] Smith's fleeting equation of the role of Christ with that of Dracula is an interesting one, but more interesting for my present purposes is a shift in tone at just this point in his remarks: "But anyway the world could use a new idea—a new Christ image, and it would be fun to sort of work that out." This pronouncement was no doubt made at least partly tongue in cheek, but, just kidding or not, the remark has a magniloquence of a kind that has often been associated with delusion—in the offhand manner in which Smith speaks of giving "the world . . . a new Christ image" as a secondary career goal, as something that "would be fun to sort of work . . . out," if and when he gets around to it. The extremely casual, possibly facetious, messianic intentions Smith expresses here may well remind the student of gay male subjectivity in this century of other, more fateful engagements between the "image" of Christ and gay self-identifications and self-representations. (Nijinsky, e.g., engaged in extensive debate with himself as to whether he was or was not Christ in the diary he kept at the time of his breakdown, the crisis that marked the end of his performing career and the onset of his ostensible madness.)[24] Far from abandoning his public self-analysis when he ceased to make films, Smith continued in his subsequent work as a performance artist to "act out" fantasies of his imaginary identities as well as critiques of these fantasies.

One should not conclude a discussion of the imaginary identities that are most important to the performances in *Flaming Creatures,* as well as to Smith's performances in such other films as Warhol's *Batman-Dracula,* without considering the figure of the vamp and the practice of vamping. The very term *vamp,* which came into wide circulation around the beginning of World War I, proclaims its derivation from *vampire,* a word and a myth that circulated wildly through mass culture in the aftermath of the success of Bram Stoker's *Dracula* (1897) and its numerous stage and film versions. The reasons for the possibly strong resonance of the figure of the vampire for the young person who comes to self-awareness in the closet (as almost all young gay people probably still do) are obvious: like Dracula, gay youngsters are driven by desires they may at least initially perceive as secret, forbidden, and even monstrous in the eyes of others.[25] Reasons for the persistence of the figure of the vamp in gay subcultures long after its general disappearance from mainstream mass culture are also not far to seek. The vamp, a figure of which Theda Bara was in her brief career the prototypical performer (she enacted the vamp in some forty feature-length film vehicles between 1915 and 1919), was an exotic woman who preyed on and ruined men.[26] The socially and sexually marginal milieu that gave rise to Smith's film practice and others like it gives it marked affinities with the vamp film, from *A Fool There Was* (1915), which starred Bara and inaugurated the subgenre, to *Blood and Sand* (1922), starring Nita Naldi and Rudolph Valentino. Thierry de Duve has noted this of Warhol's early films, which in this respect derive directly from Smith's films and from Warhol's formative interest and participation in them. De Duve writes, "Warhol didn't evolve in the plastic world of stars, but in the demimonde of vamps. His cinema plays out the bland dreams of 1950s Hollywood only to materialize the terror that the Hollywood of the '20s still knew how to signal."[27] Part of the "terror" that Smith's and Warhol's films revive is the widespread fear, in a misogynistic and homophobic culture, of recognizing some women's and gay men's high level of success at the exemplary modern urban practice of "cruising," of attracting sexual attention and response from possible partners through a command of body language, especially through the direction of a powerful, desirous-looking gaze. Judging from the intensely negative reactions of many viewers of *Flaming Creatures,* images of Smith's face, or that of his sometime star Mario Montez, gazing out at the viewer through layers of mascara and eyeshadow, scarves and veils, elicited something of the same fascinated but phobic response that Bara's and Naldi's had fifty years before, when they first signaled for a mass audience the possibility of there being sexually commanding women. That there could be sexually confident and commanding gay men, rather than only disfigured and abject victims of the closet, was powerfully manifested in Smith's and Warhol's films, and the striking enactment of this possibility in some of these films may well have renewed the "terror" of vamps—this time of openly gay male ones—that had disturbed and enthralled many viewers earlier in the century, when the "ravenous" and sup- posedly irresistible gaze of the vamp was first brought in off the street, so to speak, and developed into a classic cinematic code.

Smith's performance practice derives in obvious ways from some of the most excessive moments of early film—the screen personalities of Bara, Naldi, and Valentino and the (to our eyes) deliciously and absurdly overstaged and over- acted "orgy scenes" of which the "Babylonian" sequence of D. W. Griffith's *Intolerance* (1916) is perhaps the most notable example. Part of the success of the assault on the closet Smith's work makes is a consequence of the virtuosic fluency with which he negotiates the undulating waves of images not only across genders but also across "perversions." Successfully negotiating just such perilous perfor- mative modes—as Rubinstein in her time seems to have found ways of doing while Nijinsky did not—Smith and other featured performers in *Flaming Crea- tures* move insouciantly and triumphantly around and through a whole repertory of proscribed behaviors—transgressions that it would be reductive to describe as simply "transvestite," since a man's wearing feminine garb is only one of the numerous culturally enforced "police lines" Smith's performances frequently cross. Smith seems to have performed the roles of the "sheik" or the (presumably male) "vampire" at least as frequently as he did those of the "vamp" or "harem girl" in sixties films. He played all these roles, and directed others to play them, in ways that short-circuit their relations to the heterosexualized representational regimes from which they derive. What is compelling about these figures in Smith's films is not the sheik's enactment of virility or the harem girl's of feminin- ity; nor is it simply the reversal of these roles, as it might be if Smith's were simply another version of traditional transvestite comedy. To underestimate or dismiss the real erotic appeal Smith's "comedies" have had for many gay viewers is to ignore the primary source of their power: his films are incitements to his audience not only to play fast and loose with gender roles but also to push harder against prevailing constraints on sexuality. It therefore seems wrong to say, as Stefan

Brecht does, that "Smith does not confront heterosexuality with any other kind of sexuality: sexuality is identified as heterosexuality. . . . Homosexuality is a substitute, and Smith's art is not homosexual but transvestite."[28] The problem with Brecht's formulation lies in its reductive representation of the sexual-political landscape from the sixties forward; in this landscape, the development of behavioral and representational codes for being gay or queer in ways other than those derived from heterosexual modes of behavior and representation has been an ongoing project on a number of fronts. When commentators assert of the transgressive performance practices of the sixties, as Brecht does, that "the queerness of queerness is that it is asexual,"[29] they fail to recognize that erotic charges in a work like *Flaming Creatures* do not follow hard-wired gender lines, but move powerfully across circuits of gender and sexual identity in not altogether predictable fashions.[30]

From its inception Smith's film practice seems to have derived much of its energy from his identification with the movie star and belated vamp Maria Montez, and from what he saw as *her* identification with the definitively kitsch epics she acted in during her brief but stellar ten-year film career—the same length as Smith's of two decades later, as it turned out. Smith, like many other gay men of his generation, was particularly fascinated by the five Universal Studios vehicles in which Montez starred with the athletic but wooden leading man Jon Hall: *Arabian Nights, White Savage, Ali Baba and the Forty Thieves, Sudan,* and, above all, *Cobra Woman,* where Montez played twin "queens of the jungle," one good, one evil.[31] Smith began his career collaborating with Ken Jacobs, and their earliest joint effort appears to have been a film called *Little Cobra Dance* (the third part of *Saturday Afternoon Blood Sacrifice: TV Plug: Little Cobra Dance,* 1957), in which Smith, dressed as an "exotic" Spanish lady, launches into a wild dance, falls down, and is questioned by the police—"the last being an actual event incorporated into the film."[32] So early in Smith's career did the acting out of a pseudoexotic transvestism, combined with a manic performance of celebration and a no less manic performance of failure ("launches into a wild dance" *and* "falls down"), and culminating in ritual encounters with the police, establish themselves as the central "business" of Smith's performances.

The small body of writing Smith published is, however transgressive its content, usually grammatically and syntactically conventional, so it may well be worth noting the occasional sentence that does not conform to standard, as in the following passage from his 1962–63 essay "The Perfect Filmic Appositeness of Maria Montez": " . . . (Before a mirror is a place) is a place where it is possible to clown, to pose, to act out fantasies, to not be seen while one gives (Movie sets are sheltered, exclusive places where nobody who doesn't belong can go). . . ."³³ The repetition here, and the sentence's incoherent-looking move-ment into and out of parentheses, may seem meaningless—may, even if noticed, be easily ignored, subliminally registered as a typesetting error or at best a com-positional complexity not worth puzzling out. Consider, however, that some-thing worth noticing may be going on. This sentence, convoluted and incom-plete as it in some ways is, may be taken to be a particularly compelling statement of Smith's idea, the subject of the essay, of the "perfect appositeness" of perfor-mances like Maria Montez's and his own to what he sees as the most powerful artistic and political potentials of film. The "place" being somewhat obscurely situated in this difficult sentence is one "before a mirror," where one can see oneself without being seen by anyone else—a place somehow analogous with (or "perfectly apposite" to) the "sheltered, exclusive" movie set of Smith's fantasies, "where nobody who doesn't belong can go." One way of reading this is to imag-ine that these two "apposite" spaces, the one as small as a mirror and the other as large as a movie set, define the liminal horizons of the closet as Smith sees them. ("What's larger than a mirror but smaller than a movie set? The closet.") A better question may be: Is a closet as big as Universal Studios in the forties (home of the closed set of Smith's Montez fantasies) still a closet? Can the closet be made to cease being one if/when its bounds are extended beyond a certain point? If so, what is that point? If the closet is the place one visits or inhabits in order not "to . . . be seen while one gives," as Smith puts it, how can what is, in the space of the closet, intransitivized into objectless "giving" be retransitiv-ized—into giving what? in? out? "head"? "the finger"? pleasure? performances? For Smith, the camera is only a more complex kind of mirror, and if the mirror is sometimes the only piece of furniture in a closet, the mirror-extended-as-camera can function as an opening onto two-way streets, onto transitivity of all kinds of officially discouraged or prohibited or persecuted varieties.

The apparent wide-openness of the circuits of pleasure that energized Maria Montez's performances for herself as well as for her fans made her an exemplary figure for Smith and other gay filmmakers and filmgoers of the sixties. Ever her own greatest fan, Montez's most oft-quoted utterance, made to an interviewer in the late forties, goes, "When I see myself on the screen, I look so beautiful I want to scream with joy." For me, as I suspect for many other gay men who have relished it, the charm of that remark lies not just in what a naive interpreter might call the "childlike" openness of Montez's admiration of her larger-than-life screen image, but in its intensity—signaled by the inflection upward into the hysterical register at the sentence's end: "I want to scream with joy." And one may at least partially attribute the remark's longtime currency among the many gay men for whom American popular film of the forties and fifties—especially through its female stars—had been formative to the succinct way it brings "screen" and "scream" together. In her adoring self-critique, Montez demonstrates what Smith might call the relation of "perfect appositeness," the lexical as well as psychological near mirroring, of "screen" and "scream." Smith discovers something similar in his discussion of the related political spaces of "mirror" and "movie set"; his own politics of performance exploits the appositeness of "self-indulgent" fantasy ("screen," mirror) and disruptive public enactment ("scream," movie set). Not the least of the cultural constructs shattered by the impulse to "scream with joy" at the sight of the adorable (self-)image on the movie screen on the part of male fans of Montez or Lana Turner or Jayne Mansfield is their masculine gender identity. For how many gay men of my own and the previous generation were our earliest intimations that there might be a gap between our received gender identity and our subjective or "felt" one the consequence not of noticing our own erotic attraction to another boy or man but of enthusiastically enjoying and identifying with the performative excesses of Maria Montez rather than Jon Hall, or Lana Turner rather than Burt Lancaster, or Jayne Mansfield rather than Mickey Hargitay?

Smith, working in conjunction with Jacobs, had by 1963 articulated a full range of tentative cinematic alter egos for exploring the positions one might occupy in relation to the closet, the mirror, and the movie screen. Besides Smith's own *Flaming Creatures,* Smith and Jacobs's two most compelling collaborations, *Blonde Cobra* and *Little Stabs at Happiness,* also premiered that year. In the first of these, Smith, the "Blonde Cobra" of the title (a gesture of homage to the Brunette Cobra, Montez, as well as to the Blonde Venus of Dietrich and Sternberg) plays a character called "Jack Smith" as well as an imperious woman named Madame Nescience. In the film's central episode, the latter dreams that she is a Sadean "Mother Superior" putting down an outbreak of mass lesbian sexual activity in the girls' dormitory.

Elsewhere in the film, besides lamenting his generally degenerescent condition ("Leprosy is eating a hole in me, my teeth are falling out, my hair has turned to sauerkraut"), Smith narrates a story apparently about his childhood:

There was once a little boy, a little tweensy, microscopic little boy. . . . [. . . .] And . . . the little boy would . . . look for his Mother, but she was never there, and so he would finally pass out and just fall onto the floor and fall asleep just weary with loneliness and longing and frustration and frustrated longings, until, until when the shadows were lengthening and the sun was drooping he would hear the front door open and, and he would rush out into the hallway and there, and there was his Mother . . . and she always had little white bags from the ten-cent store and they always had certain kinds of chocolates in them, the brown, the droplet kind . . . and he would eat it and she would give him some but not much, just a little because she would save most of it for herself and ah so ah well ah and then, she'd go away again. Mother Mother Mother Mother Mother Mother and then, and there was a little boy that lived upstairs you see it was a two family apartment and ah and—a two family house! and then one day the little boy found the other little boy that lived upstairs the family who lived upstairs in the upstairs floor and the little boy who was less than seven, the lonely little boy, the lonely little boy was less than seven, I know that because we didn't leave Columbus until I was seven, I know it, I was under seven and I took a match and I lit it and I pulled out the other little boy's penis and burnt his penis with a match![34]

Reversing the narrative logic of the two "Scheherazade" stories recounted earlier, in which "orgy" is interrupted by "slaughter" and sexual "games" are violently broken up by an angry and vengeful parent or spouse, the mother of Smith's "lonely little boy" is represented as absent and withholding. This alternative version of the story culminates in an act that fuses the two principal roles and the two halves of the "Scheherazade-party" story, the "little boy" being both the initiator of a transgressive sexual game and the figure who puts an end (in this case an immediate end) to the game—with an act of violence against (in this case one of) its players. The whole story of "the lonely little boy" organizes itself along the manic lines of wild activity eventuating in failure (i.e., falling) and arrest that, as I have discussed, are the design of Smith and Jacobs's brief early collaboration, *Little Cobra Dance*. The little boy is said to be accustomed to "scamper[ing]" from room to room of the empty house looking for his mother, until he "would finally pass out and just fall onto the floor." There he sleeps until he is in turn awakened by the sound of his mother's arriving home, when he "rush[es] out and dart[s] out" to greet her. What is "arrested" at the end of this episode is both childhood sexuality and male-male sexual play, and what the subject, "the lonely little boy," is shown substituting for it is sadistic violence.

As an isolated anecdote, as a familiar kind of "confessional" story of childhood cruelty made "funny" by distance and by its belated avowal of antisocial behavior, as a shaggy-dog story with the unprepared-for punchline "and I pulled out the other little boy's penis and burnt [it] with a match"—as all of these formulations, the "lonely little boy" episode of *Blonde Cobra* may seem to conform in several ways to common conventions of largely straight male-identified styles of humor ("I was a wild and mean little boy, and here's a story to prove it"). But it figures as more than that in Smith's performance, and it does so by means of its engagement with other aspects of his work—and of this film performance in particular—that are different from and in some ways radically opposed to common conventions of straight male comic performance—whether we think of these performances as being carried out by professionals in clubs or on television or in films, or by nonprofessionals in the course of ordinary social life.

The Madame Nescience episode that immediately follows the "lonely little boy" part of *Blonde Cobra* is similarly potentially repugnant to many viewers, insofar as it fits into a familiar transvestite enactment of hostility toward women, toward women in positions of authority particularly, and toward lesbians and lesbian sexuality. Considered as an isolated episode, after all, Madame Nescience presents the viewer with a familiar butt of sexist comedy, the repressed and lascivious nun, here shown indulging in sadistic (homo)sexuality as she, in conformity with the "despotic" and homophobic "Scheherazade-party" scenario, acts out a repressive "slaughter" of her lesbian "daughters." The rest of the film, however, provides a context in which one can think "otherwise" of Smith's Madame Nescience performance. For example, following as it does on the "lonely little boy" narrative, Madame Nescience's imaginary appearance and behavior may be read as the return of the repressed mother in that episode. And if she still seems a figure of hostile male projection when seen as a displaced version of the rejecting and withholding mother of the "lonely little boy," she may seem considerably less so if her dream of disciplinary behavior toward her "daughters"—lining them up and paddling their bare bottoms with a "silver cross"—is related to the film's ultimate image. As Smith intones a line from Baudelaire—"Life swarms with innocent monsters"—the film shows him bending forward to expose his own bared buttocks with a butcher knife thrust between them, actually held high up between his thighs but placed to look as though penetrating his anus. "Ooooooooh," Smith cries in voice-over, "Sex is a pain in the ass. Sex IS a pain in the ass."

The image has something of the violent shock value of the founding image of surrealist film, that of the bisected eye in *Un chien andalou*. The butcher knife driven "up the ass" of the wailing performer is the very image of the sadistic rape of one male by another, just as it is the image of the violent sexual assault that, in homophobic fantasy, gay men both desire and "deserve." Among its other possible meanings for gay male viewers, the image, in combination with the verbal utterance that accompanies it, forcefully and comically literalizes the experience of pain in anal penetration commonly felt by inexperienced men, or by men who engage in being penetrated anally who have feelings of conscious or unconscious unwillingness or anxiety toward their partner and/or toward the idea or the reality of being penetrated.

The image of the butcher knife thrust "up the ass" of the mock-lamenting "Blonde Cobra" is only secondarily an image of male-male rape or of homophobic and sadistic contempt for gay male desire for anal connection. In the economy of the film as a whole it is primarily a comic undoing of the "lonely little boy's" burning the penis of the "other little boy" in the film's first episode and of Madame Nescience's spanking her lesbian "daughters'" bottoms with a silver cross in its central episode. Horrible as it may sound, the film's climactic image of the Cobra figure's stabbed anus is, as it actually appears in the film, more an emblematic or visual metaphysical conceit than any kind of really graphic representation of physical violation. This ostensible wound sheds no blood, nor does the viewer see the knife inserted; it will be obvious to all but the most gullible viewer from the moment of the image's appearance that what one is seeing is in a significant sense not at all a realistically simulated stabbing—no fancy special effects here—but a child's trick of concealing a knife blade in a fold of the body, combined with perhaps the clown's oldest trick for mildly shocking and amusing his audience, exposing his bottom.

The titular *Little Stabs at Happiness* of Smith and Jacobs's other 1963 collaboration are some of them, too, literal, albeit recognizably theatrical, stabs. In the first episode of that film, Smith sits in an empty bathtub, his head covered with tinfoil and his nose painted blue, hectically alternating between smoking a cigarette and gnawing the crotch of a baby doll. When he subsequently grasps the doll by the head and stubs out a cigarette in its eyes, an unsympathetic viewer may respond by thinking that Smith is simply "sick," or that his particular brand of "cinema of cruelty" is puerile in the extreme. When, in the film's final sequence, he emerges onto the roof of a building, dressed in a homemade harlequin costume looking fresh from the thrift shop, to perform a rather wan balloon dance to a recording of a forties pop tune called "Happy Bird," it is as if for once his ritualistically alternating performances of manic energy and sodden failure have met in the hitherto unavailable psychic middle to produce simple depression. In the film, the segment is entitled "The Spirit of Listlessness."

Depression, outbursts of mania, fits of hysterical anxiety, of antisocial behavior, hostility, thoughts and memories of sadistic and masochistic desires and behavior, and fantasies of the same, moods of intensely narcissistic self-indulgence (not unrelated to what Leo Bersani has called the "grave doubt resulting from homosexual desire: *the doubt about which self to adore*")[35] alternating with moods of bitter despair and self-destructive impulses: the emotional weather of Smith's performances is the emotional weather of the closet. This is not to say that gay men have any kind of monopoly on these states of mind and behavior. To do so would simply be to reinscribe the homophobic discourses that for a long time deemed (in some quarters still deem) gays "disturbed" or psychically and emotionally inadequate or damaged, and blamed our sexual and social existences as gay people for the alleged damage rather than looking to the twin institutions of homophobia and the closet, which "disturb" and damage gay and straight people both, in different ways and in differing degrees.

What Jack Smith did in his film performances and "live" performance pieces during twenty historically crucial years was to keep projecting gay subjective awareness of the political and psychological realities of the closet onto the "screen" of fantasy for collective, rather than private, recognition, inspection, and analysis. He continued to do so throughout the seventies—after Stonewall had occurred and after he himself largely stopped making and appearing in films—in a series of pieces performed in small downtown theaters or, more often, in his own loft. In sharp contrast with the spiraling trajectory of the career of his former filmmaking associate and fellow scandalmaster Andy Warhol, Smith continued to seem to court and to find failure and oblivion in his post-Stonewall, postfilm career. Incapacity and breakdown ceased to be alternative performative modes (the ritualistic "fallings" and failures of his previous work) for him, and he made the endless deferral of performance the hallmark of his work in the seventies. Audiences arriving at his loft for a midnight performance would regularly witness his fumblings with slides and slide projector for two and a half hours. Smith would then announce that owing to technical problems there would be no (further) performance that night. Hamlet, that most emblematically incapacitated and "blocked" of early modern young male inhabitants of the closet, became one of the predictable foci of an apparently endless series of Smith's performances of announcing-and-deferring-performance.

Around 1977 Smith effected what was perhaps his most successful compromise between performance in any ordinary sense and the kind of deferral that had largely replaced ordinary performance for him. He did this in his highly revisionary version of Ibsen's *Ghosts,* which Smith variously titled *The Secret of Rented Island* and *Orchid Rot of Rented Lagoon.*[36] The small group of devotees who attended the first performance were unsurprised when Smith, pleading that some of his actors had failed to appear by curtain time, invited members of the audience to "help out," and "filled in" major roles with stuffed animals from his collection. Smith played the role of Oswald, and (in the first performance) a male friend, in drag and shrouded with veils, played his mother, Mrs. Alving. Smith integrated into the production the apparently inevitable judgment that it would be an unmitigated disaster, and behaved as if he, as well as the character he was playing, was in a state of imminent mental and emotional collapse. He read his lines from the script and frequently requested help finding his place in the play from fellow cast members, who were of course most of the time as "lost" as he was. In the closing lines of the play, young Oswald's dementia, induced by a syphilitic infection inherited through his mother from his philandering but ultra-respectable father, finally manifests itself: he asks his mother to "give him the sun," and she gazes at him with the horrified realization that he has become psychotic. In Smith's production, Oswald and Mrs. Alving continued sitting side by side in silence after this climactic moment, under an intense pinlight. Mrs. Alving slowly lowered her veil, revealing a leprous face, and Oswald opened his legs, showering a heap of brilliant glitter onto the floor from his "decaying" groin. All this was performed to the sound of Doris Day's recording of "Once I Had a Secret Love."

The camp excesses of this ending, like those of Smith's earlier film work, are palpable. What is not so readily evident in this scene are the ways in which it is consistent and continuous with the political and psychological explorations of the closet I have described Smith making in his earlier work. Young men in extremis; Doris Day's songs and screen personality; the glitter that emblematized for Smith the kind of tacky glamour Maria Montez had shored up against her ruin, secret sexual desires, and afflictions; the dramatis personae and conventional apparatus of camp; the props and furniture of the closet—all are the figures and materials Smith's work tirelessly deconstructed.

Smith performed infrequently after the late seventies. When I belatedly saw him in performance in a festival of punk art in the early eighties in a storefront off Times Square, he characteristically appeared late, tinkered for a long time with props and a slide projector that was never activated, and then reclined on a couch to smoke a hookah. All the while an attractive young man and woman, both garbed in "harem pajamas," read aloud in its entirety a biography of Yvonne de Carlo (star of *Song of Scheherazade,* 1947). Beyond his silent but eloquent presence onstage, Smith restricted his contributions to the rest of the performance to a few momentary interruptions of the boy and girl odalisques, to make minute adjustments to their costumes or poses, or to correct their occasional mispronunciations of words.

Later that year I saw yet another big filmic "Scheherazade party," Pasolini's *Arabian Nights,* one of his three late productions of classic literary cluster narratives: Scheherazade's, the *Canterbury Tales,* and *The Decameron.* Pasolini subsequently repudiated the trilogy for its "liberal," optimistic "sexual pluralism," putting in its place his last completed project, the harrowing film fantasy of sexual captivity and torture under fascism called *Salò.* Although I admire some of Pasolini's films, his "Scheherazade party," the *Arabian Nights,* rehearses many of the same repugnant clichés that underlay Diaghilev's. In Pasolini's "Araby," as in so many earlier orientalizing versions of it, sex rather than survival seems to be the first priority of its denizens, and everyone except the few requisite wise old men is young, extraordinarily sexually attractive, and always available. Falling chronologically between Diaghilev's and Pasolini's *de luxe* productions, Smith's various versions of "Scheherazade" seem by contrast with these others to harbor real deconstructive potential in relation to the underlying sexual-political and nationalist-political agendas of almost all his big-budget predecessors and successors.

In the numerous political fables of the "harem" Smith directed and/or performed in, he privileges fantasies neither of Western nor of male supremacy—as so many other orientalist fantasies do—but of what he calls *moldiness*. As Madame Nescience lies on her couch, she is said to be "dreaming of old musty memories, memories that she thought that she had forgot[ten] or so she thought but you see they came up in a funky mass of ah exuding effluviums from the musty past . . . covered with moss and funk."[37] Smith calls her dream, and by extension the whole episode in which she figures, "La rêve de la purité de Madame Nescience." The manifest content of this "dream of purity," as we have seen, was one of the vigorous suppression of lesbianism in a convent by a "mother superior" who brings a suspicious degree of enthusiasm to the task. But it is not with her repressive and luridly charged "purity" that I want to close this discussion of Smith's performances, with which purity has indeed had little to do, but rather with an insistence on the paradoxically "moldy," "swampy" (to use his terms) clarity with which his work pungently represents the kind of unconscious processes that have, over the past couple of decades, fueled innumerable small- and large-scale eruptions of queer rebellion against the institutions of the closet. On these conditions, Smith's flaming performances and others like them have had wonderfully incendiary effects.

Notes

1 My discussion of the Ballets Russes *Scheherazade* is indebted to Richard Buckle's account of the planning and performance of the ballet in his biography *Nijinsky* (New York: Simon & Schuster, 1971), esp. 137–42. I wish to thank Jonathan Goldberg and Eve Kosofsky Sedgwick for their encouragement and valuable suggestions for improving earlier versions of this article and the conveners of the conference "The Closet" at Scripps College (December 1988) for the initial impetus for undertaking the project of which this article is a part.

2 Philip Kolb, ed., *Lettres à Reynaldo Hahn* (Paris, 1956), 188, quoted in Buckle, *Nijinsky*, 141–42.

3 Wollen's article has been of crucial importance to me in thinking about the kinds of continuities in gay male performance in the twentieth century that I am considering in this project (see his "Fashion/Orientalism/the Body," *New Formations*, no. 1 [Spring 1987]: 5–33). Dale Harris takes a more conventionally connoisseurial approach to the subject of the cultural impact of Ballets Russes orientalism in his "Diaghilev's Ballets Russes and the Vogue for Orientalism," in *The Art of Enchantment: Diaghilev's Ballets Russes, 1909–1929*, comp. Nancy Van Norman Baer, catalog of an exhibition held at the Fine Arts Museum of San Francisco (1988), 84–95. For accounts of the institution of the harem that tend to deconstruct Western orientalizing fantasies of it, see Malek Alloula, *The Colonial Harem*, trans. Myrna Godzich and Wlad Godzich (Minneapolis: University of Minnesota Press,

1986); and Huda Shaarawi, *Harem Years: The Memoirs of an Egyptian Feminist,* trans. and ed. Margot Badran (London: Virago, 1986).

4 Quoted in Wollen, "Fashion/Orientalism/the Body," 21.

5 The 1911 avant-garde's subversion of prevailing religious and sexual certainties was registered in, among other ways, the ban that the then archbishop of Paris placed on the performance of *The Martyrdom of Saint Sebastian.* Of the many reasons he might have put forward for this ban, he announced two: (1) d'Annunzio's identification of the saint with the pagan god Adonis, and (2) the fact that a male Christian saint was to be played by a Jewish woman. Despite the official condemnation, "the show went on," to an only middling success (see Alfred Frankenstein's liner notes for Leonard Bernstein's recording of the *Martyrdom* on Columbia Masterworks, discs M2L 353/M2S 753).

6 Bram Dijkstra, *Idols of Perversity: Fantasies of Feminine Evil in Fin-de-Siècle Culture* (New York: Oxford University Press, 1988), 53.

7 Quoted in Buckle, *Nijinsky,* 124.

8 Besides marking his performance in *Scheherazade,* the year 1910 also marks the beginning of Nijinsky's most productive period as a choreographer; it was then that he began to formulate the projects that would issue in 1912–13 in his three great inaugural modernist ballets, *L'après-midi d'un faune, Jeux,* and *Le sacre du printemps.* For a recent assessment of Nijinsky's achievements as a choreographer, see Lynn Garafola, "Vaslav Nijinsky," *Raritan* 8, no. 1 (Summer 1988): 1–27.

9 Quoted in Buckle, *Nijinsky,* 141.

10 Ibid.

11 Joan Acocella writes briefly but perceptively of the way Nijinsky was cast throughout his career in roles in which he was either "something other than human: a puppet, a god, a faun, the specter of a rose," or, if human, not so in any ordinary sense, but always in either a reduced or excessive way: "a slave, an androgyne, or some other object of sexual connoisseurship" (see her "Vaslav Nijinsky," in *The Art of Enchantment,* 110).

12 For a history of gay and lesbian political organizing and resistance in the three decades before Stonewall, see John D'Emilio, *Sexual Politics, Sexual Communities: The Making of a Homosexual Minority in the United States, 1940–1970* (Chicago: University of Chicago Press, 1983). Eve Kosofsky Sedgwick's *Epistemology of the Closet* (Berkeley and Los Angeles: University of California Press, 1990) provides a searching theoretical exploration of the ways in which an endemic crisis of homo/heterosexual definition has structured/fractured Western culture in the twentieth century.

13 Everyone interested in Jack Smith's work in film and performance is indebted to Stefan Brecht and J. Hoberman for their efforts in preserving at least some aspects of Smith's extremely fugitive performance art. Brecht gives a number of informative accounts of Smith's work from 1961 to 1977 in his valuable study *Queer Theatre* (Frankfurt: Suhrkamp, 1978), 10–27 and 157–77. Hoberman surveys Smith's performances during the same period in his article "The Theatre of Jack Smith," *Drama Review* 23, no. 1 (March 1979): 3–12. For further information about Smith and his performances, see Jonas Mekas's July 1970 *Village Voice* article "Jack Smith, or the End of Civilization," reprinted in Mekas's *Movie Journal: The Rise of a New American Cinema, 1959–1971* (New

York: Collier, 1972), 388–97. Film scholar Karel Rowe, who worked briefly as Smith's
assistant during the summer of 1972, provides useful information about Smith's film
performances as well as a Smith filmography in his book *The Baudelairean Cinema: A
Trend within the American Avant-Garde* (Ann Arbor, Mich.: UMI Research Press, 1982).
Joan Adler, in a piece entitled "On Location," gives an impressionistic account of the
making of *Normal Love,* the unfinished film project Smith undertook after *Flaming Creatures,* in Stephen Dwoskin's *Film Is: The International Free Cinema* (Woodstock, N.Y.:
Overlook, 1975), 11–21.

14 For most of the time the film has existed, it has been even more difficult to see *Flaming
Creatures* than is usual for an "underground" work. Never available for screening beyond a
very small circuit of alternative venues, the film seems to have been withdrawn from
circulation by Smith by the early seventies in angry reaction to what he considered its
misreception on the part of everyone from the New York Police Department to Susan
Sontag. Smith was antagonistic to written analyses of his work; his most frequently quoted
utterance has been, "Film critics are writers and they are hostile and uneasy in the presence
of a visual phenomenon" (quoted, e.g., in Rowe, *Baudelairean Cinema,* xiii). Given Smith's
passionate commitment to his film's being *seen* rather than being made to serve as grist for
the mill of what he saw as pseudocontroversy, it is more than ironic, it is deeply unfortunate
that *Flaming Creatures* has, owing to its general unavailability, "lived on" to the extent that
it has largely in the form of written descriptions of it. On the subject of the general
suppression of many of the most radical examples of "underground" film of the sixties, see
David E. James's eloquent prefatory statement to his recent history of noncommercial
American film of that decade, *Allegories of Cinema: American Film in the Sixties* (Princeton,
N.J.: Princeton University Press, 1979), ix. Among published descriptions of *Flaming
Creatures,* the following are particularly useful: P. Adams Sitney, *Visionary Film: The
American Avant-Garde 1943–1978,* 2d ed. (New York: Oxford University Press, 1979),
354–57; Rowe, *Baudelairean Cinema,* 49–50.

15 Rowe describes his travails in attempting to show *Flaming Creatures* in *Baudelairean
Cinema,* xi–xii; Hoberman discusses the prosecution of *Flaming Creatures* and other underground films of the period (chiefly Jean Genet's *Un chant d'amour* and Kenneth Anger's *Scorpio Rising*) in his and Jonathan Rosenbaum's *Midnight Movies* (New York: Harper & Row, 1983), 59–61.

16 Smith made this charge against his critics in his 1973 *Village Voice* review of John
Waters's *Pink Flamingos.* Brecht quotes it in *Queer Theatre,* 26n.

17 Sontag says *Flaming Creatures* "is about joy and innocence" in her essay "Jack Smith's
Flaming Creatures," reprinted in *Against Interpretation* (New York: Farrar, Straus, & Giroux, 1966), 229. Possible political meanings and consequences get thoroughly elided
from Sontag's influential account of Smith's film, which, according to her, simply eschews
moralizing in order to occupy a purely aesthetic "space": "The space in which *Flaming
Creatures* moves is not the space of moral ideas, which is where American critics have
traditionally located art. What I am urging is that there is not only moral space, by whose
laws *Flaming Creatures* would indeed come off badly; there is also aesthetic space, the space
of pleasure. Here Smith's film moves and has its being" ("Jack Smith's *Flaming Creatures,*"

231). Sontag similarly writes in "Notes on Camp": "Jews pinned their hopes for integrating into modern society on promoting the moral sense. Homosexuals have pinned their integration into society on promoting the aesthetic sense. Camp is a solvent of morality. It neutralizes moral indignation, sponsors playfulness" ("Notes on Camp," in *Against Interpretation*, 290). The problem with such extreme and extremely reductive hypostatizations is that moral and aesthetic practices cannot be rendered stable, plainly disjunct "spaces" or "senses"; categories and categorical dyads such as Jewish moral seriousness versus gay "playfulness" fall explanatorily flat, especially in view of the subsequent history of these two groups in the quarter century since Sontag's essay, during which time many of her New York Jewish liberal intellectual confrères of the mid- to late sixties have turned neoconservative and gays have been engaged in a series of political struggles that have for the most part been anything but "playful."

18 Hoberman, "The Theatre of Jack Smith," 4.

19 Quoted in ibid., 6.

20 Ibid., 4.

21 Gerard Malanga, "Interview with Jack Smith," *Film Culture*, no. 45 (1967): 15.

22 Ibid., 14.

23 Ibid., 15.

24 Romola Nijinsky, ed., *The Diary of Vaslav Nijinsky* (Berkeley: University of California Press, 1968). See, e.g., pp. 29, 51, 120, 175.

25 Norine Dresser discusses the reasons for the general appeal of the figure of the vampire to adolescents: "Teenagers find the vampire fascinating because the vampire is usually an unwilling victim of a bodily change he cannot control, a change that brings on frightening new desires and cravings, a change that sets him apart from the society he has known and makes him an outsider" (*American Vampires: Fans, Victims and Practitioners* [New York: Norton, 1989], 146). "Normal" adolescent anxieties of the kind Dresser describes are of course compounded when the young person in question is gay. Surely some of the power of the vamp/vampire comedy aspect of *Flaming Creatures* derives from the intensity of these anxieties in what may seem like the archaic past in the lives of gay viewers of the film. Smith had "rehearsed" for *Flaming Creatures* by playing "The Fairy Vampire" in a brief 1961 film collaboration with Ken Jacobs called *The Death of P'town*.

26 See chap. 3, "The Vampire," in Sumiko Higashi, *Virgins, Vamps, and Flappers: The American Silent Movie Heroine* (Montreal: Eden Press, 1978), for a compact and informative account of the cult of the film vamp ca. 1915–22.

27 Thierry de Duve, "Andy Warhol, or The Machine Perfected," *October*, no. 48 (Spring 1989): 13.

28 Brecht, *Queer Theatre*, 177n.

29 Ibid.

30 To be fair to Brecht, one should notice that while his attempts to theorize Smith's practice can be crude (as when he collapses homosexuality into heterosexuality and consigns Smith's art simply to transvestism), his descriptions and observations of Smith's work and that of other "queer artists" are more precise than anyone else's; e.g., he is the only commentator I have read who remarks that for all its apparent male-transvestite

focus, the mock rape of a female character carried out in one episode of *Flaming Creatures* culminates in a scene of lesbian affection and consolation (Brecht, *Queer Theatre*, 25n).

31 Maria Montez's other greatest admirer is Myra Breckinridge, who comes to inhabit Montez's body in the penultimate chapters of Gore Vidal's *Myron* (New York: Random House, 1974).

32 Quoted in Rowe's filmography of Ken Jacobs in *Baudelairean Cinema*, 125–26.

33 Jack Smith, "The Perfect Filmic Appositeness of Maria Montez," *Film Culture*, no. 27 (Winter 1962–63): 30.

34 Jack Smith and Ken Jacobs, "Soundtrack of *Blonde Cobra*," *Film Culture*, no. 29 (Summer 1963): 2.

35 Leo Bersani, *A Future for Astyanax: Character and Desire in Literature* (Boston: Little, Brown, 1976), 306–7.

36 My discussion of Smith's adaptation of *Ghosts* is indebted to Brecht's description of several quite different performances of it he saw (*Queer Theatre*, 157–77), and to Hoberman's remarks on the piece ("The Theatre of Jack Smith," 8–9).

37 "Soundtrack of *Blonde Cobra*," 2.

Men's

Pornography

Gay vs. Straight

Thomas Waugh

Author's Foreword, December 1992

T he following article, published in 1985, had actually been written a few
years earlier, at the height of the sex wars, and bears more than a few battle
scars.

The cultural and political context has muddied considerably since those days
of clarity in the early eighties when I was writing the piece. For one thing the
pandemic and the universal presence of home video have radically altered the
sexual landscape; though each gets a mention or two in the text, it is obvious how
this alteration requires that we look at "Men's Pornography: Gay vs. Straight" as
much as a historical document as an entry in our ongoing debates. Even Linda
Williams's much later work *Hard Core* (1989) has also been overtaken by the
video revolution in a similar way. Nevertheless, her success in legitimizing the
textual and contextual study of porn confirms that feminist scholarship around
dirty pictures has also advanced in leaps and bounds in a very short time. In fact,
it's safe to say, at least in academe, that the sex wars have been won, and Susie
Sexpert/Bright has replaced Andrea Dworkin as the footnote queen of the recent
boom in sex rep. Battle scars or not, hopefully some of my preliminary explorations may still be of use.

Outside academe, on other battlegrounds, the victory might not be so clear. In
1983–84, the publication of this piece even in a supportive and progressive
magazine like *Jump Cut* did not go without a hitch. The visual acknowledgment
of the human penis was considered so risky that the two of my illustrations
showing a mere hint of tumescence were passed through five xerox generations

(and I suspected five cycles at the laundromat) to remove the slightest indexical allure. Few struggles with censorship are so comical or inconsequential however, and since 1985, if anything, they've intensified. As just one example close to home for the author, neo-Dworkinites snuck through a fundamental change in Canadian obscenity jurisprudence earlier this year with the result that a renewed attack on lesbian and gay sexual representation has been unleashed (with Susie Sexpert/Bright its earliest victim). In the United States, one need only think of the terrible roadblocks that faced the editors of *How Do I Look?: Queer Film and Video* (Bad Object Choices, 1991), published independently and printed in Germany after *October* and American printers had panic attacks, or of my own current book-in-progress, *Hard to Imagine: Gay Male Erotic Photography and Film from Their Origins to Stonewall,* which lawyers have had stretched painfully on the rack for several years.

If the recycling of the following hoary text will contribute to the atmosphere of eternal vigilance, which we must never let down, then that alone will be adequate payment (since neither independent political magazines nor scholarly press anthologies provide any other).

The reprinting of this article is dedicated to the memory of the heroic artists mentioned therein, among them Curt McDowell, Artie Bressan, and Al Parker, who have since died of AIDS. They showed us how to love.

Introduction: Labels and Red Herrings

Taking part in a debate about pornography, I am painfully aware of contradictions involved in my position as a person to whom a great many compromising labels may be applied (in alphabetical order: academic, antipatriarchal, Canadian, cinephile, contributor-to-a-magazine-on-trial-for-obscenity, cyclist, gay, male, socialist, teacher, thirty-five, unattached, vanilla-sexual, wasp, etc.).

I belong to a cultural and political context—the urban gay male community/ ies—in which dirty pictures have a hard-won centrality, both historically and at present. I am also an individual consumer. I couldn't begin to describe the importance in my own political/personal growth of the erotic components in the work Baldwin, Genet, Pasolini, Warhol/Morrissey, Burroughs, Michelangelo, and even Gore Vidal (to begin as usual with the most respectable list), not to mention *Tomorrow's Man* (the crypto-gay physique magazine I discovered on the rack of the local newsstand as a trembling teenager in Presbyterian Ontario in the mid-sixties), and *Straight to Hell* (*STH*) (the underground folk-raunch magazine of readers' narratives I discovered as a trembling grad student in New York

City in the early seventies, when I was wondering whether marching in Gay Pride could blow my comprehensives).

How then am I to express my solidarity in words and actions with women's rightful denunciation of pornography as an instrument of antifeminist backlash, of the usurpation by industrial capitalism of the private sexual sphere, of the merchandizing and degradation of women's bodies, of the incitement of rape and violence against women? Can I do so without aping the standard liberal male guilt trip or its "we're oppressed and alienated too" refrain? Without echoing the occasional antifeminist tirades in the gay press by beleaguered men who think they see women lining up alongside the cops? Can I do so while insisting that sexual liberation is still an essential component of political liberation and that erotica has a rightful, even indispensable, place in the culture and politics of sexual liberation—gay, lesbian, feminist, and yes, straight male?

Is it enough for me to repeat that antiwoman pornography, a symptom, can only be eradicated by a fundamental transformation of society along feminist-socialist lines? And that, in the meantime, if I had time, I could support various proposed liberal stopgap measures by the bourgeois state toward curbing pornography's worst social effects, that is, *measures short of obscenity provisions in criminal codes,* such as: the use of labor and criminal codes to halt child exploitation, forced labor, nonconsensual sexual relations, and the incitement of violence; the regulation of an above-ground sex industry by means of unionization, taxation, labor codes, public visibility restrictions, in short, the kind of state intervention that regulates tobacco and alcohol (even though this kind of regulation has led in France to a kind of de facto suppression of gay culture). I also obviously support nonstate strategies of consumer resistance like boycotts and education, such as those led around "nonpornographic" films such as *Cruising, Windows,* and *Dressed to Kill* in which I have participated.

Censorship is both a red herring and a real issue, and often a means of halting debate (one Montreal writer demands that readers take a stand either for or against porn before establishing terms or definitions; a Toronto writer demands that readers choose between life and art). For me, a gay man struggling against continuing, in fact escalated, censorship of gay newspapers and films, and, in the Canadian context, resisting the most ferocious police suppression of our culture in any Western society, censorship is a real issue. Even though many of the most visible antiporn activists have repeatedly renounced legal sanctions against pornography and some have stressed the necessity of gay-lesbian rights education as part of the antiporn discourse, many mainstream spokespeople are not so careful. As just one example, in 1978, the year that the *Body Politic,* the Canadian national gay-lesbian paper, began its still ongoing struggle to survive in the obscenity courts, Canadian feminist spokespeople testified before a parliamentary committee and saw their proposals for revision of obscenity statutes (to provide for violence) manipulated and appropriated by homophobic liberals and the New Right alike. The coincidence may or may not be only symbolic, but we don't have time to wonder. In 1980, the National Organization of Women in the United States resolved that pornography is not a genuine lesbian-gay rights issue, nor are pedophilia, sadomasochism, and public sexuality (all of which overlap with the issue of pornography). All four of these issues have been central concerns within the gay male community/ies since Stonewall, and favorite pretexts for our persecution. But some feminists, straight and lesbian alike, have tended to regard them as areas where we are struggling merely to exercise our full patriarchal privileges as men (a view that has sometimes been partly justified). Within the last few years, the lesbian-feminist community has learned not only that it will not be able to resolve these issues away but also that they are of utmost pertinence to feminism and lesbian liberation, and furthermore, that (who ever would have thought?) the interests of gay men and feminists on these issues are not necessarily irreconcilable. The so-called choice between censorship and pornography, art and life, is falsely formulated: women's right to defend themselves against patriarchal violence and the right of women and sexual minorities to full cultural, sexual, and political expression are allied rights, both threatened in the current conjuncture. To prioritize or rank them on our agenda greatly damages the antipatriarchal movement (just as reproductive rights must not have less priority on the agenda than lesbian rights or vice versa).

The recent debate on sexuality within the feminist community, in the headlines of the alternative media since the *Heresies* sex issue, has already had some input from the gay men's movement. In all modesty, antipatriarchal gay men still have an important contribution to make. It may be no accident that some of the first utterances of the new feminist sexual outlaws appeared in gay newspapers with varying degrees of lesbian input, from a little (the *Advocate*), to some (the *Body Politic*), to tons (*Gay Community News*). Gay men were struck from the beginning by how much the new discourse of women's pleasure echoed but went further than the discourse of early gay liberation (in the era when gay groups used to call themselves the Gay Liberation Front instead of the National Task Force), profiting directly from two decades of feminist debate. Of course the antiporn right saw our satisfaction as patronizing and the use of our media as conspiratorial: "The lesbian S & M [*sic*] movement is a growing and organized one, especially in San Francisco. One of the leaders, Pat Califia, who has a slave, wrote the article, "The New Puritans," which was published in the paper *The Advocate*. One of her arguments is that she doesn't want anyone taking her fist fucking magazines away from her. I think it is very interesting to note that most articles on this appear in primarily gay male publications. It seems to make a lot of sense since gay men tend to like porn, have a stake in it, and reinforce these attitudes to their advantage. This is again our colonization, women being taken over by gay men instead of straight men."[1]

Regardless of the obvious rejoinder that we are too busy molesting children to have time to be "taking over" women, I would like to explore in this article our "stake" in porn, to sketch some of the contours of our contribution to the debate on sexuality and porn. Specifically, I would like to situate gay male pornography in relation to straight male pornography in terms of its uniquely contradictory mixture of progressive and reactionary characteristics in its relations of production, exhibition, consumption, and representation. Far from wishing to offer an apologetics for gay porn against homophobic dismissals from within the women's movements, both from the National Organization for Women center and the Women Against Pornography right (I realize that my refutation of such dismissals are open to being misread as defensiveness, an unnecessary attitude I may not be wholly successful in avoiding), I feel that an objective analysis of gay pornography will clarify and expand many of the terms of the current debate. The "topographical" chart in this essay is largely contemporary in its focus, that is, post-sixties, though reference is made to the historical evolution of gay pornography particularly since the establishment of embryonic modern-day gay ghettos following World War II (I also refer here and there to classical stag movies). My main object is a relatively loose comparison of gay male pornography to straight male pornography, referring wherever relevant to its major product divisions: theatrical films, hardcore and softcore; rental or mail-order video; "arcade"/adult-bookstore materials, mostly film loops and hardcore magazines; mail-order films and photographic sets (beefcake); glossy mass-distribution *Playboy*-imitation magazines like *Blueboy;* and finally, porn that may be called "artisanal," amateur or "folk," both written and visual, for example, *Straight to Hell.* (Obviously these categories sometimes overlap, as with video versions of theatrical films, and some exclusions are arbitrary—"live" performances, written materials except for the artisanal *STH*, and ancillary branches of the industry like gadgets.)

The comparison is organized in terms of relations of production (making), exhibition (showing), consumption (looking), and representation (depicting). Obviously, the chart, with its illustrations and appendages, is a work-in-progress, and I welcome any corrections or additions; it may reflect also a certain unavoidable bias and a greater expertise in the left-hand column that readers are asked to tolerate. On the sidelines, I also offer a brief reflection trying to connect the feminist conception of patriarchal public space to the gay ghetto and its pornographic cultural forms. And lastly, since we have often heard the question as to what a nonsexist pornography of the utopian future might look like, I conclude with an examination of Curt McDowell's *Loads,* a noncommercial gay pornographic film from San Francisco (recently seized in Montreal incidentally) with the idea of pondering in concrete terms how far or how near we might be to that ideal.

A Note on Definitions

Much of the debate has been a war of definitions, of distinctions between sexist pornography and nonsexist erotica, between my art and your smut, and so on. All such definitions tend to be, for reasons of semantics, ideological rather than scientific. This is true whether explicitly so (as in any definition based on values, inherent artistic merit, or political or educational effectivity), or by implication, that is, expressed as formal/aesthetic, legalistic, physiological (Auden defined pornographic as anything that gave him an erection), historical, sociological, or commercial (the definitions of pornographers themselves). I am not the first to insist that any advance in the debate must acknowledge all of the definitions currently in play since these definitions themselves are weapons in the ongoing struggle.

I will not add to the confusion by proposing a new definition (except insofar as the above caveat and a refusal to distinguish between erotica and pornography constitute a definition), since for gay people the definition imposed by police, censors, and courts at any given point will always be the determining one.

However, since discussion of pornography is becoming increasingly acrimonious and difficult, and since misunderstandings are already being translated into social and legal practice, I will make a few prescriptions. Participants in the debate must situate themselves in relation to the definitions struggle and must specify exactly what images or texts they are referring to and exactly what social remedies they are proposing, if any.

This precision is indispensable in avoiding co-optation by the book banners, the homophobes, and the Moral Majority, who have gotten so far by blurred distinctions and misleading generalizations. Next, every exclusively single-issue intervention is a step backward: connections must be established at every point between the porn debate and the other issues of the antipatriarchal struggle, especially reproductive rights, sex education, and lesbian/gay rights. I would go even further to say that every comprehensive intervention on pornography must acknowledge the existence of gay male pornography. To pass over the stacks of *Blueboy* lined up beside *Penthouse* is either homophobic (as in the case of the National Film Board of Canada's *Not a Love Story*) or misguided liberalism, misguided even if the evasion arises out of solidarity with gay people. General propositions about pornography that do not apply to gay pornography are inadmissible (e.g., does "All pornography degrades women"[2] apply to gay male pornography? if so, how? if not, why not?). Progressive gay men have nothing to fear from an open and nonhomophobic confrontation with gay pornography, nor from our own self-critical confrontation with the abuses of pornography within our community.

Finally, the following distinctions are essential to any meaningful discussion: between pornography and violent pornography, between consent and coercion, between consensual power play (SM) and violence, between images and actions, between individual sexual practices and collective sexual politics. This latter distinction is crucial. The personal may be political, but there is no such thing as a politically correct individual sexuality. By this I mean that we must support the full rights of sexual outlaws to act out their individual (consensual) desires, whether sadomasochists or drag queens or Phyllis Schlafly. Andrea Dworkin's statement that all fucking is inherently sadistic discredits her other work, some of which is useful. Specific sexual practices as depicted in a given image do not necessarily coincide with relations of exploitation or domination, nor with any other power relation. A man or woman portrayed as getting fucked cannot automatically be seen as victim; gay porn in particular, and of course gay sexuality in general, undermines the widespread assumption in the porn debate that penetration in itself is an act of political oppression. A sexual act or representation acquires ideological tenor only through its personal, social, narrative, iconographic, or larger political context.

The Ghetto: A Note on Space

One way of looking at the evolution of the gay movement since World War II is as the growth of our claims to space. Our first claim was to the inviolability of our private space (the state has no place in the bedrooms of the nation, said Trudeau, when he decriminalized consensual sodomy between two adults in 1969—a reform only a minority of American states have followed). Our next claim was for the inviolability of the ghetto, our gathering places, and neighborhoods. Our final claim was full open access to all public space of our society, and in fact, many of us insisted, to alter the terms of that society. Our claim to our media and to our culture, including our pornography, is part of all three of these claims to space.

When we talk this over with our feminist allies, we often fail to strike a sympathetic chord. The space that we have been demanding is only the space we have been conditioned to expect as men in patriarchal society, space that has been only partly withheld because we suck cock. Women have not yet achieved access to that space, either literally in terms of public territory, or metaphorically in terms of media or cultural, sexual, and political expression. In short, gay pornography profits from and aspires to the institutionalized presence of patriarchal power built on the absence/silence of women, and is thus complicit in the oppression of women.

This is true and it hurts. But it's not all of the truth. First, our claims to space, private, ghetto, or public, have not been achieved except incompletely and provisionally, always subject to invasion and revocation. Ghettoized spaces, as women have always sensed in their kitchens and church basements and offices, are no substitute for autonomous political space; they are more like enclaves of self-defense and accommodation. Our pornography, in fact, reflects the recognition of this insufficiency: of the 110 *STH* anecdotes I mention elsewhere, only eight take place in ghetto space (saunas, discos, backrooms, cinemas), whereas about forty take place in our private homes, and the rest all take place in nonghetto public space. Our greatest visibility may be in the ghetto, but our fantasies and our everyday lives are elsewhere.

Pornography has become one of our privileged cultural forms, the expression of that quality for which we are stigmatized, queer bashed, fired, evicted, jailed, hospitalized, electroshocked, disinherited, raped in prison, refused at the U.S. border, silenced, and ghettoized—that quality being our sexuality. Our pornography is shaped both by the oppression told by my long chain of participles and by our conditioning as men in patriarchy. We must direct our claim to our pornographic culture, not toward occupying our share of patriarchal space, but toward shattering that space, transforming it.

On Getting Fucked

Richard Dyer's assertion in "Male Gay Porn: Coming to Terms" about the dominance of heterosexist modes of sexuality in gay porn narrative needs some qualification: "There seems no evidence that in the predominant form of how we represent our sexuality to ourselves (in gay porn) we in any way break from the norms of male sexuality . . . the narrative is never organized around the desire to be fucked, but around the desire to ejaculate (whether or not following on from anal intercourse). Thus although at the level of public representation, gay men may be thought of as deviant and disruptive of masculine norms because we assert the pleasures of being fucked and the eroticism of the anus, in our pornography this takes a back seat." This may be true of many or even most theatrical films (though I think this requires further research—certainly lots of individual sequences I remember contradict this); however, passive penetration fantasies are extremely common as narrative principles in many noncommercial films and anecdotes I have encountered (as are fellatio fantasies, active or passive, which do not seem to be organized around the narrator's ejaculation). Perhaps the noncommercial or artisanal origin of the examples that come to mind says more about the porn industry than our erotic culture as an audience, but that remains to be seen. What does a passive penetration fantasy or a submissive fantasy look or sound like? This question is not only of academic interest. The active penetration fantasy is such a dominant one in the straight male porn industry and in patriarchal culture in general, that, in looking for alternatives, we should analyze the other side of the coin. I've talked about this with some women who, like many gay men and perhaps straight men, are aware of and often disturbed by fantasies of passive penetration, of submission, even of rape.

I propose this abridged citation from an *STH* anecdote from *Meat,* both as a footnote to Dyer's generalization, and as evidence for an investigation it may be profitable to pursue:

Air Force Guy Takes 37 Cocks Up Asshole in One Session

A.P.O. San Francisco—I heard about this construction site with a lot of horny studs. I'm 24, 6′ 1″ tall, 165 lbs, white and love to get fucked . . . gang fucked. Wore cutoffs and hung around the front gate at closing time. A dude eyed me the once over and invited me in. He was in his late 20s and was pretty rugged looking. Led me to a trailer and ripped my Levis off. My head was immediately kissing a desk top and my bare ass protruding over the desk. Talk about getting fucked rough. Heard the door open and more dudes walked in grabbing for their zippers. . . . To get guys up for it quicker I started a line in front as well as in back and sucked off dudes. Got cream in my mouth and in my ass. My asshole was raw but well-fucked, and I'd like to go back for more (from *Meat*).

Men's Pornography, Gay vs. Straight:
A Topographical Comparison

Relations of Production

Gay Male Pornography	*Straight Male Pornography*
—gay male producer employs gay male models	—straight male producer employs female models
—small-scale industrial or artisanal production and distribution base for all commercial categories, reputedly some Mafia presence in theatrical films	—large-scale industrial apparatus for production and distribution with lots of small-scale competition; pervasive presence of Mafia and other multinationals, links to other branches of sex industry.

Gay Male Pornography	*Straight Male Pornography*
—producer control, nonunion employees paid low flat rate, even for "stars"; stigma usually prevents career crossover for performers	—producer control, mostly nonunion employees with low flat rate; some performers in "legit" areas receive high rewards and occasional career crossover, e.g., Sylvia Kristel, Pets of the Year, etc.
—theatrical industry stagnant since mid-seventies with only a few dozen showcases; mail-order business strong; growth only in video area; market seems saturated in present political situation.	—still apparently a growth industry with thousands of theatrical outlets and video boom, expansion continues into "legit" films (*Lady Chatterley's Lover*), and spinoff industries.
—small capital outlay and modest profits in theaters, with budgets never exceeding $80,000 for Joe Gage's features (*L.A. Tool and Die*), all in 16mm; according to Gage, theatrical market allows only one or two major films a year; reruns endemic.	—huge capital outlays relatively common, especially in pseudolegit area, e.g., *Caligula*, where films can cross over out of the combat-zone market; huge profits.
—highly developed star system (Richard Locke, Al Parker), and brand-name auteurs (Toby Ross, Joe Gage), especially in theatrical features; also brand-name mail-order houses (Colt, Falcon).	—wide range of star and auteur recognition in legit softcore films and in "prestige" hardcore features
—overlapping of porno constituency with gay community at large, side-by-side existence within the ghetto: Artie Bressan has made political documentary, porn features, and a legit feature; porn ads appear alongside feminist women's ads in *Gay Community News*; "danglie" (danglie: a short-lived porno genre of the late sixties, after court decisions allowing nudity but before the hardcore explosion: hyperkinetic but flaccid nude males facing camera and doing a lot of jumping up and down.) mogul Pat Rocco sang in the Metropolitan Community Church choir; theatrical star Richard Locke currently campaigning for AIDS research.	—no straight equivalent; straight porn has no self-defined constituency or community base other than the straight male gender caste, extending across class, race, and zoning divisions.
—flourishing presence of nonindustrial erotica (i.e., amateur, folk, artisanal), e.g., readers' narratives in *Straight to Hell*, classified ads culture, home movies, amateur beefcake, extension of preghetto underground culture.	—straight equivalent is marginal or industry adjunct, e.g., "Playboy Forum," advice columns, *Hustler* photos of readers' partners, swingers' newsletters, cable TV. . . .
—artistic avant-garde: historically an important role as producer of gay erotica in preliberation era (police harassed Kenneth Anger and beefcake studios equally); currently a much diminished but still visible role, e.g., Curt McDowell; Barbara Hammer as source of lesbian erotica.	—artistic avant-garde: less important historical role (e.g., *Geography of the Body*, Brakhage's late-fifties fuck films); current role negligible, though Michael Snow *has* been censored in Toronto.

Relations of Exhibition

Gay Male Pornography

—commoditization of private/individual sexual space (bedside stroke mags, home video); telephone sex services a recent extension.

—theatrical, arcade, and bookstore space as social terrain, meeting place, and setting for sex

—exhibition space as liberated zone, extension of the gay ghetto, as gay refuge from heterosexist territory; favored space for anonymous contacts and for individuals who are dysfunctional in bars and saunas

—huge mail-order and rental video market is much more important than theatrical market; important glossy magazine industry. Strongest market away from gay ghettos.

—in isolated areas, straight theaters and adult bookstores service gay community; in New York and elsewhere, cheap straight theaters service poor and minority gays.

—porno theaters restricted to ghettos and combat zones; glossies are mass distributed but far less accessible than *Penthouse*.

Straight Male Pornography

—same, straight equivalent even more pervasive, e.g., pay TV, cable.

—no equivalent: theatrical exhibition space is zone of terror for unaccompanied female potential partners, except for sex industry workers

—no real equivalent in contemporary context: combat zone is extension of straight male domain. Remote equivalent to gay situation might be seen in straight male's escape from family, respectability, and suburbia. Some women have argued for similar function for women: Lisa Orlando (pornography as "first glimpse of freedom," aid in "adolescent search for validation and pleasure and sexual autonomy"); Ellen Willis (porn as "protest against the repression of nonmarital, nonprocreative sex . . . resistance to a culture that would allow women no sexual pleasure at all"); Deirdre English (porn district as "small zone of sexual freedom").[3]

—straight equivalent to mail-order market has all but disappeared except for specialty areas, e.g., fetish, SM; glossies are huge multinational industry; video is eclipsing theatrical exhibition.

—no equivalent

—pervasiveness and respectability of straight male theaters; shopping-center and neighborhood outlets in addition to combat zones; glossies omnipresent, iconography having long since seeped into popular culture and advertising.

Relations of Consumption

Gay Male Pornography

—privatized, individual masturbation aid, in all categories, including theatrical and arcade.

—accessory to sexual relations between strangers and between familiars; theaters and arcades are lively meeting and sex places, saunas often have film or video rooms

—the spectator's positions in relation to the representations are open and in flux. These include: nonviewing with the images functioning as background visual muzak; direct unmediated look at image-object, especially in solo-jerk films; look mediated by narrative—spectator's position fluctuates or is simultaneously multiple, among different characters and types, roles, etc. Spectator's identificatory entry into the narrative is not predetermined by gender divisions; mise-en-scène does not privilege individual roles, top or bottom, inserter or insertee, in any systematic way.

—gay male spectator habitually invited to identify narratively with victimization and/or penetration of the Self, i.e., of gay male, often by straight male. Eroticization of victimization or submission is most common in noncommercial porn, e.g., of 110 randomly chosen *Straight to Hell* anecdotes, 30 eroticized active role on the part of the narrator, 33 were submissive or victimized, 43 were both or interchangeable.

Straight Male Pornography

—same

—only rarely a similar phenomenon (motel movies?); probable use as accessory to prostitution?

—spectator's position tends to be rigidly gender determined; in all categories, straight male spectator looks at female image-object, *without* mediation of straight male narrative surrogates (*Penthouse* centerfolds) or *with* (narrative features). Mise-en-scène privileges women's roles and visibility, i.e., as insertee, whether active/top or passive/bottom. This is why close-up fellatio scenes (cock as prop) are far more common than male-female cunnilingus (a gynephobic taboo also operates here). Male figure has far less visual weight even in films headlining male stars such as Harry Reems. In hardcore, the privileging of women's roles is more emphatic than in classy/crossover softcore (e.g., *Private Lessons, Lady Chatterley's Lover*) because of strong narrative lines and appeal to women spectators (still such privileged male personae tend not to have cocks). (For further research: am I wrong in assuming that straight men's fantasies never flirt with forbidden corners of the text? Do they never project on/identify with the female roles? I'm afraid to ask any.)

—straight male spectator habitually invited to identify narratively with victimizer, to eroticize victimization of the Other (woman-object), only rarely of the Self, as in the specialty dominatrix subgenre (*Ilsa, Tigress of Siberia*). (Distinction must be made between passive fantasy where narrative subject is in control [almost all fellatio scenes in het porn] and submissive fantasy where narrative object is controlled or victimized, extremely rare in mainstream het porn.)

Gay Male Pornography

—gay porn functions as progressive, educative or ideological (consciousness-raising) force, as challenge to self-oppression, the closet and isolation (Oklahoma is reputedly the strongest mail-order market); gay porn often serves as isolated teenager's first link to community.

—gay porn functions as potential regressive force, valorizing sexism, looks-ism, size-ism, racism, ageism, and so on, as well as violent behaviors; reinforces the closet by providing anonymous, impersonal outlets? legitimizes straight-identified self-oppression (of 110 *STH* anecdotes, 43 valorized straight-defined men as erotic object)?

Straight Male Pornography

—no strict equivalent; historically stag movies had a loosely parallel function in sex-repressive society, as instruction and initiation for the dominant gender/sexual-orientation caste; in traditional Japanese society, pillowbooks had an important and respectable educative function.

—straight porn can/does legitimize phallocentric, gynephobic, alienated, and violent attitudes and behavior; the "throwaway" woman.

Relations of Representation: Depicted Sexual Practices

Gay Male Pornography

—gay men fuck and suck and are fucked and sucked, etc., in a wide range of combinations and roles not determined by gender; sometimes roles are defined by sexual practice, body type, age, class, race, or by the enunciation of sexual orientation (office employee short of cash for date with girl friend fucks gay boss for money), but just as often this is not so.

—no equivalent to straight convention of lesbian sex, except perhaps relations among men narratively defined as "straight"

—in longer films, overall structure is as often purely episodic as climactic, e.g., J. Brian's *First Time Around* is a narrative daisy chain (A fucks with B fucks with C fucks with D fucks with A).

—within individual sequences, usually a climactic escalation of sexual practices, i.e., fucking after sucking, with staggered ejaculations of all participants as a drawn-out climax; rigid convention of external ejaculations of all participants as a drawn-out climax; rigid convention of external ejaculation often followed by ingestion of semen. Same for loops and short films.

Straight Male Pornography

—straight man (two or more men are less common because of rigid taboo on intermale sexuality) fucks and is sucked by one or more women in a more limited gender-defined range of roles and combinations, e.g., women frequently are active partners (i.e., aggressive fellators) as well as passive insertees, but the range of roles is quite rigidly prescribed. Would nonsexist hetero porn for men or women have the role flexibility of much of gay porn?

—relations between women a routine formula, usually as prelude to entry of phallus

—features tend more often to be linear or climactic in narrative structure.

—roughly the same with ejaculation coda more compressed because of scarcity of ejaculators (the gay taboo) and limited positions; straight men come outside too. Same for loops and shorts.

Gay Male Pornography

—taboos: on male-female sex (Joe Gage's use of het coupling to establish straightness of a character is exception that proves the rule); on effeminacy, age, obesity, and drag (except in specialty materials or nonsexual roles, e.g., a drag queen in Wakefield Poole's *Bijou* leads butch construction worker down into labyrinthine sexual underworld).

—in loops or short films, narrative is often solo performance, masturbation, or just posing, which can be either or both active (tense, upright) and/or passive (supine, exposed, languid, available). Same conventions in glossy centerfolds or photo-spreads. Solo performance materials establish eye contact with spectator.

—sexual practices stigmatized and often technically illegal are standard routine component in all categories: porn shows what legit media deny, suppress, and stigmatize.

—violence and rape, consensual and nonconsensual, among gay men or perpetrated by characters defined as straight, is not uncommon.

Straight Male Pornography

—taboos: on intermale sex; also on age, obesity, deviation from perceived ideals of femininity and beauty, etc.

—same solo-stroke or posing conventions, except that poses are exclusively passive (supine, spread, seated, squatted, orifices offered, etc.). Same eye-contact conventions.

—illegal and stigmatized practices (other than violence) only in fringe subgenres such as kiddie porn or scat, etc.; het porn shows what legit media imply, simulate, or present "tastefully."

—violence and rape is common, consensual and nonconsensual, perpetrated on women by straight men, rarely vice versa, except in dominatrix subgenre; in some respectable crypto-porn, violence is perpetrated by gay man or transsexual/transvestite, e.g., *Looking for Mr. Goodbar, Dressed to Kill.*

Relations of Representation: Common Narrative Formulae

Gay Male Pornography

—5 common elements (Kathleen Barry's list quoted from Kronhausen can be applied):[4]
  —seduction (often of straight man)
  —profanation (*Straight to Hell* is full of clerical motifs, but in postclerical society the more common rendition is simple antiauthority—coach rims star athlete, sailor fucks officer)
  —incest (*Straight to Hell* is full of father and older brother fantasies; less omnipresent in commercial porn but still very common)
  —permissive-seductive parent (one film, title forgotten, depicts furtive father coming out at same time as teenage sons).

Straight Male Pornography

—these 5 elements are still basic to much straight male narrative porn, though capitalist competition has tended to expand the repertory. Profanation is less important, nuns having all but disappeared. Insatiable nymphomaniac seems to be a new formula, whether comic (*Deep Throat*) or moralistic (*Devil and Miss Jones*).

Gay Male Pornography

—defloration (in gay porn one version of this is initiation, another is the converse of the term—*being deflowered*).

—element unique to gay porn is "coming out," gay male assumption of gay identity and sexual practice; shedding of straight male identity or conversion of straight male can be part of this (Joe Gage's *Kansas City Trucking Company*).

—intranarrative voyeur or photographer is common

—doctor or sex researcher as narrative mediator

—straight-identified institutional setting, e.g., ranch, hospital, school, military, construction site (of 110 *STH* anecdotes, 30 are situated in this way); military settings especially common.

—sex for pay, especially straight hustlers and rough trade

—subversive humor (penile salute from Marines uniform in Jean-Claude von Italie's *American Cream*).

—back to nature, fucking in the forest or posing in the desert.

—documentary gimmick, e.g., Peter de Rome's Super 8 sex on the subway, or location shooting and nonprofessional actors in Toby Ross's *Boys of the Slums* with acne and failed erections.

—public sexuality a common element, e.g., glory holes of *Taxi Zum Klo* a frequent formula. 24 of 110 *STH* anecdotes take place in toilets and 38 in other public spaces such as parks, cars, and rest stops.

Straight Male Pornography

—remote equivalent without the distinct ideological tenor might be woman's realization of her true desire (*Emmanuelle*, *Deep Throat*) or young male protagonist's assumption of his patriarchal sexual prerogatives (mostly in softcore such as *Private Lessons*, *Porky's*, or *Spring Break*). Conversion formulae also present: lesbian is often converted by a good fuck; in *Roommates*, gay man is similarly converted.

—same

—same

—straight male interest in all-women institutions such as convents and brothels is related but has different ideological tenor and is now less common.

—same, especially brothels, though now less common than in classical stag films; recent twist is suburban housewife who has sex to pay bills.

—humor not so evident, either prurient (guttoral clitoris in *Deep Throat*) or flat (*Gone with the Wind*–style chorus-line rape production number in porno musical *Blond Ambition*)

—common in softcore (*Emmanuelle*, *Lady Chatterley*), less so in hardcore. Cheesecake, unlike beefcake, is usually interior.

—not common; exceptions include French feature on porn star *Exhibition*, or Vietnam brothel sequence of *Hearts and Minds*.

—no straight equivalent since straight public sexuality is accepted social norm

Gay Male Pornography	*Straight Male Pornography*
—violence/rape as vengeance (at least one example, Joe Gage's *Heatstrokes*)	—violence/rape as vengeance relatively common, e.g., Russ Meyer's *Vixen*; an exception is *Those Naughty Victorians*, where the rapist-protagonist is raped himself at the end by a (black) assailant hired by his earlier victims.
—rape of unconscious (Curt McDowell's *Nudes*) or of bound victim. Gang rape, passive fantasies of rape are common in *STH*, often with straight perpetrators	—same (woman hitchhiker trapped by car window and raped from behind); gang rape relatively less common because of intermale taboo.
—rape victim comes to like it	—extremely common in legit media as well as softcore and hardcore films
—SM, fisting, gadgets, fetishes (boots most common, followed by jock straps: rapid escalation of these motifs in seventies hardcore has apparently leveled off); a recurring minor presence in mainstream glossies (*Blueboy*), dominant in other specialized mags (*Drum* the most common SM glossy)	—SM motifs more and more common in mainstream glossies (*Hustler*) as well as stable minority proportion of hardcore magazines, arcade materials, and films; some osmosis of iconography into legit media, punk culture, high fashion, etc. Women usually bottom (e.g., *Swept Away* . . . , *The Night Porter*) but not always (*Maitresse*).
—takeoffs of legit media, especially with film titles, e.g., *Last Tango in Hollywood*	—same
—racial difference as narrative angle: rare in hardcore features where nonwhite men often appear without racial enunciation. Subgenre of beefcake and hardcore mags specializing in racial difference presumably for white clientele (but question of race of producers and consumers is for future research), e.g., "Boys of Puerto Rico." 22 of 110 *STH* anecdotes had some kind of racial enunciation, frequently with black narrator.	—several racist subgenres of hardcore and softcore films and other categories where women and men are enunciated racially, e.g., "mixed combos," dozens of Thai *Emmanuelle* spinoffs. Mainstream glossies are very white.
—class enunciation relatively common, e.g., *Boys of the Slums*; blue-collar fantasies are omnipresent.	—probably less explicit, though no less prevalent through implicit and documentary codes, especially in cheaper mags and films. Maids are much less common than in classical and European films, often replaced now by secretary fantasies.
—cock-size narrative gimmicks constructed around certain stars and in titles, e.g., *The Big Surprise*	—same with breasts (e.g., Russ Meyer) and sometimes cocks.
—as a general rule, theatrical films have a more important narrative content than straight equivalents (Wakefield Poole's *Bijou* flopped because it was criticized for "too much story.")	—narrative content relatively less important

Relations of Representation: Extracting Some Ideological Essences

Gay Male Pornography	*Straight Male Pornography*
—phallus obsession, the close-up a metaphor of corporal fragmentation and alienation; phallocentrism however not an explicit text in this fantasy universe where people not divided according to presence or absence of cock; everyone has one.	—phallocentrism: women as universally available caterers to pleasure of phallus
—self-hatred, gay eroticization of victimization of self (some *STH* anecdotes eroticize abusive homophobic "dirty talk")	—woman hatred: women as deserving and willing victims, whose victimization is eroticized
—racism: Third World beefcake constructs spectator-object relation that is exact parallel of racist organization of society	—racism: nonwhite women as exaggeratedly sexual slaves, nonwhite men as instruments of patriarchal revenge.
—ideology of gay liberation: sex-positive attitudes, valorization of "coming out," acceptance of gay identity and community, challenge to masculinism; sex industry as economic base of autonomous, prosperous ghetto and therefore of political clout.	—ideology of sexual liberation? view of straight porn as therapeutic social safety valve, as vehicle of sex-positive values, espoused by straight male apologists and profiteers, by some social scientists, by some women pro-sex or libertarian feminists.
—ideology of the closet: valorization of straight image reflect internalized homophobia, self-oppression.	—closest equivalent of self-oppression here is not in straight male pornography, which has no significant female audience, but women's romance pulp (Harlequins); men's lib line emphasizes straight male porn's oppression of men as well as of women.

Toward a Summary: Porn as Index/Echo/Prop of Political Context

Gay Male Pornography	*Straight Male Pornography*
PLUS-unlike straight male porn, gay porn does not directly and systematically replicate the heterosexist patriarchal order in its relations of production, exhibition, comsumption, or representation. Kathleen Barry's assertion "Homosexual pornography acts out the same dominant and subordinate roles of heterosexual pornography," (*Female Sexual Slavery* [New York, 1979], 206), cannot be shown to be true of any of these terms. Produced by, depicting, and consumed exclusively by gay men, the fantasy universe of gay porn resembles the gay ghetto in its hermeticism as well as in its contradictory mix of progressive and regressive values, in its occupancy of a	PLUS-porn as "liberated zone," social safety valve, as visualization of women's desire, as vehicle of the sexual revolution?

Gay Male Pornography	Straight Male Pornography
defensible enclave within heterosexist society. It subverts the patriarchal order by challenging masculinist values, providing a protected space for nonconformist, nonreproductive, and nonfamilial sexuality, encouraging many sex-positive values and declaring the dignity of gay people.	
MINUS-at the same time, the ghetto is part of as well as separate from heterosexist society. The patriarchal privilege of male sexual expression and occupancy of public space is perpetuated. The patriarchy is propped up equally by the reinforcement of the gay male spectator's self-oppression, by his ghettoization. Finally, capitalism's usurpation and commoditization of the private sphere is extended not threatened by gay commercial porn.	MINUS-gender-defined sexual roles and power imbalances, both within the narrative (woman as insertee, active or passive, woman as victim, woman as fetishized object of the camera) and outside of the narrative (woman as spectator), replicate the power relations of patriarchal capitalists and are thereby both its symptom and its reinforcement.

A Real Raw Place

I love the fact that I can't understand my films when I first make them. It feels like I'm making them out of a real raw place.[5]

Curt McDowell's *Loads* (1980) is a nineteen-minute black-and-white gay porn movie that is so hot that it makes *Kansas City Trucking Company* feel like a three-hour Marguerite Duras film projected at half speed. It is also a lot more than that, though this "more" amplifies the turn-on rather than legitimizes it.

Like most great works of eroticism, and like the erotic films of McDowell's fellow Bay Area homosexual, Barbara Hammer, *Loads* is intensely personal, autobiographical, even confessional. The diary form tends to achieve a mixture of everyday images and fantasy overtones that is highly potent. As in the first-person anecdotes of *Straight to Hell*, the authentic ring of, "This is really true. I was really there," brings a vibrancy to even the tallest tale. The diaristic form also has a documentary graininess to it that enhances the impact, the spontaneity of camera twitches, the fragility of flares; both Hammer's and McDowell's format is the low-budget independent non-sync-sound short film, an alternative form, borrowing from both documentary and experimental vocabulary, that knits well with an alternative eroticism. Slickness takes away from desire, Hefner's air-brushes notwithstanding.

Hammer and McDowell, however, live at opposite ends of the Bay. Her films have a Berkeley spirituality to them, even at her most carnal moments (the close-up labia dabbling in *Multiple Orgasms*). Maybe it comes from her habit of linking eros to nature, whether it's the garden or the desert with all their iconographic associations in our culture; maybe it's the presence of a visible lesbian community throughout her films, the pervasiveness of sisterhood for all her obsessive egotistical sublime. With San Francisco–based McDowell, a cock is a cock is a cock. His landscape is the concrete of the streets, the filtered light of his nonresidential-zone studio. But his physicality doesn't belong to the Castro, except for the overtones of camp—it belongs more to the Mission. Unlike Hammer, McDowell is usually alone. The faggot fellowship is nowhere in sight, the clone ghetto somewhere over the horizon. His love objects are the Other, the Straight Man.

In fact, in *Loads*, it's six Straight Men who swagger through the frame. The film narrates the filmmaker's encounter with each of them, on the street or in parks, his offer to film them jerking off. They all consented (though of course the filmic record doesn't include those who refused, nor any real or threatened violence incurred), and the six intermingled episodes/vignettes of the film are built from the resultant posing and sex sessions in McDowell's studio.

Suddenly spectators find themselves embarrassed voyeurs both of McDowell's tricks with the six men, and of the men's tricks with the camera. The men strut about defensively, as if taunting the camera, or they lie back invitingly, staring vulnerably, trustingly into the lens. They undress and caress themselves, or allow the filmmaker to help. The camera sometimes embodies McDowell's point of view, crawling across the floor in submission for the blow, trembling as if in echo of the spectator's excitation; or else it remains aloof on its tripod for a breather with the pretense of immediacy temporarily dropped; at other times when McDowell needs both hands, one of the subjects holds the camera, adding the frisson of subjective angle to the palpability of micro-close-ups of flesh. This is participatory camera taken as far as it will go, filmmaking as fellatio. The editing preserves the feeling of participation and spontaneity, texturing the narrative lust with the temporal patterns of memory and obsession—echoes, stuttering, flashbacks. McDowell's half-confessional, half-conspiratorial voice-over adds to the complexity of the mosaic: "I wanted to be slung on his back, fucking him as he walked down the street."

In fact, McDowell doesn't fuck any of the men. And that's the point at which the film begins to expose "the raw place" of the filmmaker's desire and of our sexual culture as gay men of the post-gay-lib era. Like all eroticism shaped by a commodity- and image-enslaved patriarchy, McDowell's eroticism is deeply troubled, and troubling. I am speaking neither of the gospel of omni-pansexuality embodied in the gay male institution of tricking, nor of the objectification inherent in the image-making process in itself—at least not here—I am referring rather to the eroticization of the Not-Gay, the Straight Man. For some, it may be gratifying that the tables are turned: the straight man becomes erotic surface, objectified, both idealized and debased, the object of erotic obsession. It is an obsession frequently present in gay male pornography, as I've noted elsewhere, and an obsession that McDowell tackles head-on, exorcizing it and analyzing it as well as indulging it and perpetuating it:

I have no idea why those straight men turn me on; I see that it's my own obsession—one of them.

My real interest lies in things, like, I want to go on expeditions, and always document the sexual aspect of things. Like National Geographic. . . .

. . . since much of (current norms of) homosexuality is based on guilt and shame, I think you can realize that guilt is what is turning you on.

. . . I'm hung up on straight men because they're like virgins. They've never done it with another guy. I like them for fantasy. But I wouldn't want to see them "turn" gay, to become my lovers.

McDowell, then, is quite deliberate in confronting the contradictions of his sexuality, of gay sexuality in its current incarnation, but he doesn't pretend to be able to understand them, nor to resolve them—without the spectator's help.

The types of men McDowell is attracted to are telling. They are macho, some bodybuilders, mostly working class, a few with tattoos—none with the idealized beauty of *Blueboy* porn—stars but in fact almost parodies of our culture's stereotype of masculinity were they not ultimately so ordinary. Their sexuality, not surprisingly, is deeply alienated. Most depend on images to masturbate to, propped on one elbow, thumbing the glossy magazine photos of women, the perfect image of the ideal sexual consumer of the post-Hefner age. One man even rubs his cock into the crack of the centerfold during and after his ejaculation. Of others, McDowell manages to capture the comic absurdity as they strut around trying to look cool with their pants down around their knees. Of still others he succeeds in registering an unexpected tenderness, a haunting vulnerability that matches his own, an openness to this experimental intermale exchange that subverts our rigid labels of sexual orientation. At the moment of his final montage of all six protracted ejaculations, McDowell adds the sound of thunder to the already exaggerated heavy breathing on the soundtrack, a hint of parody that is just the right touch to top off the "expedition," this exposure of the male sexual drive. The male body is both celebrated and decorticated, the rites of masculinity are both indulged and subverted.

As for the spectator, caught up in a mix of desire and outrage, guilt and complicity, amused distance and involvement, his disturbance remains long after the excitement has dissipated. Not your usual pornographic film, designed for easy consumption and disposal. This is the direction we must pursue if we are to attain an eroticism worthy of our political ideals. I do not mean the reworking of fuck-film formulas with ideological discourse and politically correct sexuality, nor the legitimation of eroticism "artistically" through self-reflexivity or modernist editing (though we should not exclude possibilities inherent in either of these avenues). I guess I mean an alternative practice, a grass-roots pornography to counter the industrial pornography; an eroticism that enhances our pleasure in our sexuality by starting from the raw place we're in right now and by responding to that place, without defensiveness or complacency, but with honesty, questioning, and humor; a challenge to our sexuality as well as a celebration of it.

Notes

1 "Lesbians and Pornography" (from transcript of workshop at the Pittsburgh Conference on Pornography 1980), *off our backs* (July 1980): 9.

2 Andrea Dworkin, *Pornography, Men Possessing Women* (New York, 1981), 43.

3 Lisa Orlando, "Bad Girls and 'Good' Politics," *Village Voice* (*Literary Supplement*), December 1982, 16; Ellen Willis, "Who Is a Feminist? A Letter to Robin Morgan," ibid., 17; Deirdre English, "Talking Sex: A Conversation on Sexuality and Feminism" (with Amber Hollibaugh and Gayle Rubin), *Socialist Review*, no. 58 (July/August 1981): 51.

4 Kathleen Barry, *Female Sexual Slavery* (New York, 1979), 207.

5 Quotations by Curt McDowell are taken from interviews in *Gay News* (London), no. 229, p. 47 (by Jack Babuscio); *San Francisco Chronicle Datebook*, Pink Section, 8–14 February 1981 (by Calvin Ahlgren); *Artbeat*, December 81–January 82, pp. 22–23.

Freud's "Fetishism" and

the Lesbian Dildo

Debates

Heather Findlay

From the pages of lesbian porn magazines to the meetings of the Modern Language Association, a highly organized discourse has developed around a rather unlikely object: the dildo. No other sex toy has generated the quantity or quality of discussion among mostly urban, middle-class, white lesbians than the dildo.[1] What interests me about this discourse is that a number of subcultural products (advertisements, erotic fiction, the sex toys themselves) have consistently drawn from a set of familiar conventions, thus constituting a kind of shared fantasy about lesbian dildo use. Like all fantasy, this one no doubt occludes more than it reveals about the reality of lesbian desire, whatever that may be. My focus, however, is on what the French might call the mise-en-scène of a particular dildo fantasy and its relation to the issues raised in Freud's 1927 essay on fetishism.[2] By analyzing the dildo in conjunction with Freud's text, I hope to shed light not only on the dildo debates and the feminist "sex wars" of which they are a part but also on the (perhaps paradoxical) relevance to lesbians of the psychoanalytic theory of fetishism, a "perversion" that Freud—as a number of his feminist readers have discussed in some detail[3]—claims to be exclusively male. My aim is not simply to apply psychoanalysis to lesbian sexuality but also to do what is in a sense more difficult: to reread Freud from the perspective of lesbian theory and practice and to unravel those points at which his text may be as "symptomatic" as the behavior it attempts to describe.

The Dildo Wars

To date, discourse among lesbians over the dildo has been marked by a debate divided roughly into two camps. On the one hand, some lesbians have debunked the dildo and its notorious cousin the strap-on, calling them "male identified." The most colorful, if noncanonical, spokeswomen for this position have been published in the "Letters" column of the lesbian pornographic magazine *On Our Backs*. These letters are written in protest of the fact that, as Colleen Lamos puts it, "the dildo is clearly a matter of intense interest and a focus of fetishistic desire for the readers" and publishers of the magazine.[4] For example, Daralee and Nancy, two self-described "outrageous and oversexed S/M dykes" from Birmingham, Alabama, confess that they are nonetheless puzzled about the current lesbian romance with the dildo: "What's the deal with women 'portraying' themselves as equipped with penises? We can't figure out how this could be erotic to a woman-identified-woman. If they want a dick, why are they with a woman wearing a dildo and not a man? Don't misunderstand us; we're heavily into penetration . . . but this whole life-like dildo market is baffling to us."[5] The authors' distaste for dildos, especially "lifelike" ones, is based on the conviction that a dildo represents a penis and is therefore incompatible with "woman-identified" sexuality. In fact, the letter's reference to women-identified-women situates it within a larger, radical feminist critique of sex,[6] including (as an editor at *off our backs* put it) "games that rely on paraphernalia [and] roles."[7] Ironically enough for our kinky Birmingham correspondents, the critique of the dildo has developed in tandem with radical feminist attacks on butch-femme and sado-masochism such as Sheila Jeffreys's, which hold that both practices reproduce a "heteropatriarchy" based on masculine and feminine sex roles.[8]

On the other hand, some lesbians have argued that dildos do not represent penises; rather, they are sex toys that have an authentic place in the history of lesbian subculture. This argument can be detected in Joan Nestle's writings on butch-femme sexuality[9] or, more explicitly, in the columns of self-made lesbian sexologist Susie Bright, a.k.a. Susie Sexpert. "The facts about dildos," she assures us, "aren't as controversial as their famous resemblance to the infamous 'penis' and all that *it* represents." In an attempt to downplay the "political, social, and emotional connotations of dildos," Bright writes that "a dildo can be a succulent squash, or a tender mold of silicon. Technically, it is any device you use for the pleasure of vaginal or anal penetration. . . . Penises can only be compared to dildos in the sense that they take up space."[10] As a mere "device," a sex toy that can be vegetable or mineral, a dildo has only a remote, sheerly ontological relation to the penis: like it, the dildo exists, it "takes up space" in the vagina or anus. In sum, as part of their challenge to what they see as the repressive sexual politics of radical feminism, Bright and other "prosex" feminists have defended the dildo by downplaying its referentiality, by denying that the dildo represents a penis.

Among other things, we might accuse the antidildo camp of having an unsophisticated understanding of representation. Daralee and Nancy's letter, for example, assumes that a dildo not only represents but is also the same thing as "a dick." This assumption announces itself in the quotation marks Daralee and Nancy put around "portraying"; by doubting the difference a representation can make, the authors affirm that wearing a dildo is, quite literally, equipping oneself with a penis.[11] To Bright's credit, her comments shift the burden of suspicion from the representation to the thing represented: if the lesbians from Birmingham put "portraying" in quotation marks, Bright quotes and italicizes "the infamous 'penis' and all *it* represents," thereby referring to the organ itself as if it were somebody else's peculiar idea—as if, in other words, it were already a signifier. Bright may, however, fall prey to her own brand of literalism: is it possible for a dildo to stand, as it were, only for itself? In the face of "this whole life-like dildo market" so baffling to the Birmingham lesbians—or, for that matter, the popularity of huge black dildos so troubling to *Black Lace* editor Alycee J. Lane[12]—is it possible to insist that dildos are strictly nonrepresentational, that they are not (to quote Lane) the "location" of both sexual and racial "terror and desire"?

Enter Freud with Fetish

Putting these questions aside for the moment, I would like to point out that, regardless of the speakers' feelings about psychoanalysis, the dildo debate may be said to revolve around the question of whether the dildo is a fetish in Freud's definition of the term. At the beginning of "Fetishism," Freud tells a parable about how the fetish reveals itself to be a penis replacement. According to the story, fetishism is the little boy's response to the castration anxiety he experiences on first seeing his mother's genitals: "What happened, therefore, was that the boy refused to take cognizance of the fact of his having perceived that a woman does not possess a penis. No, that could not be true: for if a woman had been castrated, then his own possession of a penis was in danger; and against that there rose in rebellion the portion of his narcissism which Nature has, as a precaution, attached to that particular organ." Freud gives his story a happy ending, at least for the boy: "To put it more plainly: the fetish is a substitute for the woman's (the mother's) penis that the little boy once believed in and—for reasons familiar to us—does not want to give up."[13] Because the fetish represents a penis, Freud argues, it allows the subject to maintain, despite evidence to the contrary, that castration is not a danger. In fact, it allows him to maintain that castration has not happened at all. I will go on to say more about this passage, but for the moment we should note that the question of whether the dildo is a penis replacement lies at the very heart of the debate I summarized above. Critics of

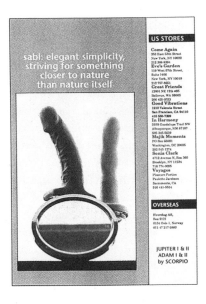

Figure I.

Scorpio products

"Sabi" advertisement.

the dildo claim that it is a penis replacement, and its proponents claim that it is not. The debate over dildo use, in other words, is a debate about the politics of fetishism.

This may seem surprising, considering that Freud's theory of fetishism seems inhospitable to lesbian experience, so exclusive is its phallo- and heterocentrism. The most glaring example of this is Freud's generic fetishist himself, who is a straight man.[14] Moreover, dildos may not be fetish objects, technically speaking. In the fetishism essay, Freud explains that fetishes, owing to unconscious censorship, most often take their form from whatever the little boy sees *just before* he witnesses the spectacle of his mother's castration: fur and velvet symbolize the mother's pubic hair, undergarments "crystalize the moment of undressing," and so on. Fetishistic desire exemplifies how (if I may refer to the oft-quoted formula) the unconscious is like a language: the fetishist finds himself representing his love object by means of contiguous associations, that is, by metonymy. Thus, to the extent that fetishes most often refer indirectly to the penis (i.e., they tend not to be obvious phallic symbols) dildos may not be "true" fetishes. Freud's essay, in fact, does not discuss them at all.

Nevertheless, recent representations of dildos in lesbian publications conform, in many ways, to Freud's paradigm. Take, for example, this advertisement for Scorpio dildo products (figure 1), which runs regularly in various pornographic magazines, including *On Our Backs*. The advertisement bases itself on a comparison between, and potential substitution of, a dildo and the penis, or

"Nature itself," according to the euphemistic language of the ad. By foregrounding the "naturalistic" dildo that looks like a penis, and contrasting it to the "nonnaturalistic" one in the background, the ad makes it clear that dildos supplement nature—indeed, they are *more* natural than nature itself—and that the natural object in question is the penis. The very terms of the ad repeat what we already find in Freud. In both cases, nature is the name for an archaic state of plenitude and satisfaction, and the penis stands as persuasive evidence of the subject's citizenship in this state. "Nature," we will remember from Freud's essay, has providentially "attached" to this organ a good measure of the boy's narcissism—so much so that nature, the organ, and narcissism seem linked indissolubly in a kind of pact. The ad also points to the very mechanism of fetishism as a form of substitution and representation: the mirror placed beneath the foregrounded dildo suggests that the fetish works precisely because it represents something else. Because the mirror tilts toward the reader, the ad further thematizes the role of fetishistic representation in the production and maintenance of an imaginary "I," an ego whose narcissistic whole is authenticated or (quite literally in this case) crowned by the phallus-fetish.

More often than not, dildo ads will deny that dildos are penis substitutes. One ad from Eve's Garden, a feminist sex boutique in New York, ends with this terse message to anyone who might be wondering: "Finally, we should add that we don't think of dildos as imitation penises"; they are "sexual accessories, not substitutes." On reading this kind of disclaimer, we may wonder if perhaps the lady doth protest too much. In the end, lesbians with uncooperative sexual tastes still market and purchase politically incorrect dildos that are shaped like penises and named after mythological patriarchs, as in the "Adam I" or the "Jupiter II." Even the conventions of English usage undermine the ad's nonsensical explanation, "We've designed (our dildos) to be factually and aesthetically pleasing." If dildos do not owe their allure to the fact that they represent penises, then how are they "factually pleasing"? For that matter, who ever says that anything is "factually pleasing"? In sum, dildo ads may cause us to conclude with Elizabeth A. Grosz that, in the case of lesbianism, "it may be possible to suggest some connection" between women and fetishism after all[15] and that the maleness of fetishism is determined more by one's subject position than by biological gender.

Yet we might want to pay close attention to this recurrent anxiety—peculiar to lesbian dildo fetishism—over conflating a representation (a dildo) with reality (a penis). For one thing, this anxiety is totally absent in gay male fetishism, where dildos (and their purveyors) strive overtly to replicate penises, even particular penises, like porn star Jeff Stryker's. The makers of the Jeff Stryker model guarantee that their dildos are cast in a mold taken directly from Stryker's erect member. Exact replication, even a kind of indexical representation, is celebrated among gay men—perhaps all too uncritically. Lesbians, on the other hand, have marketed a series of dildos that, in an obvious attempt to break the association between a piece of silicon and a penis, are shaped like dolphins, ears of corn, and even the Goddess. This urge to steer away from realism stems from the fact that these feminist dildo suppliers and their customers are suspicious of conflating a representation with reality, especially in the case of a phallus. One of the most important and repeated gestures of feminist critique has been to show how patriarchy asserts itself by making precisely this conflation, by collapsing the difference between a symbol and a real body organ.[16] In this light, being penetrated by the Goddess amounts to a defiant response to the patriarchal law that symbols of pleasure and potency always refer back to, or be somehow proper to, men's bodies. Like good Lacanians, these feminists are busily and happily disarticulating the phallus from the penis.

The Cunt We Wish Did Not Exist

But the problem of substitution is not the only issue in lesbian dildo use; nor is it the only function of the fetish for Freud. In his essay, Freud specifies further that the fetish is a representation not of just any "chance penis" but of the *mother's* penis, the penis that the boy child once imagines his mother to have had but then discovers unhappily that she has lost. Faced with the "fact" of his mother's castration, and thus the possibility of his own, the little boy replaces this image with a fetish that "remains as a token of triumph over the threat of castration and a protection against it."[17] At first glance, lesbian dildo fetishism seems to have nothing to do with mothers, castrated or not. But in Freud's account, the fetish does not refer to a real woman; it represents an imaginary, phallic one. In light of this, is not Joan Nestle's bedildoed lover in her short story "My Woman Poppa"[18] the fetishist's primal love object, the phallic woman the little boy imagines his mother to be? A more dramatic example may be a sequence from Fatale Video's pornographic collection *Clips*.[19] In this episode, set in a ranch house–style living room complete with a sonorous television, a recliner, and copies of the *Wall Street Journal*, a very femme Fanny kneels in front of her shirtless butch lover Kenny and watches as Kenny unzips her pants to reveal her pinkish-brown, "realistic" dildo. Is Fanny not taking pleasure in the fetishistic fantasy of a woman with breasts *and* a penis? Because Fanny is in the position of the spectator, is our gaze on the scene fetishistic as well? Indeed, Fanny and the spectator rehearse Freud's formula for fetishism: despite evidence to the contrary, she insists (as we also do?) on the fantasy that the penis is (still) there.

Fetishism occurs as well on the level of the video's narrative. After Kenny unzips her pants, Fanny takes her to the couch. Although the camera centers on Fanny as she sucks Kenny's dildo, we are also shown that Fanny is stimulating her lover's clitoris by rubbing her crotch with her shoulder. As she brings Kenny to orgasm, even though we know that the pleasure is clitoral, for the sake of the fantasy we believe it is phallic. In terms of recent reformulations of Freud's theory of fetishism, pleasure in this sequence conforms to Slavoj Žižek's version of fetishistic logic: she knows very well what she is doing, but she is doing it anyway.[20]

As an aside, we might also raise the issue of the dildo harness, which is sometimes the object of as much fetishistic attention as the toy it is designed to hold. Indeed, the harness may approximate the classical Freudian fetish more closely than the dildo, precisely because, as I suggest above, the fetish usually refers metonymically, rather than metaphorically, to the mother's missing penis. For the sake of testing Freud's paradigm we might say that the harness, which few lesbian fetishists ever imagine being made out of anything but the blackest of black leather, gains its allure from the fact that it is—like a woman's crotch—fleshy and dark. Even more significant may be the gaping hole at the front. Inserting and removing a dildo from this hole rehearses, in a literal manner, the traumatic primal experience of Freud's little fetishist: now she has it, now she doesn't.

Yet this function of the fetish, its use as a protective device against the mother's castration, is its most troubling one. How much do lesbians have in common with Freud's little fetishist, who believes in the "fact" that his mother—and thus all women—are lacking what he possesses, if only precariously? This question is a pressing one because, as a consequence of his belief in women's castration, the fetishist is deeply misogynist. He understands sexual difference simply in terms of women's deficiency. More concretely, Freud insists that after the fetishist represses the terrifying scenario of his mother's lack, "an aversion, which is never lacking in any fetishist, to the real female genitals remains a *stigma indelebile* of the repression which has taken place."[21] In the case of lesbian dildo fetishism, if lesbians take up the position of Freud's straight, male fetishist, how much is their pleasure accompanied by this aversion—which is supposedly never absent in any fetishist—to women and their bodies?

As light as the kind of butch-femme play in "My Woman Poppa" or *Clips* may seem, more than one lesbian has suffered from the darker undercurrents of fetishistic desire. In an article entitled "Sex, Lies, and Penetration: A Butch Finally 'Fesses Up," Jan Brown details what for her is the painful by-product of butch-femme role-playing and of the dildo that constitutes its fetishistic center. "We butches," she writes, "have a horror of the pity fuck. We cannot face the charity of the mercy orgasm or the thought of contempt in our partner's eyes when we have allowed them to convince us that they really do want to touch us, take us, that they really do want to reach behind our dick and into the cunt we both wish did not exist."[22] Brown's account reverses the usual subject/object relation and suggests that a subtle objectification is at work not of the feminine but of the masculine partner in butch-femme play. What Brown refers to sneeringly as "the sacred myth of the stone butch," a myth held in place by her holy fetish object, turns out to be a defensive construct that both partners use to veil a lack, "the cunt we both wish did not exist."

If, for Brown, the dildo allows lesbians to circumvent the question of the cunt, some feminists of color are concerned that it serves a similar function vis-à-vis racial difference. Alycee J. Lane, for example, writes that a friend once accused her of having "race issues" because she owns a dildo that, as Lane explains, is "six inches, rubbery, cheap and *mauve*." Lane defends her anatomically incorrect dildo in the tradition of "prosex" feminism: "A dildo is a dildo, not a dick. . . . The only thing that mattered, really, was the way my g-spot got worked." Yet Lane remains unsatisfied with this explanation, especially after a trip to her local sex shop reveals that "flesh-colored" dildos are actually cream-colored ("What does it *mean*," she ponders, "when white hegemony extends to the production of dildos?") and that brown dildos are hard to get because, as the cashier explains, "They sell rather quickly, you know." She is directed to another bin. "I turned and looked. They were not dildos; they were *monstrosities*. Twenty-four inches and thick as my arm. 'Big Black Dick' said the wrapper. . . . I looked around for some 'Big White Dick' or even 'Big Flesh Colored Dick.' No luck. And I seriously doubt that *they* were in high demand." Lane's experience changes her mind about the referentiality of the dildo. "Race," she concludes, "permeates American culture. A sex toy easily becomes the location for racial terror and desire, because sex itself is that location."[23]

In precisely what way, however, does a monstrous black dildo function as a signifier of racial terror and desire? When Freud claims that, in the heterosexual encounter, the fetishist's toy allows him to circumvent castration (the fetish "endows women with the attribute which makes them acceptable as sexual objects"),[24] he suggests that the fetish alleviates the fact that (to cite Jacques Lacan's dictum) there is no relation between the sexes. Similarly, it seems that the black dildo fetish can "make acceptable" a specifically racial lack—the lack, that is, under white hegemony of a relation between the races. As in the case of Freud's fetishist and his "woman," the big black dildo allows whites to carry on a relation with blacks that is, in reality, no relation at all. If sex *itself* is the location of racial terror and desire, we might say that the more general (and apparently lucrative) sexual fantasy of black superpotency—a fantasy that Jackie Goldsby accuses lesbians of sharing[25]—is another, powerful cultural fetish that allows us to circumvent the Real of racial disintegration. Behind the big black dick, in other words, is the race we wish did not exist.

The Chance Penis

I am not suggesting that all lesbian fetishism ends in this kind of aversion. Even if we go back to Freud and reread, we see that the fetishistic perspective may not be monolithic. Freud's fetishist, in fact, is guilty of some rather reckless logic, and his triumph over women's castration is not as quick and easy as it may appear. Here, in full, is the passage I have already quoted:

> When now I announce that the fetish is a substitute for the penis, I shall certainly create disappointment; so I hasten to add that it is not a substitute for any chance penis, but for a particular and quite special penis that had been extremely important in early childhood but had later been lost. . . . What happened, therefore, was that the boy refused to take cognizance of the fact of his having perceived that a woman does not possess a penis. No, that could not be true: for if a woman had been castrated, then his own possession of a penis was in danger.

First off, I am struck by the sense of urgency in Freud's rhetoric, produced perhaps by his identification with the frightened little boy. This identification is rendered most obvious when Freud speaks for the little boy and ventriloquizes his response to seeing his mother's genitals: "No, that could not be true: for if a woman had been castrated. . . ," and so on. Indeed, Freud "hastens" to erect a completed theoretical framework in the place of a lack, the "disappointment" he fears he will "certainly create" in his reader, in the same way that the little boy erects a fetish in the place of his mother's supposed castration. Emphasizing the uncanny way in which his theory doubles that of the little boy's, Freud hastens to complete it by adding, as we know, the notion of the mother's lack.

Because both Freud and his exemplary boy are in such a rush to posit the mother's castration, we might wonder if, contrary to Freud's insistence, the penis in question *may be* a "chance penis." In other words, perhaps it is not necessarily the mother's and perhaps somebody or something else might trigger the first blow to the child's narcissism. Actually, Freud describes rather circuitously the consequences of the little fetishist's sight of his mother's genitals: "What happened, therefore, was that the boy refused to take cognizance of the fact of his having perceived that a woman does not possess a penis." At this crucial moment, Freud does not write that the fetishist represses the fact of women's castration but, rather, "the fact of his having perceived" that women are castrated. The idea of women's lack, in other words, is *already* part of the boy's defensive reaction.

If everyone were not hastening to erect defenses around whatever it is we fear to lose, perhaps we might pause to consider that, in a different context, such a loss might be perceived or represented as something other than women's "fault." For example, in the context of a developed lesbian subculture, might the butch figure represent a different sort of lack, such as the absence of men like fathers and male lovers? And is it possible to imagine this lack as something other than deficiency, as something other than what my mother had in mind when she pleaded with me to "try more men"? Ideally, we might reenvision this lack as cultural difference in all its complexity. In Freud's account, this is exactly what the classic fetishistic perspective fails to do when, in its simplicity, it reduces difference to an economy of the same (to cite Jacques Derrida's formula). Faced with the alterity of the mother's body, the little boy interprets it in terms of his own body: like him, she either has or does not have a penis.

I would like to suggest a third position in the debate on lesbian dildos. If, in answer to the question of whether dildos represent penises, one camp says "yes" and the other says "no," perhaps a third position might be "yes, but. . . . " This kind of affirmation/negation is, as Sarah Kofman reminds us, the logic of fetishism itself as an "undecidable compromise."[26] In her reading of the fetishism essay, Kofman points out that Freud's subjects choose fetishes that, in the final analysis, both deny *and* affirm women's castration. For example, in the case of his patient who enjoys cutting women's hair, Freud discovers that the fetish "contains within itself the two mutually incompatible assertions: 'the woman has still got a penis' and 'my father has castrated the woman.' "[27] This undecidable compromise is also, I believe, what Fatale's video *Clips* performs, and the way that it does it is through parody: the goofy background music, the stereotypical middle-class living room, Kenny's beer drinking, even Fanny's virginal white lingerie. Through the duplicitous strategy of parody, the video audaciously inserts lesbianism into a context that still refers lovingly to the standard components of bourgeois heterosexuality—this is, after all, a video produced and consumed primarily by lesbians from more or less nuclear, middle-class families. The representation of Kenny's dildo is also inflected through parody; the video pokes fun at the association between dildo and penis, and at the same time it acknowledges and exploits its erotic power. If, as Judith Butler has proposed, such "parodic redeployment[s] of power" may have a specifically political value for lesbians,[28] we might add that parody is also a fundamentally fetishistic strategy. The makers of *Clips*, for example, know very well that what they are doing is phallocentric, but, with a subversive laugh, they are doing it anyway.

Postscript: The Safer Sex Fetish

One of the most interesting aspects of the gay response to AIDS—one that sets it apart from all other communities' responses to the epidemic—has been the invention of a whole new category of fetish objects: the safer sex fetish. In order to make safer sex erotic, AIDS activists have made great efforts to turn condoms, dental dams, and rubber gloves into sex toys. Phone sex and—as we can see in some ads for 1-900 lines—phones themselves have become fetishized qua safer sex. These ads capitalize on the familiar fetishistic association by veiling the model's groin and stringing a cord out of his fly, thus representing phones as penis substitutes. As for lesbians, the fact that they are leaping lustfully on to the bandwagon is evidenced by the fact that a company in San Francisco called Stormy Leather now sells harnesses (black, of course) that hold dental dams in place over the vagina.

Whereas Freud discusses fetishism as the psychic process of an individual, the work of AIDS activists—safer sex workshops, condom ads, porn films, and literature that foreground fetish objects as safer sex—provides us with examples of fetishism as a *cultural* labor. Because some genital sex is now threatening because it can transmit HIV, AIDS activists have begun to carry out consciously what Freud's fetishist does unconsciously, that is, to sexualize an object in the place of real genitals. In the case of condoms, the idea is to swerve the sexual drive away from direct genital contact and on to an object used to cover the penis. Take, for example, the condom ad created by the Gay Men's Health Crisis (figure 2). The ad doesn't just tell you that a condom in your pocket is your friend because it can prevent AIDS. It tells the viewer that a condom in your pocket is sexy. It tells you that a condom can be a fetish, especially for a man like this one who has already fetishized his entire appearance by working out at the gym and wearing skin-tight clothing. The sexual allure of this poster hinges on the way that it eroticizes nearly everything about the man's body except his penis; in fact, the poster tantalizingly veils the man's "lack" (i.e., his asshole) by displacing it and representing it as the suggestive little circle of the rubber in his back pocket.

It would be incorrect, actually, to speak of this cultural labor as fully conscious. Like the psychic process Freud describes, the making of the safer sex fetish is marked by its own brand of repression or at least a kind of motivated forgetting. AIDS activists have incorporated this necessary forgetfulness into the

A RUBBER IS A FRIEND
IN YOUR POCKET

UN AMIGO ES UN CONDÓN
EN EL BOLSILLO

FOR ANY INFORMATION CALL THE **GMHC** HOTLINE: 212-807-6655
PARA MÁS INFORMACIÓN LLAMA AL

Figure 2.

Ad created by Gay Men's Health Crisis.

Illustration by Michael Sabanosh.

Photograph by Paisley Currah.

design of the typical safer sex workshop: the purpose of going to one is to worry about AIDS during the workshop, and then—armed with your fetish—to forget about it during sex itself. Once again, we see the "refusal to take cognizance" at the heart of Freud's definition of the fetish.

In the case of the safer sex fetish, the threat to be repressed is not the threat of castration but the fear of contracting a terrible and probably fatal disease. Admittedly, some AIDS educational campaigns *exploit* castration fears in order to frighten people away from prostitutes and promiscuity.[29] I don't think this has been the case in the lesbian and gay response to AIDS. Queers in the age of AIDS have shunned these kinds of scare tactics, not only because they result in overt misogyny but also because members of groups like ACT UP have dedicated themselves personally and politically to the sanctity of sexual pleasure. And the fetish, it seems, is an efficient, safe, and satisfying vehicle for it. In fact, Freud opens his essay by marveling at how happy fetishists are with their toys. He writes that these well-adjusted perverts never come to analysis because they want to be cured of their fetish: "There is no need to expect that these people came to analysis on account of their fetish. For though no doubt a fetish is recognized by its adherents as an abnormality, it is seldom felt by them as the symptom of an ailment accompanied by suffering. Usually they are quite satisfied with it, or even praise the way in which it eases their erotic life."[30] In this passage, Freud seems impressed with the fetish object's accessibility, versatility, and capacity for gratification. Rather than focusing on the fear and anxiety that goes into the making of a fetish, AIDS activists have taken advantage of these, its more delightful, characteristics—all for the sake of pleasure and survival.

Notes

1 See Colleen Lamos's excellent essay on pornographic representations of the dildo, "*On Our Backs:* Taking on the Phallus" (manuscript of a talk delivered at the annual convention of the Modern Language Association, San Francisco, 28 December 1991), published as "The Postmodern Lesbian Position: *On Our Backs,*" in *The Lesbian Postmodern,* ed. Laura Doan (New York: Columbia University Press, 1994), 85–103. In general, a number of papers at the 1991 Annual Lesbian and Gay Studies Conference, including my essay and the panel entitled "Flaunting the Phallus" in which it appeared, attest to the curious increase of scholarly interest in lesbianism and the phallus, epitomized perhaps by Judith Butler's "The Lesbian Phallus and the Morphological Imaginary" (*differences* 4 [Spring 1992]: 133–71). Recent interventions by women of color in the dildo debate include Jackie Goldsby's "What It Means to Be Colored Me," *Outlook* 9 (Summer 1990): 15; and Alycee J. Lane's editorial on dildos, "What's *Race* Got to Do with It?" in the black lesbian pornographic magazine *Black Lace* (Summer 1991): 21.

2 Sigmund Freud, "Fetishism," in *The Standard Edition of the Complete Psychological Works of Sigmund Freud,* ed. James Strachey, 24 vols. (London: Hogarth, 1964), 21:153–61. All further references to Freud are from this volume. For an excellent summary of French psychoanalysis's emphasis on the "syntax" of fantasy, see Elizabeth Cowie, "Fantasia," in *The Woman in Question,* ed. Parveen Adams and Elizabeth Cowie (Cambridge, Mass.: MIT Press, 1990), 149–96.

3 Several of his feminist readers have discussed Freud's exclusion of women from fetishism. See Naomi Schor, "Female Fetishism: The Case of George Sand," in *The Female Body in Western Culture: Contemporary Perspectives,* ed. Susan Suleiman (Cambridge, Mass.: Harvard University Press, 1985), 363–72; and Elizabeth A. Grosz, "Lesbian Fetishism?" *differences* 3 (Summer 1991): 39–54.

4 Lamos, "On Our Backs," 3.

5 Daralee and Nancy, "Letters" column, *On Our Backs* (Winter 1989): 5.

6 See Anne Koedt et al., eds., *Radical Feminism* (New York: Quadrangle, 1973). Daralee and Nancy's "women-identified-women" is a catchphrase, of course, originating in part from the Radicalesbian manifesto "The Woman-Identified Woman," reprinted in *Radical Feminism,* 240–45. For a recent discussion of the radical feminist critique of sexuality, see Alice Echols's *Daring to Be Bad: Radical Feminism in America, 1967–1975* (Minneapolis: University of Minnesota Press, 1989).

7 See Fran Moira's review of a panel at the 1982 Barnard sexuality conference, "lesbian sex mafia (l s/m) speak out," *off our backs* 12 (June 1982): 24.

8 Sheila Jeffreys, "Butch and Femme: Now and Then," in *Not a Passing Phase: Reclaiming*

Lesbians in History, 1840–1985, ed. Lesbian History Group (London: Women's Press, 1989), 178.

9 See, e.g., "The Fem Question," in *Pleasure and Danger: Exploring Female Sexuality,* ed. Carole S. Vance (London: Pandora, 1989), 233; and Joan Nestle's "My Woman Poppa," in *The Persistent Desire: A Femme-Butch Reader,* ed. Joan Nestle (Boston: Alyson, 1992), 348–51.

10 Susie Bright, *Susie Sexpert's Lesbian Sex World* (Pittsburgh: Cleis, 1990), 19.

11 Similarly, radical feminist attacks on butch-femme can be accused of failing to distinguish between gender stereotyping and "gender performance" in Judith Butler's sense of the term (see Judith Butler, *Gender Trouble: Feminism and the Subversion of Identity* [New York: Routledge, 1989], 137–39), i.e., between butch-femme as a duplication of masculine/feminine sex roles and butch-femme as a performative, "erotic statement" (Joan Nestle, *A Restricted Country* [Ithaca, N.Y.: Firebrand, 1986], 100).

12 Lane, "What's *Race* Got to Do with It," 21.

13 Freud, "Fetishism," 153, 152–53.

14 He is, at least, not a homosexual. Fetishism, according to Freud, "saves the fetishist from being a homosexual by endowing women with the attribute which makes them acceptable as sexual objects" ("Fetishism," 154). In other words, the fetish object displaces the sight of the horrifying female sex organ and thus "saves" the subject from having to seek sex with other men. Interestingly, Freud pauses at this moment to admit he remains puzzled as to why a "great majority" of men are heterosexual, considering the fact that "probably no male human being is spared the fright of castration at the female genital." (See also p. 155.)

15 Grosz, "Lesbian Fetishism?" 51.

16 See, e.g., Jane Gallop's writings on the penis/phallus distinction, in particular her chapter "Beyond the Phallus" in *Thinking through the Body* (New York: Columbia University Press, 1988), 119–33.

17 Freud, "Fetishism," 154.

18 Nestle, "My Woman Poppa," 348–50.

19 "When Fanny Liquidates Kenny's Stocks," in *Clips,* directed by Nan Kinney and Debi Sundahl (Fatale Video, 1988).

20 See Slavoj Žižek, *The Sublime Object of Ideology* (London: Verso, 1989), 28–33.

21 Freud, "Fetishism," 154.

22 Jan Brown, "Sex, Lies, and Penetration: A Butch Finally 'Fesses Up," *Outlook* 7 (Winter 1990): 34 (reprinted in *The Persistent Desire,* 410–15).

23 Lane, "What's *Race* Got to Do with It?" 21.

24 Freud, "Fetishism," 154.

25 See Jackie Goldsby's critique of Susie Bright's video presentation, "All Girl Action: A History of Lesbian Erotica" (1990). Responding in part to Bright's defense of Russ Meyer's *Vixen,* which portrays a white woman getting "ram[med]" by a black woman with a "larger-than-life white dildo," Goldsby concludes that, "as Bright's lecture presented it, lesbian eroticism—its icons, its narratives, its ideologies—is white" (p. 15).

26 Sarah Kofman, *The Enigma of Woman: Woman in Freud's Writings,* trans. Catherine Porter (Ithaca, N.Y.: Cornell University Press, 1985), 88.

27 Freud, "Fetishism," 157.

28 Butler, "The Lesbian Phallus," 124.

29 See, e.g., J. D. Crowe's cartoon with the caption "DEATH FOR SALE," portraying four street prostitutes with A-I-D-S spelled over their heads (reprinted in Sander L. Gilman, "AIDS and Syphilis: The Iconography of a Disease," *October,* no. 43 [Winter 1987]: 106).

30 Freud, "Fetishism," 152.

Tom of

Finland

An Appreciation

Nayland Blake

Tom of Finland is one of the gay world's few authentic icons. For over thirty years his drawings have appeared in gay magazines and circulated in pirate editions. His men have entered the fantasy life of thousands, and his vision has influenced such artists as Robert Mapplethorpe, Bruce Weber, and Rainer Werner Fassbinder. Though his popularity has waxed and waned, he has remained modest about his work and committed to the making of it. He was born in Finland, where he worked as an illustrator and art director for an advertising firm. He first came to America in 1978, and now spends his time between Europe and California, where he has established a foundation to promote his work and an archive to preserve and protect it. [Tom of Finland has died since this essay was written—Eds.]

Tom's work is diverse. His drawings are at once a system of gay erotics, utopian documents, historical texts, formal puzzles, memories, and love letters. All of this takes place in the context of an effective pornography. This essay is an attempt to present the various ways in which Tom's work might be used to illuminate other areas of sexuality and cultural history. To do this, it is useful to use a model of several "Toms." Each might be understood to exist in separate but overlapping locations and to articulate different vantage points. Each is one-dimensional and, as such, far from any final truth about who Tom is. Taken together, however, they can indicate the diverse nature of Tom's production and the many options available to the person who looks at it.

Tom the Pornographer

Tom's work has been left on the sidelines of any debate about gay sensibility because it is pornography. Pornography remains a taboo: we consume it but will not commit to it. Yet when the history of gay images and representations is written, it will contain a large section on our pornographers. In a milieu that has produced a new connoisseurship of sexual acts, what we arouse ourselves with speaks eloquently about who we are.

Because of the marginalization of pornographic practice, Tom's work has been pirated, his earnings stolen by booksellers and art dealers, and his impact as a producer of powerful signs ignored by the same gay community he helped to create. It is time to invert the value placed on the production and consumption of pornography, and to instead look to it to provide understanding of who we are and how we are.

Tom draws. Most current discussion tends to focus on photographic pornography, treating all other forms as sidelights, or subsets of it. But there are important differences between a drawn and a photographic image. Photographic pornography operates as evidence, the documentation that certain acts took place before the camera. Drawings, however, function in a way akin to writing: they provide the props for the viewer to hang a fantasy on rather than a specific person for the viewer to be aroused by. Tom comprehends that his drawings are not renditions of reality. His "men" are machines for fucking, like exotic sofas, and they are constructed accordingly. Unlike the subject of a photograph, their brawn is not the product of endless grooming. Their bodies are not a reproach to our own, but an opportunity for luxury.

Tom constructed his ideal gay body on paper. Because of his position as a pornographer, he was able to disseminate his ideas about that body to a sympathetic underground of gay men in Europe and America, to modify and embellish it, and finally, to see it celebrated as a central fixture of gay culture.

Tom the Artist

Every work of cultural criticism has its own project. For years gay cultural critics have been locked into a project of assimilation into the dominant culture. They expect the gay community to produce figures that will stand alongside the masters by satisfying criteria of impact, technique, or seriousness of purpose. We are constantly presented with a parade of gay artists raised to mastery or snatched from the mainstream canon by their critics or publicists. In recent years we have seen this project attempted with such artists as David Hockney, George Platte

Lynnes, and Carravaggio. But the urge to "take someone seriously" and to confer respectability through placement in art history can easily be a disservice to the artist. Paul Cadmus, for instance, is an artist whose rehabilitation is complete, whose work has been successfully termed both gay and high art.

Cadmus began his career in the thirties. He was a student of Reginald Marsh and worked on several projects for the Works Progress Administration (WPA). His most famous moment came when he was commissioned to produce a painting for the U.S. Navy and presented them with a portrait of boozy sailors whoring on leave. The resulting scandal thrust him into the mainstream until the schools of postwar abstraction eclipsed his own, representational, style. In the late seventies, his reputation was revived by increased interest in the WPA period, and by his lionization in the gay press. But Cadmus's work can only be described as tangential to the entire thrust of modern art. Its overwhelming characteristic is the desire to be taken seriously, to be high art. It attempts to convince us by displaying all the signifiers of mastery: coy allusion to other paintings, meticulous rendering, a tendency to caricature divorced from any real perception, and a slavish devotion to antique craftsmanship (in his case egg tempera—which was supposed to show that the painting took a long time and wasn't easy to make). But the result of such labors is kitsch. Kitsch reassures the bourgeois audience that they are receiving their proper dosage of culture. A progressive politics cannot arise from a conservative aesthetics, and to promote Cadmus to a place within the world of museum art is to win a hollow victory for gay politics.

For Cadmus depicts gay people in an ambivalent fashion. In his early work, gay sexuality is slipped in on the sidelines, often with the artist as a knowing spectator winking at the audience. Later, history allowed him the luxury of painting beefcake. Cadmus's paintings are either social commentaries peppered with a series of grotesque homosexual "types," or in a painting like his *What I Believe,* sentimentalized hymns to a gay middlebrow heaven.

Tom cites Cadmus as an influence, but his work is different in tone and intent. He is skeptical or attempts to classify his work as high art, preferring the terms *fantasy drawings* or *dirty pictures.* His images relate to the man in the street far more than to the pantheon of great artists. His work is not an apologia for homosexuality, but a direct document of it. With Tom there are no great themes, no highblown rhetoric, but great communication. The fact that his work is utilitarian, that its aim is sexual arousal, means that it cannot make claims to distance or a transhistorical resonance. Tom sacrifices the grand for the immediate. It is his success at this that makes him a much more interesting figure in discussions of gay identity.

Tom the Craftsman

"I wanted to develop a photorealist style."

One of the most striking and transgressive features of Tom's drawings are their polish, the obsessive way in which they are rendered. The viewer's attention is shifted away from considering the quality of the line (in the way that we would speak of Matisse's line) to the object or activity that is being depicted. Rendering strives to be seamless, obscuring the process of its own making. In the twentieth century, work that has attempted to hide the process of its making has almost always been allied with extreme aesthetic and political conservatism.

Two examples of this would be Soviet socialist realism and the paintings of Norman Rockwell. They share the same concern as Tom's work does with the fetishized representation of things "as they really are." This last phrase is the most important because it is the project of this work to construct the reality it purports to depict. Such work revives the time-worn metaphor of painting as a mirror to create a fantasy reality and make us believe it as well.

Like Tom, Norman Rockwell worked for years as an illustrator and commercial artist before anyone ever claimed his work was fine art. If you tour the Rockwell Museum in Stockbridge, Massachusetts, you will be treated to endless reminders of how long the paintings took to execute, how exacting Rockwell was, how his models were drawn from the people around him. Not a word will be said about the real agenda of Rockwell's work, which is the construction of a phantom America, where people have disagreements but not differences, where social issues are the occasion for damp sympathy or sly chuckles but not action, and where every thing "feels like home." Rockwell supports a type of antihistoricism in the name of American ideals: a bumbling clerk or American soldier looks exactly like his colonial forebears; children commune with the spirit of George Washington; a young man giving a speech bears uncanny resemblance to Abraham Lincoln. His work achieves its effect by its obsessive rendering (which panders to our wish to see ourselves in the mirror it proffers) without saying it is not our image we see, but only its own distorted editorializing.

Socialist realism (the art movement promoted by Stalin in the early thirties) has a similar goal. Its aim is the creation, through their depiction, of attitudes proper to the ideal Communist state. Its style is a hybrid of nineteenth-century salon painting with the neoclassicism of late art deco. As the official government style, it succeeded in silencing some of the most important art of the twentieth century. Soviet artists moved from the vanguard of ideas in painting, filmmaking, and architecture to become obscure state functionaries. Works that treated the viewer as anything other than a passive receptor for the "correct attitudes" of the propagandists were driven underground. Like Rockwell, the Soviet artists were using arguments of naturalism and realism as a cover for their own political program, and like Rockwell, they relied on the technique of scrupulous depiction to seduce and convince the viewer. It is telling that the works produced under socialist realism began to look like those produced in Nazi Germany.

The burly workers and farmers that stride through socialist realism's paintings and sculptures are not too distant relatives of the sailors and cops whose orgies Tom lovingly depicts. Tom, too, is constructing a fantasy world, but with different aims. He is calling into being a world suffused with gay sexuality, using the power of his craft to validate his fantasies.

Tom the Narrator

Tom says, "I wanted to show a world where gays could be freer, not so afraid." He draws an idealized world of sexual courtship and activity that is at once a projection of his own private fantasies about gay behavior and a public articulation of possibilities within the gay community.

The rules of this utopia are spelled out through narrative. Tom uses narrative in two ways. The first is within the individual drawing. We see figures gesture to one another while in the background, a third is enticed toward the scene. A knot of flesh reveals itself to be a series of sexual acts, the individual articulations of which rest like beads on a strand: here a crotch is being grabbed, here a neck bitten.

Often when we feel we have solved this sexual puzzle there is an unexpected conjunction: a body is given a half twist, a foot is wedged to stroke an asshole. Such moments in the drawings are like turns in the plot. A new erotic site is revealed, and the drawings move from sexual excitement to repletion.

The second use of narrative is the linking up of various drawings into a series. In this, they begin to resemble novels or films more than photographs, displaying the possibilities for sexual conjunction between characters. We anticipate combinations—what if Kake (one of Tom's heroes) fucks this cop who is arriving? Or, if the situation reverses, is that cock sucked later on? The erotic is displaced from an object to a terrain of figures and their possible interactions. Narrative opens up the image; it denies it an authority of hierarchy.

A narrative exists throughout Tom's work as a whole. This is because certain characters have continued to appear in his work for thirty years—not only the heroes Kake and Pekka, but the bit players as well. Tom's figures are as gener-

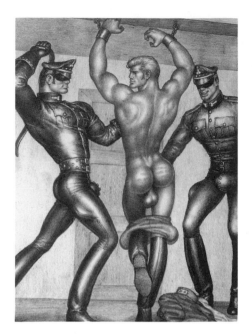

Figure 1.
Tom of Finland drawing, 1965.

alized in their appearance as they are particularized in their acts. Their similarity makes us feel at home. This is a world we recognize, but without the boundaries on our desires.

Tom the Sensualist

Tom is the poet of texture. Notice the characteristics of flesh in his work. Flesh as it is compacted into springy mass, as it pushes from between fingers, as it is ridged during fucking. Tom's men are massive, and it is this sense of the impact of flesh on flesh that provides erotic charge. His bodies are pneumatic and well upholstered, and at the same time, pouty.

In Western art, the pout is a potent sexual signifier. It is a fullness (the skin is near to bursting with the flesh that lies beneath it) and at the same time a slackening, a slight droop that connotes a leisure, a gentle lassitude. In Tom, not only the lips, but the eyes, the bellies, even the cocks seem to pout, to be packed with a sexual energy that expresses itself in a slight but significant bulging. It is this flesh that pouts, through clothes and across streets, that produces the heavy air of sex in Tom's world.

Tom is adept at portraying the texture of leather boots and jackets, the starch

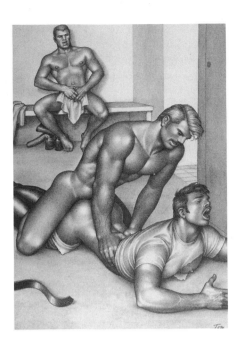

Figure 2.
Tom of Finland drawing, 1977.

of uniforms, the tension and give of denim. He admits that it was the British who first drew his attention to the world of leather, and he is perhaps its most faithful depicter. His leather is shiny and beautifully heavy, draping the men of his drawings with a sort of solemnity. This drapery frames the erotic object; clothing is often retained far into the sex act. The textures and bits of uniform are the variables that allow us to sort out who is who among Tom's generalized figures.

Tom the Voyeur

Most pornography of the image is constructed around the framework of the gaze. The gaze can be understood as the eye as phallus, a powerful and penetrative organ. In most pornography, the object presents itself to the gaze, welcomes its penetration, and is rendered passive by it. In Tom's work there is surprisingly little of the singular, phallic gaze. Instead, he presents a network of looks. Often he inserts figures observing the activities into the margins of his drawings. There is a heightened sense of people putting themselves on display.

Two fully clothed men lean against a tree. They look out onto a street where other men cruise and make gestures of sexual enticement. After a while we realize that the men are fucking. This drawing is not an invitation to us, the viewer, but it is powerfully erotic because of the combination of the men's casual looks and their position as part of an entire world of fucking. Like those of the men, our eyes are invited to roam. This allows for a double current of attraction/participation rather than the single current of gazer/object of the gaze. No longer interested in desire and its implied lack, Tom substitutes a pleasure of looking and being looked at, equating the cruising look with the sexual act.

Tom the Fascist

"Whoever designed the Nazi uniforms had to be gay. Those were the sexiest men I have ever seen in my life. . . . "

Tom's earliest sexual experiences were with German soldiers during the occupation of Helsinki. He talked about this romantic involvement in an interview with David Reed in *Christopher Street*. His first drawings were attempts to recreate those experiences and fantasies.

The first time I read the above quote two things came to mind: first, the debate then raging over the meaning of the fashion of leather and uniforms for gay men and, second, the visual similarity between Tom's drawings and the heroic neoclassicism that had been the court style under the fascist regimes of the twenties through forties.

Can Tom's work be said to provide a direct link between the *übermensch* ideals of Nazi Germany and the so-called fascist undercurrents in the gay uniform craze? And by extension, can Tom's work be called fascist?

In Tom's utopian world, roles exist, but power is fluid. He is the keenest depicter of the erotics of lubricious power. Cops may have authority, a uniformed man may begin to flog his prisoner, but these situations will soon reverse themselves as the cop bends over to be fucked, and the man in the uniform allows himself to be bound. Tom understands that the pleasure of S/M is the successful fulfillment of a role while maintaining the understanding that it is a role. "It is more playful, like acting," he says. There is also a high degree of humor in the drawings, and even when there are scenes of beating or bondage, they are suffused with an avuncular attitude that is difficult to resolve with the notion of fascism.

Some maintain that the symbol itself holds power, that to use it is to invoke all that it has stood for. At the opposite extreme are those who claim that a symbol, like the swastika, is utterly neutral and that it is the viewer's responsibility to get past any negative connotations that it may have had. Both positions contain a certain amount of self-willed naiveté. By itself, a symbol is a neutral arrangement of lines, but symbols are never by themselves. Like all signifiers, they are the product of specific historical circumstances.

After the experience of Nazi Germany, it is impossible to claim that its symbols are neutral. However, it is equally wrong to say that, once symbols acquire a meaning, that meaning is fixed forever. The meaning of phrases and images does shift depending on who uses them. While Tom's drawings utilize a style of representation popular under fascism, it would be a mistake to say that even those that contain Nazi imagery are fascist in intent or effect.

Tom himself expresses misgivings about drawings he made early in his career. "People saw them in a political way because they had Nazis in them. They thought I was a Nazi. I would not do them today because I do not want people to see them that way—they are my fantasies." Through an understanding of the traumatic effect that they have on people, Tom has removed the drawings that contain Nazi figures from circulation. This is a case in which his private fantasies were not shared by a larger public. Tom also talks about subjects that are too violent for him. "They [people with commissions] asked me to do pictures like of balls being cut off or stomachs opened with all the organs. . . . I could not do them."

A fascist art is one that seeks to silence opposition by means of its own authority, one that uses scale and impersonality to produce power. It renders the viewer mute, denying any voice other than the state. From the first, Tom has been inclusive in his work, incorporating suggestions from others, and through dialogue, coming to an understanding of its various political implications. His art does not glorify power, being all too eager to upset the balance in favor of erotic connection. It is impossible to imagine Kake as some sort of *übermensch*. He is too often on the receiving end of Tom's jokes, losing his clothes, or having his cock handcuffed to another man. Tom is too obviously delighted with the possibilities for erotic display to not invite us to join in.

Tom the Sadist

In speaking of sadism, it is important to differentiate between a garden variety of brute and someone whose work is inspired by the Marquis de Sade. Tom is a sadist, not because of any perceived violence in his work, but because he shares similar obsessions with Sade. He is a careful constructor of sexual tableaus. He is concerned with full use of the erotic zones of the body, with saturation. It is important that all orifices be filled, that figures be connected, disrupted, and connected again. In one narrative a man is pissing in a public toilet. A sailor wanders in and starts fucking him, a blond comes in and starts fucking him, and so on until there are eight people in a row. This is a typical Sadean trope; an asshole is fucked because it is there and it is important to complete the tableau. The formal demands of sexual positioning overwhelm the ideas of power relationships.

Like Sade's, Tom's work operates by an overlapping and subsequent disruption of codes. In Tom's case this is the tension between the drawn image and the photograph. His best drawings bounce between the deadpan style of the camera and the sly exaggerations of his pencil. Without the meticulous rendering, his exaggerations would fail to arouse. There is a sense of outrage with the notion of the painstaking approach to such a low aim; that one should labor so hard to produce images of men fucking.

Sade uses beautifully crafted French prose to describe the most perfidious activities. In our society, the expected result of superlative craft is the sublime. Tom, with his devotion to his fantasy, stands this expectation about highmindedness and craft on its head. His intense devotion to a pornographic labor is antiestablishment; it is a "waste" of time and talent. It disrupts society's ideas about what pornography is: cheap, thrown together, and without redeeming value.

Tom the Physique Artist

Looking at a copy of *Fizeek Art Quarterly,* it is remarkable how Tom's work stands out from the rest of the drawings that surround it—as much for what it doesn't do as for what it does. The majority of early gay pornography is dominated by a desire to return to a mythical past. Images of fauns playing lyres, gladiators, medieval knights and pages, and other never-never lands of gay desire. Tom's drawings, on the other hand, are always of contemporary subjects. Even when they portray cowboys, you know there is a pickup truck or motorcycle lurking around the corner.

This is a world of today, a world of constantly intersecting erotic gazes and gestures, where sexual activity is always a possibility. Over the years, Tom has adopted different styles of dress and hair length to maintain a contemporary look. Tom also abandons the gay figure of the ephebe, the slender hairless teen whose purity and fawn-like bearing presage the sensitive and willowy man. Tom's men are lugs, and the closest he comes to the ephebe are drawings of robust teens who ride around on motorcycles looking to get fucked.

Tom has always drawn images from his own experiences and the world around him; but as his work began to appear in the pages of America's physique magazines he began to receive suggestions for subject matter and commissions from his publishers and readers. These magazines functioned not only as a source for pinup pictures, but also as a ground for the exchange of ideas for fantasies and types of identities. They began to form the image reservoirs from which gay men were able to construct new codes for dress and behavior. They began to constitute a placeless community for gay men before physical communities existed.

The physique magazines should be seen not as cute precursors to today's hardcore porn, but as an underground press equal in importance to the first gay political magazines. Tom's drawings passed from the private fantasies of a man in Europe to the underground images that would shape a generation's ideas of how a gay man could look and act. Tom has drawn not only on the paper in front of him but on the consciousness of the men who viewed and continue to view his work.

Note

Nayland Blake would like to thank Mark Leger for his editorial insight and guidance, and Tom of Finland and Dirk Dehner for their time and patience.

Visible

Lesions

Images of the PWA

Jan Zita Grover

The camera invariably seeks out the "victims" of the most spectacular battles. Its instinct for the sensational leads it to prefer the bald and wasted AIDS patient with the feverish, haggard look, lying in his hospital bed (preferably with a few tubes up his nose), to his companion who is still able to take care of himself and speak articulately about his condition. . . . Everyone knows it's best not to give us a chance at the microphone and that pictures deceive even better than words.

—Emmanuel Dreuilhe, *Mortal Embrace: Living with* AIDS[1]

What do "the picture of health" and "the picture of sickness" look like? A stupid question, to be sure, unless we refine it: *whose* picture of health/sickness? and *for whom?* and in the service of *what?* So let's refine the question, narrow it down some: what does "the picture of health/sickness" look like in relation to AIDS within three separate discursive fields—those of medicine (directed toward physicians), newspaper and periodical photojournalism (mainstream and gay), and art photography (directed toward curators and patrons of museums and commercial galleries)?

For the sake of this argument, we will use AIDS—acquired immunodeficiency syndrome—as the measure of "sickness" by which health is defined, just as masculinity can be understood only in relation to femininity, heterosexuality in relation to its supposed opposite, homosexuality. It is through these oppositions that we can name a term, a condition.[2]

It has been almost eight years since Marcus Conant, M.D., stood outside the annual meeting of the American Academy of Dermatologists handing out a pamphlet he had produced with a $500 grant from Neutrogena, illustrated by photographs of patients with Kaposi's sarcoma (KS). This was one of the first representations of AIDS, a condition that both then and now has been partially identified with *appearances*. Photographs "of AIDS" first appeared in medical (*New England Journal of Medicine, Lancet, Journal of the American Medical Association* [JAMA]) and basic research (*Science, Nature*) journals. These photographs were not concerned with humanizing AIDS; they were largely close-ups of affected organs or microphotographs of cells, tissue, virus. They were made to identify AIDS's signs and symptoms for purposes of surveillance, diagnosis, and treatment.[3]

But as popular media became preoccupied by AIDS—most markedly, after Rock Hudson admitted his diagnosis in July 1985 and then died that October—other images of AIDS appeared, this time amid the scenes of catastrophe, celebrity, horror, and novelty that constitute mass media's photographic archives. Like many of the photographs that appear in tabloids, these "images of AIDS" were mostly unremarkable pictures in any sense: their subjects were obviously ill, usually shown seated on couches or lying in beds. It was the words surrounding these photographs that gave them their particular resonance: the words told us that these were people *doomed to die,* much as others sharing their pages told us that this unremarkable-looking boy had wed and divorced five women twice his age or that this woman had borne sextuplets or owned a three-headed cocker spaniel.

Broadcast/newspaper journalists and gallery ("art") photographers do not make their images only in response to the inherited traditions or conventions of their medium; they also incorporate their own understanding of events, authorities, and institutions related to the objects they depict. The ways that scientists and physicians understand AIDS have as great an impact on the ways that, for example, newspaper photographers depict PWAs (persons with AIDS) as existing photojournalistic conventions for depicting the chronically ill. It is only through seeing the complex relations between medical/scientific "facts" and modes of visual representation that we can assess the significance of the *choices made* by people who make images. For example,

—What does it mean in 1989, when the average life expectancy of a person diagnosed with AIDS is over twenty months, for a photographer to consistently depict PWAs as debilitated, disfigured, in extremis? Does it mean the same thing(s) as it did in 1983, when the average life expectancy of a person diagnosed with AIDS was only eight months?

—What does it mean in 1989, when there are well-organized cadres of PWAs nationwide who protest government inaction on drug trials, understaffing in clinics and hospital wards, discrimination in employment and housing, to depict PWAS *as victims?* Does it mean the same thing(s) it did in 1983?

—What did it mean in 1986–87, when the most dramatic increases in incidence of diagnosed cases of AIDS were among black and Latino women, that the plight of heterosexuals with AIDS was epitomized largely in terms of white suburbanites?

—What does it mean throughout the period 1985–89 that the number of children with AIDS (1 percent) of total U.S. AIDS cases) received more media attention than the 61 percent of diagnosed cases among gay men?

My aim here is to periodize medical-research-epidemiological events and political-cultural/media representations of AIDS in such a way that these questions can be answered. This essay is intended to propose some grounds from which they can be asked.

Most criticism of photographs treats images as if they were made and can be assessed within a continuous historical moment. As short as the history of AIDS in the United States is, there have been sufficient permutations in scientific, medical, epidemiological, political, media, and artistic responses to make historical differentiations crucial even within this brief eight-year period. What AIDS *is,* what it has been made to *mean,* and how those two interpretations have been *represented* at any given time is rather like the parable of the blind men and the elephant: everyone has an opinion of the elephant's shape, but it depends on where they are positioned in relation to it.[4]

Two premises underlie the discussion of representation that follows. The first is that media representations spiral outward from the most specialized and "authorized" (in this case, those of science) toward the most dependent and "opinionated" (i.e., those depending most heavily on the authority of representations already made at higher orders of influence). Meyrig Horton and Peter Aggleton, in their study "The Cultural Production of an AIDS Research Paradigm," make a persuasive case for this model, employing Ludwik Fleck's paradigm for the trajectory of scientific discourse (developed in Fleck's *Genesis and Development of a Scientific Fact*).[5] In Horton and Aggleton's application of Fleck (figure 1), the data published in science journals (e.g., *Science* and *Nature*) possess the greatest authority and prestige to readers who subscribe to the authority and prestige of research science. This includes not only other research scientists but also physicians, surgeons, nurses, and other health care workers, *although these may never even read the journals in question.* This group may also include newspaper and periodical science reporters and other reporters assigned to "cover" AIDS and those activists and patients for whom scientific activity is the preeminent authority on AIDS. On the other hand, for researchers, physicians, and others who reject the findings of research science (e.g., those who reject the hypothesis that HIV is the causative agent of AIDS, whether they believe it is caused by another virus or "lifestyle" factors, or because they regard the issue as moot and instead focus on, e.g., attitudinal healing), the work of journal science is not at the core of authority and prestige. Rather, the "cone of influence" is inverted: that-which-is-not-debated in the research-science model (e.g., etiologic agents other than HIV) moves to the center of debate, while what was previously the core (e.g., HIV as primary etiologic agent) moves to the periphery as that-which-is-no-longer-debated.

This paradigm is equally useful in looking at other worlds of discourse (general circulation periodicals, television news, etc.), where similar levels of dependence and influence operate. For example, within the world of general circulation weeklies, *Time* and *Newsweek* possess greater "authority" than the *National Enquirer* and the *Star,* so the latter are more likely to refer to the former as "proof" of their claims than vice versa. Similarly, the *New York Times* has greater influence as an authority publication than *USA Today,* so the latter is more likely to quote the former than the other way around.[6]

The second premise underlying this discussion is that AIDS in the United States must be differentiated year by year and locality by locality in order for us to understand it (this is, of course, true for AIDS anywhere else as well). Before 1989, AIDS in the United States was very unevenly distributed. Instead, it was concentrated—a distinctly coastal phenomenon, whether considered from an epidemiological or media coverage viewpoint. In 1986, for example, 40 percent of all reported cases of AIDS in the United States were in metropolitan New York and San Francisco.[7] These cities were closely followed by Los Angeles, Houston, and Miami. Together, these five American metropolises reported most of the country's AIDS cases. For the majority of Americans living outside these communities, AIDS appeared to be someone else's problem—something freakish and citified, related not only to an exotic homosexuality but to the corruptions of downtown city life. Despite warnings from both gay activists and the Right, before 1985 AIDS seemed unlikely to invade the (attempted) suburban refuges where most middle-class Americans lived.

Significantly, the federal Centers for Disease Control (CDC) recently announced that the greatest number of cases reported in 1989 are in communities outside the cities previously reporting the greatest caseloads. The coastal cities of the U.S. empire have now been surpassed in sheer numbers of reported cases by other metropolitan areas—Washington, D.C., Chicago, Indianapolis, Denver, Boston. By 1991, the CDC predicts that New York and San Francisco will account for only 20 percent of all reported AIDS cases.[8]

Our periodization begins by looking at the epidemic on two different fronts:

events in medicine–scientific research–epidemiology and representations in media–politics–culture. These events are described in Table 1. Anyone involved in the struggle against AIDS will have many amendments to make to the rough chronology given in Table 1. But I would argue that it is useful for beginning discussion of many strands in the evolving history of how AIDS *has been depicted*. It points out some of the push-and-pull between dominant and counter-discourses about AIDS over time. (In saying this, I am not suggesting that the many constructions placed on AIDS can be understood solely in historical terms: there is far too much of the transhistorically irrational about the shaping of AIDS to propose that.)[11] Paula Treichler's chronology of dominant media discourses is also useful and briefer for these purposes:

1. evolving biomedical understandings of AIDS (1981–1985);
2. Rock Hudson's illness and death as a turning point in national consciousness (July 1985–December 1986);
3. AIDS perceived as a pandemic disease to which sexually active heterosexuals are vulnerable (fall 1986–spring 1987)
4. diversification of discourse about women and AIDS (spring 1987–present).[12]

1981–85

In 1981, the yet-unnamed syndrome was also unimaged. Although many gay men (and, we now know, heterosexual intravenous drug abusers) in New York City and San Francisco were already suffering from inexplicable illnesses, there was no discernible pattern except for a marked increase in persistent generalized lymphadenopathy (swelling of the lymph glands, particularly in the neck and groin) that had been noted by physicians with large gay practices since 1979. In winter 1981, several of these physicians reported anomalous cases of *Pneumocystis carinii* pneumonia (PCP) and KS among their patients to the CDC in Atlanta. PCP and KS are rare conditions among young middle-class men, yet cases were showing up on both coasts. What struck CDC epidemiologists most forcibly about these cases was that all of the first patients reported were gay.[13] From this fact U.S. epidemiologists and medical researchers concluded that the condition these men suffered from was either sexually transmitted or somehow related to what came to be called "homosexual lifestyle." As Jacques Leibowitch, a French researcher immune to the peculiarly American obsession with gay-plague theory, put it, "The 'homosexual mystery' will dominate the beginning of the story: a notion that will shackle the minds of those too closely concerned with it. . . . [The] first (false) lead: the lavender peril."[14] For the next four years,

Table 1

	Medical/Epidemiological /Scientific Research	Media/Political/Culture
1981	Largely reported in gay men; epidemiologists and clinicians perceive as gay disease; names: GRID, CAID, AID, gay plague, WOG[9]	Largely medical journals
1982	CDC announces surveillance definition and name: AIDS; diagnosis of AIDS commonly precedes death by less than nine months	Meager gay press coverage; Gay Men's Health Crisis (NYC) and San Francisco Kaposi's Foundation, first of the voluntary AIDS service organizations, are formed
1983	French isolate LAV; first transfusion, hemophilia, and pediatric cases	Popular media discover AIDS; *JAMA* publishes report on "casual" transmission of AIDS; medical press covers AIDS; gay press increases coverage; voluntary AIDS service organizations formed in large U.S. cities; Advisory Committee of People with AIDS formed; first gay safer-sex publications
1984	HTLV-III argued as causative agent for AIDS; reports of transfusion and hemophiliac cases increase	Medical and gay press coverage increases
1985	HIV antibody test put on market for blood banking; begins being applied by insurance companies; first International AIDS Conference held in Atlanta	Rock Hudson dies; heterosexual panic ensues in popular media; gay press begins covering AIDS extensively; PWA Coalition formed (NYC)
1986	Heterosexual/transfusion/pediatric/IV drug cases widely publicized; drug trials in coastal cities	Heterosexual panic continues; LaRouche Initiative proposed for quarantining PWAs in CA
1987	AZT licensed for use; Presidential Commission on HIV epidemic appointed; Project Inform (San Francisco) urges people to get HIV Ab tests: aerosolized pentamidine; prophylaxis for pneumocystis pneumonia begun in NYC and SF	Helms Amendment; second LaRouche Initiative in CA; Names Project Quilt unveiled in Washington, D.C.; publication of trade and pocketbook heterosexual safer-sex guidebooks[10]
1988	Disputes over estimates of HIV-infected; Presidential Commission returns report; extent of HIV/AIDS in black and Hispanic communities becomes evident	Masters and Johnson furor; third LaRouche initiative in CA; ACT UP and other activist groups mount media actions; mainstream media highlight AIDS and the arts but otherwise back off widespread AIDS coverage

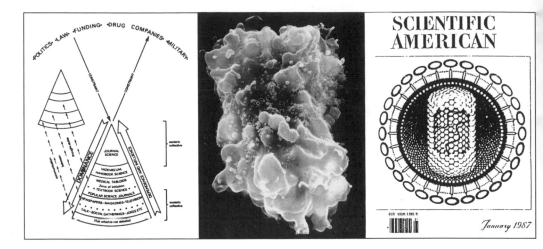

Left to right: Figure 1. Meyrig Horton and Peter Aggleton, "Preliminary Model of the Thought-Collective of the AIDS World," in *AIDS: Social Representations, Social Practices*. Figure 2. Gendered wars at the cellular level: Lennart Nilsson, 30,000 times magnification of human helper T cell (pink) "under attack by the AIDS virus (blue)" ("Our Immune System: The Wars Within," *National Geographic* 169, no. 6 [June 1986]: 707). Figure 3. "The AIDS Virus," *Scientific American* (January 1987), in Paula Treichler, "An Epidemic of Signification." Treichler calls this imaginary schematic "virus as grenade."

American medical, political, and social responses to AIDS were dominated by the hypothetical equation of AIDS and homosexuality, an association that also had long-term effects on how the syndrome was depicted visually.

In 1981–82, while AIDS as a clinical and epidemiological entity was still very much in flux, it was "visible" only in the pages of research and medical journals, where it joined other pathologic conditions as radically abstracted from the human suffering it: microscopic views of biopsy specimens, X-rays, and close-ups of KS lesions. As Horton and Aggleton, using Fleck, have argued, the pivotal influence of scientific research journals had a determining role in setting the terms of the central discourse on AIDS at the time, in the scientific press and elsewhere.

This influence, moreover, was of a distinctly Anglo-American kind: although in 1983 Luc Montagnier's group at the Pasteur Institute in Paris announced that they had isolated and named a retrovirus, LAV (lymphadenopathy-associated virus), present in cells from persons with AIDS, their discovery received little play in the pivotal U.S. scientific journals until Robert Gallo of the National Cancer Institute announced *his* discovery of HTLV-III (human T-cell lymphotropic virus type III) the following year. (This discovery was immediately followed by enter-prising Reaganite Health and Human Services director Margaret Heckler's an-nouncement that a cure for AIDS was just around the corner.)[15] These discoveries were quickly applied to the commercial production of assay kits for detecting the many-named virus[16] in blood banking, the cultural outcome of which was a profound disturbance in popular beliefs about who might be *at risk* and what they might look like (see below). Hysteria now extended not only to the visibly ill but to the invisibly ill/infected—the sick homosexual redux.

Early articles on AIDS in the gay press, which was the only other medium interested in AIDS in 1982, duplicated the visual icons of the medical, so AIDS was represented almost wholly in medicalized terms. The same microscopic views of KS lesions and PCP-infested lung tissue dominated visual coverage in gay jour-nals, making it possible for us to gauge the influence that medical/scientific discourse initially had for gay communities.[17] After the U.S. "discovery" of HTLV-III in 1985, the virus became a familiar image in both scientific/medical and popular media (figures 2, 3).

What is most striking about the nonscientific media's visual coverage of AIDS in 1981–83 is the virtual absence of the *subjects of AIDS*. Several political factors played a role here. In the years before and immediately after the virus was isolated and designated as the primary etiologic agent for the syndrome, wide-spread ignorance about how "AIDS"[18] was contracted mobilized all the old fears about toilet seats, door knobs, infected waiters and cooks, contaminated silver-ware, handshaking, and coughing strangers. As the late Nathan Fain, an AIDS activist, wrote in 1983: "The result [of mainstream media coverage] plant[s] . . . the idea in the general population that AIDS risk groups are like walking Three Mile Islands."[19] Identifiably ill PWAs (and, in the early years of the epidemic, about one-third of PWAs were diagnosed with the often visible lesions of KS) suffered employment, housing, and benefits discrimination, but there were no government statutes or ordinances as possible sources of redress until 1984. Thus PWAs' reluctance to make themselves visible to camera crews and inquiring photographers was understandable. To their credit, a number of PWAs in New York and San Francisco nonetheless chose to appear publicly on local television programs and in newspapers, although in several instances their participation was halted by nervous camera crews.[20] Their aim, perhaps naive and certainly optimistic, was to speak *for themselves* (victims are *spoken for*)[21] and to "human-ize" themselves for a public that viewed them as a threat to "the general popula-tion."

Two visual broadcast/photojournalistic conventions undercut PWAs' attempts to represent themselves and instead worked to entrench their status as threaten-ing outsiders. Broadcast television has developed conventions for depicting per-

Left to right: Figure 4. Taro Yamasaki, photograph of Ryan White, in "The Quiet Victories of Ryan White," *People Weekly* 29, no. 21 (30 May 1988): 96. Figure 5. Photograph of Kenny Ramsauer from *Photo* (Paris), reproduced in Simon Watney and Sunil Gupta, "The Rhetoric of AIDS," *Screen* 27, no. 1 (January–February 1986): 81.

sons whose identity needs to be guarded—heavy backlighting, isolation of the subject in deep shadow. These have most commonly been used with felons or potential felons—such as rapists, child abusers, drug abusers. These same conventions were often used to protect PWAs against backlash, with unintended secondary consequences: they made PWAs look *as if they had something to hide, as if they were criminals.*[22] If the PWA became in some sense more visible in such encounters, he did not become *more like "us"*: his status as pariah was, if anything, reinforced. Even when the coverage is intentionally "sympathetic," the visual tropes of isolation used in journalistic coverage emphasize the PWA's status as radically different, as cut off from life (figure 4).

In addition, television and photo journalists frequently sought out the most debilitated PWAs they could find. ABC's May 1983 *20/20* coverage of AIDS is typical of such sensationalizing coverage. The segment's producer, Joe Lovett, contacted Gay Men's Health Crisis (GMHC) in New York "and promptly found several eloquent and very ill men. They didn't *look* very sick, though. In fact, some of them looked downright handsome. Lovett kept searching until he found Kenneth Ramsauer, who at 28 was dying of Kaposi's sarcoma with an unusual—and ghastly—disfiguration of his once-winsome face."[23]

Kenny Ramsauer was subsequently featured in double-page photo spreads in *Paris Match, Photo* (Paris), and the British tabloid *Sunday People* (figure 5). The uses Kenny Ramsauer was put to are the most grotesque examples of main-stream media's penchant for seeking out the most visibly ill,[24] but similar sensa-tionalizing coverage characterized most of the media's belated "discovery" of AIDS in 1983.[25]

While there were clearly many factors involved in the new attention paid to AIDS during 1983 in mainstream media, probably the most influential was the 6 May issue of the conservative, general medicine *Journal of the American Medical Association,* which provided the "hook" on which nonmedical newspapers and networks hung their subsequent stories. *JAMA* suggested, in several articles and an editorial, that the syndrome might be transmitted through *casual* (i.e., household) contacts. If this were so, then "the general population" (i.e., hetero-sexuals) might also be "at risk" for AIDS.

All hell broke loose in popular media: AIDS briefly became a topic of wide concern. In the quarter following *JAMA*'s speculations, for example, the *New York Times* published twenty articles in May 1983, twenty-eight in June, and twenty-one in July. In the four months preceding *JAMA*'s 6 May issue, they had published a total of only twelve articles on AIDS.[26] Geraldo Rivera, with his customary restraint, upped the ante on 26 May when he proclaimed on *20/20* that "every single one of us" was at risk for AIDS from contaminated blood. "You heard right," he brayed: "There is now a steadily growing fear that the nation's entire blood supply may be threatened by AIDS."[27] From this time until Rock Hudson's death in October 1985, mainstream media found an image for the illness: the moribund *AIDS victim,* who was also (magically) a demon of sexuality, actively transmitting his condition to the "general population" even as he lay dying offstage.

During 1981–85, several kinds of images countered this mainstream one. Some were private: the loving snapshots and formal portraits, home movies, and videos made by families, lovers, and friends as someone sickened, was diag-nosed, lived on, died. Such images can be found in the archives of gay and lesbian history societies, hospital AIDS unit albums, AIDS service organizations, and family and personal albums. Unlike the mainstream media images that began to appear in this period and swelled throughout the following years, these photographs emphasized *the continuities* in a PWA's life as he moved toward and through diagnosis. They deserve our careful attention, but unfortunately they are difficult to locate and reproduce.

The major source of public counterimages between 1983 and 1985 was the gay and lesbian press and AIDS service organizations (the San Francisco Kaposi's Foundation [now the San Francisco AIDS Foundation] and Gay Men's Health Crisis [New York City], were both founded in late 1982). Representations of AIDS were addressed by these groups almost exclusively in terms of *text* in the

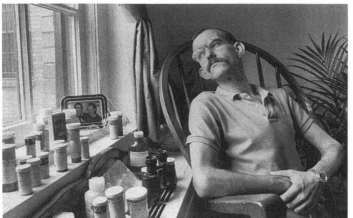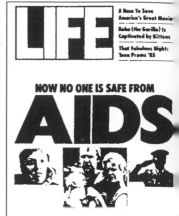

Left to right: Figure 6. Peter Sterling, photograph of David Chickadel, in "AIDS: A Diary of the Plague in America," *People Weekly* 28, no. 5 (3 August 1987): 73. Figure 7. The cover of *Life* 8, no. 8 (July 1985).

early years (their chief publications in 1983–84 were text-heavy safer-sex pamphlets) and the gay press. For them, AIDS was part of the evolution of their communities. They did not seek out subjects to picture simply because they had been diagnosed with AIDS. They were photographed because they were active, whether in gay communities at large or in emerging AIDS communities. Thus when PWAs appeared in the gay press and AIDS service organization newsletters and fund-raising appeals, they commonly appeared as whole people, not simply as *AIDS victims:* they were shown with lovers, families, caretakers. Pleasurable activities that marked their lives before and after diagnosis (gardening, weight-lifting, pets, music, leather culture) regularly figured in interviews and photographs. In gay media, PWAs' identities were not wholly collapsed into their illness as they usually were in mainstream media coverage.

This suggests some fundamental differences between mainstream media's hit-and-run approach, which records only the *current* appearance of its objects and can draw attention to their *past* only through the device of before-and-after photographs, and a community's coverage of its own. Kenny Ramsauer was quite literally *the victim* of *20/20,* which did not encourage reader identification *with* him but in fact discouraged it by reducing him to his present physical grotesqueness and contrasting that with a photograph of him *before* his illness. Community coverage by AIDS service organizations and gay newspapers, on the other hand, encouraged readers' identification with the PWA because of shared history and concerns.

Left to right: Figure 8. "Has Linda anything to fear?" (*Globe*, 13 August 1985, 20). Figure 9. Max Winter (left) and Tim Dillon (right), caption: "Ryan White (left), Matthew Kozup and his mother: The most blameless victims" ("The Social Fallout from an Epidemic," *Newsweek*, 12 August 1985, 29). Figure 10. James D. Wilson, caption: "Andrew and Helenclare: At home fighting for his life" ("A Family Gives Refuge to a Son Who Has AIDS," *Newsweek*, 12 August 1985, 24).

Such identification would of course have been possible in mainstream media's coverage; in fact, in 1985–87 it was regularly produced in covering white heterosexual PWAs and their families—AIDS's "innocent victims." It is ritually invoked every year in the ghastly "human interest," down-and-out stories that appear in city newspapers and on nighttime news between Thanksgiving and Christmas. For a single month, members of America's underclass are briefly rehabilitated as "the worthy poor," their problems treated for once as understandable and lamentable, before being returned to their usual status as invisible and incomprehensible.[28] For a host of reasons, it does not serve mainstream media's interests to regularly promote identification with the poor, gay, dying, or otherwise disenfranchised. When individual reporters do follow "victims" long enough to develop strong sympathies with them, this deviation from standard journalistic practice creates ethical problems that the more customary "hit-and-run" approach does not.[29]

1985–88

Remarkable shifts in both the quantity and nature of depictions of AIDS took place in 1985. Publicity surrounding blood banks' use of anti-HIV antibody tests because of the growing number of transfusion-related cases focused public attention on AIDS, epitomized in *Life*'s July 1985 cover story, which proclaimed, "Now No One Is Safe from AIDS" (figure 7). Rock Hudson's public admission that month that he was suffering from AIDS made the syndrome seem immediate and threatening to much of the U.S. public, for whom Hudson was a familiar figure, the quintessential manly American. If *he* could contract AIDS, couldn't anyone?[30] The fact that Hudson has continued to act—more: *to kiss* Linda Evans while taping the next season's episodes of *Dynasty* without the cast's suspecting that he was mortally ill—produced a massive outpouring of outrage and anxiety on television news and in the popular and tabloid press (figure 8).[31]

I would argue that this anxiety was a factor in producing the increasing emphasis on rigid categorizations of "risk groups" (low, high) and "*the general population*" (i.e., the population presumed *not* to be at risk). The advent of a method for detecting HTLV-III infection meant, among other things, that the threat of AIDS was no longer embodied only in people with visible lesions: it might also be your neighbor (who looked a little effeminate), your boss or secretary. . . . The invisibility of infection threw into question the comfortable categories that had kept anxieties manageable for many "low-risk" people and reinforced the need to shore them up. The anti-HTLV-III antibody assays were introduced at a time coinciding with increased reports of transfusion and hemophiliac cases of AIDS, marking the nation's invisible "carriers" of HTLV-III as internal security risks. A conservative, anti-Communist federal administration invoked containment methods recycled from ferreting out ideological impurities in the forties and fifties for purposes of epidemiologic containment: *test, test, test.*

Photographically, the (illusory) boundary between who was at risk and who was not was stressed in various ways. The media repetitiously threw up images of street prostitutes and stereotypically gay men as paradigmatic "risk group" members. "Innocent victims"—adult heterosexuals and children with AIDS—tended to be photographed surrounded by family members and animals (living or stuffed) (figure 9), as if gay men lacked both. 1985 was also the year of the first made-for-television movie about AIDS; NBC's *An Early Frost* enforced existing prejudices by returning its PWA protagonist to the bosom of his family. Evidently he lacked long-term, close-knit friends back in Manhattan; it was only after being shorn of his sexuality and his identity as a gay man that he could be returned, neutered, to his mother and father, enfolded once again within the nuclear family, and die in peace.[32] *Newsweek* also mined this rich vein of sentiment; as did countless "heartwarming" local newscasts:[33] the gay man returned to his boyhood place in the nuclear family (figure 10).

The increasing divisiveness of mainstream media coverage in 1985–86 was countered in gay communities by massive campaigns to affirm the values of gay

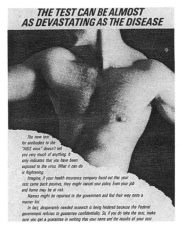

Left: Figure 11. Glenn Mansfield, "Safe Sex Calendar 1986" (Chicago: *Gay Chicago Magazine*, 1985). Middle top: Figure 12. Promotional postcard, "Join me in the Study" (New York: Gay Men's Health Crisis, 1985). Middle bottom: Figure 13. *Safer Sex Comix #2* (New York: Gay Men's Health Crisis, 1986). Right: Figure 14. Public service announcement, "The Test Can Be Almost as Devastating as the Disease" (New York: Gay Men's Health Crisis, 1985).

liberation: *re*sexualizing gay men by *re*defining sexual pleasure and sexual acts. Safer sex, as theorized by AIDS activists, could not only prevent transmission of HTLV-III (as it was still known) but also act as a cohesive force in communities increasingly under fire from the Right (now under the guise of AIDS prevention).[34] Gay safer-sex advice, begun in 1982, changed over time to accommodate new knowledge about transmission.[35] Safer-sex publications before 1985 had been exclusively textual. In 1985–86, GMHC, the San Francisco AIDS Foundation, and other AIDS service organizations began producing lively, graphically illustrated safer-sex materials. Glenn Mansfield, a Chicago gay photographer, produced a "safe sex" nude male calendar (figure 11). GMHC produced *Chance of a Lifetime* (1986), a forty-two-minute "erotic" videotape picturing a smorgasbord of safe sex (vanilla, leather, solo/masturbatory) between men of different classes, races, and what mainstream medicine and media would now term "antibody status." Recruitment materials for "The Study" (GMHC's prospective study of gay men's sexual practices) and public service announcements depicted the male body as a focus of erotic pleasure (figure 12). GMHC's series of "Safer Sex Comix" (1986), which came to public attention when Jesse Helms used them to win support for a 1987 amendment to the Senate appropriations bill to prohibit any public monies being spent on AIDS preventive education for gay men,[36] were commissioned and produced pro bono by gay artists, then distributed in New York bars (figure 13).

All these materials reaffirmed the pleasurability of gay sexuality and gay identity in the face of medicine, epidemiology, and (in their wake) popular media's massive assault on gay sexuality. At the pinnacle of medical-scientific influence, CDC epidemiologists at the first International AIDS Conference in Atlanta told gay men that they should all take the anti-HTLV-III antibody test and stop having sex with anyone whose "antibody status" differed—"as if," Cindy Patton has observed, "gay male culture is little more than a giant dating service."[37] Health and life insurance companies began calling for wholesale screening of applicants in "high-risk areas" and "high-risk occupations" (e.g., hairdressers, florists, interior designers). The military began planning their own massive screening programs of recruits and people overseas. The federal prison system began compulsory testing programs.

"Mandatory testing," the rubric under which such government programs were enacted, was in keeping with the Reagan administration's penchant for technological fixes—such as the strategic defense initiative ("Star Wars") and mandatory drug testing of federal employees. I do not intend to suggest a testing of federal employees. I do not intend to suggest a simple cause-and-effect linkage between the increased emphasis on the erotic as a *medium of information* for gay men and the distinctly chilly atmosphere created by Big Brother antibody surveillance programs in federal, state, and corporate systems: the relation between the two is much more complex. Epidemiologists, clinicians, and media "experts" advised sexually active straights and gays to find "safe" (i.e., proven antibody-negative) partners and then enter into "mutually monogamous" relationships with them. Such a model made *any* multiple-partnered sex (at this point everyone not monogamous became *promiscuous*), no matter how unrisky in terms of its practices, appear intrinsically unsafe. Heterosexual panic colored movies about marital infidelity (*Fatal Attraction*) and threatened to reduce sexual pleasure and sexual choice between men and women to the dimensions of a mortally serious job interview.[38] Yet at this time, gay institutions chose visibly to reassert the plurality and plenitude of their sexual pleasure and sexual practices *if carried out safely*. Thus the eroticized videotapes, films, and photographs that circulated increasingly after 1985 in AIDS education must be seen as a counterdiscourse to the dominant messages of science, medicine, and mainstream media.

A second counterdiscourse also became visible. People with AIDS became increasingly active in AIDS political actions and organizations, demanding that they have a voice in policy rather than being treated merely as "clients." Local PWA groups, first meeting at the annual AIDS Forum at the Lesbian and Gay Health Foundation conference in Denver, later founded the National Association of PWAs. As the need for organized opposition to draconian measures like the California LaRouche initiatives became clear,[39] PWAs led media-savvy "zaps" and other direct actions. In 1987–88, new drugs and treatments that appeared to delay the onset and severity of AIDS-related infection, that is, AZT and aerosolized pentamidine, were released slowly by the federal government and too expensive for most PWAs to purchase. ACT UP, the AIDS Coalition to Unleash Power, was founded in 1987 in reaction to federal foot dragging at the National Institutes of Health and Food and Drug Administration. It conducts AIDS direct actions in many U.S. cities. In short, the "AIDS victim" stereotype has never been less accurate (though probably in consequence of that all the more necessary: these people are *so unruly!*) than in the period extending from 1987 to the present.

As counters to mainstream media's one-note depiction of PWAs as *victims,* individual photographers working on self-assignment, as well as for leftist photojournals and AIDS service organizations, produced portraits of PWAs that were recognizably "positive images" reflecting the historical moment. The work of two women photographers suggests the sorts of uses such photographs have been put to. Gypsy Ray (Santa Cruz, Calif.) and Jane Rosett (Brooklyn, N.Y.) began making photographs of PWAs in the mid-1980s. Both Ray's and Rosett's photographs were intended primarily to serve instrumental purposes: Ray's illustrated fund-raising and other appeals for the San Francisco AIDS Foundation and Hospice of San Francisco (figure 15), and Rosett's appeared, for example, in Left press coverage of AIDS activism and the New York City PWA Coalition's valuable guide to living with AIDS, *Surviving and Thriving with AIDS* (figures 16, 17).[40]

Significantly, neither of these photographers' work was originally produced for viewing outside contexts sympathetic and committed to the struggle around AIDS. Nor were they designed to be viewed as images independent of text: Ray's were framed by the institutional message accompanying them, while Rosett's were captioned in photojournalistic style. Unlike mainstream press and television images of PWAs in 1985–88, Ray's subjects were usually photographed in domestic settings (rather than backlit against windows or silhouetted against studio backdrops), which emphasized their participation in life rather than their isolation from it.[41] Unlike mainstream mediamakers, Ray directed attention to PWAs as people living with a medical condition rather than dying from it. She also directed attention to their caregivers, the people who assisted them in living independently: health care workers, volunteers from Shanti and Hospice, lovers, and friends.

Left to right: Figure 15. Gypsy Ray, photograph used in "AIDS Home Care and Hospice Program" pamphlet (Visiting Nurses Association of San Francisco, n.d.). Figure 16. Jane Rosett, "PWA David Summers and his lover Sal Licata (center, in leather jackets and berets, L-R) join other protesters to denounce the *New York Post*'s inflammatory AIDS coverage" (in Michael Callen, *Surviving and Thriving with AIDS*, vol. 1), 88. Figure 17. Jane Rosett, "David Summers poses wearing a bizarre mask and pearls outside his hospital room at NYU Co-op Care. A mix-up in 'Davids' had caused the rumor to spread that David Summers had died. He issued the following press statement: 'Rumors of my death have been greatly exaggerated' " (in Michael Callen, *Surviving and Thriving with AIDS*, vol. 1), 98.

I don't mean to suggest that Ray's work lacked problems;[42] only that whatever problems it had derived from the tradition of formal photographic portrait that Ray used and not from an unfamiliarity with her subject or a naïveté about her photographs' possible uses.

Rosett's photographs also filled in many gaps in the mainstream's usual representations of PWAs. They documented PWAs' political and social activity: testifying before New York State legislative committees, picketing and protesting, partying, goofing off. As a counter to the widespread (I'm tempted to say definitive) media image of the PWA-at-the-window-watching-life-go-by-without-him, Rosett's photographs constituted a significant body of evidence for AIDS not as an identity, but as a condition that people live with.

The marks on the face of a leper, a syphilitic, someone with AIDS are the signs of a progressive mutation, dissolution; something organic.

—Susan Sontag, *AIDS and Its Metaphors*[43]

ALL THINGS MELLOW IN THE MIND,
A SLEIGHT OF HAND, A TRICK OF TIME
AND EVEN OUR GREAT LOVE WILL FADE
SOON WE'LL BE STRANGERS IN THE GRAVE.

THAT'S WHY THIS MOMENT IS SO DEAR,
I KISS YOUR LIPS, AND WE ARE HERE
SO LET'S HOLD TIGHT, AND TOUCH AND FEEL
FOR THIS QUICK INSTANT WE ARE REAL.

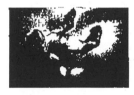

The unfortunate man could not touch the one he loved. It had been declared illegal by the government. Slowly his fingers became toes and his hands gradually became feet. He began to wear shoes on his hands to hide his shame. It never occurred to him to break the law.

Figure 18. Duane Michals, *You Are Gone* (*Christopher Street*, no. 95 [December 1984]).

It was also in 1985–86 that photographers working primarily within the artisanal system of galleries, museums, and art schools and colleges began circulating their photographs of AIDS. In the world of art, often viewed by its participants as "above" or "away from" the fray of politics, photographs expressed different things about AIDS. The photographic strategies employed by, for example, Duane Michals, Rosalind Solomon, and Nicholas Nixon were all different, as were their politics and their experience with AIDS and the mostly gay men who appeared in their AIDS photographs. But all three spoke the central discourse of modernist art photography—that the subject of art is the artist's feelings. There are undeniable attractions to such a stance at this point in time. One of the things that living on any sort of familiar terms with AIDS does is dull one's feelings, make numbness seem intermittently desirable. In theory, I have come to like the idea of photographs that court feelings, that speak to communal and personal loss. I think Michals's AIDS images are a step in this direction (figure 18)—acts of mourning, affirmations of the persistence of desire in the face of death.

This brings me to the portraits of PWAs by Nixon and Solomon (figures 19–21).[44] Critics, particularly gay ones,[45] have had a difficult time pinpointing the unease these photographs produce. During Nixon's 1988 MOMA show, members of New York's AIDS activist group, ACT UP, staged a protest in the gallery where Nixon's AIDS portraits were hung. They handed out a flyer:

NO MORE PICTURES WITHOUT CONTEXT

We believe that the representation of people with AIDS (PWAS) affects not only how viewers will perceive PWAS outside the museum, but, ultimately, crucial issues of AIDS funding, legislation, and education.

The artist's choice to produce representational work always affects more than a single artist's career, going beyond issues of curatorship, beyond the walls on which an artist's work is displayed.

Ultimately, representations affect those portrayed.

In portraying PWAS as people to be pitied or feared, as people alone and lonely, we believe that this show perpetuates general misconceptions about AIDS without addressing the realities of those of us living every day with this crisis as PWAS and people who love PWAS.

FACT. Many PWAS now live longer after diagnosis due to experimental drug treatments, better information about nutrition and holistic health care, and due to the efforts of PWAS engaged in a continuing battle to define and save their lives.

FACT: The majority of AIDS cases in New York City are among people of color, especially women. Typically, women do not live long after diagnosis because of lack of access to affordable health care, a primary care physician, or even basic information about what to do if you have AIDS.

The PWA is a human being whose health has deteriorated not simply due to a virus, but due to government inaction, the inaccessibility of affordable health care, and institutionalized neglect in the forms of heterosexism, racism, and sexism.

We demand the visibility of PWAS who are vibrant, angry, loving, sexy, beautiful, acting up and fighting back.

STOP LOOKING AT US; START LISTENING TO US.

ACT UP is undoubtedly right to challenge Nixon's motives in choosing his particular subjects, since his choice amounts to a statement that AIDS is identical to a death sentence.[46] Such a proposition is medically and historically inaccurate. It depends for its "power" on a highly selective process of choosing subjects and on people's credulity before "documentary" images. I also question the ethical value of building up a body of such single-mindedly bleak work *as a project.* "[It] may stop in a year or so . . . when I figure I have enough for a book."[47] But the challenge to Nixon's work should be aimed even deeper—at the ways that Nixon (and Solomon) use these photographs to foreground *their own experience* in photographing PWAS: they make it sound as if they were stalking rare animals at great emotional cost to themselves. The photographs then become the evidence of their bravery.

Solomon began photographing PWAS after completing projects on nursing homes and the homeless. She recalls conversations with PWAS "about art ex-

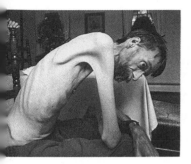 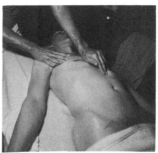 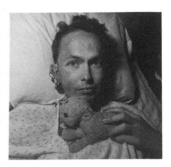

Left to right: Figure 19. Nicholas Nixon, *People with AIDS: Donald Perham* (1987). Figure 20. Rosalind Solomon, 111 (n.d.), from *Portraits in the Time of AIDS* (New York: Gray Art Gallery and Study Center, New York University, 1988). Figure 21. Rosalind Solomon, XXI (n.d.), from *Portraits in the Time of AIDS.*

hibits, rafting trips, and Fellini films. . . . There was little talk of death; the tone, the words were life."[48] How strange—Nixon found the same thing: that several of his subjects were witty, educated, enjoyable men. This discovery, of course, made the project more difficult *for him:* we are in the land here of photographs-as-mirrors-of-the-artist's-soul.

It is this, finally, that makes Solomon's and Nixon's work so inadequate, so irrelevant: it tells us nothing about the historic battles surrounding AIDS and its representation; it challenges none of the existing conventions that have led to PWAs being shunned, snubbed, hurt; it leaves us with very little to grasp but the photographer's sensibility.

But that tiny gift is precisely what art photography encourages. "Nixon has reached out to his subjects with his honesty and concern," one critic wrote, and another, "Nixon literally and figuratively moves in so close we're convinced that his subjects hold nothing back. The viewer marvels at the trust between photographer and subject."[49] Thomas Sokolowski tells us that Solomon "*enabled the sitter* not only to participate . . . but also to shed *the expected role of victim* [expected by *whom?*—my emphasis]." Solomon, he writes, "*lets* [each PWA] . . . shout out, 'I'm still here!' [my emphasis]."[50] *Photographer as lion-hearted explorer of emotional jungles, our surrogate witness to pain, enabler of victims. . . .*

The photographer may be an intrepid explorer of the unknown, but even while critics supportive of Nixon and Solomon praise them for taking us to terra not very cognita, they are quick to deny that there's anything distinctly different about the condition of the photographers' subjects: it's the *human condition,* isn't it? Owen Edwards approvingly quotes a friend looking at Nixon's work in San

Francisco: "This show isn't about AIDS, it's about mortality." Edwards himself writes, "These six people, who know they are dying, are not really much different from each of us, who are dying, too, but (if we're lucky) don't have to think about it just yet."[51] Solomon tells us, "Because all life leads inevitably to death, these pictures are about all of us,"[52] and Sokolowski, curator of her exhibition, tells us that Solomon's portraits are "portraits *of the human condition* [my emphasis]." The title to his essay on her work is "Looking in a Mirror." Precisely: this is what art photography encourages its practitioners and viewers to value—the artifact as mirror to its maker's soul.

If we accept these confused propositions at face value, we're to believe on the one hand that these photographs have merit because it took extraordinary courage to obtain them, and on the other that what they represent is something we all know and live every day. Formulations like "each of us [is] dying, too" function not to console the dying (they don't) or to acknowledge their difference but rather to cancel it out, to deny it. Critics and curators who tell us that these photographs are about all of us do so at the expense of people who are now ill and dying. Sokolowski twice quotes George Whitmore's "I see Jim—and that could be me there. It's a mirror. It's not a victim-savior relationship. We're the same person. *We're just on different sides of the fence* [my emphasis]." I would suggest that being on "different sides of the fence" is not "just" a small difference—it is a matter of great importance. Sokolowski distances himself from this fact about Solomon's subjects through formal analysis ("Solomon forces the viewer to contemplate the formal differences between the haphazard pattern of facial lesions and the thoughtful placement of the buttons fastened to the man's pullover. Each in its way, lesion or badge, is a symbol, a mark of distinction, one more indelible than the other") and through comparing them to art-historical references ("Splayed out along the picture plane, the subject recalls numerous Venuses and majas within the history of art"). Sokolowski, Solomon, and Edwards emphasize *the similarities* between PWAs and us at a time when *the differences* have serious consequences for the lives of the people in question.

These photographs belong to no current debates on the representation of the PWA, dominant or counter. They reflect no understanding of the complicated history of PWAs' attempts to *name themselves,* to assert their rights, or of the accumulated meanings surrounding mainstream media images that PWAs struggle to oppose. Their crude emphasis on physically debilitated or disfigured PWAs most closely resembles the choices made by popular media three and four years ago in emphasizing *their difference* from the rest of us. For all these reasons, their photographs are irrelevant to current attempts to define what AIDS means—whether by organized AIDS activists and PWAs, mainstream journalists, Bush administration policy makers, the federal Immigration and Naturalization Ser-

Table 2

	Agencies Who Had Employees Who Had Died from AIDS	Agencies Who Had *Not* Had Employees Who Died from AIDS
Would your agency hire an "openly homosexual" job candidate today?	78% yes	50% yes
Would you allow an HIV-infected employee with no symptoms to remain on the job?	91% yes	63% yes
If an employee exhibited AIDS symptoms, would you retain him/her?	74% yes	47% yes
Do you agree with current medical opinion that AIDS is transmitted in three ways: through sexual contact, exposure to infected blood/blood components, or prenatally from mother to unborn child?	83% yes	54% yes
Do you believe the presence of an employee with AIDS might cause coworkers to leave the agency?	13% yes	48% yes[55]

vice, the Social Security Administration, ad infinitum. Nixon's and Solomon's photographs appeal to audiences who believe that art *is* about "timeless realities," "enduring values," "the human condition"—viewers who prefer wispy abstractions to the historical and specific. The specific historical formations, for example, those of class, gender, politics, medicine, and culture, that make the position of PWAs different from mine are precisely the differences that art photography is said to transcend. These are precisely the differences that it does not.

This essay originally began here. Now it is a more fitting ending.

One of the most commonly voiced convictions among photojournalists and art photographers making portraits of PWAs is that such images can teach lessons: help other people avoid a similar fate, teach us our common fate, "humanize the disease, to make it a little bit less something that people see at arms length [*sic*]."[53]

This is a goal that has never been reached. Even in a city as saturated by media images of PWAs as San Francisco, researchers at the City and County Department of Public Health have concluded that media messages (posters, television and radio spots, billboards, newspaper advertisements) do not account for the decline of new HIV infections after 1985—watching one's friends and lovers grow sick and die was.[54] Other cities that began their AIDS prevention media campaigns earlier in the course of their epidemics have found the same thing: media messages have no significant impact on the rising incidence of AIDS in their communities. The experience of watching friends and lovers grow sick and die does.

There is no reason to think that other didactic purposes are better served by photographs. A telling example of the importance of personal experience appeared last week in *Advertising Age,* this time in relation to AIDS in the workplace. Crane Publications, *Ad Age*'s publisher, surveyed the opinions of senior executives from advertising agencies, media, and marketing companies. Ad executives' responses were divided into those from agencies who had had employees dying from AIDS and those who had not, as given in Table 2.

The survey in Table 2, like the San Francisco studies, shows that *personal experience,* not media messages (and who would have more of an investment in crediting the power of media messages than advertising executives?), makes the critical difference in changing people's beliefs and behavior.

This is not a heartening message for public-policy officials or photographers who justify making portraits of PWAs in the belief that "everyone who sees the photographs will be changed . . . and our collective understanding be advanced."[56] But it does justify our reply to all such assertions: *Then you're naive: what you want to accomplish has no basis in our experience.*

Notes

1 Emmanuel Dreuilhe, *Mortal Embrace: Living with AIDS* (New York: Hill & Wang, 1988), 122.

2 Unfortunately, the term by which sick-gay-man-(with AIDS) is opposed—i.e., healthy homosexual—has yet to be conceded in most of the fields we will look at, including the gay press. The opposite of gay PWA remains sick homosexual: the idea of healthy homosexual remains apparently inexpressible. This is no less true in gay communities (pace Susan Sontag), where psychologizing the "sick" nature of the PWA has produced *internalized homophobia, repressed anger, Type-A personality,* etc., as symptoms of the underlying (i.e., gay) illness.

3 See Jan Zita Grover, "AIDS: Keywords," *October,* no. 43 (1988): 17–30 (reprinted in *AIDS: Cultural Analysis/Cultural Activism,* ed. Douglas Crimp [Cambridge, Mass.: MIT Press, 1988], and revised in *The State of the Language,* ed. Leonard Michaels and Christo-

pher Ricks [Berkeley and Los Angeles: University of California Press, 1990]), for notes on the distinction between disease as sign and symptom of AIDS vs. sign/symptom as a disease itself.

4 Several thoughtful attempts to make sense out of the bewildering volume of data on the AIDS epidemic can be recommended: Dennis Altman's *AIDS in the Mind of America* (Garden City, N.Y.: Doubleday, 1985); Cindy Patton's *Sex and Germs: The Politics of AIDS* (Boston: South End, 1985); Randy Shilts's *And the Band Played On: Politics, People, and the AIDS Epidemic* (New York: St. Martin's, 1987), though this should be read critically in light of Shilts's method and biases; Paul Treichler's "AIDS, Homophobia, and Biomedical Discourse: An Epidemic of Signification," in *Cultural Analysis/Cultural Activism*, 31–70, and "AIDS, Gender, and Biomedical Discourse: Current Contents for Meaning," in *AIDS: The Burdens of History*, ed. Elizabeth Fee and Daniel M. Fox (Berkeley and Los Angeles: University of California Press, 1988), 190–266, are goldmines of references as well as provocative interpretations.

5 Meyrig Horton and Peter Aggleton, "Perverts, Inverts, and Experts: The Cultural Production of an AIDS Research Paradigm," in *AIDS: Social Representations and Social Practices*, ed. Peter Aggleton, Graham Hart, and Peter Davies (Barcombe, East Sussex: Falmer, 1989), 74–100. Ludwik Fleck, *Genesis and Development of a Scientific Fact* (1935; reprint, Chicago: University of Chicago Press, 1979).

6 See also Noam Chomsky and Edward Herman, *Manufacturing Consent: The Political Economy of the Mass Media* (New York: Pantheon, 1989), which comes at the same problem from a different perspective. Chomsky and Herman locate what Fleck, Horton, and Aggleton see as the prestige of related discourses as the prestige of particular experts/ authorities. This begs the question of how X becomes designated as an expert and Y does not, a question that Fleck et al.'s analysis of institutional discourses answers more effectively.

7 Institute of Medicine, National Academy of Sciences, *Confronting AIDS: Update 1988* (Washington, D.C.: National Academy Press, 1988), 4–5.

8 Ibid.

9 GRID: gay-related immune deficiency; CAID: community acquired immune deficiency; AID: acquired immune deficiency; WOG (a gay black-humor term): wrath of god.

10 See Jan Zita Grover, "Safer Sex Guidelines," *Jump Cut*, no. 33 (1987): 118–22, and "Reading AIDS," in *Social Representations and Social Practices*, 252–63.

11 Simon Watney's work on AIDS employs a psychoanalytic framework and provides some very persuasive readings of the seemingly *homophobic* reactions to AIDS as arising instead from defense of the (seemingly a)historical heterosexual family unit (see *Policing Desire: Pornography, AIDS, and the Media* [Minneapolis: University of Minnesota Press, 1987]; and Jeffrey Weeks, *Sexuality and Its Discontents: Meanings, Myths and Modern Sexualities* [London: Routledge & Kegan Paul, 1985]).

12 Treichler, "AIDS, Gender, and Biomedical Discourse," 196.

13 The whole question of what is and isn't significant in epidemiological surveillance is a fascinating subject and one explored with great subtlety by Jacques Leibowitch in his *A Strange Virus of Unknown Origin* (Paris: Flammarion, 1984; New York: Ballantine, 1985).

Leibowitch was one of the immunologists responsible for the isolation of LAV (the Pasteur Institute virus known in the United States as HTLV-III and now known internationally as HIV-1).

14 Ibid., xvi.

15 A second example of the distinctly Anglo-American (and homotropic) bias in defining AIDS in the United States was the medical-scientific establishment's dismissal of evidence from Africa and former African colonial powers (e.g., Belgium and France) that AIDS was evenly distributed between the sexes in Central Africa.

16 *Naming* in science is a means of establishing ownership, hence the multitude of names under which this retrovirus has been known: LAV (Luc Montagnier, Pasteur Institute), HTLV-III (Robert Gallo, NCI), ARV (AIDS-related virus: Jay Levy, University of California-San Francisco), IDAV (immune deficiency-associated virus), HTLV-III/LAV (an American compromise acknowledging the equivalence of the French virus to the American), and LAV/HTLV-III (a French compromise acknowledging the equivalence of the American virus to the French), culminating in that internationalist, HIV (human immunodeficiency virus), christened in 1986 as a replacement for HTLV-III/LAV and LAV/HTLV-III. Most clinicians and just about everyone else have cut right through all that to the dreaded heart of the matter: they call it the *AIDS virus*. Problems with this are discussed in Grover, "AIDS: Keywords," 21.

17 I'm not suggesting here that what publishers choose to print is necessarily what readers want or embrace. The *New York Native* is an interesting case in point. Its AIDS coverage through 1986 was far more comprehensive than that of any other gay paper and was followed closely in, e.g., San Francisco and London, despite the fact that it is basically a Manhattan "city" paper.

When its publisher's personal conviction that HIV had nothing to do with the etiology of AIDS resulted in the paper altering the emphasis of its AIDS coverage to searches for new "causes" for AIDS, including swine flu, mosquito-borne viruses, malaria, and syphilis, those readers who believed that HIV was the principal causative agent of AIDS ceased reading the paper. The *New York Native* still publishes and is still read, but the *audience* for its AIDS coverage has changed markedly. Its preeminent AIDS reporter, Ann Guiducci Fettner, who had no use for Charles Ortleb's theories, also left. Thus any account of the gay press's response to AIDS would have to factor in a complex interaction between what is published and how it is received.

18 I call attention to this term because "AIDS" is *not* itself transmissible, despite mainstream media's reckless use of such phrases as *catching AIDS, taking the AIDS test,* and *the AIDS virus* suggest. For more on this distinction, see Grover, "AIDS: Keywords."

19 Nathan Fain, "How Infectious Is AIDS?" *Advocate,* 23 June 1983. Fain's article was occasioned by the 6 May 1983 *JAMA* issue I discuss below.

20 For example, Randy Shilts, "TV Studio Turmoil over AIDS," *San Francisco Chronicle,* 15 June 1983, 8; Michael Hechtman and Jack Peritz, "TV Crew Nixes Show with an AIDS Victim," *New York Post,* 31 July 1985; Jay Sharbutt, "TV Crew Facing the AIDS Issue," *Los Angeles Times,* 10 September 1985, sec. 6, pp. 1, 8. Stuart Marshall comments sarcastically on these episodes in his important AIDS videotape *Bright Eyes* (1984).

21 See *The Denver Principles* (1983) of the group that became the National Association of People With AIDS: "We condemn attempts to label us as 'victims,' which implies defeat, and we are only occasionally 'patients,' which implies passivity, helplessness and dependence upon others. We are people with AIDS."

22 Stuart Marshall uses/inverts this device in *Bright Eyes*. See also Martha Gever's discussion of the tape, "Pictures of Sickness: Stuart Marshall's *Bright Eyes*," in *Cultural Analysis/Cultural Activism*, 122–23.

23 Nathan Fain, "AIDS and the Media: Rating the Crisis Coverage," *Advocate*, 29 September 1983. Stuart Marshall decisively deconstructed the media's use of Kenny Ramsauer in *Bright Eyes*. See also Watney's discussion in *Policing Desire*.

24 For example, Jean Carlomusto, audiovisual director of GMHC, reports that she decided to become actively involved in producing counterimages to mainstream media's after she saw a *New York Times* reporter reject the host of GMHC's New York Cable show as the subject of a PWA report "because he looked too healthy." Similarly, Michael Callen, diagnosed with AIDS in 1983, has spoken frequently of being rejected as a subject for media reportage because he "doesn't look like a PWA" (i.e., moribund).

25 See Dorothy Nelkin, *Science in the Streets: Report of the Twentieth Century Fund Task Force on the Communication of Scientific Risk* (New York: Priority, 1984), 87–95.

26 Ibid., 87.

27 Rodger Streitmatter, "The Bad-News Bearers: Lowlights of AIDS Summer '83," *Quill* 72, no. 5 (May 1984): 25.

28 The classic text discussing this in relation to photographs is Martha Rosler's "In, Around, and Afterthoughts (on Documentary Photography)," in *Martha Rosler, 3 Works* (Halifax: Press of Nova Scotia College of Art and Design, 1981), 59–89. For local examples of traditional documentary in action, see Jan Zita Grover, "The Inadequacy of Systems," *Artweek* (24 January 1987): 11, "Representing the 'Victim,' " *Artweek* (6 September 1986): 14, and "Documenting Documents and Processing Reality: the Photographs of Jim Goldberg," *In These Times* (29 January–4 February 1986).

29 Laurie Garrett, "When Death Is the End of the Story: Reporters Describe the Troubling Problems They Face in Covering the Mortally Ill," *Columbia Journalism Review* 27, no. 5 (1989): 41–42.

30 Treichler, "AIDS, Gender, and Biomedical Discourse," quotes a man "interviewed by *USA Today*," who said, "I thought AIDS was a gay disease, but if Rock Hudson can get it, I guess anyone can" (p. 205).

31 For example, "Fear & AIDS in Hollywood," *People Weekly* 23, no. 13 (23 September 1985); "AIDS Panic: Fury in Hollywood over Suspect Stars on Top Television Shows," *Star*, 10 September 1985; "Has Linda Anything to Fear?" *Globe* 13 August 1985, 20; "Linda Evans & *Dynasty* Cast Terrified—He Kissed Her on Show," *National Enquirer*, 13 August 1985; "AIDS Panic on *Dynasty* over Rock's Last Love Scenes," *Star*, 24 September 1985; "He Vows: Doctors Cleared Me for *Dynasty* Love Scenes," *Star*, 24 September 1985 (where no page numbers are given, these are cover quotations). Letters poured in to the popular newsweeklies; readers clearly felt betrayed by Hudson's suddenly changed "identity." How much of their anger was displaced from this source onto the *Dynasty* kisses (or vice versa) isn't clear.

32 For a broad survey of broadcast television and independent video work on AIDS through 1987, see Timothy Landers, "Bodies and Anti-Bodies: A Crisis in Representation," *Independent* 11, no. 1 (January–February 1988): 18–24.

33 For example, "A Family Gives Refuge to a Son Who Has AIDS," *Newsweek*, 12 August 1985, 24.

34 See Patton, *Sex and Germs,* and "Resistance and the Erotic: Reclaiming History, Setting Strategy as We Face AIDS," *Radical America* 20, no. 6 (September 1987): 68–78; and Douglas Crimp, "How to Have Promiscuity in an Epidemic," in *Cultural Analysis/Cultural Activism,* 237–70.

35 Richard Berkowitz, Michael Callen, and Richard Dworkin's *How to Have Sex in an Epidemic* (New York: News from the Front, 1983), Lawrence Mass, M.D.'s, several editions of *Medical Answers about AIDS* (New York: Gay Men's Health Crisis, 1983), and GMHC's *AIDS Newsletter* (1983, 1984) provide documentary evidence of the sophistication of gay men in evolving safer sexual practices without benefit of the federal government's testing programs.

36 See Grover, "Safer Sex Guidelines."

37 Patton, "Resistance and the Erotic," 69.

38 A striking feature of the pop "safer-sex" manuals written for heterosexuals after 1986 is their emphasis on the necessity of "interviewing" sexual prospects. Dr. Art Ulene ("The Today Show's Physician") actually provides "the questions you should ask to help determine just how risky your partner is for the AIDS virus" (pp. 34–35), hypothetical cases to test your savvy at risk assessment (pp. 39–53), and a table for "Estimating a Sex Partner's Risk for AIDS" (pp. 64–65), in *Safe Sex in a Dangerous World* (New York: Vintage, 1987). Helen Singer Kaplan jumps through similar hoops in *The Real Truth about Women and AIDS: How To Eliminate the Risks without Giving Up Love and Sex* (New York: Fireside/ Simon & Schuster, 1987).

39 These were proposed measures for mandatory testing and reporting and optional quarantine of PWAs that appeared on the general election ballots in California in 1986 (Proposition 69), 1987 (Proposition 64), and 1988 (Proposition 96 and 102). All but Proposition 96 were voted down by California voters by resounding majorities.

40 Michael Callen, ed., *Surviving and Thriving with AIDS,* vol. 2 (New York: PWA Coalition, 1988); vol. 1 was published in 1987 and is out of print.

41 I spent six months working with Tom Waddell, founder of the Gay Games, after his diagnosis with AIDS. Because of Waddell's prominence in San Francisco's gay community, he was frequently interviewed, taped, and photographed. Waddell's house was a huge turn-of-the-century turnverein in the Mission District—a distinctive and novel home, with the old gymnasium serving as a living room used for many fund-raising and political events.

When the *San Francisco Examiner* sent a reporter and photographer to interview Waddell about four months before he died, the photographer chose to seat Tom in front of a backlit, venetian-blinded window, posed at a right angle to the window. Although I could see the classic *AIDS victim* shot that the photographer was setting up, I had no right to intervene in the shoot. I can't describe the peculiar pain it gave me to know what was happening and yet to say nothing. The resulting photograph showed a gaunt man in high, Rembrandt-like sidelighting with the bars of the blinds cutting dramatically across his face and upper body.

42 See my review of Gypsy Ray's work in Grover, "Representing the 'Victim.' "

43 Susan Sontag, *AIDS and Its Metaphors* (New York: Farrar, Straus, Giroux, 1989), 41.

44 Nicholas Nixon's photographs of PWAs appeared in his retrospective exhibition at the Museum of Modern Art last fall as well as at his dealers' galleries. One series of these appears in *Nicholas Nixon: Pictures of People* (Boston: Little, Brown/New York Graphic Society, 1988). Rosalind Solomon's photographs of PWAs appeared in a May–July 1988 exhibition at the Gray Art Gallery, New York University. A selection appears in the catalog *Portraits in the Time of AIDS* with text by Thomas W. Sokolowski (New York: Gray Art Gallery and Study Center, New York University, 1988).

45 Here I am speaking of Douglas Crimp, Robert Atkins, Deborah Bright, and myself.

46 In an informal talk at MOMA last October, Nixon said that he had turned down some of the PWAs who had contacted him about participating in his project because he didn't find them interesting looking. If his exhibition is any indication, *interesting* PWAs are ones who bear visible signs of their mortality.

47 Nixon, audiotape made at MOMA, 11 October 1988.

48 Solomon, artist's statement, *Portraits in the Time of AIDS*, n.p.

49 Quoted by Douglas Crimp at the conference "AIDS: Crisis and Criticism," University of Western Ontario, London, Canada, 10–12 November 1988.

50 Sokolowski, "Looking in a Mirror," in *Portraits in the Time of AIDS*, n.p.

51 Owen Edwards, "Mortal Vision: Nicholas Nixon Shows Us the Condition We're In," *American Photographer* 21, no. 6 (December 1988): 19.

52 Solomon, *Portraits in the Time of AIDS*, n.p.

53 Nicholas Nixon, artist's statement, "*People with AIDS: Donald Perhan* (1987)," in *AIDS: The Artists' Response*, ed. Jan Zita Grover (exhibition catalog) (Columbus: University Gallery of Fine Arts, Ohio State University, 1988), 45.

54 Patricia E. Evans, G. W. Rutherford, J. W. Amory, and N. A. Hessol, "Does Health Education Work? Publicly Funded AIDS Education in San Francisco" (paper presented at the Fourth International AIDS Conference, Stockholm, 1988), 1:364 (Abstract 6044). See also Stephen F. Morin, "Behavior Change and Prevention of Sexual Transmission of HIV" (paper presented at the Fourth International AIDS Conference, Stockholm, 1988), 1:368 (Abstract 6058), which found "perceived threat" the most critical early factor in gay men's changes in sexual behavior.

55 Questions paraphrased to save space. Thomas J. Tyrer, "AIDS: AA Survey Shows Workplace Concern," *Advertising Age* 60, no. 15 (3 April 1989): 1, 22, 27.

56 Sokolowski, "Looking in a Mirror," n.p.

Pee Wee Herman

The Homosexual Subtext

Bruce La Bruce

An examination of contemporary issues of comedy would be incomplete without taking into consideration the meaning behind Pee Wee Herman, a comedian who, amid the macho posturing of the current male Hollywood stars, has somehow managed to generate a phenomenal mystique around his unique reworking of the classic ninety-eight-pound weakling image. In direct opposition to the despicably hypermasculine bravado of the other comedy superstar of the present era, Eddie Murphy, whose notorious homophobia, rivaling Anita Bryant's, has become an obligatory part of his screen persona (his annoying, mincing fag imitations), Pee Wee champions the milquetoast quarter, providing a hero who's not afraid to cry when his bike gets stolen, and who actually uses his pantywaist status to the utmost advantage, outsmarting any number of lumbering hulks with his wacky, unpredictable, and, most importantly, "sexually suspect" antics. Pee Wee is the new underdog whose sexual ambivalence both places him squarely in this position, and serves as his greatest strength, his secret, naughty world penetrating the unconscious of a rigid and repressed popular audience that doesn't quite grasp the insurrectionary purposes behind the Pee Wee pose.

I want to concentrate mostly on the sexual significance of the Pee Wee Herman persona, a dimension largely avoided (or altogether missed) by "serious" critics and pop reviewers alike, and the way he uses comedy as a strategy of rebellion. To this end, Freud's *Wit and Its Relation to the Unconscious,* a work, itself, not without a sense of humor, will provide a useful theoretical background for the analysis of Pee Wee.

The failure of critics to come to terms with Pee Wee Herman can be partly attributed to a reluctance to deal with the implications of an implicitly gay icon who is adored by children, and whose appeal cuts across a surprisingly wide range of youth subcultures—punks, skateboard and BMX kids, even the black rap faction, rappers Joeski Love immortalizing him in their "Pee Wee's Dance" record and video. Pee Wee makes parents (and critics) nervous because he is strange, perverse, aberrant—not only an adult who acts, resolutely, like a smart alecky kid, but an androgynous one as well, who wears pancake makeup, rouge, and a hint of lipstick, and talks in a weird falsetto—hardly a role model for the sensible youth of today. Critics shy away from acknowledging the homosexual connotations; a typical response from *Film Comment* suggests that " . . . if Pee Wee has to have an inordinate number of handsome young men on the show, that's his business. You just have to take *Pee Wee's Playhouse* [his Saturday morning kid's show] at face value."[1] Most accounts of Pee Wee I've read[2] restrict themselves to describing the comedian's crazy behavior and the décor of his television show set, or digress into a nostalgia about the writer's own childhood, expressing relief that Pee Wee's silliness permits them to forgo any ideological analysis. There is also an aspect of resentment at work over not having access to the lexicon that Pee Wee has developed—an aggressive mixture of childspeak and gay references that confounds critical reading—a good measure of the success of Pee Wee's radical project.

It should be made clear that when I speak of Pee Wee Herman's "gayness," it's not the actual sexual status of Paul Reubens, the comedian behind the persona, that is, particularly, at issue (or Pee Wee's, either, for that matter), but rather the "homosexual subtext," the disguised allusions to a gay sensibility that inform both Pee Wee's television show and his first big screen vehicle, *Pee Wee's Big Adventure*. In the tradition of classical Hollywood, Reubens maintains his star image (as Pee Wee) whenever he is in the public eye (talk shows, interviews, etc.), never allowing the private person to emerge, a "strategy" that has, itself, become a subject of controversy and promoted much conjecture. It might be assumed, then, that Reubens (like Rock Hudson, e.g.) is concealing something (like homosexuality) that might impede his career, or jeopardize his popular acceptance, particularly as the host of a nationally broadcast children's show. This does not, however, prevent the hidden personality, or the significance of its "repression," from making itself felt in the constructed persona, the split between the private and the public becoming, in fact, an important aspect of it. Reubens has chosen to have both his own sexuality, and that of his comic creation, remain ambiguous; the proof of a gay point of reference lies in the images he presents us with.

As the reviewer from *Film Comment* nervously points out, Pee Wee does surround himself with attractive men on his show, a fact not necessarily revealing in itself until one realizes that each represents a specific gay male icon, prominent fantasy figures in homosexual pornography (although in the context of the Play-house, made human and friendly), including the sailor (Captain Carl), the black cowboy (Cowboy Curtis), and the muscular, scantily clad lifeguard (Tito), not to mention the escaped con (Mickey) in *Pee Wee's Big Adventure*. The latter example in particular provides an explicit reference to gay fantasy as Pee Wee, hitchhiking on a deserted highway, is picked up by the handsome, swarthy Mickey, reckless and ready for anything after a long stretch in the big-house. The two quickly establish a complicity in their contempt for the law before a police roadblock conveniently provides Pee Wee with the opportunity to dress up as Mickey's girlfriend to confound the authorities. This instance of drag, along with his brief appearance as a nun near the end of the film, takes Pee Wee's sexual ambivalence to its logical extreme, the nun, in particular, a dead giveaway in its appeal to the irreverent gay camp aesthetic. That the character, in the context of the narrative, is a "boy" named Pee Wee who uses drag to retrieve his stolen bike, his most precious possession, adds a disturbing twist to the "conventional" campiness of cross-dressing, presenting it, instead, as another aspect of Pee Wee's rebellion against authority. For those who think the idea of a homosexual subtext in Pee Wee Herman is an instance of "reading into" the material, con-sider Mickey's lascivious smile, looking him up and down, as Pee Wee flounces in his "cute little outfit" (as the policeman calls it) long after the roadblock has been passed, or Pee Wee, at the end of the film, giving Mickey, behind bars once more, a hotdog, saying "one footlong," and winking coyly. Sure, there's a file in it, but the double entendre is unmistakable.

The camp sensibility extends beyond these small but significant instances of drag, encompassing, also, Pee Wee's love of the world of retro objects and extra-neous gizmos (which fill his Playhouse and his home in the *Big Adventure*) and the Pee Wee persona itself. Camp, according to Susan Sontag, relies on the extravagant, the exaggerated, and the theatrical, all of which apply to Pee Wee and his playthings, and on a certain innocence, such that it "discloses innocence, but also, when it can, corrupts it."[3] This quality is essential to Pee Wee, behind whose naivety and ingenuousness always lurks a naughty understanding of his own seditious behavior. Sontag also points to androgyny and a lack of character development as standard earmarks of the camp icon, both of which apply to Pee Wee, and to the predominantly gay impetus behind camp in general, a tradition from which Pee Wee/Reubens borrows strongly. And, of course, one can't over-look Jambi, the fey genie-in-a-box on the "Playhouse," who camps it up for kids to an alarming extreme. So although Pee Wee transcends the apolitical restric-tions of camp, which I'll get to shortly, his affinity with the sensibility is an important dimension of the gay subtext.

Pee Wee's problematic relationship with "girls" in *Big Adventure* presents another gay reference, his identification with the boy or teen role becoming probably his most outrageous and disquieting characteristic. In one of his "Playhouse" episodes, on receiving a present from his many friends, Pee Wee blurts out, "I'm the luckiest boy in the whole world." It's shocking to hear not merely a fully grown man, but an epicine dandy, refer to himself as a boy; one can imagine parents' eyebrows raising all across the country. In his movie, Pee Wee is confronted with the necessity, according to cinematic convention, of having a love interest, forcing him into the position of dealing with the reality of girls, more specifically Dottie, the one who works at Chuck's Bike-o-rama. Here his boy pose dictates the classic behavior of male adolescents who dislike girls interested in romance; but consistent with the double-edged meaning of his persona, Pee Wee's lack of interest in this area also signifies something "different." When Dottie tries to get Pee Wee to take her to the drive-in, he announces "I like you, Dottie," then yells "*Like,*" emphasizing his preference for a platonic relationship. Next he tells her, "There's a lot of things you don't know about me. Things you wouldn't understand. Things you couldn't understand," then, adding cryptically, "Things you *shouldn't* understand." The reference is obvious, something that, like much of Pee Wee Herman, is lost on kids, but can't be avoided by adults. Finally, Pee Wee gets out of the proposed date by parodying his own rebellious stance: "You don't want to get mixed up with a guy like me. I'm a loner, Dottie, a rebel." That these exact words are used later on by Mickey, the escaped con, to dump Pee Wee, and delivered by James Brolin, playing Pee Wee Herman to Morgan Fairchild's Dottie, in the final film within a film based on Pee Wee's adventure, suggests how absurd the idea of Pee Wee Herman conforming to conventional notions of romantic, heterosexual love really is. His relationship in the film with Dottie, and with Simone, the sexy French waitress, remains one strictly between good friends, and is not, incidentally, characterized by the misogyny one might expect from a camp figure.

Some other indications of a homosexual significance to Pee Wee take the form of classic gay "jokes" or stereotypes. For example, in *Pee Wee's Big Adventure,* the hero steps on a scale which points, automatically, to the ninety-eight-pound mark, a sure sign of the "sissy." Then there's Pee Wee's sarcastic mincing that causes him to knock over the row of motorcycles, putting him in hot water with the bike gang. Or on an episode of the "Playhouse," Pee Wee cuts in on a couple on the dance floor and starts dancing with the man before laughing it off and setting things straight by turning to the woman. It's significant that in most of these instances of humor based on a kind of sexual transgression, Pee Wee places himself in the self-acknowledged "rebel" position, as the bratty kid who refuses to play by the rules of adult conduct. The connection, for kids, is profound.

Of course Pee Wee couldn't get away with any of this if it wasn't all in the name of comedy. In *Wit and Its Relation to the Unconscious,* Freud discusses how humor "makes use of a means of connection which is rejected by, and carefully avoided in serious thinking,"[4] exactly the dynamic that gives Pee Wee the room to be so abnormal. As the grown man in a suit and bow tie who acts childish, even, at times, infantile, Pee Wee eludes reason, returning us to a state of mind where anything goes. Freud describes how play is stopped by the advent of reason, so that the only access to such release in adulthood is through humor; the purpose of jokes, then, is "to remove inhibitions and thereby, render productive those pleasure-sources which have become inaccessible."[5] Pee Wee is all about this kind of "regression," encouraging a living out of fantasies, impulsive behavior, and the pleasure of pure nonsense that stimulates us through confusion.[6] This freedom from logic and "alleviation from the pressure of reason"[7] induced by Pee Wee's playworld (which will soon become, from all reports, an actual geographical site, like Disney's, such is the popularity of Pee Wee), a state in which contradictions can be easily accommodated, may also explain the acceptance of his "sexual difference," situated, as it is, before the constraints of a repressed, adult sexual identity.

Freud also points to a more "sinister" side of the comic impulse coming out of this uninhibited play state, a manifestation of humor "in the service of hostile aggression."[8] There is definitely an edge to Pee Wee, as when, in both television show and movie, he wraps scotch tape around his face in front of a mirror, then rips it off, watching his own startled expression of pain, delighted by the sensation and his naughtiness. What are parents to make of this kind of onanistic, masochistic act performed in the privacy of the bathroom? The secret word of the "Playhouse," which children must greet with screaming and yelling at its mention all day long (Pee Wee enlisting children in his schemes for far more than the thirty minutes of air time) serves a similarly antagonistic purpose, promoting a rebellion against authority that Freud describes as another function of humor.[9] This strategy of comedy, then, aggressively confounding reason and seriousness, combined with the playful elusiveness of camp and the sexual ambiguity it entails, constitutes a veiled attack on the conventional values kids are supposed to assume: Pee Wee attempts to intervene before the big package is bought. As in "Penny," the animated short seen on each "Playhouse" episode, the message is, unequivocally, kids have rights too.

There is one more gap in the critical appraisal of Pee Wee Herman that I want to address: little, if anything, has been made of the obvious affinities between Pee Wee and Jerry Lewis, a connection that puts the comedian in a more meaningful context. To begin with, Lewis, like Herman, appealed to children as much as adults, his sublimely silly and juvenile character even picked up by the comics.

Lewis's ape-like caricature as a comic book hero presented a more masculine, sexualized figure than Pee Wee, but both have the same quality of a grown-up masquerading as a kid, adopting similarly irritating voices and crazy, spastic dances. Both personas also tend to undercut masculinity, Pee Wee by feminizing it, Lewis by parodying the he-man role, particularly in *The Nutty Professor* as the intellectual wimp who makes a Jekyll and Hyde transformation into the virile crooner, Buddy Love (a travesty of the swaggering, lady-killer persona of Lewis's former partner, Dean Martin), and in *The Ladies' Man*, as Herbert, playing a shy, innocent houseboy in a thinly disguised bordello. Both also use drag to this end, Lewis, for example, playing his own female back-up trio in *The Patsy*.

Pee Wee consciously plays on his identification with Jerry Lewis, to the extent that *Pee Wee's Big Adventure* is designed very much as a Lewis vehicle of the sixties. Like the self-directed Lewis films, *Big Adventure* (although not directed, and only co-written, by Paul Reubens) is composed of a series of loosely connected and uneven gags, some working, some misfiring, providing the hero with scenarios in which he can adopt various disguises. The other most obvious quality shared by the films is that both are full of self-conscious filmic references, their own star images wackily breaking out of the diegesis for shock value. In *The Bellboy*, Jerry Lewis plays himself as a big star arriving at the hotel where, within the context of the "plot," he is employed as a bellboy. To complicate things, Milton Berle, in a cameo, plays himself as another star registered at the same hotel, as well as another bellboy. In the *Big Adventure*, Pee Wee pays homage to this exact joke, playing a bellboy himself in the film within a film that stars James Brolin as Pee Wee, the film proper also featuring a cameo by Milton Berle. The end of Lewis's *The Patsy* provides a similar reference point, in which Lewis as Stanley Belt, the failed "King of Comedy" (as he is referred to in the film), steps out of character to undermine the traditional cinematic union of the couple. After falling out the window that he is backed up to by his love interest, Ellen/Ina Balin, Stanley/Lewis pops up to reveal the entire set as merely a Hollywood sound stage, saying, "I can't die. I have to make more movies," and asking "Miss Balin" to join him for lunch. It's the same kind of send-up of filmic convention that Pee Wee Herman appropriates for his first starring vehicle, spoofing the romantic coupling of himself and Dottie by having them embodied by two somewhat sleazy television personalities in the final drive-in movie within a movie.

This tentative comparison of the two comedians is meant to indicate that Pee Wee Herman is very aware of his comic project, engaging the same kind of techniques and strategies that Jerry Lewis pioneered in the sixties. *Pee Wee's Big Adventure* is certainly nowhere as complex and accomplished as any of the Lewis films of that period; it remains to be seen whether Pee Wee/Reubens, with future films (the next to be set at the circus) will produce works as exciting and brilliant as *The Nutty Professor, The Ladies' Man,* and *The Patsy.* He has already asserted a different kind of genius with *Pee Wee's Playhouse.*

The most exciting aspect of Pee Wee Herman, so far, remains his role as vindicator of the sissies, the reluctant hero who outsmarts bullies and worms his way out of impossible situations. In *Big Adventure,* the weird ritual of his "Tequila dance," performed in vintage camp seventies platform shoes, so impresses the surly bikers that they make him an honorary member of their gang. And in his most heroic act, the rescue of all the animals in the pet shop fire, he even saves the snakes that boys are supposed to like, but which Pee Wee finds loathsome and disgusting. That's exactly the kind of hero we need to see more of.

Notes

1 Jack Barth, "Pee Wee TV," *Film Comment* 22, no. 6 (November–December 1986), 79.
2 *Rolling Stone, Graffiti, Impulse,* etc.
3 Susan Sontag, "Notes on Camp," in *Against Interpretation* (New York: Delta, 1981), 283.
4 Sigmund Freud, *Wit and Its Relation to the Unconscious,* from *The Basic Writings of Sigmund Freud,* ed. A. A. Brill (New York: Random House, 1966), 713.
5 Ibid., 721.
6 Ibid., 727.
7 Ibid., 719.
8 Ibid., 698.
9 Ibid., 699.

"In Living Color"

Toms, Coons, Mammies, Faggots, and Bucks

Essex Hemphill

"Homey don't play that!"

On a recent trip to Washington, D.C., to participate as a panelist in a public forum regarding the issues of "sex, politics and art," I came face-to-face with the dangerous consequences of misrepresentation.

As I entered Union Station from the train platform, I was immediately approached by a white man. He was an officer of the law. I was questioned and harassed by him as I headed through the station to the taxi stand. I was in no mood to be toyed with, particularly by a white man with a badge and a gun. I refused to stop and answer his questions, and I told him that if he wanted to question me he would have to do so as we walked. His suspicion—that I was a drug courier—was aroused because I was dressed in jeans, a down jacket and a Raiders baseball cap—the standard attire of what we call the "butch queen" look, the home-boy look, the look of the ghetto. I refused to cooperate with the officer because I knew it was my *look* that made him feel he could single me out to receive his intimidating tactics. I angrily suggested that if he wanted to search me, then he would also have to search some of the white women and men who were on the train with me because they could be smuggling cocaine, guns, and bombs in the linings of their fur coats or in the pockets of their suits and briefcases. The officer then said that I could be a wanted man, and I snidely said, "I am wanted by most men and some women." This only caused him to escalate his aggression. He then said, "I stop people everyday who are carrying automatic weapons and illegal firearms." I then added, "Unfortunately, I'm not carrying weapons today."

When we reached the taxi stand, I really kicked into my resistance by raising my voice and generally drawing attention to the harassment that I was being subjected to. My strategy caused a white man to rush up to me with a pen, paper, and his business card. He instructed me to take down the officer's name and badge number. He said that he would serve as my witness if I needed one, then he rushed into a cab and was gone. The officer working my nerves was not working alone. An unobtrusive, mousey looking black man standing to my left was also an officer. I turned to him and said, "Since *you're* not doing anything, why don't you get out there and get me a cab!"

I was angry enough to have turned Union Station into a pile of rubble. The image I was giving is one every nightly news show projects of young, black males, who are seen in attire similar to my own but often with handcuffs on their wrists or sheets being drawn up over their bullet-riddled bodies. Had I been carrying my briefcase and dressed in slacks and trench coat, as I sometimes am, I doubt if they would have given me the blues.

How many other black males, dressed like me, have endured this, while others, white and black, have sailed through the station without being harassed because they were not dressed like a home boy, dressed in the attire we often see on the nightly news and have come to associate with drugs? How many have had to endure this because they are black and male and wearing a Raiders baseball cap?

As I walk the streets of Hollywood Boulevard
Thinkin' how hard it was for those that starred
In the movies portrayin' the roles
Of butlers and maids, slaves and hoes
Many intelligent Black men seemed to look uncivilized
When on the screen
Like a guess I figure you to play some jigaboo
On the plantation, what else can a nigger do. . . .
—"Burn Hollywood Burn"
from *Fear of a Black Planet,* Public Enemy

"In Living Color" has now been on the air for two seasons. The Fox Broad-casting Network provides the home for the program. Keenen Ivory Wayans, the twenty-three-year-old black producer of the program, recently appeared on Phil Donahue's talk show with members of the cast to discuss, among other matters, the program's controversy. To the credit of Wayans and the cast, "In Living Color" won this year's Emmy Award for outstanding comedy/variety show based on its first season. The show is totally irreverent. They have spoofed everyone from Mike Tyson to Oprah Winfrey, Little Richard to Captain Kirk, Della Reese to Louis Farrakhan, and a host of other characters including homeless men, illiterates, gossips, and thieving televangelists.

The program's best skits deftly reveal that pointed political commentary can occur in the context of comedy, and the exceptionally talented cast delivers the comedic goods. When the comedy is on, it's fresh, but at it's worst, the program simply serves up the same old stereotypes that have long plagued the disempowered.

Donahue challenged Wayans and the cast to speak to the Gay and Lesbian Alliance against Defamation's, or GLAAD's, assertions that the program's portrayal of black gay men in the popular skit "Men on Film" is less than flattering, given the way AIDS, gay bashing, and other sorts of violence have put the gay and lesbian community in a position of increased vulnerability.

Wayan's response was, "Well, first off, all the sketches on the show have to be looked at within the context of the show, and it's not as though we isolate any particular group. We make fun of everybody, and so I don't think that anybody should have a chip on their shoulder—when it's a free-for-all. And the other thing, too, is, the sketch is not a bashing sketch. We don't do jokes about any issues related to gay people. It's really a play on the extremes of the stereotype, and that's it."

One then wonders how well do these obviously talented actors understand the potential danger of stereotypes? GLAAD and Gay Men of African Descent, or GMAD, have taken the lead in speaking out against the show. In a recent interview with *New York* magazine regarding the "Men on . . . " segment of the program—with its two sharp-tongued effeminate SNAP! queens—El Gates, the executive director of GMAD said, "For the whole image to be trivializing, petty and sex-obsessed plays into the hands of homophobes. It allows European Americans to laugh at qualities that have been *assigned* to African Americans."

Additionally, some of the people I interviewed raised questions such as, "What is politically correct comedy?" Can there be such a thing in the context of entertainment? Can entertainment for the sake of entertainment exist in an oppressive society? When do gays, lesbians, women, the homeless, the illiterate, and the generally oppressed cease being funny? Is it at the point that we no longer care about the plights of these groups, and we then feel no genuine concern for issues like rape, AIDS, gay bashing, inadequate education, poverty, sexism, and a host of other conditions? Or are the stereotypes funny to the extent that we are enlightened and motivated to make changes in this society that will render some of these conditions intolerable? And finally, what is the value of laughter if it is driven by the profit motives of a network seeking to gain prominence and by the ambitions of a producer who claims he wants to be an "entity"? At whose expense is this to occur?

When I was offered the opportunity to write this piece about "In Living Color," and specifically about "Men on . . . ," I wasn't sure that I wanted to take on such a challenge. I knew that it would be necessary to get commentary from filmmakers such as Marlon Riggs and Michele Parkerson. I would need to talk to Ron Simmons, assistant professor in the Department of Radio, TV, and Film at Howard University, and I would need to speak with Jacquie Jones, editor of the *Black Film Review*. As I cast my net out, I realized that Alan Bell, publisher of the national black gay and lesbian news magazine, *BLK,* and black gay community organizer Tyrone Smith of Philadelphia, president of Unity, Inc., would also need to be queried about their responses to "In Living Color." What began to emerge from these queries was a picture that critically dismantles "In Living Color" and the "Men on . . . " skits.

But that was not enough. I decided to go to BJP's, a lesbian-owned black entertainment complex located in West Philadelphia that caters to gays and lesbians. The staff was very gracious in allowing me to camp down for three hours to interview patrons. When word went out in the bar about what I was doing, people freely volunteered and waited in line to say their piece—pro or con—about "In Living Color."

Freddie Kruger, 20, BJP's Employee

The first thing, I think, is that they're two queens, honey. But they give it to you right, honey. The girls give it to you right. They tell you the right things, honey. They tell you how the mens gonna do, honey, especially the episode they did where they went away on this tour around the world or something, honey; the girls, they snapped they fingers and clicked they feets. They just did it the right way, honey. "In Living Color" is dynamite. They've got enough queens to work that show, honey. They need some queens from Philadelphia, though. They definitely need some queens from Philly. We've got a couple of queens here at BJP's that we would *love* to get on that show. I'm one of them, honey! The show is lovely. I think it's dynamite. And them two queens, again, honey, they get three circles in a SNAP!

Marlon Riggs, 33, Filmmaker

I feel very ambivalent about "Men on. . . . " It plays into the stereotypes the dominant culture has of us, but that's not my concern, not that they're queens— they're camp queens—but rather it's an image of queens who function in a way that justifies all of the very traditional beliefs about black gay sexuality and allows a larger public—beyond gay and lesbian people—to box gay people into this category that allows them to deal with them by not really dealing with them. For me, the skits are particularly troublesome because of the portrayals of gay men as misogynist and buffoonish in a way that's close to caricature—not camp, but caricature. And again, it's not just that it's—for me—a vicious image in this sort of dichotomous positive/negative sense, but rather it plays into a notion of black *gay* sexuality held by the black community and now being embraced by the larger dominant community. A notion that black gay men are sissies, ineffectual, ineffective, womanish in a way that signifies inferiority rather than empowerment.

It's easy to take delight in their portrayals because they do speak to an experience that we are very much familiar with and understand. What we have to keep in mind regarding "Men on . . . " is that it is intended not for *our* consumption but for the consumption by mass audiences who have no understanding of us, no desire to understand us, and to the degree that they have any desire or understanding at all, it's being informed by skits such as "Men on . . . " in a way that continues to perjure what we're about in terms of our humanity.

Anthony Owens, 31, BJP's Patron

"Men on . . . "—I love it. I think it's a parody, and it should be taken as such. It's not a representation of gay folks as a whole, and it shouldn't be taken as that; it should just be taken as parody. Politically speaking, perhaps it can be a bit overwhelming for those that aren't enlightened, and I can understand that, but you've also got to take it, as I said before, for what it's worth. Simply take it as a parody and nothing more. If anybody is really that stupid to think that "Men on . . . " is a representation of all gay folks, then they've got a problem.

I love the show [as a whole] because it's the first time that we—meaning black folks—have really gotten a chance to just put our comedy out there. It doesn't bother white folks when they make fun of themselves. Why should it bother us when we make fun of ourselves?

Amiel Bares, BJP's Patron

They say hugs are therapeutic, but laughter is the best form of medicine. And they keep me laughing. They never cease to amaze me. They come up with some of the damnedest lines that I would never think of, and I'm one for lines, you know. I can part a line [SNAP!] as fast as you can change your drawers or brush your teeth, OK?

At my last job, when "In Living Color" first came out with they SNAPS!, that's all the kids were doing, you know. They were straight, and I used to sit there and laugh, you know, 'cause it was like they didn't really know what they were doing. Then, when I started doing all these terrible SNAPS! on them, they bust out laughing, you know. I came up with a "Bewitched" SNAP! You snap and then you roll your hands up in the air—you know, the Endora SNAP! They thought it was funny!

Glen Johnson, 36, BJP's Patron

Every day, as a black man, I fight the misrepresentations that white people have of me from watching the news and so forth. No, I may not talk like your so-called average black, but that doesn't mean I'm trying to be like you, either. I'm multi-faceted. Our whole race is multifaceted, so it's the ignorance of those who watch this who want to take this and use it as a tool to say, "Well, this is the way all gay people are, and this is why I don't want to be bothered." I know what I am. I'm proud of who I am. I'm a black homosexual, and I'm proud of that. "In Living Color" nor anything else is not going to destroy my image of myself. If anything, it will help me. Every place I've worked at has known that I am gay. I'm proud of myself. I don't have to snap my fingers. In a way, I'm acting Jew. A Jew told me a long time ago, "I'm just like you, except for one thing: I can change my last name, I can hide the fact that I'm Jewish, but you can't hide the fact that you're black." With my gaiety, I feel like a Jewish man. If I feel like I want to hide it, I can, but I don't. I don't overtly express it either. Just like a Jew may not go around saying, "I'm Jewish, but, hey, if you find out, that's on you." But by the time you find out that I'm something that you may not particularly agree with, you've gotten to know me. You've gotten to like me. You've gotten to respect me, and in time you realize it doesn't really matter what I am.

Alan Bell, Publisher and Editor of *BLK*, the National Black Lesbian and Gay Newsmagazine

Well, I have dual feelings. I think that it's frightfully funny, and I enjoy looking at it, but at the same time I recognize that these portrayals are going out to people who don't have another context to put them in. I, and most black gay men, have another context, and so, in that sense, "Men on . . . " is negative.

Yvette Vasquez, Thirtysomething, BJP's Employee

I think "Men on . . . " is unique. They're one of a kind. They remind me of a lot of my customers here at the bar. They tend to have faggotry—what we call faggotry around here—down pat, OK. They give you *more* than two snaps and more than a couple of circles. I think they're really good. It's not homophobic, which is, I think, one of the best things.

Tess Burruss, BJP's Patron

I don't particularly care for their portrayals of homosexuals. I think it's too flamboyant. I think gay people have been stereotyped enough without having a black program castrating black men. For example, when they scream. Nobody screams anymore. We're not flamey. We're trying to be productive in society, and we don't need black folk denigrating us.

Do you find the portrayal of women offensive?

No, I don't find it offensive because they don't portray women, they portray a man's viewpoint of what womanhood means to a man. They have no concept of what a woman is. They're more or less ridiculing black people on all levels in this show. I find it hilarious. It's just embarrassing to me that it's black people. If it was Dean Martin and Jerry Lewis, I'd really laugh. But there's nothing funny about black life. There's nothing funny about gay life. There's nothing funny about life, period. I think black people in this country have been portrayed too long as buffoons. There should be a program where blacks can be themselves without having to resort to that type of *Imitation of Life*.

Betty "Brandy" Randolph, 54, Co-owner of BJP's, "the Only Lesbian-owned, Black Gay Entertainment Complex in the Delaware Valley, SNAP!"

I think that "In Living Color" is exquisite fun. I really do. I think that the two guys in the portrayal of two gay males do something that is just wonderful for our community. They present a great deal of humor and a great deal of truisms. During the time that this particular segment is on TV, the juke box is turned off, unplugged, and the entire group, everyone—in the bar, in the restaurant and the disco—*all* stop to watch "In Living Color."

Jacquie Jones, Editor, *Black Film Review*

I'm not gay. I'm not lesbian. "Men on . . . ," along with the portrayals of the West Indian family on the show "The Hedleys," are two of the least hostile skits—in terms of the way that characters are presented. I have more problems with the use and the roles of women in the [entire] show. I think "Men on . . . " is explosive in the sense that it puts black homosexuality out there, and rather unabashedly out there, which, I think, in a lot of ways, is important because it forces people to deal with it and to think about it.

I think that the use of these half-naked dancing girls [on the show] is just reprehensible. All kudos to Rosie Perez—I'm sure she is a wonderful choreographer—but to have these women dancing to open the show is clearly about objectification. It just continues the woman-as-backdrop mentality that I have a big problem with, especially when they introduce Keenen Wayans, and the women surround him, and he's *obviously* fully clothed. In addition to that, I have a lot of issues about the way that they portray women in terms of weight and size. They seem to be really hard on fat people or people that are obese. I think everything *is* fair game for comedy. They have the right to have whatever their opinions may be, but I think that there is a kind of hostility in that show, when it comes to dealing with women, that places women in a traditional context: Be beautiful, be thin, dance. I think that there's a current of hostility in general in TV programming. I think that we're looking at a popular culture that is hostile. When you listen to rap music, a lot of what these brothers have to say is right on, but, my God, it's like: *Get in my face, I will bust your lip, I will fuck you up, I'm a black man,* you know, whatever. So understanding "In Living Color" in regard to the rest of popular culture, I don't think it's unusually hostile in the context of a general hostility in popular culture. What the show wants to do is have a very biting, satirical kind of commentary which, I think, it has had in a lot of really, really good skits. So, to have issues addressed is very important. But then I think there is also an underlying strain to the show, as there is in rap music, of a very misogynist attitude.

Michelle Parkerson, Filmmaker

I think that [the "Men on . . ." skit] compares a lot to images of blacks in film prior to the sixties. In other words, what's dangerous about that particular segment is that there are no alternatives to images of black gay men. They're always represented as these kinds of caricatures, these kinds of "coonisms," and if there were an alternative to it, it would be OK, but this is all a lot of people (*most* people, I would venture to say) absorb regarding images of black gay men. It's always this same regurgitation of a SNAP! queen or a suicidal queen, you know. That's what's very dangerous about "Men on . . . " Now on the other side of it, some of the reads that the brothers give are so on that they cannot be denied in their own validity in terms of the statements that are being made; it's the accuracy with which they caricature black gay queens.

I think that the reference for the "Men on . . . " section comes more out of heterosexism than it does out of homophobia. In other words, it's a heterosexist reflection or a heterosexist caricature of black gay SNAP! queens, as opposed to one that's steeped in the fear or hatred of gay people. It's all of *their* references and stereotypes come alive, based on and entrenched in, what is nonhetero, down to the costumes that are worn and the furniture that they sit in; so, I think it connotes more about the danger of heterosexism than it does homophobia, which is equally as dangerous.

What is the parallel for them in terms of stereotypical imagery of black women?

It's a bitchiness that parallels Sapphire in terms of the black female imagery and stereotype that's pervasive. It's akin to that particular category of black people being dangerous with language and attitude more so than having any real power. That's comfortable for television. By and large, TV comedy is not geared toward spoofing even human complexity. It's not about that. It's about boiling everything down to the common denominator and the pervasive joke and the big stereotype. So you wouldn't expect "In Living Color" to provide those kind of alternative images that I'm saying are lacking.

What I do appreciate about "In Living Color" is its commitment to irreverence, in that sense that it'll strip stuff down to caricature and prod and spoof anyone, white or black. No one is safe—from Obsession [perfume] to Jesse Jackson to Mayor Barry to Calvin Klein—no one is safe. I appreciate that daring because the purity of that kind of daring is sorely lacking in television. But the images are awfully dangerous when they're not mediated by other alternatives.

Eugene Townsend, 42, BJP's Employee

I'm not gay. I'm friendly with everybody in here. I can deal with anybody. I have no discrepancies here whatsoever.

Personally, I don't feel that "Men on . . . " is offensive in any way. I feel that it's a form of art. When you look at it in an overall picture, it's not a program that's singling out any specific group. All through the entire show they hit everybody— from the president to the lowly housewife—they hit everybody. They're not focused on any one group or ethnic group of people or whatever. I think it's marvelous, and it's a tribute to our race to have that type of talent that can be that versatile.

As a straight man, do you find the images of the two gay men in "Men on . . . " true in any way?

I can't really say that's the true image, but like I say, it's a form of art. It's like watching a cartoon. The cat eats the fish, and then they put it in reverse, and the fish might eat the cat. So, it's how *you,* the individual, perceive what's projected before you.

Charles Harpe, 37, Founder and President of Baldwin/Hughes

I'm not an ardent fan of the show; I don't see it every Sunday, but on the occasions that I have seen it, I've enjoyed it—for the most part. I feel that black people, at this stage of the game—in terms of our affirmations that we receive as being a valid culture or society in the context of America—comes when we're able to see ourselves on the screen, be it on the television screen or on the movie screen. I don't think satirization takes away from the importance of institutions and the value of them in terms of perpetuating our community. To my knowledge, this may be the first time that black gay men are portrayed in any way on television, and the fact that the two men who play those characters take on some of the more flamboyant stereotypical kinds of behavior of gay people as a whole, and black gay men specifically, I have not taken that as a point of offense, yet. I'm open to the possibility that I will, but not as yet.

Tyrone Smith, 50, President of Unity, Inc., a Philadelphia-based Advocacy Group for African-American Gay Men

I find it somewhat disappointing that they take African-American gay men and make humor out of them. We are not to be humored. We are not a thing of humor. We are more than that. We are professionals. We are teachers, doctors, lawyers. We are a very positive part of the African-American community. I think that they depict us in a very lax and a very negative presentation. The thing that I find somewhat appalling is the fact that we come off as always snapping our fingers, being nonproductive, silly queens, and that's not true for all African gay men. We are very productive individuals.

Regina Alexander, 33, BJP's Patron

Well, I love "Men on . . . " They're exciting. They're real. But I'm thinking about the three children of my lover. The children will forsake whatever treat they're going to get that night to get home in time for "In Living Color."

Their mother, my lover, before she was maybe twelve, had decided her lifestyle basically would be a lesbian lifestyle—therefore, the children understand. In fact they laugh, kid, and enjoy the hell out of the two snaps in a circle. They have been very saddened this season by the fact that "Men on . . . " does not come on as regularly.

Their uncle, who has been taken away through the deadly disease of AIDS, was in fact a gay man, and they loved him. They *loved* him. That relationship is one they shall always miss and always treasure. So they have a very positive memory as well as a day-to-day idea of what the gay black man is all about.

Ron Simmons, Ph.D., 40, Assistant Professor, Department of Radio, TV, and Film, Howard University

There are some who say that they like the characters, that the characters are real, and that everybody knows that it's just a joke, it's all meant in fun. Then there are others, like myself, who think that those characters are ultimately dangerous and that a lot of people do not realize the difference between those characters and real life. The characters are dangerous in a time when gay bashing is on the rise and people are being shot and killed for small things. To further stereotype and to further objectify and dehumanize people, I think, feeds into those people being perceived as something that one can easily get rid of—who cares? That's what bothers me. It's also divisive in that it feeds into the idea that gay men are misogynist. People assume that gay men don't like women. Whenever "Men on . . . " critiques a female work, they say, "Hated it." That's a running joke. A country that's known for females they hate. A book about females they hate. A movie about females they hate. They had the audacity to call a black woman a "fish" in a recent segment, then they turned around after calling her a fish and cruised the crotch of some white guy. Now why couldn't a black guy have walked by in bikini briefs for them to cruise?

I'm not impressed with black men being the producers of this show because it's not the fact that they're producing it, it's the fact that TV is allowing it on the air. TV would not allow it on the air if it were a threat. So the fact that we now have enough black people who are educated, creative, and talented enough, and the system is liberal enough to let us now get on the air and attack our own people, that does not impress me. Our people are still being attacked.

If we're going to laugh at people, then let's laugh at those who have the power. And if we're going to laugh at ourselves, let's educate ourselves as we laugh at ourselves, but "Men on . . . " does no educating whatsoever—*none*. If anything, it further adds to the ignorance of people not knowing what gay men really are about. Black people are at war with the U.S. power structure, at war with the ruling elite—those who brought us here in chains and have been living off our labor since day one. We are in a state of war with them, which they are winning, by the fact that we are now worse off than we were back in the sixties. Forty-two percent of American black children are living in poverty. Clearly they are winning. The number of black men in jail is more than [the number] in college. *They are winning.* If history was to record that while all this was going on, black folks were sitting in their homes laughing at some stupid-ass shit like "Men on . . . ," you see, it's almost like watching TV on the Titanic. That's what really scares me. That's why I say "In Living Color" is dangerous.

As these responses indicate, the representation of sexual, racial, ethnic, and gender identities in the context of media is one of the most critical debates the marginalized, the oppressed, and the disenfranchised groups in this country will contend with during this decade. These debates, these efforts to claim and re-claim identity are not new, particularly for black Americans. Throughout this century we have challenged the images others have presented of us. Perhaps now, more so than at any other time in our history, the images of blacks por-trayed in the media are being rigorously interrogated, and simultaneously, there is an increased effort to bring accuracy and truth to these portrayals, either through reappropriating and reinscribing the images with the power to point the way to our liberation or, conversely, the images that have only served to affirm the mechanisms and conditions of our oppression are being righteously de-stroyed.

These efforts are not occurring exclusively among black Americans; lesbians, gays, women, the physically challenged, and other ethnic groups and nation-alities are at work creating images that affirm and empower, while simultaneously destroying those that confine and injure. Each and every one of us is an active or passive participant in this process.

Representation is not to be viewed solely in the context of mass media; televi-sion, Hollywood, and the realm of the printed word are all areas where these debates and battles are escalating. They are also occurring in the realm of what can be deemed the "personal," which I would define as being the realms of family, intimate and community relationships, and I would also include relation-ships that occur in a business context such as the relationship between an em-ployer and employee. How does each one see the other? In each of these areas, and others, representation is critical to the extent that your identity is respected, and you are not victimized by the representation someone else creates of you.

As predominately passive consumers of mass-media representations of blacks, women, gays, Hispanics, and others, we would be wise to understand that we do not have to submit to, or accept, what is served to us, even when it is supposed to be a reflection or a parody of our lives. Television is ubiquitous and powerful only to the extent that we allow it to enter into our homes and create chaos while we literally sit and watch.

Black gay men and black lesbians need to then understand that the longer we stay in the closet, the longer we will be victimized by buffoonish depictions of our lives—as in the case of the SNAP! queens portrayed on "In Living Color." We should not expect sympathetic nonhomo black Americans to go forth and advocate for portrayals of our lives in contexts other than cheap humor. We have to take an aggressive lead in that battle. Too often our own people have exploited our identities as a means to obtain a fast buck and celebrity status. The complexity of the misrepresentations we confront is exacerbated by the ability of satellites to instantaneously beam disparaging depictions of our lives to any place the signal can be received, including beyond this solar system. Living in a closet is thus that much more frightening than ever, for to do so is to surrender our sexual identity to the hands of people who would be just as satisfied if our silence was absolute either by way of us being dead or by way of us disappearing.

Dossier on Popular Music

Introduction

Corey K. Creekmur

I f you "can't tell" by looking, can *listening* provide more reliable clues? Richard Dyer prefaces his groundbreaking analysis of the gay adoration of Judy Garland with Joe Orton's observation that a collection of Garland records clinched one's suspicion that their owner was a "friend of Dorothy." But, in the 1990s, *Northern Exposure*'s homophobic Maurice Minnifield is horrified when his sexual orientation is misidentified on the basis of his superb collection of Broadway soundtracks, especially strong on Ethel Merman. While there may be queer "tendencies" in the consumption of popular music, gay and lesbian listening habits may be somewhat less consistent than sexual preferences. Nevertheless, popular music has functioned as far more than "mere" entertainment in the lives of modern lesbians and gays, even at times playing a fundamental role in establishing gay self-identity and maintaining community solidarity.

Whether in the forms of opera, musical theater, blues, "women's music," disco, or "homocore," gays and lesbians have relied on popular music to express both personal desires and political demands, recognizing themselves in songs ranging from Judy Garland's affirmative "The Man That Got Away" to Tom Robinson's anthemic "Glad to Be Gay." Music has also provided a shared soundtrack for lesbian and gay communities, whether meeting clandestinely in bars and cabarets or publicly at marches, pride parades, or music festivals. In the liberationist seventies, women's music festivals and gay discos were key meeting grounds for lovers and activists, whose bodies—electric, erotic, and politic—responded to Cris Williamson and Donna Summer, Ferron and Sylvester. More recently, queer culture has generated the politically outspoken and musically diverse Jimmy Somerville, Erasure, Two Nice Girls, and Pansy Division, as well as the teasing—and thus often annoying—ambisexuality of Morrissey, the Pet

Shop Boys, and Suede. In fact, the popular music accompanying queer pleasure and politics has continually occupied a key position in the shifting constellation of popular activities and styles marking the cultural identity of gay and lesbian communities in this century.

'I'he full history of music and homosexuals—as composers, performers, and listeners—remains to be written, but, for much of the twentieth century, the often stereotyped but undeniably important gay love of popular music was necessarily a camp relationship, simultaneously indulging in and distanced from Broadway and Tin Pan Alley's conventional musical representations of heterosexual romance. Even great gay composers of American popular song like Cole Porter and Lorenz Hart wrote lyrics in straight drag, although often demonstrating a mastery of innuendo and double entendre. Perhaps because musicals as a form acknowledge performance and reject bourgeois realism or allow the vibrant vocal expression of private thoughts and feelings, gays have historically been especially attracted to this otherwise heterocentric genre, even if through the ironic twist of camp. Debates around the politics of camp after gay liberation have emphasized camp's inherent ambivalence, its construction of elitist, "inside" knowledge for an audience otherwise forced "outside" the mainstream, and its sometimes desperate appropriation of the scraps of a culture that demands conformist assimilation. If the practice of camp now seems an artifact of the closet, its contradictory love-hate quality nonetheless continues to structure gay and lesbian relationships to mass culture in general and to popular music in particular.

All the essays in this section emphasize the ambivalences experienced by any marginal or oppositional group in relation to mass culture, where popularity is often secured through conformity and defined by the cash register. Although many queer performers no longer write and sing in hetero drag and their audiences no longer listen through the fine-tuning of camp, these essays recognize that popular music remains circumscribed by the contradictions of mass media circulation. These essays therefore ask specific but interpenetrating questions: Can the consumption of commercial music ever serve radical, liberatory ends? Does a lesbian or gay performer's mainstream success inevitably require "selling out," the pop fan's worst condemnation, and "staying in," the queer fan's worst nightmare? Can a popular star—perhaps the most popular in the world—generate, acknowledge, and maintain a queer following without condescending to or disappointing her fans? And, in American popular music especially, can the dominant culture's assimilation of a sexual subculture's style be isolated from racial crossover, or does commercialization whitewash as it straightens?

Richard Dyer's "defense" of disco argues for the positive, if not radical, potential of disco (as he notes, as much a sensibility as a kind of music) for gay culture. While disco was the soundtrack for the liberation-era urban gay male, it was also an ostentatiously capitalist product, and Dyer's essay investigates how resistance may be figured (and limited) by gay culture's consumption of this blatantly commercial form. Arlene Stein's essay on recent women's music looks in quite the opposite direction, asking how music generated by a communal, folk environment may be affected by the threat of commercial success; unlike the popular musical forms appropriated by gay men, the lesbian community has often produced and supported music separated from the hit-driven music industry, recorded for independent labels like Olivia and distributed through the network of feminist bookstores and at women's music festivals. Stein's essay describes an ideological and generational crisis in women's music, where identity politics and separatist ideals seem challenged by financial reward and larger audiences, but where figures like k. d. lang also suggest that such oppositions can be creatively negotiated.

Michael Musto's campy essay updates a classic gay subject, the cult worship of the pop diva, for a contemporary queer cultural context, where, among other changes, queer adoration of the icon is openly acknowledged and solicited, and conventional gay identification *with* the female star is balanced by lesbian desire *for* the star. Madonna's status as the "post-Stonewall Judy Garland" also invites Musto's investigation into the context for fandom in contemporary culture, where gay and lesbian consumers are desired and celebrated rather than merely (economically) tolerated. One of Madonna's explicitly gay-influenced songs and videos, "Vogue," might be recalled in relation to Anthony Thomas's historical account of the gay black origins of contemporary dance music. Thomas's survey restores the racial as well as sexual contexts of disco and house music, demonstrating, like Dyer, how subcultural identity can be acknowledged within commercial forms. Although Thomas chronicles white and straight appropriations of gay black musical forms, he also affirms the elements of house music that resist mainstream commercialization and inappropriate evaluation. Like all these writers, Thomas finally locates the real value of popular music in its cultural context and use rather than in its artistic form. (In retrospect, the "disco sucks" bumperstickers and record-burning rallies of the late seventies look more racist and homophobic than they first appeared since the musical style of disco has survived under other names through countless new wave, pop, and "alternative" dance bands.)

In the early nineties, openly gay performers Jimmy Somerville, Marc Almond, and Erasure are heard in clubs as well as on the radio, and once-closeted mainstream performers Johnny Mathis, Elton John, Melissa Etheridge, Janis Ian, and k. d. lang are now out, with lang generating "lesbian Beatlemania" at her concerts; stunning black drag queen "supermodel" RuPaul is on the pop charts and

MTV, and the postpunk homocore and riot grrrl movements have produced queer bands like Pansy Division and C.W.A. (Cunts with Attitude), who have recorded "Only Straight Girls Wear Dresses." But Sylvester, Freddie Mercury, and Oscar-winning lyricist Howard Ashman have died from AIDS; rappers like Heavy D. and Big Daddy Kane and metal rockers Guns N' Roses proudly fag bash in word if not in deed; and reggae singer Buju Banton's "Boom Bye Bye" threatens that "When Buju Banton arrives / Faggots have to run / Or get a bullet in the head." Whether in the musical margins or mainstream, alternative to or assimilated by a popular music industry at once more gay-positive and openly homophobic than ever, the ongoing relation between queers and music continues to underscore the contemporary intersection between sexuality, politics, and culture.

In Defense

of Disco

Richard Dyer

All my life I've liked the wrong music. I never liked Elvis and rock 'n' roll; I always preferred Rosemary Clooney. And since I became a socialist, I've often felt virtually terrorized by the prestige of rock and folk on the Left. How could I admit to two Petula Clark LPs in the face of miners' songs from the North East and the Rolling Stones? I recovered my nerve partially when I came to see show-biz music as a key part of gay culture, which, whatever its limitations, was a culture to defend. And I thought I'd really made it when I turned on to Tamla Motown, sweet soul sounds, disco. Chartbusters already, and I like them! Yet the prestige of folk and rock, and now punk and (rather patronizingly, I think) reggae, still holds sway. It's not just that people whose politics I broadly share don't *like* disco; they manage to imply that it is politically beyond the pale to like it. It's against this attitude that I want to defend disco (which otherwise, of course, hardly needs any defense).

I'm going to talk mainly about disco *music,* but there are two preliminary points I'd like to make. The first is that disco is more than just a form of music, although certainly the music is at the heart of it. Disco is also kinds of dancing, club, fashion, film—in a word, a certain *sensibility,* manifest in music, clubs, and so forth, historically and culturally specific, economically, technologically, ideologically, and aesthetically determined—and worth thinking about. Second, as a sensibility in music it seems to me to encompass more than what we would perhaps strictly call disco music, and include a lot of soul, Tamla, and even the later work of mainstream and jazz artists like Peggy Lee and Johnny Mathis.

My defense is in two parts: first, a discussion of the arguments against disco in terms of its being "capitalist" music and, second, an attempt to think through the—ambivalently, ambiguously, contradictorily—positive qualities of disco.

Disco and Capital

Much of the hostility to disco stems from the equation of it with capitalism. Both in how it is produced and in what it expresses, disco is held to be irredeemably capitalistic.

Now it is unambiguously the case that disco is produced by capitalist industry, and since capitalism is an irrational and inhuman mode of production, the disco industry is as bad as all the rest. Of course. However, this argument has assumptions behind it that are more problematic. These are of two kinds. One assumption concerns *music as a mode of production,* and has to do with the belief that it is possible in a capitalist society to produce things (e.g., music, such as rock and folk) that are outside of the capitalist mode of production. Yet quite apart from the general point that such a position seeks to elevate activity outside of existing structures rather than struggles against them, the two kinds of music most often set against disco as a mode of production are not really convincing.

One is folk music—in the United Kingdom, people might point to Gaelic songs and industrial ballads—the kind of music often used, or reworked, in Left fringe theater. These, it is argued, are not, like disco (and pop music in general), produced *for* the people, but *by* them. They are "authentic" people's music. So they are—or, rather, were. The problem is that we don't live in a society of small, technologically simple communities such as produce such art. Preserving such music at best gives us a historical perspective on peasant and working-class struggle, at worst leads to a nostalgia for a simple, harmonious community existence that never even existed. More bluntly, songs in Gaelic or dealing with nineteenth-century factory conditions, beautiful as they are, don't mean much to most English-speaking people today.

The other kind of music most often posed against disco, and "pap pop" at the level of how it is produced, is rock (including Dylan-type folk and everything from early rock 'n' roll to progressive concept albums). The argument here is that rock is easily produced by nonprofessionals—all that is needed are a few instruments and somewhere to play—whereas disco music requires the whole panoply of recording studio technology, which makes it impossible for non-professionals (the kid on the streets) to produce. The factual accuracy of this observation needs supplementing with some other observations. Quite apart from the very rapid—but then bemoaned by some purists—move of rock into elaborate recording studios, even when it is simple and produceable by non-professionals, the fact is that rock is still quite expensive, and remains in practice largely the preserve of the middle class, who can afford electric guitars, music lessons, and the like. (You have only to look at the biographies of those now professional rock musicians who started out in a simple nonprofessional way—

the preponderance of public school- and university-educated young men in the field is rivaled only by their preponderance in the Labour party cabinet.) More important, this kind of production is wrongly thought of as being generated from the grassroots when, except perhaps at certain key historical moments, non-professional music making, in rock as elsewhere, bases itself, inevitably, on professional music. Any notion that rock emanates from "the people" is soon confounded by the recognition that what "the people" are doing is trying to be as much like professionals as possible.

The second kind of argument based on the fact that disco is produced by capitalism concerns *music as an ideological expression*. Here it is assumed that capitalism as a mode of production necessarily and simply produces "capitalist" ideology. The theory of the relation between the mode of production and the ideologies of a particular society is too complicated and unresolved to be gone into here, but we can begin by remembering that capitalism is about profit. In the language of classical economics, capitalism produces commodities, and its interest in commodities is their exchange value (how much profit they can realize) rather than their use value (their social or human worth). This becomes particularly problematic for capitalism when dealing with an expressive commodity—such as disco—since a major problem for capitalism is that there is no necessary or guaranteed connection between exchange value and use value. In other words, capitalism as productive relations can just as well make a profit from something that is ideologically opposed to bourgeois society as something that supports it. As long as a commodity makes a profit, what does it matter? Indeed, it is because of this dangerous, anarchic tendency of capitalism that ideological institutions—the church, the state, education, the family—are necessary. It is their job to make sure that what capitalism produces is in capitalism's longer-term interests. However, since they often don't know that that is their job, they don't always perform it. Cultural production within capitalist society is, then, founded on two profound contradictions—the first between production for profit and production for use; the second, within those institutions whose job it is to regulate the first contradiction. What all this boils down to, in terms of disco, is that the fact that disco is produced by capitalism does not mean that it is automatically, necessarily, simply supportive of capitalism. Capitalism constructs the disco experience, but it does not necessarily know what it is doing, apart from making money.

I am not now about to launch into a defense of disco music as some great subversive art form. What the arguments above lead me to is, first, a basic point of departure in the recognition that cultural production under capitalism is necessarily contradictory, and, second, that it may well be the case that capitalist cultural products are most likely to be contradictory at just those points—such as disco—where they are most commercial and professional, where the urge to profit is at its strongest. Third, this mode of cultural production has produced a commodity, disco, that has been taken up by gays in ways that may well not have been intended by its producers. The anarchy of capitalism throws up commodities that an oppressed group can take up and use to cobble together its own culture. In this respect, disco is very much like another profoundly ambiguous aspect of male gay culture, camp. It is a "contrary" use of what the dominant culture provides, it is important in forming a gay identity, and it has subversive potential as well as reactionary implications.

The Characteristics of Disco

Let me turn now to what I consider to be the three important characteristics of disco—eroticism, romanticism, and materialism. I'm going to talk about them in terms of what it seems to me they mean within the context of gay culture. These three characteristics are not in themselves good or bad (any more than disco music as a whole is), and they need specifying more precisely. What is interesting is how they take us to qualities that are not only key ambiguities within gay male culture, but have also traditionally proved stumbling blocks to socialists.

Eroticism   It can be argued that all popular music is erotic. What we need to define is the specific way of thinking and feeling erotically in disco. I'd like to call it "whole body" eroticism, and to define it by comparing it with the eroticism of the two kinds of music to which disco is closest—popular song (i.e., the Gershwin, Cole Porter, Burt Bacharach type of song) and rock.

Popular song's eroticism is "disembodied": it succeeds in expressing a sense of the erotic that yet denies eroticism's physicality. This can be shown by the nature of tunes in popular songs and the way they are handled.

Popular song's tunes are rounded off, closed, self-contained. They achieve this by adopting a strict musical structure (AABA) in which the opening melodic phrases are returned to and, most important, the tonic note of the song is also the last note of the tune. (The tonic note is the note that forms the basis for the key in which the song is written; it is therefore the harmonic "anchor" of the tune, and closing on it gives precisely a feeling of "anchoring," coming to a settled stop.) Thus although popular songs often depart from their melodic and harmonic beginnings—especially in the middle section (B)—they also always return to them. This gives them—even at their most passionate, as in Cole Porter's "Night and Day"—a sense of security and containment. The tune is not allowed to invade the whole of one's body. Compare the typical disco tune, which is often little more than an endlessly repeated phrase that drives beyond itself, is not "closed off." Even when disco music uses a popular song standard, it often turns it into a simple phrase. Gloria Gaynor's version of Porter's "I've Got You under My Skin," for instance, is in large part a chanted repetition of "I've got you."

Popular song's lyrics place its tunes within a conceptualization of love and passion as emanating from "inside," the heart or the soul. Thus the yearning cadences of popular song express an erotic yearning of the inner person, not the body. Once again, disco refuses this. Not only are the lyrics often more directly physical and the delivery more raunchy (e.g., Grace Jones's "I Need a Man"), but, most important, disco is insistently rhythmic in a way that popular song is not.

Rhythm, in Western music, is traditionally felt as being more physical than other musical elements such as melody, harmony, and instrumentation. This is why Western music is traditionally so dull rhythmically—nothing expresses our Puritan heritage more vividly. It is to other cultures that we have had to turn—above all to Afro-American culture—to learn about rhythm. The history of popular songs since the late nineteenth century is largely the history of the white incorporation (or ripping off) of black music—ragtime, the Charleston, the tango, swing, rock 'n' roll, rock. Now what is interesting about this incorporation or ripping off is what it meant and means. Typically, black music was thought of by the white culture as being both more primitive and more "authentically" erotic. Infusions of black music were always seen as (and often condemned as) sexual and physical. The use of insistent black rhythms in disco music, recognizable by the closeness of the style to soul and reinforced by such characteristic features of black music as the repeated chanted phrase and the use of various African percussion instruments, means that it inescapably signifies (in this white context) physicality.

However, rock is as influenced by black music as disco is. This then leads me to the second area of comparison between the eroticism of disco and rock. The difference between them lies in what each "hears" in black music. Rock's eroticism is thrusting, grinding—it is not whole body, but phallic. Hence it takes from black music the insistent beat and makes it even more driving; rock's repeated phrases trap you in their relentless push, rather than releasing you in an open-ended succession of repetitions as disco does. Most revealing perhaps is rock's instrumentation. Black music has more percussion instruments than white, and it knows how to use them to create all sorts of effects—light, soft, lively, as well as heavy, hard, and grinding. Rock, however, hears only the latter and develops the percussive qualities of essentially nonpercussive instruments to increase this, hence the twanging electric guitar and the nasal vocal delivery. One can see how, when rock 'n' roll first came in, this must have been a tremendous liberation from popular song's disembodied eroticism—here was a really physical music, and not just mealy-mouthed physical, but quite clear what it was about—cock. But rock confines sexuality to cock (and this is why, no matter how progressive the lyrics and even when performed by women, rock remains indelibly phallocentric music). Disco music, on the other hand, hears the physicality in black music and its range. It achieves this by a number of features, including the sheer amount going on rhythmically in even quite simple disco music (for rhythmic clarity with complexity, listen to the full-length version of the Temptations' "Papa Was a Rolling Stone"); the willingness to play with rhythm, delaying it, jumping it, countering it rather than simply driving on and on (e.g., Patti Labelle, Isaac Hayes); the range of percussion instruments used and their different effect (e.g., the spiky violins in Quincy Jones and Herbie Hancock's "Tell Me a Bedtime Story"; the gentle pulsations of George Benson). This never stops being erotic, but it restores eroticism to the whole of the body and for both sexes, not just confining it to the penis. It leads to the expressive, sinuous movement of disco dancing, not just that mixture of awkwardness and thrust so dismally characteristic of dancing to rock.

Gay men do not intrinsically have any prerogative over whole-body eroticism. We are often even more cock oriented than nongays of either sex, and it depresses me that such phallic forms of disco as Village People should be so gay identified. Nonetheless, partly because many of us have traditionally not thought of ourselves as being "real men," and partly because gay ghetto culture is also a space where alternative definitions, including those of sexuality, can be developed, it seems to me that the importance of disco in scene culture indicates an openness to a sexuality that is not defined in terms of cock. Although one cannot easily move from musical values to personal ones, or from personal ones to politically effective ones, it is at any rate suggestive that gay culture should promote a form of music that denies the centrality of the phallus while at the same time refusing the nonphysicality that such a denial has hitherto implied.

Romanticism   Not all disco music is romantic. The lyrics of many disco hits are either straightforwardly sexual—not to say sexist—or else broadly social (e.g., Detroit Spinners' "Ghetto Child," Stevie Wonder's "Living in the City"), and the hard drive of Village People or Labelle is positively antiromantic. Yet there is nonetheless a strong strain of romanticism in disco. This can be seen in the lyrics, which often differ little from popular song standards, and indeed often are standards (e.g., "What a Difference a Day Made" by Esther Phillips, "La vie en rose" by Grace Jones). More impressively, it is the instrumentation and arrangements of disco music that are so romantic.

The use of massed violins takes us straight back, via Hollywood, to Tchaikovsky, to surging, outpouring emotions. A brilliant example is Gloria Gaynor's

"I've Got You under My Skin," where in the middle section the violins take a hint from one of Porter's melodic phrases and develop it away from this tune in an ecstatic, soaring movement. This "escape" from the confines of popular song into ecstasy is very characteristic of disco music, and nowhere more consistently than in such Diana Ross classics as "Reach Out" and "Ain't No Mountain High Enough." This latter, with its lyrics of total surrender to love, its heavenly choir, and sweeping violins, is perhaps one of the most extravagant reaches of disco's romanticism. But Ross is also a key figure in the gay appropriation of disco.

What Ross's records do—and I'm thinking basically of her work up to *Greatest Hits* volume 1 and the *Touch Me in the Morning* albums—is express the intensity of fleeting emotional contacts. They are all-out expressions of adoration that yet have built on to them the recognition of the (inevitably) temporary quality of the experience. This can be a straightforward lament for having been let down by a man, but more often it is both a celebration of a relationship and the almost willing recognition of its passing and the exquisite pain of its passing—"Remember me / As a sunny day / That you once had / Along the way"; "If I've got to be strong / Don't you know I need to have tonight when you're gone / When you go I'll lie here / And think about / the last time that you / Touch me in the morning." This last number, with Ross's "unreally" sweet, porcelain fragile voice and the string backing, concentrates that sense of celebrating the intensity of the passing relationship that haunts so much of her work. No wonder Ross is (was?) so important in gay male scene culture, for she both reflects what that culture takes to be an inevitable reality (that relationships don't last) and at the same time celebrates it, validates it.

Not all disco music works in this vein, yet in both some of the more sweetly melancholy orchestrations (even in lively numbers, like "You Should Be Dancing" from *Saturday Night Fever*) and some of the lyrics and general tone (e.g., Donna Summer's *Four Seasons of Love* album), there is a carryover of this emotional timbre. At a minimum, then, disco's romanticism provides an embodiment and validation of an aspect of gay culture.

But romanticism is a particularly paradoxical quality of art to come to terms with. Its passion and intensity embody or create an experience that negates the dreariness of the mundane and everyday. It gives us a glimpse of what it means to live at the height of our emotional and experiential capacities—not dragged down by the banality of organized routine life. Given that everyday banality, work, domesticity, ordinary sexism, and racism are rooted in the structures of class and gender of this society, the flight from that banality can be seen as a flight from capitalism and patriarchy as lived experiences.

What makes this more complicated is the actual situation within which disco occurs. Disco is part of the wider to and fro between work and leisure, alienation and escape, boredom and enjoyment that we are so accustomed to (and that *Saturday Night Fever* plugs into so effectively). Now this to and fro is partly the mechanism by which we keep going, at work, at home—the respite of leisure gives us the energy to work, and anyway we are still largely brought up to think of leisure as a "reward" for work. This circle locks us into it. But what happens in that space of leisure can be profoundly significant; it is there that we may learn about an alternative to work and to society as it is. Romanticism is one of the major modes of leisure in which this sense of an alternative is kept alive. Romanticism asserts that the limits of work and domesticity are not the limits of experience.

I don't say that romanticism, with its passion and intensity, is a political ideal we could strive for—I doubt it is humanly possible to live permanently at that pitch. What I do believe is that the movement between banality and something "other" than banality is an essential dialectic of society, a constant keeping open of a gap between what is and what could or should be. Herbert Marcuse in the currently unfashionable *One-Dimensional Man: Studies in the Ideology of Advanced Industrial Society* argues that our society tries to close that gap, to assert that what is all that there could be, is what should be. For all its commercialism and containment within the to and fro between work and leisure, I think disco romanticism is one of the things that can keep the gap open, that can allow the *experience of contradiction* to continue. Since I also believe that political struggle is rooted in experience (though utterly doomed if left at it), I find this dimension of disco potentially positive. (A further romantic/utopian aspect of disco is realized in the noncommercial discos organized by gay and women's groups. Here a moment of community can be achieved, often in circle dances or simply in the sense of knowing people as people, not anonymous bodies. Fashion is less important, and sociability correspondingly more so. This can be achieved in smaller clubs, perhaps especially outside the center of London, which, when not just grotty monuments to self-oppression, can function as supportive expressions of something like a gay community.)

Materialism   Disco is characteristic of advanced capitalist societies simply in terms of the scale of money squandered on it. It is a riot of consumerism, dazzling in its technology (echo chambers, double and more tracking, electric instruments), overwhelming in its scale (banks of violins, massed choirs, the limitless range of percussion instruments), lavishly gaudy in the mirrors and tat of discotheques, the glitter and denim flash of its costumes. Its tacky sumptuousness is well evoked in *Thank God It's Friday*. Gone are the restraint of popular song, the sparseness of rock and reggae, the simplicity of folk. How can a socialist, or someone trying to be a feminist, defend it?

In certain respects, it is doubtless not defensible. Yet socialism and feminism are both forms of materialism—why is disco, a celebration of materialism if ever there was one, not therefore the appropriate art form of materialist politics?

Partly, obviously, because materialism in politics is not to be confused with mere matter. Materialism seeks to understand how things are in terms of how they have been produced and constructed in history, and how they can be better produced and constructed. This certainly does not mean immersing oneself in the material world—indeed, it includes deliberately stepping back from the material world to see what makes it the way it is and how to change it. But materialism is also based on the profound conviction that politics is about the material world, and indeed that human life and the material world are all there is; there is no God, there are no magic forces. One of the dangers of materialist politics is that it is in constant danger of spiritualizing itself, partly because of the historical legacy of the religious forms that brought materialism into existence, partly because materialists have to work so hard not to take matter at face value that they often end up not treating it as matter at all. Disco's celebration of materialism is only a celebration of the world we are necessarily and always immersed in. Disco's materialism, in technological modernity, is resolutely historical and cultural—it can never be, as most art claims for itself, an "emanation" outside of history and of human production.

Disco's combination of romanticism and materialism effectively tells us—lets us experience—that we live in a world of materials, that we can enjoy them but that the experience of materialism is not necessarily what the everyday world assures us it is. Its eroticism allows us to rediscover our bodies as part of this experience of materialism and the possibility of change.

If this sounds over the top, let one thing be clear—disco can't change the world or make the revolution. No art can do that, and it is pointless to expect it to. But partly by opening up experience, partly by changing definitions, art and disco can be used. To which one might risk adding the refrain, if it feels good, *use* it.

Crossover

Dreams

Lesbianism and Popular Music since the 1970s

Arlene Stein

L esbians broadly constitute what Herbert Gans has called a "taste public."[1] We are a heterogeneous group of individuals who, like all members of society, wish to see aspects of our lives reflected in the films, books, music, and other cultural goods we consume. We comprise a "partial culture," that is, we share some basic interests that separate us from the rest of society, but we also belong to mainstream society.[2]

One would hardly know this from listening to popular music, however. Writing in 1990, pop critic Jon Savage noted that while "popular music acknowledges the sign of 'gayness', there is not yet a whisper of female sexual autonomy, of lesbianism."[3] Because images of heterosexuality and, more specifically, female sexual accessibility, are central to pop music's appeal, out lesbians are not generally thought to be "crossover" material. Driven by big hits and anticipating the specter of meager sales (or outraged moralists), commercial record companies steer away from potential controversy.

A performer who makes her lesbianism known typically becomes categorized as a "lesbian artist," and is doomed to marginality. Consequently, performers, who labor under the competitive pressures of the market, engage in self-censorship, fashioning their words and images to achieve "universal" appeal, or at least what they interpret as such. The "crossover artist," who embraces lesbian identifications while achieving mainstream success, simultaneously acknowledging both lesbian marginality and membership in the dominant culture, is a rare specimen indeed.

But while images of heterosexuality dominate popular music, they do not go unchallenged. For example, women have always found ways to "read" popular music against the grain, by changing the pronouns of songs in their heads and projecting their fantasies of identification and desire upon female icons. In addition, out lesbians have for at least twenty years struggled for greater participation in popular music production, both by explicitly encoding lesbian references into their music, and by using more implicit, ambiguous coding. In what follows, I look at lesbian efforts to influence popular music production, focusing upon recent experience in the United States.

Sing This Song All Together

Lesbian performers have long participated in the creation of popular music in North America. However, the social movements of the seventies provided, for the first time, impetus for many women to openly incorporate their sexual identities into their creative work. In the early seventies, young women who "came out through feminism," as the saying went, attempted to transform lesbianism from a medical condition, or at best, a sexual "preference," into a collective identity that transcended rampant individualism and its excesses, as well as compulsory sexual and gender roles. Central to this movement was a belief in what Michel Foucault and others have called "reverse affirmation," the reclaiming and affirming of stigmatized identities, such as homosexuality.[4]

Lesbian feminism spawned the most vibrant and visible lesbian culture that had ever existed in the United States, or indeed the world. It encouraged women to develop their own fiction, visual art and music. "Women's music" was an important product of this period of cultural innovation. Though usually not explicitly lesbian, women's music was created and performed primarily by lesbian/feminists. It defined itself as popular music that drew upon lesbian/feminist iconography and imagery, and dealt with themes which were of interest primarily to lesbian/feminists. Like other forms of women's culture at the time, women's music was imbued with a belief in a universal female sensibility, expressed in the idea of "woman-identification."[5]

This identity was defined, in large part, by its opposition to masculinist forms of culture, such as mainstream rock and roll—"cock rock." In 1974, *Ms.* magazine asked "Can a Feminist Love the World's Greatest Rock and Roll Band?" and critic Robin Morgan replied with a resolute "No!" She warned that lesbian feminists who listened to the Rolling Stones were no better than those who advocated non-monogamy and accepted transsexuals as allies: they had all adopted a "male style" that would destroy the movement.

Women's music also was rooted in the populist tradition of social protest and in the belief that small and simple was best.[6] For the American Left, at least since the thirties, folk music provided an antidote to an alienated mass culture in which cultural objects became isolated from the communities and traditions that initially gave them shape and meaning. Women's music, which grew partially out of this Left critique, sought to achieve a more authentic form of cultural expression for women, a goal that was embodied in the organization of the women's music industry itself. In addition to encouraging innovation in terms of musical content, women's music politicized the *process* of musical production.

Olivia, the pioneering women's record company formed in the early seventies, comprised the backbone of the women's music industry. It, like most of the women's music industry, was founded on the belief that it was important to erase the distinctions between industry, performers, and audience—distinctions that were central to commercial music.[7] Even more important, perhaps, women's music sought to redress the fact that women in general, and lesbians in particular, had been shut out of positions of power in commercial music. Within alternative music organizations such as Olivia, women were offered opportunities— as performers, singers, producers, and promoters—never before available to them. As singer-songwriter Holly Near explained in retrospect:

Women's music was not just music being done by women. It was music that was challenging the whole system, a little different from disco, a little different from David Bowie playing with androgyny. . . . We were dealing with a lot of issues David Bowie wasn't dealing with, questions his management wasn't asking. So it was not just the music. It was like taking a whole look at systems and societies and letting a music rise out of those systems.[8]

The vision of women's music was an ambitious one. In positively valuing women's (and lesbian) lives and accomplishments, and serving as an organizing tool, it played an important role in the development of lesbian feminist culture. However, the narrow way in which women's music was defined—as music produced by, of, and for feminists—may have inadvertently limited its appeal.

Women of color charged that women's music had become firmly entrenched in what was, for the most part, a European tradition. Confirming their suspicions was the fact that albums and tours by black artists on women's music labels failed to attract much-needed sales. Criticism also came from women in punk which, like women's music, made a politics of disrupting gender and sexual codes, debunking "male" technique and expertise, and posing a critique of glamour.[9] But unlike women's music, punk refused to position itself as the affirmative expression of either feminism or gay liberation, and its brash style was at odds with the folkiness of women's music. As one of the founders of Boston's Rock Against Sexism, a cultural activist group comprised of "closet rock-and-roll fans" in the women's community, explained: "Women's music is really peaceful, not raunchy or angry; it doesn't really excite me or turn me on or get me energized."[10]

In the eighties, the viability of women's music was thrown into question by a crisis of identity. The "decentering" of lesbian feminism, related at least in part to generational changes and to the critique posed by women of color, called into question the prior belief that women's music could reflect an "essential" femaleness. The notion of identity constructed by a century of scientific "experts" implied that all lesbians were alike, united by a common deviance. Removing its basis in biology, lesbian feminists attempted to universalize the possibility of lesbian experience, but in its place they often created rigid ideological prescriptions about who belonged in the lesbian community, and what lesbian culture should look and sound like.[11]

In the end, women's music was revealed to be the expression of a particular generation of activist women. But its undercapitalization prevented it from branching out into other directions. Sales lagged, and many women's music producers responded by moving away from their lesbian-feminist roots.[12] In 1988, as Olivia Records celebrated its fifteenth anniversary with a series of concerts throughout the United States, its records languished in the "women's music" section in the rear of record stores, if they were there at all. But at that very moment a new generation of women performers were entering the mainstream.

Androgyny Goes Pop

In 1988, American music journalists pronounced the arrival of a "new breed of women" in popular music. Tracy Chapman, k. d. lang, Michelle Shocked, the Indigo Girls, and Melissa Etheridge, among others, were noted for defying conventions of femininity in popular music, and moving "back to the basics" away from artifice and role-playing into authenticity.[13]

It was a movement that confounded the critics. "Neither their songs," one critic wrote, "nor the images they project, cater to stereotypical male fantasies of female pop singers." Another proclaimed:

The most astounding thing of all is that Tracy Chapman et al., even happened. Since when did the industry that insisted its strongest women play cartoon characters . . . allow a serious, powerful, flesh and blood female to stand firm on a concert stage?[14]

The answer, as any informed observer could say, was rather simple: the "new breed" of pop women emerged once the industry was convinced that they were marketable. Tracy Chapman became a household name in 1988, selling more than ten million albums, because she was "just so real," according to an Elektra Records executive.

Subcultures have long fueled musical innovation: hugely successful commercial disco and house music, for example, had its origins in the black gay dance floors of Chicago and New York. Likewise, on the heels of the feminist movement, female performers and fans became commercially important "properties" and "markets," giving them a new position of power to define what they did and demand what they wanted. The trail was blazed by such performers as Cyndi Lauper and Madonna—whose messages, though at times contradictory, affirmed an empowered female sexuality practically unseen in commercial pop. In 1983, Lauper released the single "Girls Just Want to Have Fun," described by Lisa Lewis as a "powerful cry for access to the privileged realm of male adolescent leisure and fun."[15] Madonna, probably *the* most successful female star of the contemporary period, exuded sexual power and invincibility, at times making allusions to lesbianism, as on her "Justify My Love" video, which was banned by MTV at the end of 1990.[16]

While there had been, at least since the early seventies, women in popular music who defied conventions of femininity—Patti Smith, Pat Benatar, Janis Joplin, Annie Lennox were among the most central figures—what was new about the eighties wave of androgyny was that its proponents, though not always lesbian-identified, tended to be rooted, at least partially, in lesbian subcultures. Tracy Chapman made the rounds in women's music festivals in 1986 and 1987, while Melissa Etheridge, k. d. lang, Michelle Shocked, and the others knocked around lesbian and "alternative" clubs in Austin, Atlanta, San Francisco, and New York City.

Though influenced by feminism, and frequently women's music, they were convinced that it was necessary to work within the constraints of the industry to get their message across, and saw mainstreaming as an act no less subversive than the feminist disaffection from the industry a decade earlier. Los Angeles-based singer-songwriter Phranc, whose 1989 album *I Enjoy Being a Girl* sported her in a flat-top haircut (alongside a blurb that sang her praises as a "little daughter of bilitis"), toured as the opening act for the Smiths and other popular post-punk acts, playing for mixed audiences because, she said, "it's important to reach out to the kids." As a member of Austin, Texas's 2 Nice Girls, put it: "We don't want to be found only in the speciality bin at the record store. We want to be in your face."[17]

But the most ambitious of these performers carefully constructed their personae to assert a strong, sexually ambiguous female presence. Studiously avoiding male pronouns in romantic ballads, through the subtleties of self-presentation, which were often indecipherable to those who weren't cued into the codes, they made themselves objects of female as well as male desire. Swaggering in a man's western suit, k. d. lang proclaimed: "Yeah, sure, the boys can be attracted to me, the girls can be attracted to me, your mother . . . your uncle, sure. It doesn't really matter to me." On Michelle Shocked's 1989 album, *Captain Swing*, one had to listen closely to "Sleep Keeps Me Awake" to make out the fact that it was a love song to a woman. Even as they were being applauded by the critics for their fresh, unencumbered simplicity and their return to "honesty" and "naturalness," many of these artists constructed their songs and their images with an ambiguity that at times verged on camp.

The arrival of the new breed of androgynous women in pop in the eighties, propelled in large part by an increasingly self-conscious lesbian audience, evidenced the fact that some women could finally defy conventions of femininity in popular music and still achieve mainstream success. But the classic dilemma persisted: a performer either became known as a "lesbian artist" and was doomed to marginality, or she watered down her lesbianism in order to appeal to a mass audience. Lesbian performers were only "safe" (read: marketable) if their sexuality was muted—a woman singing a love song to another woman was still taboo.[18]

The Politics of Ambiguity

Some who had made an explicit politics of their lesbianism charged that the cultural revolution that had begun in the early 1970s had been stalled, gobbled up and incorporated by "the industry." As Phranc sang:

Everybody wants to be a folk singer. They want to be hip and trendy. They want to make sensitive videos and sing about politics. Androgyny is the ticket or at least it seems to be. Just don't wear a flat-top and mention sexuality, and girl you'll go far, you'll get a record contract and be a star.[19]

Women's music, which was created in the context of lesbian institutions and communities, had linked lesbian/feminist authorship to feminist content and audience. With the arrival of the "androgynous pop star," some argued that women's music had been replaced by music that blandly played with lesbian signifiers like clothes and hairstyle in order to gain commercial acceptance, but never really identified itself as lesbian.[20] While such criticisms were perhaps overstated, it was true that, shorn from its community base, lesbian music emerged in the mainstream as a series of floating signifiers, linked to feminist/lesbian sensibilities, but having no real loyalty or commitment to an organized subculture or movement.

Industry constraints were at least partially behind the apparent prohibition against "speaking" lesbianism. In the eighties, the belief in an undifferentiated mass market was replaced in favor of marketing appeals targeted to niches geared to specific racial, ethnic, and "lifestyle" groups of various sorts. Yet it was rare for a commercial record company to acknowledge the existence of the lesbian audience possessing a specific location and particular tastes. When record companies recognized the existence of such a market, they often saw it as a liability rather than as an asset. In marketing an out-lesbian musician such as Phranc, a spokesman for Island Records acknowledged that a performer who makes her lesbianism a central part of her act (that is, she mentions it at all) may have a "limited consumer base."[21]

But if many of these emerging performers were ambiguous about their identities, it was not simply because of industry constraints—it was also because, frequently, their identities *were* ambiguous. Historically, artists have often resisted the demands of identity politics, preferring instead to place their art above loyalties to any one particular group. In the eighties, the "decentring" of lesbian feminism called into question the tendency to make lesbianism a "dominant" or "master" identity. Audre Lorde wrote in 1979:

As a Black lesbian feminist comfortable with the many different ingredients of my identity . . . I find I am constantly being encouraged to pluck out some one aspect of myself and present this as the meaningful whole, eclipsing or denying the other parts of self.[22]

Following from this, one can imagine that Tracy Chapman, a black woman, is a complex personality possessing commitments to more than just the lesbian community. So too is Michelle Shocked, who eventually became involved with a man. In the seventies, Holly Near often hid her bisexuality in order to appeal to a women's audience, in the interest of providing a united front. Ten years later, there appeared to be greater tolerance for ambiguity, and even a certain attraction to *not* really knowing the "truth."

Anyway, what *was* the truth? The eighties, after all, was a decade in which "pleasure," said critic Larry Grossberg, "was replacing understanding."[23] David Letterman, the American baby boomers' late-night talk-show host of choice, celebrated alienation with a mocking self-referentiality, as MTV blurred the boundaries of pop music and advertising. Quick-change, recombinant pop jumped from style to style, integrating new sounds and textures, new identities and images and blurring cultural categories of all sorts. A rap song sampled the theme from the television series *Gilligan's Island;* Peter Gabriel and Paul Simon borrowed from African traditional music. Comedian Sandra Bernhard mixed and matched identities, alluding at times to her lesbianism without ever really embracing it. "I would never make a declaration of anything," she proclaimed. "It's so stupid. Who even cares? It's so presumptuous."[24]

Indeed, for many audience members, particularly younger ones, it seemed, this ambiguity was part of the appeal. As one nineteen-year-old lesbian told me:

I like "cock rock" and women's music. I like both. But I like mainstream women's music the best. Music that speaks to women but isn't only of women. . . . They don't use pronouns, proper nouns. To us that's cool. And we notice that men don't really listen to that music.

As Barbara Bradby has convincingly shown, the fantasies lesbians construct about particular performers' identities, and about themselves in relation to these performers, are a collectively shaped and shared part of lesbian experience.[25] Sexual ambiguity allows for the double appeal of the music—to the subculture, as well as to the mass audience. It allows performers to communicate with lesbian and feminist members of its audience without pledging allegiance to the norms of the subcultures, or becoming spokespersons for them. It allows audience members to listen to music which they consider, secretly, to be lesbian, with the knowledge that millions of other people are also listening to it.

In the end, perhaps it was a testimony to the maturity of feminist and lesbian culture that performers, as well as members of their audience, no longer saw it necessary to make their lesbianism the central overriding feature of their work. In the eighties, as feminist styles were incorporated into popular culture and the boundaries between the mainstream and women's culture blurred, some performers found an unprecedented degree of freedom to construct their images, and their music, as they pleased.

But this strategy also had its limitations. While the new wave of androgynous women in pop achieved mass appeal beyond the already-converted audience of women's music, they were reliant on the existence of a savvy audience to read their codes. Young lesbians could finally see images in the mainstream that closely resembled them, but since lesbianism was still unspoken and since the vast majority lacked the necessary knowledge to cue into these codes, the heterosexual norm remained, for the most part, unchallenged.

Crossover Dreams, Marginal Realities?

In the early nineties, a few women were able to "cross over" and achieve mainstream success as out lesbians, integrating their sexuality into their art without allowing it to become either *the* salient fact, or else barely acknowledged. k. d.

lang and Melissa Etheridge, who had previously coded their sexuality as androgyny, came out as lesbians to great fanfare within lesbian/gay circles and even greater commercial success. Their coming out was highly significant, in part because it was certain to have a ripple effect, encouraging others to follow suit.

Still, it would be unwise to view this development as evidence of the unmitigated march of progress. While these artists were able to (partially) incorporate their lesbianism into their music and images, they did so only after they had achieved considerable commercial success. It was much more difficult, and perhaps even impossible, to do the opposite, to "cross over" from margin to mainstream, and come out while one's career was still at the early stages of development.

Moreover, as I have tried to show, the representation of lesbianism in popular music is a far more complex matter than the sum of individuals who "come out." Lesbian representation in popular music has occurred through the interaction between performers, music industry, and audiences. Artists attempt to achieve popularity while maximizing their creative autonomy, frequently against the imperatives of both the recording industry and a demanding public. The music industry, a source of both conservatism and innovation, tries to keep abreast of trends and emerging "taste publics" without alienating existing audience members. Audiences are constantly in flux, shaped by cultural trends and social movements (such as feminism and gay liberation) that create subcultures that in turn influence popular tastes.[26]

Furthermore, lesbian representation is not simply a matter of making lesbianism visible. Increasingly, as Biddy Martin has argued, the "irreducibly complex and contested nature of identity has itself been made more visible."[27] Women of the baby-boom generation, the founders of women's music and culture, believed that they could construct a collective sense of what it meant to be a lesbian, and also develop representations of that collective identity. Today's emergent generation, much more aware of the limitations of identity politics, seemingly does not. While this indeterminacy is deeply troubling to many women, particularly those who once held the hope of constructing a lesbian-feminist movement that was culturally and ideologically unified, a "decentered" lesbian identity and culture may present new democratic potential. For one thing, many women who felt excluded by an earlier model of identity and culture now feel that they can finally participate on their own terms.

During the last two decades, female pop stars, a good number of whom are lesbians, have worked within these constraints, utilizing different strategies to bring their message to an increasingly self-conscious and sophisticated female audience. The influence of feminism on mainstream culture has meant that many performers are able to exercise a greater degree of control over their image and their music. Popular music is today performed by self-identified lesbians and sympathetic others, drawing upon lesbian iconography and/or subcultural sensibilities, and addressing an audience which at least partially consists of lesbians. And while the dream of a body of music and art that expresses lesbian experience(s) openly and honestly has not yet come to pass in the mainstream, in the meantime, lesbian performers and audiences are struggling in various ways to construct positions from which to speak that acknowledge both lesbian marginality *and* membership in the dominant culture.

Notes

1 Herbert Gans, *Popular Culture and High Culture* (New York: Basic, 1974). See also Angela McRobbie's comments on the importance of looking at "identity-in-culture," in "Post-Marxism and Cultural Studies: A post-script," in *Cultural Studies,* eds. Lawrence Grossberg, Cary Nelson and Paula Treichler (London: Routledge, 1992).

2 Gans, *Popular Culture,* 95. Stuart Hall's "Cultural Identity and Cinematic Representation," in *Framework,* No. 36, is also relevant to this discussion.

3 Jon Savage, "Tainted Love: The Influence of Male Homosexuality and Sexual Divergence on Pop Music and Culture Since the War," in *Consumption, Identity and Style,* ed. Alan Tomlinson (London: Routledge, 1990).

4 Michel Foucault, *The History of Sexuality, Vol. 1* (New York: Random House, 1978).

5 See also Bonnie Zimmerman's study of lesbian feminist fiction, *The Safe Sea of Women: Lesbian Fiction 1969–1989* (Boston: Beacon, 1990).

6 On the "massification" of authentic cultures, see Walter Benjamin, *Illuminations* (New York: Harcourt, 1968).

7 On the history of women's music and its relationship to American radical feminism, see Alice Echols, *Daring to Be Bad: Radical Feminism in America* (Minneapolis: University of Minnesota Press, 1989). For a history of women in music that places women's music in a larger historical perspective, see Gillian Gaar, *She's a Rebel: The History of Women in Rock and Roll* (Seattle: Seal, 1992).

8 Holly Near, interviewed by Gillian Gaar in *She's a Rebel,* 154.

9 In Simon Frith, *Music for Pleasure* (London: Routledge, 1988).

10 Arlene Stein, "Androgyny Goes Pop," in *Sisters, Sexperts, Queers: Beyond the Lesbian Nation,* ed. Arlene Stein (New York: Plume, 1993), 101.

11 Arlene Stein, "Sisters and Queers: the Decentering of Lesbian Feminism," *Socialist Review* (January–March, 1992).

12 For example, Olivia Records turned down overtures from Melissa Etheridge before she was signed to a major label. Redwood Records, the label that Holly Near founded, tried to sign Tracy Chapman when she was still in school in Boston, but could not compete with Elektra.

13 This was the reverse of an earlier embrace of androgyny by male pop stars like David Bowie, influenced by gay drag's tradition of artifice and costume.

14 Susan Wilson, "Talkin' 'bout a revolution for women in pop?" *Boston Sunday Globe* (20 November, 1988).

15 Lisa Lewis, *Gender Politics and MTV: Voicing the Difference* (Philadelphia: Temple University Press, 1990).

16 On the Madonna phenomenon and its relationship to lesbian/gay subcultures, see *The Madonna Connection: Representational Politics, Subcultural Identities and Cultural Theory,* ed. Cathy Schwichtenberg (Boulder, Colo.: Westview, 1993).

17 Stein, "Androgyny Goes Pop," 103.

18 In a rare acknowledgment of the lesbian roots of the late 1980s folk boom, Michelle Shocked, upon accepting the award for Folk Album of the Year at the 1989 New Music Awards in New York (nominated along with Phranc, Tracy Chapman, and the Indigo Girls) quipped "This category should have been called 'Best Lesbian Vocalist.' " But she later complained to an interviewer about being lumped together with all the other emerging women performers, while others avoided the subject entirely, refusing to be interviewed by lesbian/gay or feminist publications.

19 "Folksinger," by Phranc, from *I Enjoy Being a Girl,* Island Records, 1989.

20 Ginny Z. Berson, "Who owes what to whom? Building and maintaining lesbian culture," *Windy City Times* (22 June, 1989).

21 Interview with author, 1991.

22 "Age, Race, Class and Sex: Women Redefining Difference," in Audre Lorde, Sister Outsider (New York: Crossing, 1984).

23 Lawrence Grossberg, "MTV: Swinging on the (Postmodern) Star," in *Cultural Politics in Contemporary America,* eds. Ian Angus and Sut Jhally (London: Routledge, 1989).

24 Stein, "Androgyny Goes Pop," 108.

25 Barbara Bradby, "Lesbians and Popular Music: Does It Matter Who is Singing?" in *Outwrite: Lesbianism and Popular Culture,* ed. Gabriele Griffin (London: Pluto, 1993).

26 Holly Kruse, "Subcultural Identity in Alternative Music Culture," *Popular Music* 12. (January 1993).

27 Biddy Martin, "Sexual Practice and Changing Lesbian Identities," in *Destabilizing Theory: Contemporary Feminist Debates* (Stanford: Stanford University Press, 1992).

Immaculate

Connection

Michael Musto

She stands before the queer nation Madonna Louise Veronica Ciccone Penn—our mother confessor, mistress, master, virgin, whore, wiser sister, nastier daughter, siren, strumpet, couturier, and material girl for those in the market for lace, chiffon, and any other material that provocatively reveals bare flesh. She writhes in our daymares, touches herself in our daydreams, shuns us in our nightmares, undulates and ovulates in the tabloids that we devour to get closer to this glittering enigma, knowing that even half-truths about her will inevitably be more compelling than irrevocable facts about, say, Pebbles or Sheena Easton.

She shimmies into our fag imagination, spreads her legs for our dyke approbation, grabs us by the pudenda, and makes us face things we didn't think it was possible to learn from pop music. After an hour's private session with her, we're aroused but wearing condoms, mad at her for ripping us off, but somehow thanking her for noticing us, legitimizing us, pulling us by our bootstraps up out of hiding and into the public pleasure dome of scrutiny and success. As with no other star before her, we've ceased to be just an audience watching, like Bette Midler's higher being, from a distance (the distance Bette herself has studiously maintained since her baths days). Deliriously, we imagine we're sitting *with* her in the arena—not cheering from the bleachers, but laughing alongside her on-stage and sharing in the kudos from the throngs who recognize that we're a big part of her triumph—even if any real attempt to get near our lady of the poses would have a bouncer dragging us out by the necks as she sang "keep people together" with her usual twisted sense of irony.

But Madonna has nothing, and everything, to do with realness. Aloof, pre-packaged, and encased in the heavy artillery of superstar merchandising, she somehow pierces through the machinery to bare her intentions so frankly we feel intimate with her, breaking down barriers between audience and performer as she brings her deepest secrets into our homes with diary-like immediacy. She's both untouchable and alarmingly accessible—the icon next door, the best friend in a glass booth—and all the contradictions feed into our burgeoning interest, fueling the flames of fascination for someone who's brought crass exploitation to new levels of art, and art to new depths of entertaining debasement.

We don't even know this girl, but we spend more time talking about her than about our real friends, devote more hours to analyzing every cut of her gowns than to our own personal problems. She wears a man's suit and monocle and grabs her crotch in the "Express Yourself" video, and suddenly that becomes the most pressing issue of the week, surpassing any scheduled root-canal work, rent payments, or international skirmish. She says (jokingly?) on national television that she goes to the lesbian bar The Cubby Hole, and that's all anyone of any age group or walk of life can talk about—for two years now! The obsession grows to scary, almost pathological heights, feeding on itself to become more and more ravenously consuming, and we don't try to curb it; this is the healthiest of our vices, after all. However seemingly trivial, it helps us confront religious guilt, purges us of libidinal inhibitions, and forces us to rethink the limitations of gender, intercourse, and responsibility—all with a good beat that you can dance to.

By now, we finally seem willing to release Judy Garland from her afterlife responsibility of being our quintessential icon. And in the land of the living, career stagnation has robbed Diana, Liza, and Barbra of their chances, while Donna thumped the Bible on our heads in a way that made it bounce back into her face. That leaves Madonna as Queer Queen, and she merits the title as someone who isn't afraid to offend straight America, if it does the rest of us some good. *She'd* never use the Bible against queers, but she just might use queers against the Bible. And unlike past icons, she's not a vulnerable toy, but a master of her own fate who's only chained to a bed when she chains herself, and who only cuts loose when some rich, powerful man decides to come up with a bauble to make it worth her while. She's not the lip-quivering, tragic, and overpowered figure Marilyn Monroe was—now and then she just pretends to be before tossing it off for the next fabulous guise.

It's all calculated, controlled, temporary, and autoerotic. Madonna doesn't strip for anyone else, she uncorks herself for the sheer pleasure she takes in her own physicality, enjoying the nuances of her own body even more than we do. Her pride, flamboyance, and glamour reach out to gay guys as much as her butch/femme dichotomy and her refusal to be victimized strikes a chord in lesbians. As a result, Madonna—the great leveler, a breath mint and a candy mint—is the first superstar to appeal equally to both camps. It's not the divisive old Judy story, with guys weeping along with the diva as she longs to go over the rainbow and track down the man that got away, while women cringe. *We all* cheer Madonna as she climbs barefoot over the rainbow, grabs the pot of gold, and forces that man to trade it in for the world's largest diamond ring. The whole scenario is so appealing that, sick as it is, straights like it too.

Why do we all worship at this person's throne so devoutly, even when we're fed up and want her to leave us alone with all the old guilts and repressions? Because, like, you know, she's so articulate? Because, like, you know, she's so underexposed? Because she's the only singer/actress to juggle both nude centerfolds and Lincoln Center ("I'm not ashamed," she announced, presumably about both career moves)?

No, as with everything else in the transparent world of pop, it has to do with sex—the sex the star delivers, withholds, and sells. Everything, admits Madonna, relates to sex—without it she wouldn't be here in the first place. And with her, the sex is right there on the surface, not in any withering, subliminal message that we can subtly pick up between the lines. It's flagrant, shameless, and constant. And a lot of times, thank God—from a distance—it's gay.

She's unafraid to venture into gay territory—not only not fearing, but almost relishing the consequences the way no other straight star is daring enough to do. Performers who are insecure about their own sexuality notoriously steer clear of gay and lesbian associations because they're nervous about what those associations might say about themselves. But Madonna—who seems awesomely secure in her sexuality and all the forms that it may take—is as far from the valley of Richard Simmons (who won't allow gay humor on a talk show he's on because he has "an image problem") as you can get on the axis of *People* magazine celebs. Madonna *wants* an image problem. Blatantly rubbing her desires in the faces of the petit bourgeoisie, she plays with gender roles in ways that any middle-of-the-road performer would toss into the career-move trash heap (where Shelley Long's decision to leave *Cheers* festers).

But—irony of ironies—Madonna's refusals to conform *become* career moves. With each controversy, she emerges more famous and salable, allusions to lesbianism (to name one "scandal") serving only to make her even more desirable to her fans. Reinventing herself constantly, in the way the rapidly aging MTV generation seemingly requires, she's elevated "What next?" to an art form. We collectively gasp over each new shock and brace ourselves for the next, slightly larger one (until snuff looms as the only remaining frontier). In her publicity-seeking quest for thrills, isn't she just using us to advance her own notoriety? Probably, but isn't that infinitely better than a star (Andrew Dice Clay, for example) who uses homophobia to the same end? And hasn't she accorded us our own share of good press, not just bilked us for her own good? With Madonna, you tend to answer a lot of questions with a lot of other questions.

Madonna's gay images exploit us, but it's an exploitation we enjoy. We *want* to be visible in videos, milked for eroticism, pandered to as an audience. We *want* representations of pop music to have same-sex stuff going on, at least as much as goes on in real life (since David Geffen has admitted to being bisexual, shouldn't his company's videos be half-straight and half-gay?). To leave the element out of human experience has always been strangely unnatural, as though no thin people or children with blue eyes were allowed to penetrate the sanctum of music television.

Madonna makes everything permissible, and even if the censors knock her down, she ultimately beats them at their own game. In the sexist context of MTV, she's like a slap of realness from the next century. MTV, remember, is the land where *all* hard-rock videos have to include fast motor vehicles and scantily clad girls jiggling around or striking dehumanized, zombiesque poses. Songs like "Cherry Pie" and "Simply Irresistible" render females as furniture-like objects, alluring accessories for the pubescent straight male audience to whack their puds over and dispose of. The format can hardly be described as a parade of feminism (even Madonna's brand). Yet our self-righteous queen of causes, Sinead O'Connor—who recently boycotted the Grammys because she refuses to be part of a "sexist" and "materialistic" business—gleefully accepted several MTV awards last year, as if this were the highest accolade from a world where women, gays, and people of color run free.

MTV, my dears, is a land that is just starting to wake up to gay issues (some of which were well covered in their "Sex in the '90s" special). But it's got as far to go in that endeavor as it does in portraying women as independent of their bikinis. To this day, anyone who is too eccentric (i.e., gay) doesn't cut it as an on-air regular; an ACT UP "Read My Lips" T-shirt that shows same-sex kissing gets computer scrambled; and while 2 Live Crew's controversial utterances are discussed endlessly, no mention of the grossly homophobic rap group Audio Two manages to seep into airtime. Recently, a network rep wouldn't even consider placing a picture of me in drag (as Madonna, of course) on the air—though she desperately wanted to—as if cross-dressing were somehow against FCC regulations.

MTV's still so regimented in the way it clings to hoary, misguided values of decency and acceptability that anyone who challenges them seems revolutionary. While Sinead did try to shake things up—with the boys dancing together in her video from *Red Hot and Blue*—more than anyone it's Madonna who's dissolved the network's prejudices, often by feeding right into them, then throwing them a whammy.

It's into this stagnant world that she's force-injected beefcake for equal time's sake—the frolicking mermen of "Cherish," the sinewy, *Metropolis*-like laborers of "Express Yourself," even (are we allowed to lust over him?) the hot, if brutally abusive, dad of "Oh, Father." The woman who introduced Herb Ritts to video is definitely someone doing gay men a favor. And for the ladies, at the center of it all is Madonna—twirling half-nakedly and writhing endlessly in gondolas, on dirt roads, on altars—but shrewdly, not "like a" zombie. Her message, projected while twirling, is for women to shamelessly use their wiles to get whatever respect and appliances they want from men. It's not exactly the most advanced brand of feminism, but it may be the most realistic; society puts women at a disadvantage, she's saying, and it's up to them to use every trick imaginable to overcome that and make men their slaves. Like gay activists who vow to get their point across "by any means necessary," Madonna will do anything to get an edge over her male counterparts. She's not fighting for equality within the system, but for superiority through deviousness and manipulation. You can almost see her taking over *Nightline* on the air à la ACT UP; her mission: to force Ted Koppel to bark (or, worse, recite this line: "*Shanghai Surprise* was far and away the best movie of the eighties"). But of course, she *did* take over *Nightline* already.

There are problems with Madonna's somewhat stunted agenda—yes, she *chose* to lick milk out of a bowl, but couldn't she have chosen something else?—yet I'm pretty much sold. She explains "Express Yourself" by giggling, "Pussy rules the world," and if having a pussy can get that many greased muscle studs turning cartwheels around you, then I want one.

Beyond serving as a purveyor of fine *boef*, Madonna throws seemingly limitless other curves into the stasis of contemporary life. Several of the male suitors fawning over her in the "Material Girl" video looked a lot more interested in getting into her red dress than into her. The courtesans in her Marie Antoinette version of "Vogue" emitted enough gay resonances to make the excitable Arsenio Hall extremely nervous (he couldn't resist putting down their foppish outfits on his show, presumably forgetting that he himself has appeared in full drag). And her even more outlandish male backup dancers prancing around in full-figure Gaultier bras (on her "Blond Ambition" tour) were a busty touch that one probably wouldn't expect at a Mariah Carey show.

But then you wouldn't expect Mariah to anonymously coproduce drag-performer Lypsinka's show, or to hang out at the drag-rendezvous bar Edelweiss, either. The club—an atmospheric love-dive set in a German restaurant where all three genders compete for wiener schnitzel—was recently descended on by Madonna, Liza Minnelli, and Naomi Campbell—together—in a priceless meeting of queen bees and wannabes. Most of the transsexual regulars were atwitter, but not happy; they'd been upstaged in their own natural habitat by the very women they were trying to become. I hear the place hasn't been the same since.

The video equivalent of Edelweiss, "Justify My Love" shattered rules in the most self-aggrandizing—but ultimately liberating—way. With its scenes of voyeurism, lesbianism, and cross-dressing, it may have been a typical night on the town for most of us, but to MTV, it was a visit from another planet bearing everything they find repugnant. Especially since a topless girl in suspenders wanders through the sexy murk, it was bound to be banned by the network—only to end up for sale around the country amid a hailstorm of controversy, attention, and money-money-money. It seemed Madonna deliberately played into MTV's homophobia, *hoping* the product would offend them enough to be blacklisted, so she could then serve it up, for a price, to a hungry public nursed on hype. And eventually, I've heard, MTV *will* show it (maybe with a few cuts)—so everybody ends up rich and happy, except for those who realize they didn't have to buy it after all.

But what a product. Clutching her throbbing head as she shuffles through a dank corridor, Madonna has so many fantasies to stop in and visit on the way to the nipples at the end that the video becomes a veritable shrimp-and-salad bar of taboo thrills. Suggestions of S/M, sapphism (Madonna kisses a male-looking female as boyfriend Tony Ward looks on intently), interracial sex (shades of "Like a Prayer"), and androgyny pile up, and you wonder why she didn't have time to throw in a willing sheep or two, or at least a two-headed dildo. "I want to kiss you in Paris," she coos, but you know if she did, her boyfriend would be watching with one hand on his crotch.

The video was the clearest proof that Tony Ward is the perfect partner in Madonna's love crimes; she couldn't have auditioned a boyfriend to better serve her purposes of scandal and sensationalism. An alleged bisexual (the *Star*'s Janet Charlton told a talk-show host that Tony will sleep with apparently anything that's put in front of him—now if I could only get in front of him), Tony's been both engaged and married to other women, but—not your typical spouse—was known to dress as Madonna, and also fantasize about the star watching him having sex. He's always been obsessed with Madonna just like she's always been obsessed with Madonna.

Supposedly, when they first combusted at a party (he'd been in her "Like a Prayer" video, but she'd hardly noticed), Madonna put a cigarette out on Tony, and it was love at first burn. She quickly found that the publicity he generated—he was a gay-porn magazine model, etc., etc.—created even more steam in ways that the highest paid publicist couldn't have dreamed up. The ultimate freewheeling, pansexual plaything, he's the ideal human brooch for Madonna, who apparently enjoys having a love slave a lot more than she enjoyed supposedly being tied to a chair by Sean Penn. Whether or not the relationship's still sizzling (we hear Tony's backing off a bit from her ego), he appeals to all our fascination with Madonna's gay love, as we sit and wonder endlessly who straps what on and does what to whom. And we should thank Madonna for giving us the chance to wonder. While most stars would have tried to suppress such a boyfriend's gay/drag associations or dumped him completely, Madonna just basks in the bad mouthing.

And the controversies keep coming. This May expect a concert documentary called *Truth or Dare,* which in bootleg versions making the rounds on both coasts have already caused more tongue wagging than even the version of *Peter Pan* (*Hook*) (with Julia Roberts as Tinkerbell) turdballing our way. This is not another *Bring on the Night,* where the biggest revelation is Sting being a little snippy to a musician. It's a sensationally private peek at a truly complex, outrageous creature who's always acting up in order to be the center of attention—a very real glimpse at the startling games she plays, made all the more delicious by her having approved every second of it. Out of control, doing things anyone else would have exercised their power to edit out (though she still might), Madonna once again questions our views of what is and isn't acceptable star, and human, behavior.

Growing up in a large family in which she competed for her father's attention, Madonna must have rehearsed her nasty-girl act for years, because in the film, as a bad seed trapped in a woman's body, she's got it down pat. The *Truth or Dare* Madonna is proud of her naughtiness, and exults in it so involuntarily that sometimes she even shocks herself (like when she explains how as a girl she'd crawl into bed with Dad to sleep better, which she did—she laughs—"after he fucked me"). At one point, she's seen deep-throating an Evian bottle just because she can ("And honey, she swallows," her backup singer says). She also plays Truth or Dare with her male dancers, asking truths like, "Have you ever gotten butt-fucked?" and dares like, "Show me your dick." Has Whitney Houston ever made that demand of anyone?

As Warren Beatty skulks through the background of the film trying not to be noticed, Madonna takes center stage, horsing around with her dancers (all but one of whom are gay) trying to resolve the sexuality clashes that unexpectedly erupt. The token straight dancer, it seems, has never been exposed to gay people before, and he's a bit freaked, especially since they've been promising to nail his ass on the tour. A voguing fish out of water, he tells Madonna, "I'm not used to being around fags and stuff," and she tells him to get over it. Then, efficiently enough, she instructs the other backup dancers to lighten up because the guy hasn't been around long enough to build up the defense mechanisms they have. Her handling of the whole mess seems pretty intelligent for a superstar, though of course the ultimate gay-positive thing to do would have been to say, "Ah, let them nail you. Maybe you'll like it."

In a scene where she's performing at a benefit for the Keith Haring Foundation, Madonna frustratedly announces that she's trying to unite thousands against homophobia and bigotry "and I can't even unify seven dancers." Her willingness to even try is kind of touching. More crassly, Madonna says in the film, "I'd kill fags who hate women." (More likely, they'd kill her first.) But then she's lovable again, making the lesbian revelation we've all dreamed of, as she admits that an old girlfriend of hers—who's now married with children—used to finger-fuck her when they were kids (Justify my glove . . .). This isn't a joke, either. In a crosscutting sequence, Madonna is shown describing the episode delightedly as the friend, who admits to having done a lot of drugs back then, tries to remember it, ultimately taking Madonna's word. No value judgment is made of the act—no fingers are pointed, as it were—it's just another cute admission served up to unnerve the complacent public and exacerbate Madonna's reputation for opening her heart, her mouth, and our eyes. In its nonchalance, it both shocks and satisfies.

Even Sandra Bernhard—who's not a dyke, yes she is, no she's not—talks openly on camera about her girlfriend, making one wonder if perhaps she's a dyke again. We also can't help thinking that she's now decided to be an acknowledged lesbian because she's been pressured to be, or if she's only pulling this as another filthy stunt to later deny. The sight of her brings back all that "Letterman" brouhaha, when Madonna and Sandra carried on like girlfriends and confessed to being Cubby Hole regulars, only to then spend two years trying to live it down—as if it were something they *had* to live down (it only made them that much more famous and talked about). No one said, "I'm not going to see *Without* You *I'm Nothing* or *Dick Tracy* because those girls are lesbians." And if Sandra or Madonna have convinced themselves that people did say that, then they're using their own homophobia to rationalize their shortcomings.

Seemingly desperate to go from the fringe to mainstream—and her rambunctious talent merits the leap—Sandra hasn't been able to decide how to keep her gay audience while amassing a larger one. Instead, she spites gays, then still finds that doesn't help advance her career. Like Boy George, who cloaked himself in fake bisexuality and ended up becoming the kind of drug-abusing, hotel room–trashing rock star he so loathed, Sandra runs the risk of developing into what she once made fun of. Clothed in designer duds, lunching with Isaac Mizrahi, changing her sexuality every five minutes, she's treacherously close to being the climbing vine she's not supposed to respect. Hopefully, she's learned from Madonna that keeping your edge may be the best way to go forward.

The whole self-loathing "Letterman" episode continues to leave a foul taste, as if we'd been teased into thinking these were our friends, then repeatedly clubbed over the head by their alarm at being considered so. Still, it's important to remember that it was Sandra, not Madonna, who later said they'd been dragged into a "cesspool of degradation" by being labeled lesbians. It was Sandra, not Madonna, who told the inquisitive press to "kiss my fat butt." It was Sandra, not Madonna, who announced, "I'm not a lesbian, and I'm sick of being called one."

And besides, it somehow seems more acceptable for a woman who's not a lesbian (Madonna) to say, "We were just kidding. I'm not really," than a woman who is (Sandra) to do the same. And yet—ah, the tangled thoughts—while not as damagingly as Sandra, Madonna did let us down. She could have responded to queries with, "Well, maybe I do go to the Cubby Hole and maybe I don't," and continued to act as if there would be nothing wrong with that. She could have chosen that moment to bring up those misty finger-fucking memories. She could have said, "Yes, Sandra and I dive on each other nightly," whether or not they really do (and I have my own thoughts on that subject). But she reneged, and for once we did feel like we'd been had.

The using issue came up again last year when Madonna released "Vogue"—at a time when we jaded New York folk were sure the trend was way over—and once again proved that her timing was impeccable. Middle America was all primped and ready for it, legs akimbo and arms in a formation. In accessorizing herself with a black/Hispanic, gay/drag art form for mass success, Madonna was doing her usual shtick of taking something bubbling under the surface and putting it over in a big way. She was inviting public perception to a movement that seemed to have become slick enough to warrant a commercial venue. And she was, quite blatantly, ripping it off. What Madonna does best is exploit what she sees on the street, and since gay blacks are at the forefront of so much of that, it was probably inevitable that they'd end up being the targets of her co-opting frenzy. Whether they should feel grateful or raped is another issue.

While most voguers struggle through their low-income lives, becoming powerful real men and women only in the contrived world of the voguing balls, Madonna approached the phenomenon from the opposite direction, as a well-off, pampered celebrity slumming up in Harlem for effect. She's that rare voguer who can both strike a pose and also strike a multimillion deal with a record and movie company. By saturating the airwaves with voguing, she certainly helped it, and voguers in general, become more visible, but that's like saying Vanilla Ice did blacks a favor by making rap more visible.

Of course, another argument is that Madonna did employ gay people of color in her video and on her tour. But wasn't that just to add authenticity to her well-researched attempt at currency? The questions don't quit, especially in light of rumors that the song's lyrics—"It makes no difference if you're black or white, if you're a boy or a girl"—were supposed to include references to gays, but in the final whitewashed version, glaringly didn't. Ultimately, we won and lost on the "Voguing" issue; it was Madonna's nod to this creative underground and her subtle stab in its back. As with many of her exploitative choices, she ended up helping herself more than anybody.

Fortunately, she's proven herself to be a good friend to the gay and AIDS community, doing enough selfless things to perhaps ameliorate the memory of the debatable ones. Someone who has kids chanting along with her, "Hey you, don't be silly, put a rubber on your willy," is far more valuable an ally than say, a Sebastian Bach, who asks his audience to chirp along with "AIDS Kills Fags Dead." Madonna's assumed more than her share of responsibility in the AIDS crisis, a crisis that's divided the entertainment world into moralists (Axl Rose), self-aggrandizers (Dionne Warwick), people who'd like to help but feel it wouldn't be good for the career (fill in the blank), and a handful of outspoken leaders. Madonna has a personal stake in the crisis; her old New York roommate Martin Burgoyne died of AIDS (and she quietly assumed a lot of his expenses), and so did her dance teacher and mentor Christopher Flynn, prompting the tabs to report, "Madonna Heartbroken as Her First Love Dies of AIDS." Propelled by these losses (and Keith Haring's), she determined to make it in vogue to fight an otherwise unpopular, unfabulous battle. Recently, she told the BBC, "I have such a youthful following and a very large gay following that since I have that ear, it's very important for me to be a spokesperson."

And for someone who clawed her way to the top half-naked and made a career eking glamour out of cold, grasping greed, she's been very generous. While the organizers of one recent AIDS drag ball complained that she withdrew participation, it's hard to argue with what she has done, and ridiculous to expect her to put her name on every charity opportunity offered. To her credit, she was the first star to put safer-sex information in her records, she's talked openly against the church's AIDS policies and in favor of condoms, and she's donated large sums to AIDS charities, always keeping the subject in the public eye despite the government's attempts to render it invisible. Fortunately, as a role model and evocator of change, Madonna is right now more powerful than the government.

The House

the Kids Built

The Gay Black Imprint on American Dance Music

Anthony Thomas

America's critical establishment has yet to acknowledge the contributions made by gay Afro-Americans. Yet black (and often white) society continues to adopt cultural and social patterns from the gay black subculture. In terms of language, turns of phrase that were once used exclusively by gay Afro-Americans have crept into the vocabulary of the larger black society: singer Gladys Knight preaches about unrequited love to her "girlfriend" in the hit "Love Overboard"; and college rivals toss around "Miss Thing" in Spike Lee's film "School Daze."

What's also continued to emerge from the underground is the dance music of gay black America. More energetic and polyrhythmic than the sensibility of straight African-Americans, and simply more African than the sensibility of white gays, the musical sensibility of today's "house" music—like that of disco and club music before it—has spread beyond the gay black subculture to influence broader musical tastes.

What exactly is house music? At a recording session for DJ International, a leading label of house music, British journalist Sheryl Garratt posed that question to the assembled artists. A veritable barrage of answers followed: "I couldn't begin to tell you what house is. You have to go to the clubs and see how people react when they hear it. It's more like a feeling that runs through, like old time religion in the way that people jus' get happy and screamin'. . . . It's happening! . . . It's Chicago's own sound. . . . It's rock till you drop. . . . You might go and seek religion afterwards! It's gonna be hot, it's gonna be sweaty, and it's gonna be great. It's honest-to-goodness, get down, low down gutsy, grabbin' type music."[1]

Like the blues and gospel, house is very Chicago. Like rap out of New York and go-go out of D.C., house is evidence of the regionalization of black Ameri-can music. Like its predecessors, disco and club, house is a scene as well as a music, black as well as gay.

But as house music goes pop, so slams the closet door that keeps the facts about its roots from public view. House, disco, and club are not the only black music that gays have been involved in producing, nor is everyone involved in this music gay. Still, the sound, the beat, and the rhythm *have* risen up from the dancing sensibilities of urban gay Afro-Americans.

The music, in turn, has provided one of the underpinnings of the gay black subculture. Dance clubs are the only popular institutions of the gay black com-munity that are separate and distinct from the institutions of the straight black majority. Unlike their white counterparts, gay black Americans, for the most part, have not redefined themselves—politically or culturally—apart from their majority community. Although political and cultural organizations of gay Afro-Americans have formed in recent years, membership in these groups remains very small and represents only a tiny minority of the gay black population. Lesbian and gay Afro-Americans still attend black churches, join black frater-nities and sororities, and belong to the NAACP.

Gay black dance clubs, like New York's Paradise Garage and Chicago's Ware-house (the birthplace of house music), have staked out a social space where gay black men don't have to deal with the racist door policies at predominantly white gay clubs or the homophobia of black straight clubs. Over the last twenty years the soundtrack to this dancing revolution has been provided by disco, club, and now—house music.

Playback: The Roots of House

Although disco is most often associated with gay white men, the roots of the music actually go back to the small underground gay black clubs of New York City. During the late sixties and early seventies, these clubs offered inexpensive all-night entertainment where DJs, in order to accommodate the dancing urgen-cies of their gay black clientele, overlapped soul and Philly (Philadelphia Inter-national) records, phasing them in and out, to form uninterrupted soundtracks for nonstop dancing. The Temptations' 1969 hit "I Can't Get Next To You" and the O'Jays' "Back Stabbers" are classic examples of the genre of songs that were manipulated by gay black DJs. The songs' up-tempo, polyrhythmic, Latin percussion-backed grooves were well suited for the high energy, emotional, and physical dancing sensibility of the urban gay black audience.

In African and African-American music, new styles are almost always built from simple modifications of existing and respected musical styles and forms. By mixing together the best dance elements of soul and Philly records, DJs in gay black clubs had taken the first steps in the creative process that music critic Iain Chambers interprets as a marker of disco's continuity with the rhythm and blues tradition: "[In disco] the musical pulse is freed from the claustrophobic interiors of the blues and the tight scaffolding of R&B and early soul music. A looser, explicitly polyrhythmic attack pushes the blues, gospel and soul heritage into an apparently endless cycle where there is no beginning or end, just an ever-present 'now.' Disco music does not come to a halt . . . restricted to a three-minute single, the music would be rendered senseless. The power of disco . . . lay in saturating dancers and the dance floor in the continual explosion of its presence."[2]

Although the disco pulse was born in the small gay black clubs of New York, disco music only began to gain commercial attention when it was exposed to the dance floor public of the large, predominantly white gay discos. *Billboard* only introduced the term *disco-hit* in 1973, years after disco was a staple among gay Afro-Americans, but—as music historian Tony Cummings has noted—only one year after black and white gay men began to intermingle on the dance floor.

By the mid-seventies disco music production was in high gear, and many soul performers (such as Johnny Taylor with his 1976 hit "Disco Lady") had switched camps to take advantage of disco's larger market. Records were now being recorded to accomplish what DJs in gay black clubs had done earlier. Gloria Gaynor scored a breakthrough in disco technique with her 1974 album, *Never Can Say Goodbye*. The album treated the three songs on side one ("Honey Bee," "Never Can Say Goodbye," and "Reach Out, I'll Be There") as one long suite delivered without interrupting the dance beat—a ploy that would become a standard disco format and the basis of house music's energy level.

As the decade progressed, disco music spread far beyond its gay black origins and went on to affect the sound of pop. In its journey from this underground scene, however, disco was whitewashed. The massive success of the 1978 film *Saturday Night Fever* convinced mainstream America that disco was a new fad, the likes and sound of which had never been seen before. White gay men latched onto the "Hi NRG" Eurodisco beat of Donna Summer's post–"Love to Love You" recordings and the camp stylings of Bette Midler.

Indeed, the dance floor proved to be an accurate barometer of the racial differences in the musical tastes of white and black gays and the variation in dancing sensibilities between gay and straight Afro-Americans. Quick to recognize and exploit the profit-making potential of this phenomenon, independent producers began to put out more and more records reflecting a gay black sound.

Starting in 1977, there was an upsurge in the production of disco-like records with a soul, rhythm and blues, and gospel feel: club music was born. The most significant difference between disco and club was rhythm. Club rhythms were more complex and more Africanized. With club music, the gay black subculture reappropriated the *disco impulse,* as demonstrated by the evolution in disco superstar Sylvester's music.

In 1978 Sylvester had a big hit with "Disco Heat"; in 1980 he released another smash, "Fever." "Disco Heat" was a classic example of the type of disco popular among gay Afro-Americans. At 136 beats per minute it combined the high energy aspect of white gay disco with the orchestral flourishes of contemporary soul. The song also contained the metronomic bass drum that characterized all disco. It was only the gospel and soul-influenced vocals of Sylvester and his back-up singers, Two Tons o' Fun, that distinguished the music from whiter genres of disco.

"Fever," on the other hand, more clearly reflects a black/African sensibility. To begin with, the song starts with the rhythmic beating of cowbells. Sylvester also slowed the beat down to a funkier 116 beats per minute and added polyrhythmic conga and bongo drumming. The drumming is constant throughout the song and is as dominant as any other sound in it. Just as significant, in terms of Africanizing the music, was the removal of the metronomic bass drum that served to beat time in disco. In African music there is no single main beat; the beat emerges from the relation of cross-rhythms and is provided by the listener or dancer, not the musician. By removing the explicit time-keeping bass of disco, Sylvester had reintroduced the African concept of the "hidden rhythm."

While most black pop emphasizes vocals and instrumental sounds, club music tends to place more emphasis on a wide array of percussive sounds (many of which are electronically produced) to create complex patterns of cross-rhythms. In the best of club music, these patterns change very slowly; some remain stable throughout the song. It is this characteristic of club music, above all, that makes it an African-American dance music par excellence.

Like disco, club also moved beyond the gay black underground scene. Gay clubs helped spread the music to a "straight" black audience on ostensibly "straight" Friday nights. And some club artists, like Grace Jones, Colonel Abrams, and Gwen Guthrie, achieved limited success in the black pop market.

For most of its history, though, club music largely has been ignored by black-oriented radio stations. Those in New York, for instance, were slow to start playing club music with any regularity; finally WBLS and WRKS began airing dance mixes at various intervals during the day. In the early eighties, the two black-oriented FM radio outlets in Chicago, WBMX and WGCI, began a similar programming format that helped give rise to the most recent variation of gay black music: house.

Pumping Up the Volume

The house scene began, and derived its name from Chicago's now defunct dance club The Warehouse. At the time of its debut in 1977, the club was the only after-hours dance venue in the city, opening at midnight Saturday and closing after the last dancers left on Sunday afternoon. On a typical Saturday night, two to five thousand patrons passed through its doors.

The Warehouse was a small three-story building—literally an abandoned warehouse with a seating area upstairs, free juice, water, and munchies in the basement, and a dimly lit, steamy dance floor in between. You only could reach the dance floor through a trap door from the level above, adding to the underground feeling of the club.

A mixed crowd (predominantly gay—male and female) in various stages of undress (with athletic wear and bare flesh predominating) was packed into the dance space, wall to wall. Many actually danced hanging from water pipes that extended on a diagonal from the walls to the ceiling. The heat generated by the dancers would rise to greet you as you descended, confirming your initial impression that you were going down into something very funky and "low."

What set the Warehouse apart from comparable clubs in other cities was its economically democratic admission policy. Its bargain admission price of four dollars made it possible for almost anyone to attend. The Paradise Garage in New York, on the other hand, was a private club that charged a yearly membership fee of seventy-five dollars, plus a door price of eight dollars. The economic barriers in New York clubs resulted in a less "low" crowd and atmosphere, and the scene there was more about who you saw and what you looked like than in Chicago.

For the Warehouse's opening night in 1977, its owners lured one of New York's hottest DJs, Frankie Knuckles, to spin for the "kids" (as gay Afro-Americans refer to each other). Knuckles found out that these Chicagoans would bring the roof down if the number of beats per minute weren't sky high: "That fast beat [had] been missing for a long time. All the records out of New York the last three years [had] been mid- or down-tempo, and the kids here [in Chicago] won't do that all night long, they need more energy."[3]

Responding to the needs of their audience, the DJs in Chicago's gay black clubs, led by Knuckles, supplied that energy in two ways: by playing club tunes and old Philly songs (like MFSB's "Love Is the Message") with a faster, boosted rhythm track, and by mixing in the best of up-tempo avant-garde electronic dance music from Europe. Both ploys were well received by the kids in Chicago; the same was not true of the kids in New York.

As Knuckles points out, many of the popular songs in Chicago were big in

New York City, "but one of the biggest cult hits, 'Los Ninos' by Liasons Dangereuses, only got played in the punk clubs there." *Dance Music Report* noted that for most of the eighties, Chicago has been the most receptive American market for avant-garde dance music. The Windy City's gay black clubs have a penchant for futuristic music, and its black radio stations were the first in the United States to give airplay to Kraftwerk's "Trans Europe Express" and Frankie Goes to Hollywood's "Two Tribes." The Art of Noise, Depeche Mode, David Byrne and the Talking Heads, and Brian Eno were all popular in Chicago's gay black circles.

What's also popular in Chicago is the art of mixing. In an interview with Sheryl Garratt, Farley Keith Williams (a.k.a. "Farley Jackmaster Funk"), one of house music's best known DJ/producers, says: "Chicago is a DJ city. . . . If there's a hot record out, in Chicago they'll all buy two copies so they can mix it. We have a talent for mixing. When we first started on the radio there weren't many [DJs], but then every kid wanted two turntables and a mixer for Christmas. . . . And if a DJ can't mix, they'll boo him in a minute because half of them probably known [*sic*] how to do it themselves."

What was fresh about house music in its early days was that folks did it themselves; it was "homemade." Chicago DJs began recording rhythm tracks, using inexpensive synthesizers and drum machines. Very soon, a booming trade developed in records consisting solely of a bassline and drum patterns. As music critic Carol Cooper notes, "basement and home studios sprang up all over Chicago."

DJs were now able to create and record music and then expose it to a dance floor public all their own, completely circumventing the usual process of music production and distribution. These homespun DJs-cum-artists/producers synthesized the best of the avant-garde electronic dance music (Trilogy's "Not Love," Capricorn's "I Need Love," and Telex's "Brain Washed") with the best loved elements of classic African-American dance cuts, and wove it all through the cross-rhythms of the percussion tracks, creating something unique to the character of gay black Chicago.

There are so many variants of house that it is difficult to describe the music in general terms. Still, there are two common traits that hold for all of house: the music is always a brisk 120 bpm or faster; and percussion is everything. Drums and percussion are brought to the fore, and instrumental elements are electronically reproduced. In Western music, rhythm is secondary in emphasis and complexity to harmony and melody. In house music, as in African music, this sensibility is reversed.

Chip E., producer of the stuttering, stripped-down dance tracks "Like This" and "Godfather of House" characterizes house's beat as "a lot of bottom, real heavy kick drum, snappy snare, bright hi-hat and a real driving bassline to keep the groove. Not a lot of lyrics—just a sample of some sort, a melody [just] to remind you of the name of the record."[4]

That's all you can remember—the song's title—if you're working the groove of house music, because house is pure dance music. Don't dismiss the simple chord changes, the echoing percussion lines, and the minimalist melody: in African music the repetition of well-chosen rhythms is crucial to the dynamism of the music. In the classic *African Rhythm and African Sensibility,* John Chernoff remarks that "repetition continually re-affirms the power of the music by locking that rhythm, and the people listening or dancing to it, into a dynamic and open structure." It is precisely the recycling of well-chosen rhythmic patterns in house that gives the music a hypnotic and powerfully kinetic thrusting, permitting dancers to extract the full tension from the music's beat.

Chernoff argues that the power and dynamic potential of African music is in the gaps between the notes, and that it is there that a creative participant will place his contribution. By focusing on the gaps rather than the beats, the dancers at the Warehouse found much more freedom in terms of dancing possibilities, a freedom that permitted total improvisation.

The result was a style of dancing dubbed "jacking" that more closely resembled the spasmodic up and down movements of people possessed than it did the more choreographed and fluid "vogueing" movement of the dancers at other clubs like New York's Paradise Garage. Dancers at The Warehouse tended to move faster, quirkier, more individualistically, and deliberately off-beat. It's not that the kids had difficulty getting the beat; they simply had decided to move beyond it—around, above, and below it. Dancing on the beat was considered too normal. To dance at the Warehouse was to participate in a type of mass possession: hundreds of young black kids packed into the heat and darkness of an abandoned warehouse in the heart of Chicago during the twilight hours of Sunday morning, jacking as if there would be no tomorrow. It was a dancing orgy of unrivaled intensity, as Frankie Knuckles recalls: "It was absolutely the only club in the city to go to . . . it wasn't a polished atmosphere—the lighting was real simplistic, but the sound system was intense and it was about what you heard as opposed to what you saw."[5]

No Way Back: House Crosses Over

Like disco and club, house music is rapidly moving beyond the gay black underground scene, thanks in part to a boost from radio play. As early as 1980, Chicago's black-oriented radio stations WBMX and WGCI rotated house music into their programming by airing dance mixes. WBMX signed on a group of street

DJs, the "Hot Mix 5," whose ranks included two of the most prolific and important house producers/artists—Ralph Rosario and Farley Jackmaster Funk. When the Hot Mix crew took to the air on Saturday nights, their five-hour show drew an estimated audience of 250,000 to 1,000,000 Chicagoans.

Now in Chicago, five-year-olds are listening to house and jacking. Rocky Jones, president of the DJ International recording label, points out that "[in Chicago, house] appeals to kids, teenagers, blacks, whites, hispanics, straights, gays. When McDonald's HQ throws a party for its employees, they hire house DJs."

Outside of Chicago, house sells mainly in New York, Detroit, D.C., and other large urban/black markets in the Northeast and Midwest. As in Chicago, the music has moved beyond the gay black market and is now very popular in the predominantly white downtown scene in New York, where it regularly is featured in clubs like Boy Bar and the World. But the sound also has traveled uptown, into the boroughs (and even into New Jersey) by way of increased airplay on New York's black radio stations; house can now be heard blasting forth from the boom boxes of b-boys and b-girls throughout the metropolitan area. It has also spread south and west to gay clubs like the Marquette in Atlanta and Catch One in Los Angeles. Even Detroit is manufacturing its own line, tagged "techno-house."

House music has a significant public in England as well, especially in London. In reporting on the house scene in Chicago, the British music press scooped most of its American counterparts (with the notable exception of *Dance Music Report*) by more than a year. So enthusiastic has been the British response to house that English DJs and musicians (both black and white) are now producing their own variety of house music, known as "acid" house.

House music, however, is not without its critics. Like disco and club, it has been either ignored or libeled by most in the American music press. In a recent *Village Voice* article hailing the popularity of rap music, Nelson George perfunctorily dismisses the music as "retro-disco." Other detractors of house have labeled the music "repetitive" and "unoriginal."[6]

Because of its complex rhythmic framework, though, house should not be judged by Western music standards but by criteria similar to those used to judge African music. House is retro-disco in the same way and to the same extent that rap is "retro-funk."

The criticism that this music is unoriginal stems from the fact that many house records are actually house versions of rhythms found in old soul and Philly songs. Anyone familiar with African-American musical idioms is aware that the remaking of songs is a time-honored tradition. As John Chernoff has documented, truly original style in African and African-American music often consists in subtle modifications of perfected and strictly respected forms. Thus, Africans remain "curiously" indifferent to what is an important concern of Western culture: the issue of artistic origins.

Each time a DJ plays at a club, it is a different music-making situation. The kids in the club are basically familiar with the music and follow the DJ's mixing with informed interest. So, when a master DJ flawlessly mixes bits and pieces of classic soul, Philly, disco, and club tunes with the best of more recent house fare to form an evenly pumping groove, or layers the speeches of political heroes (Martin Luther King, Jr., Malcolm X, or Jesse Jackson) or funky Americana (a telephone operator's voice or jingles from old television programs) over well-known rhythm tracks, the variations stand out clearly to the kids and can make a night at the club a special affair.

To be properly appreciated, house must be experienced in a gay black club. As is true of other African music, it is a mistake "to listen" to house because it is not set apart from its social and cultural context. "You have to go to the clubs and see how people react when they hear it . . . people jus' get happy and screamin.'" When house really jacks, it is about the most intense dance music around. Wall-flowers beware: you have to move to understand the power of house.

Notes

1 Sheryl Garrat, "Let's Play House," *The Face* (September 1986), 18–23.

2 Iain Chambers, *Urban Rhythms: Pop Music and Popular Culture* (New York: St. Martin's, 1985), 187–88.

3 Simon Wiffer, "House Music," *i–d* (September 1986).

4 Garrat, "Let's Play House," 23.

5 Wiffer, "House Music."

6 Nelson George, "Nationwide: America Raps Back," *Village Voice* 4, 19 January 1988, p. 32–33.

Children

of Paradise

A Brief History of Queens

Mark Thompson

In contemporary Western society, few figures are held in greater contempt, or considered more useless or perverse, than the drag queen. But in many non-Christian and preindustrialized cultures, those who bridged the genders were placed in a position of honor and ritual purpose. As Judy Grahn points out in *Another Mother Tongue: Gay Words, Gay Worlds* (Beacon Press, 1984): "In tribal/pagan realms cross-dressing often meant entering a magical state involving taking on a persona or spirit of a god being for public ceremonial purposes." Cross-dressed men and women assumed a variety of roles: healers and mediators of spiritual life, as well as daily life within their community.

The magical role of the gay shaman has been recorded in many cultures around the world. Among the Ambo people of South West Africa they were known as the *omasenge;* in Polynesia they were called the *mahu;* in Central and North American Indian tribes they were referred to as the *berdache,* a term European colonizers used to generalize the many names the native tribes had for their sacred transvestites. The Oglala called their gay magic men *winkte.* The Crow Indians of Montana used *bote,* meaning "not-man, not-woman." Among the Zuni of New Mexico, men of the tribe who pursued the skills and activities of the opposite sex—for example, those who became potters or weavers—were called *Lhamana.* And the Navajo named their gay shamans *nadle.* A Navajo elder once said, "I believe when all the *nadle* have passed away, it will be the end of the Navajo culture."

In the Americas, as in the pre-Christian and indigenous cultures of Europe, an uninhibited expression of homosexuality was often applied to sacred ritual, an understanding about sex and spirit that has long since been obliterated through centuries of genocide and cruel repression of pagan sensibilities.

Today, the religious role of those who bridge gender has been reduced to a tragic and trivialized cipher, a faint echo of the symbolic importance it once had in human culture. Yet, in many societies around the world, some gay men continue to cross-dress. But unlike the many heterosexual men who do so largely with guilt and shame, gay transvestites wear their adornment as public celebration. By doing so they release the feminine energy that's usually kept locked within the male psyche and set free laughter that can empower hearts and minds more than any rigid devotion to the protocol of gender. As Holly Woodlawn once said, "Man or woman? What difference does it make as long as you look fabulous!"

For gay men, drag is still theater, a form of public ritual. And while seemingly divorced from any spiritual or social context, it is still possible to scrape away layers of cultivated Christian dogma and glimpse a small example of the useful ways in which cross-dressing can serve a community. We'll begin with one summer night in San Francisco, not too many years ago.

The word is out at the corner of Powell and Columbus. It's midnight, and a large theater marquee spelling *Palace* illuminates the milling crowd below in gaudy neon hues. There are men in rouge and green eyeshadow and women wearing black leather jackets and bowler hats. Inside, the theater is packed to capacity, and cheap wine and joints are freely passed from row to row.

Backstage, confusion is equally rife. Performers stand in front of mirrors and tug on costumes pieced together from moulting boas, old satin dresses, and papier-mâché hats. Nearby, a naked man dusts his body with silver glitter, while a woman, some months pregnant, rehearses the words to "I Want a Little Sugar in My Bowl." Curtain time has come and gone, and the audience roars its good-natured impatience. The lights suddenly dim, and a voice booms through the dark, "Ladies and gentlemen! The all-new, all-singing, all-electric, all cardboard Cockettes!" The troupe enters to cheers, a spectacle of rouged nipples, dime-store jewelry, and lamé codpieces. Goldie Glitters, playing a fiendish gossip columnist, Vedda Viper, steps forward and screeches, "All the dirt, all the stars, no matter whose life I fuck up!"

Later, while a bearded torch singer croons "Can't Help Loving That Man of Mine," a backdrop of cardboard calla lilies in bloom begins to collapse. Cast, crew, and even a few audience members rush on stage to rescue the sagging set piece. But the balance is lost, and the lilies exit in a cloud of dust. Someone on stage stamps his foot. "I'm tired of this. Let's do something else."

And they did.

"The lobby of the Palace Theater was a beautiful place to be gay," one observer of the times said. "It was crowded with the extraordinary, the bizarre decadents who created an underground renaissance." It was 1970, and radical drag—"gender fuck"—was in vogue. The first angry howls of gay revolt were still reverberating across the land, and the national tragedies and creative liberation of the previous decade were finding perspective. That a small band of gay men on the West Coast had taken to wearing dresses and beards at the same time seemed, to some people, a needless confusion of the issues at hand. A few critics dismissed the glittery phenomenon as a quaint last gasp of the hippie counterculture, and others thought it made some sort of polymorphous perverse political statement about the future. The men in question couldn't have cared less. Almost no one perceived the sensation for what it really was—a form of gay consciousness asserting itself.

"We were exploding the myth of romance and glamour, the myth of success," I would be told years later by Martin Worman, who had gone on from the troupe to direct theater in New York. "Of course, it was political, but no one among us verbalized it. We had no need of rhetoric. We were madcap chefs cooking up a storm and the ingredients were magic and tribal anarchy."

The Cockettes were symptomatic of an entire generation flipping out from a lifetime of popular culture—a gut-wrenching angst combined, in this case, with a budding gay sensibility. Conceived on the back seat of a 1953 pink Cadillac parked at the intersection of Hollywood Boulevard and Madison Avenue, weaned on the junky excrement of television, they saw American culture in full circle. And, recognizing themselves, they let out a cry of chaos and rage.

"Among the other myths, we were also exploding nostalgia," said Worman. "We never took the poses and ambience of another decade seriously; we were pointing up the absurdities. But in our wake, old clothes and old songs became ends in themselves. Nostalgia became an insidious tool used by mass marketeers to cover up the shortages of spirit, imagination and raw materials in the post-Vietnam and post-Watergate bankruptcy." The Cockettes *were* outrageous because their theater was a pastiche of every used-up myth, fable, and lie they had ever watched, read, or been taught. And their audience laughed, as if looking into a crazy-house mirror.

Poet Allen Ginsberg, who fondly remembers the Cockettes, told me that the notoriety of the group "affected the entire suburban culture" that was to follow. "Kids who wanted some way to express difference from the homogenized television culture adopted the plumage of these [radical transvestites]. The Cockettes were part of a large-scale spiritual liberation movement and reclamation of self from the homogenization of the military state. They were expressing themselves as actual people with their own natures and tendencies, rather than being ashamed—and doing it with humor."

The role of the fool, the trickster, the *contrary one* capable of turning a situation inside out, is one of the most enduring of all archetypes. Often cross-dressed or adorned with both masculine and feminine symbols, these merry pranksters chase through history, holding up a looking glass to human folly. Confidants to kings and commoners, teller of truths, and cloaked in many disguises, these queer figures seem to spring from the shadow realm that lies between the worlds of above and below. It is a role that seems particularly suited to gay men, and in San Francisco it is possible to trace a succession of such men playing the role with glee.

On the more tolerant West Coast, men dressed as women have always been a recognized part of the social landscape. Men cross-dressed in the rough-hewn frontier of the mid-nineteenth century, before most women would make the long and dangerous trip from the East. And drag performers in Barbary Coast music halls were not uncommon later, echoing other cultures' use of men in feminine roles, as in Greece, England, and Japan. During the fifties, Jose Sarria reigned as San Francisco's most celebrated drag queen. Ensconced at the Black Cat, a bohemian bar in North Beach not too many blocks from the venerable Palace Theater, Sarria would enact madcap, one-man parodies of such classic operas as *Carmen* to packed houses.

"I decided that if I was going to be labeled a queen, I would be the biggest, best queen there was," he would say to me twenty-five years later. There was a method to his mayhem, and raising gay self-esteem during a time of near-unanimous moral and legal sanctions against homosexuality was a conscious act on Sarria's part. The husky chanteuse would conclude each performance at the famous bar with a brief talk on gay rights, and then lead the entire audience in a rousing version of "God Bless Us Nellie Queens." In 1961, Sarria was the first person to run for public office in the United States as an openly gay candidate. His tally of nearly six thousand voters—for a seat on the city's governing board—sent shock waves through San Francisco's political establishment. The election also necessitated Sarria's first suit of men's clothing.

"Our humor is our key. If we lose that we're dead," he said. "The cross-dressing was part of our humor. Yes, it was our camp. I dressed at the Black Cat to show some of the absurdities expected of women. I poked fun to make gay people laugh, but when they started to laugh too hard I turned the joke around on them. I played one against the other. I wanted the queens to see how ridiculous they were, too."

During those early days there "were maybe twenty-five who dressed like me" in San Francisco, said Sarria, but those uninhibited individuals seemed to give permission for many others to follow. Thirty years later, an extensive network of cross-dressed "Royal Courts"—with Sarria crowned its first empress—had developed throughout the western United States, involving hundreds of gay men in dozens of cities, from Seattle to San Diego, Denver to Monterey. However, among other gay organizations, "We continue to be the most controversial, the most misunderstood and the most disliked," said one prominent member of the drag community. "One can compare the gay court system to the Shriners, Elks or other similar social community-service organizations. No one personally receives monetary gain from the tens of thousands of dollars raised at our functions every year. The money goes directly back into the community."

Bold drag queens have always been the revolutionaries of the gay movement: disfranchised, near the bottom of any community's pecking order (including their own), but empowered with lessons of nonattachment and the realization that they stand with those who have the least to lose in their fight against social injustice. Over the last several decades the confrontational, campy words and images created by public drag personas such as Sarria at the Black Cat, Michelle at the Village Club, Charles Pierce at the Gilded Cage ("Drag is dirty work, but someone has to do it!"), and Doris Fish all over town have inspired their audiences. That's not to mention the vertiginous effect made within their community by a virtual constellation of drag title holders—duchesses and dukes, empresses and emperors, and dowager queens—and the hundreds of other cross-dressed men who have filled San Francisco streets with Gay Pride celebration in June and on other occasions throughout the year; each man standing—politically, at least—center stage.

"In the early days [the fifties] we really had to stick together," recalled Sarria, "and we'd often meet to talk about police harassment and how to cope with it. When police officers came in you'd telephone the next bar down the line and say, 'Watch out—he's wearing a trenchcoat and a pair of green slacks—and headed your way.'

"That bar would then be alerted. Tell a queen and you tell the world! The law said that an officer had to make himself known. Well, by the time he got to the Black Cat we'd play the national anthem for him and all stand up. He'd always leave just furious."

The Black Cat was internationally known before it was forced to close its doors on Halloween of 1963, when its liquor license was revoked. "There was nobody who came to San Francisco who did not go there," said Sarria. "And I always told them that being homosexual was nothing to be ashamed of and how important it was to be proud and united." As with the clichés of gender role, it was men in dresses who took society's other warped expectations to absurd extremes; making these impositions on the primacy of self transparent for all to see—and thus easier, ultimately, to shed.

It was the so-called effeminate men—those who cross-dressed—who were among the first to fill the front ranks of San Francisco's gay civil rights movement. Such was the case in New York City as well, most notably during the Stonewall riots in late June 1969 that, more than any event, have come to symbolize the modern-day struggle for homosexual equality. One reporter of the three-day riots, which were ignited by routine police harassment of a Village gay bar called the Stonewall Inn, observed that "those usually put down as 'sissies' and 'swishes' showed the most courage and sense during the action. Their bravery and daring saved many people from being hurt, and their sense of humor and 'camp' helped keep the crowds from getting nasty or too violent."

Despite their historic posture, the queens in the East remained largely shunned, economically and socially downcast, even by fellow gays. In San Francisco, the queens continued to provide much of the community nurturing and fundraising savvy needed to fuel the burgeoning movement—traditional feminine skills. But, for the most part, they remained resolutely middle class, even while a new and outwardly classless drag sensibility was beginning to assert itself.

By the late sixties, a younger generation of gay men were learning how to organize themselves: angry, well-educated, and politically astute, often espousing socialist ideals, they viewed drag queens with resigned embarrassment—a barely understood social inheritance. San Francisco was then sweeping up the Haight-Ashbury neighborhood and its ragtag leftovers from the Summer of Love. And while drug dealers and runaway youths were clearly not welcomed, the gay people who had been such an integral part of the counterculture scene there simply moved elsewhere in the city. This was a decade before a frenzy of downtown highrise construction would inflate rents and living costs to a record level, making San Francisco one of the most expensive urban habitats in the nation. The city then was an enchanted place, still habitable for artists and free spirits of all stripes, alive with exploration on many fronts. The Cockettes were simply a group of gay men who decided to get together and put on a show.

"Their productions were transvestite-glitter-fairie-theatric masques," recalled Ginsberg. "Transsexual dressing is a gay contribution to the realization that we're not a hundred percent masculine or feminine, but a mixture of hormones— and not being afraid of that natural self which the hormones dictate. The Cockettes just brought out into the street what was in the closet, in terms of theatric dress and imaginative theater."

"I don't think any of us were aware of the politics of what we were doing," former Cockette John Rothermel told me some years later. "Since we were so open to interpretation, we were used by radical factions and distorted well beyond what our statement really was—that we were simply having a party. As a statement it was naïve, but it was oh, so fresh and very guileless. It took someone else to come along and say, 'Hey that's outrageous.' Because I think that in being truly outrageous you can't have a self-conscious attitude that betrays what you're doing. At that moment, you lose the spark."

It was only a matter of time before the international press descended on the colorful and irreverent troupe, issuing profiles, celebrity reviews, and important magazine covers headlining the "decadence" of it all. Meanwhile, this small band of Aquarian-age drag queens went about their business; living freely, canvassing secondhand stores for props and costumes to adorn their midnight shows, and covering everything with a patina of glitter. "About the only thing we paid money for was the glitter," said Rothermel. "We ransacked the city for it.

"The glitter was about the idea of the ages of light. The whole thing was some sort of rainbow-colored depiction of what it's like to have hallucinogenic experience. It's what we were trying to exemplify in one way or another. We had had numerous enlightening experiences in our lifestyle, and people who have had such experiences usually say that when they find peace of mind or their greatest self-realization, something magical happens—like a great white light that descends on them or exudes from them. It's sort of like that story about Jesus and the twelve disciples, when the flames appeared on their heads. It was like the idea of having a halo, of being aware of your aura, your magnetism."

The Cockettes were truly ingenuous, but the harsh glare of hype and expectation undermined their fragile magic. They gave their last performance in the autumn of 1972. "The time, the mood, the people were changing," said Worman. "The camaraderie started to deteriorate into dish. The light that had sailed cometlike across the San Francisco sky to illuminate the arrival of the new androgynous Aquarian Age was moving on."

Today, most gay men who remember the group view its ambiguous message as an anachronistic relic from another era—scarcely relevant. But the troupe's tinseled theatrics ignited imaginations, awakened a consciousness in all those they touched in their vain attempt to resurrect innocence, rearrange reality. No doubt unwittingly, they had probed a vital nerve, decorated a rite of passage still remembered and deeply felt by some.

Yet the tradition of radical drag persisted in the city with another group, the Angels of Light. More underground, and perhaps more serious minded about their craft, the Angels still used glitter and campy routines. But their shows seemed to have more of a point: opposition to the ruling class was the message of their 1975 dada musical extravaganza, *Paris Sights under the Bourgeois Sea;* a warning about imperialism was implicit in *Sci-Clones,* an audacious and often breathtaking mix of Chinese folk opera, Balinese mask drama, and science fiction epic; and themes of spiritual quest and attainment were interwoven with Hindu mythology and lavish song and dance routines in 1980s *Holy Cow!* Men and women in the group explained in 1979, "The Angels of Light are an expression that represents an inward dream and vision. It means a positiveness, an idea of sharing the things that are important in uplifting people." Employing great imagination and ingenuity over the years, the Angels' elaborate, baroque productions were mounted with little funds and offered to audiences without charge.

One of the most astute observations about the Angels' ability to move their audiences in ways rare to contemporary theater was offered to me by Adrian Brooks, a poet, novelist, performer, and playwright-in-residence with the Angels of Light from 1975 to 1980. Six years after his principal involvement with the group had come to an end, Brooks had the following words to say about the spirit that resonated deep beneath the glitter: "Perhaps, in some way, the Angels of Light danced in the circus arena for all gay people and, in our own unique fashion, exhibited the joy of a spontaneous, childlike self-discovery that was illuminating. The fascination with everything incandescent and luminous, the glorification of the present tense, the suspension of disbelief in the melange of whirling colors and forms—all these things were more than individual creators, more than solo performers taking a star turn. It was its own self-evident proof of existence, its own tapestry and common parable. Not simply invented or used for effect, but gathered up as one collects ample harvest, arms full of the bounty, a tribal celebration that surpasses the mere fact of survival and becomes, in and of itself, a kind of ancient religion that must be discovered afresh by any mystic or dervish.

"We were all dervishes, then, and we knew it even at the time. The fact that the productions were complex but based on simple morality tales, meant that their very creation involved a synthesis which went far beyond the venue of a theatrical presentation. It was incumbent on me—as playwright-in-residence for the group—to suspend formal discipline, abandon judicious editing, circumvent the reflexive application of a writer in order not to impede the free flow of spirit. This was a choice, and it had to be made (and made again and again), despite academic criticism, despite reviewers who failed to understand that camp was taking its place beside other time-honored forms of theater: dance, mask drama, vaudeville, burlesque, commedia dell'arte, guignol. That it was a spirit beyond the rules and could only be entertained by creating a vehicle. Within that vessel, the whorl would come to pass. But if it was ever burdened (as it came to be) by spirit denial or self-consciousness, like love itself it would become crippled, mutant, deformed and lost in its own crazy-house mirror.

"Thus, both the theater and the participants themselves enacted a ritual spirit dance, most remarkable for the fact that it never sought to codify the soul life of the community but, rather, welcomed the outsider as insider and accepted the haphazard as synchronistic. In doing this, the actors themselves—and all who participated—performed offstage psychic roles as well as onstage characters. The most fascinating thing of all was that there was an inversion of self-portrayal, the shadow side of individuals, the minor mask of Janus flitting across the stage—directly contrary to the offstage personality and its effect on the theater as a company. Throughout the course of the theater's life, the company thus represented an intense experiment in self-discovery—for it had profound psychic resonance for the players that surpassed the public face presented. With this curious and mysterious loop, the Angels became as mystical and totemic for the people involved as the theater itself was for the community it served as beacon, spur, paper lantern and, ultimately, overburdened blossom."

Exploration around the issues of gender, dress, and androgyny were not only being contained on the city's stages. In the late seventies, a small circle of gay men came together to reclaim the powerful epithet of *sissy*. Chanted, implied, and denied, few words in the male lexicon seem so universally to hit the emotional bottom line. It is a word most gay men grew up with, praying that it didn't mean them, although it usually did, leaving long-remembered wounds.

"It's important to break down sex roles," a member of the outspoken and visible circle said at the time, "and putting on a dress is one of the most obvious ways to do that. The first time I put one on was to attend a political rally." Another "sissy"-identified man told me, "The main reason I wear a dress is because I like the feel of it. I like expressing my kinship with the people I've learned from." But for those in the group there was a deeper meaning to cross-dressing, beyond political confrontation and gender solidarity.

"There's an historical precedent of effeminate men being spiritual leaders all over the world. People are just now becoming aware of that history," one of the men in the group said. "When a man is feminine and a woman masculine, I think that person is more in touch with the total range of human experience. They are more receptive, they have a broader range of sensibility and awareness. It goes far beyond the boundaries of sex roles.

"Sex roles are one of the primary ways in which we identify ourselves. If you could break out of that, I think it would be easy to see how you could break out of other restraints—to think that there is more to the world than what we can see. I'm learning to trust my feelings, and for me that's a spiritual development. That's what magic is. I see my life becoming increasingly shamanistic, but it's a quality that doesn't even apply to this culture."

By the early eighties, the idea of applying spiritual purpose to cross-dressing was a concept seized, quite literally, by another group of gay men who dubbed themselves the Sisters of Perpetual Indulgence. Controversial even within the gay community and often provoking outrage, especially from the middle-aged burghers of the by-then well-entrenched gay commercial establishment, the Sisters flaunted themselves throughout the city in the distinctive black and white habits of nuns. "Our mission is much bigger than we could ever have imagined," the well-publicized group admitted in 1981. "Our ministry is one of public manifestation and habitual penetration. Our motto is 'Give up the guilt.' And we're going to do that through any form at our means—theater, dance, spiritual expression and therapy."

In the tradition of actual nuns, the Sisters dedicated themselves to service to their community: fundraising, educating on the issues of health and sexuality, staging public healing rituals, and participating in political protest, including one demonstration honoring the slain nuns and laywomen of El Salvador. In fact, they involved themselves with the type of work that had always seemed the stock in trade of the city's queens. And like their predecessors, they found the greatest opposition to their cross-dressing coming from other gay men. At the Central American vigil, for instance, it was the gay monitors of the march who cajoled and threatened them to leave for fear of negative publicity. "One man said we were an embarrassment," a Sister said, "but I've been one most of my life anyway. They couldn't understand that we weren't making fun of nuns, that we're adding more to the nunhood than had been added in the recent past, and that it was an outreach toward the other Christian groups participating—who, by the way, made no comment on their own."

Keeping whimsy, mockery, and outrage alive was probably the Sisters' most significant accomplishment—sustaining qualities that were rapidly diminishing as the gay community's self-consciousness and power grew. "So much of the political movement has become narrow," one of the Sisters said. "We might be the answer to the evolution of coming out as a gay person."

"Humor and sexuality are at the roots of spirituality," they explained to me. "They are the transcendental experiences that take us beyond morality. Through humor and sexuality we can realize visions and feelings beyond everyday life. The truest religion in the world is theater, or ritual. On a broad philosophical range, we are being religious in the truest sense, but merely by definition. Being nuns is a practical application of our spiritual feelings as gay men."

The Sisters of Perpetual Indulgence kept their communal vows for a few years, and then splintered. Some members continued to wear their habits, standing out against the city's changing panorama as lone—almost totemic—figures. Many of the Sisters were already active in the newly created fairie movement, where the interplay of ritual, androgyny, and pagan spirituality seemed to be intuitively understood and less hidebound by cultural convention and dogma.

In this brief history, cross-dressed men appear as the rude and anarchical element disrupting the surface of society's status quo. And to all these men, one *feeling* has seemed central: that cross-dressing is a natural, almost instinctive gesture, a remnant of some misunderstood and long-forgotten tradition. When compared to the cross-dress of shamans in other cultures, the drag worn by the men described here could be viewed as a ritual-fetish-power object, enabling catharsis in themselves and others. Prescribed forms of dress codified around gender roles is the most pervasive means of social control—a tacit spell that cross-dressing immediately shatters.

But to understand this better, let's return to the stage of the Palace Theater and, in particular, a life. This young man is central to the legacy of radical drag on the West Coast, which he eventually left. So in spring 1981, I traveled to New York City to catch up with this errant angel of light, and here is his story.

He discovered his name in a Jean Cocteau novel. Somewhere, he says, there is a line about a blood-red hibiscus: a flower that blooms briefly and then shrivels. "That interested me very much."

I'm sitting on a park bench in Sheridan Square playing with the sound of the word, letting it pass between my lips. "Hi-bis-cus." The word has a powerful, almost passionate, connotation for me—representing, as it does, a fantastic period in gay history. A wrinkle in time that, sadly, bears as much relevance to the lives of gay people today as a chapter from *The Wizard of Oz*.

Hibiscus. Spawned in New York, bred in San Francisco and on the road in the rest of the world. I'm staring at his name now on a billboard high above the square, set in hundreds of tiny red sequins stitched in place by a team of elderly women in Brooklyn. The slightly ludicrous, and very gay, icon glitters over the blasé midday crowds, advertising a new act. The whole thing reminds me of a not-too-distant past when being gay meant something different. But I resist sentiment and remind myself that glitter—and all that it reflected—had its day. I express no laments but entertain a curiosity.

I find Hibiscus in a spacious West Village loft apartment littered with gaudy props, bamboo furniture from the forties, and other nostalgic knickknacks. I'm startled when he answers the door. I did not expect this handsome young man, more likely to peer from the pages of a fashion magazine than down from a glittered billboard on Sheridan Square. He adjusts a wool cravat, and I wonder to what extent his dress and careful manner are calculated. I indulge a shift of setting and drag and—for a moment—am amused to find myself playing Louella Parsons to his Jayne Mansfield. "I've always been fascinated by her," he later admits. "I love her entire life. She had heart-shaped everything."

Like his environment, Hibiscus's life has been eclectic, a collection of odd events. He's been a performer all his life, a passion that has led him to some very strange places, from performing at Black Panther headquarters in blackface to singing and dancing "under a Mafia whip" in Paris.

"I was born in Bronxville, in Westchester," he begins. "Then my family moved to Florida. My parents lost everything in the subdivisions that sank." His father decided to pursue a career in acting and returned to New York. Eventually, the rest of the family followed, and "We lived in an apartment on First Avenue and Ninth Street that cost twenty-eight dollars a month and had sloping floors. We camped out in sleeping bags. It was interesting."

Both his parents became regulars at the Caffe Cino and other off-off-Broadway theaters. Hibiscus, then George Harris, worked as a child model in commercials and played bit parts at the Cino, La Mama, and other showcases. It was the early sixties. He was thirteen when he left home to live with another man. "My parents were very liberal and, considering the financial situation at the time, very understanding. There was never any question about my gayness. I mean, my mother told me that I was. I always knew that I was different."

According to Allen Ginsberg, the precocious young actor had a circle of friends that included Irving Rosenthal, who had edited William Burroughs's *Naked Lunch* at Grove Press, and filmmaker Jack Smith, whose *Flaming Creatures* remains a classic of independent cinema. Both men espoused controversial and visionary points of view through their work. "Jack Smith's film involved dressing people up in transsexual costumes with great adornment; veils and spangles and beautiful makeup. And Irving had the theory of having everything free," said Ginsberg. "So Hibiscus brought all that new culture west."

When he was seventeen, Hibiscus had an offer to drive to California with Peter Orlovsky and another friend. "I was still very Brooks Brothers—you know, short hair and lots of madras shirts. I was lucky to catch the whole love-child bit just in time.

"We arrived in San Francisco, and one of my friends decided he was going to start a printing commune in Japantown. I started to grow my hair and became a vegetarian. I lived the life of an angel there. I was celibate and started to wear long robes and headdresses. I'd go down to Union Square and pick roses out of the garbage and run around singing all my old Broadway favorites: 'You Are Beautiful,' 'If I Loved You.'" The headdresses kept getting bigger and bigger.

"Everything was free then. Free medical care; a free newspaper, the *Kaliflower;* and we even used to distribute free food to the needy. I had also been doing this show at various communes around town—the Kitchen Sluts Floor Show. I'd go with a couple of other friends and scrub down their entire kitchen, then present cum bread. The making of the bread was rather controversial. It was a whole spiritual thing for me at the time, although a lot of people didn't like it."

The city was alive with counterculture entertainment. The Grateful Dead and the Jefferson Airplane gave regular concerts in the parks, and groups like the Committee and the Floating Light Opera attracted large followings. A small movie theater in North Beach, the Palace, was also featuring Nocturnal Dream Shows at midnight. "I wanted to do a New Year's show," Hibiscus recalls, "and the Palace invited me to do it there. About eight of us—including Dusty Dawn, Scrumbly, Goldie Glitters and Kreemah Ritz—got up on the stage in drag and danced to an old recording of 'Honky Tonk Woman.' The audience surged toward the stage, screaming. I was dumbfounded." The seventies had begun; the Cockettes were born.

A bit of worldly sophistication, a touch of transplanted glamour, and years of practical experience—even at such an early age—were all elements of Hibiscus's carpetbag brought west. San Francisco then seemed like a romantic but somewhat faded European town. Lacking much formal education ("I went to the school of hard knocks"), Hibiscus nevertheless projected an undefinable authority through his soft-focus persona. "I feel that I have always had a certain energy at my fingertips, a spirit for bringing creative people together," he says. "It must have come from some other place. It's a well I've always drawn from."

The foundling troupe took its cue from Hibiscus and dipped into the inchoate pastiche of popular American culture, then so abundantly at their disposal. The Cockettes exposed and played with the sexual and cultural confusion of the times and emerged, if not with diamonds, then at least with rhinestones. "Our second show was *Paste on Paste*," Hibiscus recalls. "It opened with Kreemah Ritz showing a novice how to put on coconut breasts and closed with the entire cast singing 'You'll Never Walk Alone' to the Virgin Mary." The group staged one revue per week, usually with a budget of less than twenty dollars. Backdrops were painted sheets; sets were fashioned out of cardboard and castoff junk from the streets. "You could do things like that then."

Gone with the Showboat to Oklahoma, Myth Thing, Pearls over Shanghai followed in rapid succession, and the group began to attract widespread attention. Janis Joplin, John Lennon, and Truman Capote were among the celebrities who sent notes backstage. *Rolling Stone, Paris Match,* and other major periodicals published feature articles; the troupe was featured in several underground movies; and the theater was packed to the chandeliers every Saturday night. "No one had seen anything like it before. It was totally freeform," explains Hibiscus. "Instead of dressing in drag, I was dressing more as gods. We were all creating mythic figures."

"It was a revolution in theater," recalls Sylvester, who left a church choir in nearby Oakland to join the motley group—a significant step toward his career as an international pop music star.

Smart-alecky pluck, a "let's-put-on-a-show" attitude, and plenty of glitter: an ingenuous fantasy had fermented into a show-biz phenomenon. But the scene began to attract adults more stony than stoned out, and their somber appraisal of the group's commercial potential meant that Hibiscus's days at the Palace were numbered.

One night after a performance of *Madama Butterfly,* he came home to find his apartment building burned down. He took off for the country to recover from his loss, but stayed too long. On his return he discovered that he had been voted out of the troupe. His insistence that their shows be free did not agree with the group's newfound ambitions to seek fame and fortune in New York.

The Cockettes took off (with someone else dressed as their founding figure) and opened 5 November 1971 amid great hoopla at the Anderson Theater in the East Village. The group had been taken up by New York's cultural avant-garde, and even the *Washington Post* said that their debut was the biggest off-Broadway opening the city had ever seen. Still, the group failed miserably; a classic case of too much, too soon. It was while hastily exiting at intermission with other attending celebrities that Gore Vidal said, "No talent is not enough," offering a premonition of headlines to come: COAST TRANSVESTITE TROUPE A DRAG, FOR THIS THEY HAD TO COME FROM FRISCO? Other critics argued that their impact would be felt for decades. Nevertheless, the troupe soon returned home, and despite another year of performances for an enthusiastic hometown audience, its inner light was never to shine quite as bright.

Meanwhile, Hibiscus remained in San Francisco and continued to pursue his ideal of free theater. While in the mountains, he had met a stranger who had told him that he was an angel—or at least one in training—and so he called his new group the Angels of Light.

Their first performance was Christmas 1971 atop the city's staid Nob Hill. With he and a lover dressed as Mary and Joseph and friends dressed as angels, the troupe enacted a mock Nativity scene in Grace Cathedral, as a counterpoint to high mass. "Everyone there kind of liked us," Hibiscus explained, "but the police came anyway." It was the troupe's first show, and many others were to follow, including performances in ghetto neighborhoods where more than one rock was hurled through a theater window.

"We did shows like *Flamingo Stampede* and *Moroccan Operetta,* which was like *Kabuki* in Balinese drag. Allen Ginsberg did his first drag onstage in *Blue Angel Cabaret.*" Ginsberg remembers that performance well. "I dressed up as a sort of Shakespearean nurse with a long cone hat with the moon and stars pasted on it and a blue gown, which was appropriate to Blake's 'Nurse's Song.' Hibiscus and I were lovers at the time. He was a very beautiful man, was very kind to me, and gave me a place to do an act—to sing Blake, actually. He had a kind of angelic imagination."

Eventually Hibiscus left San Francisco and returned home to New York, where he was reunited with his family. With parents, siblings, and a lover, Angel Jack (discovered while hanging from a cross), Hibiscus began to perform as an East Coast incarnation of the Angels. Once again he attracted notoriety, including the interest of Belgian choreographer Maurice Bejart, who financed the group's first European tour. The troupe spent much of the rest of the seventies traveling throughout the Continent in various shows and configurations, always with a strong cult following.

He's been back on home ground for some time now, determined to stay put with a new cabaret act—at least for a while. The concept of free theater is still a precious one for him, but these are leaner times than the late sixties. Today, even sparkle has its price.

For Hibiscus, the world is a somewhat more serious place. Gaiety, in all senses of the word, and especially within the homosexual milieu, seems posed on the edge of exhaustion. "I'm afraid I'll slip and say something that will outrage a million mad queens," he suddenly blurts out in the middle of the interview. An impish grin interjects. "But then, there aren't many mad queens left anymore." There's something happening within the gay movement today that worries him, a growing attitude almost too intangible for him to express satisfactorily.

"I don't know if I'm going to say this right, but I have to: I'm scared to death of what's emerging in the gay middle class. I was at the Saint [a trendy, high-tech disco] in costume the other night and I was petrified. I felt like Jezebel when she came into the room with a scarlet dress. No one wanted to go near me. Everyone was so afraid to be different. I call it a gay middle-class vacuum. This conformity is a dangerous thing.

"I think that people who are gay verge on being angels, or wayward angels. Gayness is a gift. I know a lot of people who feel that gay men, in particular, can be the most powerful force for transformation within our society. Gay men have often pushed society to new limits, such as with the Cockettes. All I really want to say is that the gay middle class can track you down."

Try as they may, it would be a futile task for anyone to track down Hibiscus. "My idea is to be a fifties drag queen for today," he says in a sudden change of mood, "a kind of Liberace for the eighties. I want to take the act back to Europe. And, of course, to San Francisco; I lived so intensely there, every street has a haunting memory. I guess I still have a semiaudience out there, although most of them seem to have moved to Oregon."

Most creative people know that to dissect inner compulsions is to destroy the soul of their work. The content of Hibiscus's art seems ephemeral: camp humor, secondhand glamour, and a child's perennial delight. He may be a trickster with a tacky mirror, but somehow it's impossible not to take a look.

I had planned to return for another visit after our first talk that April afternoon, but I never got the chance. A year later, in May 1982, George Harris was dead. He was among the first in a legion of angels to die from AIDS.

The Politics of Drag

Jeffrey Hilbert

The radical drag underground. The Wigstock generation. Drag post*moderne*. Whatever it's called, there is a new generation of drag performers who have no desire to coddle their audience with the umpteenth rendition of Marilyn. Spurred on by both homophobia and AIDS phobia, this drag is fresh, fierce, and fighting mad. These performers have fashioned their own personae and are often found at the forefront of AIDS fund-raisers, Queer Nation stings, public-access cable broadcasts, alternative-magazine manifestos, and live guerrilla theater.

But not all drag performers see false eyelash to false eyelash on the activist power of donning a dress. There are those performers, both male and female, who use cross-gender guise to bring attention to their political forum and those who do it strictly for entertainment value. The division clearly separates drag into two camps.

While Atlanta drag performer Lurleen and Los Angeles drag Vaginal Creme Davis are out on the front lines, involved in groups such as the AIDS Coalition to Unleash Power (ACT UP), and giving benefit performances for the fight against AIDS, others, such as John Epperson as Lypsinka, see their roles simply as entertainers.

"AIDS has forced gay people to think about who we are and what our relationship with straight society really is," says the strawberry-blond Lurleen. "It's hard to be an apolitical person these days. I'm no strident Marxist, but when there is a reactionary government in power, it's kind of hard to get up onstage and lip-synch Barbra Streisand and then say, 'Drink up, everybody.' "

Lypsinka, who hopes to cross over from the stage into mainstream network television, disagrees. "Some people opt to do that [be political]. I don't. I set out to entertain."

A Reemerging Past

The disagreements over style and form between Lypsinka, Lurleen, Vaginal Creme Davis, and legions of other drag queens—politics versus entertainment—are not new, having emerged during the tumultuous times of the late sixties, when gays and lesbians were beginning the fight for basic civil rights.

At the 1969 Stonewall riots, drag queens were the first to pitch stones and rip up parking meters in a battle against New York police over harassment of gay bar patrons. The riots and the ensuing gay liberation movement smashed preconceived notions of sexuality and behavorial conformity. While countless drag performers from coast to coast were still doing unthreatening impersonations of Judy Garland, a handful of cross-dressers were fighting the system.

The Judy Garlands of the drag queen world, however, became the unquestioned norm during the heady disco days of the seventies and eighties, when drag bars blossomed throughout the country. Although there were several drag troupes, such as the Sisters of Perpetual Indulgence and the Cockettes in San Francisco, who maintained a high profile at parades and demonstrations, it was not until the late eighties and the acceleration of the AIDS crisis that drag again embraced a political message.

"Basically, drag had to get hipper or else just be so square," says film director John Waters, who brought the world the late great drag diva Divine in movies like *Pink Flamingos, Female Trouble,* and *Hairspray.* "The old idea of what drag queens were is incredibly corny and square in the nineties. The ones who do Carol Channing are really like what Uncle Tom used to be."

Clearly, today's drag artists have a lot more on their minds than tight wigs. "[Political] drag is absolutely, unquestioningly experiencing a comeback," claims Martin Worman, aka Philthee Ritz, one of the original members of the Cockettes. "The Cockettes didn't have a dogma. Now drag has an edge and a conscience because of AIDS."

Although most drag queens recognize the influence of their predecessors, they feel they've taken the movement a step further. "We've all been influenced by old-line drag," admits Lurleen, a self-described cross between Sandra Bernhard and Daisy Duke. "Traditionally drag has been a form of escapist entertainment, like the alternative version of TV—sitcoms for fags.

"The difference between old-line drag and new drag is that those performers take *themselves* seriously," continues Lurleen. "That's tedious in any form of self-expression. What we do reflects the mentality of our generation. We approach serious causes with humor and react to what's going on in our culture and society."

Rebirth of Political Drag

The setting for this rebirth can probably be traced to the Pyramid Club in Manhattan's East Village, where acts like the band Now Explosion and performers such as Hapi Phace, Tabboo! and the late Ethyl Eichelberger-honed their considerable talents in front of an audience that included New York's intellectual and social elite.

"The Pyramid was the center of it all," says New York drag figurehead Lady Bunny. "In the early eighties everyone wore black, and it was all gloom, doom, gothic punk sensibility. But we made it more upbeat, loud, colorful, and trashy, which reflected our outlook on life.

"Now drag is about trying new things," explains Bunny. "It isn't limited to lip-synching. There is a new generation of queers whose icons aren't Barbra, Judy, and Eartha." Instead, blaxploitation films, seventies sitcoms, glitter-rock bands, or parodies of other drags are now de rigueur inspirations.

Lady Bunny went to New York in 1982 with fellow performers Lahoma, RuPaul, and Larry T. when their Atlanta-based band, Now Explosion, had a gig at the Pyramid. They decided to stay. Two years later, as a lark "to see the drags of the New York club world in the daylight," Bunny coorganized the first annual Wigstock.

The event, now in its seventh year, attracts thousands to Tompkins Square Park in New York's East Village on Labor Day as an end-of-the-summer gay love-in teeming with bouffants, bell-bottoms, platforms, and, most important, media visibility. Even Manhattan borough president Ruth Messinger declared 3 September 1990 as Wigstock Day.

Owing to Wigstock's success and the increasing visibility of drags, the Washington, D.C.–based media-watchdog group National Gay and Lesbian Task Force (NGLTF) plans to present a forum addressing the power of politics and cross-dressing at its next Creating Change Conference in November. NGLTF director Robert Bray's suggested title for the forum: "Drag Activism—Work It, Girl."

"The camp and irony evoked by drag have carried our movement through some rough times," says Bray. "We're seeing more and more participation of drag queens on the front lines of the movement. Who could ever calculate how much money has been raised by queens for the AIDS epidemic?"

"Drag adds an element of fun to politics so that it's not all Maoist uniforms and being glum and gray," says the platform-heeled Lurleen. "Hopefully it makes thinking about politics more palatable."

Confront or Coddle?

A division remains over whether the entertainers should confront or pamper their audiences.

Lypsinka, whose lightning-paced lip-synch revue *I Could Go on Lip-Synching!* has had tremendous financial success on both coasts, says that although he has performed at AIDS and gay-related fund-raisers, he sees himself as "not political at all. The closest I get to a political comment in my show is with Shirley Bassey singing "This Is My Life' and suddenly cutting to Norma Zimmer singing 'This Is My Country' and then abruptly cutting into Tallulah Bankhead asking, '*What* have you been doing? What *have* you been doing?' "

"A Lypsinka kind of performer will probably appeal to more people," says self-described "blacktress" Vaginal Creme Davis, who uses an aggressive, abrasive, in-your-face style to reach his audience.

"It's easier to digest Lypsinka's kind of performance," explains Vaginal. "It's safer, and people aren't challenged. But when people see an African American in this feminized role, they realize that there's a whole spectrum of being out there and that the black experience or the queer experience is not just limited to one aspect."

Unlike most drags, Vaginal and his heavy-metal thrash-parody band Pedro, Muriel, and Ester tend to confront, not cater to their audience. Their shows are often permeated with a sense of danger, with the audience becoming frenzied and involved in the sometimes dangerous practice of slam dancing.

"The whole controversy over using the term *queer* or *gay and lesbian* is so heated right now," explains Vaginal, editor of *Fertile La Toyah Jackson Magazine,* a gay parody of supermarket tabloids, "because people who want to be identified as gay and lesbian want everyone to like them. Someone with a queer identification doesn't want that kind of acceptance."

Even those performers with an agenda have a hard time considering themselves political, much less agreeing on how their politics connect. For the most part, these performers see themselves as channelers for the voice of an activist generation.

"Nobody puts on a dress just to be political, but once the motivation is there, a lot of people answer the call," says Los Angeles-based performer Gender, whose naughty, bawdy patter and ridiculous tap-dancing routines are combined with a concern over the growing power of the Far Right and their attacks on the First Amendment.

"I mean, how political can a piece of clothing be?" Gender asks. "But then I suppose it can be. Drag queens were out there pitching rocks at Stonewall because they had the most to lose. Now there is this timely episode of activism, and since drag queens are so visual, they are out there *doing*. At least some of them are. In that way drag is political."

"The queens are better at PR than they were before," says Les Simpson, editor of *My Comrade/Sister,* an alternative publication chronicling the East Village scene. "It goes hand in hand with gay people building more confidence, being louder, and being more out there."

Hitting the Airwaves

"The Brenda and Glennda Show," hosted by Brenda Sexual and Glennda Orgasm, takes the queer cause over the airwaves on Manhattan Cable every Monday night.

"We take the talk-show format out of the studio and into unlikely places where you're never sure what will happen," Glennda continues. "We confront people on the street and don't care if they like us. We're not out there to make friends."

Brenda and Glennda met at Wigstock in 1989 and that December took part in the now-legendary ACT UP demonstration at St. Patrick's Cathedral, in which protesters interrupted Cardinal John O'Connor's mass.

"We dressed up as clowns—the religious right—and were arrested," Glennda recalls. "That's when I realized that street theater and AIDS and gay activism were what I wanted to do."

Using their video camera as a weapon, Brenda, Glennda, and entourage take to the streets, recording homophobia, AIDS phobia, and drag phobia in the general public. A show filmed aboard a Buffalo, N.Y., rail line profiled a group of fellow train passengers—"black Baptist Bible thumpers," according to Glennda, who were chanting, "Adam and Eve! Not Adam and Steve!" A road trip to Donald Trump's Atlantic City, N.J., casino, the Taj Mahal, focused on the alleged discrimination Brenda and Glennda faced there. They were barred entrance to the gambling floor by security. The reason given: too much makeup.

"People need to be educated about gay issues and gay politics and about AIDS and activism," Glennda says. "The way to reach people is to make them laugh and, at the same time, make them think about more serious issues. The people I see at our shows are not the people I see at ACT UP or Queer Nation meetings, but they do listen to what we're talking about because we are entertaining.

"We try to incorporate AIDS activism with our show to make people aware that all issues are connected," continues Glennda. "The AIDS crisis, gay visibility, antigay violence, women's issues, reproductive issues—they're all connected. They're all about what we do with our bodies. And drag is just another choice of what we do with our bodies."

Like Brenda and Glennda and the Cockettes before them, Ggreg Deborah Taylor (his legal name) and his pal Jerome of San Francisco perform what Taylor calls "drag outreach to fight gay invisibility." Taylor and company take their outreach on the road and into mainstream America.

When the group descended on the Serramonte shopping mall in northern California for a Hello Kitty coloring contest last winter, mall security was not amused and called in the police, who saw nothing wrong, leaving the gang to color to their hearts' content. The event was reported in the *San Francisco Examiner* under the headline HELLO KITTY CORNERED: DRAG QUEENS, PUNKS JOIN IN THE FUN.

Drag Kings

Of course, drag performance is not strictly the domain of men. San Francisco is also home to Leigh Crow, whose character, Elvis Herselvis, puts an ironic spin on Elvis impersonators, discussing the King's drug problem and making copious references to "little girls in white cotton panties." Herselvis, a hit among both the city's gay and lesbian communities, performs at ACT UP benefits and joins in on Taylor's outings.

Shelly Mars's male characters have a somewhat harder edge. The New York performer's best-known character is Martin, a leering, cigar-chomping man in a baggy suit who performs a striptease, fondles his dick (a beer bottle, which she shakes up), and ejaculates over the audience. By the end of the performance, Martin transforms into a woman, and the idea comes full circle.

Mars's newest male character, Peter, is a person with AIDS who is slightly psychotic from medication and dementia. Modeled after people she met through ACT UP and friends who have died of the disease, Mars's Peter elicits very powerful reactions from her audience.

"It's a scary character to do," says Mars. "You never know what kind of response you are going to get. Some people think that since I am portraying an insane character, I am making fun of him or saying all people with AIDS are this way. That narrow-mindedness comes from their own denial.

"AIDS dementia is kind of closeted and not really talked about much," Mars continues. "We don't talk about how someone lost his mind, and it happens a lot. AIDS is a very fucked-up disease.

"It's very heavy for people to see their friends go through dementia and then die," she explains. "Hopefully my performance brings up a voice to talk about this. To get people talking is the most important thing."

The Pride and the Prejudice

Beyond politics and the divisions it engenders, there is a common thread running through the drag community: the desire to get audiences thinking about their own sexuality.

"We challenge gender roles," explains Glennda of "The Brenda and Glennda Show." "And even though it's a campy parody, it goes beyond that. A lot of gay men are bothered by their own femininity. Like 'I'm gay, but I'm not feminine, I'm not a fag. I'm a man, even though I like to suck cock.' Seeing a drag queen confronts all those fears. That's why we do drag."

"There is a certain amount of prejudice within the gay community," says Los Angeles's Gender. "A form of denial—that whole straight-acting/straight-appearing complex. Some of these gays are more effeminate than the drag queens I know. Of course, they would never dream of putting on a dress. Not that they should! But it makes me wonder where their heads are."

"I understand the objection to drag from gays within the system who are working on gay and lesbian issues that way," says Lurleen, "and yet I think that's wrong. The issue is diversity and tolerance for people who are different and not just people who are different 'our way.' All oppressed people have something in common and need to work together."

Still, drags continue to don their wigs, apply their makeup, and take to the stage in support of a community that, more often than not, tends to reject rather than embrace them.

Perhaps the message this new drag best reflects is one of SILENCE=DEATH.

Black Macho Revisited

Reflections of a Snap! Queen

Marlon Riggs

Negro faggotry is in fashion.

SNAP!

Turn on your television and camp queens greet you in living color.

SNAP!

Turn to cable and watch America's most bankable modern minstrel expound on getting "fucked in the ass" or his fear of faggots.

SNAP!

Turn off the TV, turn on the radio: rotund rapper Heavy D, the self-styled "overweight lover MC," expounds on how *his* rap will make you "happy like a faggot in jail." Perhaps to pre-empt questions about how he would know—you might wonder what kind of "lover" he truly is—Heavy D reassures us that he's just "extremely intellectual, not bisexual." (*BLK,* March 1990)

Jelly-roll SNAP!

N egro faggotry *is* in vogue. Madonna commodified it into a commercial hit. Mapplethorpe photographed it, and art galleries drew fire and record crowds in displaying it. Black macho movie characters dis'—or should we say dish?—their antagonists with unkind references to it. Indeed references to, and representations of, Negro faggotry seem a rite of passage among contemporary black male rappers and filmmakers. Observe the pageantry.

Snap-swish-and-dish divas have truly arrived, giving beauty shop drama center stage, performing the read-and-snap two-step as they sashay across the movie screen, entertaining us in the castles of our homes—like court jesters, like eunuchs—with their double entendres and dead-end lusts, and above all, their relentless hilarity in the face of relentless despair. Negro faggotry is the rage!

Black gay men are not. For in the cinematic and television images of and from black America as well as the words of music and dialogue that now abound and *seem* to address my life as a black gay man, I am struck repeatedly by the determined, unreasoning, often irritational desire to discredit my claim to blackness and hence to black manhood.

In consequence the terrain black gay men navigate in the quest for self and social identity is, to say the least, hostile. What disturbs—no, enrages—me is not so much the obstacles set before me by whites, which history conditions me to expect, but the traps and pitfalls planted by my so-called brothers, who because of the same history should know better.

I am a Negro faggot, if I believe what movies, television, and rap music say of me. My life is game for play. Because of my sexuality, I cannot be black. A strong, proud, "Afrocentric" black man is resolutely heterosexual, not *even* bisexual. Hence I remain a Negro. My sexual difference is considered of no value; indeed it's a testament to weakness, passivity, the absence of real guts—balls. Hence I remain a sissy, punk, faggot. I cannot be a black gay man because by the tenets of black macho, black gay man is a triple negation. I am consigned, by these tenets, to remain a Negro faggot. And as such I am game for play, to be used, joked about, put down, beaten, slapped, and bashed, not just by illiterate homophobic thugs in the night, but by black American culture's best and brightest.

In a community where the dozens, signifying, dis'ing, and *dishing* are revered as art form, I ask myself: What does this obsession with Negro faggotry signify? What is its significance?

What lies at the heart, I believe, of black America's pervasive cultural homophobia is the desperate need for a convenient Other *within* the community, yet not truly *of* the community, an Other onto which blame for the chronic identity crises afflicting the black male psyche can be readily displaced, an indispensable Other that functions as the lowest common denominator of the abject, the base line of transgression beyond which a black man is no longer a man, no longer black, an essential Other against which black men and boys maturing, struggling with self-doubt, anxiety, feelings of political, economic, social, and sexual inadequacy—even impotence—can always measure themselves and by comparison seem strong, adept, empowered, superior.

Indeed the representation of Negro faggotry disturbingly parallels and reinforces America's most entrenched racist constructions around African American identity. White icons of the past signifying "blackness" share with contemporary icons of Negro faggotry a manifest dread of the deviant Other. Behind the Sambo and the Snap queen lies a social psyche in torment, a fragile psyche threatened by deviation from its egocentric/ethnocentric construct of self and society. Such a psyche systematically defines the Other's "deviance" by the essential characteristics which make the Other distinct, then invests those differences with intrinsic defect. Hence: blacks are inferior because they are not white. Black gays are unnatural because they are not straight. Majority representation of both affirm the view that blackness and gayness constitute a fundamental rupture in the order of things, that our very existence is an affront to nature and humanity.

For black gay men, this burden of (mis)representation is compounded. We are saddled by historic caricatures of the black male, now fused with newer notions of the Negro faggot. The resultant dehumanization is multilayered and profound.

What strikes me as most insidious, and paradoxical, is the degree to which popular African American depictions of us as black gay men so keenly resonate in American majority depictions of us, as black people. Within the black gay community, for example, the Snap! contains a multiplicity of coded meanings: as in—SNAP!—"Got your point!" Or—SNAP!—"Don't even try it." Or—SNAP!—"You *fierce!*" Or—SNAP!—"Get out of my face." Or—SNAP!—"Girlfriend, pleeeease." The snap can be as emotionally and politically charged as a clenched fist, can punctuate debate and dialogue like an exclamation point, a comma, an ellipsis, or altogether negate the need for words among those who are adept at decoding its nuanced meanings.

But the particular appropriation of the snap by Hollywood's Black Pack deflates the gesture into rank caricature. Instead of a symbol of communal expression and, at times, cultural defiance, the snap becomes part of a simplistically reductive Negro faggot identity: it functions as a mere signpost of effeminate, cute, comic homosexuality. Thus robbed of its full political and cultural dimension, the snap, in this appropriation, descends to stereotype.

Is this any different from the motives and consequences associated with the legendary white dramatist T. D. Rice, who more than 150 years ago appropriated the tattered clothes and dance style of an old crippled black man, then went on stage and imitated him, thus shaping in the popular American mind an indelible image of blacks as simplistic and poor yet given, without exception, to "natural" rhythm and happy feet?

A family tree displaying dominant types in the cultural iconography of black men would show, I believe, an unmistakable line of descent from Sambo to the Snap queen, and in parallel lineage, from the brute negro to the AIDS-infected black homo-con-rapist.

What the members of this pantheon share in common is an extreme displacement and distortion of sexuality. In Sambo and the Snap queen sexuality is repressed, arrested. Laughter, levity, and a certain child-like disposition cement their mutual status as comic eunuchs. Their alter egos, the brute black and the homo con, are but psychosocial projections of an otherwise tamed sexuality run amuck, bestial, promiscuous, pathological.

Contemporary proponents of black macho thus converge with D. W. Griffith in their cultural practice, deploying similar devices toward similarly dehumanizing ends. In their constructions of "unnatural" sexual aggression, the infamous chase scene in *Birth of a Nation* displays a striking aesthetic kinship to the homophobic jail rap—or should I say, attempted rape?—in Reginald and Warrington Hudlin's *House Party*.

The resonances go deeper.

Pseudo-scientific discourse fused with popular icons of race in late nineteenth-century America to project a social fantasy of black men, not simply as sexual demons, but significantly, as intrinsically corrupt. Diseased, promiscuous, destructive—of self and others—our fundamental nature, it was widely assumed, would lead us to extinction.

Against this historical backdrop consider the highly popular comedy routines of Eddie Murphy, which unite Negro faggotry, "Herpes Simplex 10"—and AIDS—into an indivisible modern icon of sexual terrorism. Rap artists and music videos resonate with this perception, fomenting a social psychology that blames the *victim* for his degradation and death.

The sum total of prime-time fag pantomines, camp queens as culture critics, and the proliferating bit-part swish-and-dish divas who, like ubiquitous black maids and butlers in fifties Hollywood films, move along the edges of the frame, seldom at the center, manifests the persistent psychosocial impulse toward control, displacement, and marginalization of the black gay Other. This impulse, in many respects, is no different than the phobic, distorted projections that motivated blackface minstrelsy.

This is the irony: there are more black male filmmakers and rap artists than ever, yet their works display a persistently narrow, even monolithic construction of black male identity.

"You have to understand something," explained Professor Griff of the controversial and highly popular rap group Public Enemy in an interview. "In knowing and understanding black history, African history, there's not a word in any African language which describes homosexual, y'understand what I'm saying? You would like to make them part of the community, but that's something brand new to black people."

And so black macho appropriates African history, or rather, a deeply reductive, mythologized view of African history, to rationalize homophobia. Pseudo-academic claims of "Afrocentricity" have now become a popular invocation when black macho is pressed to defend its essentialist vision of the race. An inheritance from black cultural nationalism of the late sixties, and Negritude before that, today's Afrocentrism, as popularly theorized, premises an historical narrative which runs thus: Before the white man came, African men were strong, noble, protectors, providers, and warriors for their families and tribes. In pre-colonial Africa, men were truly men. And women—were women. Nobody was lesbian. Nobody was feminist. Nobody was gay.

This distortion of history, though severe, has its seductions. Given the increasingly besieged state of black men in America, and the nation's historic subversion of an affirming black identity, it is no wonder that a community would turn to pre-Diasporan history for metaphors of empowerment. But the embrace of the African warrior ideal—strong, protective, impassive, patriarchal—has cost us. It has set us down a perilous road of cultural and spiritual redemption, and distorted or altogether disappeared from historical record the multiplicity of identities around color, gender, sexuality, and class, which inform the African and African American experience.

It is to me supremely revealing that in black macho's popular appropriation of Malcolm X (in movies, music, rap videos) it is consistently Malcolm *before Mecca*—militant, Macho, "by any means necessary" Malcolm—who is quoted and idolized, not Malcolm *after* Mecca, when he became more critical of himself and exclusivist Nation of Islam tenets, and embraced a broader, multicultural perspective on nationalist identity.

By the tenets of black macho, true masculinity admits little or no space for self-interrogation or multiple subjectivities around race. Black Macho prescribes an inflexible ideal: strong black men—"Afrocentric" black men—don't flinch, don't weaken, don't take blame or shit, take charge, step-to when challenged, and defend themselves without pause for self-doubt.

Black Macho counterpoises this warrior model of masculinity with the emasculated Other: the Other as punk, sissy, Negro Faggot, a status with which any man, not just those who, in fact, are gay, can be and are branded should one deviate from rigidly prescribed codes of hypermasculine conduct.

"When I say Gamma, you say Fag. Gamma. Fag. Gamma. Fag." In the conflict between the frat boys and the "fellas" in Spike Lee's *School Daze,* verbal fag-bashing becomes the weapon of choice in the fellas' contest for male domination. In this regard Lee's movie not only resonates a poisonous dynamic in contemporary black male relations, but worse, Lee glorifies it.

Spike Lee and others like him count on the complicit silence of those who know better, who know the truth of their own lives as well as the diverse truths which inform the total black experience.

Notice is served.

Our silence has ended.

SNAP!

Note

This essay was first delivered as a talk at the conference "African-American Film and Media Culture: A Re-Examination" at the Whitney Museum of American Art in June 1990. It also appears in *Brother to Brother: New Writings by Black Gay Men,* ed. Essex Hemphill (Boston: Alyson, 1991), 253–57, and in *Black American Literature Forum* 25 no. 2 (Summer 1991), 389–94, a special issue on black film edited by Camille Billops, Valerie Smith, and Ada Gay Griffin.

All Dressed Up, But No Place to Go?

Style Wars and the New Lesbianism

Arlene Stein

The women feel that in their choice of clothing they are striking a blow against the consumerism of a capitalist society as well as leveling class distinctions that might exist in the community. Their clothing mostly comes from "free boxes," in which people discard their still usable clothing to be recycled by anyone who wants it. Typical clothing consists of Levis or other sturdy pants, t-shirts, workshirts . . .[1]

A s I read these words, from an account of San Francisco's lesbian community circa 1978, I find myself wondering whether the author, in her wildest imagination, could possibly have pictured that in 1988, the hottest lesbian club in town would unabashedly display dolled-up go-go dancers on pedestals, patrons clad in leather miniskirts, with nary a flannel shirt in the house.

Lesbian communities, in San Francisco and elsewhere, have undergone tremendous shifts in tone and emphasis during the past decade. A younger generation of lesbians, who have come of age in a period of relative conservatism, are constructing sexual identities that draw on elements of seventies lesbian-feminism, fifties butch-femme, punk, and assorted other influences. In the battle for the redefinition of lesbianism in the eighties, style, along with sex (and the two are perhaps closely related), has become a central battleground.

When boyish girls make their way onto the pages of *Glamour*, Madonna blurts out to a bemused David Letterman that she and actress friend Sandra Bernhard frequent a certain lesbian bar in New York, and five cute dykes go on "Donahue" to proudly proclaim their sexuality, something is going on. Suddenly, almost imperceptibly, lesbianism is becoming a more visible part of our cultural landscape.

It is a very different public face than that which came before. The man-hating, bra-burning, rabble-rousing dyke—the butt of Fellini's satire in "City of Women" and the object of ridicule for many others—long coexisted with an image of lesbian sensuality that was the stuff of pornographic fantasy. When they do appear, those images increasingly are replaced by real-life symbols of androgynous strength (Martina Navratilova) or quirky artiness (Sandra Bernhard or k. d. lang)—which isn't to say they appear very often. And those few times that they do, the "L-word" is almost always conspicuous by its absence.

These trends probably don't signify a generalized thawing of homophobia or sexism as much as they represent the commercialization and popularization of feminist culture and the avant-garde art world—which many lesbians populate in discrete and not-so-discrete ways. Every day millions of us still fight internal and external battles just to claim the freedom of sexual choice. But in a few particularly tolerant areas of the nation, and increasingly among the young, hip, and artsy, it's almost (but not quite) cool to be queer. It is in these pockets, and to a lesser extent other areas of the nation, that the new lesbian fashion is incubating.

The lesbian look has never been monolithic; it's always reflected a rich combination of cultural forms and styles—local and national, underground and commercial, multicolored and polyethnic. But generally speaking, the "new lesbian" face peeking through today's mass culture is young, white, and alluring, fiercely independent, and nearly free of the anger that typed her predecessors as shrill and humorless. To tell whether she is *really* one of us, your radar must be finely tuned. For better or for worse, this is the public face that many younger women who have come out in the eighties are seeing and taking as their models.

What is the meaning of style for contemporary lesbian identity and politics? Are today's lesbian style wars skin-deep, or do they reflect a changed conception of what it means to be a dyke? If a new lesbian has in fact emerged, is she all flash and no substance, or is she at work busily carving out new lesbian politics that strike at the heart of dominant notions of gender and sexuality?

The Elements of (Lesbian) Style

"They loved it! People weren't used to seeing women look the way they looked—dressed up. After that they wouldn't go to a club unless it had a dress code. . . . Before it was really sad. We really had no place to go."
—Caroline Clone, owner of a San Francisco club for "lipstick lesbians."[2]

In the seventies, lesbian-feminists fashioned themselves as antifashion, flying in the face of reigning standards of femininity, beauty, and respectability. Wearing a flannel shirt and baggy pants was an affront to the dominant culture that liked to keep its women glossy and available, as well as a way for dykes to identify one another. In a world where feminist energies were channeled into the creation of battered women's shelters, antipornography campaigns, or women's music festivals, primping and fussing over your hair was strictly taboo.

Lesbian-feminist antistyle was an emblem of refusal, an attempt to strike a blow against the twin evils of capitalism and patriarchy, the fashion industry and the female objectification that fueled it. The flannel-and-denim look was not so much a style as it was antistyle—an attempt to replace the artifice of fashion with a supposed naturalness, free of gender roles and commercialized pretense.

Situated in this framework, today's self-conscious embrace of high-heels, short skirts, and other utterly feminine trappings—along with a general revival of interest in fashion and appearance among many lesbians—have been interpreted by some as a plainly regressive set of developments. When lesbian-feminists see young femmes strutting around in makeup and panty hose, they may see women intent on fitting in, assimilating into the straight world, shedding their anger, and forgetting their roots. It's somewhat like the clash between dark- and light-skinned blacks described by poet Langston Hughes in the twenties: "The younger blacks were obsessed by money and position, fur coats and flashy cars; their ideals seemed most Nordic and un-Negro." Replace *Nordic* with *straight,* *Negro* with *lesbian,* and you get the picture.

Many lesbians also associate the resurgence of gendered fashion with a return to butch-femme roles and forbidden love in smoky bars. Roles were a central and highly valued feature of lesbian culture—until they were given a bad rep by feminists and consequently stamped out as vestiges of a patriarchal past.

Today, roles *are* enjoying a renaissance among younger dykes, women who never fully parted with their butch and femme identities, and feminists who are finally recognizing the error of their ways. Many women have found that roles are an erotic charge, a way of understanding sexual preferences, and of identifying and attracting potential lovers and friends. But it's clear that roles mean something very different today than they once did.

Joan Nestle, co-founder of the Lesbian Herstory Archives, has written that butch-femme in the fifties was "a conspicuous flag of rebellion" in a highly stigmatized, secretive world, a means of survival in an age when gender rules were heavy as lead weights. Being a butch was an assertion of strength against very narrow conceptions of what it meant to be a woman. Wearing a leather jacket and slicking back short hair wasn't simply an experiment with style—it was an embrace of one's "true nature" in the face of the dominant culture's notions of what it meant to be a woman: feminine and coy.[3]

Butch-femme roles, at least in their prefeminist incarnation, linked sexuality, appearance and, frequently, economic position in a highly ritualized way. Dress was a reflection of sexual style, a signal to potential sexual and nonsexual partners, a clue to one's sensibility on a range of related issues, and a pretty good indicator of whether you worked as a secretary or an elevator operator.

Implicit within that old notion of roles was a great deal of permanence and consistency. One's identity as butch or femme was an essential part of one's being. Once a femme, always a femme. The same for butches. By imposing rules and placing limits on self-expression, roles eroticized difference, providing security and regularity in a tenuous, secretive world. They were often proud statements of lesbian resistance, but they were also the expression of an oppressed minority faced with a paucity of alternatives.

Today's embrace of roles, though, is not a throwback to the fifties. For many women, adopting a role is more a matter of play than necessity; roles are more ambiguous and less naturalized. Many dykes still identify more strongly with one role than the other, but now there is a greater possibility of choice. Eighties butch-femme—if it accurately can be termed as such—is a self-conscious aesthetic that plays with style and power, rather than an embrace of one's "true" nature against the constraints of straight society. Gone is the tightly constructed relation between personal style, erotic preference, and economic position—the hallmark of roles during the prefeminist era.

There is no longer a clear one-to-one correspondence between fashion and identity. For many, clothes are transient, interchangeable; you can dress as a femme one day and a butch the next. You can wear a crew-cut along with a skirt. Wearing high heels during the day does not mean you're a femme at night, passive in bed, or closeted on the job. "Different communities have their own styles," commented Joan Nestle recently, "but on a good bar night the variety of self presentation runs the whole gamut from lesbian separatist drag, to full fem regalia, to leather and chains."

The new lesbianism is defining itself against the memory of the old by rejecting the antistyle of the past. As the owner of a new lesbian nightclub in San Francisco implies when she praises the fact that women are "finally dressing up," lesbians are feeling good about themselves today (implying that they didn't in the past). Even the *Wall Street Journal* reports that "lipstick" lesbians are clashing with flannel-shirted "crunchies" in the hallowed halls of Yale. Lesbian-feminism is on the wane, and lifestyle lesbianism—particularly among younger, urban dykes, is on the rise.

Lifestyle versus Politics

Popularized by advertising and marketing experts, *lifestyle* has become one of the buzzwords of the eighties; it is used to refer to yuppies, gay men, and others thought to possess greater-than-average amounts of disposable income, or those who are at least willing to part with what they have to create the illusion that they do. Implicit in the use of this terminology is the belief that *lifestyle* is opposed to *politics:* you are either self-absorbed and obsessed with Things and Style, *or* you are ascetic and devoted to Higher Ends.

The American Dream, that manifestly apolitical vision, is predicated on buying a home, filling it with consumer durables, and insulating it as best as you can from outside intrusions. Laboring in dull jobs during the day, we should live for the weekend, for freedom, for shiny objects. The market and its plastic pretensions have pervaded all corners of our lives, distorting our needs and shaping our desires.

Lesbian-feminism, born of the counterculture, was partially conceived as a challenge to this crass materialism. Throughout the seventies, while some gay men were busily carving out commercial niches in urban centers, many lesbians scoffed at such activities, and chose instead to build a nonsexist, antimaterialistic world. The asceticism and political correctness that frequently accompanied these pursuits may have been the unintended consequence of a defensive separatism. But politicizing every aspect of personhood, many later discovered, was just too tall an order to live with.

In 1970, the Radicalesbians declared, "A lesbian is the rage of all women condensed to the point of explosion." Today, we've lightened up. Witness the new lesbian comedians and novelists who convey a sense of lesbian life, warts and all, by constructing characters driven by anger, jealousy, and revenge—as well as love and community. The sex debates of the early eighties, coupled with the increasing acknowledgment of racial, ethnic, and other forms of difference, have broken down the idea of a seamless, transhistorical lesbian identity that we all share.

While lesbian communities are perhaps less politically organized, less cohesive, and less homogeneous in thought and action than they were ten years ago, activism hasn't completely vanished though. The recent emergence of the Lesbian Agenda for Action, a city-wide political organization in San Francisco, is a testament to this, as is the recent National Lesbian Rights Conference sponsored by NOW or even the large number of dykes who staff numerous AIDS-related organizations. But it is a lot more difficult to pack an auditorium with women committed to any one issue than it was in the seventies. There is a seeming multiplication of diverse subcultural pockets and cliques—corporate dykes, arty dykes, dykes of color, clean and sober dykes—of which political lesbians are but one among many.

What does it mean that often the most visible players in our communities today are lipstick lesbians, given that lesbian communities are more fragmented, that it's harder to scrounge for a living, and that—for many women—political involvements fail to provide the sort of personal sustenance they once did? The rise of the femme and the new ambiguity of lesbian style could be interpreted as a sign of retrenchment. It could be argued that lifestyle lesbianism promotes assimilation over separation, style over substance, and is a sign of our growing conservatism.

Yet many lesbians today don't see it that way. Instead, they experience this new attention to lifestyle as a freedom, a testament to the fact that their identity is now a matter of personal choice rather than political compulsion. As a once-fervent activist remarked recently, "After years of holding myself back and dressing to hide myself, shopping, I've found out, can be a real joy."

Calling the new lesbianism a retrenchment or embracing it as a freedom both appear to reflect popular sentiments. Is there a way to reconcile them without lapsing into a simplistic plea to smash style, or a lamentation that politics is oh-so-boring so why not shop til we drop? Can we transcend the puritanism (shared by the Left and the Right in this country) that one has to suffer to be noble, without depoliticizing lesbian identity?

Politics in a New Lesbian World

"You can analyze me to death, but it's just that I grew up as a tomboy and I prefer my hair being short and I love Nudie suits. Yeah, sure, the boys can be attracted to me, the girls can be attracted to me, your mother . . . your uncle, sure. It doesn't really matter to me."
    —Country-western singer k. d. lang[4]

My friends and I are all rabid fans of k. d. lang, a Canadian who sings traditional torch ballads tongue-in-cheek, appears regularly on Johnny Carson sporting a butch haircut, cowgirl skirt, and no makeup, and defies every prescription of what a woman in country music—and indeed pop music—should be. To most of her straight fans, k. d. lang is simply a quirky, tomboyish character, a performer whose powerful voice and compelling originality compensate for her lack-of-fit in a musical genre where it's usually easy to tell the boys from the girls. But to her legions of dyke devotees she is divine. When a newly formed k. d. lang fan club sponsored a video night at one of the oldest dyke bars in San Francisco recently, the place was packed tighter than I ever can remember having seen it—testimony, perhaps, to how starved we are for media images of lesbianism, and to how attractive her image is to many of us.

She is one of a new breed of performers, all in their twenties, who came of age when women's music was au courant, but who've rejected that genre in favor of mainstream exposure. Without identifying themselves as dykes, they experiment with style and self-presentation, pushing up against the boundaries of what is acceptable for women. I've spent hours with friends discussing the pros and cons of whether k. d. and the others should come out, whether or not it really matters since, after all, *we* all know. Or is it all a big sellout? When she calls herself a tomboy, and says that she doesn't care whether men or women are attracted to her, is it simply a ploy to maintain her cover?

This dilemma lies at the heart of the new lesbianism.

On the one hand, the new lesbianism deconstructs the old, perhaps overly politicized or prescriptive notion of lesbianism by refusing ghettoization, acknowledging internal group differences, and affirming the value of individual choice when it comes to style and political and sexual expression. On the other hand, it comes perilously close to depoliticizing lesbian identity and perpetuating our invisibility by failing, frequently, to name itself to others.

Some might argue that if we define politics broadly as a series of contests between competing cultural images—of what it means to be a woman or a lesbian, for example—then the new lesbian style can be seen as a political act, a public assertion of lesbian identity. Yet this new political strategy of cultural visibility, if it can be called that, is paradoxical, because it emerges at a point in our history when lesbian identity is in the process of reformulation.

If lesbianism ceases to be the defining aspect of identity for many women and becomes simply an image, and if notions of what a lesbian looks like break down as fashion codes change and recombine, will we lose sight of what it means to be a lesbian in a largely heterosexual world? As cultural critic Stuart Ewen argues, when power is at stake, a politics of images is no substitute for a "politics of substance." Images are too easily manipulated, their meanings complex and evanescent.

By skirting the issue of power (no pun intended), the new lifestyle lesbianism comes perilously close to giving credence to the liberal belief that today, any sexual choice is possible. While the fragmentation of lesbian identity and decoding of lesbian style may be justifiable responses to an overpoliticization of the personal, they run the risk of erasing the political dimension of lesbian communities. It may be easier to be a dyke today than even a decade ago, but the sobering truth remains that, in a heterosexist, male-dominated society, lesbianism is still not freely chosen. As Margaret Cerullo observed recently, the "hundred lifestyles" strategy, a strategy that calls for a pluralism of sexual choice, "doesn't represent an adequate response to the one lifestyle that has all the power"—heterosexuality.[5]

A little history lesson could go a long way. In the trenches of the style wars, it's easy to forget that political lesbianism paved the way for lifestyle lesbianism.

Lacking a sense of history, the new lesbian defines herself against those who came before her, unaware of the fact that greater choice is possible today because lesbians (as well as many straight feminists) fought long and hard for it. By struggling to destigmatize lesbianism, and by forging institutional spaces within which it could flourish, lesbian-feminism was largely responsible for creating the conditions under which a new, more mainstream, and less radical lesbianism would eventually take root. That many women experience the new lesbianism as freedom is perhaps testimony to the success, rather than the failure, of the old.

Recognizing this doesn't mean the old political models don't need revising. If the emergence of lifestyle lesbianism tells us anything, it is that we need a political language that acknowledges our diversity as well as our commonality, that embodies playfulness along with rage, and that faces outward as well as inward. Lesbian style may be one of the central battlegrounds for the reformulation of lesbian identity today, but style itself is an insufficient basis for a lesbian politic.

That doesn't mean we should all discard our newly purchased dresses and cowboy boots and begin to boycott the hair salon once again. Rather, it suggests we should embrace style—along with anger—to forge a lesbianism that can take on the new, more complex realities of the eighties and nineties.

Notes

1 Deborah Wolf, *The Lesbian Community* (Berkeley and Los Angeles: University of California Press, 1979), 85–86.

2 Karen Everett, "Lipstick Lesbians Love the Night Life," *San Francisco Sentinel,* 28 October 1988.

3 Joan Nestle, "Butch-Fem Relationships: Sexual Courage in the 1950s," *Heresies, No. 12 (1981).* See also Pat Califia, "GenderBending," *Advocate,* 15 September 1983.

4 Burt Kearns, "Canadian Cowpie," *Spin Magazine,* September 1988.

5 Margaret Cerullo, "Night Visions: Toward a Lesbian/Gay Politics for the Present," *Radical America,* vol. 21 (March–April 1987).

Commodity

Lesbianism

Danae Clark

A commodity appears, at first sight, a very trivial thing, and easily understood. Its analysis shows that it is, in reality, *a very queer thing.*
—Karl Marx, *Capital*[1]

n an effort to articulate the historical and social formation of female subjectivity under capitalism, feminist investigations of consumer culture have
addressed a variety of complex and interrelated issues, including the construction of femininity and desire, the role of consumption in media texts, and the
paradox of the woman/commodity relation. Implicit in these investigations,
however, has been an underlying concern for the heterosexual woman as consuming subject.[2] Perhaps because, as Jane Gaines notes, "consumer culture
thrives on heterosexuality and its institutions by taking its cues from heterosexual 'norms,'"[3] theories *about* consumerism fall prey to the same normalizing
tendencies. In any event, analyses of female consumerism join a substantial body
of other feminist work that "assumes, but leaves unwritten, a heterosexual context for the subject" and thus contributes to the continued invisibility of lesbians.[4]

But lesbians too are consumers. Like heterosexual women they are major
purchasers of clothing, household goods, and media products. Lesbians have
not, however, been targeted as a separate consumer group within the dominant
configuration of capitalism, either directly through the mechanism of advertising
or indirectly through fictional media representations; their relation to consumerism is thus necessarily different. This "difference" requires a careful look at the
relation between lesbians and consumer culture, representations of lesbianism
and consumption in media texts, and the role of the lesbian spectator as consum-

ing subject. Such an investigation is especially timely since current trends in both advertising and commercial television show that lesbian viewers (or at least some segments of the lesbian population) are enjoying a certain pleasure as consumers that was not available to them in the past. An analysis of these pleasures should therefore shed light not only on the place that lesbians occupy within consumer culture, but on the identificatory processes involved in lesbian reading formations.

Dividing the Consumer Pie

Lesbians have not been targeted as consumers by the advertising industry for several historical reasons. First, lesbians as a social group have not been economically powerful; thus, like other social groups who lack substantial purchasing power (e.g., the elderly), they have not been attractive to advertisers. Second, lesbians have not been easily identifiable as a social group anyway. According to the market strategies commonly used by advertisers to develop target consumer groups, four criteria must be met. A group must be (1) identifiable, (2) accessible, (3) measurable, and (4) profitable.[5] In other words, a particular group must be "knowable" to advertisers in concrete ways. Lesbians present a problem here because they exist across race, income, and age (three determinants used by advertisers to segment and distinguish target groups within the female population). To the extent that lesbians are not identifiable or accessible, they are not measurable and, therefore, not profitable. The fact that many lesbians prefer not to be identified because they fear discrimination poses an additional obstacle to targeting them. Finally, most advertisers have had no desire to identify a viable lesbian consumer group. Advertisers fear that by openly appealing to a homosexual market their products will be negatively associated with homosexuality and will be avoided by heterosexual consumers. Thus, although homosexuals (lesbians and gay men) reputedly compose 10 percent of the overall U.S. market population—and up to 20–22 percent in major urban centers such as New York and San Francisco—advertisers have traditionally stayed in the closet when it comes to peddling their wares.[6]

Recently, however, this trend has undergone a visible shift—especially for gay men. According to a 1982 review in the *New York Times Magazine* called "Tapping the Homosexual Market," several of today's top advertisers are interested in "wooing . . . the white, single, well-educated, well-paid man who happens to be homosexual." This interest, prompted by surveys conducted by the *Advocate* between 1977 and 1980 that indicated that 70 percent of their readers aged twenty to forty earned incomes well above the national median, has led companies such as Paramount, Seagram, Perrier, and Harper and Row to advertise in gay male publications like *Christopher Street* and the *Advocate*. Their ads are tailored specifically for the gay male audience. Seagram, for example, ran a "famous men of history" campaign for Boodles Gin that pictured men "purported to be gay."[7]

A more common and more discreet means of reaching the gay male consumer, however, is achieved through the mainstream (predominately print) media. As one marketing director has pointed out, advertisers "really want to reach a bigger market than just gays, but [they] don't want to alienate them" either. Thus, advertisers are increasingly striving to create a dual marketing approach that will "speak to the homosexual consumer in a way that the straight consumer will not notice." As one observer explains, "It used to be that gay people could communicate to one another, in a public place, if they didn't know one another, only by glances and a sort of *code behavior* . . . to indicate to the other person, but not to anybody else, that you, too, were gay. Advertisers, if they're smart, can do that too" (emphasis added). One early example of this approach was the Calvin Klein jeans series that featured "a young, shirtless blond man lying on his stomach" and, in another ad, "a young, shirtless blond man lying on his side, holding a blue-jeans jacket." According to Peter Frisch, a gay marketing consultant, one would "have to be comatose not to realize that it appeals to gay men" (I presume he is referring to the photographs' iconographic resemblance to gay pornography). Calvin Klein marketing directors, however, denied any explicit gay element: "We did not try *not* to appeal to gays. We try to appeal, period. With healthy, beautiful people. If there's an awareness in that community of health and grooming, they'll respond to the ads."[8]

This dual marketing strategy has been referred to as "gay window advertising." Generally, gay window ads avoid explicit references to heterosexuality by depicting only one individual or same-sexed individuals within the representational frame. In addition, these models bear the signifiers of sexual ambiguity or androgynous style. But "gayness" remains in the eye of the beholder: gays and lesbians can read into an ad certain subtextual elements that correspond to experiences with or representations of gay/lesbian subculture. If heterosexual consumers do not notice these subtexts or subcultural codes, then advertisers are able to reach the homosexual market along with the heterosexual market without ever revealing their aim.

The metaphor of the window used by the advertising industry to describe gay marketing techniques is strikingly similar to feminist descriptions of women's relation to consumer culture and film representation. Mary Ann Doane, for example, remarks that "the film frame is a kind of display window and spectatorship consequently a form of window shopping."[10] Jane Gaines likewise suggests that cinema going is "analogous to the browsing-without-obligation-to-buy pioneered by the turn-of-the-century department store, where one could, with no offense to the merchant, enter to peruse the goods, exercising a kind of *visual connoisseurship,* and leave without purchase" (emphasis added). Gaines further argues that the show window itself is "a medium of circulation" and that "commodification seems to facilitate circulation by multiplying the number of possible contexts."[11] The metaphor of the window, in other words, posits an active reader as well as a multiple, shifting context of display.

The notion of duality that characterizes gay window advertising's marketing strategy is also embodied in various theoretical descriptions and approaches to consumer culture in general. Within the Frankfurt School, for example, Adorno speaks of the dual character or dialectic of luxury that "opens up consumer culture to be read as its opposite," and Benjamin suggests that consumer culture is a dual system of meaning whereby "the economic life of the commodity imping[es] upon its life as an object of cultural significance."[12] More recently, a duality has been located in feminist responses to consumer culture and fashion culture in particular. As Gaines notes, the beginning of the Second Wave of feminist politics and scholarship was marked by a hostility toward fashion, perceiving it as a patriarchal codification and commodification of femininity that enslaved women and placed their bodies on display. But this "antifashion" position is now joined by a feminist perspective that sees fashion culture as a site of female resistance, masquerade, and self-representation.[13] At the heart of this "fabrication," says Gaines, is a gender confusion and ambiguity that disrupts and confounds patriarchal culture.[14]

Lesbians have an uneasy relation to this dual perspective on fashion. First of all, lesbians have a long tradition of resisting dominant cultural definitions of female beauty and fashion as a way of separating themselves from heterosexual culture politically and as a way of signaling their lesbianism to other women in their subcultural group. This resistance to or reformulation of fashion codes thus distinguished lesbians from straight women at the same time that it challenged patriarchal structures. As Arlene Stein explains in an article on style in the lesbian community, "Lesbian-feminist anti-style was an emblem of refusal, an attempt to strike a blow against the twin evils of capitalism and patriarchy, the fashion industry and the female objectification that fueled it. The flannel-and-denim look was not so much a style as it was anti-style—an attempt to replace the artifice of fashion with a supposed naturalness, free of gender roles and commercialized pretense."[15] Today, however, many lesbians, particularly younger, urban lesbians, are challenging this look, exposing the constructedness of "natural" fashion, and finding a great deal of pleasure in playing with the possibilities of fashion and beauty.

This shift, which is not total and certainly not without controversy, can be attributed to a number of factors. First of all, many lesbians are rebelling against a lesbian-feminist credo of political correctness that they perceive as stifling. As a *Village Voice* writer observes, "A lesbian can wag her fingers as righteously as any patriarchal puritan, defining what's acceptable according to what must be ingested, worn, and especially desired. . . . In a climate where a senator who doesn't like a couple of photographs tries to do away with the National Endowment for the Arts, censorious attacks within the lesbian community begin to sound a lot like fundamentalism. . . . They amount to a policing of the lesbian libido."[16] Stein thus notes that while the old-style, politically correct(ing) strain of lesbian feminism is on the wane, "lifestyle" lesbianism is on the rise. Lifestyle lesbianism is a recognition of the "diverse subcultural pockets and cliques—corporate dykes, arty dykes, dykes of color, clean and sober dykes—of which political lesbians are but one among many."[17] But it may also be a response to the marketing strategies of consumer culture.

The predominate research trend in U.S. advertising for the past two decades has been VALS (values and lifestyles) research. By combining information on demographics (sex, income, educational level), buying habits, self-image, and aspirations, VALS research targets and, in the case of yuppies, effectively *creates* consumer lifestyles that are profitable to advertisers.[18] Given lesbian-feminism's countercultural, anticapitalist roots, it is not surprising that lesbians who "wear" their lifestyles or flaunt themselves as "material girls" are often criticized for trading in their politics for a self-absorbed materialism. But there is more to "lipstick lesbians" or "style nomads" than a freewheeling attitude toward their status as consumers or a boredom with the relatively static nature of the "natural look" (fashion, after all, implies change). Fashion-conscious dykes are rebelling against the idea that there is a clear one-to-one correspondence between fashion and identity. As Stein explains, "You can dress as a femme one day and a butch the next. You can wear a crew-cut along with a skirt. Wearing high heels during the day does not mean you're a femme at night, passive in bed, or closeted on the job."[19] Seen in this light, fashion becomes an assertion of personal freedom as well as political choice.

The new attitudes of openness toward fashion, sexuality, and lifestyle would not have been possible, of course, without the lesbian-feminist movement of recent decades. Its emergence may also have an economic explanation. According to a recent survey in *Out/look*, a national gay and lesbian quarterly, the average annual income for individual lesbians (who read *Out/look*) is $30,181; the average lesbian household income is approximately $58,000.[20] Since lesbians as a group are beginning to raise their incomes and class standing, they are now in a position to afford more of the clothing and "body maintenance" that was once beyond their financial capabilities. Finally, some credit for the changing perspectives on fashion might also be given to the recent emphasis on masquerade and fabrication in feminist criticism and to the more prominent role of camp in lesbian criticism. At least within academic circles these factors seem to affect, or to be the effect of, lesbian theorists' fashion sensibilities.

But regardless of what has *caused* this shift, or where one stands on the issue of fashion, advertisers in the fashion industry have begun to capitalize on it. Given the increasing affluence and visibility of one segment of the lesbian population—the predominantly white, predominantly childless, middle-class, educated lesbian with disposable income—it appears that advertisers are now interested in promoting "lesbian window advertising." (Even while recognizing the highly problematic political implications of such a choice, I will continue to use the term *gay* instead of *lesbian* when referring to this marketing strategy since *gay window advertising* is the discursive phrase currently employed by the advertising industry.) In fashion magazines such as *Elle* and *Mirabella,* and in mail-order catalogs such as *Tweeds, J. Crew,* and *Victoria's Secret,* advertisers (whether knowingly or not) are capitalizing on a dual market strategy that packages gender ambiguity and speaks, at least indirectly, to the lesbian consumer market. The representational strategies of gay window advertising thus offer what John Fiske calls "points of purchase" or points of identification that allow readers to make sense of cultural forms in ways that are meaningful or pleasurable to them.[21] The important question here is how these consumer points of purchase become involved in lesbian notions of identity, community, politics, and fashion.

When Dykes Go Shopping . . .

In a recent issue of *Elle,* a fashion layout entitled "Male Order" shows us a model who, in the words of the accompanying ad copy, represents "the zenith of masculine allure." In one photograph the handsome, short-haired model leans against the handlebars of a motorcycle, an icon associated with bike dyke culture. Her man-styled jacket, tie, and jewelry suggest a butch lesbian style that offers additional points of purchase for the lesbian spectator. In another photograph from the series, the model is placed in a more neutral setting, a café, that is devoid of lesbian iconography. But because she is still dressed in masculine attire and, more important, exhibits the "swaggering" style recommended by the advertisers, the model incorporates aspects of lesbian style. Here, the traditional "come-on" look of advertising can be read as the look or pose of a cruising dyke. Thus, part of the pleasure that lesbians find in these ads might be what Elizabeth Ellsworth calls "lesbian verisimilitude," or the representation of body language, facial expression, and general appearance that can be claimed and coded as "lesbian" according to current standards of style within lesbian communities.[22]

A fashion layout from *Mirabella,* entitled "Spectator," offers additional possibilities for lesbian readings. In this series of photographs by Deborah Turbeville, two women (not always the same two in each photograph) strike poses in a fashionable, sparsely decorated apartment. The woman who is most prominently featured has very short, slicked-back hair, and, in three of the photographs, she is wearing a tank top (styled like a man's undershirt) and baggy trousers. With her confident poses, her broad shoulders, and strong arms (she obviously pumps iron), this fashion model can easily be read as "high-style butch." The other women in the series are consistently more "femme" in appearance, though they occasionally wear masculine-style apparel as well. The lesbian subtext in this fashion layout, however, is not limited to the models' appearances. The adoption of butch and femme *roles* suggests the possibility of interaction or a "playing out" of a lesbian narrative. Thus, while the women are physically separated and do not interact in the photographs,[23] their stylistic role-playing invites the lesbian spectator to construct a variety of (butch-femme) scenarios in which the two women come together. The eroticism of these imaginary scenes is enhanced by compositional details such as soft lighting and a rumpled bedsheet draped over the apartment window to suggest a romantic encounter. The variation of poses and the different combination of models also invites endless possibilities for narrative construction. Have these two women just met? Are they already lovers? Is there a love triangle going on here? and so on.

Much of what gets negotiated, then, is not so much the contradictions between so-called dominant and oppositional readings, but the details of the subcultural reading itself. Even so, because lesbians (as members of a heterosexist culture) have been taught to read the heterosexual possibilities of representations, the "straight" reading is never entirely erased or replaced. Lesbian readers, in other words, know that they are not the primary audience for mainstream advertising, that androgyny is a fashionable and profitable commodity, and that the fashion models in these ads are quite probably heterosexual. In this sense, the dual approach of gay window advertising can refer not only to the two sets of readings formulated by homosexuals and heterosexuals, but to the dual or multiple interpretations that exist *within* lesbian reading formations. The straight readings, however, do not simply exist alongside alternative readings, nor do they necessarily diminish the pleasure found in the alternate readings. As "visual connoisseurs" lesbians privilege certain readings (styles) over others, or, in the case of camp readings, the straight reading itself forms the basis of (as it becomes twisted into) a pleasurable interpretation.

Here, as Sue-Ellen Case might argue, is the locus of a true masquerade of readership.[24] Lesbians are accustomed to playing out multiple styles and sexual roles as a tactic of survival and thus have learned the artifice of invention in defeating heterosexual codes of naturalism: "The closet has given us the lie; and the lie has given camp—the style, the discourse, the mise-en-scène of butch-femme roles. The survival tactic of hiding and lying [has] produced a camp discourse . . . in which gender referents are suppressed, or slip into one another, fictional lovers are constructed, [and] metaphors substitute for literal descriptions." I would not argue, as Case does, that "the butch-femme couple inhabit the [lesbian] subject position together"[25] since the butch-femme aesthetic is a historically specific (and even community and lifestyle specific) construct that ranges from the rigid butch-femme roles of the fifties to the campy renaissance of today's butch-femme role-playing, and thus cannot represent a consistent subject position. But a lesbian subject's recognition of the butch-femme binarism, as it has been historically styled by lesbian communities, is an essential component of a reading practice that distances, subverts, and plays with both heterosexist representations and images of sexual indeterminacy. Another aspect of reading that must be considered is the pleasure derived from seeing the dominant media "attempt, but fail, to colonize 'real' lesbian space." Even in representations that capitalize on sexual ambiguity there are certain aspects of lesbian subculture that remain (as yet) inaccessible or unappropriated. By claiming this unarticulated space as something distinct and separable from heterosexual (or heterosexist) culture, lesbian readers are no longer outsiders, but insiders privy to the inside jokes that create an experience of pleasure and solidarity with other lesbians "in the know." Thus, as Ellsworth notes, lesbians "have responded to the marginalization, silencing, and debasement" found in dominant discourse "by moving the field of social pleasures . . . to the center of their interpretive activities" and reinforcing their sense of identity and community.[26]

This idea assumed concrete dimensions for me during the course of researching and presenting various versions of this paper. Lesbians across the country were eager to talk about or send copies of advertisements that had *dyke appeal* (and there was a good deal of consensus over how that term was interpreted). A number of lesbians admitted to having an interest in *J. Crew* catalogs because of a certain model they looked forward to seeing each month. Another woman told me of several lesbians who work for a major fashion publication as if to reassure me that gay window fashion photography is not an academic hallucination or a mere coincidence. Gossip, hearsay, and confessions are activities that reside at the center of lesbian interpretive communities and add an important discursive dimension to lesbians' pleasure in looking.

This conception of readership is a far cry from earlier (heterosexist) feminist analyses of advertising that argued that "advertisements help to endorse the powerful male attitude that women are passive bodies to be endlessly looked at, waiting to have their sexual attractiveness matched with *active* male sexual desire," or that women's relation to advertisements can only be explained in terms of anxiety or "narcissistic damage."[27] These conclusions were based on a conspiracy theory that placed ultimate power in the hands of corporate patriarchy and relegated no power or sense of agency to the female spectator. Attempts to modify this position, however, have created yet another set of obstacles around which we must maneuver with caution. For in our desire and haste to attribute agency to the spectator and a means of empowerment to marginal or oppressed social groups, we risk losing sight of the interrelation between reading practices and the political economy of media institutions.

In the case of gay window advertising, for example, appropriation cuts both ways. While lesbians find pleasure (and even validation) in that which is both accessible and unarticulated, the advertising industry is playing on a material and ideological tension that simultaneously appropriates aspects of lesbian subculture and positions lesbian reading practices in relation to consumerism. As John D'Emilio explains, "This dialectic—the constant interplay between exploitation and some measure of autonomy—informs all of the history of those who have lived under capitalism." According to D'Emilio's argument that capitalism and the institution of wage labor have created the material conditions for homosexual desire and identity, gay window advertising is a logical outgrowth of capitalist development, one that presumably will lead to more direct forms of marketing in the future. But the reasons behind this development can hardly be attributed to a growing acceptance of homosexuality as a legitimate lifestyle. Capitalist enterprise creates a tension: materially it "weakens the bonds that once kept families together," but ideologically it "drives people into heterosexual families." Thus, "while capitalism has knocked the material foundations away from family life, lesbians, gay men, and heterosexual feminists have become the scapegoats for the social instability of the system."[28] The result of this tension is that capitalists welcome homosexuals as consuming subjects but not as social subjects. Or, as David Ehrenstein remarks, "the market is there for the picking, and questions of 'morality' yield ever so briefly to the quest for capital."[29]

The sexual indeterminancy of gay window advertising's dual market approach thus allows a space for lesbian identification, but must necessarily deny the representation of lesbian identity politics. This is a point that has so far been overlooked in the ongoing feminist and lesbian/gay debates over the issue of identity politics.[30] At the core of these debates is the poststructuralist challenge to essentialist definitions of identity. While theorists and activists alike agree that some shared sense of identity is necessary to build a cohesive and visible political community, some theorists argue that any unified conception of gay/lesbian identity is reductive and ahistorical. They thus opt for a historically constructed notion of *identities* that is contradictory, socially contingent, and rooted in progressive sexual politics. But while the controversies are raging over whether gay/lesbian identity is essential or constructed, media industries are producing texts that deny the very politics feminists and lesbians are busy theorizing.

Mainstream media texts employ representational strategies that generally refer to gays and lesbians in *antiessentialist* terms. That is, homosexuals are not depicted as inherently different from heterosexuals; neither does there exist a unified or authentic "gay sensibility." As Mark Finch observes, "The most recuperable part of the gay movement's message is that gay people are individuals."[31] The result is a liberal gay discourse that embraces humanism while rejecting any notion of a separate and authentic lesbian/gay subject. The homosexual, says John Leo, is thus "put together from disarticulating bits and pieces of the historical discourse on homosexual desire, which become a narrative pastiche for middle-class 'entertainment.'"[32] As a mode of representation that lacks any clear positioning toward what it shows, pastiche embodies "the popular" in the sense that people are free to make their own meanings out of the cultural bits and ideological pieces that are presented to them.

But this postmodern, antiessentialist (indeed, democratic) discourse could also be interpreted as a homophobic response. As Jeffrey Weeks ironically points out, "The essentialist view lends itself most effectively to the defense of minority status."[33] (For example, if homosexuality were to be classified by the courts as biologically innate, discrimination would be more difficult to justify. By contrast, when a sense of lesbian or gay identity is lost, the straight world finds it easier to ignore social and political issues that directly affect gays and lesbians as a group.) The constructionist strategies of the media are thus not as progressive as antiessentialist theorists (or media executives) might have us believe. The issue is not a matter of choosing between constructionism or essentialism, but a matter of examining the political motivations involved in each of these approaches—whether they appear in theory or media texts.

If we take politics as our starting point, then media and advertising texts can be analyzed in terms of their (un)willingness or (in)ability to represent the identity politics of current lesbian communities. Gay window advertising, as suggested earlier, consciously disavows any explicit connection to lesbianism for fear of offending or losing potential customers. At the same time, an appropriation of lesbian styles or appeal to lesbian desires can also assure a lesbian market. This dual approach is effective because it is based on two key ingredients of marketing success: style and choice. As Dick Hebdige has noted, "It is the subculture's stylistic innovations which first attract the media's attention."[34] Because style is a cultural construction, it is easily appropriated, reconstructed, and divested of its original political or subcultural signification. Style as resistance becomes commodifiable as chic when it leaves the political realm and enters the fashion world. This simultaneously diffuses the political edge of style. Resistant trends (such as wearing men's oversized jackets or oxford shoes—which, as a form of masquerade, is done in part for fun, but also in protest against the fashion world's insistence on dressing women in tightly fitted garments and dangerously unstable footwear) become restyled as high-priced fashions.

In an era of "outing" (the practice of forcing gay and lesbian public figures to come out of the closet as a way to confront heterosexuals with our ubiquity as well as our competence, creativity, or civic-mindedness), gay window advertising can be described as a practice of "ining." In other words, this type of advertising invites us to look *into* the ad to identify with elements of style, invites us *in* as consumers, invites us to be part of a fashionable "*in* crowd," but negates an identity politics based on the act of "coming out." Indeed, within the world of gay window advertising, there is no lesbian community to come out to, no lesbian community to identify with, no indication that lesbianism or "lesbian style" is a political issue. This stylization furthermore promotes a liberal discourse of choice that separates sexuality from politics and connects them both with consumerism. Historically, this advertising technique dates back to the twenties, as Roland Marchand explains: "The compulsion of advertising men to relegate women's modernity to the realm of consumption and dependence found expression not only in pictorial styles but also in tableaux that sought to link products with the social and political freedoms of the new woman. Expansive rhetoric that heralded women's march toward freedom and equality often concluded by proclaiming their victory only in the narrower realm of consumer products."[35] Just as early twentieth-century advertisers were more concerned about women's votes in the marketplace than their decisions in the voting booth, contemporary advertisers are more interested in lesbian consumers than lesbian politics. Once stripped of its political underpinnings, lesbianism can be represented as a style of consumption linked to sexual preference. Lesbianism, in other words, is treated as merely a sexual style that can be chosen—or not chosen—just as one chooses a particular mode of fashion for self-expression.

But within the context of consumerism and the historical weight of heterosexist advertising techniques, "choice" is regulated in determinate ways. For example, gay window advertising appropriates lesbian subcultural style, incorporates its features into commodified representations, and offers it back to lesbian consumers in a packaged form cleansed of identity politics. In this way, it offers lesbians the opportunity to solve the "problem" of lesbianism: by choosing to clothe oneself in fashionable ambiguity, one can pass as "straight" (in certain milieux) while still choosing lesbianism as a sexual preference; by wearing the privilege of straight culture, one can avoid political oppression. Ironically, these ads also offer heterosexual women an alternative as well. As Judith Williamson notes, "The bourgeois always wants to be in disguise, and the customs and habits of the oppressed seem so much more fascinating than his [sic] own."[36] Thus, according to Michael Bronski, "When gay sensibility is used as a sales pitch, the strategy is that gay images imply distinction and non-conformity, granting straight consumers a longed-for place outside the humdrum mainstream."[37] The seamless connections that have traditionally been made between heterosexuality and consumerism are broken apart to allow straight and lesbian women alternative choices. But these choices, which result in a rearticulated homogenized style, deny the differences among women as well as the potential antagonisms that exist between straight and lesbian women over issues of style, politics and sexuality. As Williamson might explain, "Femininity needs the 'other' in order to function . . . even as politically [it] seek[s] to eliminate it."[38]

Similar contradictions and attempts at containment occur within the discourses surrounding women's bodybuilding. As Laurie Schulze notes, "The deliberately muscular woman disturbs dominant notions of sex, gender, and sexuality, and any discursive field that includes her risks opening up a site of contest and conflict, anxiety and ambiguity." Thus, within women's fashion magazines, bodybuilding has been recuperated as a normative ideal of female beauty that promotes self-improvement and ensures attractiveness to men. This discourse "also assures women who are thinking about working out with weights that they need not fear a loss of privilege or social power; despite any differences that may result from lifting weights, they will still be able to 'pass.'" The assurances in this case are directed toward heterosexual women who fear that bodybuilding will bring the taint of lesbianism. The connection between bodybuilding and lesbianism is not surprising, says Schulze, for "the ways in which female bodybuilders and lesbians disturb patriarchy and heterosexism . . . draw very similar responses from dominant culture."[39] Both the muscular female and the butch lesbian are accused of looking like men or wanting to be men. As Annette Kuhn puts it, "Muscles are rather like drag."[40] Lesbian style, too, tends toward drag, masquerade, and the confusion of gender. Thus, both are subjected to various forms of control that either refuse to accept their physical or sexual "excesses" or otherwise attempt to domesticate their threat and fit them into the dominant constructions of feminine appearances and roles.

Both bodybuilders and lesbians, in other words, are given opportunities to "pass" in straight feminine culture. For bodybuilders, this means not flexing one's muscles while walking down the street or, in the case of competitive bodybuilders, exhibiting the signs of conventional feminine style (e.g., makeup, coiffed hair, and string bikinis) while flexing on stage.[41] For lesbians, as discussed earlier, this means adopting more traditionally feminine apparel or the trendy accoutrements of gender ambiguity. But within these passing strategies are embodied the very seeds of resistance. As Schulze argues, muscle culture is a "terrain of resistance/refusal" as well as a "terrain of control."[42] It's simply a matter of how much muscle a woman chooses to flex. Within bodybuilding subculture, flexing is encouraged and admired; physical strength is valorized as a new form of femininity. Lesbians engage in their own form of "flexing" within lesbian subcultures (literally so for those lesbians who also pump iron) by refusing to pass as straight.

This physical and political flexing calls the contradictions of women's fashion culture into question and forces them out of the closet. It thus joins a long history of women's subversive and resistant responses to consumer culture in general. Although consumer culture has historically positioned women in ways that benefit heterosexist, capitalist patriarchy, women have always found ways to exert their agency and create their own pleasures and spaces. Fiske, for example, discusses the way that shopping has become a "terrain of guerrilla warfare" where women change price tags, shoplift, or try on expensive clothing without the intent of purchase.[43] The cultural phenomenon of shopping has also provided a homosocial space for women (e.g., mothers and daughters, married and single adult women, teenage girls) to interact and bond. Lesbians have been able to extend this pleasure by shopping with their female lovers or partners, sharing the physical and erotic space of the dressing room, and, afterward, wearing/exchanging the fashion commodities they purchase. Within this realm, the static images of advertising have even less control over their potential consumers. Gay window advertising, for example, may commodify lesbian masquerade as legitimate high-style fashion, but lesbians are free to politicize these products or reappropriate them in combination with other products/fashions to act as new signifiers for lesbian identification or ironic commentaries on heterosexual culture.

This is not to suggest that there exists an authentic "lesbian sensibility" or that all lesbians construct the same, inherently progressive, meanings in the realm of consumption. One must be wary of the "affirmative character" of a cultural studies that leans toward essentialist notions of identity at the same time as it tends to overestimate the freedom of audience reception.[44] Since lesbians are never simply lesbians but also members of racial groups, classes, and so on, their consumption patterns and reading practices always overlap and intersect those of other groups. In addition, there is no agreement within lesbian communities on the "proper" response or relation to consumer culture. This is precisely why the lesbian "style wars" have become a topic of such heated debate. Arlene Stein pinpoints the questions and fears that underlie this debate: "Are today's lesbian style wars skin-deep, or do they reflect a changed conception of what it means to be a dyke? If a new lesbian has in fact emerged, is she all flash and no substance, or is she at work busily carving out new lesbian politics that strike at the heart of dominant notions of gender and sexuality?"[45] The answers are not simple, not a matter of binary logic. Some lesbians choose to mainstream. Others experience the discourse of fashion as an ambivalence—toward power, social investment, and representation itself.[46] Still others engage a camp discourse or masquerade that plays on the lesbian's ambivalent position within straight culture. These responses, reading practices, interpretive activities—whatever one might call them—are as varied as the notions of lesbian identity and lesbian community.

Given the conflicts that lesbians frequently experience within their communities over issues of race, class, and lifestyle, lesbians are only too aware that a single, authentic identity does not exist. But, in the face of these contradictions, lesbians are attempting to forge what Stuart Hall calls an *articulation,* "a connection, a linkage that can establish a unity among different elements within a culture, under certain conditions."[47] For lesbians, the conditions are *political.* Lesbian identity politics must therefore be concerned with constructing political agendas and articulating collective identities that take into account our various needs and differences as well as our common experiences and oppressions *as a social group.* So too a theory of lesbian reading practices rooted in identity politics must stretch beyond analyses of textual contradictions to address the history of struggle, invisibility, and ambivalence that positions the lesbian subject in relation to cultural practices.

Ironically, now that our visibility is growing, lesbians have become the target of "capitalism's constant search for new areas to colonize."[48] This consideration must remain central to the style debates. For lesbians are not simply forming a new relation with the fashion industry, *it* is attempting to forge a relation with us. This imposition challenges us and is forcing us to renegotiate certain aspects of identity politics. (I can't help but think, e.g., that the fashion controversy may not be about "fashion" at all but has more to do with the fact that it is the femmes who are finally asserting themselves.) In the midst of this challenge, the butch-femme aesthetic will undoubtedly undergo realignment. We may also be forced to reconsider the ways in which camp can function as a form of resistance. For once "camp" is commodified by the culture industry, how do we continue to camp it up?

The only assurance we have in the shadow of colonization is that lesbians *as lesbians* have developed strategies of selection, (re)appropriation, resistance, and subversion in order to realign consumer culture according to the desires and needs of lesbian sexuality, subcultural identification, and political action. Lesbian reading/social practices, in other words, are informed by an identity politics, however that politics may be formulated historically by individuals or by larger communities. This does not mean that the readings lesbians construct are always "political" in the strictest sense of the term (e.g., one could argue that erotic identification is not political, and there is also the possibility that lesbians will identify with mainstreaming). Nonetheless, the discourses of identity politics—which arise out of the lesbian's marginal and ambivalent social position—have *made it possible* for lesbians to consider certain contradictions in style, sexual object choice, and cultural representation that inform their reading practices, challenge the reading practices of straight culture, and potentially create more empowered, or at least pleasurable, subject positions as lesbians. Because identities are always provisional, lesbians must also constantly assert themselves. They must replace liberal discourse with camp discourse, make themselves visible, foreground their political agendas and their politicized subjectivities.

This may explain why feminists have avoided the issue of lesbian consumerism. Lesbians may present too great a challenge to the heterosexual economy in which they are invested, or lesbians may be colonizing the theoretical and social spaces they wish to inhabit. As long as straight women focus on the relation between consumer culture and women in general, lesbians remain invisible, or are forced to pass as straight, while heterosexual women can claim for themselves the oppression of patriarchal culture or the pleasure of masquerade that offers them "a longed for place outside the humdrum mainstream." On the other hand, straight feminists may simply fear that lesbians are better shoppers. When dykes go shopping in order to "go camping," they not only subvert the mix 'n' match aesthetic promoted by dominant fashion culture, they do it with very little credit.

Notes

1 Karl Marx, *Capital,* vol. I (London: Lawrence & Wishart, 1970), 71.

2 For a recent overview of the literature, see Lynn Spigel and Denise Mann, "Women and Consumer Culture: A Selective Bibliography," *Quarterly Review of Film and Video* 11, no. 1 (1989): 85–105. Spigel and Mann's compilation does not so much reproduce as *reflect* the heterosexual bias of scholarship in this field.

3 Jane Gaines, "The Queen Christina Tie-Ups: Convergence of Show Window and Screen," *Quarterly Review of Film and Video,* 11, no. 1 (1989): 50. Gaines is one of the few feminist critics who acknowledge gays and lesbians as consuming subjects.

4 Sue-Ellen Case, "Toward a Butch-Femme Aesthetic," *Discourse* 11, no. 1 (1988–89): 56.

5 Roberta Astroff, "Commodifying Cultures: Latino Ad Specialists as Cultural Brokers"

(paper presented at the Seventh International Conference on Culture and Communication, Philadelphia, 1989).

6 Karen Stabiner, "Tapping the Homosexual Market," *New York Times Magazine*, 2 May 1982, 79, 80.

7 Ibid., 75.

8 Ibid., 80, 81.

9 Ibid., 80.

10 Mary Ann Doane, "The Economy of Desire: The Commodity Form in/of the Cinema," *Quarterly Review of Film and Video* 11, no. 1 (1989): 27.

11 Gaines, "The Queen Christina Tie-Ups," 35, 56.

12 Jane Gaines, "Introduction: Fabricating the Female Body," in *Fabrications: Costume and the Female Body*, ed. Jane Gaines and Charlotte Herzog (New York: Routledge, 1990), 12–13.

13 Ibid., 3–9. Also see Kaja Silverman, "Fragments of a Fashionable Discourse," in *Studies in Entertainment: Critical Approaches to Mass Culture*, ed. Tania Modleski (Bloomington: Indiana University Press, 1986), 139–52.

14 Gaines, "Fabricating the Female Body," 27.

15 Arlene Stein, "All Dressed Up, But No Place to Go? Style Wars and the New Lesbianism," *Out/look* 1, no. 4 (1989): 37. (Reprinted in this volume.)

16 Alisa Solomon, "Dykotomies: Scents and Sensibility in the Lesbian Community," *Village Voice*, 26 June 1990, 40.

17 Stein, "All Dressed Up," 39.

18 Stan LeRoy Wilson, *Mass Media/Mass Culture* (New York: Random House, 1989), 279.

19 Stein, "All Dressed Up," 38.

20 "*Out/look* Survey Tabulations," Queery #10, Fall 1990.

21 John Fiske, "Critical Response: Meaningful Moments," *Critical Studies in Mass Communication* 5 (1988): 247.

22 Elizabeth Ellsworth, "Illicit Pleasures: Feminist Spectators and *Personal Best*," *Wide Angle* 8, no. 2 (1986): 54.

23 Cathy Griggers, "A Certain Tension in the Visual/Cultural Field: Helmut Newton, Deborah Turbeville and the *Vogue* Fashion Layout," *differences* 2, no. 2 (1990): 87–90. Griggers notes that Turbeville's trademark is photographing women (often in pairs or groups) who "stand or sit like pieces of sculpture in interiors from the past in [a] grainy, nostalgic soft-focused finish."

24 Case, "Butch-Femme Aesthetic," 64.

25 Case, 60, 58.

26 Ellsworth, "Illicit Pleasures," 54.

27 Jane Root, *Pictures of Women* (London: Pandora, 1984), 68; Rosalind Coward, *Female Desires* (New York: Grove, 1985), 80.

28 John D'Emilio, "Capitalism and Gay Identity," in *Powers of Desire: The Politics of Sexuality*, ed. Ann Snitow, Christine Stansell, and Sharon Thompson (New York: Monthly Review Press, 1983), 102, 109.

29 David Ehrenstein, "Within the Pleasure Principle or Irresponsible Homosexual Propaganda," *Wide Angle* 4, no. 1 (1980): 62.

30 See, e.g., Teresa de Lauretis, "The Essence of the Triangle or, Taking the Risk of Essentialism Seriously: Feminist Theory in Italy, the U.S., and Britain," *differences* 1, no. 2 (1989): 3–37; Diana Fuss, *Essentially Speaking* (New York: Routledge, 1989); Diana Fuss, "Reading Like a Feminist," *differences* 1, no. 2 (1989): 72–92; Carol Vance, "Social Construction Theory: Problems in the History of Sexuality," in *Which Homosexuality?* (London: GMP, 1989), 13–34; Jeffrey Weeks, "Against Nature," in *Which Homosexuality?* 99–213, and *Sexuality and Its Discontents* (London: Routledge, 1985).

31 Mark Finch, "Sex and Address in 'Dynasty,'" *Screen* 27, no. 6 (1986): 36.

32 John R. Leo, "The Familialism of 'Man' in American Television Melodrama," *South Atlantic Quarterly* 88, no. 1 (1989): 42.

33 Weeks, *Sexuality,* 200.

34 Dick Hebdige, *Subculture: The Meaning of Style* (London: Methuen, 1979), 93.

35 Roland Marchand, *Advertising the American Dream* (Berkeley and Los Angeles: University of California Press, 1985), 186.

36 Judith Williamson, "Woman Is an Island: Femininity and Colonization," in *Studies in Entertainment,* 116.

37 Michael Bronski, *Culture Clash: The Making of Gay Sensibility* (Boston: South End, 1984), 187.

38 Williamson, "Woman Is an Island," 109, 112.

39 Laurie Schulze, "On the Muscle," in *Fabrications,* 59, 63, 73.

40 Annette Kuhn, "The Body and Cinema: Some Problems for Feminism," *Wide Angle* 11, no. 4 (1989): 56.

41 Schulze, "On the Muscle," 68.

42 Ibid., 67.

43 John Fiske, *Reading the Popular* (Boston: Unwin Hyman, 1989), 14–17. Fiske cites the research of M. Pressdee, "Agony or Ecstasy: Broken Transitions and the New Social State of Working-Class Youth in Australia," Occasional Papers, S. Australian Centre for Youth Studies, S.A. College of A.E., Magill, S. Australia, 1986.

44 Mike Budd, Robert M. Entman, and Clay Steinman, "The Affirmative Character of U.S. Cultural Studies," *Critical Studies in Mass Communication* 7, no. 2 (1990): 169–84.

45 Stein, "All Dressed Up," 37.

46 Griggers, "A Certain Tension," 101.

47 Jacqueline Bobo, "*The Color Purple:* Black Women as Cultural Readers," in *Female Spectators,* ed. E. Deidre Pribram (London: Verso, 1988), 104–5. See also Stuart Hall, "Race, Articulation and Societies Structured in Dominance," in *Sociological Theories: Race and Colonialism* (Unesco, 1980), 305–45.

48 Williamson, "Woman Is an Island," 116.

Gay, Lesbian, and Queer Popular

Culture Bibliography

Corey K. Creekmur and Alexander Doty

T his bibliography collects lesbian, gay, and queer materials in popular culture (film, television, video, photography, music, dance, fashion, drag, camp, etc.) and excludes most material more accurately classified as anthropology, history, sociology, literary criticism, psychology, etc., although these disciplinary boundaries are obviously frequently blurred and crossed. Major general bibliographies include Wayne Dyne, *Homosexuality: A Research Guide* (New York: Garland, 1987); Cal Gough and Ellen Greenblatt, eds., *Gay and Lesbian Library Service* (Jefferson, N.C.: McFarland, 1990); Dolores Maggiore, *Lesbianism: An Annotated Bibliography and Guide to the Literature, 1976–1991* (Metuchen, N.J.: Scarecrow, 1992); and William Parker, *Homosexuality: A Selective Bibliography of over 3,000 Items* (Metuchen, N.J.: Scarecrow, 1985); *Homosexuality Bibliography, Second Supplement 1976–1982* (Metuchen, N.J.: Scarecrow, 1985); *Homosexuality Bibliography: Supplement 1970–1975* (Metuchen, N.J.: Scarecrow, 1977). Although extensive, the following bibliography is of course not exhaustive. Especially underrepresented here are the regular and often groundbreaking articles, reviews, and interviews appearing in the lesbian, gay, and queer press, community newspapers, and underground 'zines; such materials are rarely indexed and, unfortunately, remain difficult to locate in even major research libraries. For access to primary source materials, see Alan V. Miller, *Directory of the International Association of Lesbian and Gay Archives and Libraries* (Toronto: Canadian Gay Archives, 1987).

Abelove, Henry, Michele Aina Barale, and David Halperin, eds. *The Lesbian and Gay Studies Reader.* New York: Routledge, 1993.

Adam, Margie. "Greta Garbo's 'Mysterious' Private Life." *Out/Look* 3:2 (Fall 1990): 25.

Aitken, Will. "Twenty-eight Minutes of Genius." *Gay News* 205 (1980–81): 11–12. (On Genet's *Un chant d'amour.*)

——. "Erect in the Dark." *Gay News* (Winter Extra, December–January 1981–82): 15–20.

Alcock, Beverly, and Jocelyn Robson. "Cagney and Lacey Revisited." *Feminist Review* 35 (Summer 1990): 42–52.

Als, Hilton. "Negro Faggotry." *Black Film Review* 5:3 (Summer 1989): 18–19.

Arbuthnot, Lucie, and Gail Seneca. "Pre-Text and Text in *Gentlemen Prefer Blondes*." *Film Reader* 5 (Winter 1981): 15–23.

Arroyo, Jose. "Pedro Almodovar: Law and Desire." *Descant* 20, nos. 1–2 (Spring–Summer 1989): 53–70.

Attig, R. Brian. "The Gay Voice in Popular Music: A Social Value Model Analysis of 'Don't Leave Me This Way.'" In *Gay People, Sex, and the Media,* ed. Michelle A. Wolf and Alfred P. Kielwasser. Binghamton, N.Y.: Harrington Park/Hayworth, 1991.

Atwell, L. "Homosexual Themes in the Cinema." *Tangents* (March and April 1966): 4–10, 4–9.

——. "*Word Is Out* and *Gay USA*." *Film Quarterly* 32 (Winter 1982): 50–57.

Babuscio, Jack. "Camp and the Gay Sensibility." In *Gays and Film,* ed. Richard Dyer. London: BFI, 1977. Rev. ed., New York: New York Zoetrope, 1984.

Bader, Eleanor. "Coping and Caring: Films on the AIDS Crisis." *Cineaste* 17:1 (1989): 18–19.

Bad Object-Choices, eds. *How Do I Look? Queer Film and Video.* Seattle: Bay Press, 1991.

Banneker, Revon Kyle. "Marlon Riggs Untied." *Out/look* 10 (3:2, 1990): 14–18.

Barton, Sabrina. "'Criss-Cross': Paranoia and Projection in *Strangers on a Train*." *Camera Obscura* 25–26 (January/May 1991): 75–100. (Reprinted in this volume.)

Beauvais, Y. "Barbara Hammer." *Spiral* 6 (January 1986): 33–38.

Becquer, Marcos. "Snap!thology and Other Discursive Practices in *Tongues Untied*." *Wide Angle* 13:2 (April 1991): 6–17.

Bell-Metereau, Rebecca. *Hollywood Androgyny.* New York: Columbia University Press, 1986.

Belton, Don. "Young Soul Rebel: A Conversation with Issac Julien." *Out/Look* 16 (Spring 1992): 15–19.

Bensinger, Terralee. "Lesbian Pornography: The Re/Making of (a) Community." *Discourse* 15:1 (Fall 1992): 69–93.

Bergman, David. "Strategic Camp: The Art of Gay Rhetoric." In *Gaiety Transfigured: Gay Self-Representation in American Literature.* Madison: University of Wisconsin Press, 1991.

Bergman, David, ed. *Camp Grounds: Style and Homosexuality.* Amherst: University of Massachusetts Press, 1993.

Blachford, Gregg. "Looking at Pornography." *Gay Left* 6 (1978): 16–20.

Blake, Nayland. "Tom of Finland: An Appreciation." *Out/Look* 1:3 (Fall 1988): 36–45. (Reprinted in this volume.)

Block, A. "*An Early Frost:* The Story Behind NBC's AIDS Drama." *Advocate* (26 November 1985): 43–47.

Bociurkiw, Marusia. "Territories of the Forbidden: Lesbian Culture, Sex and Censorship." *Fuse* (March–April 1988): 27–32.

Boffin, Tessa, and Jean Fraser, eds. *Stolen Glances: Lesbians Take Photographs*. London: Pandora, 1991.

Booth, Mark. *Camp*. New York: Quartet, 1983.

Bordowitz, Gregg, and Jean Carlomusto. "Do It! Safer Sex Pornography for Girls and Boys Comes of Age." *Outweek* (28 August 1989): 38–41.

Brasell, R. Bruce. "*My Hustler:* Gay Spectatorship as Cruising." *Wide Angle* 14:2 (April 1992): 54–64.

Bravmann, Scott. "Issac Julien's *Looking for Langston:* Hughes, Biography, and Queer(ed) History." *Cultural Studies* 7:2 (May 1993): 311–23.

Brett, Philip, Elizabeth Wood, and Gary Thomas, eds. *Queering the Pitch: The New Gay and Lesbian Musicology*. New York: Routledge, 1993.

Britton, Andrew. "For Interpretation: Notes against Camp." *Gay Left* 7 (1978–79): n.p.

——. "Cary Grant: Comedy and Male Desire." *CineAction!* 7 (December 1986): 36–51. Originally published by Tyneside Press, 1984.

Bronski, Michael. *Culture Clash: The Making of Gay Sensibility*. Boston: South End, 1984.

——. "Gay Men and Movies: Reel to Real." In *Gay Life: Leisure, Love, and Living for the Contemporary Gay Male,* ed. E. E. Rofes. Garden City, N.Y.: Dolphin/Doubleday, 1986.

Bruce, Bryan. "Pee Wee Herman: The Homosexual Subtext." *CineAction!* 9 (July 1987): 3–7. (Reprinted in this volume under author's name Bruce La Bruce.)

——. "Rosa Von Praunheim in Theory and Practice." *CineAction!* 9 (July 1987): 25–31.

——. "Whipping It Up: Gay Sex in Film and Video." *CineAction!* 10 (October 1987): 38–44.

——. "Modern Diseases: Gay Self-Representation in the Age of AIDS." *CineAction!* 15 (December 1988): 29–38.

Burger, John R. *One-Handed Stories: Popular Memory and the Eroto Politics of Gay Male Video Pornography*. Binghamton, N.Y.: Hayworth, 1993.

Burgess, Marilyn. "*Proudly She Marches:* Wartime Propaganda and the Lesbian Spectator," *CineAction* 23 (Winter 1990–91): 22–27.

Butler, Alison. "'She Must Be Seeing Things': An Interview with Sheila McLaughlin." *Screen* 28:4 (Autumn 1987): 20–29.

Butler, Judith. "The Force of Fantasy: Feminism, Mapplethorpe, and Discursive Excess." *differences* 2:2 (1990), 105–25.

——. *Gender Trouble: Feminism and the Subversion of Identity*. New York: Routledge, 1990.

——. "Imitation and Gender Insubordination." In *Inside/Out: Lesbian Theories, Gay Theories,* ed. Diana Fuss. New York: Routledge, 1991.

——. "Gender Is Burning: Questions of Appropriation and Subversion." In *Bodies That Matter: On the Discursive Limits of "Sex."* New York: Routledge: 1993.

Carter, E., et al. "Interview with Ulrike Ottinger." *Screen Education* 41 (Winter/Spring 1982): 34–42.

Carter, Erica, and Simon Watney, eds. *Taking Liberties: AIDS and Cultural Politics*. London: Serpent's Tail, 1989.

Case, Sue-Ellen. "Towards a Butch-Femme Aesthetic." *Discourse* 11:1 (Fall–Winter

1988–89): 55–73. Reprinted in *Making a Spectacle: Feminist Essays on Contemporary Women's Theatre,* ed. Lynda Hart. Ann Arbor: University of Michigan Press, 1989.

——. "Tracking the Vampire." *differences* 3:2 (1991): 1–20.

Castiglia, Christopher. "Rebel without a Closet." In *Engendering Men: The Question of Male Feminist Criticism,* ed. Joseph A. Boone and Michael Cadden. New York: Routledge, 1990.

Castle, Terry. *The Apparitional Lesbian: Female Homosexuality and Modern Culture.* New York: Columbia University Press, 1993.

Chapman, Rowena, and Jonathan Rutherford, eds. *Male Order: Unwrapping Masculinity.* London: Lawrence & Wishart, 1989.

Chauncey, George. *Gay New York: Gender, Urban Culture, and the Makings of the Gay Male World, 1890–1940.* New York: Basic Books, 1994.

Cheseboro, James W., and Kenneth L. Klenk. "Gay Masculinity in the Gay Disco." In *Gayspeak: Gay Male and Lesbian Communication,* ed. James W. Cheseboro. New York: Pilgrim, 1981.

Chin, Daryl. "Super-8 Films and the Aesthetics of Intimacy." *Jump Cut* 37 (1992): 78–81.

Chinn, Sarah, and Kris Franklin. "'I Am What I Am' (or Am I?): The Making and Unmaking of Lesbian and Gay Identity in *High Tech Gays.*" *Discourse* 15:1 (Fall 1992): 11–26.

Chris, Cynthia. "Policing Desire (*Urinal*)." *Afterimage* 17:5 (December 1989): 19–20.

Chua, Lawrence. "Queer n' Asian." *Cinevue* (Winter 1993): n.p.

Citron, Michelle. "The Films of Jan Oxenberg: Comic Critique." In *Films for Women,* ed. Charlotte Brundson. London: BFI, 1986. Edited version of essay originally in *Jump Cut* 24/25 (1981): 31–32.

Clarens, Carlos. "Masculine/Feminine, Feminine/Masculine." *Film Comment* 18, no. 3 (May/June 1982): 18–19.

——. "The Secret Life of George Cukor" (interviewed by John Hofsess). *Stallion* (August 1983): n.p.

Clark, Danae. "Commodity Lesbianism." *Camera Obscura* 25–26 (January/May 1991): 181–201. (Reprinted in this volume.)

Clayton, D. "Put the Blame on *Mame:* The Movie Characters That Made Us Gay." *Advocate* (8 November 1988): 47–51.

Cohen, Derek, and Richard Dyer. "The Politics of Gay Culture." In *Homosexualities, Power and Politics,* ed. Gay Left Collective. London: Allison & Busby, 1980.

Cohan, Steven, and Ina Rae Hark, eds. *Screening the Male: Exploring Masculinities in the Hollywood Cinema.* New York: Routledge, 1993.

Collins, M. "A History of Homosexuality in the Movies." *Drum* 27 (1967): 12–21, 30–32.

Connor, E. "Film in Drag: Transvestism on the Screen." *Films in Review* 32 (1981): 398–405.

Considine, David M. "What a Difference a Gay Makes." In *The Cinema of Adolescence.* Jefferson, N.C.: McFarland, 1985.

Coon, E. O. "Homosexuality in the News." *Archives of Criminal Psychodynamics* 2:4 (1957): 843–65.

Corber, Robert J. *In the Name of National Security: Hitchcock, Homophobia, and the Political Construction of Gender in Postwar America.* Durham, N.C.: Duke University Press, 1993.

Core, Philip. *Camp: The Lie That Tells the Truth.* New York: Delilah, 1984.

Corzine, H. J. "The Gay Press." Ph.D. diss., Washington University, 1977.

Crimp, Douglas. "Fassbinder, Franz, Fox, Elvira, Erwin, Armin, and All the Others." *October* 21 (Summer 1982): 63–81.

——, ed. *AIDS: Cultural Analysis/Cultural Activism.* Cambridge, Mass.: MIT Press, 1988.

——. "Portraits of People with AIDS." In *Cultural Studies,* ed. Lawrence Grossberg, Cary Nelson, and Paula Treichler. New York: Routledge, 1991.

——. "Right On, Girlfriend!" *Social Text* 33 (1992): 2–18.

Crisp, Quentin. *How to Go to the Movies.* New York: St. Martin's, 1989. (Essays and reviews originally published in *Christopher Street.*)

Danzig, Alexis. "Acting Up: Independent Video and the AIDS Crisis." *Afterimage* 16:10 (May 1989): 5–7.

Davy, Kate. "Constructing the Spectator: Reception, Context, and Address in Lesbian Performance." *Performing Arts Journal* 10:2 (1987): 43–52.

D'Emilio, John. *Sexual Politics, Sexual Communities: The Making of a Homosexual Minority in the United States, 1940–1970.* Chicago: University of Chicago Press, 1983.

——. "Capitalism and Gay Identity." In *Powers of Desire: The Politics of Sexuality,* ed. Ann Snitow, Christine Stansell, and Sharon Thompson. New York: Monthly Review Press, 1983. Reprinted in *Making Trouble: Essays on Gay History, Politics, and the University.* New York: Routledge, 1992.

De Lauretis, Teresa. "Sexual Indifference and Lesbian Representation." *Theatre Journal* 40:2 (May 1988): 155–77.

——. "Film and the Visible." In *How Do I Look? Queer Film and Video,* ed. Bad Object-Choices. Seattle: Bay, 1991.

——. "Guerrilla in the Midst: Women's Cinema in the 80s." *Screen* 31:1 (Spring 1990): 6–25.

Del Valle, Desi. "The Grandmother of Lesbian Film: An Interview with Barbara Hammer." *On Our Backs* (May/June 1993): 20–22, 38–40.

De Stefano, George. "Does *GQ* Hate Gay Men?" *Advocate* (17 September 1985): 26–31.

——. "A Wank through History." *Outweek* 45 (9 May 1990): 38–42. (On skin magazines.)

Diawara, Manthia. "The Absent One: The Avant-Garde and the Black Imaginary in *Looking for Langston.*" *Wide Angle* 13, nos. 3/4 (July–October 1991): 96–109.

DiCaprio, Lisa. "*Lianna:* Liberal Lesbianism." *Jump Cut* 29 (1984): 45–47.

Dickens, Homer. *What a Drag: Men as Woman and Women as Men in the Movies.* New York: Quill, 1984.

Dorenkamp, Monica. "Sisters Are Doin' It. . . . " *Outweek* 62 (5 September 1990): 40–47.

Doty, Alexander. "The Sissy Boy, the Fat Ladies, and the Dykes: Queerness and/as Gender in Pee-Wee's World." *Camera Obscura* 25–26 (January/May 1991): 125–43.

——. *Making Things Perfectly Queer: Interpreting Mass Culture.* Minneapolis: University of Minnesota Press, 1993.

——. "Whose Text Is It Anyway? Queer Cultures, Queer *Auteurs,* and Queer Authorship." *Quarterly Review of Film and Video* 15:1 (1993): 41–54.

——. "Queerness, Comedy, and *The Women,*" in *Classical Hollywood Comedy,* ed. Kristine Brunovska Karnic and Henry Jenkins III, New York: Routledge, 1994, 332–347.

Duggan, Lisa. "The Anguished Cry of an 80s Fem: 'I Want to Be a Drag Queen.'" *Out/Look* 1:1 (Spring 1988): 62–65.

DuMont, Howard, and Jeffrey Escoffier. "*Word Is Out:* An Interview with the Mariposa Film Group." *Cineaste* 8:4 (1979): 8–11.

Dyer, Richard. "Homosexuality and Film Noir." *Jump Cut* 16 (1977): 18. Reprinted in *The Matter of Images: Essays on Representations.* New York: Routledge, 1993.

——. "Pasolini and Homosexuality." In *Pier Paolo Pasolini,* ed. Paul Willemen. London: BFI, 1977.

——. "*Victim:* Hermeneutic Project." *Film Form* 1 (1977): 3–22. Reprinted in *The Matter of Images: Essays on Representations.* New York: Routledge, 1993.

——. "Gays in Film." *Jump Cut* 18 (1978): 15–16.

——. "Resistance through Charisma: Rita Hayworth and *Gilda.*" In *Women and Film Noir,* ed. E. Ann Kaplan. London: BFI, 1978, 1980.

——. "Reading Fassbinder's Sexual Politics." In *Fassbinder,* 2d ed., ed. Tony Rayns. London: BFI, 1979.

——. "Don't Look Now: The Instabilities of the Male Pin-Up." *Screen* 23, nos. 3–4 (1982): 61–73. Reprinted in *Only Entertainment.* New York: Routledge, 1992.

——. "Review Essay: Vito Russo and *The Celluloid Closet.*" *Studies in Visual Communication* 9:2 (Spring 1983): 52–56.

——. "Seen to Be Believed: Some Problems in the Representation of Gay People as Typical." *Studies in Visual Communication* 9:2 (Spring 1983): 2–19. Reprinted in *The Matter of Images: Essays on Representations.* New York: Routledge, 1993.

——, ed. *Gays and Film.* Rev. ed. New York: New York Zoetrope, 1984. Originally published London: BFI, 1980.

——. "Male Gay Porn: Coming to Terms." *Jump Cut* 30 (1985): 27–29. Reprinted as "Coming to Terms: Gay Pornography." In *Only Entertainment.* New York: Routledge, 1992.

——. *Heavenly Bodies: Film Stars and Society.* New York: St. Martin's, 1986.

——. "Children of the Night: Vampirism as Homosexuality, Homosexuality as Vampirism." In *Sweet Dreams: Sexuality, Gender and Popular Fiction,* ed. Susannah Radstone. London: Lawrence & Wishart, 1988.

——. "A Conversation about Pornography." In *Coming on Strong: Gay Politics and Culture,* ed. Simon Shepherd and Mick Wallis. London: Unwin Hyman, 1989.

——. "In Defense of Disco." In *On Record: Rock, Pop, and the Written Word,* ed. Simon Frith and Andrew Goodwin. New York: Pantheon, 1990. Reprinted in *Only Entertainment.* New York: Routledge, 1992. (Reprinted in this volume.)

——. "Less and More than Women and Men: Lesbian and Gay Cinema in Weimar Germany." *New German Critique* 51 (Fall 1990): 5–60.

——. *Now You See It: Studies on Lesbian and Gay Film.* New York: Routledge, 1990.

——. "Believing in Fairies: The Author and the Homosexual." In *Inside/Out: Lesbian Theories, Gay Theories,* ed. Diana Fuss. New York: Routledge, 1991.

——. "It's Being So Camp as Keeps Us Going." In *Only Entertainment.* New York: Routledge, 1992. Originally published in *Playguy* (1976) and reprinted in the *Body Politic* 36 (1977).

——. *Only Entertainment.* New York: Routledge, 1992.

——. *The Matter of Images: Essays on Representations.* New York: Routledge, 1993.

Edelman, Lee. *Homographesis: Essays in Gay Literary and Cultural Theory.* New York: Routledge, 1994.

Edelson, Stuart. "Of Torture and Tangents: Consequences of the Robert Mapplethorpe Exhibition." *Out/Look* 2:3 (Winter 1990): 52–53.

Ehrenstein, David. "The Filmmaker as Homosexual Hipster: Andy Warhol Contextualized." *Arts Magazine* 63:10 (Summer 1989): 61–64.

Ehrenstein, David. "Within the Pleasure Principle or Irresponsible Homosexual Propaganda." *Wide Angle* 4:1 (1980): 62–65.

——. "Homophobia in Hollywood II: The Queer Empire Strikes Back." *Advocate* 600 (7 April 1992): 36–43.

Elliot, Beth. "Holly Near and Yet So Far." In *Closer to Home: Bisexuality and Feminism,* ed. Elizabeth Reba Weise. Seattle: Seal, 1992.

Ellenzweig, Allen. "Picturing the Homoerotic: Gay Images in Photography." *Out/Look* 2:3 (Winter 1990): 44–51.

——. *The Homoerotic Photograph.* New York: Columbia University Press, 1992.

Ellsworth, Elizabeth. "Illicit Pleasures: Feminist Spectators and *Personal Best.*" *Wide Angle* 8:2 (1986): 45–56.

Facets Multimedia. *Facets Gay and Lesbian Video Guide.* Chicago: Academy Chicago, 1993.

Faderman, Lillian. *Odd Girls and Twilight Lovers: A History of Lesbian Life in Twentieth-Century America.* New York: Columbia University Press, 1991.

Fain, N. "Rating the Crisis Coverage: AIDS and the Media." *Advocate* (29 September 1983): 24–26, 74.

Fani-Kayode, Rotimi. "Traces of Ecstasy." *Ten. 8* 28 (Summer 1988): 36–43.

Fassbinder, Rainer Werner. *The Anarchy of the Imagination: Interviews, Essays, Notes.* Baltimore: PAJ, 1992.

Ferguson, Ann. "Is There a Lesbian Culture?" In *Lesbian Philosophies and Cultures,* ed. Jeffner Allen. Albany: SUNY Press, 1990.

Ferris, Lesley, ed. *Crossing the Stage: Controversies on Cross-Dressing.* New York: Routledge, 1993.

Finch, Mark. "Uncovering the Very First Gay Film." *Body Politic* 107 (October 1984). (On *Wings,* 1916.)

——. "Sex and Address in *Dynasty.*" *Screen* 27:6 (November–December 1986): 24–42.

——. "Mauritz Stiller's *The Wings* and Early Scandinavian Gay Cinema." *European Gay Review* 2 (1987): 26–31.

——. "Business as Usual: Substitution and Sex in *Prick Up Your Ears* and other Recent

Gay-Themed Movies." In *Coming on Strong: Gay Politics and Culture,* ed. Simon Shepherd and Mick Wallis. London: Unwin Hyman, 1989.

Finch, Mark, and Richard Kwietniowski. "Melodrama and *Maurice:* Homo Is Where the Het Is." *Screen* 29:3 (Summer 1988): 72–80.

Findlay, Heather. "Freud's 'Fetishism' and the Lesbian Dildo Debates." *Feminist Studies* 18:3 (Fall 1992): 563–79. (Reprinted in this volume.)

Fischer, Lucy. "Women in Love: The Theme of Lesbianism." In *Shot/Countershot: Film Tradition and Women's Cinema.* Princeton, N.J.: Princeton University Press, 1989.

Fisher, Hal. *Gay Semiotics: A Photographic Study of Visual Coding among Homosexual Men.* San Francisco: NSF, 1977.

Frank, Lisa, and Paul Smith, eds. *Madonnarama: Essays on Sex and Popular Culture.* Pittsburgh: Cleis, 1993.

Fraser, B. "Coming Out in the Comics." *Body Politic* (July/August 1984): 31–34.

Frechette, David. "What's Wrong with This Picture." *Black Film Review* 5:3 (Summer 1989): 22–23.

Friedrich, Su. "Radical Form: Radical Content." *Millenium Film Journal* 22 (1989): 117–23.

Fung, Richard. "Looking for My Penis: The Eroticized Asian in Gay Porn Video." In *How Do I Look? Queer Film and Video,* ed. Bad Object-Choices. Seattle: Bay, 1991.

Fuss, Diana, ed. *Inside/Out: Lesbian Theories, Gay Theories.* New York: Routledge, 1991.

——. "Fashion and the Homospectatorial Look." *Critical Inquiry* 18:4 (Summer 1992): 713–37.

Gaines, Jane M. "Competing Glances: Who Is Reading Robert Mapplethorpe's *Black Book?*" *New Formations* 16 (1992): 24–39.

——. "Dorothy Arzner's Trousers." *Jump Cut* 37 (1992): 88–98.

Garber, Eric. "Gladys Bentley: The Bulldagger Who Sang the Blues." *Out/Look* 1:1 (Spring 1988): 52–61.

Garber, Marjorie. *Vested Interests: Cross-Dressing and Cultural Anxiety.* New York: Routledge, 1992.

Garfield, K. "*Desert Hearts:* A Lesbian Love Story Heats Up the Silver Screen." *Advocate* (18 February 1986): 43–47.

——. "Carrying the Torch." *Advocate* (10 October 1988): 45–49.

——. "Where the Boys Were." *Advocate* (8 May 1990): 34–38.

Gates, Henry Louis, Jr., "The Black Man's Burden." In *Black Popular Culture: A Project by Michelle Wallace,* ed. Gina Dent. Seattle: Bay, 1992. (On Issac Julien's *Looking for Langston.*)

Gay/Lesbian Task Force. Council of Social Education Work. *Annotated Filmography of Selected Films with Lesbian/Gay Content.* New York: ERIC Document Reproduction Service no. ED 250 230, 1984.

Gerson, P. "Homosexuality on Television." *Christopher Street* 2:2 (August 1977): 47–49.

Gever, Martha. "Pictures of Sickness: Stuart Marshall's *Bright Eyes.*" *October* 43 (1987): 109–26. Reprinted in *AIDS: Cultural Analysis/Cultural Activism,* ed. Douglas Crimp. Cambridge, Mass.: MIT Press, 1988.

——. "Where We Are Now." *Art in America* 75:7 (July 1987): 43–49.

——. "Girl Crazy: Lesbian Narratives in *She Must Be Seeing Things* and *Damned If You Don't.*" *Independent* 11:6 (July 1988): 14–18.

——. "The Names We Give Ourselves." In *Out There: Marginalization and Contemporary Cultures,* ed. Russell Ferguson, Martha Gever, Trinh T. Minh-ha, and Cornel West. Cambridge, Mass.: MIT Press, 1990.

——. "Invisibility Made Visible." *Art in America* (April 1991): 57–63.

Gever, Martha, and Nathalie Magnan. "The Same Difference: On Lesbian Representation." *Exposure* 24:2 (1986): 27–35. Reprinted in *Stolen Glances: Lesbians Take Photographs,* ed. Tessa Boffin and Jean Fraser. London: Pandora, 1991.

Gever, Martha, Pratibha Parmar, and John Greyson, eds. *Queer Looks: Perspectives on Lesbian and Gay Film and Video.* New York: Routledge, 1993.

Giles, Jane. *The Cinema of Jean Genet: Un chant d'amour.* London: BFI, 1991.

Gilman, Sander. "Strauss, the Pervert, and Avant-Garde Opera of the Fin de Siècle." *New German Critique* 43 (Winter 1988): 35–68.

Ginsberg, Terri. "Nazis and Drifters: The Containment of Radical (Sexual) Knowledge in Two Italian Neorealist Films." *Journal of the History of Sexuality* 1:2 (1990): 241–61.

Goldberg, Jonathan. "Recalling Totalities: The Mirrored Stages of Arnold Schwarzenegger." *differences* 4:1 (1992): 172–204.

Goldin, Nan. *The Other Side.* New York: Scalo, 1992. (Photographs of cross-dressers.)

Goldsby, Jackie. "What It Means to Be Colored Me." *Out/Look* 9 (Summer 1990): 8–17.

Goldstein, Richard. "The Gay New Wave." *Village Voice* (22 April 1986): 51–53.

Gould, R. E., and C. W. Davenport. "Homosexuality on Television." *Medical Aspects of Human Sexuality* 7 (October 1973): 116–27.

Gomez, Gabriel. "*Wild Life:* Collaborative Process and Gay Identity." *Jump Cut* 37 (1992): 82–87.

Goodwin, Joseph P. *More Man Than You'll Ever Be: Gay Folklore and Acculturation in Middle America.* Bloomington: Indiana University Press, 1989.

Graham, Allison. "*Outrageous* and *Boys in the Band:* The Possibilities and Limitations of 'Coming Out.'" *Film Criticism* 5:1 (Fall 1980): 36–42.

Gregg, Ronald. "PBS and AIDS." *Jump Cut* 37 (1992): 64–71.

Gregg, Stephen. "Comics in the Closet: The Subtext in Captain America." *Out/Look* 1:2 (Summer 1988): 80–84.

Greyson, John. "Homo Video." *Jump Cut* 30 (1985): 36–38.

——. "Two Men Embracing: Gay Video Images." *Video Guide* 8:4 (December 1986): 10–11.

——. "Proofing." In *AIDS: The Artist's Response,* ed. Jan Zita Grover. Columbus: Ohio State University Press, 1989.

——. "Compromised Strategies: AIDS and Alternative Video Practices." In *Voices of Dissent,* ed. Mark O'Brian and Craig Little. Bloomington: Indiana University Press, 1990.

Grisham, Therese. "Twentieth Century *Theatrum mundi:* Ulrike Ottinger's *Johanna d'Arc of Mongolia*" and "An Interview with Ulrike Ottinger." *Wide Angle* 14:2 (April 1992): 22–36.

Gross, Larry. "The Cultivation of Intolerance: Television, Blacks, and Gays." In *Cultural Indicators: An International Symposium,* ed. G. MeLischek, K. E. Rosengren, and J. Stappers. Vienna: Verlag Ossterriechschen Akademie der Wissenschaftern, 1984.

——. "The Ethics of (Mis)Representation." In *Image Ethics: The Moral Rights of Subjects in Photographs, Film and Television,* ed. L. Gross, J. S. Katz, and J. Ruby. New York: Oxford University Press, 1988.

——. "Out of the Mainstream: Sexual Minorities and the Media." In *Remote Control: Television, Audiences, and Cultural Power.* ed. E. Seiter, H. Borchers, G. Kreutzner, and E. Warth. New York: Routledge, 1989.

——. *Contested Closets: The Politics and Ethics of Outing.* Minneapolis: University of Minnesota Press, 1993.

——. "What Is Wrong with This Picture: Lesbian Women and Gay Men on Television." In *Queer Words, Queer Images: Communication and the Construction of Homosexuality.* ed. R J Ringer. New York: New York University Press, 1994.

Grosz, Elizabeth A. "Lesbian Fetishism?" *differences* 3:2 (Summer 1991): 39–54.

Grover, Jan Zita. "Visible Lesions: Images of the PWA," *Afterimage* 17:1 (Summer 1989): 10–16. (Reprinted in this volume.)

Grover, Jan Zita, ed. *AIDS: The Artist's Response.* Catalog for exhibition/conference. Columbus: Hoyt L. Sherman Gallery, Ohio State University, 1989.

Guthman, E. "The *Cruising* Controversy: William Friedkin vs. the Gay Community." *Cineaste* 10:3 (1980): 2–8.

——. "*Dynasty:* The Behind-the-Scene-Story of a Television Phenomenon." *Advocate* (7 January 1986): 43–49.

——. "Prime-Time Pillow Talk." *Advocate* (2 January 1990): 50–52.

Gup, T. "Identifying Homosexuals: What Are the Rules?" *Washington Journalism Review* 10:8 (1988): 30–33.

Hachem, Samir. "Inside the Tinseled Closet." *Advocate* (17 March 1987): 42–49.

Hadleigh, Boze. *Conversations with My Elders.* New York: St. Martin's, 1986.

——. "Hollywood Square Comes Out: A Conversation with Comedian Paul Lynde." *Out/Look* 2:2 (Fall 1989): 24–27.

——. *The Vinyl Closet: Gays in the Music World.* San Diego: Los Hombres, 1991.

——. *The Lavender Screen: The Gay and Lesbian Films: Their Stars, Makers, Characters and Critics.* New York: Citadel, 1993.

Haines, Fred. "Art in Court: City of Angels vs. *Scorpio Rising.*" In *The Movies in Our Midst,* ed. Gerald Mast. Chicago: University of Chicago Press, 1982. Originally appeared in *Nation* (September 1964).

Hake, Sabine. "'Gold, Love, Adventure': The Postmodern Piracy of *Madame X.*" *Discourse* 11:1 (1988–89): 88–110.

Halberstam, Judith. "Some Like It Hot: The New Sapphic Cinema." *Independent* 15:9 (November 1992): 26–29, 43.

Hamilton, Godfrey. "Anger." *Gay News* 116 (1977): 22–23.

Hammer, Barbara. "Use of Time in Women's Cinema." *Heresies* 3 (1977): 86–69.

——. "The Invisible Screen: Lesbian Cinema." *Center Quarterly* (Spring 1988): n.p.

——. "Risk Taking as Alternative Living/Art-Making or Why I Moved to the Big City." *Millenium Film Journal* 22 (1989): 127–29.

Hanlon, Lindley. "Female Rage: The Films of Su Friedrich." *Millenium Film* 12 (1982–83): 79–86.

Hanna, Judith Lynne. *Dance, Sex, and Gender: Signs of Identity, Dominance, Defiance, and Desire.* Chicago: University of Chicago Press, 1988.

Hansen, Miriam. "Visual Pleasure, Fetishism, and the Problem of Feminine Feminist Discourse: Ulrike Ottinger's *Ticket of No Return.*" *New German Critique* 31 (Winter 1984): 95–108.

Hardy, Robin. "Kenneth Anger: Master in Hell." *Body Politic* no. 82 (April 1982): 29–32.

Hart, Lynda. *Fatal Women: Lesbian Sexuality and the Mark of Aggression.* Princeton, N.J.: Princeton University Press, 1994.

Hayles, Nancy K., and Kathryn Dohrmann Rindskopf. "The Shadow of Violence." *Journal of Popular Film and Television* 8:2 (1980): 2–8. (On *Cruising.*)

Hemphill, Essex. "Brother to Brother." *Black Film Review* 5:3 (Summer 1989): 14–17. (Interview with Issac Julien.)

——. "*In Living Color:* Toms, Coons, Mammies, Faggots and Bucks." *Outweek* 78 (26 December 1990): 32–40. (Reprinted in this volume.)

——, ed. *Brother to Brother: New Writings by Black Gay Men.* Boston: Alyson, 1991.

Henderson, Lisa. "Justify Our Love: Madonna and the Politics of Queer Sex." In *The Madonna Connection: Representational Politics, Subcultural Identities, and Cultural Theory,* ed. Cathy Schwichtenberg. Boulder, Colo.: Westview, 1993.

Hepworth, John. "Hitchcock's Homophobia." *Christopher Street* 6:4 (1982): 42–49. (Reprinted in this volume.)

Hilbert, Jeffrey. "The Politics of Drag." *Advocate* 575 (23 April 1991): 42–47.

Holleran, Andrew. "New York Notebook: Rock's Life." *Christopher Street* (December 1989): 4–19. (On Rock Hudson.)

Holmlund, Christine. "I Love Luce: The Lesbian, Mimesis, and Masquerade in Irigaray, Freud, and Mainstream Film." *New Formations* 9 (Winter 1989): 105–23.

——. "Visible Difference and Flex Appeal: The Body, Sex, Sexuality and Race in the *Pumping Iron* Films." *Cinema Journal* 28:4 (Summer 1989): 38–51.

——. "When Is a Lesbian Not a Lesbian? The Lesbian Continuum and the Mainstream Femme Film." *Camera Obscura* 25–26 (January/May 1991): 145–78.

hooks, bell. "*Looking for Langston.*" *Z Magazine* (May 1990): 75–77. Reprinted as "Seductive Sexualities: Representing Blackness in Poetry and on Screen." In *Yearning: Race, Gender, and Cultural Politics.* Boston: South End, 1990.

——. "*Is Paris Burning?*" *Z Magazine* (June 1991): 60–64. Reprinted in *Black Looks: Race and Representation.* Boston: South End, 1992.

Horne, Larry, and John Ramirez. "Conference Report: The UCLA Gay and Lesbian Media Conference." *Camera Obscura* 11 (1983): 120–31.

Howe, Gregg. "On Identifying with Judy Garland" and "A Dozen Women We Adore." In *Gay Life,* ed. Eric E. Rofes. New York: Doubleday, 1986.

Howes, Keith. *Broadcasting It: An Encyclopaedia of Homosexuality on Film, Radio, and TV in the U.K. 1923–1993*. London: Cassell, 1993.

Hughes, Walter. "Feeling Mighty Real: Disco as Discourse and Discipline." *Village Voice Rock and Roll Quarterly* (Summer 1993): 7, 10–11, 21.

Humphries, Martin, ed. *Tongues Untied*. London: GMP, 1987.

Huston, John. "All My Friends Are Girls Wrapped in Boys: Gender in Pop." *Christopher Street* 144 (12:12, 1989): 16–23.

Jackson, Ed, and Stan Persky, eds. *Flaunting It! A Decade of Gay Journalism from the Body Politic*. Vancouver/Toronto: New Star/Pink Triangle, 1982. (Includes essays on the *Cruising* protests.)

Jahr, C. "Gay Movies for Straight People." *Village Voice* (30 June 1975): 12–13.

Jarman, Derek. *Derek Jarman's Caravaggio: The Complete Film Script and Commentaries*. London: Thames & Hudson, 1986.

———. *War Requiem*. London: Faber & Faber, 1989.

———. *Queer Edward II*. Bloomington: Indiana University Press, 1992.

———. *At Your Own Risk: A Saint's Testament*. Woodstock, N.Y.: Overlook, 1993.

———. *Dancing Ledge*. Woodstock, N.Y.: Overlook, 1993.

———. *Wittgenstein: The Terry Eagleton Script, the Derek Jarman Film*. London: BFI, 1993.

Jay, K., and A. Young, eds. *Lavender Culture*. New York: Jove/Harcourt Brace Jovanovich, 1978.

Julien, Issac, and Pratibha Parmar. "In Conversation." In *Ecstatic Antibodies: Resisting the* University Press, 1992.

Julien, Issac, and Kobena Mercer. "True Confessions: A Discourse on Images of Black Masculinity." In *Male Order: Unwrapping Masculinity*, ed. Rowena Chapman and Jonathan Rutherford. London: Lawrence & Wishart, 1988.

Julian, Issac, and Pratibha Parmar. "In Conversation." In *Ecstatic Antibodies: Resisting the AIDS Mythology*, ed. Tessa Boffin and Sunil Gupta. London: River Oram, 1990.

Kalin, Tom. "Identity Crisis: The Lesbian and Gay Experimental Film Festival." *Independent* (January/February 1989): 27–31.

Kelly, Keith. "The Sexual Politics of Rosa von Praunheim." *Millenium Film Journal* 3 (1979): 115–18.

Kennedy, Elizabeth Lapovsky and Madeline D. Davis. *Boots of Leather, Slippers of Gold: The History of a Lesbian Community*. New York: Routledge, 1993.

Kilday, Gregg. "Hollywood's Homosexuals." *Film Comment* 22:2 (March–April 1986): 40–43.

Kielwasser, Alfred P., and Michelle A. Wolf. "Mainstream Television, Adolescent Homosexuality, and Significant Silence." *Critical Studies in Mass Communication* 9:4 (December 1992): 350–73.

King, Katie. "Audre Lorde's Lacquered Layerings: The Lesbian Bar as a Site of Literary Production." *Cultural Studies* 2:3 (October 1988): 321–42.

Kipnis, Laura. "She-Male Fantasies and the Aesthetics of Pornography." In *Dirty Looks: Women, Pornography, Power*, ed. Pamela Church Gibson and Roma Gibson. London: BFI, 1993.

Kirk, Kris, and Ed Heath. *Men in Frocks*. London: GMP, 1984.

Kirkham, Pat, and Janet Thumin, eds. *You Tarzan: Masculinity, Movies, and Men*. New York: St. Martin's, 1993.

Kleinberg, Seymour. *Alienated Affections: Being Gay in America*. New York: St. Martin's, 1980.

Knapp, Lucretia. "The Queer Voice in *Marnie*," *Cinema Journal* 32:4 (Summer 1993): 6–23. (Reprinted in this volume.)

Koestenbaum, Wayne. *The Queen's Throat: Opera, Homosexuality, and the Mystery of Desire*. New York: Poseidon, 1993.

Kotz, Liz. "Across the Sexual Divide: The San Francisco International Lesbian and Gay Film Festival." *Independent* (October 1989): 31–33.

Kuhn, Annette. "Encounter between Two Cultures: A Discussion with Ulrike Ottinger." *Screen* 28:4 (Autumn 1987): 74–79.

———. "Sexual Disguise in the Cinema." In *The Power of the Image: Essays on Representation and Sexuality*. London: Routledge, 1985.

Landers, Timothy. "Bodies and Anti-Bodies: A Crisis in Representation." *Independent* 11:1 (January–February 1988): 18–24.

Lang, Robert. "Batman and Robin: A Family Romance." *American Imago* 47, nos. 3–4 (Fall–Winter 1990): 293–319.

LaValley, Al. "The Great Escape." *American Film* 10:6 (April 1985): 28–34, 70–71. (Reprinted in this volume.)

Lebow, Alisa. "Lesbians Make Movies." *Cineaste* 20, no. 2 (December 1993): 18–23.

Leo, John R. "The Familialism of 'Man' in American Television Melodrama." In *Displacing Homophobia: Gay Male Perspectives in Literature and Culture*, ed. Ronald R. Butters, John M. Clum, and Michael Moon. Durham, N.C.: Duke University Press, 1989.

Lesage, Julia. "*Celine and Julie Go Boating*: Subversive Fantasy." *Jump Cut* 24–25 (1981): 36–43.

Lesbian and Gay Media Advocates. *Talk Back! The Gay Person's Guide to Media Action*. Boston: Alyson, 1982.

Leyland, Winston, ed. *Physique: A Pictorial History of the Athletic Model Guild*. San Francisco: Gay Sunshine, 1982.

Lightning, Robert K. "Spike Lee's Homophobia," *CineAction* 29 (August 1992): 35–39.

Limbacher, James L. *Sexuality in World Cinema*. Metuchen, N.J.: Scarecrow, 1983.

Lind, Earl. *The Female Impersonators* (1922). Reprint. New York: Arno, 1975.

Lippe, Richard. "Gay Visibility: Contemporary Images." *CineAction!* 7 (December 1986): 81–88.

———. "Gender and Destiny: George Cukor's *A Star Is Born*." *CineAction!* 3/4 (January 1986): 46–57.

———. "Rock Hudson: His Story." *CineAction!* 10 (October 1987): 46–54.

———. "Montgomery Clift: A Critical Disturbance." *CineAction!* 17 (September 1989): 36–42.

———. "Authorship and Cukor: A Reappraisal." *CineAction!* 21/22 (November 1990): 21–34.

Longfellow, Brenda. "Love Letters to the Mother: The Works of Chantal Akerman." *Canadian Journal of Political and Social Theory* 13, nos. 1–2 (1989): 73–90.

Lord, Catherine. "Plotting Queer Culture." *Artpaper* 9:7 (March 1990): 16–17.

Lowry, Ed. "The Appropriation of Signs in *Scorpio Rising*." *Velvet Light Trap* 20 (1983): 41–47.

MacBean, James Roy. "Between Kitsch and Fascism: Notes on Fassbiner, Pasolini, and Homosexual Politics." *Cineaste* 13:4 (1984): 12–19.

MacDonald, Scott. "Su Friedrich: Reappropriations." *Film Quarterly* 41, no. 2 (Winter 1987–88): 34–43.

——. "*Damned If You Don't:* An Interview with Su Friedrich." *Afterimage* 15:10 (May 1988): 6–10.

MacDowall, Cyndra. "Sapphic Scenes: Looking through a History." *Fuse Magazine* 14:4 (Spring 1991): 24–39.

MacKinnon, Kenneth. *The Politics of Popular Representation: Reagan, Thatcher, AIDS, and the Movies.* Madison, N.J.: Fairleigh Dickinson Press, 1992.

Mangin, Daniel. "College Course File: The History of Lesbians and Gays on Film." *Journal of Film and Video* 41:3 (Fall 1989): 50–66.

Marks, Jim. "Looking for Issac." *Outweek* 1 (October 1989): 30–33. (On Issac Julien's *Looking for Langston*.)

Marshall, Stuart. "*Taxi zum Klo*." *Undercut* 3–4 (March 1982): 1–3.

——. "Picturing Deviancy." In *Ecstatic Antibodies: Resisting the AIDS Mythology,* ed. Tessa Boffin and Sunil Gupta. London: River Oram, 1990.

Matthews, Peter. "Garbo and Phallic Motherhood—a 'Homosexual' Visual Economy." *Screen* 29:3 (Summer 1988): 14–39.

Mayne, Judith. "Murnau's *Nosferatu:* Dracula in the Twilight." In *German Literature and Film: Adaptations and Transformations,* ed. Eric Rentschler. New York: Methuen, 1986.

——. "*L.A. Law* and Prime-Time Feminism." *Discourse* 10, no. 2 (Spring–Summer 1988): 30–47.

——. *The Woman at the Keyhole: Feminism and Women's Cinema.* Bloomington: Indiana University Press, 1990.

——. "Lesbian Looks: Dorothy Arzner and Female Authorship." In *How Do I Look? Queer Film and Video,* ed. Bad Object-Choices. Seattle: Bay, 1991.

——. "A Parallax View of Lesbian Authorship." In *Inside/Out: Lesbian Theories, Gay Theories,* ed. Diana Fuss. New York: Routledge, 1991.

——. *Cinema and Spectatorship.* New York: Routledge, 1993.

——. "Julie Zando's Primal Scene and Lesbian Representation." *Quarterly Review of Film and Video* 15:1 (November 1993): 15–26.

McAllister, Matthew P. "Comic Books and AIDS." *Journal of Popular Culture* 26:2 (Fall 1992): 1–24.

McCay, Anne. *Wolf Girls at Vassar: Lesbian and Gay Experiences, 1930–1990.* New York: St. Martin's, 1993.

McDonald, Boyd. *Cruising the Movies: A Sexual Guide to "Oldies" on TV.* New York: Gay Presses of New York, 1985.

McDowell, Cyndra, and Lee Waldorf. "Close-Up: A Conversation with Toronto Film-maker Midi Onodera." *Body Politic* (March 1986): 34–35.

McGann, Nadine L. "A Kiss Is Not a Kiss: An Interview with John Greyson." *Afterimage* 19:6 (January 1992): 10–13.

Medhurst, Andy. "*Victim:* Text as Context." *Screen* (July/August 1984): 22–35.

——. "Batman, Deviance and Camp." in *The Many Lives of the Batman: Critical Approaches to a Superhero and His Media,* ed. Roberta E. Pearson and William Uricchio. New York: Routledge, 1991.

——. "That Special Thrill: *Brief Encounter,* Homosexuality, and Authorship." *Screen* 32:2 (Summer 1991): 197–208.

Mellen, Joan. "Lesbianism in the Movies." In *Women and Their Sexuality in the New Film.* New York: Dell, 1973.

Mercer, Kobena. "Imaging the Black Man's Sex." In *Photography/Politics: Two,* ed. Pat Holland, Jo Spence, and Simon Watney. London: Comedia/Methuen, 1987.

——. "Dark and Lovely: Notes on Black Gay Image Making." *Ten .8* (1991): n.p.

——. "Reading Racial Fetishism: The Photographs of Robert Mapplethorpe." In *Fetishism: Gender, Commodity, Vision,* ed. Emily Apter and Bill Pietz. Ithaca, N.Y.: Cornell University Press, 1991.

——. "Skin Head Sex Thing: Racial Differences and the Homoerotic Imaginary." *New Formations* 16 (1992): 1–23. Reprinted in *How Do I Look? Queer Film and Video,* ed. Bad Object-Choices. Seattle: Bay, 1991.

Mercer, Kobena, Jacqueline Rose, Gayatri Spivak, and Angela McRobbie. "Sexual Identities: Questions of Difference." *Undercut* 17 (Spring 1988): 19–30.

Merck, Mandy. "*Lianna* and the Lesbians of Art Cinema." In *Films for Women,* ed. Charlotte Brunsdon. London: BFI, 1986.

——. "Desert Hearts." *Independent* 10:6 (July 1987): 15–17.

——. "Difference and Its Discontents." *Screen* 28:1 (Winter 1987): 2–9.

——, ed. *The Sexual Subject: Screen Reader in Sexuality.* New York: Routledge, 1992.

——. *Perversions: Deviant Readings.* New York: Routledge, 1993.

Meyer, Moe, ed. *The Politics and Poetics of Camp.* New York: Routledge, 1994.

Meyer, Richard. "Imagining Sadomasochism: Robert Mapplethorpe and the Masquerade of Photography." *Qui Parle* 4:1 (1990): 62–78.

——. "Rock Hudson's Body." In *Inside/Out: Lesbian Theories, Gay Theories,* ed. Diana Fuss. New York: Routledge, 1991.

Miller, D. A. "Anal *Rope.*" *Representations* 32 (Fall 1990): 114–33. Reprinted in *Inside/Out: Lesbian Theories, Gay Theories,* ed. Diana Fuss. New York: Routledge, 1991.

Mitchell, Pam, ed. *Pink Triangles: Radical Perspectives on Gay Liberation.* Boston: Alyson, 1980.

Modleski, Tania. *Feminism without Women: Culture and Criticism in a "Postfeminist" Age.* New York: Routledge, 1991.

Montero, Oscar. "Lipstick Vogue: The Politics of Drag." *Radical America* 22:1 (January–February 1988): 35–42.

Montgomery, Jennifer. "Lesbian Viewing and Perversity." *Jump Cut* 37 (1992): 74–78.

Montgomery, K. "Gay Activists and the Networks." *Journal of Communication* 31:3 (1981): 49–57.

Moon, Michael. "Flaming Closets." *October* 51 (Winter 1989): 19–54. (Reprinted in this volume.)

——. "A Small Boy and Others: Sexual Disorientation in Henry James, Kenneth Anger, and David Lynch." In *Comparative American Identities: Race, Sex, and Nationality in the Modern Text*, ed. Hortense J. Spillers. New York: Routledge, 1991.

——. "Outlaw Sex and the 'Search for America': Representing Male Prostitution and Perverse Desire in Sixties Film (*My Hustler* and *Midnight Cowboy*)." *Quarterly Review of Film and Video* 15:1 (November 1993): 27–40.

Moon, Michael, and Eve Kosofsky Sedgwick. "Divinity: A Dossier, a Performance Piece, a Little-Understood Emotion." *Discourse* 13:1 (Fall–Winter 1990–91): 12–39. Reprinted in Eve Kosofsky Sedgwick. *Tendencies*. Durham: Duke University Press, 1993.

Moritz, M J. "American Television Discovers Gay Women: The Changing Context of Programming Decisions at the Networks." *Journal of Communication Inquiry* 13:2 (1989): 62–78.

Mueller, R. "Interview with Ulrike Ottinger." *Discourse* 4 (Winter 1981/1982): 108–26.

Mullins, Greg. "Nudes, Prudes, and Pigmies: The Desirability of Disavowal in *Physical Culture*." *Discourse* 15:1 (Fall 1992): 27–48.

Musto, Michael. "Immaculate Connection." *Outweek* 90 (20 March 1991): 35–41, 62. (Reprinted in this volume.)

——. "Old Camp, New Camp." *Out* 5 (April/May 1993): 32–39.

National Gay Task Force. *What Can Gay People Do about the Media?* New York: NGTF, n.d.

Navarro, Ray, and Catherine Saalfield. "Not Just Black and White: AIDS Media and People of Color." *Independent* 12:6 (July 1989): 18–23.

——. "Shocking Pink Praxis: Race and Gender on the ACT UP Frontlines." In *Inside/Out: Lesbian Theories, Gay Theories*, ed. Diana Fuss. New York: Routledge, 1991.

Nelson, Jeffrey. "Homosexuality in Hollywood Films: A Contemporary Paradox." *Critical Studies in Mass Communication* 2:1 (1985): 54–64.

Nestle, Joan, ed. *The Persistent Desire: A Femme-Butch Reader*. Boston: Alyson, 1991.

Nestle, Joan. "The Fem Question." In *Pleasures and Dangers: Exploring Female Sexuality*, ed. Carol Vance. London: Pandora, 1989.

"New Queer Cinema." *Sight and Sound*, suppl. (September 1992): 30–39. (Essays by B. Ruby Rich, Derek Jarman, Pratibha Parmar, Issac Julien, Constantine Giannaris, Seun Okewole, Amy Taubin, and Cherry Smith.)

Newton, Esther. *Mother Camp: Female Impersonators in America*. Chicago: University of Chicago Press, 1972; reprint, 1979.

——. *Cherry Grove, Fire Island: Sixty Years in America's First Gay and Lesbian Town*. Boston: Beacon, 1993.

Norden, Martin F. "Sexual References in James Whale's *Bride of Frankenstein*." In *Eros in the Mind's Eye: Sexuality and the Fantastic in Art and Film*, ed. Donald Palumbo. New York: Greenwood, 1986.

Noriega, Chon. " 'SOMETHING'S MISSING HERE!': Homosexuality and Film Reviews during the Production Code Era, 1934–1962." *Cinema Journal* 30:1 (Fall 1990): 20–41.

Nunokawa, Jeff. " 'All the Sad Young Men': AIDS and the Work of Mourning." *Yale Journal of Criticism* 4:2 (1991): 1–12.

Olson, Ray. "Gay Film Work (1972–77): Affecting but Too Evasive." *Jump Cut* 20 (1979): 9–12.

O'Neil, S. "The Role of the Mass Media and Other Socialization Agents in the Identity Formation of Gay Males." In *Studies in Communication,* vol. 1, *Studies in Mass Communication and Technology,* ed. S. Thomas. Norwood, N.J.: Ablex, 1984.

O'Pray, Michael. "Derek Jarman's Cinema: Eros and Thanatos." *Afterimage* 12 (1985): 6–15.

Ortleb, Charles. "The Context of *Cruising*." In *The Christopher Street Reader,* ed. Michael Denney, Charles Ortleb, and Thomas Steele. New York: Perigee, 1983.

Oswald, Laura. "The Perversion of I/Eye in *Un chant d'amour*." *Enclitic* 7:2 (Fall 1983): 106–14.

Packman, D. "Jack Smith's *Flaming Creatures*." *Film Culture* 63 (1977): 51–56.

Pajaczkowska, Claire. "The Heterosexual Presumption: A Contribution to the Debate on Pornography." *Screen* 22:1 (1981): 79–92.

Pally, Marcia. "When the Gaze Is Gay: Women in Love." *Film Comment* 22:2 (March/April 1986): 35–39.

Parkerson, Michelle. "Diva under Glass." *Heresies* 16 (1983): 11.

——. "Beyond Chiffon: The Making of *Storme*." In *Blasted Allegories: An Anthology of Writings by Contemporary Artists,* ed. Brian Wallis. Cambridge, Mass.: MIT Press, 1987.

Parmar, Pratibha. "Black Feminism: The Politics of Representation." In *Identity: Community, Culture, Difference,* ed. Jonathan Rutherford. London: Lawrence & Wishart, 1990.

Patlevich, JoAnn. "Muscling the Mainstream: Lesbian Murder Mysteries and Fantasies of Justice." *Discourse* 15:1 (Fall 1992): 94–111.

Patton, Cindy. "The Cum Shot: Three Takes on Lesbian and Gay Sexuality." *Out/Look* 1:3 (Fall 1988): 72–77.

——. "Hegemony and Orgasm, or The Instability of Heterosexual Pornography." *Screen* 30:3 (Fall 1989): 72–77.

——. *Inventing AIDS.* New York: Routledge, 1990.

——. "Safe Sex and the Pornographic Vernacular." In *How Do I Look? Queer Film and Video,* ed. Bad Object-Choices. Seattle: Bay, 1991.

——. "Unmediated Lust?" In *Stolen Glances: Lesbians Take Photographs,* ed. Tessa Boffin and Jean Fraser. London: Pandora, 1991.

——. "Visualizing Safe Sex: When Pedagogy and Pornography Collide." In *Inside/Out: Lesbian Theories, Gay Theories,* ed. Diana Fuss. New York: Routledge, 1991.

Pearce, Frank. "How to Be Immoral and Ill, Dangerous and Pathetic, All at the Same Time: Mass Media and Homosexuality." In *The Manufacture of News,* ed. Stanley Cohen and Jock Young. London: Constable, 1973.

Penley, Constance, and Sharon Willis, eds. *Male Trouble.* Minneapolis: University of Minnesota Press, 1993.

Pepper, Rachel. "Into the Woods." *Outweek* 64 (19 September 1990): 36–41. (On the Michigan Women's Music Festival.)

Picano, Felice. "Imitation of Life: Interview with Vito Russo." In *The Christopher Street Reader,* ed. Michael Denney, Charles Ortleb, and Thomas Steele. New York: Perigee, 1983.

Price, Theodore. *Hitchcock and Homosexuality: His 50-Year Obsession with Jack the Ripper and the Superbitch Prostitute—a Psychoanalytic View.* Metuchen, N.J.: Scarecrow, 1992.

Ramirez, John, and Larry Horne. "Report: UCLA Gay and Lesbian Media Conference." *Jump Cut* 29 (1984): 66–68.

"Reel to Real: A Conversation between Jennie Livingston and Todd Haynes." *Outweek* 94 (17 April 1991): 32–44.

Reid, Mark A. "The Photography of Rotimi Fani-Kayode." *Wide Angle* 14:2 (April 1992): 38–51.

Rich, B. Ruby. "From Repressive Tolerance to Erotic Liberation: *Mädchen in Uniform.*" In *Re-Vision: Essays in Feminist Film Criticism,* ed. Mary Ann Doane, Patricia Mellencamp, and Linda Williams. Los Angeles: American Film Institute, 1984. (Reprinted in this volume.)

——. "The New Queer Cinema." *Sight and Sound* (September 1992): 30–35.

——. "Reflections on a Queer Screen." *GLQ* 1:1 (1993): 83–91.

Riggs, Marlon T. "Black Macho Revisited: Reflections on a Snap! Queen." *Independent* 14:3 (April 1991): 32–34. (Reprinted in this volume.)

——. "Ruminations of a Snap Queen: What Time Is It?" *Out/Look* 3:3 (Spring 1991): 12–19.

——. "Unleash the Queen." In *Black Popular Culture: A Project by Michelle Wallace,* ed. Gina Dent. Seattle: Bay, 1992.

Rist, Darrell Yates. "Fear and Loving and AIDS." *Film Comment* 22:2 (March–April 1986): 44–50.

Robertson, Pamela. " 'The Kinda Comedy That Imitates Me': Mae West's Identification with the Feminist Camp." *Cinema Journal* 32:2 (Winter 1993): 57–72. Reprinted in *Camp Grounds: Style and Homosexuality,* ed. David Bergman. Amherst: University of Massachusetts Press, 1993.

Robinson, David. "Homosexual Images in Contemporary Cinema." *European Gay Review* 2 (1987): 8–24.

Robinson, Tom. "A Conversation about Rock, Politics, and Gays." In *Coming on Strong: Gay Politics and Culture,* ed. Simon Shepherd and Mick Wallis. London: Unwin Hyman, 1989.

Roen, Paul. *High Camp: A Gay Guide to Camp and Cult Films.* San Francisco: Leyland, 1994.

Rolfes, Eric E., ed. *Gay Life: Leisure, Love, and Living for the Contemporary Gay Male.* New York: Doubleday, 1986. (Section on culture and leisure.)

Rolland, Howard. "Homosexuality as a Vehicle for Masochism Symbolized in the Film *Fireworks.*" *Mattachine Review* 7:7 (1961): 6–8.

Ross, Andrew. "Uses of Camp." *Yale Journal of Criticism* 2:1 (1988): 1–24. Reprinted in *No Respect: Intellectuals and Popular Culture.* New York: Routledge, 1989.

Rubenstein, Anne. "Designing Women." *Outweek* 48 (30 May 1990): 44–53. (On lesbian cartoonists.)

Russo, Vito. "Camp." In *Gay Men: The Sociology of Male Homosexuality,* ed. Martin P. Levine. New York: Harper & Row, 1979.

——. *The Celluloid Closet: Homosexuality in the Movies* (1981). Rev. ed. New York: Harper & Row, 1987.

——. "Gay Films: Gay Reality vs. Political Correctness." *Advocate* (4 September 1984): 38.

——. "A State of Being." *Film Comment* 22:2 (March–April 1986): 32–34.

Ryan, James, and G. Luther Whitington. "Homophobia in Hollywood." *Advocate* 573 (26 March 1991): 32–44.

Saalfield, Catherine. "Positive Propaganda: Jean Carlomusto and Gregg Bordowitz on AIDS Media." *Independent* 13:10 (December 1990): 19–21.

Sartin, Hank. "Bugs Bunny: Queer as a Three-Dollar Bill." *Windy City Times* (Chicago), 24 June 1993, sec. 2, 79.

Satuloff, Bob. "Homophobia Goes to the Movies." *Christopher Street* 14:19 (25 May 1992): 13–17.

Sausser, Gail. "Movie and T.V. Heart-Throbs." In *Lesbian Etiquette.* Trumansburg, N.Y.: Crossing, 1986.

Savage, Jon. "Tainted Love: The Influence of Male Homosexuality and Sexual Divergence on Pop Music and Culture since the War." In *Consumption, Identity, Style,* ed. Alan Tomlinson. New York: Routledge, 1990.

Scholar, Nancy. "*Madchen in Uniform.*" In *Sexual Stratagems: The World of Women and Film,* ed. Patricia Erens. New York: Horizon, 1979.

Schwartz, Deb. "Madonna and Sandra: Like We Care." In *Desperately Seeking Madonna,* ed. Adam Sexton. New York: Delta, 1993.

Schwichtenburg, Cathy. "*Near the Big Chakra:* Vulvar Conspiracy and Protean Film/Text." *Enclitic* 4:2 (1980): 78–90.

Sedgwick, Eve Kosofsky. *Tendencies.* Durham, N.C.: Duke University Press, 1993.

Sharrett, Christopher. "The Last Stranger: *Querelle* and Cultural Simulation." *Canadian Journal of Political and Social Theory* 13, nos. 1–2 (1989): 115–28.

Shaviro, Steven. *The Cinematic Body.* Minneapolis: University of Minnesota Press, 1993.

Shaw, Nancy. "On a Trumped-Up Charge: Two Video Films." *Vanguard* 18:3 (Summer 1989): 20–25.

Sheldon, Caroline. "Lesbians and Film: Some Thoughts." In *Gays and Film,* rev. ed., ed. Richard Dyer. New York: New York Zoetrope, 1984.

Shepherd, Simon, and Mick Wallis, eds. *Coming on Strong: Gay Politics and Culture.* London: Unwin Hyman, 1989.

Siebenand, Paul Alcuin. *The Beginnings of Gay Cinema in Los Angeles: The Industry and the Audience.* Ann Arbor, Mich.: UMI Press, 1980.

Signorile, Michelangelo. *Queer in America: Sex, the Media, and the Closets of Power.* New York: Random House, 1993.

Silverman, Kaja. *Male Subjectivity at the Margins.* New York: Routledge, 1992.

Simmons, Ron. "Other Options." *Black Film Review* 5:3 (Summer 1989): 20–22.

Simms, Steven A. "Gay Images on Television." In *Gayspeak: Gay Male and Lesbian Communication,* ed. James W. Chesebro. New York: Pilgrim, 1981.

Simpson, Mark. *Male Impersonators: Men Performing Masculinity.* New York: Routledge, 1994.

Smith, Jack. "The Perfect Filmic Appositeness of Maria Montez." *Film Culture* 27 (1962–63): 28–32.

——. "The Memoirs of Maria Montez, or Wait for Me at the Bottom of the Pool." *Film Culture* 31 (Winter 1963/1964): 3–4.

——. "Taboo of Jingola: The Art of the Audience." *Village Voice* (21 December 1972): 75. ("Review" of *Reefer Madness.*)

——. " 'Pink Flamingo' Formulas in Focus." *Village Voice* (19 July 1973): 69. ("Review" of *Pink Flamingos.*)

Smith, Paul. "Action Movie Hysteria, or Eastwood Bound." *differences* 1:5 (Fall 1989): 88–107.

——. *Clint Eastwood: A Cultural Production.* Minneapolis: University of Minnesota Press, 1993.

Smith, Paul Julian. *Desire Unlimited: The Cinema of Pedro Almodovar.* London: Verso, 1994.

——. *Laws of Desire: Questions of Homosexuality in Spanish Writing and Film, 1960–90.* New York: Oxford University Press, 1992.

Smyth, Cherry. "The Pleasure Threshold: Looking at Lesbian Pornography on Film." *Feminist Review* 34 (Spring 1990): 152–59.

Snyder, Stephen. "*Cruising:* The Semiotics of S & M." *Canadian Journal of Political and Social Theory* 13:1–2 (1989): 102–14.

"Special Section: Gays and Film." *Jump Cut* 16 (1977): 13–28. (Includes Thomas Waugh, "Films by Gays for Gays"; Richard Dyer, "Homosexuality and Film Noir"; Bob Cant, "Fassbinder's *Fox and His Friends*"; Andrew Britton, "Foxed: A Reply to Cant"; Will Aitken, "Leaving the Dance: Bertolucci's Gay Images"; and Tom Waugh and Chuck Kleinhans, "A Dialogue: Gays and Straights, Film and the Left.")

"Special Section: Lesbians and Film." *Jump Cut* 24/25 (1981): 17–50. (Includes Edith Becker, Michelle Citron, Julia Lesage, and B. Ruby Rich, "Introduction" [reprinted in this volume]; Andrea Weiss, with help from Altermedia, Women Make Movies, and Greta Schiller, "Filmography of Lesbian Works"; Bonnie Zimmerman, "Lesbian Vampires"; Claudette Charboneau and Lucy Winer, "Lesbians in 'Nice' Films"; Jacquelyn Zita, "The Films of Barbara Hammer"; Andrea Weiss, "*Women I Love* and *Double Strength* (Barbara Hammer, 1976 and 1978)"; Michelle Citron, "The Films of Jan Oxenberg"; Judy Whitaker, "Hollywood Transformed"; Julia Lesage, "*Celine and Julie Go Boating* (Jacques Rivette, 1974)"; B. Ruby Rich, "*Maedchen in Uniform* (Leontine Sagan, 1931).")

Stacey, Jackie. "Desperately Seeking Difference." *Screen* 28:1 (Winter 1987): 48–61.

Staiger, Janet. "The Logic of Alternative Readings: A Star Is Born." In *Interpreting Films: Studies in the Historical Reception of American Cinema*. Princeton, N.J.: Princeton University Press, 1992.

Steakley, James. "Gay Film and Censorship: A 1919 Case Study." In *Homosexuality, Which Homosexuality?* Conference Papers, Free University of Amsterdam, Literature and Art Volume 2 (1987).

Stein, Arlene. "All Dressed Up, But No Place to Go? Style Wars and the New Lesbianism." *Out/Look* 1:4 (Winter 1989): 34–42. (Reprinted in this volume.)

——. "Androgony Goes Pop: But Is It Lesbian Music?" *Out/Look* 3:3 (Spring 1991): 26–33. Reprinted in *Sisters, Sexperts, Queers: Beyond the Lesbian Nation*, ed. Arlene Stein. New York: Plume/Penguin, 1993.

——. "Crossover Dreams: Lesbianism and Popular Music Since the 1970s." In *The Good, The Bad, and The Gorgeous: Popular Culture's Romance with Lesbianism*, eds. Diane Hamer and Belinda Budge. London: Pandora, 1994. (Reprinted in this volume.)

Stein, Arlene, ed. *Sisters, Sexperts, Queers: Beyond the Lesbian Nation*. New York: Plume/Penguin, 1993.

Steven, Peter. "Gay and Lesbian Cinema." In *Jump Cut: Hollywood, Politics, and Counter Cinema*, ed. Peter Steven. New York: Praeger, 1985.

——. "The Bourgeoisie Is Not My Audience: An Interview with John Greyson," *Cine-Action* 23 (Winter 1990–91): 40–45.

Stevens, Robin. "Creating a Bisexual Comic Heroine: An Interview with Jaimie Hernandez." *Out/Look* 4:4 (Spring 1992): 32–35.

Straayer, Chris. "The Hypothetical Lesbian Heroine: *Voyage en douce* (Michele Deville, 1980), *Entre nous* (Diane Kurys, 1983)." *Jump Cut* 35 (1990): 50–57. (Reprinted in this volume.)

——. "*Personal Best:* Lesbian/Feminist Audience." *Jump Cut* 29 (1984): 40–44.

——. "The She-Man: Postmodern Bi-Sexed Performance in Film and Video." *Screen* 31:3 (Autumn 1990): 262–280.

——. "Redressing the 'Natural': The Temporary Transvestite Film." *Wide Angle* 14:1 (January 1992): 36–55.

——. "Sample Syllabus." *Quarterly Review of Film and Video* 15:1 (November 1993): 79–88.

——. "The Seduction of Boundaries: Feminist Fluidity in Annie Sprinkle's Art/Education/Sex." In *Dirty Looks: Women, Pornography, Power*, ed. Pamela Church Gibson and Roma Gibson. London: BFI, 1993.

Tartaglia, Jerry. "The Gay Sensibility in American Avant-Garde Film." *Millenium Film Journal* 4–5 (1979): 53–58.

Taylor, Fran. "*Word Is Out* but Still Tongue-Tied." *Jump Cut* 21 (1979): 27–28. Reprinted from *Off Our Backs* (May 1978).

Thomas, Anthony. "The House the Kids Built: The Gay Black Imprint on American Dance Music." *Out/Look* 2:1 (Summer 1989): 24–33. (Reprinted in this volume.)

Thompson, Mark. "Children of Paradise: A Brief History of Queens." In *Gay Spirit: Myth and Meaning,* ed. Mark Thompson. New York: St. Martin's, 1987. (Reprinted in this volume.)

Traub, Valerie. "The Ambiguities of 'Lesbian' Viewing Pleasure: The (Dis)articulations of *Black Widow.*" In *Body Guards: The Cultural Politics of Gender Ambiguity,* ed. Julia Epstein and Kristina Straub. New York: Routledge, 1991. (Reprinted in this volume.)

Turan, Kenneth, and Stephen F. Zito. *Sinema: American Pornographic Films and the People Who Make Them.* New York: Praeger, 1974.

Turim, Maureen. "Gentlemen Consume Blondes." In *Movies and Methods,* vol. 2, ed. Bill Nichols. Berkeley and Los Angeles: University of California Press, 1985. Originally in *Wide Angle* 1:1 (1979), reprinted with addendum considering lesbianism.

Tyler, Carole-Anne. "The Supreme Sacrifice? TV, 'TV,' and the Renee Richards Story." *differences* 1:5 (Fall 1989): 160–86.

——. "Boys Will Be Girls: The Politics of Gay Drag." In *Inside/Out: Lesbian Theories, Gay Theories,* ed. Diana Fuss. New York: Routledge, 1991.

Tyler, Parker. *The Hollywood Hallucination.* New York: Creative Arts, 1944.

——. *Magic and Myth of the Movies.* New York: Holt, 1947.

——. *The 3 Faces of the Film: The Art, the Dream, the Cult* (1960). S. Brunswick, N.J.: Barnes, 1967.

——. *Sex Psyche Etcetera in the Film.* New York: Horizon, 1969.

——. *Underground Film: A Critical History.* New York: Grove, 1969.

——. *Screening the Sexes: Homosexuality in the Movies.* New York: Holt, Rinehart & Winston, 1972.

——. *A Pictorial History of Sex in Films.* Seacaucus, N.J.: Citadel, 1974.

Vandervelden, M. "Changing Gay Images on the Screen: Alliance for Gay and Lesbian Artists." *Advocate* (20 January 1987): 10–11, 20.

Ventura, Jan. "Barbara Hammer: Woman of Vision." *High Performance* 41–42 (Spring–Summer 1988): 18–19.

Vida, Ginny. "The Lesbian Image in the Media." In *Our Right to Love: A Lesbian Resource Book,* ed. Ginny Vida. Englewood Cliffs, N.J.: Prentice-Hall, 1976.

Walters, Barry. "Gay Culture: The Underground Influence Sinks Deep Roots." *Au Courant* 7:37 (31 July 1989): 1, 7, 9.

Walters, Suzanna Danuta. "As Her Hand Crept Slowly Up Her Thigh: Ann Bannon and the Politics of Pulp." *Social Text* 23 (1989): 83–101.

Warner, Michael, ed. *Fear of a Queer Planet: Queer Politics and Social Theory.* Minneapolis: University of Minnesota Press, 1993.

Watney, Simon. "Hollywood's Homosexual World." *Screen* 23, nos. 3–4 (September–October 1982): 107–21.

——. "The Rhetoric of AIDS," *Screen* (January/February 1986): 72–85.

——. *Policing Desire: Pornography, AIDS, and the Media.* Minneapolis: University of Minnesota Press, 1987.

——. "Stellar Studies." *Screen* 28:3 (Summer 1987): 110–14. (Review of Richard Dyer's *Heavenly Bodies.*)

Waugh, Thomas. "Films by Gays for Gays," *Jump Cut* 16 (1977): 14–16.

——. "The Gay Cultural Front." *Jump Cut* 18 (1978): 36–7.

——. "Murnau: The Films Behind the Man." *Body Politic* (March/April 1979): 31–34.

——. "A Heritage of Pornography: On the Gay Film Collection of the Kinsey Institute." *Body Politic* 90 (January 1983): 29–33.

——. "Photography, Passion and Power: On the Gay Still-Photo Collection of the Kinsey Institute." *Body Politic* 101 (March 1984): 29–33.

——. "Men's Pornography: Gay versus Straight." *Jump Cut* 30 (1985): 30–35. (Updated version reprinted in this volume.)

——. "Gay Male Visual Culture in North America during the Fifties: Emerging from the Underground." *Parallelogramme* 12:1 (Fall 1986): 63–67.

——. "Hard to Imagine: Gay Erotic Cinema in the Postwar Era." *CineAction!* 10 (October 1987): 65–72.

——. "Lesbian and Gay Documentary: Minority Self-Imaging, Oppositional Film Practice, and the Question of Image Ethics." In *Image Ethics: The Moral Rights of Subjects in Photographs, Film, and Television,* ed. Larry Gross, John Stuart Katz, and Jay Ruby. New York: Oxford University Press, 1988.

——. "Homoerotic Representation in the Stag Film, 1920–1940: Imagining an Audience." *Wide Angle* 14:2 (April 1992): 4–19.

Weiermair, Peter. *The Hidden Image: Photographs of the Male Nude in the Nineteenth and Twentieth Centuries.* Cambridge, Mass.: MIT Press, 1988.

Weise, Elizabeth Reba. "Bisexuality, *The Rocky Horror Picture Show,* and Me." In *Bi Any Other Name: Bisexual People Speak Out,* ed. Loraine Hutchins and Lani Kaahumanu. Boston: Alyson, 1991.

Weiss, Andrea. "Lesbian as Outlaw: New Forms and Fantasies in Women's Independent Cinema." *Conditions* 11:12 (1985): 117–31.

——. "From the Margins: New Images of Gays in the Cinema." *Cineaste* 15:1 (1986): 4–8.

——. *Vampires and Violets: Lesbians in Film.* New York: Penguin, 1993.

Weiss, Andrea, and Greta Schiller. *Before Stonewall: The Making of a Gay and Lesbian Community.* Tallahassee: Naiad, 1988. (Book version of documentary film.)

Whetmore, Edward Jay. *Androgyny and Sex Role Perception in Television Situation Comedies.* Eugene: University of Oregon Press, 1976.

Whitaker, Claire. "Hollywood Transformed: Interviews with Lesbian Viewers." In *Jump Cut: Hollywood, Politics, and Counter-Cinema,* ed. Peter Steven. New York: Praeger, 1985. Originally in *Jump Cut* 24/25 (1981) under author's name Judy Whitaker.

White, Armond. "Outing the Past." *Film Comment* 28:4 (July–August 1992): 21–25.

White, Patricia. "Madame X of the China Seas." *Screen* 28:4 (1987): 80–95.

——. "Female Spectator, Lesbian Spectre: *The Haunting.*" In *Inside/Out: Lesbian Theories, Gay Theories,* ed. Diana Fuss. New York: Routledge, 1991.

Williams, Linda. "*Personal Best:* Women in Love." *Jump Cut* 27 (1982): 1, 11–12.

Wolf, Michelle A., and Alfred P. Kielwasser, eds. *Gay People, Sex and the Media.* Binghamton, N.Y.: Harrington Park/Haworth, 1991. Originally in *Journal of Homosexuality* 21, nos. 1/2 (1990).

Wood, Robin. "Responsibilities of a Gay Film Critic." *Film Comment* 14:1 (January–

February 1978): 12–17. Reprinted in *Movies and Methods,* vol. 2, ed. Bill Nichols. Berkeley and Los Angeles: University of California Press, 1985. (Reprinted in this volume.)

——. "The Dark Mirror: Murnau's *Nosferatu.*" In *The American Nightmare,* ed. Richard Lippe and Robin Wood. Toronto: Festival of Festivals, 1979.

——. "*Cruising* and Gay Life." *Canadian Forum* (May 1980): 41.

——. "The Dyer's Hand: Stars and Gays." *Film Comment* 16:1 (January–February 1980): 70–72.

——. "Burying the Undead: The Use and Obsolescence of Count Dracula." *Mosaic* 16, nos. 1–2 (Winter/Spring 1983): 175–87.

——. "Is There Camp after *Cruising?*" *Films and Filming* (June 1983): 26–29.

——. *Hollywood from Vietnam to Reagan.* New York: Columbia University Press, 1986.

——. "Notes for the Exploration of Hermosillo." *CineAction!* 5 (May 1986): 32–38.

——. *Hitchcock's Films Revisited.* New York: Columbia University Press, 1989. (Portion reprinted in this volume.)

Worth, Fabienne. "Of Gayzes and Bodies: A Bibliographical Essay on Queer Theory, Psychoanalysis and Archeology." *Quarterly Review of Film and Video* 15:1 (November 1993): 1–14.

——. "Towards Alternative Film Histories: Lesbian Films, Spectators, Filmmakers and the French Cinematic/Cultural Apparatus." *Quarterly Review of Film and Video* 15:1 (November 1993): 55–78.

Wyatt, Justin. "Cinematic/Sexual Transgression: An Interview with Todd Haynes." *Film Quarterly* 46:3 (Spring 1993): 2–8.

Yarborough, Jeff. "Heart of Stone." *Advocate* 600 (7 April 1992): 44–49. (Interview with Oliver Stone on *JFK.*)

Zimmerman, Bonnie. "*Daughters of Darkness:* Lesbian Vampires." *Jump Cut* 24/25 (1981): 23–24.

Acknowledgments

of

Copyright

B. Ruby Rich, "From Repressive Tolerance to Erotic Liberation: *Mädchen in Uniform*," originally appeared in *Re-Vision: Essays in Feminist Film Criticism*, ed. Mary Ann Doane, Patricia Mellencamp, and Linda Williams (Los Angeles: American Film Institute, 1984), 100–30. Reprinted by permission of the author.

Corey K. Creekmur, "Acting Like a Man: Masculine Performance in *My Darling Clementine*," reprinted by permission of the author.

John Hepworth, "Hitchcock's Homophobia," originally appeared in *Christopher Street* 64 (6.4, 1982): 42–49. Reprinted by permission of *Christopher Street* and the author.

Robin Wood, "Letter to the Editor," and John Hepworth's response originally appeared in *Christopher Street* 66 (6.6, 1982): 4–5. Reprinted by permission of *Christopher Street* and the authors.

Robin Wood, "The Murderous Gays: Hitchcock's Homophobia," originally appeared in *Hitchcock's Films Revisited* (New York: Columbia University Press, 1989), 336–57. Reprinted by permission of Columbia University Press and the author.

Sabrina Barton, " 'Crisscross': Paranoia and Projection in *Strangers on a Train*," originally appeared in *Camera Obscura* 25–26 (January/May 1991), 75–100. Reprinted by permission of *Camera Obscura*, Indiana University Press, and the author.

Rhona J. Berenstein, " 'I'm not the sort of person men marry': Monsters, Queers, and Hitchcock's *Rebecca*," originally appeared in *CineAction* 29 (August 1992), 82–96. Reprinted by permission of *CineAction* and the author.

Lucretia Knapp, "The Queer Voice in *Marnie*," originally appeared in *Cinema Journal* 32.4 (Summer 1993): 6–23. Reprinted by permission of *Cinema Journal* and the author.

Michael Moon, "Flaming Closets," originally appeared in *October* 51 (Winter 1989): 19–54. Reprinted by permission of *October*, Massachusetts Institute of Technology Press, and the author.

Thomas Waugh, "Men's Pornography: Gay vs. Straight," originally appeared in *Jump Cut* 30 (1985), 30–35. Updated version reprinted by permission of *Jump Cut* and the author.

Heather Findlay, "Freud's 'Fetishism' and the Lesbian Dildo Debates," originally appeared in *Feminist Studies* 18.3 (Fall 1992): 563–579. Reprinted by permission of the author and *Feminist Studies* Inc., c/o Women's Studies Program, University of Maryland, College Park, MD 20742.

Nayland Blake, "Tom of Finland: An Appreciation," originally appeared in *Out/Look* 1.3 (Fall 1988): 36–45. Reprinted by permission of the author; illustrations by permission of the Tom of Finland Foundation, P.O. Box 26658, Los Angeles, CA 90026.

Jan Zita Grover, "Visible Lesions: Images of the PWA," originally appeared in *Afterimage* 17.1 (Summer 1989): 10–16. Reprinted by permission of *Afterimage* and the author.

Bruce La Bruce, "Pee Wee Herman: The Homosexual Subtext," originally appeared in *CineAction!* 9 (Summer 1987): 3–6. Reprinted by permission of *CineAction!* and the author.

Essex Hemphill, "*In Living Color:* Toms, Coons, Mammies, Faggots, and Bucks," originally appeared in *Outweek* 78 (26 December 1990): 32–40. Reprinted by permission of the author.

Richard Dyer, "In Defense of Disco," originally appeared in *On Record: Rock, Pop, and the Written Word,* ed. Simon Frith and Andrew Goodwin (New York: Pantheon, 1990), 410–16. Reprinted by permission of the author.

Arlene Stein, "Crossover Dreams: Lesbianism and Popular Music Since the 1970s," originally appeared in *The Good, The Bad, and The Gorgeous: Popular Culture's Romance with Lesbianism,* eds. Diane Hamer and Belinda Budge (London: Pandora, 1994). Reprinted by permission of Pandora and the author.

Michael Musto, "Immaculate Connection," originally appeared in *Outweek* 90 (20 March 1991): 35–41, 62. Reprinted by permission of the author.

Anthony Thomas, "The House the Kids Built: The Gay Black Imprint on American Dance Music," originally appeared in *Out/Look* 2.1 (Summer 1989): 24–33.

Mark Thompson, "Children of Paradise: A Brief History of Queens," originally appeared in *Gay Spirit: Myth and Meaning,* ed. Mark Thompson (New York: St. Martin's Press, 1987), 49–68. Reprinted by permission of St. Martin's Press and the author.

Jeffrey Hilbert, "The Politics of Drag," originally appeared in *The Advocate* 575 (23 April 1991): 42–47. Reprinted by permission of *The Advocate,* the national gay and lesbian newsmagazine.

Marlon Riggs, "Black Macho Revisited: Reflections of a Snap! Queen," originally appeared in *The Independent* 14.3 (April 1991), 32–34. Reprinted by permission of the estate of Marlon Riggs.

Arlene Stein, "All Dressed Up, But No Place To Go? Style Wars and the New Lesbianism," originally appeared in *Out/Look* 1.4 (Winter 1989): 34–42. Reprinted by permission of the author.

Danae Clark, "Commodity Lesbianism," originally appeared in *Camera Obscura* 25–26 (January/May 1991): 181–201. Reprinted by permission of *Camera Obscura,* Indiana University Press, and the author.

Contributors

Sabrina Barton is Assistant Professor in the Department of English at the University of Texas, Austin. She is currently working on a book about how the woman's psychothriller stages encounters between "real" and "performative" identities.

Edith Becker is a filmmaker in New York. In September 1993 she started a new cable channel for the City of New York to provide basic education and employment programs for adults.

Rhona J. Berenstein is Assistant Professor in Film Studies at the University of California, Irvine. She is the author of *Attack of the Leading Ladies: Gender, Sexuality and Performance in Classic Horror Cinema* (forthcoming, Columbia University Press), and has published essays in *The Canadian Journal of Political and Social Theory, CineAction!, Film History, Frame-work,* and *The Journal of Popular Culture.* She is the coproducer and codirector of the award-winning Satori Productions documentary *Voices of Choice.*

Nayland Blake is an artist and illustrator. He currently lives and works in San Francisco. His pieces are in the collections of the Whitney Museum, the San Francisco Museum of Modern Art, the Newport Harbor Art Museum, and the Des Moines Museum of Art. He is the copublisher, with Camille Roy, Doug Ischar, and Wayne Smith, of *Dear World,* an anthology of gay and lesbian writing, and has collaborated on two books: *Low* (with Kathy Acker) and *Jerk* (with Dennis Cooper).

Michelle Citron, Associate Professor and Chair of the Department of Radio/Television/Film, Northwestern University, is an independent filmmaker whose work includes *Parthenogenesis, Daughter Rite* and *What You Take For Granted . . . .* She is currently working on a feature film about female sexuality, the family, and incest.

Danae Clark is Associate Professor of Media Studies in the Department of Communication at the University of Pittsburgh. Her book *Star Power: The Cultural Politics of Actors' Labor* is forthcoming from the University of Minnesota Press.

Corey K. Creekmur is Assistant Professor of English at Wayne State University, where he teaches film and cultural studies. He has published essays and reviews in *Wide Angle, Film*

Quarterly, Arachne, Discourse and other journals. His work in progress, *Cattle Queens and Lonesome Cowboys,* concerns representations of gender and sexuality in the Western.

Alexander Doty is Associate Professor of English at Lehigh University, where he teaches film, American literature, and mass culture. He has written *Making Things Perfectly Queer* (Minnesota, 1993) and would like to write one of those cute BFI monographs on *Gentlemen Prefer Blondes.*

Richard Dyer teaches film studies at the University of Warwick. In 1977 he organized the first season of lesbian and gay films at the National Film Theatre in London. His books include *Stars, Heavenly Bodies, Now You See It, Only Entertainment, The Matter of Images,* and *Brief Encounter.*

Heather Findlay completed her Ph.D. at Cornell University, worked as the editor of *On Our Backs,* and is currently editor of *Girlfriends.*

Jan Zita Grover worked at San Francisco General Hospital from 1986–88. In 1989, she curated "AIDS: The Artists' Response" for Ohio State University. She lives in Minneapolis, Minnesota and Wascott, Wisconsin. She dedicates this reprinting of her essay to the late Stuart Marshall and his survivor, Royston Edwards.

Essex Hemphill is editor of *Brother to Brother: New Writings by Black Gay Men* (1991) and author of *Ceremonies: Prose and Poetry* (1992). His work is featured in the films *Tongues Untied* and *Looking for Langston.*

John Hepworth is a Montreal painter and writer. He was a contributing editor for *Christopher Street* for a number of years. He is currently at work on a novel which—he assures us—threatens to take on kaleidoscopic proportions.

Jeffrey Hilbert has contributed articles to *The Advocate.*

Lucretia Knapp is a still photographic and video artist and an independent filmmaker. Her works have been exhibited nationally and internationally. She has taught video production, still photography, computer graphics and film theory at Ohio State University and Cable 21, the public access station in Columbus.

Bruce La Bruce is a farm boy who went to film school, dropped out, hung out with undesirable elements, got brainwashed by Marxist feminists, then got deprogrammed and now makes post-feminist, super-sexist, gay cult movies like *No Skin Off My Ass.* He lives with his pit bull Cookie, and needs money for future films—so send him some.

Al LaValley teaches film studies at Dartmouth. He is the author of *Carlyle and the Idea of the Modern* (1968), and editor of *Focus on Hitchcock* (1972), the screenplays of *Mildred Pierce* (1980), and *Invasion of the Body Snatchers* (1989).

Julia Lesage teaches at the University of Oregon, is a cofounder and editor of *Jump Cut,* and an independent filmmaker.

Michael Moon is the author of *Disseminating Whitman: Revision and Corporeality in Leaves of Grass* (Harvard, 1991), and of a forthcoming study of queer performance that will include the essay in this volume. He teaches gay studies and American literature at Duke University.

Michael Musto writes the column "La Dolce Musto" for the *Village Voice* and is the author of *Downtown* (1986).

B. Ruby Rich is a San Francisco-based critic and Associate Editor of *Jump Cut*. Her work has appeared in *Jump Cut*, the *Village Voice, Sight and Sound, Heresies, Feminist Review*, and many other publications. She has also worked as Director of the Film Program at the New York State Council on the Arts, and a collection of her essays is forthcoming.

Marlon Riggs, who died in 1994, taught in the Graduate School of Journalism at the University of California, Berkeley, and was the director of *Anthem, Affirmations, Tongues Untied, Ethnic Notions*, and *Color Adjustment,* among other award-winning videotapes.

Arlene Stein is the editor of *Sisters, Sexperts, and Queers: Beyond the Lesbian Nation* (1993), and has recently taught in the Department of Sociology at the University of Essex.

Chris Straayer teaches cinema studies at New York University. Her book *Deviant Eyes/Deviant Bodies: Lesbian, Gay and Queer Discourse in Film and Video* is being published by Columbia University Press.

Anthony Thomas has worked as a DJ and, at last report, was completing law school in Chicago.

Mark Thompson, former Senior Editor of *The Advocate,* is the editor of *Gay Spirit: Myth and Meaning* (1987), *Leatherfolk: Radical Sex, People, Politics and Practice* (1991), and *Long Road to Freedom: The Advocate History of the Gay and Lesbian Movement* (1994). Currently working on a retelling of the Gilgamesh myth for gay men, he lives in Los Angeles with his life partner, Episcopal priest and author Malcolm Boyd.

Valerie Traub is Associate Professor of Renaissance Drama and Gender Studies at Vanderbilt University. She is the author of *Desire and Anxiety: Circulations of Sexuality in Shakespearean Drama* (Routledge, 1992), and is currently working on issues of female erotic pleasure and embodiment in early modern England.

Thomas Waugh, professor of film studies at Concordia University, Montreal, is most recently the author of *Hard to Imagine: Gay Male Eroticism in Photography and Film from their Beginnings to Stonewall* (Columbia University Press, 1995). In addition to the anthology *"Show Us Life": Towards a History and Aesthetics of the Committed Documentary* (1984) and publications in such periodicals as *Jump Cut, The Body Politic,* and *CineAction!,* his areas of research, teaching and publication include lesbian and gay film and video, Canadian and Indian national cinema, and documentary. He is currently teaching an interdisciplinary undergraduate course on cultural, social, and scientific aspects of HIV/AIDS.

Patricia White is Assistant Professor in the Department of English Literature at Swarthmore College, where she teaches film and lesbian and gay studies. She is completing a book on lesbian representability and classical Hollywood cinema and co-editing a collection of essays on feminist independent cinema.

Robin Wood is the author of *Hollywood from Vietnam to Reagan* (1986) and *Hitchcock's Films Revisited* (1989), among many other books. He is a founding member of the *CineAction!* editorial collective, and is currently writing fiction and working on screenplays with Jaime Humberto Hermosillo. He lives in Toronto with Richard Lippe.

Index